POETRY:
AN INTRODUCTION

POETRY:
AN INTRODUCTION

MICHAEL MEYER

University of Connecticut

BEDFORD BOOKS OF ST. MARTIN'S PRESS

BOSTON

For Bedford Books
President and Publisher: Charles H. Christensen
General Manager and Associate Publisher: Joan E. Feinberg
Managing Editor: Elizabeth M. Schaaf
Developmental Editor: Karen S. Henry
Production Editor: Anne Benaquist
Production Assistant: Karen Baart
Copyeditor: Cynthia Benn
Text Design: Sandra Rigney, The Book Department, Inc.
Cover Design: Hannus Design Associates
Cover Art: Along the Shore, ca. 1921, by Maurice Prendergast. Oil on canvas, 23¼″ × 34″.
Columbus Museum of Art, Ohio. Gift of Ferdinand Howald.

Acknowledgments

M. H. Abrams. "The Speakers in 'Ode on a Grecian Urn'" from *Literature and Belief: English Institute Essays* by M. H. Abrams. Copyright © 1958, Columbia University Press, New York. Reprinted by permission of the publishers.

Diane Ackerman. "A Fine, A Private Place" from *Lady Faustus* by Diane Ackerman. Copyright © 1983 by Diane Ackerman. Reprinted by permission of the author.

Claribel Alegría. "I Am Mirror" from *Sobrevivo* by Claribel Alegría. Reprinted by permission of the author.

Paula Gunn Allen. "Pocahontas to Her English Husband, John Rolfe" from *Skin and Bones* by Paula Gunn Allen. West End Press, Inc. 1988. Reprinted by permission.

A. R. Ammons. "Coward." Reprinted from *Diversifications: Poems by A. R. Ammons* by A. R. Ammons with permission of W. W. Norton & Company, Inc. Copyright © 1975 by A. R. Ammons.

Charles R. Anderson. "Eroticism in 'Wild Nights — Wild Nights!'" from *Emily Dickinson's Poetry: Stairway of Surprise* by Charles R. Anderson. Copyright 1960 by Holt, Rinehart, and Winston. Reprinted by permission of the author.

Maya Angelou. "My Arkansas" from *And I Still Rise* by Maya Angelou. Copyright © 1978 by Maya Angelou. Reprinted by permission of Random House, Inc.

Richard Armour. "Going to Extremes" from *Light Armour* by Richard Armour. Reprinted by permission of Kathleen S. Armour.

John Ashbery. "Paradoxes and Oxymorons" from *The Shadow Train* by John Ashbery. Copyright © 1981 by John Ashbery. Reprinted by permission of Georges Borchardt, Inc.

Margaret Atwood. "You Fit Into Me" from *Power Politics* by Margaret Atwood (Toronto: House of Anansi Press, 1971). Reprinted by permission of Stoddart Publishing Co. Limited (Don Mills, Ontario) and Margaret Atwood, © 1980. "Spelling" from *True Stories* by Margaret Attwood. Copyright © Margaret Atwood 1981. Reprinted by permission of the author and Oxford University Press Canada.

W. H. Auden. "The Unknown Citizen," "As I Walked Out One Evening," "Lay Your Sleeping Head, My Love," and "Musée des Beaux Arts" from *W. H. Auden: Collected Poems* by W. H. Auden. Copyright 1940 and renewed 1968 by W. H. Auden. Reprinted by permission of Random House, Inc. and Faber and Faber Ltd.

Regina Barreca. "Nighttime Fires" in *The Minnesota Review* (Fall 1986). Reprinted by permission of the author.

Matsuo Bashō. "Under cherry trees" from *Japanese Haiku*, trans. by Peter Beilenson, Series I, © 1955–56, Peter Beilenson, Editor. Reprinted by permission of Peter Pauper Press, Inc.

Michael L. Baumann. "The 'Overwhelming Question' for Prufrock," excerpt from "Let Us Ask 'What Is It?'" in *Arizona Quarterly* 37 (Spring 1981) 47–58. Reprinted by permission of the author.

John Berryman. "Dream Song 14" from *The Dream Songs* by John Berryman. Copyright © 1959, 1962, 1963, 1964, 1965, 1966, 1967, 1968, 1969 by John Berryman. Reprinted by permission of Farrar, Straus & Giroux, Inc.

Mei-Mei Berssenbrugge. "Jealousy" reprinted by permission of Station Hill Press.

Preface for Instructors

Poetry: An Introduction is an innovative new book that — paradoxically — has been successfully used for a number of years by instructors and students. Drawn from the widely adopted *Bedford Introduction to Literature,* this first edition of *Poetry* has many distinctive features that have already been class-tested in hundreds of literature courses and carefully revised over three editions. With its balance of classic and contemporary, traditional, and multicultural works, along with its in-depth treatment of selected poets, provocative secondary materials, and its pervasive concern with critical reading, thinking, and writing, *Poetry* addresses all the requirements of the contemporary poetry course. Like its predecessor, *Poetry: An Introduction* reflects the assumptions that understanding enhances the enjoyment of literature and that reading literature offers a valuable and unique means of apprehending life in its richness and diversity. The book also reflects the hope that the selections included will encourage students to become lifelong readers of imaginative literature. Designed to accommodate a variety of teaching styles, the collection of 423 poems represents a wide range of periods, nationalities, ethnicities, and voices. Each selection has been carefully chosen for its appeal to students today and for its usefulness in demonstrating the effects, significance, and pleasures of poetry.

Poetry: An Introduction is designed for the introductory poetry course as it is taught today, which varies — from school to school and from instructor to instructor — more than ever before. Even the traditional course emphasizing the elements of poetry and a broad range of works from the Western canon is changing in response to important developments in literary studies and, more generally, in higher education and in American society. The course is now viewed by many teachers as an opportunity to supplement classics of Western literature with the work of writers previously excluded from the traditional canon. Increasingly, it now also serves as an introduction to the discipline of literary study, a challenging development which brings to the undergraduate classroom important trends in literary theory and provocative new readings of both familiar and unfamiliar texts. Finally, introduction to poetry is now frequently taught as a second course in composition in which the critical thinking and writing that students do are as important as the reading that they do. *Poetry: An Introduction* responds to these developments with distinctive features that address the needs of instructors who teach a traditional course but who are also concerned about canonical issues, literary theory, and writing about literature.

Selected Major Authors Treated in Depth

The book includes an extensive selection of poems, seventeen by John Keats, thirty-seven by Emily Dickinson, and nineteen by Robert Frost. Substantial introductions provide useful biographical and critical information about each of these important writers. A selection of "Perspectives" — excerpts from letters, journals, and critical commentaries — follows each writer's works to provide a context for discussion and writing. "Considerations for Critical Thinking and Writing" follow both selections and "Perspectives"; these questions for discussion or writing encourage critical thinking and provide stimulating opportunities for student essays.

In addition, "Two Complementary Critical Readings" on a particular work by each of the three major authors offer students examples of the variety of approaches they can take in reading and writing about poetry. The two readings on Dickinson, for instance, focus on the eroticism of "Wild Nights — Wild Nights!" and its relationship to nineteenth-century popular sensationalist literature. By reading commentaries by two critics who argue competing ideas about one text or who illuminate different aspects of that text, students can see immediately that there is no single way to read a work of literature, an important and necessary step for learning how to formulate their own critical approaches in their essays.

Albums of Contemporary and World Literature

An album of contemporary selections offers some of the most interesting and lively poems published in the last decade or so, including works by Amy Clampitt, Louise Erdrich, Galway Kinnell, Yusef Komunyakaa, Sharon Olds, and Cathy Song. Biographical information about the album authors is included in the text in order to introduce instructors and students to these important but, perhaps, unfamiliar writers.

In addition, an album of world literature offers students a sampling of poems from other cultures, including the work of Claribel Alegría (Salvadoran), Faiz Ahmed Faiz (Pakistani), Vinícius De Moraes (Brazilian), Wole Soyinka (Nigerian), Wislawa Szymborska (Polish), and Tomas Transtromer (Swedish), among others. Over a third of the poems in this edition are by women and minority writers and writers from other cultures. Finally, an album of Canadian poems provides a selection by such poets as Margaret Atwood, Roo Borson, George Bowering, and David Donnell in order to whet students' appetites for Canadian poetry.

"Connections to Other Selections" consist of questions that link the selections in the albums of contemporary and world literature to more traditional selections in the text. For example, Amy Clampitt's "Nothing Stays Put" is linked with William Wordsworth's "The World Is Too Much with Us" and Wole Soyinka's "Future Plans" is connected to Dylan Thomas's "The Hand That Signed the Paper." These questions provide engaging writing opportunities and provocative topics for class discussion. "Connections to Other Selections" questions also appear after many of the works in the chapters on the elements of poetry.

Perspectives on Literature

"Perspectives" — journal notes, letters, classic and contemporary theoretical essays, interviews, and student responses — have proven to be extremely useful for class discussion and student writing. These "Perspectives" are included in five different places in the text: in the chapters treating major authors in depth; in a chapter-length collection in "A Critical Case Study" on T. S. Eliot's "The Love Song of J. Alfred Prufrock"; at the end of Chapter 14, on literary theory; and, finally, throughout the text's discussion chapters. Individual "Perspectives" in these chapters follow the works to which they refer and, in many cases, discuss a poem in terms of the element of literature for which it serves as an illustration in order to teach students how to think critically and write effectively about poetry.

Focus on Critical Reading and Thinking

To further encourage critical reading and thinking, a discussion of how to read imaginative literature appears in Chapter 1. This offers practical advice about the kinds of questions active readers ask themselves as they read. In addition, Chapter 14, "Critical Strategies for Reading," deepens the introductory discussions of active reading by focusing on the different reading strategies employed by contemporary literary theorists. This chapter, which can be assigned at any point in the course, introduces students to eight major contemporary theoretical approaches — formalist, biographical, psychological, historical, sociological (including Marxist and feminist strategies), mythological, reader-response, and deconstructionist. In brief examples the approaches are applied in analyzing Robert Frost's "Mending Wall," as well as other works, so that students will have a sense of how to use these strategies in their own reading and writing. A selected bibliography for the approaches and a set of "Perspectives" by contemporary literary critics conclude this unique chapter.

Although the emphasis in this text is on critical reading and understanding rather than on critical terminology, terms such as *symbol, irony,* and *metaphor* are defined and illustrated to equip students with a basic working vocabulary for discussing and writing about poetry. When first defined in the text, these terms appear in boldface type. An "Index of Terms" appears inside the back cover of the book for easy reference.

Writing about Poetry

The book's concern with helping students write about poetry is pervasive. The chapters treating major figures in depth, the albums of contemporary and world literature, the "Connections to Other Selections" questions, the "Perspectives," and the "Critical Case Study" — which gathers four critical "Perspectives" about T. S. Eliot's "The Love Song of J. Alfred Prufrock" in order to illustrate the variety of approaches available to students — all provide intriguing writing opportunities designed to provoke students' interest, sharpen their critical thinking, and help them improve their writing skills. "Considerations for Critical Thinking and Writing" (questions and suggestions useful for class discussion or writing assignments) accompany virtually every selection in the discussion chapters and all the "Perspectives." In addition to the assignments, the final section of the book, "Critical Thinking and Writing," offers a practical discussion of writing about poetry, including advice about how to read a work closely, take notes, and develop a topic into a thesis. A section titled "Arguing about Literature" discusses how arguments on literary topics can be generated and made persuasive. A list of questions based on the critical approaches covered in the chapter titled "Critical Strategies for Reading" helps students to discover the significant issues regarding a poem that may be arguable. Furthermore, an annotated list of important reference sources for literary research is provided. There is also useful information on revising and editing a paper. Student examples illustrate the entire process and offer concrete models of the different types of papers usually assigned in an introductory poetry course, including explication, analysis, and comparison-contrast. A detailed chapter on the literary research paper, with a student example, concludes the section. In short, the integrated coverage of critical reading and thinking enables students to master the critical strategies necessary for writing with confidence about literary experiences.

Connections between "Popular" and "Literary" Culture

Poetry: An Introduction draws carefully on examples from popular culture to explain the elements of poetry, inviting students to make connections between what they already know and what they will encounter in subsequent selections. Comparisons between popular culture and more canonical literary selections offer excellent writing opportunities, and suggestions are provided after each popular culture example. The examples include greeting card verse and contemporary song lyrics.

Resources for Teaching *Poetry: An Introduction*

This thorough and practical instructor's manual — about 300 pages long and spiral bound — discusses virtually every selection and suggests answers to the questions posed in the text, along with providing additional questions and writing assignments. The manual also offers questions and writing assignments for the collection of poems in Chapter 12. It includes biographical information for many authors whose backgrounds are not discussed in the text and offers selected bibliographies for authors treated in depth, as well as a bibliography of articles on teaching literature. Finally, the manual provides an annotated list of videos, films, and recordings related to the works of literature in the text.

Classic and Contemporary Poems

An audiotape of poetry selections from the book is available to instructors who adopt *Poetry: An Introduction*. Poems linked by "Connections to Other Selections" questions are read together to offer an added resource for class discussion. In addition, the tape features the work of poets treated in depth (Keats, Dickinson, and Frost); poems that serve as good examples of the elements of poetry discussed in the book; and, finally, a rich selection of classic and contemporary poems.

Acknowledgments

This book has benefited from the ideas, suggestions, and corrections of scores of careful readers who helped transform various stages of an evolving manuscript into a finished book and into subsequent editions. I remain grateful to those I have thanked in prefaces of *The Bedford Introduction to Literature,* particularly Robert Wallace of Case Western Reserve University. In addition, many instructors who have used *The Bedford Introduction to Literature* responded to a questionnaire on the book. For their valuable comments and advice I am grateful to Janet Abramson, Lansing Community College; Helen J. Aling, Northwestern College; Barbara Barnard, Hunter College, CUNY; Claudia A. Basha, Victor Valley College; Srileka Bell, University of New Haven; Stephen Benz, Barry University; Paul R. Brandt, Kent State University; Sister Anne Denise Brennan, College of Mount St. Vincent; Jon C. Burton, Northern Virginia Community College; Laura L. Bush, Ricks College; Ruth A. Cameron, Eastern Nazarene College; J. Rocky Colavito, Central Arizona College/Winkelman; Debra Conner, West Virginia University/Parkersburg; Janice Reynolds Cooke, University of New Orleans; Joan Kuzma Costello, Inver Hills Community College; Albert C. DeCiccio, Merrimack College; Emeric DeLuca, Harrisburg Area Community College; George Dennis, Southeastern Illinois College; Brian Dillon, Eastern Montana College; Paul M. Dombrowski, Ohio University; Olivia Carr Edenfield, Georgia Southern University; David L. Elliott, Keystone Junior College; Audrey Elwood, Merritt College; James P. Erickson, Wichita State University; Irene R. Fairley, Northeastern University; Jacqueline Fuller, University of Southern Maine; Marshall Bruce Gentry, University of Indianapolis; Christopher Golden, Kennesaw State College; Rosalie Hewitt, Northern Illinois University; M. Jean Jones, Columbia State Community College; AnnLouise Keating, Eastern New Mexico University; Carolyn Kipnis, Montgomery County Community College; Bernard M. Knab, Chemeketa Community College; Robert S. Kunzinger, Tidewater

Community College; Dr. Harvey Lehman, La Guardia Community College; G. T. Lenard, Stockton State College; Marcia P. Lin; Edgar J. Lovelady, Grace College; Sandra Marshburn, West Virginia State College; John J. McKenna, University of Nebraska/Omaha; Chris McKinnon, Lansing Community College; Gayle H. Miller, Western Carolina University; Scott Moncrieff, Andrews University; Janice T. Moore, Young Harris College; Dr. Michael Olendzenski, Cape Cod Community College; Richard J. Panofsky, University of Massachusetts/N. Dartmouth; Christopher M. Patterson, Iona College, Adelphi University; Richard A. Peacock, Birmingham-Southern College; Julie Pember, University of Rhode Island; Timothy K. Rice, University of Toledo; David Schelhaas, Dordt College; Allen Schwab, Washington University; Susan Seyfarth, Valdosta State College; Margaret C. Sims, Delta State University; Dennis P. Slattery, Incarnate Word College; Ernest Smith, University of Central Florida; Marianne Taylor, Fullerton College; Pamela Thoma, Colorado State University; Dr. Larry Thompson, Ricks College; Marilyn Price Voss, Western Illinois University; William B. Watterson, Lees-McRae College; Thomas A. Westerfield, University of Northern Iowa; Brett Westbrook; Isabelle White, Eastern Kentucky University; Andrew Woolf, Northern Essex Community College; and Karen Wunsch, Queensboro College.

I am also indebted to those who cheerfully answered questions and generously provided miscellaneous bits of information. What might have seemed to them like inconsequential conversations turned out to be important leads. Among these friends and colleagues are Raymond Anselment, Ann Charters, Irving Cummings, William Curtin, Herbert Goldstone, Patrick Hogan, Lee Jacobus, Greta Little, George Monteiro, William Moynihan, Brenda Murphy, Joel Myerson, Thomas Recchio, William Sheidley, Milton Stern, Kenneth Wilson, and the dedicated reference librarians at the Homer Babbidge Library, University of Connecticut.

I continue to be grateful for what I have learned from teaching my students and for the many student papers I have received over the years that I have used in various forms to serve as good and accessible models of student writing. I am particularly indebted to Kathleen Drowne for her diligent help on this project.

At Bedford Books, my debts once again require more time to acknowledge than the deadline allows. Charles H. Christensen and Joan Feinberg initiated this project and launched it with their intelligence, energy, and sound advice. Karen Henry tirelessly steered this as well as earlier editions of *The Bedford Introduction to Literature* through rough as well as becalmed moments; her work was as first-rate as it was essential. Verity Winship oversaw *Resources for Teaching Poetry: An Introduction* with clear-headedness and perseverance. The difficult tasks of production were skillfully managed by Anne Benaquist. (I also thank Karen Baart for her assistance with these tasks.) Cynthia Benn provided careful copyediting, and Mary Lou Wilshaw did more than meticulous proofreading. Ellen Kuhl deftly arranged the permissions, and all the people at Bedford Books — including Donna

Lee Dennison, Adrian Harris, and Jennifer Henning — helped to make this formidable project a manageable one.

Finally, I am grateful to my sons Timothy and Matthew for all kinds of help, but mostly I'm just grateful they're my sons. And for making all the difference, I thank my wife, Regina Barreca.

Brief Contents

Contents

4. Figures of Speech   88

5. Symbol, Allegory, and Irony   108

13. Perspectives on Poetry   497

POETRY:
AN INTRODUCTION

INTRODUCTION

Reading
Imaginative Literature

THE NATURE OF LITERATURE

Literature does not lend itself to a single tidy definition, because the making of it over the centuries has been as complex, unwieldy, and natural as life itself. Is literature everything that is written, from ancient prayers to graffiti? Does it include songs and stories that were not written down until many years after they were recited? Does literature include the television scripts from *The Cosby Show* as well as Shakespeare's *King Lear?* Is literature only that which has permanent value and continues to move people? Must literature be true or beautiful or moral? Should it be socially useful?

Although these kinds of questions are not conclusively answered in this book, they are implicitly raised by the poems included here. No definition of literature, particularly a brief one, is likely to satisfy everyone, because definitions tend to weaken and require qualification when confronted by the uniqueness of individual works. In this context it is worth recalling Herman Melville's humorous use of a definition of a whale in *Moby-Dick* (1851). In the course of the novel Melville presents his imaginative and symbolic whale as inscrutable, but he begins with a quotation from Georges Cuvier, a French naturalist who defines a whale in his nineteenth-century study *The Animal Kingdom* this way: "The whale is a mammiferous animal without hind feet." Cuvier's description is technically correct, of course, but there is little wisdom in it. Melville understood that the reality of the whale (which he describes as the "ungraspable phantom of life") cannot be caught by isolated facts. If the full meaning of the whale is to be understood, it must be sought on the open sea of experience, where the whale itself is, rather than in exclusionary definitions. Facts and definitions are helpful; however, they do not always reveal the whole truth.

Despite Melville's reminder that a definition can be too limiting and even comical, it is useful for our purposes to describe literature as a fiction consisting of carefully arranged words designed to stir the imagination. Stories, poems, and plays are fictional. They are made up — imagined —

even when based upon actual historic events. Such imaginative writing differs from other kinds of writing because its purpose is not primarily to transmit facts or ideas. Imaginative literature is a source more of pleasure than of information, and we read it for basically the same reasons we listen to music or view a dance: enjoyment, delight, and satisfaction. Like other art forms, imaginative literature offers pleasure and usually attempts to convey a perspective, mood, feeling, or experience. Writers transform the facts the world provides — people, places, and objects — into experiences that suggest meanings.

Consider, for example, the difference between the following factual description of a snake and a poem on the same subject. Here is *Webster's Ninth New Collegiate Dictionary* definition:

> any of numerous limbless scaled reptiles (suborder Serpentes or Ophidia) with a long tapering body and with salivary glands often modified to produce venom which is injected through grooved or tubular fangs.

Contrast this matter-of-fact definition with Emily Dickinson's poetic evocation of a snake in "A narrow Fellow in the Grass":

A narrow Fellow in the Grass
Occasionally rides —
You may have met Him — did you not
His notice sudden is —

The Grass divides as with a Comb —   5
A spotted shaft is seen —
And then it closes at your feet
And opens further on —

He likes a Boggy Acre
A floor too cool for Corn —   10
Yet when a Boy, and Barefoot —
I more than once at Noon
Have passed, I thought, a Whip lash
Unbraiding in the Sun
When stooping to secure it   15
It wrinkled, and was gone —

Several of Nature's People
I know, and they know me —
I feel for them a transport
Of cordiality —   20

But never met this Fellow
Attended, or alone
Without a tighter breathing
And Zero at the Bone —

The dictionary provides a succinct, anatomical description of what a snake is, while Dickinson's poem suggests what a snake can mean. The definition offers facts; the poem offers an experience. The dictionary would probably allow someone who had never seen a snake to sketch one with reasonable accuracy. The poem also provides some vivid subjective descriptions — for example, the snake dividing the grass "as with a Comb" — yet it offers more than a picture of serpentine movements. The poem conveys the ambivalence many people have about snakes — the kind of feeling, for example, so evident on the faces of visitors viewing the snakes at a zoo. In the poem there is both a fascination with and a horror of what might be called snakehood; this combination of feelings has been coiled in most of us since Adam and Eve.

That "narrow Fellow" so cordially introduced by way of a riddle (the word *snake* is never used in the poem) is, by the final stanza, revealed as a snake in the grass. In between, Dickinson uses language expressively to convey her meaning. For instance, in the line "His notice sudden is," listen to the *s*-sound in each word and note how the verb *is* unexpectedly appears at the end, making the snake's hissing presence all the more "sudden." And anyone who has ever been surprised by a snake knows the "tighter breathing / And Zero at the Bone" that Dickinson evokes so successfully by the rhythm of her word choices and line breaks. Perhaps even more significant, Dickinson's poem allows those who have never encountered a snake to imagine such an experience.

A good deal more could be said about the numbing fear that undercuts the affection for nature at the beginning of this poem, but the point here is that imaginative literature gives us not so much the full, factual proportions of the world as some of its experiences and meanings. Instead of defining the world, literature encourages us to try it out in our imaginations.

THE VALUE OF LITERATURE

Mark Twain once shrewdly observed that a person who chooses not to read has no advantage over a person who is unable to read. In industrialized societies today, however, the question is not who reads, because nearly everyone can and does, but what is read. Why should anyone spend precious time with literature when there is so much reading material available that provides useful information about everything from the daily news to personal computers? Why should a literary artist's imagination compete for attention that could be spent on the firm realities that constitute everyday life? In fact, national best-seller lists much less often include collections of stories, poems, or plays than they do cookbooks and, not surprisingly, diet books. Although such fare may be filling, it doesn't stay with you. Most people have other appetites too.

Certainly one of the most important values of literature is that it nourishes our emotional lives. An effective literary work may seem to speak directly to us, especially if we are ripe for it. The inner life that good writers reveal in their characters often gives us glimpses of some portion of ourselves. We can be moved to laugh, cry, tremble, dream, ponder, shriek, or rage with a character by simply turning a page instead of turning our lives upside down. Although the experience itself is imagined, the emotion is real. That's why the final chapters of a good adventure novel can make a reader's heart race as much as a 100-yard dash or why the repressed love of Hester Prynne in *The Scarlet Letter* by Nathaniel Hawthorne is painful to a sympathetic reader. Human emotions speak a universal language regardless of when or where a work was written.

In addition to appealing to our emotions, literature broadens our perspectives on the world. Most of the people we meet are pretty much like ourselves, and what we can see of the world even in a lifetime is astonishingly limited. Literature allows us to move beyond the inevitable boundaries of our own lives and culture because it introduces us to people different from ourselves, places remote from our neighborhoods, and times other than our own. Reading makes us more aware of life's possibilities as well as its subtleties and ambiguities. Put simply, people who read literature experience more life and have a keener sense of a common human identity than those who do not. It is true, of course, that many people go through life without reading imaginative literature, but that is a loss rather than a gain. They may find themselves troubled by the same kinds of questions that reveal Daisy Buchanan's restless, vague discontentment in F. Scott Fitzgerald's *The Great Gatsby:* "What'll we do with ourselves this afternoon?" cried Daisy, "and the day after that, and the next thirty years?"

Sometimes students mistakenly associate literature more with school than with life. Accustomed to reading it in order to write a paper or pass an examination, students may perceive such reading as a chore instead of a pleasurable opportunity, something considerably less important than studying for the "practical" courses that prepare them for a career. The study of literature, however, is also practical, because it engages you in the kinds of problem solving important in a variety of fields, from philosophy to science and technology. The interpretation of literary texts requires you to deal with uncertainties, value judgments, and emotions; these are unavoidable aspects of life.

People who make the most significant contributions to their professions — whether in business, engineering, teaching, or some other area — tend to be challenged rather than threatened by multiple possibilities. Instead of retreating to the way things have always been done, they bring freshness and creativity to their work. F. Scott Fitzgerald once astutely described the "test of a first-rate intelligence" as "the ability to hold two opposed ideas in the mind at the same time, and still retain the ability to function." People with such intelligence know how to read situations, shape questions, interpret details, and evaluate competing points of view. Equipped with a healthy respect for facts, they also understand the value of pursuing hunches and exercising their imaginations. Reading literature encourages a suppleness of mind that is helpful in any discipline or work.

Once the requirements for your degree are completed, what ultimately matters are not the courses listed on your transcript but the sensibilities and habits of mind that you bring to your work, friends, family, and, indeed, the rest of your life. A healthy economy changes and grows with the times; people do too if they are prepared for more than simply filling a job description. The range and variety of life that literature affords can help you to interpret your own experiences and the world in which you live.

To discover the insights that literature reveals requires careful reading and sensitivity. One of the purposes of a college introduction to literature is to cultivate the analytic skills necessary for reading well. Class discussions often help establish a dialogue with a work that perhaps otherwise would not speak to you. Analytic skills can also be developed by writing about what you read. Writing is an effective means of clarifying your responses and ideas, because it requires you to account for the author's use of language as well as your own. This book is based on two premises: that reading literature is pleasurable, and that the more sensitively a work is read and understood by thinking, talking, or writing about it the more pleasurable the experience of it is.

Understanding its basic elements — such as point of view, symbol, theme, tone, irony, and so on — is a prerequisite to an informed appreciation of literature. This kind of understanding allows you to perceive more in a literary work in much the same way that a spectator at a tennis match sees more if he or she understands the rules and conventions of the game. But literature is not simply a spectator sport. The analytic skills that open up literature also have their uses when you watch a television program or film, and, more important, when you attempt to sort out the significance of the people, places, and events that constitute your own life. Literature enhances and sharpens your perceptions. What could be more lastingly practical as well as satisfying?

THE CHANGING LITERARY CANON

Perhaps the best reading is that which creates some kind of change in us: we see more clearly; we're alert to nuances; we ask questions that previously didn't occur to us. Henry Thoreau had that sort of reading in mind when he remarked in *Walden* that the books he valued most were those that caused him to date "a new era in his life from the reading." Readers are sometimes changed by literature, but it is also worth noting that the life of a literary work can also be affected by its readers. Melville's *Moby-Dick,* for example, was not valued as a classic until the 1920s, when critics rescued the novel from the obscurity of being cataloged in many libraries (including Yale's) not under fiction but under cetology, the study of whales. Indeed, many poets contemporary to Melville who were important and popular in the nineteenth century — William Cullen Bryant, Henry Wadsworth Longfellow, and James Russell Lowell, to name a few — are now mostly unread; their names appear more often on elementary schools built early in this century than in anthologies. Clearly, literary reputations and what is valued as great literature change over time and in the eyes of readers.

Such changes have accelerated during the past thirty years as the literary *canon* — those works considered by scholars, critics, and teachers to be the most important to read and study — has undergone a significant series of shifts. Writers who previously were overlooked, undervalued, neglected, or studiously ignored have been brought into focus in an effort to create a more diverse literary canon, one that recognizes the contributions of the many cultures that make up American society. Since the 1960s, for example, some critics have reassessed writings by women, who had been left out of the standard literary traditions dominated by male writers. Many more female writers are now read alongside the male writers who traditionally populated literary history. This kind of enlargement of the canon also resulted from another reform movement of the 1960s. The civil rights movement sensitized literary critics to the political, moral, and aesthetic necessity of rediscovering African-American literature, and more recently Asian and Hispanic writers are making their way into the canon. Moreover, on a broader scale the canon is being revised and enlarged to include the works of writers from parts of the world other than the West, a development that reflects the changing values, concerns, and complexities of the past several years, when literary landscapes have shifted as dramatically as the political boundaries of Eastern Europe and what was once the Soviet Union.

No semester's reading list — or anthology — can adequately or accurately echo all the new voices competing to be heard as part of the mainstream literary canon, but recent efforts to open up the canon attempt to sensitize readers to the voices of women, minorities, and writers from all over the world. This development has not occurred without its urgent advocates or passionate dissenters. It's no surprise that issues about race, gender, and class often get people off the fence and on their feet (these controversies are discussed further in Chapter 14, "Critical Strategies for Reading"). Although what we regard as literature — whether it's called great, classic, or canonical — continues to generate debate, there is no question that such controversy will continue to reflect readers' values as well as the writers they admire.

POETRY

1. Reading Poetry

READING POETRY RESPONSIVELY

Perhaps the best way to begin reading poetry responsively is not to allow yourself to be intimidated by it. Come to it, initially at least, the way you might listen to a song on the radio. You probably listen to a song several times before you hear it all, before you have a sense of how it works, where it's going, and how it gets there. You don't worry about analyzing a song when you listen to it, even though after repeated experiences with it you know and anticipate a favorite part and know, on some level, why it works for you. Give yourself a chance to respond to poetry. The hardest work has already been done by the poet, so all you need to do at the start is listen for the pleasure produced by the poet's arrangement of words.

Try reading the following poem aloud. Read it aloud before you read it silently. You may stumble once or twice, but you'll make sense of it if you pay attention to its punctuation and don't stop at the end of every line where there is no punctuation. The title gives you an initial sense of what the poem is about.

MARGE PIERCY (b. 1936)
The Secretary Chant   1973

My hips are a desk.
From my ears hang
chains of paper clips.
Rubber bands form my hair.
My breasts are wells of mimeograph ink.   5
My feet bear casters.
Buzz. Click.
My head is a badly organized file.

My head is a switchboard
where crossed lines crackle.   10
Press my fingers
and in my eyes appear
credit and debit.
Zing. Tinkle.
My navel is a reject button.   15
From my mouth issue canceled reams.
Swollen, heavy, rectangular
I am about to be delivered
of a baby
Xerox machine.   20
File me under W
because I wonce
was
a woman.

What is your response to this secretary's chant? The point is simple
enough — she feels dehumanized by her office functions — but the pleasures are manifold. Piercy makes the speaker's voice sound mechanical by
using short bursts of sound and by having her make repetitive, flat, matter-
of-fact statements ("My breasts . . . My feet . . . My head . . . My navel").
"The Secretary Chant" makes a serious statement about how such women
are reduced to functionaries. The point is made, however, with humor since
we are asked to visualize the misappropriation of the secretary's body — her
identity — as it is transformed into little more than a piece of office equipment, which seems to be breaking down in the final lines, when we learn
that she "wonce / was / a woman." Is there the slightest hint of something
subversive in this misspelling of "wonce"? Maybe so, but the humor is clear
enough, particularly if you try to make a drawing of what this dehumanized
secretary has become.

The next poem creates a different kind of mood. Think about the title,
"Those Winter Sundays," before you begin reading the poem. What associations do you have with winter Sundays? What emotions does the phrase
evoke in you?

ROBERT HAYDEN (1913–1980)
Those Winter Sundays   1962

Sundays too my father got up early
and put his clothes on in the blueblack cold,
then with cracked hands that ached
from labor in the weekday weather made
banked fires blaze. No one ever thanked him.   5

I'd wake and hear the cold splintering, breaking,
When the rooms were warm, he'd call,
and slowly I would rise and dress,
fearing the chronic angers of that house,

Speaking indifferently to him,   10
who had driven out the cold
and polished my good shoes as well.
What did I know, what did I know
of love's austere and lonely offices?

Did the poem match the feelings you have about winter Sundays? Either way your response can be useful in reading the poem. For most of us Sundays are days at home; they might be cozy and pleasant experiences or they might be dull and depressing. Whatever they are, Sundays are more evocative than, say, Tuesdays. Hayden uses that response to call forth a sense of missed opportunity in the poem. The person who reflects on those winter Sundays didn't know until much later how much he had to thank his father for "love's austere and lonely offices." This is a poem about a cold past and a present reverence for his father — elements brought together by the phrase "Winter Sundays." *His* father? You may have noticed that the poem doesn't use a masculine pronoun; hence the voice could be a woman's. Does the sex of the voice make any difference to your reading? Would it make any difference about which details are included or what language is used?

What is most important about your initial readings of a poem is that you ask questions. If you read responsively, you'll find yourself asking all kinds of questions about the words, descriptions, sounds, and structures of a poem. The specifics of those questions will be generated by the particular poem. We don't, for example, ask how humor is achieved in "Those Winter Sundays" because there is none, but it is worth asking what kind of tone is established by the description of "the chronic angers of that house." The remaining chapters in this part will help you to formulate and answer questions about a variety of specific elements in poetry, such as speaker, image, metaphor, symbol, rhyme, and rhythm. For the moment, however, read the following poem several times and note your response at different points in the poem. Then write down a half dozen questions or so about what produces your response to the poem. In order to answer questions it's best to know first what the questions are, and that's what the rest of this chapter is about.

JOHN UPDIKE (b. 1932)
Dog's Death   1969

She must have been kicked unseen or brushed by a car.
Too young to know much, she was beginning to learn
To use the newspapers spread on the kitchen floor
And to win, wetting there, the words, "Good dog! Good dog!"

We thought her shy malaise was a shot reaction.   5
The autopsy disclosed a rupture in her liver.
As we teased her with play, blood was filling her skin
And her heart was learning to lie down forever.

Monday morning, as the children were noisily fed
And sent to school, she crawled beneath the youngest's bed.   10
We found her twisted and limp but still alive.
In the car to the vet's, on my lap, she tried

To bite my hand and died. I stroked her warm fur
And my wife called in a voice imperious with tears.
Though surrounded by love that would have upheld her,   15
Nevertheless she sank and, stiffening, disappeared.

Back home, we found that in the night her frame,
Drawing near to dissolution, had endured the shame
Of diarrhoea and had dragged across the floor
To a newspaper carelessly left there. *Good dog.*   20

Here's a simple question to get started with your own questions: what
would its effect have been if Updike had titled the poem "Good Dog" instead
of "Dog's Death"?

THE PLEASURE OF WORDS

The impulse to create and appreciate poetry is as basic to human experience as language itself. Although no one can point to the precise origins
of poetry, it is one of the most ancient of the arts, because it has existed
ever since human beings discovered pleasure in language. The tribal ceremonies of peoples without written language suggest evidence that the earliest
primitive cultures incorporated rhythmic patterns of words into their rituals.
These chants, very likely accompanied by the music of a simple beat and
the dance of a measured step, expressed what people regarded as significant
and memorable in their lives. They echoed the concerns of the chanters and
the listeners by chronicling acts of bravery, fearsome foes, natural disasters,
mysterious events, births, deaths, and whatever else brought people pain or

pleasure, bewilderment or revelation. Later cultures, such as the ancient Greeks, made poetry an integral part of religion.

Thus, from its very beginnings, poetry has been associated with what has mattered most to people. These concerns — whether natural or super-natural — can, of course, be expressed without vivid images, rhythmic patterns, and pleasing sounds, but human beings have always sensed a magic in words that goes beyond rational, logical understanding. Poetry is not simply a method of communication; it is a unique kind of experience in itself.

What is special about poetry? What makes it valuable? Why should we read it? How is reading it different from reading prose? To begin with, poetry pervades our world in a variety of forms, ranging from advertising jingles to song lyrics. These may seem to be a long way from the chants heard around a primitive camp fire, but they serve some of the same purposes. Like poems printed in a magazine or book, primitive chants, catchy jingles, and popular songs attempt to stir the imagination through the carefully measured use of words.

Although reading poetry usually makes more demands than does the kind of reading used to skim a magazine or newspaper, the appreciation of poetry comes naturally enough to anyone who enjoys playing with words. Play is an important element of poetry. Consider, for example, how the following words appeal to the children who gleefully chant them in play-grounds.

> I scream, you scream
> We all scream
> For ice cream.

These lines are an exuberant evocation of the joy of ice cream. Indeed, chanting the words turns out to be as pleasurable as eating ice cream. In poetry, the expression of the idea is as important as the idea expressed.

But is "I scream . . ." poetry? Some poets and literary critics would say that it certainly is one kind of poem, because the children who chant it experience some of the pleasures of poetry in its measured beat and repeated sounds. However, other poets and critics would define poetry more narrowly and insist, for a variety of reasons (some of which are included among the definitions in Chapter 13), that this isn't true poetry but merely ***doggerel,*** a term used for lines whose subject matter is trite and whose rhythm and sounds are monotonously heavy-handed.

Although probably no one would argue that "I scream . . ." is a great poem, it does contain some poetic elements that appeal, at the very least, to children. Does that make it poetry? The answer depends on one's definition, but poetry has a way of breaking loose from definitions. Because there are nearly as many definitions of poetry as there are poets, Edwin Arlington Robinson's succinct observations are useful: "poetry has two outstanding characteristics. One is that it is undefinable. The other is that it is eventually unmistakable."

This comment places more emphasis on how a poem affects a reader than on how a poem is defined. By characterizing poetry as "undefinable," Robinson acknowledges that it can include many different purposes, subjects, emotions, styles, and forms. What effect does the following poem have on you?

WILLIAM HATHAWAY (b. 1944)
Oh, Oh   1982

My girl and I amble a country lane,
moo cows chomping daisies, our own
sweet saliva green with grass stems.
"Look, look," she says at the crossing,
"the choo-choo's light is on." And sure   5
enough, right smack dab in the middle
of maple dappled summer sunlight
is the lit headlight — so funny.
An arm waves to us from the black window.
We wave gaily to the arm. "When I hear   10
trains at night I dream of being president,"
I say dreamily. "And me first lady," she
says loyally. So when the last boxcars,
named after wonderful, faraway places,
and the caboose chuckle by we look   15
eagerly to the road ahead. And there,
poised and growling, are fifty Hell's Angels.

Hathaway's poem serves as a convenient reminder that poetry can be full of surprises. Even on a first reading there is no mistaking the emotional reversal created by the last few words of this poem. With the exception of the final line, the poem's language conjures up an idyllic picture of a young couple taking a pleasant walk down a country lane. Contented as "moo cows," they taste the sweetness of the grass, hear peaceful country sounds, and are dazzled by "dappled summer sunlight." Their future together seems to be all optimism as they anticipate "wonderful, faraway places" and the "road ahead." Full of confidence, this couple, like the reader, is unprepared for the shock to come. When we see those "fifty Hell's Angels," we are confronted with something like a bucket of cold water in the face.

But even though our expectations are abruptly and powerfully reversed, we are finally invited to view the entire episode from a safe distance — the distance provided by the delightful humor in this poem. After all, how seriously can we take a poem that is titled "Oh, Oh"? The poet has his way with us, but we are brought in on the joke too. The terror takes on comic proportions as the innocent couple is confronted by no fewer than *fifty* Hell's Angels. This is the kind of raucous overkill that informs a short animated film produced some years ago titled *Bambi Meets Godzilla:* you might not have seen it, but you know how it ends. The poem's good humor comes through when we realize how pathetically inadequate the response of "Oh, Oh" is to the circumstances.

As you can see, reading a description of what happens in a poem is not the same as experiencing a poem. The exuberance of "I scream . . ." and the surprise of Hathaway's "Oh, Oh" are in the hearing or reading rather than in the retelling. A *paraphrase* is a prose restatement of the central ideas of a poem in your own language. Consider the difference between the following poem and the paraphrase that follows it. What is missing from the paraphrase?

ROBERT FRANCIS (1901–1987)
Catch   1950

Two boys uncoached are tossing a poem together,
Overhand, underhand, backhand, sleight of hand, every hand,
Teasing with attitudes, latitudes, interludes, altitudes,
High, make him fly off the ground for it, low, make him stoop,
Make him scoop it up, make him as-almost-as-possible miss it,   5
Fast, let him sting from it, now, now fool him slowly,
Anything, everything tricky, risky, nonchalant,
Anything under the sun to outwit the prosy,
Over the tree and the long sweet cadence down,
Over his head, make him scramble to pick up the meaning,   10
And now, like a posy, a pretty one plump in his hands.

Paraphrase: A poet's relationship to a reader is similar to a game of catch. The poem, like a ball, should be pitched in a variety of ways to challenge and create interest. Boredom and predictability must be avoided if the game is to be engaging and satisfying.

A paraphrase can help us achieve a clearer understanding of a poem, but, unlike a poem, it misses all the sport and fun. It is the poem that "outwit[s] the prosy," because the poem serves as an example of what it suggests poetry should be. Moreover, the two players — the poet and the reader — are "uncoached." They know how the game is played, but their expectations do not preclude spontaneity and creativity or their ability to surprise and be surprised. The solid pleasure of the workout — of reading poetry — is the satisfaction derived from exercising your imagination and intellect.

That pleasure is worth emphasizing. Poetry uses language to move and delight even when it includes a cast of fifty Hell's Angels. The pleasure is in having the poem work its spell on us. For that to happen, it is best to relax and enjoy poetry rather than worrying about definitions of it. Pay attention to what the poet throws you. We read poems for emotional and intellectual discovery — to feel and experience something about the world and ourselves. The ideas in poetry — what can be paraphrased in prose — are important, but the real value of a poem consists in the words that work their magic by allowing us to feel, see, and be more than we were before. Perhaps the best way to approach a poem is similar to what Francis's "Catch" implies: expect to be surprised; stay on your toes; and concentrate on the delivery.

Write a paraphrase of this next poem. How does your prose statement differ from the effects produced by the language in the poem? Which descriptions seem particularly vivid?

X. J. KENNEDY (b. 1929)
First Confession   1961

Blood thudded in my ears. I scuffed,
    Steps stubborn, to the telltale booth
Beyond whose curtained portal coughed
    The robed repositor of truth.

The slat shot back. The universe   5
    Bowed down his cratered dome to hear
Enumerated my each curse,
    The sip snitched from my old man's beer,

My sloth pride envy lechery,
    The dime held back from Peter's Pence°   *Catholic offering*   10
With which I'd bribed my girl to pee
    That I might spy her instruments.

Hovering scale-pans when I'd done
    Settled their balance slow as silt
While in the restless dark I burned   15
    Bright as a brimstone in my guilt

Until as one feeds birds he doled
    Seven Our Fathers and a Hail
Which I to double-scrub my soul
    Intoned twice at the altar rail   20

Where Sunday in seraphic light
    I knelt, as full of grace as most,
And stuck my tongue out at the priest:
    A fresh roost for the Holy Ghost.

Innocence, piety, anxiety, humor, and irreverence tumble out of this confession booth, along with the boy's conscience and not entirely repentant attitude. Kennedy's description of the boy's first confession reveals the boy as well as redeems him.

Poets often remind us that beauty can be found in unexpected places. What is it that Elizabeth Bishop finds so beautiful about the "battered" fish she describes in the following poem?

ELIZABETH BISHOP (1911–1979)
The Fish   1946

I caught a tremendous fish
and held him beside the boat
half out of water, with my hook
fast in a corner of his mouth.
He didn't fight.   5
He hadn't fought at all.
He hung a grunting weight,
battered and venerable
and homely. Here and there
his brown skin hung in strips   10
like ancient wall-paper,
and its pattern of darker brown
was like wall-paper:
shapes like full-blown roses
stained and lost through age.   15
He was speckled with barnacles,
fine rosettes of lime,
and infested
with tiny white sea-lice,
and underneath two or three   20
rags of green weed hung down.
While his gills were breathing in
the terrible oxygen
— the frightening gills,
fresh and crisp with blood,   25
that can cut so badly —
I thought of the coarse white flesh
packed in like feathers,
the big bones and the little bones,
the dramatic reds and blacks   30
of his shiny entrails,
and the pink swim-bladder
like a big peony.
I looked into his eyes

which were far larger than mine   35
but shallower, and yellowed,
the irises backed and packed
with tarnished tinfoil
seen through the lenses
of old scratched isinglass.   40
They shifted a little, but not
to return my stare.
— It was more like the tipping
of an object toward the light.
I admired his sullen face,   45
the mechanism of his jaw,
and then I saw
that from his lower lip
— if you could call it a lip —
grim, wet, and weapon-like,   50
hung five old pieces of fish-line,
or four and a wire leader
with the swivel still attached,
with all their five big hooks
grown firmly in his mouth.   55
A green line, frayed at the end
where he broke it, two heavier lines,
and a fine black thread
still crimped from the strain and snap
when it broke and he got away.   60
Like medals with their ribbons
frayed and wavering,
a five-haired beard of wisdom
trailing from his aching jaw.
I stared and stared   65
and victory filled up
the little rented boat,
from the pool of bilge
where oil had spread a rainbow
around the rusted engine   70
to the bailer rusted orange,
the sun-cracked thwarts,
the oarlocks on their strings,
the gunnels — until everything
was rainbow, rainbow, rainbow!   75
And I let the fish go.

Considerations for Critical Thinking and Writing

1. Which lines in this poem provide especially vivid details of the fish? What makes these descriptions effective?
2. How is the fish characterized? Is it simply a weak victim because it "didn't fight"?

3. Comment on lines 65–76. In what sense has "victory filled up" the boat, given that the speaker finally lets the fish go?

The speaker in Bishop's "The Fish" ends on a triumphantly joyful note. The *speaker* is the voice used by the author in the poem; like the narrator in a work of fiction, the speaker is often a created identity rather than the author's actual self. The two should not automatically be equated. Contrast the attitude toward life of the speaker in "The Fish" with that of the speaker in the following poem.

PHILIP LARKIN (1922–1985)
A Study of Reading Habits   1964

When getting my nose in a book
Cured most things short of school,
It was worth ruining my eyes
To know I could still keep cool,
And deal out the old right hook   5
To dirty dogs twice my size.

Later, with inch-thick specs,
Evil was just my lark:
Me and my cloak and fangs
Had ripping times in the dark.   10
The women I clubbed with sex!
I broke them up like meringues.

Don't read much now: the dude
Who lets the girl down before
The hero arrives, the chap   15
Who's yellow and keeps the store,
Seem far too familiar. Get stewed:
Books are a load of crap.

What the speaker sees and describes in "The Fish" is close if not identical to Bishop's own vision and voice. The joyful response to the fish is clearly shared by the speaker and the poet, between whom there is little or no distance. In "A Study of Reading Habits," however, Larkin distances himself from a speaker whose sensibilities he does not wholly share. The poet — and many readers — might identify with the reading habits described by the speaker in the first twelve lines, but Larkin uses the last six lines to criticize the speaker's attitude toward life as well as reading. The speaker recalls in lines 1–6 how as a schoolboy he identified with the hero, whose virtuous strength always triumphed over "dirty dogs," and in lines 7–12 he recounts how his schoolboy fantasies were transformed by adolescence into a fascination with violence and sex. This description of early reading habits is pleasantly amusing, because most readers of popular fiction will probably recall having moved through similar stages, but at the end of the poem the speaker provides more information about himself than he intends to.

As an adult the speaker has lost interest in reading, because it is no longer an escape from his own disappointed life. Instead of identifying with heroes or villains, he finds himself identifying with minor characters who are irresponsible and cowardly. Reading is now a reminder of his failures, so he turns to alcohol. His solution, to "Get stewed," because "Books are a load of crap," is obviously self-destructive. The speaker is ultimately exposed by Larkin as someone who never grew beyond fantasies. Getting drunk is consistent with the speaker's immature reading habits. Unlike the speaker, the poet understands that life is often distorted by escapist fantasies, whether through a steady diet of popular fiction or through alcohol. The speaker in this poem, then, is not Larkin but a created identity whose voice is filled with disillusionment and delusion.

The problem with Larkin's speaker is that he misreads books as well as his own life. Reading means nothing to him unless it serves as an escape from himself. It is not surprising that Larkin has him read fiction rather than poetry, because poetry places an especially heavy emphasis upon language. Fiction, indeed any kind of writing, including essays and drama, relies upon carefully chosen and arranged words, but poetry does so to an even greater extent. Notice, for example, how Larkin's deft use of trite expressions and slang characterizes the speaker so that his language reveals nearly as much about his dreary life as what he says. Larkin's speaker would have no use for poetry.

What is "unmistakable" in poetry (to use Robinson's term again) is its intense, concentrated use of language — its emphasis on individual words to convey meanings, experiences, emotions, and effects. Poets never simply process words; they savor them. Words in poems frequently create their own tastes, textures, scents, sounds, and shapes. They often seem more sensuous than ordinary language, and readers usually sense that a word has been hefted before making its way into a poem. Although poems are crafted differently from the ways a painting, sculpture, or musical composition is created, in each form of art the creator delights in the medium. Poetry is carefully orchestrated so that the words work together as elements in a structure to sustain close, repeated readings. The words are chosen to interact with one another in order to create the maximum desired effect, whether the purpose is to capture a mood or feeling, create a vivid experience, express a point of view, narrate a story, or portray a character.

Here is a poem that looks quite different from most *verse,* a term used for lines composed in a measured rhythmical pattern, which are often, but not necessarily, rhymed.

ROBERT MORGAN (b. 1944)
Mountain Graveyard

for the author of "Slow Owls"

Spore Prose

stone	notes
slate	tales
sacred	cedars
heart	earth
asleep	please
hated	death

Though unconventional in its appearance, this is unmistakably poetry because of its concentrated use of language. The poem demonstrates how serious play with words can lead to some remarkable discoveries. At first glance "Mountain Graveyard" may seem intimidating. What, after all, does this list of words add up to? How is it in any sense a poetic use of language? But if the words are examined closely, it is not difficult to see how they work. The wordplay here is literally in the form of a game. Morgan uses a series of *anagrams* (words made from the letters of other words, such as *read* and *dare*) to evoke feelings about death. "Mountain Graveyard" is one of several poems that Morgan has called "Spore Prose" (another anagram) because he finds in individual words the seeds of poetry. He wrote the poem in honor of the fiftieth birthday of another poet, Jonathan Williams, the author of "Slow Owls," whose title is also an anagram.

The title, "Mountain Graveyard," indicates the poem's setting, which is also the context in which the individual words in the poem interact to provide a larger meaning. Morgan's discovery of the words on the stones of a graveyard is more than just clever. The observations he makes among the silent graves go beyond the curious pleasure a reader experiences in finding the words *sacred cedars,* referring to evergreens common in cemeteries, to consist of the same letters. The surprise and delight of realizing the connection between heart and earth is tempered by the more sober recognition that everyone's story ultimately ends in the ground. The hope that the dead are merely asleep is expressed with a plea that is answered grimly by a hatred of death's finality.

Little is told in this poem. There is no way of knowing who is buried or who is looking at the graves, but the emotions of sadness, hope, and pain are unmistakable — and are conveyed in fewer than half the words of this sentence. Morgan takes words that initially appear to be a dead, prosaic list and energizes their meanings through imaginative juxtapositions.

The following poem also involves a startling discovery about words.

With the peculiar title "l(a," the poem cannot be read aloud, so there is no sound, but is there sense, a ***theme***, a central idea or meaning, in the poem?

e. e. cummings (1894–1962)
l(a   1958

l(a

le
af
fa

ll

s)
one
l

iness

Considerations for Critical Thinking and Writing

1. Discuss the connection between what appears inside and outside the parentheses in this poem.
2. What does cummings draw attention to by breaking up the words? How do this strategy and the poem's overall shape contribute to its theme?
3. Which seems more important in this poem — what is expressed, or the way it is expressed?

Although "Mountain Graveyard" and "l(a" do not resemble the kind of verse that readers might recognize immediately as poetry on a page, both are actually a very common type of poem, called the *lyric,* usually a brief poem that expresses the personal emotions and thoughts of a single speaker. Lyrics are often written in the first person but sometimes — as in "Spore Prose" and "l(a" — no speaker is specified. Lyrics present a subjective mood, emotion, or idea. Very often they are about love or death, but almost any subject or experience that evokes some intense emotional response can be found in lyrics. In addition to brevity and emotional intensity, lyrics are also frequently characterized by their musical qualities. The word *lyric* derives from the Greek word *lyre,* meaning a musical instrument that originally accompanied the singing of a lyric. Lyric poems can be organized in a variety of ways, such as the sonnet, elegy, and ode (see Chapter 8), but it is enough to point out here that lyrics are an extremely popular kind of poetry with writers and readers.

The following anonymous lyric was found in a sixteenth-century manuscript.

ANONYMOUS
Western Wind

c. 1500

Western wind, when wilt thou blow,
The small rain down can rain?
Christ, if my love were in my arms,
And I in my bed again!

This speaker's intense longing for his lover is characteristic of lyric poetry. He impatiently addresses the western wind that brings spring to England and could make it possible for him to be reunited with the woman he loves. We do not know the details of these lovers' lives, because this poem focuses on the speaker's emotion. We do not learn why the lovers are apart or if they will be together again. We don't even know if the speaker is a man. But those issues are not really important. The poetry gives us a feeling rather than a story.

A poem that tells a story is called a ***narrative poem***. Narrative poetry may be short or very long. An ***epic***, for example, is a long narrative poem on a serious subject chronicling heroic deeds and important events. Among the most famous epics are Homer's *Iliad* and *Odyssey*, the Old English *Beowulf*, Dante's *Divine Comedy*, and John Milton's *Paradise Lost*. More typically, however, narrative poems are considerably shorter, such as the following poem, which tells the story of a child's memory of her father.

REGINA BARRECA (b. 1957)
Nighttime Fires

1986

When I was five in Louisville
we drove to see nighttime fires. Piled seven of us,
all pajamas and running noses, into the Olds,
drove fast toward smoke. It was after my father
lost his job, so not getting up in the morning   5
gave him time: awake past midnight, he read old newspapers
with no news, tried crosswords until he split the pencil
between his teeth, mad. When he heard
the wolf whine of the siren, he woke my mother,
and she pushed and shoved   10
us all into waking. Once roused we longed for burnt wood
and a smell of flames high into the pines. My old man liked
driving to rich neighborhoods best, swearing in a good mood
as he followed fire engines that snaked like dragons
and split the silent streets. It was festival, carnival.   15

If there were a Cadillac or any car

in a curved driveway, my father smiled a smile
from a secret, brittle heart.
His face lit up in the heat given off by destruction
like something was being made, or was being set right.   20
I bent my head back to see where sparks
ate up the sky. My father who never held us
would take my hand and point to falling cinders that
covered the ground like snow, or, excited, show us
the swollen collapse of a staircase. My mother   25
watched my father, not the house. She was happy
only when we were ready to go, when it was finally over
and nothing else could burn.
Driving home, she would sleep in the front seat
as we huddled behind. I could see his quiet face in the   30
rearview mirror, eyes like hallways filled with smoke.

This narrative poem could have been a short story if the poet had
wanted to say more about the "brittle heart" of this unemployed man whose
daughter so vividly remembers the desperate pleasure he took in watching
fire consume other people's property. Indeed, a reading of William Faulkner's famous short story "Barn Burning" suggests how such a character can
be further developed and how his child responds to him. The similarities
between Faulkner's angry character and the poem's father, whose "eyes [are]
like hallways filled with smoke," are coincidental, but the characters' sense
of "something . . . being set right" by flames is worth comparing. Although
we do not know everything about this man and his family, we have a much
firmer sense of their story than we do of the story of the couple in "Western
Wind."

Although narrative poetry is still written, short stories and novels have
largely replaced the long narrative poem. Lyric poems tend to be the predominant type of poetry today. Regardless of whether a poem is a narrative
or a lyric, however, the strategies for reading it are somewhat different from
those for reading prose. Try these suggestions for approaching poetry.

SUGGESTIONS FOR APPROACHING POETRY

1. Assume that it will be necessary to read a poem more than once.
   Give yourself a chance to become familiar with what the poem has
   to offer. Like a piece of music, a poem becomes more pleasurable
   with each encounter.
2. Do pay attention to the title; it will often provide a helpful context
   for the poem and serve as an introduction to it. Larkin's "A Study
   of Reading Habits" is precisely what its title describes.
3. As you read the poem for the first time, avoid becoming entangled

in words or lines that you don't understand. Instead, give yourself a chance to take in the entire poem before attempting to resolve problems encountered along the way.

4. On a second reading, identify any words or passages that you don't understand. Look up words you don't know; these might include names, places, historical and mythical references, or anything else that is unfamiliar to you.

5. Read the poem aloud (or perhaps have a friend read it to you). You'll probably discover that some puzzling passages suddenly fall into place when you hear them. You'll find that nothing helps, though, if the poem is read in an artificial, exaggerated manner. Read in as natural a voice as possible, with slight pauses at line breaks. Silent reading is preferable to imposing a te-tumpty-te-tum reading on a good poem.

6. Read the punctuation. Poems use punctuation marks — in addition to the space on the page — as signals for readers. Be especially careful not to assume that the end of a line marks the end of a sentence, unless it is concluded by punctuation. Consider, for example, the opening lines of Hathaway's "Oh, Oh."

> My girl and I amble a country lane,
> moo cows chomping daisies, our own
> sweet saliva green with grass stems.

Line 2 makes little or no sense if a reader stops after "own." Keeping track of the subjects and verbs will help you find your way among the sentences.

7. Paraphrase the poem to determine whether you understand what happens in it. As you work through each line of the poem, a paraphrase will help you to see which words or passages need further attention.

8. Try to get a sense of who is speaking and what the setting or situation is. Don't assume that the speaker is the author; often it is a created character.

9. Assume that each element in the poem has a purpose. Try to explain how the elements of the poem work together.

10. Be generous. Be willing to entertain perspectives, values, experiences, and subjects that you might not agree with or approve. Even if you loathe baseball, you should be able to comprehend its imaginative use in Francis's "Catch."

11. Try developing a coherent approach to the poem that helps you to shape a discussion of the text. See Chapter 14, Critical Strategies for Reading (p. 1080), to review formalist, biographical, historical, psychological, feminist, and other possible critical approaches.

12. Don't expect to produce a definitive reading. Many poems do not

resolve all the ideas, issues, or tensions in them, and so it is not always possible to drive their meaning into an absolute corner. Your reading will explore rather than define the poem. Poems are not trophies to be stuffed and mounted. They're usually more elusive. And don't be afraid that a close reading will damage the poem. Poems aren't hurt when we analyze them; instead, they come alive as we experience them and put into words what we discover through them.

A list of more specific questions employing the literary terms and concepts discussed in the following chapters begins on page 342. That list, like the suggestions just made, raises issues and questions that can help you to read just about any poem closely. These strategies should be a useful means for getting inside poems to understand how they work. Furthermore, because reading poetry inevitably increases sensitivity to language, you're likely to find yourself a better reader of words in any form — whether in a novel, a newspaper editorial, an advertisement, a political speech, or a conversation — after having studied poetry. In short, many of the reading skills that make poetry accessible also open up the world you inhabit.

You'll probably find some poems amusing or sad, some fierce or tender, and some fascinating or dull. You may find, too, some poems that will get inside you. Their kinds of insights — the poet's and yours — are what Emily Dickinson had in mind when she defined poetry this way: "If I read a book and it makes my whole body so cold no fire can ever warm me, I know that it is poetry. If I feel physically as if the top of my head were taken off, I know that it is poetry." Dickinson's response may be more intense than most — poetry was, after all, at the center of her life — but you too might find yourself moved by poems in unexpected ways. In any case, as Edwin Arlington Robinson knew, poetry is, to an alert and sensitive reader, "eventually unmistakable."

POETRY IN POPULAR FORMS

Before you try out these strategies for reading on a few more poems, it is worth acknowledging that the verse which enjoys the widest readership appears not in collections, magazines, or even anthologies for students, but in greeting cards. A significant amount of the personal daily mail delivered in the United States consists of greeting cards. That represents millions of lines of verse going by us on the street and in planes over our heads. These verses share some similarities with the poetry included in this anthology, but there are also important differences that indicate the need for reading serious poetry closely rather than casually.

The popularity of greeting cards is easy to explain: just as many of us have neither the time nor the talent to make gifts for birthdays, weddings, anniversaries, graduations, Valentine's Day, Mother's Day, and other holidays, we are unlikely to write personal messages when cards conveniently say them for us. Though impersonal, cards are efficient and convey an important message no matter what the occasion for them: I care. These greetings are rarely serious poetry; they are not written to be. Nevertheless, they demonstrate the impulse in our culture to generate and receive poetry.

In a handbook for greeting-card free-lancers, a writer and past editor of such verse began with this advice:

> Once you determine what you want to say — and in this regard it is best to stick to one basic idea — you must choose your words to do several things at the same time:
>
> 1. Your idea must be expressed as a complete idea; it must have a beginning, a middle, and an end.
> 2. There must be coherence in your verse. Every line must be linked logically and smoothly with its neighbors.
> 3. Your expressions . . . must be conversational. High-flown language rarely comes off successfully in greeting card writing.
> 4. You must write with emphasis — and something else: enthusiasm. It's necessary to create interest in that all-important first line. From that point on, writing your verse is a matter of developing your idea and bringing it to a peak of emphasis in the last line. Occasionally you will find that you have shot your wad too early in the verse, and whatever you say after that point sounds like an afterthought.
> 5. You must do all of the above and at the same time make everything come out right in the meter-and-rhyme department.[1]

This advice is followed by a list of approximately fifty of the most frequently used rhyme sounds accompanied by rhyming words, such as *love, of, above* for the sound *uv.* The point of these prescriptions is that the verse must be written so that it is immediately accessible — consumable — by both the buyer and the recipient. Writers of these cards are expected to avoid any complexity.

Compare the following greeting-card verse with the poem that comes after it. "Magic of Love," by Helen Farries, has been a longtime favorite in a major greeting-card company's "wedding line"; with different endings it has been used also in valentines and friendship cards.

[1]Chris Fitzgerald, "Conventional Verse: The Sentimental Favorite," *The Greeting Card Writer's Handbook,* ed. H. Joseph Chadwick (Cincinnati: Writer's Digest, 1975): 13, 17.

HELEN FARRIES
Magic of Love

date unknown

There's a wonderful gift that can give you a lift,
It's a blessing from heaven above!
It can comfort and bless, it can bring happiness —
It's the wonderful MAGIC OF LOVE!

Like a star in the night, it can keep your faith bright,   5
Like the sun, it can warm your hearts, too —
It's a gift you can give every day that you live,
And when given, it comes back to you!

When love lights the way, there is joy in the day
And all troubles are lighter to bear,   10
Love is gentle and kind, and through love you will find
There's an answer to your every prayer!

May it never depart from your two loving hearts,
May you treasure this gift from above —
You will find if you do, all your dreams will come true,   15
In the wonderful MAGIC OF LOVE!

JOHN FREDERICK NIMS (b. 1913)
Love Poem

1947

My clumsiest dear, whose hands shipwreck vases,
At whose quick touch all glasses chip and ring,
Whose palms are bulls in china, burs in linen,
And have no cunning with any soft thing

Except all ill-at-ease fidgeting people: 5
The refugee uncertain at the door
You make at home; deftly you steady
The drunk clambering on his undulant floor.

Unpredictable dear, the taxi drivers' terror,
Shrinking from far headlights pale as a dime   10
Yet leaping before red apoplectic streetcars —
Misfit in any space. And never on time.

A wrench in clocks and the solar system. Only
With words and people and love you move at ease.
In traffic of wit expertly maneuver   15
And keep us, all devotion, at your knees.

Forgetting your coffee spreading on our flannel,
Your lipstick grinning on our coat,

So gaily in love's unbreakable heaven
Our souls on glory of spilt bourbon float.

20

Be with me, darling, early and late. Smash glasses —
I will study wry music for your sake.
For should your hands drop white and empty
All the toys of the world would break.

Considerations for Critical Thinking and Writing

1. Read these two works aloud. Characterize their differences.
2. To what extent does the advice to would-be greeting-card writers apply to each work?
3. Compare the two speakers. Which do you find more appealing? Why?
4. How does Nims's description of love differ from Farries's?

In contrast to poetry, which transfigures and expresses an emotion or experience through an original use of language, the verse in "Magic of Love" relies upon *clichés,* ideas or expressions that have become tired and trite from overuse, such as describing love as "a blessing from heaven above." Clichés anesthetize readers instead of alerting them to the possibility of fresh perceptions. They are used to draw out *stock responses,* predictable, conventional reactions to language, characters, symbols, or situations; God, heaven, the flag, motherhood, hearts, puppies, and peace are some often-used objects of stock responses. Advertisers manufacture careers from this sort of business.

Clichés and stock responses are two of the major ingredients of sentimentality in literature. *Sentimentality* exploits the reader by inducing emotional responses that exceed what the situation warrants. This pejorative term should not be confused with *sentiment,* which is synonymous with *emotion* or *feeling.* Sentimentality cons readers into falling for the mass murderer who is devoted to stray cats, and it requires that we not think twice about what we're feeling, because those tears shed for the little old lady, the rage aimed at the vicious enemy soldier, and the longing for the simple virtues of poverty might disappear under the slightest scrutiny. The experience of sentimentality is not unlike biting into a swirl of cotton candy; it's momentarily sweet but wholly insubstantial.

Clichés, stock responses, and sentimentality are generally the hallmarks of weak writing. Poetry — the kind that is unmistakable — achieves freshness, vitality, and genuine emotion that sharpen our perceptions of life.

Although the most widely read verse is found in greeting cards, the most widely *heard* poetry appears in song lyrics. Not all songs are poetic, but a good many share the same effects and qualities as poems. Consider these lyrics by Tracy Chapman.

TRACY CHAPMAN (b. 1964)

Fast Car

1987

You got a fast car
I want a ticket to anywhere
Maybe we make a deal
Maybe together we can get somewhere
Anyplace is better   5
Starting from zero got nothing to lose
Maybe we'll make something
But me myself I got nothing to prove

You got a fast car
And I got a plan to get us out of here   10
I been working at the convenience store
Managed to save just a little bit of money
We won't have to drive too far
Just 'cross the border and into the city
You and I can both get jobs   15
And finally see what it means to be living

You see my old man's got a problem
He live with the bottle that's the way it is
He says his body's too old for working
I say his body's too young to look like his   20
My mama went off and left him
She wanted more from life than he could give
I said somebody's got to take care of him
So I quit school and that's what I did

You got a fast car   25
But is it fast enough so we can fly away
We gotta make a decision
We leave tonight or live and die this way

I remember we were driving driving in your car
The speed so fast I felt like I was drunk   30
City lights lay out before us
And your arm felt nice wrapped 'round my shoulder
And I had a feeling that I belonged
And I had feeling I could be someone, be someone, be someone

You got a fast car   35
And we go cruising to entertain ourselves
You still ain't got a job
And I work in a market as a checkout girl
I know things will get better
You'll find work and I'll get promoted   40
We'll move out of the shelter
Buy a big house and live in the suburbs

You got a fast car
And I got a job that pays all our bills
You stay out drinking late at the bar   45
See more of your friends than you do of your kids
I'd always hoped for better
Thought maybe together you and me would find it
I got no plans I ain't going nowhere
So take your fast car and keep on driving   50

You got a fast car
But is it fast enough so you can fly away
You gotta make a decision
You leave tonight or live and die this way

Considerations for Critical Thinking and Writing

1. Characterize the speaker in this song lyric. What sort of life does she live? How does she want to change it?
2. What is the effect of the repetition of "You got a fast car"? Describe the man in the song. What does his "fast car" come to represent to the speaker?
3. Why isn't punctuation necessary to read these lyrics?
4. Explain whether you think this song can be accurately called a narrative poem.

PERSPECTIVE

ROBERT FRANCIS (1901–1987)
On "Hard" Poetry   1965

When Robert Frost said he liked poems hard he could scarcely have meant he liked them difficult. If he had meant difficult he would have said he didn't like them easy. What he said was that he didn't like them soft.

Poems can be soft in several ways. They can be soft in form (invertebrate). They can be soft in thought and feeling (sentimental). They can be soft with excess verbiage. Frost used to advise one to squeeze the water out of a poem. He liked poems dry. What is dry tends to be hard, and what is hard is always dry, except perhaps on the outside.

Yet though hardness here does not mean difficulty, some difficulty naturally goes with hardness. A hard poem may not be hard to read but is hard to write. Not too hard, preferably. Not so hard to write that there is no flow in the writer. But hard enough for the growing poem to meet with some healthy resistance. Frost often found this healthy resistance in a tight rhyme scheme and strict meter. There are other ways of getting good resistance, of course.

And in the reader too, a hard poem will bring some difficulty. Preferably not too much. Not enough difficulty to completely baffle him. Ideally a hard poem should not be too hard to make sense of, but hard to exhaust its meaning and its beauty.

"What I care about is the hardness of the poems. I don't like them soft, I want them to be little pebbles, but placed where they won't dislodge easily. And I'd like them to be little pebbles of precious stone — precious, or semiprecious" (interview with John Ciardi, *Saturday Review,* March 21, 1959).

Here is hard prose talking about hard poetry. Frost was never shrewder or more illuminating. Here, as well as in anything else he ever said, is his flavor.

What contemporary of his can you imagine saying this or anything like it?

In 1843 Emerson jotted in his journal: "Hard clouds and hard expressions, and hard manners, I love."

From *The Satirical Rogue on Poetry*

Considerations for Critical Thinking and Writing

1. What is the distinction between "hard" and "soft" poetry?
2. Given Francis's brief essay and his poem "Catch" (p. 17), write a review of Helen Farries's "Magic of Love" (p. 30) as you think Francis would.
3. Explain whether you would characterize Chapman's "Fast Car" as hard or soft.

POEMS FOR FURTHER STUDY

ALBERTO RÍOS (b. 1952)
Seniors   1985

William cut a hole in his Levi's pocket
so he could flop himself out in class
behind the girls so the other guys
could see and shit what guts we all said.
All Konga wanted to do over and over   5
was the rubber band trick, but he showed
everyone how, so nobody wanted to see
anymore and one day he cried, just cried
until his parents took him away forever.
Maya had a Hotpoint refrigerator standing   10
in his living room, just for his family to show
anybody who came that they could afford it.

Me, I got a French kiss, finally, in the catholic
darkness, my tongue's farthest half vacationing
loudly in another mouth like a man in Bermudas,   15
and my body jumped against a flagstone wall,
I could feel it through her thin, almost
nonexistent body: I had, at that moment, that moment,
a hot girl on a summer night, the best of all
the things we tried to do. Well, she   20
let me kiss her, anyway, all over.

Or it was just a flagstone wall
with a flaw in the stone, an understanding cavity

for burning young men with smooth dreams —
the true circumstance is gone, the true   25
circumstances about us all then
are gone. But when I kissed her, all water,
she would close her eyes, and they into somewhere
would disappear. Whether she was there
or not, I remember her, clearly, and she moves   30
around the room, sometimes, until I sleep.

I have lain on the desert in watch
low in the back of a pick-up truck
for nothing in particular, for stars, for
the things behind stars, and nothing comes   35
more than the moment: always now, here in a truck,
the moment again to dream of making love and sweat,
this time to a woman, or even to all of them
in some allowable way, to those boys, then,
who couldn't cry, to the girls before they were   40
women, to friends, me on my back, the sky over me
pressing its simple weight into her body
on me, into the bodies of them all, on me.

Considerations for Critical Thinking and Writing

1. Comment on the use of slang in the poem. How does it serve to characterize the speaker?
2. How does language of the final stanza differ from that of the first stanza? To what purpose?
3. Write an essay that discusses the speaker's attitudes toward sex and life. How are they related?

Connections to Other Selections

1. Compare the treatment of sex in this poem with that in Sharon Olds's "Sex without Love" (p. 492).
2. Think about "Seniors" as a kind of love poem and compare the speaker's voice here with the one in T. S. Eliot's "The Love Song of J. Alfred Prufrock" (p. 330). How are these two voices used to evoke different cultures? Of what value is love in these cultures?

TED KOOSER (b. 1939)
Selecting a Reader   1974

First, I would have her be beautiful,
and walking carefully up on my poetry
at the loneliest moment of an afternoon,
her hair still damp at the neck
from washing it. She should be wearing   5

a raincoat, an old one, dirty
from not having money enough for the cleaners.
She will take out her glasses, and there
in the bookstore, she will thumb
over my poems, then put the book back   10
up on its shelf. She will say to herself,
"For that kind of money, I can get
my raincoat cleaned." And she will.

Considerations for Critical Thinking and Writing

1. What do the descriptive details in this poem reveal about the kind of reader the
   poet desires?
2. Based on this description of the poet's desired reader, write a one-paragraph
   description of the poem's speaker. Try to include some imaginative details that
   suggest his personality.

JOHN DONNE (1572–1631)
The Sun Rising   c. 1633

    Busy old fool, unruly sun,
      Why dost thou thus,
Through windows, and through curtains, call on us?
Must to thy motions lovers' seasons run?
    Saucy pedantic wretch, go chide   5
      Late schoolboys, and sour prentices,
  Go tell court-huntsmen that the king will ride,
  Call country ants° to harvest offices;   *farm workers*
Love, all alike, no season knows, nor clime,
Nor hours, days, months, which are the rags of time.   10

    Thy beams, so reverend and strong
      Why shouldst thou think?
I could eclipse and cloud them with a wink,
But that I would not lose her sight so long:
    If her eyes have not blinded thine,   15
      Look, and tomorrow late, tell me
  Whether both the Indias° of spice and mine   *East and West Indies*
  Be where thou left'st them, or lie here with me.
Ask for those kings whom thou saw'st yesterday,
And thou shalt hear, all here in one bed lay.   20

    She is all states, and all princes I,
      Nothing else is.
Princes do but play us; compared to this,
All honor's mimic, all wealth alchemy.
    Thou, sun, art half as happy as we,   25
      In that the world's contracted thus;

Thine age asks ease, and since thy duties be
To warm the world, that's done in warming us.
Shine here to us, and thou art every where;
This bed thy center° is, these walls thy sphere.   *of orbit*   30

Considerations for Critical Thinking

1. What is the situation in this poem? Why is the speaker angry with the sun? What does he urge the sun to do in the first stanza?
2. What claims does the speaker make about the power of love in stanzas 2 and 3? What does he mean when he says, "Shine here to us, and thou art every where"?
3. Are any of the speaker's exaggerations in any sense true? How?

Connection to Another Selection

1. Compare this lyric poem with Richard Wilbur's "A Late Aubade" (p. 58). What similarities do you find in the ideas and emotions expressed in each?

NIKKI GIOVANNI (b. 1943)
Nikki-Rosa   1968

childhood remembrances are always a drag
if you're Black
you always remember things like living in Woodlawn
with no inside toilet
and if you become famous or something   5
they never talk about how happy you were to have your mother
all to yourself and
how good the water felt when you got your bath from one of those
big tubs that folk in chicago barbecue in
and somehow when you talk about home   10
it never gets across how much you
understood their feelings
as the whole family attended meetings about Hollydale
and even though you remember
your biographers never understand   15
your father's pain as he sells his stock
and another dream goes
and though you're poor it isn't poverty that
concerns you
and though they fought a lot   20
it isn't your father's drinking that makes any difference
but only that everybody is together and you
and your sister have happy birthdays and very good christmasses
and I really hope no white person ever has cause to write about me
because they never understand Black love is Black wealth and they'll   25
probably talk about my hard childhood and never understand that
all the while I was quite happy

Considerations for Critical Thinking and Writing

1. How does reading this poem aloud help to convey its meaning and characterize the speaker? How does the lack of punctuation contribute to our image of the speaker?
2. Is this poem addressed primarily to whites, blacks, or both? Why?
3. Does the speaker describe his or her childhood as positive or negative?
4. Is this a sentimental treatment of childhood memories? Why or why not?

Connections to Other Selections

1. Compare the feelings evoked by the "childhood remembrances" in Giovanni's poem with those in Regina Barreca's "Nighttime Fires" (p. 25).
2. Write an essay contrasting the attitude toward the past expressed in "Nikki-Rosa" with the black man's attitude in M. Carl Holman's "Mr. Z" (p. 386).

LOUIS SIMPSON (b. 1923)
American Poetry   1963

Whatever it is, it must have
A stomach that can digest
Rubber, coal, uranium, moons, poems.

Like the shark, it contains a shoe.
It must swim for miles through the desert
Uttering cries that are almost human.

Considerations for Critical Thinking and Writing

1. According to Simpson, what kind of appetite should American poetry have for life?
2. Consider whether you think any limits should be placed on the subject matter of poetry. Explain why or why not.

MAXINE KUMIN (b. 1925)
Morning Swim   1965

Into my empty head there come
a cotton beach, a dock wherefrom

I set out, oily and nude
through mist, in chilly solitude.

There was no line, no roof or floor   5
to tell the water from the air.

Night fog thick as terry cloth
closed me in its fuzzy growth.

I hung my bathrobe on two pegs.
I took the lake between my legs.   10

Invaded and invader, I
went overhand on that flat sky.

Fish twitched beneath me, quick and tame.
In their green zone they sang my name

and in the rhythm of the swim   15
I hummed a two-four-time slow hymn.

I hummed *Abide with Me*. The beat
rose in the fine thrash of my feet,

rose in the bubbles I put out
slantwise, trailing through my mouth.   20

My bones drank water; water fell
through all my doors. I was the well

that fed the lake that met my sea
in which I sang *Abide with Me*.

Considerations for Critical Thinking and Writing

1. How does the description of swimming reveal the speaker's feelings about the morning swim?
2. What is the significance of the hymn's title, "Abide with Me"? How is it related to the central point of the poem?

LI HO (791–817)
A Beautiful Girl Combs Her Hair
TRANSLATED BY DAVID YOUNG

Awake at dawn
she's dreaming
by cool silk curtains

fragrance of spilling hair
half sandalwood, half aloes   5

windlass creaking at the well
singing jade

the lotus blossom wakes, refreshed

her mirror
two phoenixes   10
a pool of autumn light

standing on the ivory bed
loosening her hair
watching the mirror

one long coil, aromatic silk   15
a cloud down to the floor

drop the jade comb — no sound

delicate fingers
pushing the coils into place
color of raven feathers   20

shining blue-black stuff
the jewelled comb will hardly hold it

spring wind makes me restless
her slovenly beauty upsets me

eighteen and her hair's so thick   25
she wears herself out fixing it!

she's finished now
the whole arrangement in place

in a cloud-patterned skirt
she walks with even steps   30
a wild goose on the sand

turns away without a word
where is she off to?

down the steps to break a spray of
          cherry blossoms   35

Considerations for Critical Thinking and Writing

1. How does the speaker use sensuous language to create a vivid picture of the girl?
2. What are the speaker's feelings toward the girl? Do they remain the same throughout the poem?
3. Why would it be difficult to capture the essence of this poem in a paraphrase?

Connections to Other Selections

1. Compare the description of hair in this poem with that in Cathy Song's "The White Porch" (p. 493). What significant similarities do you find?
2. Write an essay that explores the differing portraits in this poem and in Theodore Roethke's "I Knew a Woman" (p. 417). Which portrait is more interesting to you? Explain why.

2. Word Choice, Word Order, and Tone

DICTION

Like all good writers, poets are keenly aware of *diction,* their choice of words. Poets, however, choose words especially carefully, because the words in poems call attention to themselves. Characters, actions, settings, and symbols may appear in a poem, but in the foreground, before all else, is the poem's language. Also, poems are usually briefer than other forms of writing. A few inappropriate words in a two-hundred-page novel (which would have about 100,000 words) create fewer problems than they would in a 100-word poem. Functioning in a compressed atmosphere, the words in a poem must convey meanings gracefully and economically. Readers therefore have to be alert to the ways in which those meanings are released.

Although poetic language is often more intensely charged than ordinary speech, the words used in poetry are not necessarily different from everyday speech. Inexperienced readers may sometimes assume that language must be high-flown and out of date to be included in a poem: instead of reading about a boy "enjoying a swim," they expect to read about a boy "disporting with pliant arm o'er a glassy wave." During the eighteenth century this kind of *poetic diction* — the use of elevated language over ordinary language — was highly valued in English poetry, but since the nineteenth century poets have generally overridden the distinctions that were once made between words used in everyday speech and those used in poetry. Today all levels of diction can be found in poetry.

A poet, like any writer, has several levels of diction from which to choose; they range from formal to middle to informal. *Formal diction* consists of a dignified, impersonal, and elevated use of language. Notice, for example, the formality of Thomas Hardy's description of the sunken luxury liner *Titanic* in this stanza from "The Convergence of the Twain" (the entire poem appears on p. 60):

In a solitude of the sea
Deep from human vanity,
And the Pride of Life that planned her, stilly couches she.

There is nothing casual or relaxed about these lines. Hardy's use of *stilly*, meaning "quietly" or "calmly," is purely literary; the word rarely, if ever, turns up in everyday English.

The language used in Richard Wilbur's "A Late Aubade" (p. 58) represents a less formal level of diction; the speaker uses a ***middle diction*** spoken by most educated people. Consider how Wilbur's speaker tells his lover what she might be doing instead of being with him.

You could be sitting now in a carrel
Turning some liver-spotted page,
Or rising in an elevator-cage
Toward Ladies' Apparel.

The speaker elegantly enumerates his lover's unattractive alternatives to being with him — reading old books in a library or shopping in a department store — but the wit of his description lessens its formality.

Informal diction is evident in Philip Larkin's "A Study of Reading Habits" (p. 21). The speaker's account of his early reading is presented *colloquially*, in a conversational manner that in this instance includes slang expressions not used by the culture at large.

When getting my nose in a book
Cured most things short of school,
It was worth ruining my eyes
To know I could still keep cool,
And deal out the old right hook
To dirty dogs twice my size.

This level of diction is clearly not that of Hardy's or Wilbur's speakers.

Poets may also draw on another form of informal diction, called ***dialect***. Dialects are spoken by definable groups of people from a particular geographic region, economic group, or social class. New England dialects are often heard in Robert Frost's poems, for example. Gwendolyn Brooks employs a black dialect in "We Real Cool" (p. 62) to characterize a group of pool players. Another form of diction related to particular groups is ***jargon***, a category of language defined by a trade or profession. Sociologists, photographers, carpenters, baseball players, and dentists, for example, all use words that are specific to their fields. e. e. cummings manages to get quite a lot of mileage out of automobile jargon in "she being Brand" (p. 47).

Many levels of diction are available to poets. The variety of diction to be found in poetry is enormous, and that is how it should be. No language is foreign to poetry, because it is possible to imagine any human voice as the speaker of a poem. When we say a poem is formal, informal, or some-where in between, we are making a descriptive statement rather than an evaluative one. What matters in a poem is not only which words are used but how they are used.

DENOTATIONS AND CONNOTATIONS

One important way that the meaning of a word is communicated in a poem is through sound: snakes *hiss,* saws *buzz.* This and other matters related to sound are discussed in Chapter 6. Individual words also convey meanings through denotations and connotations. *Denotations* are the literal, dictionary meanings of a word. For example, *bird* denotes a feathered animal with wings (other denotations for the same word include a shuttlecock, an airplane, or an odd person), but in addition to its denotative meanings *bird* also carries *connotations,* associations and implications that go beyond a word's literal meanings. Connotations derive from how the word has been used and the associations people make with it. Therefore, the connotations of *bird* might include fragility, vulnerability, altitude, the sky, or freedom, depending on the context in which the word is used. Consider also how different the connotations are for the following types of birds: hawk, dove, penguin, pigeon, chicken, peacock, duck, crow, turkey, gull, owl, goose, coot, and vulture. These words have long been used to refer to types of people as well as birds. They are rich in connotative meanings.

Connotations derive their resonance from a person's experiences with a word. Those experiences may not always be the same, especially when the people having them are in different times and places. *Theater,* for instance, was once associated with depravity, disease, and sin, while today the word usually evokes some sense of high culture and perhaps visions of elegant opulence. In several ethnic communities in the United States many people would find *squid* appetizing, but elsewhere the word is likely to produce negative connotations. Readers must recognize, then, that words written in other times and places may have unexpected connotations. Annotations usually help in these matters, which is why it makes sense to pay attention to them when they are available.

Ordinarily, though, the language of poetry is accessible, even when the circumstances of the reader and the poet are different. Although connotative language may be used subtly, it mostly draws on associations experienced by many people. Poets rely on widely shared associations rather than the idiosyncratic response that an individual might have to a word. Someone who has received a severe burn from a fireplace accident may associate the word *hearth* with intense pain instead of home and family life, but that reader must not allow a personal experience to undermine the re-sponse the poet intends to evoke. Connotative meanings are usually public meanings.

Perhaps this can be seen most clearly in advertising, where language is also used primarily to convey moods and feelings rather than information. For instance, our recent efforts to get in shape have created a collective consciousness that advertisers have capitalized on successfully. Knowing that we want to be slender or lean or slim (not spare or scrawny and certainly not gaunt), advertisers have created a new word to describe beers, wines, sodas, cheeses, canned fruits, and other products that tend to overload what used to be called sweatclothes and sneakers. The word is *lite*. The assumed denotative meaning of *lite* is low in calories, but as close readers of ingredient labels know, some *lites* are heavier than regularly prepared products. There can be no doubt about the connotative meaning of *lite,* however. Whatever is *lite* cannot hurt you; less is more. Even the word is lighter than *light;* there is no unnecessary droopy *g* or plump *h*. *Lite* is a brilliantly manufactured use of connotation.

Connotative meanings are valuable to poets because they allow them to be economical and suggestive simultaneously. In this way emotions and attitudes are carefully woven into the texture of the poem's language. Read the following poem and pay close attention to the connotative meanings of its words.

RANDALL JARRELL (1914–1965)
The Death of the Ball Turret Gunner   1945

From my mother's sleep I fell into the State
And I hunched in its belly till my wet fur froze.
Six miles from earth, loosed from its dream of life,
I woke to black flak and the nightmare fighters.
When I died they washed me out of the turret with a hose.

The title of this poem establishes the setting and the speaker's situation. Like the setting of a short story, the setting of a poem is important when the time and place influence what happens. "The Death of the Ball Turret Gunner" is set in the midst of a war and, more specifically, in a ball turret — a Plexiglas sphere housing machine guns on the underside of a bomber. The speaker's situation obviously places him in extreme danger; indeed, his fate is announced in the title.

Although the poem is written in the first-person singular, its speaker is clearly not the poet. Jarrell employs a *persona,* a speaker created by the poet. In this poem the persona is a disembodied voice that makes the gunner's story all the more powerful. What is his story? A paraphrase might read something like this:

After I was born, I grew up to find myself at war, cramped into the turret of a bomber's belly some 31,000 feet above the ground. Below me were exploding shells from antiaircraft guns and attacking fighter planes. I was killed, but the bomber returned to base, where my remains were cleaned out of the turret so the next man could take my place.

This paraphrase is accurate, but its language is much less suggestive than the poem's. The first line of the poem has the speaker emerge from his "mother's sleep," the anesthetized sleep of her giving birth. The phrase also suggests the comfort, warmth, and security he knew as a child. This safety was left behind when he "fell," a verb that evokes the danger and involuntary movement associated with his subsequent "State" (*fell* also echoes, perhaps, the fall from innocence to experience related in the Bible).

Several dictionary definitions appear for the noun *state;* it can denote a territorial unit, the power and authority of a government, a person's social status, or a person's emotional or physical condition. The context provided by the rest of the poem makes clear that "State" has several denotative meanings here: Because it is capitalized it certainly refers to the violent world of a government at war, but it also refers to the gunner's vulnerable status as well as his physical and emotional condition. By having "State" carry more than one meaning, Jarrell has created an intentional ambiguity. *Ambiguity* allows for two or more simultaneous interpretations of a word, phrase, action, or situation, all of which can be supported by the context of a work. Through his ambiguous use of "State," Jarrell connects the horrors of war not just to bombers and gunners but to the governments that control them.

Related to this ambiguity is the connotative meaning of "State" in the poem. The context demands that the word be read with a negative charge. The word is not used with patriotic pride but to suggest an anonymous, impersonal "State" that kills rather than nurtures the life in its "belly." The state's "belly" is a bomber, and the gunner is "hunched" like a fetus in the cramped turret, where, in contrast to the warmth of his mother's womb, everything is frozen, even the "wet fur" of his flight jacket (newborn infants have wet fur too). The gunner is not just 31,000 feet from the ground but "six miles from earth." *Six miles* has roughly the same denotative meaning as 31,000 feet, but Jarrell knew that the connotative meaning of *six miles* makes the speaker's position seem even more remote and frightening.

When the gunner is born into the violent world of war, he finds himself waking up to a "nightmare" that is all too real. The poem's final line is grimly understated, but it hits the reader with the force of an exploding shell: what the State-bomber-turret gives birth to is a gruesome death that is merely one of an endless series. It may be tempting to reduce the theme of this poem to the idea that "war is hell"; but Jarrell's target is more specific. He implicates the "State," which routinely executes such violence, and he does so without preaching or hysterical denunciations. Instead, his use of language conveys his theme subtly and powerfully. Consider how this next poem uses connotative meanings to express its theme.

e. e. cummings (1894–1962)
she being Brand

1926

she being Brand

-new;and you
know consequently a
little stiff i was
careful of her and(having   5

thoroughly oiled the universal
joint tested my gas felt of
her radiator made sure her springs were O.

K.)i went right to it flooded-the-carburetor cranked her

up,slipped the   10
clutch(and then somehow got into reverse she
kicked what
the hell)next
minute i was back in neutral tried and

again slo-wly;bare,ly nudg.   ing (my   15

lev-er Right-
oh and her gears being in
A 1 shape passed
from low through
second-in-to-high like   20
greasedlightning) just as we turned the corner of Divinity

avenue i touched the accelerator and give

her the juice,good

                         (it

was the first ride and believe i we was   25
happy to see how nice she acted right up to
the last minute coming back down by the Public
Gardens i slammed on

the
internalexpanding   30
&
externalcontracting
brakes Bothatonce and

brought allofher tremB
-ling   35
to a:dead.

stand-
;Still)

Considerations for Critical Thinking and Writing

1. How does cummings's arrangement of the words on the page help you to read this poem aloud? What does the poem describe?
2. What ambiguities in language does the poem ride on? At what point were you first aware of these double meanings?
3. Explain why you think the poem is primarily serious or humorous.
4. Find some advertisements for convertibles or sports cars in magazines and read them closely. What similarities do you find in the use of connotative language in them and in cummings's poem? Write a brief essay explaining how language is used to convey the theme of one of the advertisements and the poem.

WORD ORDER

Meanings in poems are conveyed not only by denotations and connotations but also by the poet's arrangement of words into phrases, clauses, and sentences to achieve particular effects. The ordering of words into meaningful verbal patterns is called *syntax*. A poet can manipulate the syntax of a line to place emphasis on a word; this is especially apparent when a poet varies normal word order. In Emily Dickinson's "A narrow Fellow in the Grass" (p. 4), for example, the speaker says about the snake that "His notice sudden is." Ordinarily, that would be expressed as "his notice is sudden." By placing the verb *is* unexpectedly at the end of the line, Dickinson creates the sense of surprise we feel when we suddenly come upon a snake. Dickinson's inversion of the standard word order also makes the final sound of the line a hissing *is*.

Cummings uses one long sentence in "she being Brand" to take the reader on a ride that begins with a false start but accelerates quickly before coming to a halt. The jargon creates an exuberantly humorous mood that is helped along by the poem's syntax. How do cummings's ordering of words and sentence structure reinforce the meaning of the lines?

TONE

Tone is the writer's attitude toward the subject, the mood created by all the elements in the poem. Writing, like speech, may be characterized as serious or light, sad or happy, private or public, angry or affectionate, bitter or nostalgic, or any other attitudes and feelings that human beings experience. In Jarrell's "The Death of the Ball Turret Gunner," the tone is clearly serious; the voice in the poem even sounds dead. Listen again to the persona's final words: "When I died they washed me out of the turret with a hose." The brutal, restrained matter-of-factness of this line is effective because the reader is called on to supply the appropriate anger and despair, a strategy that makes those emotions all the more convincing.

Consider how tone is used to convey meaning in the next poem, inspired by the poet's contemplating Chinese silk shoes in a museum.

RUTH FAINLIGHT (b. 1931)
Flower Feet
1989

(SILK SHOES IN THE WHITWORTH ART GALLERY,
MANCHESTER, ENGLAND)

Real women's feet wore these objects
that look like toys or spectacle cases stitched
from bands of coral, jade, and apricot silk
embroidered with twined sprays of flowers.
Those hearts, tongues, crescents, and disks, leather   5
shapes an inch across, are the soles of shoes
no wider or longer than the span of my ankle.

If the feet had been cut off and the raw stumps
thrust inside the openings, surely
it could not hurt more than broken toes, twisted   10
back and bandaged tight. An old woman,
leaning on a cane outside her door
in a Chinese village, smiled to tell how
she fought and cried, how when she stood on points
of pain that gnawed like fire, nurse and mother   15
praised her tottering walk on flower feet.
Her friends nodded, glad the times had changed.
Otherwise, they would have crippled their daughters.

Considerations for Critical Thinking and Writing

1. Why did the Chinese bind feet?
2. How is the speaker's description of the process of binding feet in lines 8–16 different from the description of the shoes in lines 1–7?
3. Describe the poem's tone. Does it remain the same throughout the poem, or does it change? Explain your response.

Connections to Other Selections

1. How do you think the neighbor in this poem would respond to Dickinson's idea of imagination in "To make a prairie it takes a clover and one bee" (p. 256)?
2. What similarities and differences does the neighbor have with the people Frost describes in "Neither Out Far nor In Deep" (p. 311)?
3. Write an essay discussing the speakers' sensibilities in this poem and Amy Clampitt's "Nothing Stays Put" (p. 477).

The next work is a ***dramatic monologue,*** a type of poem in which a character — the speaker — addresses a silent audience in such a way as to reveal unintentionally some aspect of his or her temperament or personality. What tone is created by Machan's use of a persona?

KATHARYN HOWD MACHAN (b. 1952)
Hazel Tells LaVerne   1976

last night
im cleanin out my
howard johnsons ladies room
when all of a sudden
up pops this frog   5
musta come from the sewer
swimmin aroun an tryin ta
climb up the sida the bowl
so i goes ta flushm down
but sohelpmegod he starts talkin   10
bout a golden ball
an how i can be a princess
me a princess
well my mouth drops
all the way to the floor   15
an he says
kiss me just kiss me
once on the nose
well i screams
ya little green pervert   20
an i hitsm with my mop
an has ta flush
the toilet down three times
me
a princess   25

Considerations for Critical Thinking and Writing

1. What do you imagine the situation and setting are for this poem?
2. What creates the poem's humor? How does Hazel's use of language reveal her personality? Is her treatment of the frog consistent with her character?
3. Although it has no punctuation, this poem is easy to follow. How does the arrangement of the lines organize Hazel's speech for clarity and emphasis?
4. What is the theme? Is it conveyed through denotative or connotative language?
5. Write what you think might be LaVerne's reply to Hazel. First, write LaVerne's response as a series of ordinary sentences, and then try editing and organizing them into poetic lines.

Connection to Another Selection

1. Although Robert Browning's "My Last Duchess" (p. 126) is a more complex poem than Machan's, both use dramatic monologues to reveal character. How are the strategies in each poem similar?

WILLIAM TROWBRIDGE (b. 1941)
Enter Dark Stranger 1985

In "Shane," when Jack Palance first appears,
a stray cur takes one look and slinks away
on tiptoes, able, we understand, to recognize
something truly dark. So it seems when we
appear, crunching through the woods. A robin   5
cocks her head, then hops off,
ready to fly like hell and leave us the worm.
A chipmunk, peering out from his hole beneath
a maple root, crash dives when he hears
our step. The alarm sounds everywhere. Squirrels,   10
finches, butterflies flee for their lives. Imagine
a snail picking up the hems of his shell
and hauling ass for cover. He's studied carnivores,
seen the menu, noticed the escargots.

But forget Palance, who would have murdered Alabama   15
just for fun. Think of Karloff's monster,
full of lonely love but too hideous
to bear; or Kong, bereft with Fay Wray
shrieking in his hand: the flies buzz our heads
like angry biplanes, and the ants hoist pitchforks   20
to march on our ankles as we watch the burgher's daughter
bob downstream in a ring of daisies.

Considerations for Critical Thinking and Writing

1. How does a human's presence change the tone of nature in the first stanza?
2. How does the shift from Jack Palance in the first stanza to Boris Karloff and King Kong in the second stanza reflect a different tone in the speaker's assessment of humankind in nature?
3. How do the references to popular films affect the overall tone of the poem?

Connections to Other Selections

1. Write an essay that considers the relationship between humankind and nature in Trowbridge's poem and in William Stafford's "Traveling through the Dark" (p. 118).
2. Compare the speaker's tone in "Enter Dark Stranger" with the speaker's tone in

"Hazel Tells LaVerne" (p. 50). How does the humor in each poem affect your sense of its meaning?

How do the speaker's attitude and tone change during the course of this next poem?

MAXINE KUMIN (b. 1925)
Woodchucks

1972

Gassing the woodchucks didn't turn out right.
The knockout bomb from the Feed and Grain Exchange
was featured as merciful, quick at the bone
and the case we had against them was airtight,
both exits shoehorned shut with puddingstone,°   5
but they had a sub-sub-basement out of range.

Next morning they turned up again, no worse
for the cyanide than we for our cigarettes
and state-store Scotch, all of us up to scratch.
They brought down the marigolds as a matter of course   10
and then took over the vegetable patch
nipping the broccoli shoots, beheading the carrots.

The food from our mouths, I said, righteously thrilling
to the feel of the .22, the bullets' neat noses.
I, a lapsed pacifist fallen from grace   15
puffed with Darwinian° pieties for killing,
now drew a bead on the littlest woodchuck's face.
He died down in the everbearing roses.

Ten minutes later I dropped the mother. She
flipflopped in the air and fell, her needle teeth   20
still hooked in a leaf of early Swiss chard.
Another baby next. O one-two-three
the murderer inside me rose up hard,
the hawkeye killer came on stage forthwith.

There's one chuck left. Old wily fellow, he keeps   25
me cocked and ready day after day after day.
All night I hunt his humped-up form. I dream
I sight along the barrel in my sleep.
If only they'd all consented to die unseen
gassed underground the quiet Nazi way.   30

5 *puddingstone:* Pebbles cemented together.   16 *Darwinian:* Charles Darwin (1809–1882), an English naturalist associated with the ideas of evolution and natural selection.

Considerations for Critical Thinking and Writing

1. How does the word *airtight* help create the tone of the first stanza?
2. How does the speaker's attitude toward the woodchucks change in the second stanza? How does that affect the tone in lines 13–24?
3. What competing emotions are present in the speaker's descriptions of the woodchucks' activities and the descriptions of killing them?
4. Given that "Gassing" begins the poem, why does the speaker withhold the description of the woodchucks being "gassed underground the quiet Nazi way" until the final line?
5. Explain how line 15 suggests, along with the final stanza, the theme of the poem.

DICTION AND TONE IN FOUR LOVE POEMS

The first three of these love poems share the same basic situation and theme: a male speaker addresses a female (in the first poem it is a type of female) urging that love should not be delayed because time is short. This theme is as familiar in poetry as it is in life. In Latin this tradition is known as *carpe diem,* for "seize the day." Notice how the poets' diction helps create a distinctive tone in each poem, even though the subject matter and central ideas are similar (though not identical) in all three.

ROBERT HERRICK (1591–1674)
To the Virgins, to Make Much of Time   1648

Gather ye rose-buds while ye may,
    Old Time is still a-flying;
And this same flower that smiles today,
    Tomorrow will be dying.

The glorious lamp of heaven, the sun,   5
    The higher he's a-getting,
The sooner will his race be run,
    And nearer he's to setting.

That age is best which is the first,
    When youth and blood are warmer;   10
But being spent, the worse, and worst
    Times still succeed the former.

Then be not coy, but use your time,
    And while ye may, go marry;
For having lost but once your prime,   15
    You may for ever tarry.

Considerations for Critical Thinking and Writing

1. Would there be any change in meaning if the title of this poem were "To Young Women, to Make Much of Time"? Do you think the poem can apply to young men too?
2. What do the virgins have in common with the flowers (lines 1–4) and the course of the day (5–8)?
3. How does the speaker develop his argument? What will happen to the virgins if they don't "marry"? Paraphrase the poem.
4. What is the tone of the speaker's advice?

The next poem was also written in the seventeenth century, but it includes some words that have changed in usage and meaning over the past three hundred years. The title of Andrew Marvell's "To His Coy Mistress" requires some explanation. *Mistress* does not refer to a married man's illicit lover but to a woman who is loved and courted — a sweetheart. Marvell uses *coy* to describe a woman who is reserved and shy rather than coquettish or flirtatious. Often such shifts in meanings over time are explained in the notes that accompany reprintings of poems. You should keep in mind, however, that it is helpful to have a reasonably thick dictionary available when you are reading poetry. The most thorough is the *Oxford English Dictionary* (*OED*), which provides histories of words. The *OED* is a multi-volume leviathan, but there are other useful unabridged dictionaries as well as desk dictionaries.

Knowing its original meaning can also enrich your understanding of why a contemporary poet chooses a particular word. Elizabeth Bishop begins "The Fish" this way: "I caught a tremendous fish." We know immediately in this context that *tremendous* means very large. In addition, given that the speaker clearly admires the fish in the lines that follow, we might even understand *tremendous* in the colloquial sense of wonderful and extraordinary. But a dictionary gives us some further relevant insights. Because, by the end of the poem, we see the speaker thoroughly moved as a result of the encounter with the fish ("everything/was rainbow, rainbow, rainbow!"), the dictionary's additional information about the history of *tremendous* shows why it is the perfect adjective to introduce the fish. The word comes from the Latin *tremere* (to tremble) and therefore once meant "such as to make one tremble." That is precisely how the speaker is at the end of the poem: deeply affected and trembling. Knowing the origin of *tremendous* gives us the full heft of the poet's word choice.

Although some of the language in "To His Coy Mistress" requires annotations for the modern reader, this poem continues to serve as a powerful reminder that time is a formidable foe, even for lovers.

ANDREW MARVELL (1621–1678)

To His Coy Mistress

1681

Had we but world enough, and time,
This coyness, lady, were no crime.
We would sit down, and think which way
To walk, and pass our long love's day.
Thou by the Indian Ganges'° side   5
Shouldst rubies find; I by the tide
Of Humber° would complain.° I would   *write love songs*
Love you ten years before the Flood,
And you should, if you please, refuse
Till the conversion of the Jews.   10
My vegetable love should grow°
Vaster than empires, and more slow;
An hundred years should go to praise
Thine eyes and on thy forehead gaze,
Two hundred to adore each breast,   15
But thirty thousand to the rest:
An age at least to every part,
And the last age should show your heart.
For, lady, you deserve this state,
Nor would I love at lower rate.   20
   But at my back I always hear
Time's wingèd chariot hurrying near;
And yonder all before us lie
Deserts of vast eternity.
Thy beauty shall no more be found,   25
Nor in thy marble vault shall sound
My echoing song; then worms shall try
That long preserved virginity,
And your quaint honor turn to dust,
And into ashes all my lust.   30
The grave's a fine and private place,
But none, I think, do there embrace.
   Now, therefore, while the youthful hue
Sits on thy skin like morning dew,
And while thy willing soul transpires°   *breathes forth* 35
At every pore with instant fires,
Now let us sport us while we may,
And now, like amorous birds of prey,
Rather at once our time devour
Than languish in his slow-chapped° power.   *slow-jawed* 40

---

5 *Ganges:* A river in India sacred to the Hindus.   7 *Humber:* A river that flows through Marvell's native town, Hull.   11 *My vegetable love . . . grow:* A slow, unconscious growth.

Let us roll all our strength and all
Our sweetness up into one ball,
And tear our pleasures with rough strife
Thorough° the iron gates of life.   *through*
Thus, though we cannot make our sun   45
Stand still, yet we will make him run.

Considerations for Critical Thinking and Writing

1. This poem is divided into a three-part argument. Briefly summarize each section:
   if (lines 1–20), but (21–32), therefore (33–46).
2. What is the speaker's tone in lines 1–20? How much time would he spend adoring
   his mistress? Is he sincere? How does he expect his mistress to respond to these
   lines?
3. How does the speaker's tone change beginning with line 21? What is his view of
   time in lines 21–32? What does this description do to the lush and leisurely sense
   of time in lines 1–20? How do you think his mistress would react to lines 21–32?
4. In the final lines of Herrick's "To the Virgins, to Make Much of Time," the speaker
   urges the virgins to "go marry." What does Marvell's speaker urge in lines 33–46?
   How is the pace of these lines (notice the verbs) different from that of the first
   twenty lines of the poem?
5. This poem is sometimes read as a vigorous but simple celebration of flesh. Is
   there more to the theme than that?

PERSPECTIVE

BERNARD DUYFHUIZEN (b. 1953)
"To His Coy Mistress": On How a Female
Might Respond   1988

Clearly a female reader of "To His Coy Mistress" might have trouble identifying with the poem's speaker; therefore, her first response would be to identify
with the listener-in-the-poem, the eternally silent Coy Mistress. In such a reading
she is likely to recognize that she has heard this kind of line before although
maybe not with the same intensity and insistence. Moreover, she is likely to
(re)experience the unsettling emotions that such an egoistic assault on her
virginal autonomy would provoke. She will also see differently, even by contemporary standards, the plot beyond closure, the possible consequences—both
physical and social—that the Mistress will encounter. Lastly, she is likely to be
angered by this poem, by her marginalization in an argument that seeks to
overpower the core of her being.

From "Textual Harassment of Marvell's Coy Mistress:
The Institutionalization of Masculine Criticism,"
College English, April 1988

Considerations for Critical Thinking and Writing

1. Explain whether you find convincing Duyfhuizen's description of a female's potential response to the poem. How does his description compare with your own response?
2. Characterize the silent mistress of the poem. How do you think the speaker treats her? What do his language and tone suggest about his relationship to her?
3. Does the fact that this description of a female response is written by a man make any difference in your assessment of it? Explain why or why not.

The third in this series of *carpe diem* poems is a twentieth-century work. The language of Wilbur's "A Late Aubade" is more immediately accessible than that of Marvell's "To His Coy Mistress"; a dictionary will quickly identify any words unfamiliar to a reader, including the allusion to Arnold Schoenberg, the composer, in line 11. An *allusion* is a brief reference to a person, place, thing, event, or idea in history or literature. Allusive words, like connotative words, are both suggestive and economical; poets use allusions to conjure up biblical authority, scenes from Shakespeare's plays, historic figures, wars, great love stories, and anything else that might serve to deepen and enrich their own work. The speaker in "A Late Aubade" makes an allusion that an ordinary dictionary won't explain. He tells his lover: "I need not rehearse/The rosebuds-theme of centuries of verse." True to his word, he says no more about this for her or the reader. The lines refer, of course, to the *carpe diem* theme as found familiarly in Herrick's "To the Virgins, to Make Much of Time." Wilbur assumes that his reader will understand the allusion.

Allusions imply reading and cultural experiences shared by the poet and reader. Literate audiences once had more in common than they do today because more people had similar economic, social, and educational backgrounds. But a judicious use of specialized dictionaries, encyclopedias, and other reference tools can help you decipher allusions that grow out of this body of experience. See page 592 for a list of useful reference works for students of literature. As you read more, you'll be able to make connections based on your own experiences with literature. In a sense, allusions make available what other human beings have deemed worth remembering, and that is certainly an economical way of supplementing and enhancing your own experience.

Wilbur's version of the *carpe diem* theme is on the next page. What strikes you as particularly modern about it?

RICHARD WILBUR (b. 1921)

A Late Aubade   1968

You could be sitting now in a carrel
Turning some liver-spotted page,
Or rising in an elevator-cage
Toward Ladies' Apparel.

You could be planting a raucous bed   5
Of salvia, in rubber gloves,
Or lunching through a screed of someone's loves
With pitying head,

Or making some unhappy setter
Heel, or listening to a bleak   10
Lecture on Schoenberg's serial technique.
Isn't this better?

Think of all the time you are not
Wasting, and would not care to waste,
Such things, thank God, not being to your taste.   15
Think what a lot

Of time, by woman's reckoning,
You've saved, and so may spend on this,
You who had rather lie in bed and kiss
Than anything.   20

It's almost noon, you say? If so,
Time flies, and I need not rehearse
The rosebuds-theme of centuries of verse.
If you *must* go,

Wait for a while, then slip downstairs   25
And bring us up some chilled white wine,
And some blue cheese, and crackers, and some fine
Ruddy-skinned pears.

Considerations for Critical Thinking and Writing

1. An *aubade* is a song about lovers parting at dawn, but in this "late aubade," "It's almost noon." Is there another way of reading the adjective *late* in the title?
2. How does the speaker's diction characterize both him and his lover? What sort of lives do they live? What does the casual allusion to Herrick's poem (line 23) reveal about them?
3. What is the effect of using "liver-spotted page," "elevator-cage," "raucous bed," "screed," "unhappy setter," and "bleak Lecture" to describe the woman's activities?

1. How does the man's argument in "A Late Aubade" differ from the speakers' in Herrick's and Marvell's poems? Which of the three arguments do you find most convincing?
2. Explain how the tone of each poem is suited to its theme.

This fourth love poem is by a woman. Listen to the speaker's voice. Does it sound different from the way the men speak in the previous three poems?

EDNA ST. VINCENT MILLAY (1892–1950)
Never May the Fruit Be Plucked   1923

Never, never may the fruit be plucked from the bough
And gathered into barrels.
He that would eat of love must eat it where it hangs.
Though the branches bend like reeds,
Though the ripe fruit splash in the grass or wrinkle on the tree,   5
He that would eat of love may bear away with him
Only what his belly can hold,
Nothing in the apron,
Nothing in the pockets.
Never, never may the fruit be gathered from the bough   10
And harvested in barrels.
The winter of love is a cellar of empty bins,
In an orchard soft with rot.

Considerations for Critical Thinking and Writing

1. Compare the meaning of the fruit in this poem with that of the rosebuds in Herrick's "To the Virgins, to Make Much of Time."
2. Explain the consequences of "eat[ing] of love" in lines 3–5.
3. Why can't love be gathered or harvested into barrels? Is this a *carpe diem* poem? Why or why not?
4. Explain why you think this poem is addressed to men, women, or both.
5. Discuss the tone of the final two lines. Do you think this poem is closer in tone to "To the Virgins, to Make Much of Time," Marvell's "To His Coy Mistress," or Wilbur's "A Late Aubade"? Why?

Connections to Other Selections

1. Write an essay comparing Millay's view of love with that of e. e. cummings in "since feeling is first" (p. 371).
2. Discuss how the idea of passionate abandon is central to Millay's poem and Emily

Dickinson's "Wild Nights—Wild Nights!" (p. 265). Consider whether the tones of these poems are similar or different.

3. Contrast the ideal of love presented by Millay with that offered by John Keats in "Ode on a Grecian Urn" (p. 237).

POEMS FOR FURTHER STUDY

THOMAS HARDY (1840–1928)
The Convergence of the Twain   1912

Lines on the Loss of the "Titanic"°

I

     In a solitude of the sea
     Deep from human vanity,
And the Pride of Life that planned her, stilly couches she.

II

     Steel chambers, late the pyres
     Of her salamandrine fires,°   5
Cold currents thrid,° and turn to rhythmic tidal lyres.   *thread*

III

     Over the mirrors meant
     To glass the opulent
The sea-worm crawls—grotesque, slimed, dumb, indifferent.

IV

     Jewels in joy designed   10
     To ravish the sensuous mind
Lie lightless, all their sparkles bleared and black and blind.

V

     Dim moon-eyed fishes near
     Gaze at the gilded gear
And query: "What does this vaingloriousness down here?"   15

VI

     Well: while was fashioning
     This creature of cleaving wing,
The Immanent Will that stirs and urges everything

VII

     Prepared a sinister mate
     For her—so gaily great—   20
A Shape of Ice, for the time far and dissociate.

Titanic: A luxurious ocean liner, reputed to be unsinkable, which sank after hitting an iceberg on its maiden voyage in 1912. Only a third of the 2,200 passengers survived.   5 *salamandrine fires:* Salamanders were, according to legend, able to survive fire; hence, the ship's fires burned even though under water.

VIII

> And as the smart ship grew
> In stature, grace, and hue,
> In shadowy silent distance grew the Iceberg too.

IX

> Alien they seemed to be: 25
> No mortal eye could see
> The intimate welding of their later history,

X

> Or sign that they were bent
> By paths coincident
> On being anon twin halves of one august event,   30

XI

> Till the Spinner of the Years
> Said "Now!" And each one hears,
> And consummation comes, and jars two hemispheres.

Considerations for Critical Thinking and Writing

1. How do the words used to describe the ship in this poem reveal the speaker's attitude toward the *Titanic?*
2. The diction of the poem suggests that the *Titanic* and the iceberg participate in something like an arranged marriage. What specific words imply this?
3. Who or what causes the disaster? Does the speaker assign responsibility?

DAVID R. SLAVITT (b. 1935)
Titanic   1983

Who does not love the *Titanic?*
If they sold passage tomorrow for that same crossing,
who would not buy?

To go down . . . We all go down, mostly
alone. But with crowds of people, friends, servants,   5
well fed, with music, with lights! Ah!

And the world, shocked, mourns, as it ought to do
and almost never does. There will be the books and movies
to remind our grandchildren who we were
and how we died, and give them a good cry.   10

Not so bad, after all. The cold
water is anesthetic and very quick.
The cries on all sides must be a comfort.

We all go: only a few, first-class.

Considerations for Critical Thinking and Writing

1. What, according to the speaker in this poem, is so compelling about the *Titanic?*
2. Discuss the speaker's tone. Why would it be inaccurate to describe it as solemn and mournful?
3. What is the effect of the poem's final line? What emotions does it produce in you?

Connections to Another Selection

1. How does "Titanic" differ in its attitude toward opulence from "The Convergence of the Twain"?
2. Which poem is more emotionally satisfying to you? Explain why.
3. Compare the speakers' tones in "Titanic" and "The Convergence of the Twain."
4. Hardy wrote his poem in 1912, the year the *Titanic* went down, but Slavitt wrote his more than seventy years later. How do you think Slavitt's poem would have been received if it had been published in 1912? Write an essay explaining why you think what you do.

GWENDOLYN BROOKS (b. 1917)
We Real Cool   1960

The Pool Players.
Seven at the Golden Shovel.

We real cool. We
Left school. We

Lurk late. We   5
Strike straight. We

Sing sin. We
Thin gin. We

Jazz June. We
Die soon.   10

Considerations for Critical Thinking and Writing

1. How does the speech of the pool players in this poem help to characterize them? What is the effect of the pronouns coming at the ends of the lines? How would the poem sound if the pronouns came at the beginnings of lines?
2. What is the author's attitude toward the players? Is there a change in tone in the last line?
3. How is the pool hall's name related to the rest of the poem and its theme?

MARGE PIERCY (b. 1936)

A Work of Artifice

1973

The bonsai tree
in the attractive pot
could have grown eighty feet tall
on the side of a mountain
till split by lightning.   5
But a gardener
carefully pruned it.
It is nine inches high.
Every day as he
whittles back the branches   10
the gardener croons,
It is your nature
to be small and cozy,
domestic and weak;
how lucky, little tree,   15
to have a pot to grow in.
With living creatures
one must begin very early
to dwarf their growth:
the bound feet,   20
the crippled brain,
the hair in curlers,
the hands you
love to touch.

Considerations for Critical Thinking and Writing

1. What is a bonsai tree? How is it likened to a woman in this poem? At what point
   in the poem does the comparison become apparent?
2. What attitudes are revealed by the language of the gardener's song? Which words
   have especially strong connotative values?
3. The final two lines ("the hands you/love to touch") allude to a soap commercial.
   Explain the effect this allusion has on your understanding of the poem's theme.

Connections to Other Selections

1. Write an essay comparing the tone of this poem with that of Stevie Smith's
   "Valuable" (p. 64).
2. How does Piercy's theme compare with Ruth Fainlight's treatment of binding feet
   in "Flower Feet" (p. 49)?
3. Contrast the attitudes expressed about women in Piercy's poem with those in
   Conrad Hilberry's "The Frying Pan" (p. 116).

STEVIE SMITH (1902–1971)
Valuable

1962

After reading two paragraphs in a newspaper.

All these illegitimate babies . . .
Oh girls, girls,
Silly little cheap things,
Why do you not put some value on yourselves,
Learn to say, No?   5
Did nobody teach you?
Nobody teaches anybody to say No nowadays,
People should teach people to say No.

Oh poor panther,
Oh you poor black animal,   10
At large for a few moments in a school for young children in Paris,
Now in your cage again,
How your great eyes bulge with bewilderment,
There is something there that accuses us,
In your angry and innocent eyes,   15
Something that says:
I am too valuable to be kept in a cage.

Oh these illegitimate babies!
Oh girls, girls,
Silly little valuable things,   20
You should have said, No, I am valuable,
And again, It is because I am valuable
I say, No.

Nobody teaches anybody they are valuable nowadays.

Girls, you are valuable,   25
And you, Panther, you are valuable,
But the girls say: I shall be alone
If I say 'I am valuable' and other people do not say it of me,
I shall be alone, there is no comfort there.
No, it is not comforting but it is valuable,   30
And if everybody says it in the end
It will be comforting. And for the panther too,
If everybody says he is valuable
It will be comforting for him.

Considerations for Critical Thinking and Writing

1. Which words are repeated in the poem? What is the effect of these repetitions?
2. What relationship does the speaker establish between the girls and the panther?
3. Describe the speaker's voice. How does it produce the poem's overall tone?

DIANE ACKERMAN (b. 1948)

A Fine, A Private Place

1983

He took her one day
under the blue horizon
where long sea fingers
parted like beads
hitched in the doorway   5
of an opium den,
and canyons mazed the deep
reef with hollows,
cul-de-sacs, and narrow boudoirs,
and had to ask twice   10
before she understood
his stroking her arm
with a marine feather
slobbery as aloe pulp
was wooing, or saw the octopus   15
in his swimsuit
stretch one tentacle
and ripple its silky bag.

While bubbles rose
like globs of mercury,   20
they made love
mask to mask, floating
with oceans of air between them,
she his sea-geisha
in an orange kimono   25
of belts and vests,
her lacquered hair waving,
as Indigo Hamlets
tattooed the vista,
and sunlight   30
cut through the water,
twisting its knives
into corridors of light.

His sandy hair
and sea-blue eyes,   35
his kelp-thin waist
and chest ribbed wider
than a sandbar
where muscles domed
clear and taut as shells   40
(freckled cowries,
flat, brawny scallops
the color of dawn),

his sea-battered hands
gripping her thighs   45
like tawny starfish
and drawing her close
as a pirate vessel
to let her board:
who was this she loved?   50

Overhead, sponges
sweating raw color
jutted from a coral arch,
Clown Wrasses°   *brightly colored tropical fish*
hovered like fireworks,   55
and somewhere an abalone opened
its silver wings.
Part of a lusty dream
under aspic, her hips rolled
like a Spanish galleon,   60
her eyes swam
and chest began to heave.
Gasps melted on the tide.
Knowing she would soon be
breathless as her tank,   65
he pumped his brine
deep within her,
letting sea water drive it
through petals
delicate as anemone veils   70
to the dark purpose
of a conch-shaped womb.
An ear to her loins
would have heard the sea roar.

When panting ebbed,   75
and he signaled *Okay?*
as lovers have asked,
land or waterbound
since time heaved ho,
he led her to safety: 80
shallower realms,
heading back toward
the boat's even keel,
though ocean still petted her
cell by cell, murmuring   85
along her legs and neck,
caressing her
with pale, endless arms.

Later, she thought often
of that blue boudoir,   90

pillow-soft and filled
with cascading light,
where together
they'd made a bell
that dumbly clanged   95
beneath the waves
and minutes lurched
like mountain goats.
She could still see
the quilted mosaics   100
that were fish
twitching spangles overhead,
still feel the ocean
inside and out, turning her
evolution around.   105

She thought of it miles
and fathoms away, often,
at odd moments: watching
the minnow snowflakes
dip against the windowframe,   110
holding a sponge
idly under tap-gush,
sinking her teeth
into the cleft
of a voluptuous peach.   115

Considerations for Critical Thinking and Writing

1. Read Andrew Marvell's "To His Coy Mistress" (p. 55). To what does Ackerman's title allude in Marvell's poem? Explain how the allusion to Marvell is crucial to understanding Ackerman's poem.
2. Comment on the descriptive passages of "A Fine, A Private Place." Which images seem especially vivid to you? How do they contribute to the poem's meanings?
3. What are the speaker's reflections upon her experience in lines 106–115? What echoes of Marvell do you hear in these lines?

Connections to Another Selection

1. Write an essay comparing the tone of Ackerman's poem with that of Marvell's "To His Coy Mistress." To what extent are the central ideas in the poems similar?
2. Compare the speaker's voice in Ackerman's poem with the voice you imagine for the coy mistress in Marvell's poem.

MARTÍN ESPADA (b. 1958)

Tiburón°

1987

East 116th
and a long red car
stalled with the hood up
roaring salsa
like a prize shark   5
mouth yanked open
and down in the stomach
the radio
of the last fisherman
still tuned   10
to his lucky station

Tiburón: "Shark" in Spanish.

Considerations for Critical Thinking and Writing

1. East 116th Street is in Spanish Harlem. How does this information about the
   setting affect your reading of the poem?
2. Describe the tone of this poem.

3. Images

POETRY'S APPEAL TO THE SENSES

A poet, to borrow a phrase from Henry James, is one of those on whom nothing is lost. Poets take in the world and give us impressions of what they experience through images. An ***image*** is language that addresses the senses. The most common images in poetry are visual; they provide verbal pictures of the poets' encounters — real or imagined — with the world. But poets also create images that appeal to our other senses. Richard Wilbur arouses several senses when he has the speaker in "A Late Aubade" gently urge his lover to linger in bed with him instead of getting on with her daily routines and obligations.

> Wait for a while, then slip downstairs
> And bring us up some chilled white wine,
> And some blue cheese, and crackers, and some fine
> Ruddy-skinned pears.

These images are simultaneously tempting and satisfying. We don't have to literally touch that cold, clear glass of wine (or will it come in a green bottle beaded with moisture?) or smell the cheese or taste the crackers to appreciate this vivid blend of colors, textures, tastes, and fragrances.

Images give us the physical world to experience in our imaginations. Some poems, like the following one, are written to do just that; they make no comment about what they describe.

WILLIAM CARLOS WILLIAMS (1883–1963)
Poem   1934

As the cat
climbed over
the top of

the jamcloset
first the right   5
forefoot

carefully
then the hind
stepped down

into the pit of   10
the empty
flowerpot

This poem defies paraphrase because it is all an image of agile movement. No statement is made about the movement; the title, "Poem" — really no title — signals Williams's refusal to comment on the movements. To impose a meaning on the poem, we'd probably have to knock over the flowerpot.

We experience the image in Williams's "Poem" more clearly because of how the sentence is organized into lines and groups of lines, or stanzas. Consider how differently the sentence is read if it is arranged as prose.

As the cat climbed over the top of the jamcloset, first the right forefoot
carefully then the hind stepped down into the pit of the empty flowerpot.

The poem's line and stanza division transforms what is essentially an awkward prose sentence into a rhythmic verbal picture. Especially when the poem is read aloud, this line and stanza division allows us to feel the image we see. Even the lack of a period at the end suggests that the cat is only pausing.

Images frequently do more than offer only sensory impressions, however. They also convey emotions and moods, as in the following lyric.

BONNIE JACOBSON (b. 1933)
On Being Served Apples   1989

Apples in a deep blue dish
            are the shadows of nuns

Apples in a basket
            are warm red moons on Indian women

Apples in a white bowl
            are virgins waiting in snow

Beware of apples on an orange plate:
            they are the anger of wives

The four images of apples in this poem suggest a range of emotions. How would you describe these emotions? How does the meaning of the apples change depending upon the context in which they are served? In this poem we are given more than just images of the world selected by the poet; we are also given her feelings about them.

What mood is established in this next poem's view of Civil War troops moving across a river?

WALT WHITMAN (1819–1892)
Cavalry Crossing a Ford   1865

A line in long array where they wind betwixt green islands,
They take a serpentine course, their arms flash in the sun — hark to the musical clank,
Behold the silvery river, in it the splashing horses loitering stop to drink,
Behold the brown-faced men, each group, each person, a picture, the negligent rest on the saddles,
Some emerge on the opposite bank, others are just entering the ford — while,
Scarlet and blue and snowy white,
The guidon flags flutter gaily in the wind.

Considerations for Critical Thinking and Writing

1. What effect do the colors and sounds have in establishing the mood of this poem?
2. How would the poem's mood have been changed if Whitman had used *look* or *see* instead of *behold* (lines 3, 4)?
3. Where is the speaker as he observes this troop movement?
4. Does *serpentine* in line 2 have an evil connotation in this poem? Explain your answer.

Whitman seems to capture momentarily all the troop's actions, and through carefully chosen, suggestive details — really very few — he succeeds in making "each group, each person, a picture." Specific details, even when few are provided, give us the impression that we see the entire picture; it is as if those are the details we would remember if we had viewed the scene ourselves. Notice too that the movement of the "line in long array" is emphasized by the continuous winding syntax of the poem's lengthy lines.

Poets choose details the way they choose the words to present those details: only telling ones will do. Consider the images Theodore Roethke uses in "Root Cellar."

THEODORE ROETHKE (1908–1963)
Root Cellar

1948

Nothing would sleep in that cellar, dank as a ditch,
Bulbs broke out of boxes hunting for chinks in the dark,
Shoots dangled and drooped,
Lolling obscenely from mildewed crates,
Hung down long yellow evil necks, like tropical snakes.   5
And what a congress of stinks!
Roots ripe as old bait,
Pulpy stems, rank, silo-rich,
Leaf-mold, manure, lime, piled against slippery planks.
Nothing would give up life: 10
Even the dirt kept breathing a small breath.

Considerations for Critical Thinking and Writing

1. What senses are engaged by the images in this poem? Is the poem simply a series of sensations, or do the detailed images make some kind of point about the root cellar?
2. What controls the choice of details in the poem? Why isn't there, for example, a rusty shovel leaning against a dirt wall or a worn gardener's glove atop one of the crates?
3. Look up *congress* in a dictionary for its denotative meanings. Explain why "congress of stinks" is especially appropriate given the nature of the rest of the poem's imagery.
4. What single line in the poem suggests a theme?

The tone of the images and mood of the speaker are consistent in Roethke's "Root Cellar." In Matthew Arnold's "Dover Beach," however, they shift as the theme is developed.

MATTHEW ARNOLD (1822–1888)
Dover Beach

1867

The sea is calm tonight.
The tide is full, the moon lies fair
Upon the straits; — on the French coast the light
Gleams and is gone; the cliffs of England stand,
Glimmering and vast, out in the tranquil bay.   5
Come to the window, sweet is the night-air!
Only, from the long line of spray
Where the sea meets the moon-blanched land,
Listen! you hear the grating roar
Of pebbles which the waves draw back, and fling,   10

At their return, up the high strand,
Begin, and cease, and then again begin,
With tremulous cadence slow, and bring
The eternal note of sadness in.

Sophocles long ago   15
Heard it on the Aegean, and it brought
Into his mind the turbid ebb and flow
Of human misery;° we
Find also in the sound a thought,
Hearing it by this distant northern sea.   20

The Sea of Faith
Was once, too, at the full, and round earth's shore
Lay like the folds of a bright girdle furled.
But now I only hear
Its melancholy, long, withdrawing roar,   25
Retreating, to the breath
Of the night-wind, down the vast edges drear
And naked shingles° of the world.   *pebble beaches*

Ah, love, let us be true
To one another! for the world, which seems   30
To lie before us like a land of dreams,
So various, so beautiful, so new,
Hath really neither joy, nor love, nor light,
Nor certitude, nor peace, nor help for pain;
And we are here as on a darkling plain   35
Swept with confused alarms of struggle and flight,
Where ignorant armies clash by night.

15–18 *Sophocles long ago . . . misery:* In *Antigone,* lines 557–66, Sophocles likens the disasters that
beset the house of Oedipus to a "mounting tide."

Considerations for Critical Thinking and Writing

1. Contrast the images in lines 4–8 and 9–13. How do they reveal the speaker's mood? To whom is he speaking?
2. What is the cause of the "sadness" in line 14? What is the speaker's response to the ebbing "Sea of Faith"? Is there anything to replace his sense of loss?
3. What details of the beach seem related to the ideas in the poem? How is the sea used differently in lines 1–14 and lines 21–28?
4. Describe the differences in tone between lines 1–8 and 35–37. What has caused the change?

Connections to Other Selections

1. Explain how the images in Wilfred Owen's "Dulce et Decorum Est" (p. 76) develop further the ideas and sentiments suggested by Arnold's final line concerning "ignorant armies clash[ing] by night."

2. Write an essay comparing Arnold's reflections on faith with Thomas Hardy's in "The Oxen" (p. 150).
3. Contrast Arnold's images with those of Anthony Hecht in his parody "The Dover Bitch" (p. 384). How do Hecht's images create a very different mood from that of "Dover Beach"?

POEMS FOR FURTHER STUDY

EAMON GRENNAN (b. 1941)
Bat   1991

With no warning and only the slightest whishing sound
it was in the room with me, trapped and flying
wall to wall, a wild heart out of its element: flat
black leather wings that never stop, body
bunched as a baby's fist, the tiny head peering   5
blindly, out of its mouth a piercing
inaudible pulse-scream that sets its course
and keeps it beating, barely grazing the painted
walls, the wardrobe, desk, chest of drawers (all
smelling of outdoors, I suppose — walnut, maple,   10
oak — and sending it, surely, round the bend)
while I try to keep track of its dodgy swerves,
ducking when it flutters at me, springing after
with my eyes. All this is happening
in a fathomless silence that binds us   15
to one another for a hypnotized little while,
making me feel as the creature circles and circles
as if I'd been kissed repeatedly in sleep, lips
lightly brushing, gone. In the end, by
luck, it seems, not navigation, it goes   20
through the window I've scrambled open, leaving
me in another kind of silence
to watch its stuttering flight over bright green grass —
by light afflicted, desperate for the dark. I keep
to myself that other, unseamed silence   25
in which it went about its woeful task, trying
to find a way to friendly shade, its own
crepuscular and insect-humming haven, those
jinking missions in the homely dark, its own
heartbeat keeping it one with an everyday world   30
of intoxicating scents and glimmers, almost infinite
possibilities. Gone for good. It's the sheer
stoic silence (to my ears) of the whole operation
that stays with me, teaching me how to behave
in a tight corner: hold your tongue, keep moving, try   35

everything more than once, steer by brief kisses and
the fleeting grace of dark advances, quick retreats,
until you find lying in your way the window, open.

Considerations for Critical Thinking and Writing

1. Explain which images are particularly effective in capturing the desperation of the trapped bat.
2. How does the speaker's description of the bat serve to characterize the speaker?
3. In the final seven lines what does the speaker report learning from the bat's movements?
4. Given that this poem is about more than just a bat, why do you think it's entitled "Bat"? What alternative titles would appropriately sum up the poem?

Connections to Other Selections

1. Compare the description of images of flight in this poem with Emily Dickinson's "A Bird came down the Walk — " (p. 136).
2. Write an essay discussing the use of images to express confinement and freedom in this poem and in Rainer Maria Rilke's "The Panther" (p. 81).

H. D.
[HILDA DOOLITTLE] (1886–1961)
Heat   1916

O wind, rend open the heat,
cut apart the heat,
rend it to tatters.

Fruit cannot drop
through this thick air —   5
fruit cannot fall into heat
that presses up and blunts
the points of pears
and rounds the grapes.

Cut the heat —   10
plough through it,
turning it on either side
of your path.

Considerations for Critical Thinking and Writing

1. What physical properties are associated with heat in this poem?
2. Explain the effect of the description of fruit in lines 4–9.
3. Why is the image of the cutting plow especially effective in lines 10–13?

WILLIAM BLAKE (1757–1827)

London   1794

I wander through each chartered° street,   *defined by law*
Near where the chartered Thames does flow,
And mark in every face I meet
Marks of weakness, marks of woe.

In every cry of every man,   5
In every Infant's cry of fear,
In every voice, in every ban,
The mind-forged manacles I hear.

How the Chimney-sweeper's cry
Every black'ning Church appalls;   10
And the hapless Soldier's sigh
Runs in blood down Palace walls.

But most through midnight streets I hear
How the youthful Harlot's curse
Blasts the new-born Infant's tear,   15
And blights with plagues the Marriage hearse.

Considerations for Critical Thinking and Writing

1. How do the visual images in this poem suggest a feeling of being trapped?
2. What is the predominant sound heard in the poem?
3. What is the meaning of line 8? What is the cause of the problems that the speaker sees and hears in London? Does the speaker suggest additional causes?
4. The image in lines 11–12 cannot be read literally. Comment on its effectiveness.
5. How does Blake's use of denotative and connotative language enrich this poem's meaning?
6. An earlier version of Blake's last stanza appeared this way:

   > But most the midnight harlot's curse
   > From every dismal street I hear,
   > Weaves around the marriage hearse
   > And blasts the new-born infant's tear.

   Examine carefully the differences between the two versions. How do Blake's revisions affect his picture of London life? Which version do you think is more effective? Why?

WILFRED OWEN (1893–1918)

Dulce et Decorum Est   1920

Bent double, like old beggars under sacks,
Knock-kneed, coughing like hags, we cursed through sludge,
Till on the haunting flares we turned our backs,

And towards our distant rest began to trudge.
Men marched asleep. Many had lost their boots,   5
But limped on, blood-shod. All went lame, all blind;
Drunk with fatigue; deaf even to the hoots
Of gas-shells dropping softly behind.

Gas! GAS! Quick, boys! — An ecstasy of fumbling,
Fitting the clumsy helmets just in time,   10
But someone still was yelling out and stumbling
And flound'ring like a man in fire or lime. —
Dim through the misty panes and thick green light,
As under a green sea, I saw him drowning.

In all my dreams before my helpless sight   15
He plunges at me, guttering, choking, drowning.

If in some smothering dreams, you too could pace
Behind the wagon that we flung him in,
And watch the white eyes writhing in his face,
His hanging face, like a devil's sick of sin,   20
If you could hear, at every jolt, the blood
Come gargling from the froth-corrupted lungs
Bitter as the cud
Of vile, incurable sores on innocent tongues, —
My friend, you would not tell with such high zest   25
To children ardent for some desperate glory,
The old lie: *Dulce et decorum est
Pro patria mori.*

Considerations for Critical Thinking and Writing

1. The Latin quotation in lines 27–28 is from Horace: "It is sweet and fitting to die
   for one's country." Owen served as a British soldier during World War I and was
   killed. Is this poem unpatriotic? What is its purpose?
2. Which images in the poem are most vivid? To which senses do they speak?
3. Describe the speaker's tone. What is his relationship to his audience?
4. How are the images of the soldiers in this poem different from the images that
   typically appear in recruiting posters?

ELIZABETH BARRETT BROWNING (1806–1861)
Grief   1844

I tell you, hopeless grief is passionless;
That only men incredulous of despair,
Half-taught in anguish, through the midnight air

Beat upward to God's throne in loud access
Of shrieking and reproach. Full desertness,   5
In souls as countries, lieth silent-bare
Under the blanching, vertical eye-glare
Of the absolute Heavens. Deep-hearted man, express
Grief for thy Dead in silence like to death —
Most like a monumental statue set   10
In everlasting watch and moveless woe
Till itself crumble to the dust beneath.
Touch it; the marble eyelids are not wet.
If it could weep, it could arise and go.

Considerations for Critical Thinking and Writing

1. What images does Browning use to describe grief?
2. What is the effect of the poem's first words, "I tell you"? How do they serve to characterize the speaker?
3. Describe the emotional tone of this poem.

ROBERT LOWELL (1917–1977)
Skunk Hour   1959

For Elizabeth Bishop

Nautilus Island's hermit
heiress still lives through winters in her Spartan cottage;
her sheep still graze above the sea.
Her son's a bishop. Her farmer
is first selectman in our village;   5
she's in her dotage.

Thirsting for
the hierarchic privacy
of Queen Victoria's century,
she buys up all   10
the eyesores facing her shore,
and lets them fall.

The season's ill —
we've lost our summer millionaire,
who seemed to leap from an L. L. Bean°   15
catalogue. His nine-knot yawl
was auctioned off to lobstermen.
A red fox stain covers Blue Hill.

And now our fairy
decorator brightens his shop for fall;   20

15 *L. L. Bean:* A famous Maine mail-order store specializing in outdoor clothes and equipment.

his fishnet's filled with orange cork,
orange, his cobbler's bench and awl;
there is no money in his work,
he'd rather marry.

One dark night,   25
my Tudor Ford climbed the hill's skull;
I watched for love-cars. Lights turned down,
they lay together, hull to hull,
where the graveyard shelves on the town. . . .
My mind's not right.   30

A car radio bleats,
"Love, O careless Love. . . ." I hear
my ill-spirit sob in each blood cell,
as if my hand were at its throat. . . .
I myself am hell;   35
nobody's here —

only skunks, that search
in the moonlight for a bite to eat.
They march on their soles up Main Street:
white stripes, moonstruck eyes' red fire   40
under the chalk-dry and spar spire
of the Trinitarian Church.

I stand on top
of our back steps and breathe the rich air —
a mother skunk with her column of kittens swills the garbage pail.   45
She jabs her wedge-head in a cup
of sour cream, drops her ostrich tail,
and will not scare.

Considerations for Critical Thinking and Writing

1. How does the speaker in this poem characterize life in this Maine coastal town? Which images suggest his attitude toward the town?
2. What is the significance of the title? How is it related to the description of the town?
3. Comment on lines 32–35. What is the speaker's state of mind? How is it reflected throughout the poem?
4. What is the effect of the skunks' appearance at the end of the poem? What does the speaker's attitude toward them reveal about the speaker?
5. Work up a series of a dozen or so images that capture your impressions of a town or city with which you are familiar. Then summarize in a few sentences the overall tone the images evoke.

JOHN REPP (b. 1953)

Cursing the Hole in the Screen, Wondering
at the Romance Some Find in Summer   1986

Interminable as a slug inching up
the mildewed wall of a chicken coop
left to fall down or be wrecked some
wrung-out night by boys marking the new
swell in their balls with ruin —   5
summer shambles on, its random tiny horrors
hatch, sting, copulate, die, all
in these rooms. Kitchen? Midges throng
to every orifice. Bathroom? Wasps lumber
down from the sill. Bedroom? Mosquitoes   10
sing like autistic children.
             Run out
to the pond with no clothes on and bob
in the tepid wet, a hellish middle C
penetrating everything. And bellicose   15
frogs feasting in chorus so dissonant
it puts to shame all the postmodernist°
harumping of hoarse tubas and hubcaps
loved by believers in naturalism
and the culturally symptomatic.   20
               Night wrings
its filthy washcloth as the first coil
of heat unwinds, the few dewdrops steam away,
here dust on the marigolds, there a cat sprawled
in the willow's crackling shade, no Artemis,°   25
no Mark Twain Mississippi River, no veranda,
just the *pop* of a billion eggs falling open.

17 *postmodernist:* A term that refers to the interest in contemporary arts in experimental forms.
25 *Artemis:* A Greek goddess of hunting, healing, and fertility.

Considerations for Critical Thinking and Writing

1. What feelings do you associate with summer? How does this poem make you feel about summer? Do the poem's images confirm or challenge your associations with summer?
2. Describe the poem's speaker. How does the voice of lines 1–8 compare with that of lines 15–20? What do the diction and allusions tell you about the speaker?
3. Comment on the appropriateness of the poem's title. Explain whether you think it is helpful or intrusive.
4. Select an image from the poem and expand on it by writing a brief essay developing further what the image mentions.

1. Explain which image of heat you find more effective, Repp's or H. D.'s in "Heat" (p. 75).
2. Write a response to William Shakespeare's "Shall I compare thee to a summer's day?" (p. 181) from the point of view of Repp's speaker. Try to capture the speaker's vivid use of images.

RICHMOND LATTIMORE (b. 1906)
The Crabs   1972

There was a bucket full of them. They spilled,
crawled, climbed, clawed: slowly tossed
and fell: precision made: cold iodine color of their own
world of sand and occasional brown weed, round stone
chilled clean in the chopping waters of their coast.   5
One fell out. The marine thing on the grass
tried to trundle off, barbarian and immaculate and to be killed
with his kin. We lit water: dumped the living mass
in: contemplated tomatoes and corn: and with the good cheer of civilized man,
cigarettes, that is, and cold beer, and chatter,   10
waited out and lived down the ten-foot-away clatter
of crabs as they died for us inside their boiling can.

Considerations for Critical Thinking and Writing

1. How is the reader's initial attitude toward the crabs in this poem controlled by references to them as "precision made," "marine thing[s]," and "barbarian"?
2. How do the later images of the crabs as a "living mass" and their "clatter" as they are boiled compete with the images of them in lines 1–8?
3. What is the effect of the images describing the humans? How do you feel about these people?
4. The diction of this poem is informal and chatty, but it conveys a dark theme. Do you think the level of diction is appropriate for the theme?
5. Write a short essay that develops some point about the "chatter" of "civilized man" and the "clatter" of the crabs.

RAINER MARIA RILKE (1875–1926)
The Panther   1927
TRANSLATED BY STEPHEN MITCHELL

His vision, from the constantly passing bars,
has grown so weary that it cannot hold
anything else. It seems to him there are
a thousand bars; and behind the bars, no world.

As he paces in cramped circles, over and over,   5
the movement of his powerful soft strides
is like a ritual dance around a center
in which a mighty will stands paralyzed.

Only at times, the curtain of the pupils
lifts, quietly —. An image enters in,   10
rushes down through the tensed, arrested muscles,
plunges into the heart and is gone.

Considerations for Critical Thinking and Writing

1. What kind of "image enters in" the heart of the panther in the final stanza?
2. How are images of confinement achieved in the poem? Why doesn't Rilke describe
   the final image in lines 10–12?

Connections to Other Selections

1. Write an essay explaining how a sense of movement is achieved by the images
   and rhythms in this poem and in Emily Dickinson's "A Bird came down the
   Walk —" (p. 136).
2. Discuss the idea of confinement in "The Panther" and Eamon Grennan's "Bat"
   (p. 74).

MARGARET HOLLEY (b. 1944)
The Fireflies   1991

Sparks from a bonfire,
desire's half-hidden furnace,
drift in the black meadow,

pulsing shrimps,
their candles flaring,   5
each comma carrying its own lantern.

You remain indoors
reading by lamplight, glowworm,
larva whose labor is to eat,

molt,   10
and feverishly expand before
the newly secreted chitin hardens.

This is the fire in between
the first awareness
of desire   15

and its denouement,
the time of craving unfulfilled,
a bright transparency

of the verb "to want"
in all its conjugations.   20
For now, your cocoon of pages

keeps you as quiet
as the pupa, the doll,
that seems to just hang around

doing nothing,   25
while under the exoskeleton
a major transformation occurs.

What can I say to you,
except that out here at night
the body becomes an intermittent torch   30

finally consenting to burn,
consenting to know what it is
one wants

and may or may not have,
to walk in the dark by one's own light,   35
ablaze, transparent,

and as transient
as these, their minute lamps
making a silent firework of praise.

Considerations for Critical Thinking and Writing

1. What does this poem say about desire?
2. How does the speaker describe the reader who remains indoors? Does the speaker offer advice or simply make an observation?
3. How might this poem's images be regarded as a "firework of praise"?

SALLY CROFT (b. 1935)
Home-Baked Bread   1981

Nothing gives a household a greater sense of stability and common comfort than the aroma of cooling bread. Begin, if you like, with a loaf of whole wheat, which requires neither sifting nor kneading, and go on from there to more cunning triumphs.
— The Joy of Cooking

What is it she is not saying?
Cunning triumphs. It rings
of insinuation. Step into my kitchen,
I have prepared a cunning triumph

for you. Spices and herbs   5
sealed in this porcelain jar,

a treasure of my great-aunt
who sat up past midnight
in her Massachusetts bedroom
when the moon was dark. Come,   10
rest your feet. I'll make
you tea with honey and slices

of warm bread spread with peach butter.
I picked the fruit this morning
still fresh with dew. The fragrance   15
is seductive? I hoped you would say that.
See how the heat rises
when the bread opens. Come,

we'll eat together, the small flakes
have scarcely any flavor. What cunning   20
triumphs we can discover in my upstairs room
where peach trees breathe their sweetness
beside the open window and
sun lies like honey on the floor.

Considerations for Critical Thinking and Writing

1. Why does the speaker in this poem seize upon the phrase "cunning triumphs" from *The Joy of Cooking* excerpt?
2. Distinguish between the voice we hear in lines 1–3 and the second voice in lines 3–24. Who is the "you" in the poem?
3. Why is "insinuation" an especially appropriate word choice in line 3?
4. How do the images in lines 20–24 bring together all the senses evoked in the preceding lines?
5. Write a paragraph that describes the sensuous (and perhaps sensual) qualities of a food you enjoy.

CAROLYN KIZER (b. 1925)
Food for Love   1984

> *Eating is touch carried to the bitter end.*
>   – Samuel Butler II

I'm going to murder you with love;
I'm going to suffocate you with embraces;
I'm going to hug you, bone by bone,
Till you're dead all over.
Then I will dine on your delectable marrow.   5

You will become my personal Sahara;
I'll sun myself in you, then with one swallow
Drain your remaining brackish well.
With my female blade I'll carve my name
In your most aspiring palm   10
Before I chop it down.
Then I'll inhale your last oasis whole.

But in the total desert you become
You'll see me stretch, horizon to horizon,
Opulent mirage!   15
Wisteria balconies dripping cyclamen.
Vistas ablaze with crystal, laced in gold.

So you will summon each dry grain of sand
And move towards me in undulating dunes
Till you arrive at sudden ultramarine: 20
A Mediterranean to stroke your dusty shores;
Obstinate verdure, creeping inland, fast renudes
Your barrens; succulents spring up everywhere,
Surprising life! And I will be that green.

When you are fed and watered, flourishing   25
With shoots entwining trellis, dome and spire,
Till you are resurrected field in bloom,
I will devour you, my natural food,
My host, my final supper on the earth,
And you'll begin to die again.   30

Considerations for Critical Thinking and Writing

1. What's going on here? Is this a love poem? Explain why or why not.
2. What does the epigraph from Samuel Butler contribute to your understanding of
   the poem?
3. Contrast the speaker's relationship with her "personal Sahara" in lines 1–12 and
   in lines 13–30.

Connections to Other Selections

1. Write a reply to this poem—in poetry or prose—as you think the speaker of
   Andrew Marvell's "To His Coy Mistress" (p. 55) would respond.
2. Discuss the relationship between food and love in Kizer's poem and Sally Croft's
   "Home-Baked Bread" (p. 83).
3. Write an essay comparing the tone of "Food for Love" and Elaine Magarrell's "The
   Joy of Cooking" (p. 106).

SAPPHO (c. 612–c. 580 B.C.)
With his venom

TRANSLATED BY MARY BARNARD

With his venom

Irresistible
and bittersweet

that loosener
of limbs, Love

reptile-like
strikes me down

Considerations for Critical Thinking and Writing

1. In what sense is love both "Irresistible and bittersweet" in this poem?
2. Consider the sounds in this poem. How are they related to their meanings?
3. Does it make sense to use a snakebite as an image of love? Explain why or why not.

Connections to Other Selections

1. How does your response to the images of love in this poem compare with the response evoked by the images in Cathy Song's "The White Porch" (p. 493).
2. Discuss the attitudes toward love expressed by Sappho and by Edna St. Vincent Millay in "I Too beneath Your Moon, Almighty Sex" (p. 402).

EZRA POUND (1885–1972)
In a Station of the Metro°   1913

The apparition of these faces in the crowd;
Petals on a wet, black bough.

Metro: Underground railroad in Paris.

Considerations for Critical Thinking and Writing

1. What kind of mood does the image in the second line convey?
2. Why is "apparition" a better word choice than, say, "appearance" or "sight"?

T. E. HULME (1883–1917)
On the Differences between Poetry and Prose   1924

In prose as in algebra concrete things are embodied in signs or counters which are moved about according to rules, without being visualized at all in the process. There are in prose certain type situations and arrangements of words, which move as automatically into certain other arrangements as do functions in algebra. One only changes the X's and the Y's back into physical things at the end of the process. Poetry, in one aspect at any rate, may be considered as an effort to avoid this characteristic of prose. It is not a counter language, but a visual concrete one. It is a compromise for a language of intuition which would hand over sensations bodily. It always endeavors to arrest you, and to make you continuously see a physical thing, to prevent you gliding through an abstract process. It chooses fresh epithets and fresh metaphors, not so much because they are new, and we are tired of the old, but because the old cease to convey a physical thing and become abstract counters. A poet says a ship "coursed the seas" to get a physical image, instead of the counter word "sailed." Visual meanings can only be transferred by the new bowl of metaphor; prose is an old pot that lets them leak out. Images in verse are not mere decoration, but the very essence of an intuitive language. Verse is a pedestrian taking you over the ground, prose—a train which delivers you at a destination.

From "Romanticism and Classicism," in *Speculations,*
edited by Herbert Read

Considerations for Critical Thinking and Writing

1. What distinctions does Hulme make between poetry and prose? Which seems to be the most important difference?
2. Write an essay that discusses Hulme's claim that poetry "is a compromise for a language of intuition which would hand over sensations bodily."

4. Figures of Speech

Figures of speech are broadly defined as a way of saying one thing in terms of something else. An overeager funeral director might, for example, be described as a vulture. Although figures of speech are indirect, they are designed to clarify, not obscure, our understanding of what they describe. Poets frequently use them because, as Emily Dickinson said, the poet's work is to "Tell all the truth but tell it slant" in order to capture the reader's interest and imagination. But figures of speech are not limited to poetry. Hearing them, reading them, or using them is as natural as using language itself.

Suppose that in the middle of a class discussion concerning the economic causes of World War II your history instructor introduces a series of statistics by saying, "Let's get down to brass tacks." Would anyone be likely to expect a display of brass tacks for students to examine? Of course not. To interpret the statement literally would be to wholly misunderstand the instructor's point that the time has come for a close look at the economic circumstances leading to the war. A literal response transforms the statement into the sort of hilariously bizarre material often found in a sketch by Woody Allen.

The class does not look for brass tacks, because, to put it in a nutshell, they understand that the instructor is speaking figuratively. They would understand, too, that in the preceding sentence *in a nutshell* refers to brevity and conciseness rather than to the covering of a kernel of a nut. Figurative language makes its way into our everyday speech and writing as well as into literature because it is a means of achieving color, vividness, and intensity.

Consider the difference, for example, between these two statements.

Literal: The diner strongly expressed anger at the waiter.
Figurative: The diner leaped from his table and roared at the waiter.

The second statement is more vivid because it creates a picture of ferocious anger by likening the diner to some kind of wild animal, such as a lion or tiger. By comparison, "strongly expressed anger" is neither especially strong nor especially expressive; it is flat. Not all figurative language avoids this kind of flatness, however. Figures of speech such as "getting down to brass tacks" and "in a nutshell" are clichés because they lack originality and freshness. Still, they suggest how these devices are commonly used to give language some color, even if that color is sometimes a bit faded.

There is nothing weak about William Shakespeare's use of figurative language in the following passage from *Macbeth*. Macbeth has just learned that his wife is dead, and he laments her loss as well as the course of his own life.

WILLIAM SHAKESPEARE (1564–1616)
From *Macbeth (Act V, Scene v)*   1605–06

Tomorrow, and tomorrow, and tomorrow
Creeps in this petty pace from day to day
To the last syllable of recorded time;
And all our yesterdays have lighted fools
The way to dusty death. Out, out, brief candle!
Life's but a walking shadow, a poor player,
That struts and frets his hour upon the stage,
And then is heard no more. It is a tale
Told by an idiot, full of sound and fury,
Signifying nothing.

This passage might be summarized as "life has no meaning," but such a brief paraphrase does not take into account the figurative language that reveals the depth of Macbeth's despair and his view of the absolute meaninglessness of life. By comparing life to a "brief candle," Macbeth emphasizes the darkness and death that surround human beings. The light of life is too brief and unpredictable to be of any comfort. Indeed, life for Macbeth is a "walking shadow," futilely playing a role that is more farcical than dramatic, because life is, ultimately, a desperate story filled with pain and devoid of significance. What the figurative language provides, then, is the emotional force of Macbeth's assertion; his comparisons are disturbing because they are so apt.

The remainder of this chapter discusses some of the most important figures of speech used in poetry. A familiarity with them will help you to understand how poetry achieves its effects.

SIMILE AND METAPHOR

The two most common figures of speech are simile and metaphor. Both compare things that are ordinarily considered unlike each other. A *simile* makes an explicit comparison between two things by using words such as *like, as, than, appears,* or *seems:* "A sip of Mrs. Cook's coffee is like a punch in the stomach." The force of the simile is created by the differences between the two things compared. There would be no simile if the comparison were stated this way: "Mrs. Cook's coffee is as strong as the cafeteria's coffee." This is a literal comparison because Mrs. Cook's coffee is compared with something like it, another kind of coffee. Consider how simile is used in this poem.

MARGARET ATWOOD (b. 1939)
you fit into me   1971

you fit into me
like a hook into an eye

a fish hook
an open eye

    If you blinked on a second reading, you got the point of this poem, because you recognized that the simile "like a hook into an eye" gives way to a play on words in the final two lines. There the hook and eye, no longer a pleasant domestic image of fitting closely together, become a literal, sharp fishhook and a human eye. The wordplay qualifies the simile and drastically alters the tone of this poem by creating a strong and unpleasant surprise.

    A *metaphor,* like a simile, makes a comparison between two unlike things, but it does so implicitly, without words such as *like* or *as:* "Mrs. Cook's coffee is a punch in the stomach." Metaphor asserts the identity of dissimilar things. Macbeth tells us that life *is* a "brief candle," life *is* a "walking shadow," life *is* a "poor player," life *is* a "tale / Told by an idiot." Metaphor transforms people, places, objects, and ideas into whatever the poet imagines them to be, and if metaphors are effective, the reader's experience, understanding, and appreciation of what is described are enhanced. Metaphors are frequently more demanding than similes because they are not signaled by particular words. They are both subtle and powerful.

    Here is a poem about presentiment, a foreboding that something terrible is about to happen.

EMILY DICKINSON (1830–1886)
Presentiment — is that long Shadow — on the lawn —   c. 1863

Presentiment — is that long Shadow — on the lawn —
Indicative that Suns go down —

The notice to the startled Grass
That Darkness — is about to pass —

The metaphors in this poem define the abstraction *presentiment*. The sense of foreboding that Dickinson expresses is identified with a particular moment, the moment when darkness is just about to envelop an otherwise tranquil ordinary scene. The speaker projects that fear onto the "startled Grass" so that it seems any life must be frightened by the approaching "Shadow" and "Darkness" — two richly connotative words associated with death. The metaphors obliquely tell us ("tell it slant" was Dickinson's motto, remember) that presentiment is related to a fear of death, and, more important, the metaphors convey the feelings which attend that idea.

Some metaphors are more subtle than others, because their comparison of terms is less explicit. Notice the difference between the following two metaphors, both of which describe a shaggy derelict refusing to leave the warmth of a hotel lobby. "He was a mule standing his ground" is a quite explicit comparison. The man is a mule; X is Y. But this metaphor is much more covert: "He brayed his refusal to leave." This second version is an *implied metaphor,* because it does not explicitly identify the man with a mule. Instead, it hints at or alludes to the mule. Braying is associated with mules and is especially appropriate in this context because of those animals' reputation for stubbornness. Implied metaphors can slip by readers, but they offer the alert reader the energy and resonance of carefully chosen, highly concentrated language.

Some poets write extended comparisons in which part or all of the poem consists of a series of related metaphors or similes. Extended metaphors are more common than extended similes. In "Catch" (p. 17), Robert Francis creates an *extended metaphor* that compares poetry to a game of catch. The entire poem is organized around this comparison, just as all of the elements in e. e. cummings's "she being Brand" (p. 47) are clustered around the extended comparison of a car and a woman. Because these comparisons are at work throughout the entire poem, they are called *controlling metaphors.* Extended comparisons can serve as a poem's organizing principle; they are also a reminder that in good poems metaphor and simile are not merely decorative but inseparable from what is expressed.

Notice the controlling metaphor in this poem, written by a woman whose contemporaries identified her more as a wife and mother than as a poet. Anne Bradstreet's first volume of poetry, *The Tenth Muse,* was published by her brother-in-law in 1650 without her prior knowledge.

ANNE BRADSTREET (c. 1612–1672)
The Author to Her Book 1678

Thou ill-formed offspring of my feeble brain,
Who after birth did'st by my side remain,
Till snatched from thence by friends, less wise than true,
Who thee abroad exposed to public view;
Made thee in rags, halting, to the press to trudge,   5
Where errors were not lessened, all may judge.
At thy return my blushing was not small,
My rambling brat (in print) should mother call;
I cast thee by as one unfit for light,
Thy visage was so irksome in my sight;   10
Yet being mine own, at length affection would
Thy blemishes amend, if so I could:
I washed thy face, but more defects I saw,
And rubbing off a spot, still made a flaw.
I stretched thy joints to make thee even feet,   15
Yet still thou run'st more hobbling than is meet;
In better dress to trim thee was my mind,
But nought save homespun cloth in the house I find.
In this array, 'mongst vulgars may'st thou roam;
In critics' hands beware thou dost not come;   20
And take thy way where yet thou are not known.
If for thy Father asked, say thou had'st none;
And for thy Mother, she alas is poor,
Which caused her thus to send thee out of door.

The extended metaphor likening her book to a child came naturally to Bradstreet and allowed her to regard her work both critically and affectionately. Her conception of the book as her child creates just the right tone of amusement, self-deprecation, and concern.

OTHER FIGURES

Perhaps the humblest figure of speech — if not one of the most familiar — is the pun. A *pun* is a play on words that relies on a word having more than one meaning or sounding like another word. For example, "A fad is in one era and out the other" is the sort of pun that produces obligatory groans. But most of us find pleasant and interesting surprises in puns. Here's one that has a slight edge to its humor.

EDMUND CONTI (b. 1929)
Pragmatist

1985

Apocalypse soon
Coming our way
Ground zero at noon
Halve a nice day.

Grimly practical under the circumstances, the pragmatist divides the familiar cheerful cliché by half. As simple as this poem is, its tone is mixed because it makes us laugh and wince at the same time.

Puns can be used to achieve serious effects as well as humorous ones. Although we may have learned to underrate puns as figures of speech, it is a mistake to underestimate their power and the frequency with which they appear in poetry. A close examination, for example, of Henry Reed's "Naming of Parts" (p. 124), Robert Frost's "Design" (p. 311), or almost any lengthy passage from a Shakespeare play will confirm the value of puns.

Synecdoche is a figure of speech in which part of something is used to signify the whole: a neighbor is a "wagging tongue" (a gossip); a criminal is placed "behind bars" (in prison). Less typically, synecdoche refers to the whole used to signify the part: "Germany invaded Poland"; "Princeton won the fencing match." Clearly, certain individuals participated in these activities, not all of Germany or Princeton. Another related figure of speech is **metonymy**, in which something closely associated with a subject is substituted for it: "She preferred the silver screen [motion pictures] to reading." "At precisely ten o'clock the paper shufflers [office workers] stopped for coffee."

Synecdoche and metonymy may overlap and are therefore sometimes difficult to distinguish. Consider this description of a disapproving minister entering a noisy tavern: "As those pursed lips came through the swinging door, the atmosphere was suddenly soured." The pursed lips signal the presence of the minister and are therefore a synecdoche, but they additionally suggest an inhibiting sense of sin and guilt that makes the bar patrons feel uncomfortable. Hence, the pursed lips are also a metonymy, since they are in this context so closely connected with religion. Although the distinction between synecdoche and metonymy can be useful, when a figure of speech overlaps categories, it is usually labeled a metonymy.

Knowing the precise term for a figure of speech is, finally, less important than responding to its use in a poem. Consider how metonymy and synecdoche convey the tone and meaning of the following poem.

DYLAN THOMAS (1914–1953)
The Hand That Signed the Paper   1936

The hand that signed the paper felled a city;
Five sovereign fingers taxed the breath,
Doubled the globe of dead and halved a country;
These five kings did a king to death.

The mighty hand leads to a sloping shoulder,   5
The finger joints are cramped with chalk;
A goose's quill has put an end to murder
That put an end to talk.

The hand that signed the treaty bred a fever,
And famine grew, and locusts came;   10
Great is the hand that holds dominion over
Man by a scribbled name.

The five kings count the dead but do not soften
The crusted wound nor stroke the brow;
A hand rules pity as a hand rules heaven;   15
Hands have no tears to flow.

The "hand" in this poem is a synecdoche for a powerful ruler, because it is a part of someone used to signify the entire person. The "goose's quill" is a metonymy that also refers to the power associated with the ruler's hand. By using these figures of speech, Thomas depersonalizes and ultimately dehumanizes the ruler. The final synecdoche tells us that "Hands have no tears to flow." It makes us see the political power behind the hand as remote and inhuman. How is the meaning of the poem enlarged when the speaker says, "A hand rules pity as a hand rules heaven"?

One of the ways writers energize the abstractions, ideas, objects, and animals that constitute their created worlds is through **personification**, the attribution of human characteristics to nonhuman things: temptation pursues the innocent; trees scream in the raging wind; mice conspire in the cupboard. We are not explicitly told that these things are people; instead, we are invited to see that they behave like people. Perhaps it is human vanity that makes personification a frequently used figure of speech. Whatever the reason, personification, a form of metaphor that connects the nonhuman with the human, makes the world understandable in human terms. Consider this concise example from William Blake's *The Marriage of Heaven and Hell,* a long poem that takes delight in attacking conventional morality: "Prudence is a rich ugly old maid courted by Incapacity." By personifying prudence, Blake transforms what is usually considered a virtue into a comic figure hardly worth emulating.

Often related to personification is another rhetorical figure called **apostrophe,** an address either to someone who is absent and therefore cannot hear the speaker or to something nonhuman that cannot comprehend. Apostrophe provides an opportunity for the speaker of a poem to think aloud, and often the thoughts expressed are in a formal tone. John Keats, for example, begins "Ode on a Grecian Urn" (p. 237) this way: "Thou still unravished bride of quietness." Apostrophe is frequently accompanied by intense emotion that is signaled by phrasing such as "O Life." In the right hands — such as Keats's — apostrophe can provide an intense and immediate voice in a poem, but when it is overdone or extravagant it can be ludicrous. Modern poets are more wary of apostrophe than their predecessors, because apostrophizing strikes many self-conscious twentieth-century sensibilities as too theatrical. Thus modern poets tend to avoid exaggerated situations in favor of less charged though equally meditative moments, as in this next poem, with its amusing, half-serious cosmic twist.

JANICE TOWNLEY MOORE (b. 1939)
To a Wasp   1984

You must have chortled
finding that tiny hole
in the kitchen screen. Right
into my cheese cake batter
you dived,   5
no chance to swim ashore,
no saving spoon,
the mixer whirring
your legs, wings, stinger,
churning you into such   10
delicious death.
Never mind the bright April day.
Did you not see
rising out of cumulus clouds
That fist aimed at both of us?   15

Moore's apostrophe "To a Wasp" is based on the simplest of domestic circumstances; there is almost nothing theatrical or exaggerated in the poem's tone until "That fist" in the last line, when exaggeration takes center stage. As a figure of speech exaggeration is known as **overstatement** or **hyperbole** and adds emphasis without intending to be literally true: "The teenage boy ate everything in the house." Notice how the speaker of Andrew Marvell's "To His Coy Mistress" (p. 55) exaggerates his devotion in the following overstatement.

An hundred years should go to praise
Thine eyes and on thy forehead gaze,
Two hundred to adore each breast,
But thirty thousand to the rest:

That comes to 30,500 years. What is expressed here is heightened emotion, not deception.

The speaker also uses the opposite figure of speech, **understatement,** which says less than is intended. In the next section he sums up why he cannot take 30,500 years to express his love.

> The grave's a fine and private place,
> But none, I think, do there embrace.

The speaker is correct, of course, but by deliberately understating — saying "I think" when he is actually certain — he makes his point that death will overtake their love all the more emphatic. Another powerful example of understatement appears in the final line of Randall Jarrell's "The Death of the Ball Turret Gunner" (p. 45), when the disembodied voice of the machine-gunner describes his death in a bomber: "When I died they washed me out of the turret with a hose."

Paradox is a statement that initially appears to be self-contradictory but that, on closer inspection, turns out to make sense: "The pen is mightier than the sword." In a fencing match, anyone would prefer the sword, but if the goal is to win the hearts and minds of people, the art of persuasion can be more compelling than swordplay. To resolve the paradox, it is necessary to discover the sense that underlies the statement. If we see that "pen" and "sword" are used as metonymies for writing and violence, then the paradox rings true. *Oxymoron* is a condensed form of paradox in which two contradictory words are used together. Combinations such as "sweet sorrow," "silent scream," "sad joy," and "cold fire" indicate the kinds of startling effects that oxymorons can produce. Paradox is useful in poetry because it arrests a reader's attention by its seemingly stubborn refusal to make sense, and once a reader has penetrated the paradox, it is difficult to resist a perception so well earned. Good paradoxes are knotty pleasures. Here is a simple but effective one.

MICHAEL CADNUM (b. 1949)
Cat Spy   1985

He closes both eyes
and watches.

Anyone familiar with feline behavior knows the truth of this apparent contradiction.

The following poems are rich in figurative language. As you read and study them, notice how their figures of speech vivify situations, clarify ideas, intensify emotions, and engage your imagination. Although the terms for the various figures discussed in this chapter are useful for labeling the particular devices used in poetry, they should not be allowed to get in the way of your response to a poem. Don't worry about rounding up examples of figurative language. First relax and let the figures work their effects on you. Use the terms as a means of taking you further into poetry, and they will serve your reading well.

POEMS FOR FURTHER STUDY

ERNEST SLYMAN (b. 1946)
Lightning Bugs

1988

In my backyard,
They burn peepholes in the night
And take snapshots of my house.

Considerations for Critical Thinking and Writing

1. Explain why the title is essential to this poem.
2. What makes the description of the lightning bugs effective? How do the second and third lines complement each other?
3. As Slyman has done, take a simple, common fact of nature and make it vivid by using a figure of speech to describe it.

MARK IRWIN (b. 1953)
Icicles

1987

Slender beards of light
hang from the railing.

My son shows me
their array of sizes:

one oddly shaped,   5
its queer curve

a clear walrus tooth,
illumined, tinseled.

We watch crystal cones
against blue sky.   10

Suddenly some break loose,
an echo of piano notes.

The sun argues
ice to liquid.

Tiny buds of water   15
pendent on dropper tips

push to pear shapes,
prisms that shiver silver

in a slight wind
before falling.   20

Look, he says laughing,
a pinocchio nose,

and grabs one
in his small hand,

touching the clear carrot,   25
cold to his lips.

Considerations for Critical Thinking and Writing

1. What role does the son serve in this poem?
2. Identify the metaphors in this poem. How do the metaphors help to create the
   tone?

SYLVIA PLATH (1932–1963)
Mirror   1963

I am silver and exact. I have no preconceptions.
Whatever I see I swallow immediately
Just as it is, unmisted by love or dislike.
I am not cruel, only truthful —
The eye of a little god, four-cornered.   5
Most of the time I meditate on the opposite wall.
It is pink, with speckles. I have looked at it so long
I think it is a part of my heart. But it flickers.
Faces and darkness separate us over and over.

Now I am a lake. A woman bends over me,   10
Searching my reaches for what she really is.
Then she turns to those liars, the candles or the moon.
I see her back, and reflect it faithfully.
She rewards me with tears and an agitation of hands.
I am important to her. She comes and goes.   15
Each morning it is her face that replaces the darkness.
In me she has drowned a young girl, and in me an old woman
Rises toward her day after day, like a terrible fish.

Considerations for Critical Thinking and Writing

1. What is the effect of the personification in this poem? How would our view of the aging woman be different if she, rather than the mirror, told her story?
2. What is the mythical allusion in "Now I am a lake" (line 10)?
3. In what sense can "candles or the moon" be regarded as "liars"? Explain this metaphor.
4. Discuss the effectiveness of the simile in the final line of the poem.

WILLIAM WORDSWORTH (1770–1850)
London, 1802

1802

Milton!° thou should'st be living at this hour:
England hath need of thee: she is a fen
Of stagnant waters: altar, sword, and pen,
Fireside, the heroic wealth of hall and bower,
Have forfeited their ancient English dower   5
Of inward happiness. We are selfish men;
Oh! raise us up, return to us again;
And give us manners, virtue, freedom, power.
Thy soul was like a star, and dwelt apart:
Thou hadst a voice whose sound was like the sea: 10
Pure as the naked heavens, majestic, free,
So didst thou travel on life's common way,
In cheerful godliness; and yet thy heart
The lowliest duties on herself did lay.

1 *Milton:* John Milton (1608–1674), poet, famous especially for his religious epic *Paradise Lost* and his defense of political freedom.

Considerations for Critical Thinking and Writing

1. Explain the metonymies in lines 3–6 of this poem. What is the speaker's assessment of England?
2. How would the effect of the poem be different if it were in the form of an address to Wordsworth's contemporaries rather than an apostrophe to Milton? What qualities does Wordsworth attribute to Milton by the use of figurative language?

JIM STEVENS (b. 1922)
Schizophrenia

1992

It was the house that suffered most.

It had begun with slamming doors, angry feet scuffing the carpets,
dishes slammed onto the table,
greasy stains spreading on the cloth.

Certain doors were locked at night,   5
feet stood for hours outside them,
dishes were left unwashed, the cloth
disappeared under a hardened crust.

The house came to miss the shouting voices,
the threats, the half-apologies, noisy   10
reconciliations, the sobbing that followed.

Then lines were drawn, borders established,
some rooms declared their loyalties,
keeping to themselves, keeping out the other.
The house divided against itself.   15

Seeing cracking paint, broken windows,
the front door banging in the wind,
the roof tiles flying off, one by one,
the neighbors said it was a madhouse.

It was the house that suffered most.   20

Considerations for Critical Thinking and Writing

1. What is the effect of the personification in this poem?
2. How are the people characterized who live in the house? What does their behavior reveal about them? How does the house respond to them?
3. Comment on the title. If the title were missing what, if anything, would be missing from the poem? Explain your answer.

WALT WHITMAN (1819–1892)
A Noiseless Patient Spider   1868

A noiseless patient spider,
I mark'd where on a little promontory it stood isolated,
Mark'd how to explore the vacant vast surrounding,
It launch'd forth filament, filament, filament, out of itself,
Ever unreeling them, ever tirelessly speeding them.   5

And you O my soul where you stand,
Surrounded, detached, in measureless oceans of space,
Ceaselessly musing, venturing, throwing, seeking the spheres to connect them,
Till the bridge you will need be form'd, till the ductile anchor hold,
Till the gossamer thread you fling catch somewhere, O my soul.   10

Considerations for Critical Thinking and Writing

1. Spiders are not usually regarded as pleasant creatures. Why does the speaker in this poem liken his soul to one? What similarities are there in the poem between spider and soul? Are there any significant differences?

2. How do the images of space relate to the connections made between the speaker's soul and the spider?

Connection to Another Selection

1. Read the early version of "A Noiseless Patient Spider" printed below. Which version is more unified by its metaphors? Which do you prefer? Why? Write an essay about the change of focus from the early version to the final one.

WALT WHITMAN (1819–1892)
The Soul, reaching, throwing out for love c. 1862

The Soul, reaching, throwing out for love,
As the spider, from some little promontory, throwing out filament after filament,
    tirelessly out of itself, that one at least may catch and form a link, a bridge,
    a connection
O I saw one passing along, saying hardly a word — yet full of love I detected
    him, by certain signs
O eyes wishfully turning! O silent eyes!
For then I thought of you o'er the world,
O latent oceans, fathomless oceans of love!
O waiting oceans of love! yearning and fervid! and of you sweet souls perhaps
    in the future, delicious and long:
But Death, unknown on the earth — ungiven, dark here, unspoken, never born:
You fathomless latent souls of love — you pent and unknown oceans of love!

JOHN DONNE (1572–1631)
A Valediction: Forbidding Mourning 1611

As virtuous men pass mildly away,
    And whisper to their souls to go,
While some of their sad friends do say,
    The breath goes now, and some say, no:

So let us melt, and make no noise,   5
    No tear-floods, nor sigh-tempests move;
'Twere profanation of our joys
    To tell the laity our love.

Moving of th' earth° brings harms and fears,   *earthquakes*
    Men reckon what it did and meant,   10
But trepidation of the spheres,°
    Though greater far, is innocent.

11 *trepidation of the spheres:* According to Ptolemaic astronomy, the planets sometimes moved violently, like earthquakes, but these movements were not felt by people on earth.

Dull sublunary° lovers' love
    (Whose soul is sense) cannot admit
Absence, because it doth remove   15
    Those things which elemented° it.   *composed*

But we by a love so much refined,
    That ourselves know not what it is,
Inter-assured of the mind,
    Care less, eyes, lips, and hands to miss.   20

Our two souls therefore, which are one,
    Though I must go, endure not yet
A breach, but an expansion,
    Like gold to airy thinness beat.

If they be two, they are two so   25
    As stiff twin compasses are two;
Thy soul the fixed foot, makes no show
    To move, but doth, if th' other do.

And though it in the center sit,
    Yet when the other far doth roam,   30
It leans, and hearkens after it,
    And grows erect, as that comes home.

Such wilt thou be to me, who must
    Like th' other foot, obliquely run;
Thy firmness makes my circle just,°   35
    And makes me end, where I begun.

13 *sublunary:* Under the moon; hence mortal and subject to change.   35 *circle just:* The circle is a
traditional symbol of perfection.

Considerations for Critical Thinking and Writing

1. A valediction is a farewell. Donne wrote this poem for his wife before leaving on
   a trip to France. What kind of "mourning" is the speaker forbidding?
2. Explain how the simile in lines 1–4 is related to the couple in lines 5–8. Who is
   described as dying?
3. How does the speaker contrast the couple's love to "sublunary lovers' love" (line
   13)?
4. Explain the similes in lines 24 and 25–36.

ABRAHAM COWLEY (1618–1667)
Drinking

1656

The thirsty earth soaks up the rain,
And drinks, and gapes for drink again.
The plants suck in the earth, and are
With constant drinking fresh and fair;
The sea itself — which one would think   5
Should have but little need of drink —
Drinks ten thousand rivers up,
So filled that they o'erflow the cup.
The busy sun — and one would guess
By's drunken fiery face no less —   10
Drinks up the sea, and when he's done,
The moon and stars drink up the sun:
They drink and dance by their own light;
They drink and revel all the night.
Nothing in nature's sober found,   15
But an eternal health goes round.
Fill up the bowl then, fill it high,
Fill up the glasses there; for why
Should every creature drink but I;
Why, man of morals, tell me why?   20

Considerations for Critical Thinking and Writing

1. What is the purpose of the poet's survey of nature's drinking?
2. Consider the nature of the speaker. Explain whether you think his argument should be taken seriously or lightly.

MAY SWENSON (b. 1927)
The Secret in the Cat

1964

I took my cat apart
to see what made him purr.
Like an electric clock
or like the snore

of a warming kettle,   5
something fizzed and sizzled in him.
Was he a soft car,
the engine bubbling sound?

Was there a wire beneath his fur,
or humming throttle?   10

I undid his throat.
Within was no stir.

I opened up his chest
as though it were a door:
no whisk or rattle there.   15
I lifted off his skull:

no hiss or murmur.
I halved his little belly
but found no gear,
no cause for static.   20

So I replaced his lid,
laced his little gut.
His heart into his vest I slid
and buttoned up his throat.

His tail rose to a rod   25
and beckoned to the air.
Some voltage made him vibrate
warmer than before.

Whiskers and a tail:
perhaps they caught   30
some radar code
emitted as a pip, a dot-and-dash

of woolen sound.
My cat a kind of tuning fork? —
amplifier? — telegraph? —   35
doing secret signal work?

His eyes elliptic tubes:
there's a message in his stare.
I stroke him
but cannot find the dial.   40

Considerations for Critical Thinking and Writing

1. What is the secret in the cat? Does the poem answer this question? Explain why
   or why not.
2. What kinds of things is the cat compared to? What do they have in common? Why
   are they appropriate comparisons?

Connection to Another Selection

1. Write an essay comparing Swenson's response to her cat with John Updike's
   treatment in "Dog's Death" (p. 14). How does each writer manage to evoke what
   is essential about the nature of the animal described in the poem?

LINDA PASTAN (b. 1932)
Marks 1978

My husband gives me an A
for last night's supper,
an incomplete for my ironing,
a B plus in bed.
My son says I am average, 5
an average mother, but if
I put my mind to it
I could improve.
My daughter believes
in Pass/Fail and tells me 10
I pass. Wait 'til they learn
I'm dropping out.

Considerations for Critical Thinking and Writing

1. Explain the appropriateness of the controlling metaphor in this poem. How does
   it reveal the woman's relationship to her family?
2. Discuss the meaning of the title.
3. How does the last line serve as both the climax of the woman's story and the
   controlling metaphor of the poem?

Connection to Another Selection

1. Compare the tone of this poem with that of Mark Halliday's "Graded Paper"
   (p. 484).

LUCILLE CLIFTON (b. 1936)
come home from the movies 1974

come home from the movies,
black girls and boys,
the picture be over and the screen
be cold as our neighborhood.
come home from the show, 5
don't be the show.
take off some flowers and plant them,
pick us some papers and read them,
stop making some babies and raise them.
come home from the movies 10

black girls and boys,
show our fathers how to walk like men,
they already know how to dance.

Considerations for Critical Thinking and Writing

1. What are the "movies" a metaphor for?
2. What advice does the speaker urge upon "black girls and boys"?
3. Explain the final two lines. Why do they come last?

ELAINE MAGARRELL (b. 1928)
The Joy of Cooking   1988

I have prepared my sister's tongue,
scrubbed and skinned it,
trimmed the roots, small bones, and gristle.
Carved through the hump it slices thin and neat.
Best with horseradish   5
and economical — it probably will grow back.
Next time perhaps a creole sauce
or mold of aspic?

I will have my brother's heart,
which is firm and rather dry,   10
slow cooked. It resembles muscle
more than organ meat
and needs an apple-onion stuffing
to make it interesting at all.
Although beef heart serves six   15
my brother's heart barely feeds two.
I could also have it braised
and served in sour sauce.

Considerations for Critical Thinking and Writing

1. How are the tongue and heart used to characterize the sister and brother in this poem?
2. Describe the speaker's tone. What effect does the title have on your determining the tone?

Connection to Another Selection

1. Write an essay that explains how cooking becomes a way of talking about something else in this poem and in Sally Croft's "Home-Baked Bread" (p. 83).

TRUMBULL STICKNEY (1874–1904)
Sir, say no more

Sir, say no more,
Within me 'tis as if
The green and climbing eyesight of a cat
Crawled near my mind's poor birds.

Considerations for Critical Thinking and Writing

1. What kind of experience does the speaker describe in this poem?
2. Why is this poem especially difficult to paraphrase?

PERSPECTIVE

JOHN R. SEARLE (b. 1932)
Figuring Out Metaphors

1979

If you hear somebody say, "Sally is a block of ice," or, "Sam is a pig," you are likely to assume that the speaker does not mean what he says literally, but that he is speaking metaphorically. Furthermore, you are not likely to have very much trouble figuring out what he means. If he says, "Sally is a prime number between 17 and 23," or "Bill is a barn door," you might still assume he is speaking metaphorically, but it is much harder to figure out what he means. The existence of such utterances — utterances in which the speaker means metaphorically something different from what the sentence means literally — poses a series of questions for any theory of language and communication: What is metaphor, and how does it differ from both literal and other forms of figurative utterances? Why do we use expressions metaphorically instead of saying exactly and literally what we mean? How do metaphorical utterances work, that is, how is it possible for speakers to communicate to hearers when speaking metaphorically inasmuch as they do not say what they mean? And why do some metaphors work and others do not?

From *Expression and Meaning*

Considerations for Critical Thinking and Writing

1. Searle poses a series of important questions. Write an essay that explores one of these questions, basing your discussion on the poems in this chapter.
2. Try writing a brief poem that provides a context for the line "Sally is a prime number between 17 and 23" or the line "Bill is a barn door." Your task is to create a context so that either one of these metaphoric statements is as readily understandable as "Sally is a block of ice" or "Sam is a pig." Share your poem with your classmates and explain how the line generated the poem you built around it.

5. Symbol, Allegory, and Irony

SYMBOL

A *symbol* is something that represents something else. An object, person, place, event, or action can suggest more than its literal meaning. A handshake between two world leaders might be simply a greeting, but if it is done ceremoniously before cameras it could be a symbolic gesture signifying unity, issues resolved, and joint policies that will be followed. We live surrounded by symbols. When a seventy-thousand-dollar Mercedes-Benz comes roaring by in the fast lane, we get a quick glimpse of not only an expensive car but an entire life-style that suggests opulence, broad lawns, executive offices, and power. One of the reasons some buyers are willing to spend roughly the cost of five Chevrolets for a single Mercedes-Benz is that they are aware of the car's symbolic value. A symbol is a vehicle for two things at once: it functions as itself and it implies meanings beyond itself.

The meanings suggested by a symbol are determined by the context in which they appear. The Mercedes could symbolize very different things depending upon where it was parked. Would an American political candidate be likely to appear in a Detroit blue-collar neighborhood with such a car? Probably not. Although a candidate might be able to afford the car, it would be an inappropriate symbol for someone seeking votes from all the people. As a symbol, the German-built Mercedes would backfire if voters perceived it as representing an entity partially responsible for layoffs of automobile workers or, worse, as a sign of decadence and corruption. Similarly, a huge statue of Mao Tse-tung conveys different meanings to residents of Beijing than it would to farmers in Prairie Center, Illinois. Because symbols depend on contexts for their meaning, literary artists provide those contexts so that the reader has enough information to determine the probable range of meanings suggested by a symbol.

In the following poem the speaker describes walking at night. How is the night used symbolically?

ROBERT FROST (1874–1963)

Acquainted with the Night

1928

I have been one acquainted with the night.
I have walked out in rain — and back in rain.
I have outwalked the furthest city light.

I have looked down the saddest city lane.
I have passed by the watchman on his beat   5
And dropped my eyes, unwilling to explain.

I have stood still and stopped the sound of feet
When far away an interrupted cry
Came over houses from another street,

But not to call me back or say good-by;   10
And further still at an unearthly height
One luminary clock against the sky

Proclaimed the time was neither wrong nor right.
I have been one acquainted with the night.

In approaching this or any poem, you should read for literal meanings first, and then allow the elements of the poem to invite you to symbolic readings, if they are appropriate. Here the somber tone suggests that the lines have symbolic meaning too. The flat matter-of-factness created by the repetition of "I have" (lines 1–5, 7, 14) understates the symbolic subject matter of the poem, which is, finally, more about the "night" located in the speaker's mind or soul than it is about walking away from a city and back again. The speaker is "acquainted with the night." The importance of this phrase is emphasized by Frost's title and by the fact that he begins and ends the poem with it. Poets frequently use this kind of repetition to alert readers to details that carry more than literal meanings.

The speaker in this poem has personal knowledge of the night but does not indicate specifically what the night means. To arrive at the potential meanings of the night in this context, it is necessary to look closely at its connotations, along with the images provided in the poem. The connotative meanings of night suggest, for example, darkness, death, and grief. By drawing upon these connotations, Frost uses a ***conventional symbol***, something that is recognized by many people to represent certain ideas. Roses conventionally symbolize love or beauty; laurels, fame; spring, growth; the moon, romance. Poets often use conventional symbols to convey tone and meaning.

Frost uses the night as a conventional symbol, but he also develops it into a ***literary*** or ***contextual symbol,*** which goes beyond traditional, public meanings. A literary symbol cannot be summarized in a word or two. It tends to be as elusive as experience itself. The night cannot be reduced or equated with darkness or death or grief, but it evokes those associations and more. Frost took what perhaps initially appears to be an overworked, conventional symbol and prevented it from becoming a cliché by deepening and extending its meaning.

The images in "Acquainted with the Night" lead to the poem's symbolic meaning. Unwilling, and perhaps unable, to explain to the watchman (and to the reader) what the night means, the speaker nevertheless conveys feelings about it. The brief images of darkness, rain, sad city lanes, the necessity for guards, the eerie sound of a distressing cry coming over rooftops, and the "luminary clock against the sky" proclaiming "the time was neither wrong nor right" all help to create a sense of anxiety in this tight-lipped speaker. Although we cannot know what unnamed personal experiences have acquainted the speaker with the night, the images suggest that whatever the night means, it is somehow associated with insomnia, loneliness, isolation, coldness, darkness, death, fear, and a sense of alienation from humanity and even time. Daylight — ordinary daytime thoughts and life itself — seems remote and unavailable in this poem. The night is literally the period from sunset to sunrise, but, more important, it is an internal state being felt by the speaker and revealed through the images.

Frost used symbols rather than an expository essay that would explain the conditions that cause these feelings, because most readers can provide their own list of sorrows and terrors that evoke similar emotions. Through symbol, the speaker's experience is compressed and simultaneously expanded by the personal darkness that each reader brings to the poem. The suggestive nature of symbols makes them valuable for poets and evocative for readers.

ALLEGORY

Unlike expansive, suggestive symbols, *allegory* is a narration or description usually restricted to a single meaning because its events, actions, characters, settings, and objects represent specific abstractions or ideas. Although the elements in an allegory may be interesting in themselves, the emphasis tends to be on what they ultimately mean. Characters may be given names such as Hope, Pride, Youth, and Charity; they have few if any personal qualities beyond their abstract meanings. These personifications are a form of extended metaphor, but their meanings are severely restricted. They are not symbols because, for instance, the meaning of a character named Charity is precisely that virtue.

There is little or no room for broad speculation and exploration in allegories. If Frost had written "Acquainted with the Night" as an allegory, he might have named his speaker Loneliness and had him leave the City of Despair to walk the Streets of Emptiness, where Crime, Poverty, Fear, and other characters would define the nature of city life. The literal elements in an allegory tend to be deemphasized in favor of the message. Symbols, however, function both literally and figuratively, so that "Acquainted with the Night" is about both a walk and a sense that something is terribly wrong.

Allegory especially lends itself to **didactic poetry,** which is designed to teach an ethical, moral, or religious lesson. Many stories, poems, and plays are concerned with values, but didactic literature is specifically created to convey a message. "Acquainted with the Night" does not impart advice or offer guidance. If the poem argued that city life is self-destructive or sinful, it would be didactic; instead, it is a lyric poem that expresses the emotions and thoughts of a single speaker.

Although allegory is often enlisted in didactic causes because it can so readily communicate abstract ideas through physical representations, not all allegories teach a lesson. Here is a poem describing a haunted palace while also establishing a consistent pattern that reveals another meaning.

EDGAR ALLAN POE (1809–1849)
The Haunted Palace   1839

I
In the greenest of our valleys,
    By good angels tenanted,
Once a fair and stately palace —
    Radiant palace — reared its head.
In the monarch Thought's dominion —   5
    It stood there!
Never seraph spread a pinion
    Over fabric half so fair.

II
Banners yellow, glorious, golden,
    On its roof did float and flow;   10
(This — all this — was in the olden
    Time long ago)
And every gentle air that dallied,
    In that sweet day,
Along the ramparts plumed and pallid,   15
    A winged odor went away.

III
Wanderers in that happy valley
    Through two luminous windows saw
Spirits moving musically

To a lute's well-tunèd law,   20
Round about a throne, where sitting
    (Porphyrogene!)°   *born to purple, royal*
In state his glory well befitting,
    The ruler of the realm was seen.

IV

And all with pearl and ruby glowing   25
    Was the fair palace door,
Through which came flowing, flowing, flowing
    And sparkling evermore,
A troop of Echoes whose sweet duty
    Was but to sing,   30
In voices of surpassing beauty,
    The wit and wisdom of their king.

V

But evil things, in robes of sorrow,
    Assailed the monarch's high estate;
(Ah, let us mourn, for never morrow   35
    Shall dawn upon him, desolate!)
And, round about his home, the glory
    That blushed and bloomed
Is but a dim-remembered story
    Of the old time entombed.   40

VI

And travelers now within that valley,
    Through the red-litten windows see
Vast forms that move fantastically
    To a discordant melody;
While, like a rapid ghastly river,   45
    Through the pale door,
A hideous throng rush out forever,
    And laugh — but smile no more.

    On one level this poem describes how a once happy palace is desolated by "evil things." If the reader pays close attention to the diction, however, an allegorical meaning becomes apparent on a second reading. A systematic pattern develops in the choice of words used to describe the palace, so that it comes to stand for a human mind. The palace, banners, windows, door, echoes, and throng are equated with a person's head, hair, eyes, mouth, voice, and laughter. That mind, once harmoniously ordered, is overthrown by evil, haunting thoughts that lead to the mad laughter in the poem's final lines. Once the general pattern is seen, the rest of the details fall neatly into place to strengthen the parallels between the surface description of a palace and the allegorical representation of a disordered mind.

    Modern writers generally prefer symbol over allegory because they tend to be more interested in opening up the potential meanings of an experience instead of transforming it into a closed pattern of meaning. Perhaps the major difference is that while allegory may delight a reader's imagination, symbol challenges and enriches it.

IRONY

Another important resource writers use to take readers beyond literal meanings is *irony*, a technique that reveals a discrepancy between what appears to be and what is actually true. Here is a classic example in which appearances give way to the underlying reality.

EDWIN ARLINGTON ROBINSON (1869–1935)
Richard Cory   1897

Whenever Richard Cory went down town,
We people on the pavement looked at him:
He was a gentleman from sole to crown,
Clean favored, and imperially slim.

And he was always quietly arrayed,   5
And he was always human when he talked;
But still he fluttered pulses when he said,
"Good-morning," and he glittered when he walked.

And he was rich — yes, richer than a king —
And admirably schooled in every grace: 10
In fine, we thought that he was everything
To make us wish that we were in his place.

So on we worked, and waited for the light,
And went without the meat, and cursed the bread;
And Richard Cory, one calm summer night,   15
Went home and put a bullet through his head.

Richard Cory seems to have it all. Those less fortunate, "the people on the pavement," regard him as well bred, handsome, tasteful, and richly endowed with both money and grace. Until the final line of the poem, the reader, like the speaker, is charmed by Cory's good fortune, so quietly expressed in his decent, easy manner. That final, shocking line, however, shatters the appearances of Cory's life and reveals him to have been a desperately unhappy man. While everyone else assumes that Cory represented "everything" to which they aspire, the reality is that he could escape his miserable life only as a suicide. This discrepancy between what appears to be true and what actually exists is known as *situational irony*: what happens is entirely different from what is expected. We are not told why

Cory shoots himself; instead, the irony in the poem shocks us into the recognition that appearances do not always reflect realities.

Words are also sometimes intended to be taken at other than face value. *Verbal irony* is saying something different from what is meant. After reading "Richard Cory," to say "That rich gentleman sure was happy" is ironic. The tone of voice would indicate that just the opposite was meant; hence, verbal irony is usually easy to detect in spoken language. In literature, however, a reader can sometimes take literally what a writer intends ironically. The remedy for this kind of misreading is to pay close attention to the poem's context. There is no formula that can detect verbal irony, but contradictory actions and statements as well as the use of understatement and overstatement can often be signals that verbal irony is present.

Consider how verbal irony is used in the next poem.

KENNETH FEARING (1902–1961)
AD   1938

Wanted: Men;
Millions of men are *wanted at once* in a big new field;
New, tremendous, thrilling, great.
If you've ever been a figure in the chamber of horrors,
If you've ever escaped from a psychiatric ward,   5
If you thrill at the thought of throwing poison into wells, have heavenly visions
    of people, by the thousands, dying in flames —

You are the very man we want
We mean business and our business is *you*
Wanted: A race of brand-new men.

Apply: Middle Europe;   10
No skill needed;
No ambition required; no brains wanted and no character allowed;

Take a permanent job in the coming profession
Wages: *Death.*

This poem was written as Nazi troops stormed across Europe at the start of World War II. The advertisement suggests on the surface that killing is just an ordinary job, but the speaker indicates through understatement that there is nothing ordinary about the "business" of this "*coming profession.*" Fearing uses verbal irony to indicate how casually and mindlessly people are prepared to accept the horrors of war.

"AD" is a *satire,* an example of the literary art of ridiculing a folly or vice in an effort to expose or correct it. The object of satire is usually some human frailty; people, institutions, ideas, and things are all fair game for satirists. Fearing satirizes the insanity of a world mobilizing itself for war:

his irony reveals the speaker's knowledge that there is nothing *"New, tremendous, thrilling,* [or] *great"* about going off to kill and be killed. The implication of the poem is that no one should respond to advertisements for war. The poem serves as a satiric corrective to those who would troop off armed with unrealistic expectations; wage war and the wages consist of death.

Dramatic irony is used when a writer allows a reader to know more about a situation than a character does. This creates a discrepancy between what a character says or thinks and what the reader knows to be true. Dramatic irony is often used to reveal character. In the following poem the speaker delivers a public speech that ironically tells us more about him than it does about the patriotic holiday he is commemorating.

e. e. cummings (1894–1962)
next to of course god america i   1926

"next to of course god america i
love you land of the pilgrims' and so forth oh
say can you see by the dawn's early my
country 'tis of centuries come and go
and are no more what of it we should worry   5
in every language even deafanddumb
thy sons acclaim your glorious name by gorry
by jingo by gee by gosh by gum
why talk of beauty what could be more beautiful than these heroic happy dead   10
who rushed like lions to the roaring slaughter
they did not stop to think they died instead
then shall the voice of liberty be mute?"

He spoke. And drank rapidly a glass of water

This verbal debauch of chauvinistic clichés (notice the run-on phrases and lines) reveals that the speaker's relationship to God and country is not, as he claims, one of love. His public address suggests a hearty mindlessness that leads to "roaring slaughter" rather than to reverence or patriotism. Cummings allows the reader to see through the speaker's words to their dangerous emptiness. What the speaker means and what cummings means are entirely different. Like Fearing's "AD," this poem is a satire that invites the reader's laughter and contempt in order to deflate the benighted attitudes expressed in it.

When a writer uses God, destiny, or fate to dash the hopes and expectations of a character or humankind in general, it is called *cosmic irony.* In "The Convergence of the Twain" (p. 60), for example, Thomas Hardy describes how "The Immanent Will" brought together the *Titanic* and a deadly iceberg. Technology and pride are no match for "the Spinner of the Years." Here's a painfully terse version of cosmic irony.

STEPHEN CRANE (1871–1900)
A Man Said to the Universe 1899

A man said to the universe:
"Sir, I exist!"
"However," replied the universe,
"The fact has not created in me
A sense of obligation."

Unlike in "The Convergence of the Twain," there is the slightest bit of humor in Crane's poem, but the joke is on us.

Irony is an important technique that allows a writer to distinguish between appearances and realities. In situational irony a discrepancy exists between what we expect to happen and what actually happens; in verbal irony a discrepancy exists between what is said and what is meant; in dramatic irony a discrepancy exists between what a character believes and what the reader knows to be true; and in cosmic irony a discrepancy exists between what a character aspires to and what universal forces provide. With each of these forms of irony, we are invited to move beyond surface appearances and sentimental assumptions to see the complexity of experience. Irony is often used in literature to reveal a writer's perspective on matters that previously seemed settled.

POEMS FOR FURTHER STUDY

CONRAD HILBERRY (b. 1928)
The Frying Pan 1978

My mark is my confusion.
If I believe it, I am
another long-necked girl
with the same face.
I am emptiness reflected
in a looking glass, a head   5

kept by a collar and leash,
a round belly with something
knocking to get in.

But cross the handle   10
with a short stroke
and I am Venus, the old
beauty. I am both the egg
and the pan it cooks in,
the slow heat, the miraculous   15
sun rising.

Considerations for Critical Thinking and Writing

1. Discuss the meanings of the "mark" in the first stanza. Can you think of any potential readings of it not mentioned by the speaker?
2. How is the pan transformed into an entirely different kind of symbol in the second stanza? How do the images of lines 13–16 create powerful symbolic values?
3. Discuss the significance of the poem's title.
4. The speaker of this poem is a woman, but the author is a man. Write an essay explaining whether knowing this makes any difference in your appreciation or understanding of the poem.

WILLIAM BLAKE (1757–1827)
The Sick Rose   1794

O Rose, thou art sick!
The invisible worm
That flies in the night,
In the howling storm,

Has found out thy bed
Of crimson joy,
And his dark secret love
Does thy life destroy.

Considerations for Critical Thinking and Writing

1. How does the use of personification in this poem indicate that the speaker laments the fate of more than a rose?
2. Discuss some of the possible meanings of the rose. How does the description of the worm help to explain the rose?
3. Is this poem to be read allegorically or symbolically? Can it be read literally?

PAUL LAURENCE DUNBAR (1872–1906)
We Wear the Mask

1896

We wear the mask that grins and lies,
It hides our cheeks and shades our eyes, —
This debt we pay to human guile;
With torn and bleeding hearts we smile,
And mouth with myriad subtleties.   5

Why should the world be overwise,
In counting all our tears and sighs?
Nay, let them only see us, while
    We wear the mask.

We smile, but, O great Christ, our cries   10
To thee from tortured souls arise.
We sing, but oh the clay is vile
Beneath our feet, and long the mile;
But let the world dream otherwise,
    We wear the mask!   15

Considerations for Critical Thinking and Writing

1. What does the mask symbolize? What kind of behavior does it represent?
2. Dunbar was a black man. Does awareness of that fact affect your reading of the poem? Explain why or why not.

Connection to Another Selection

1. Write an essay on oppression as explored in "We Wear the Mask" and William Blake's "The Chimney Sweeper" (p. 127).

WILLIAM STAFFORD (1914–1993)
Traveling through the Dark

1962

Traveling through the dark I found a deer
dead on the edge of the Wilson River road.
It is usually best to roll them into the canyon:
that road is narrow; to swerve might make more dead.

By glow of the tail-light I stumbled back of the car   5
and stood by the heap, a doe, a recent killing;
she had stiffened already, almost cold.
I dragged her off; she was large in the belly.

My fingers touching her side brought me the reason —
her side was warm; her fawn lay there waiting,   10

alive, still, never to be born.
Beside that mountain road I hesitated.

The car aimed ahead its lowered parking lights;
under the hood purred the steady engine.
I stood in the glare of the warm exhaust turning red;   15
around our group I could hear the wilderness listen.

I thought hard for us all — my only swerving —
then pushed her over the edge into the river.

Considerations for Critical Thinking and Writing

1. Notice the description of the car in this poem: the "glow of the tail-light," the "lowered parking lights," and how the engine "purred." How do these and other details suggest symbolic meanings for the car and the "recent killing"?
2. Discuss the speaker's tone. Does the speaker seem, for example, tough, callous, kind, sentimental, confused, or confident?
3. What is the effect of the last stanza's having only two lines rather than the established four lines of the previous stanzas?
4. Discuss the appropriateness of this poem's title. In what sense has the speaker "thought hard for us all"? What are those thoughts?
5. Is this a didactic poem?

RICHARD EBERHART (b. 1904)
The Groundhog   1936

In June, amid the golden fields,
I saw a groundhog lying dead.
Dead lay he; my senses shook,
And mind outshot our naked frailty.
There lowly in the vigorous summer   5
His form began its senseless change,
And made my senses waver dim
Seeing nature ferocious in him.
Inspecting close his maggots' might
And seething caldron of his being,   10
Half with loathing, half with a strange love,
I poked him with an angry stick.
The fever arose, became a flame
And Vigor circumscribed the skies,
Immense energy in the sun,   15
And through my frame a sunless trembling.
My stick had done nor good nor harm.
Then stood I silent in the day
Watching the object, as before;

And kept my reverence for knowledge   20
Trying for control, to be still,
To quell the passion of the blood;
Until I had bent down on my knees
Praying for joy in the sight of decay.
And so I left; and I returned   25
In Autumn strict of eye, to see
The sap gone out of the groundhog,
But the bony sodden hulk remained.
But the year had lost its meaning,
And in intellectual chains   30
I lost both love and loathing,
Mured° up in the wall of wisdom.   *walled*
Another summer took the fields again
Massive and burning, full of life,
But when I chanced upon the spot   35
There was only a little hair left,
And bones bleaching in the sunlight
Beautiful as architecture;
I watched them like a geometer,
And cut a walking stick from a birch.   40
It has been three years, now.
There is no sign of the groundhog.
I stood there in the whirling summer,
My hand capped a withered heart,
And thought of China and of Greece,   45
Of Alexander° in his tent;
Of Montaigne° in his tower,
Of Saint Theresa° in her wild lament.

46 *Alexander:* Alexander the Great (356–323 B.C.), Macedonian king famous for conquering much of the world.   47 *Montaigne:* Michel de Montaigne (1533–1592), French essayist who commented on human affairs.   48 *Saint Theresa:* Saint Theresa of Avila (1515–1582), a mystic who founded a religious order.

Considerations for Critical Thinking and Writing

1. The speaker in this poem makes several visits to view the groundhog. Describe his changing feelings about the dead animal. What does the groundhog mean to the speaker?
2. How are the final four lines related to the speaker's response to the groundhog?
3. Why is a groundhog — rather than, say, a raccoon — an especially appropriate animal for the thematic purposes of this poem?
4. Explain whether you think this is an optimistic or pessimistic poem. Or is it somewhere in between?

Connections to Other Selections

1. Both "The Groundhog" and Stafford's "Traveling through the Dark" (p. 118) have as their subjects the death of an animal. Discuss how that death affects the speaker in each poem.

2. Write an essay that compares the symbolic meanings of the images of decay in "The Groundhog" and Theodore Roethke's "Root Cellar." (p. 72).
3. Compare and contrast the views of nature presented in "The Groundhog," "Traveling through the Dark," and D. H. Lawrence's "Snake" (below). How does each poem represent an effort to understand the nature of nature? Which view of nature do you find most convincing? Why?

D. H. LAWRENCE (1885–1930)
Snake   1923

A snake came to my water-trough
On a hot, hot day, and I in pajamas for the heat,
To drink there.

In the deep, strange-scented shade of the great dark carob-tree
I came down the steps with my pitcher   5
And must wait, must stand and wait, for there he was at the trough before me.

He reached down from a fissure in the earth-wall in the gloom
And trailed his yellow-brown slackness soft-bellied down, over the edge of the
    stone trough
And rested his throat upon the stone bottom,
And where the water had dripped from the tap, in a small clearness,   10
He sipped with his straight mouth,
Softly drank through his straight gums, into his slack long body,
Silently.

Someone was before me at my water-trough,
And I, like a second comer, waiting.   15

He lifted his head from his drinking, as cattle do,
And looked at me vaguely, as drinking cattle do,
And flickered his two-forked tongue from his lips, and mused a moment,
And stooped and drank a little more,
Being earth-brown, earth-golden from the burning bowels of the earth   20
On the day of Sicilian July, with Etna° smoking.   *a volcano*
The voice of my education said to me
He must be killed,
For in Sicily the black, black snakes are innocent, the gold are venomous.

And voices in me said, If you were a man   25
You would take a stick and break him now, and finish him off.

But must I confess how I liked him,
How glad I was he had come like a guest in quiet, to drink at my water-trough
And depart peaceful, pacified, and thankless,
Into the burning bowels of this earth?   30

Was it cowardice, that I dared not kill him?
Was it perversity, that I longed to talk to him?
Was it humility, to feel so honored?

I felt so honored.

And yet those voices: 35
If you were not afraid, you would kill him!

And truly I was afraid, I was most afraid,
But even so, honored still more
That he should seek my hospitality
From out the dark door of the secret earth.   40

He drank enough
And lifted his head, dreamily, as one who has drunken,
And flickered his tongue like a forked night on the air, so black,
Seeming to lick his lips,
And looked around like a god, unseeing, into the air,   45
And slowly turned his head,
And slowly, very slowly, as if thrice adream,
Proceeded to draw his slow length curving round
And climb again the broken bank of my wall-face.

And as he put his head into that dreadful hole,   50
And as he slowly drew up, snake-easing his shoulders, and entered farther,
A sort of horror, a sort of protest against his withdrawing into that horrid black
     hole,
Deliberately going into the blackness, and slowly drawing himself after,
Overcame me now his back was turned.

I looked round, I put down my pitcher,   55
I picked up a clumsy log
And threw it at the water-trough with a clatter.

I think it did not hit him,
But suddenly that part of him that was left behind convulsed in undignified
     haste.
Writhed like lightning, and was gone   60
Into the black hole, the earth-lipped fissure in the wall-front,
At which, in the intense still noon, I stared with fascination.

And immediately I regretted it.
I thought how paltry, how vulgar, what a mean act!
I despised myself and the voices of my accursed human education.   65

And I thought of the albatross,
And I wished he would come back, my snake.

For he seemed to me again like a king,
Like a king in exile, uncrowned in the underworld,
Now due to be crowned again.   70

And so, I missed my chance with one of the lords
Of life.
And I have something to expiate;
A pettiness.

Considerations for Critical Thinking and Writing

1. Do you think Lawrence uses the snake in this poem as a conventional symbol of evil, or does he go beyond the traditional meanings associated with snakes? Consider the images used to describe the snake.
2. What is the "voice of my education" (line 22)? What is the conflict the speaker feels about the snake?
3. Identify the allusion to the albatross (line 66).
4. Explain why the speaker wishes the snake would return (lines 67–70). Why do you think the snake is described as "one of the lords / Of life" (71–72)?

JAMES MERRILL (b. 1926)
Casual Wear   1984

Your average tourist: Fifty. 2.3
Times married. Dressed, this year, in Ferdi Plinthbower
Originals. Odds 1 to 9
Against her strolling past the Embassy

Today at noon. Your average terrorist: 5
Twenty-five. Celibate. No use for trends,
At least in clothing. Mark, though, where it ends.
People have come forth made of colored mist

Unsmiling on one hundred million screens
To tell of his prompt phone call to the station,   10
"Claiming responsibility" — devastation
Signed with a flourish, like the dead wife's jeans.

Considerations for Critical Thinking and Writing

1. What is the effect of the statistics in this poem?
2. Describe the speaker's tone. Is it appropriate for the subject matter? Explain why or why not.
3. Comment on the ironies that emerge from the final two lines. How are the tourist and terrorist linked by the speaker's description? Explain why you think the speaker sympathizes more with the tourist or terrorist — or with neither.

Connections to Other Selections

1. Compare the satire in this poem with that in Peter Meinke's "The ABC of Aerobics" (p. 491). What is satirized in each poem? Which satire is more pointed from your perspective?
2. Write an essay comparing this poem's profiles of the "average tourist" and "terrorist" with either W. H. Auden's "The Unknown Citizen" (p. 355) or Howard Nemerov's "Life Cycle of Common Man" (p. 405). How are these profiles made convincing?

HENRY REED (1914–1986)
Naming of Parts   1946

Today we have naming of parts. Yesterday,
We had daily cleaning. And tomorrow morning,
We shall have what to do after firing. But today,
Today we have naming of parts. Japonica
Glistens like coral in all of the neighboring gardens,   5
        And today we have naming of parts.

This is the lower sling swivel. And this
Is the upper sling swivel, whose use you will see,
When you are given your slings. And this is the piling swivel,
Which in your case you have not got. The branches   10
Hold in the gardens their silent, eloquent gestures,
        Which in our case we have not got.

This is the safety-catch, which is always released
With an easy flick of the thumb. And please do not let me
See anyone using his finger. You can do it quite easy   15
If you have any strength in your thumb. The blossoms
Are fragile and motionless, never letting anyone see
        Any of them using their finger.

And this you can see is the bolt. The purpose of this
Is to open the breech, as you see. We can slide it   20
Rapidly backwards and forwards: we call this
Easing the spring. And rapidly backwards and forwards
The early bees are assaulting and fumbling the flowers:
        They call it easing the Spring.

They call it easing the Spring: it is perfectly easy   25
If you have any strength in your thumb: like the bolt,
And the breech, and the cocking-piece, and the point of balance,
Which in our case we have not got; and the almond-blossom
Silent in all of the gardens and the bees going backwards and forwards,
        For today we have naming of parts.   30

Considerations for Critical Thinking and Writing

1. Characterize the two speakers in this poem. Identify the lines spoken by each.
   How do their respective lines differ in tone?
2. What is the effect of the last line of each stanza?
3. How do ambiguities and puns contribute to the poem's meaning?
4. What symbolic contrast is made between the rifle instruction and the gardens?
   How is this contrast ironic?

JOHN CIARDI (1916–1986)
Suburban

1978

Yesterday Mrs. Friar phoned. "Mr. Ciardi,
   how do you do?" she said. "I am sorry to say
this isn't exactly a social call. The fact is
   your dog has just deposited — forgive me —
a large repulsive object in my petunias."   5

I thought to ask, "Have you checked the rectal grooving
   for a positive I.D.?" My dog, as it happened,
was in Vermont with my son, who had gone fishing —
   if that's what one does with a girl, two cases of beer,
and a borrowed camper. I guessed I'd get no trout.   10

But why lose out on organic gold for a wise crack?
   "Yes, Mrs. Friar," I said, "I understand."
"Most kind of you," she said. "Not at all," I said.
   I went with a spade. She pointed, looking away.
"I always have loved dogs," she said, "but really!"   15

I scooped it up and bowed. "The animal of it.
   I hope this hasn't upset you, Mrs. Friar."
"Not really," she said, "but really!" I bore the turd
   across the line to my own petunias
and buried it till the glorious resurrection   20

when even these suburbs shall give up their dead.

Considerations for Critical Thinking and Writing

1. How does the speaker transform Mrs. Friar into a symbolic figure of the suburbs?
2. Why do you suppose Ciardi focuses on this particular incident to make a comment upon the suburbs? What is the speaker's attitude toward suburban life?
3. Write a one-paragraph physical description of Mrs. Friar that captures her character for you.

Connection to Another Selection

1. Compare the speaker's voices in "Suburban" and in John Updike's "Dog's Death" (p. 14).

ROBERT BROWNING (1812–1889)

My Last Duchess   1842

Ferrara°

That's my last Duchess painted on the wall,
Looking as if she were alive. I call
That piece a wonder, now: Frà Pandolf's° hands
Worked busily a day, and there she stands.
Will't please you sit and look at her? I said   5
"Frà Pandolf" by design, for never read
Strangers like you that pictured countenance,
The depth and passion of its earnest glance,
But to myself they turned (since none puts by
The curtain I have drawn for you, but I)   10
And seemed as they would ask me, if they durst,
How such a glance came there; so, not the first
Are you to turn and ask thus. Sir, 'twas not
Her husband's presence only, called that spot
Of joy into the Duchess' cheek: perhaps   15
Frà Pandolf chanced to say "Her mantle laps
Over my lady's wrist too much," or "Paint
Must never hope to reproduce the faint
Half-flush that dies along her throat": such stuff
Was courtesy, she thought, and cause enough   20
For calling up that spot of joy. She had
A heart — how shall I say? — too soon made glad,
Too easily impressed; she liked whate'er
She looked on, and her looks went everywhere.
Sir, 'twas all one! My favor at her breast,   25
The dropping of the daylight in the West,
The bough of cherries some officious fool
Broke in the orchard for her, the white mule
She rode with round the terrace — all and each
Would draw from her alike the approving speech,   30
Or blush, at least. She thanked men, — good! but thanked
Somehow — I know not how — as if she ranked
My gift of a nine-hundred-years-old name
With anybody's gift. Who'd stoop to blame
This sort of trifling? Even had you skill   35
In speech — which I have not — to make your will
Quite clear to such an one, and say, "Just this
Or that in you disgusts me; here you miss,
Or there exceed the mark" — and if she let
Herself be lessoned so, nor plainly set   40

Ferrara: In the sixteenth century, the duke of this Italian city arranged to marry a second time after
the mysterious death of his very young first wife.   3 *Frà Pandolf:* A fictitious artist.

Her wits to yours, forsooth, and made excuse,
— E'en then would be some stooping; and I choose
Never to stoop. Oh sir, she smiled, no doubt,
Whene'er I passed her; but who passed without
Much the same smile? This grew; I gave commands;   45
Then all smiles stopped together. There she stands
As if alive. Will't please you rise? We'll meet
The company below, then. I repeat,
The Count your master's known munificence
Is ample warrant that no just pretense   50
Of mine for dowry will be disallowed;
Though his fair daughter's self, as I avowed
At starting, is my object. Nay, we'll go
Together down, sir. Notice Neptune, though,
Taming a sea-horse, thought a rarity,   55
Which Claus of Innsbruck° cast in bronze for me!

56 *Claus of Innsbruck:* Also a fictitious artist.

Considerations for Critical Thinking and Writing

1. To whom is the duke addressing his remarks about the duchess in this poem? What is ironic about the situation?
2. Why was the duke unhappy with his first wife? What does this reveal about the duke? What does the poem's title suggest about his attitude toward women in general?
3. What seems to be the visitor's response (lines 53–54) to the duke's account of his first wife?
4. What do you think happened to the Duchess?

Connection to Another Selection

1. Write an essay describing the ways in which the speakers of "My Last Duchess" and "Hazel Tells LaVerne" (p. 50) by Katharyn Howd Machan inadvertently reveal themselves.

WILLIAM BLAKE (1757–1827)
The Chimney Sweeper   1789

When my mother died I was very young,
And my father sold me while yet my tongue
Could scarcely cry " 'weep! 'weep! 'weep! 'weep!"
So your chimneys I sweep, and in soot I sleep.

There's little Tom Dacre, who cried when his head,   5
That curled like a lamb's back, was shaved: so I said

"Hush, Tom! never mind it, for when your head's bare
You know that the soot cannot spoil your white hair."

And so he was quiet, and that very night,
As Tom was a-sleeping, he had such a sight!   10
That thousands of sweepers, Dick, Joe, Ned, and Jack,
Were all of them locked up in coffins of black.

And by came an Angel who had a bright key,
And he opened the coffins and set them all free;
Then down a green plain leaping, laughing, they run,   15
And wash in a river, and shine in the sun.

Then naked and white, all their bags left behind,
They rise upon clouds and sport in the wind;
And the Angel told Tom, if he'd be a good boy,
He'd have God for his father, and never want joy.   20

And so Tom awoke; and we rose in the dark,
And got with our bags and our brushes to work.
Though the morning was cold, Tom was happy and warm;
So if all do their duty they need not fear harm.

Considerations for Critical Thinking and Writing

1. Characterize the speaker in this poem, and describe his tone. Is his tone the same
   as the poet's? Consider especially lines 7–8 and 24.
2. What is the symbolic value of the dream in lines 11–20?
3. Why is irony central to the meaning of this poem?
4. Discuss the validity of this statement: " 'The Chimney Sweeper' is a sentimental
   poem about a shameful eighteenth-century social problem; such a treatment of
   child abuse cannot be taken seriously."

TESS GALLAGHER (b. 1932)
Black Silk   1984

She was cleaning — there is always
that to do — when she found,
at the top of the closet, his old
silk vest. She called me
to look at it, unrolling it carefully   5
like something live
might fall out. Then we spread it
on the kitchen table and smoothed
the wrinkles down, making our hands
heavy until its shape against Formica   10
came back and the little tips
that would have pointed to his pockets

lay flat. The buttons were all there.
I held my arms out and she
looped the wide armholes over   15
them. "That's one thing I never
wanted to be," she said, "a man."
I went into the bathroom to see
how I looked in the sheen and
sadness. Wind chimes   20
off-key in the alcove. Then her
crying so I stood back in the sink-light
where the porcelain had been staring. Time
to go to her, I thought, with that
other mind, and stood still.   25

Considerations for Critical Thinking and Writing

1. Why is "Black Silk" an appropriate title?
2. Explain whether you think this poem is sentimental. Why or why not?
3. How are the speaker's emotions revealed? What is she feeling as she observes the
   other woman?

Connection to Another Selection

1. Write an essay comparing "Black Silk" with Emily Dickinson's "The Bustle in a
   House" (p. 275).

HOWARD NEMEROV (1920–1991)
The Fourth of July   1958

Because I am drunk, this Independence Night,
I watch the fireworks from far away,
From a high hill, across the moony green
Of lakes and other hills to the town harbor,
Where stately illuminations are flung aloft,   5
One light shattering in a hundred lights
Minute by minute. The reason I am crying,
Aside from only being country drunk,
That is, may be that I have just remembered
The sparklers, rockets, roman candles, and   10
So on, we used to be allowed to buy
When I was a boy, and set off by ourselves
At some peril to life and property.
Our freedom to abuse our freedom thus
Has since, I understand, been remedied   15
By legislation. Now the authorities
Arrange a perfectly safe public display

To be watched at a distance; and now also
The contribution of all the taxpayers
Together makes a more spectacular   20
Result than any could achieve alone
(A few pale pinwheels, or a firecracker
Fused at the dog's tail). It is, indeed, splendid:
Showers of roses in the sky, fountains
Of emeralds, and those profusely scattered zircons   25
Falling and falling, flowering as they fall
And followed distantly by a noise of thunder.
My eyes are half-afloat in happy tears.
God bless our Nation on a night like this,
And bless the careful and secure officials   30
Who celebrate our independence now.

Considerations for Critical Thinking and Writing

1. What is the central irony of this poem?
2. Why do you think Nemerov makes the speaker drunk? How are the speaker's
   reflections affected by his drinking?
3. Write an essay on the idea of freedom expressed in this poem.

Connections to Other Selections

1. Discuss the speakers in "The Fourth of July" and in John Ciardi's "Suburban"
   (p. 125). How do the poets ensure that readers will be sympathetic to the two
   speakers?
2. Write an essay that compares the "careful and secure officials" in Nemerov's poem
   with the public official in e. e. cummings's "next to of course god america i"
   (p. 115). What is the poet's attitude toward officialdom in each work?

PERSPECTIVE

EZRA POUND (1885–1972)
On Symbols   1912

I believe that the proper and perfect symbol is the natural object, that if a
man use "symbols" he must so use them that their symbolic function does not
obtrude; so that *a* sense, and the poetic quality of the passage, is not lost to
those who do not understand the symbol as such, to whom, for instance a hawk
is a hawk.

From "Prolegomena," *Poetry Review,* February 1912

Considerations for Critical Thinking and Writing

1. Discuss whether you agree with Pound that the "perfect symbol" is a "natural object" that does not insist on being read as a symbol.
2. Write an essay in which you discuss Eamon Grennan's "Bat" (p. 74) as an example of the "perfect symbol" Pound proposes.
3. Do you think the poems by Pound in this anthology (see the index) fit his requirements for the way a symbol should function in a poem? Explain why or why not.

6. Sounds

Poems yearn to be read aloud. Much of their energy, charm, and beauty comes to life only when they are heard. Poets choose and arrange words for their sounds as well as for their meanings. Most poetry is best read with your lips, teeth, and tongue, because they serve to articulate the effects that sound may have in a poem. When a voice is breathed into a good poem, there is pleasure in the reading, the saying, and the hearing.

LISTENING TO POETRY

The earliest poetry — before writing and painting — was chanted or sung. The rhythmic quality of such oral performances served two purposes: it helped the chanting bard remember the lines, and it entertained audiences with patterned sounds of language, which were sometimes accompanied by musical instruments. Poetry has always been closely related to music. Indeed, as the word suggests, lyric poetry evolved from songs. "Western Wind" (p. 25), an anonymous Middle English lyric, survived as song long before it was written down. Had Robert Frost lived in a nonliterate society, he probably would have sung some version — a very different version to be sure — of "Acquainted with the Night" (p. 109) instead of writing it down. Even though Frost creates a speaking rather than a singing voice, the speaker's anxious tone is distinctly heard in any careful reading of the poem.

Like lyrics, early narrative poems were originally part of an anonymous oral folk tradition. A *ballad* such as "Bonny Barbara Allan" (p. 346) told a story that was sung from one generation to the next until it was finally transcribed. Since the eighteenth century, this narrative form has sometimes been imitated by poets who write *literary ballads*. John Keats's "La Belle Dame sans Merci" (p. 231) is, for example, a more complex and sophisticated nineteenth-century reflection of the original ballad traditions that developed in the fifteenth century and earlier. In considering poetry as sound, we should not forget that poetry traces its beginnings to song.

These next lines exemplify poetry's continuing relation to song. What poetic elements can you find in this song, which was popular in the 1960s?

LEONARD COHEN (b. 1934)
Suzanne   1966

Suzanne takes you down
to her place near the river,
you can hear the boats go by
you can stay the night beside her.
And you know that she's half crazy   5
but that's why you want to be there
and she feeds you tea and oranges
that come all the way from China.
Just when you mean to tell her
that you have no gifts to give her,   10
she gets you on her wave-length
and she lets the river answer
that you've always been her lover.
    And you want to travel with her,
    you want to travel blind   15
    and you know that she can trust you
    because you've touched her perfect body
    with your mind.

Jesus was a sailor
when he walked upon the water   20
and he spent a long time watching
from a lonely wooden tower
and when he knew for certain
only drowning men could see him
he said All men will be sailors then   25
until the sea shall free them,
but he himself was broken
long before the sky would open,
forsaken, almost human,
he sank beneath your wisdom like a stone.   30
    And you want to travel with him,
    you want to travel blind
    and you think maybe you'll trust him
    because he touched your perfect body
    with his mind.   35

Now Suzanne takes your hand
and she leads you to the river,
she is wearing rags and feathers
from Salvation Army counters,
and the sun pours down like honey   40
on our lady of the harbour,
and she shows you where to look
among the garbage and the flowers.
There are heroes in the seaweed,
there are children in the morning,   45
they are leaning out for love
and they will lean that way forever
while Suzanne holds the mirror.
  And you want to travel with her,
  you want to travel blind   50
  and you know that you can trust her
  because she's touched your perfect body
  with her mind.

Considerations for Critical Thinking and Writing

1. What parallels are drawn between Jesus and Suzanne in this song? What do the images reveal about each of them? Which images are used metaphorically?
2. Who is the "you" of the song?
3. What is indicated by the changing pronouns in lines 17–18, 34–35, and 51–52?
4. What is the tone of this song?
5. Choose a contemporary song that you especially like and examine the lyrics. Write an essay explaining whether or not you consider the lyrics poetic.

Of course reading Cohen's "Suzanne" is not the same as hearing it. Like the lyrics of a song, many poems must be heard — or at least read with listening eyes — before they can be fully understood and enjoyed. The sounds of words are a universal source of music for human beings. This has been so from ancient tribes to bards to the two-year-old child in a bakery gleefully chanting "Cuppitycake, cuppitycake!"

Listen to the sound of the following poem as you read it aloud. How do the words provide, in a sense, their own musical accompaniment?

JOHN UPDIKE (b. 1932)
Player Piano   1958

My stick fingers click with a snicker
And, chuckling, they knuckle the keys;
Light-footed, my steel feelers flicker
And pluck from these keys melodies.

My paper can caper; abandon
Is broadcast by dint of my din,
And no man or band has a hand in
The tones I turn on from within.

At times I'm a jumble of rumbles,
At others I'm light like the moon,
But never my numb plunker fumbles,
Misstrums me, or tries a new tune.

The speaker in this poem is a piano that can play automatically by means of a mechanism that depresses keys in response to signals on a perforated roll. Notice how the speaker's voice approximates the sounds of a piano. In each stanza a predominant sound emerges from the carefully chosen words. How is the sound of each stanza tuned to its sense?

Like Updike's "Player Piano," the next poem is also primarily about sounds.

MAY SWENSON (b. 1919)
A Nosty Fright   1984

The roldengod and the soneyhuckle,
the sack eyed blusan and the wistle theed
are all tangled with the oison pivy,
the fallen nine peedles and the wumbleteed.

A mipchunk caught in a wobceb tried
to hip and skide in a dandy sune
but a stobler put up a EEP KOFF sign.
Then the unfucky lellow met a phytoon

and was sept out to swea. He difted for drays
till a hassgropper flying happened to spot
the boolish feast all debraggled and wet,
covered with snears and tot.

Loonmight shone through the winey poods
where rushmooms grew among risted twoots.
Back blats flew betreen the twees
and orned howls hounded their soots.

A kumkpin stood with tooked creeth
on the sindow will of a house
where a icked wold itch lived all alone
except for her stoombrick, a mitten and a kouse.

"Here we part," said hassgropper.
"Pere we hart," said mipchunk, too.

They purried away on opposite haths,
both scared of some "Bat!" or "Scoo!"

October was ending on a nosty fright   25
with scroans and greeches and chanking clains,
with oblins and gelfs, coaths and urses,
skinning grulls and stoodblains.

Will it ever be morning, Nofember virst,
skue bly and the snappy hun, our friend?   30
With light breaves of wall by the fayside?
I sope ho, so that this oem can pend.

At just the right moments Swenson transposes letters to create amusing
sound effects and wild wordplays. Although there is a story lurking in "A
Nosty Fright," any serious attempt to interpret its meaning is confronted with
"a EEP KOFF sign." Instead, we are invited to enjoy the delicious sounds the
poet has cooked up.

Few poems revel in sound so completely. More typically, the sounds of
a poem contribute to its meaning rather than become its meaning. Consider
how sound is used in the next poem.

EMILY DICKINSON (1830–1886)
A Bird came down the Walk —   c. 1862

A Bird came down the Walk —
He did not know I saw —
He bit an Angleworm in halves
And ate the fellow, raw,

And then he drank a Dew   5
From a convenient Grass —
And then hopped sidewise to the Wall
To let a Beetle pass —

He glanced with rapid eyes
That hurried all around —   10
They looked like frightened Beads, I thought —
He stirred his Velvet Head

Like one in danger, Cautious,
I offered him a Crumb
And he unrolled his feathers   15
And rowed him softer home —

Than Oars divide the Ocean,
Too silver for a seam —

Or Butterflies, off Banks of Noon
Leap, plashless as they swim.   20

  This description of a bird offers a close look at how differently a bird
moves when it hops on the ground than when it flies in the air. On the
ground the bird moves quickly, awkwardly, and irregularly as it plucks up a
worm, washes it down with dew, and then hops aside to avoid a passing
beetle. The speaker recounts the bird's rapid, abrupt actions from a somewhat superior, amused perspective. By describing the bird in human terms
(as if, for example, it *chose* to eat the worm "raw"), the speaker is almost
condescending. But when the attempt to offer a crumb fails and the frightened bird flies off, the speaker is left looking up instead of down at the bird.
  With that shift in perspective the tone shifts from amusement to awe in
response to the bird's graceful flight. The jerky movements of lines 1–13
give way to the smooth motion of lines 15–20. The pace of the first three
stanzas is fast and discontinuous. We tend to pause at the end of each line,
and this reinforces a sense of disconnected movements. In contrast, the final
six lines are to be read as a single sentence in one flowing movement,
lubricated by various sounds.
  Read again the description of the bird flying away. Several *o*-sounds
contribute to the image of the serene, expansive, confident flight, just as the
s-sounds serve as smooth transitions from one line to the next. Notice how
these sounds are grouped in the following vertical columns:

unrolled	softer	too	his	Ocean	Banks
rowed	Oars	Noon	feathers	silver	plashless
home	Or		softer	seam	as
Ocean	off		Oars	Butterflies	swim

This blending of sounds (notice how "Leap, plashless" brings together the
p- and *l*-sounds without a ripple) helps convey the bird's smooth grace in
the air. Like a feathered oar, the bird moves seamlessly in its element.
  The repetition of sounds in poetry is similar to the function of the tones
and melodies that are repeated, with variations, in music. Just as the patterned
sounds in music unify a work, so do the words in poems, which have been
carefully chosen for the combinations of sounds they create. These sounds
are produced in a number of ways.
  The most direct way in which the sound of a word suggests its meaning
is through **onomatopoeia**, which is the use of a word that resembles the
sound it denotes: *quack, buzz, rattle, bang, squeak, bowwow, burp, choo-
choo, ding-a-ling, sizzle.* The sound and sense of these words are closely
related, but they represent a very small percentage of the words available to
us. Poets usually employ more subtle means for echoing meanings.
  Onomatopoeia can consist of more than just single words. In its broadest
meaning the term refers to lines or passages in which sounds help to convey
meanings, as in these lines from Updike's "Player Piano":

My stick fingers click with a snicker
And, chuckling, they knuckle the keys.

The sharp crisp sounds of these two lines approximate the sounds of a piano; the syllables seem to "click" against one another. Contrast Updike's rendition with the following lines:

My long fingers play with abandon
And, laughing, they cover the keys.

The original version is more interesting and alive, because the sounds of the words are pleasurable and reinforce the meaning through a careful blending of consonants and vowels.

Alliteration is the repetition of the same consonant sounds at the beginnings of nearby words: "*d*escending *d*ewdrops"; "*l*uscious *l*emons." Sometimes the term is also used to describe the consonant sounds within words: "tres*p*asser's re*p*roach"; "we*dd*ed la*d*y." Alliteration is based on sound rather than spelling. "*K*ean" and "*c*ar" alliterate, but "*c*ar" does not alliterate with "*c*ite." Rarely is heavy-handed alliteration effective. Used too self-consciously, it can be distracting instead of strengthening meaning or emphasizing a relation between words. Consider the relentless *h*'s in this line: "Horrendous horrors haunted Helen's happiness." Those *h*'s certainly suggest that Helen is being pursued, but they have a more comic than serious effect because they are overdone.

Assonance is the repetition of the same vowel sound in nearby words: "asl*ee*p under a tr*ee*"; "t*i*me and t*i*de"; "h*au*nt" and "*aw*esome"; "*ea*ch *e*vening." Both alliteration and assonance help to establish relations among words in a line or a series of lines. Whether the effect is **euphony** — lines that are musically pleasant to the ear and smooth, like the final lines of Dickinson's "A Bird came down the Walk — " — or the effect is **cacophony** — lines that are discordant and difficult to pronounce, like the claim that "never my numb plunker fumbles" in Updike's "Player Piano" — the sounds of words in poetry can be as significant as the words' denotative or connotative meanings.

The next poem provides a feast of sounds. Read the poem aloud and try to determine the effects of its sounds.

GALWAY KINNELL (b. 1927)
Blackberry Eating   1980

I love to go out in late September
among the fat, overripe, icy, black blackberries
to eat blackberries for breakfast,
the stalks very prickly, a penalty
they earn for knowing the black art   5

of blackberry-making; and as I stand among them
lifting the stalks to my mouth, the ripest berries
fall almost unbidden to my tongue,
as words sometimes do, certain peculiar words
like *strengths* or *squinched,*   10
many-lettered, one-syllabled lumps,
which I squeeze, squinch open, and splurge well
in the silent, startled, icy, black language
of blackberry-eating in late September.

Considerations for Critical Thinking and Writing

1. Underline the alliteration and circle the assonance throughout this poem. What is the effect of these sounds?
2. How do lines 4–6 fit into the poem? What does this prickly image add to the poem?
3. Explain what you think the poem's theme is.
4. Write an essay that considers the speaker's love of blackberry eating along with the speaker's appetite for words. How are the two blended in the poem?

RHYME

Like alliteration and assonance, **rhyme** is a way of creating sound patterns. Rhyme, broadly defined, consists of two or more words or phrases that repeat the same sounds: *happy* and *snappy*. Rhyme words often have similar spellings, but that is not a requirement of rhyme; what matters is that the words sound alike: *vain* rhymes with *reign* as well as *rain*. Moreover, words may look alike but not rhyme at all. In *eye rhyme* the spellings are similar but the pronunciations are not, as with *bough* and *cough*, or *brow* and *blow*.

Not all poems employ rhyme. Many great poems have no rhymes, and many weak verses use rhyme as a substitute for poetry. These are especially apparent in commercial messages and greeting-card lines. At its worst, rhyme is merely a distracting decoration that can lead to dullness and predictability. But used skillfully, rhyme creates lines that are memorable and musical.

Following is a poem using rhyme that you might remember the next time you are in a restaurant.

RICHARD ARMOUR (1906–1989)
Going to Extremes   1954

Shake and shake
　The catsup bottle
None'll come —
　And then a lot'll.

　The experience recounted in Armour's poem is common enough, but
the rhyme's humor is special. The final line clicks the poem shut, an effect
that is often achieved by the use of rhyme. That click provides a sense of a
satisfying and fulfilled form. Rhymes have a number of uses: they can emphasize words, direct a reader's attention to relations between words, and
provide an overall structure for a poem.
　Rhyme is used in the following poem to imitate the sound of cascading
water.

ROBERT SOUTHEY (1774–1843)
From *The Cataract of Lodore*   1820

　　　　"How does the water
　　　　Come down at Lodore?"
　　. . . . .
From its sources which well
　In the tarn on the fell;
　　　From its fountains   5
　　　In the mountains,
　　Its rills and its gills;
Through moss and through brake,
　　It runs and it creeps
　　For awhile, till it sleeps   10
　　In its own little lake.
　And thence at departing,
　Awakening and starting,
　It runs through the reeds
　　And away it proceeds,   15
Through meadow and glade,
　In sun and in shade,
And through the wood-shelter,
　Among crags in its flurry,
　　　Helter-skelter,   20
　　　Hurry-scurry.

Here it comes sparkling,
And there it lies darkling;
Now smoking and frothing
Its tumult and wrath in,   25
Till in this rapid race
On which it is bent,
It reaches the place
Of its steep descent.

The cataract strong   30
Then plunges along,
Striking and raging
As if a war waging
Its caverns and rocks among:
Rising and leaping,   35
Sinking and creeping,
Swelling and sweeping,
Showering and springing,
Flying and flinging,
Writhing and ringing,   40
Eddying and whisking,
Spouting and frisking,
Turning and twisting,
Around and around
With endless rebound!   45
Smiting and fighting,
A sight to delight in;
Confounding, astounding,
Dizzying and deafening the ear with its sound.
· ·
Dividing and gliding and sliding,   50
And falling and brawling and spawling,
And driving and riving and striving,
And sprinkling and twinkling and wrinkling,
And sounding and bounding and rounding,
And bubbling and troubling and doubling,   55
And grumbling and rumbling and tumbling,
And clattering and battering and shattering;
Retreating and beating and meeting and sheeting,
Delaying and straying and playing and spraying,
Advancing and prancing and glancing and dancing,   60
Recoiling, turmoiling and toiling and boiling,
And gleaming and streaming and steaming and beaming,
And rushing and flushing and brushing and gushing,
And flapping and rapping and clapping and slapping,
And curling and whirling and purling and twirling,   65
And thumping and plumping and bumping and jumping,
And dashing and flashing and splashing and clashing;

And so never ending, but always descending,
Sounds and motions forever and ever are blending,
All at once and all o'er, with a mighty uproar;   70
And this way the water comes down at Lodore.

This deluge of rhymes consists of "Sounds and motions forever and ever . . . blending" (line 69). The pace quickens as the water creeps from its mountain source and then descends in rushing cataracts. As the speed of the water increases, so do the number of rhymes, until they run in fours: "dashing and flashing and splashing and clashing." Most rhymes meander through poems instead of flooding them; nevertheless, Southey's use of rhyme suggests how sounds can flow with meanings. "The Cataract of Lodore" has been criticized, however, for overusing onomatopoeia. Some readers find the poem silly; others regard it as a brilliant example of sound effects. What do you think?

A variety of types of rhyme is available to poets. The most common form, *end rhyme,* comes at the ends of lines.

It runs through the reeds
    And away it proceeds,
Through meadow and glade,
    In sun and in shade.

Internal rhyme places at least one of the rhymed words within the line, as in "Dividing and gliding and sliding" or, more subtly, in the fourth and final words of "In mist or cloud, on mast or shroud."

The rhyming of single-syllable words such as *grade* and *shade* is known as *masculine rhyme.*

Loveliest of trees, the cherry now
Is hung with bloom along the bough.
                    —A. E. Housman

Rhymes using words of more than one syllable are also called masculine when the same sound occurs in a final stressed syllable, as in *defend, contend; betray, away.* A *feminine rhyme* consists of a rhymed stressed syllable followed by one or more rhymed unstressed syllables, as in *butter, clutter; gratitude, attitude; quivering, shivering.*

Lord confound this surly sister,
Blight her brow and blotch and blister.
                    —John Millington Synge

All the examples so far have been *exact rhymes,* because they share the same stressed vowel sounds as well as any sounds that follow the vowel. In *near rhyme* (also called *off rhyme, slant rhyme,* and *approximate rhyme*), the sounds are almost but not exactly alike. There are several kinds of near rhyme. One of the most common is *consonance,* an identical consonant sound preceded by a different vowel sound: *home, same; worth, breath; trophy, daffy.* Near rhyme can also be achieved by using different vowel sounds with identical consonant sounds: *sound, sand; kind, conned; fellow, fallow.* The dissonance of *blade* and *blood* in the following lines helps to reinforce their grim tone.

> Let the boy try along this bayonet-blade
> How cold steel is, and keen with hunger of blood.
> —Wilfred Owen

Near rhymes greatly broaden the possibility for musical effects in English, a language that, compared with Spanish or Italian, contains few exact rhymes. Do not assume, however, that a near rhyme represents a failed attempt at exact rhyme. Near rhymes allow a musical subtlety and variety, and can avoid the sometimes overpowering jingling effects that exact rhymes may create.

These basic terms hardly exhaust the ways in which the sound in poems can be labeled and discussed, but the terms can help you to describe how poets manipulate sounds for effect. Read "God's Grandeur" (p. 144) aloud and try to determine how the sounds of the lines contribute to their sense.

PERSPECTIVE

DAVID LENSON (b. 1945)
On the Contemporary Use of Rhyme   1988

One impediment to a respectable return to rhyme is the popular survival of "functional" verse; greeting cards, pedagogical and mnemonic devices ("Thirty days hath September"), nursery rhymes, advertising jingles, and of course song lyrics. Pentameters, irregular rhymes, and free verse aren't much use in songwriting, where the meter has to be governed by the time signature of the music.

Far from universities, there has been a revival of rhymed couplets in Rap music, in which, to the accompaniment of synthesizers, vocalists deliver lengthy first-person narratives in tetrameter. While most writing teachers would dismiss such lyrics as doggerel, the aim of the songs is really not so far from that of Alexander Pope: to use rhyme to sharpen social insight, in the hope that the world may be reordered.

From *The Chronicle of Higher Education,* February 24, 1988

Considerations for Critical Thinking and Writing

1. Read some contemporary song lyrics from a wide range of groups or vocalists. Is Lenson correct in his assessment that irregular rhyme is not much use in songwriting?

2. Examine the rhymed couplets of some rap music. Discuss whether they are used "to sharpen social insight." What is the effect of using rhymes in rap music?
3. What is your own response to rhymed poetry? Do you like yours with or without? What do you think informs your preference?

SOUND AND MEANING

GERARD MANLEY HOPKINS (1844–1889)
God's Grandeur   1877

The world is charged with the grandeur of God
  It will flame out, like shining from shook foil;°   *shaken gold foil*
  It gathers to a greatness, like the ooze of oil
Crushed.° Why do men then now not reck his rod?°
Generations have trod, have trod, have trod;   5
  And all is seared with trade; bleared, smeared with toil;
  And wears man's smudge and shares man's smell: the soil
Is bare now, nor can foot feel, being shod.

And for all this, nature is never spent;
  There lives the dearest freshness deep down things;   10
And though the last lights off the black West went
  Oh, morning, at the brown brink eastward, springs —
Because the Holy Ghost over the bent
  World broods with warm breast and with ah! bright wings.

4 *Crushed:* Olives crushed in their oil; *reck his rod:* Obey God.

The subject of this poem is announced in the title and the first line: "The world is charged with the grandeur of God." The poem is a celebration of the power and greatness of God's presence in the world, but the speaker is also perplexed and dismayed by people who refuse to recognize God's authority and grandeur as they are manifested in the creation. Instead of glorifying God, "men" have degraded the earth through meaningless toil and cut themselves off from the spiritual renewal inherent in the beauty of nature. The relentless demands of commerce and industry have blinded people to the earth's natural and spiritual resources. In spite of this abuse and insensitivity to God's grandeur, however, "nature is never spent"; the morning light that "springs" in the east redeems the "black West" of the night and is a sign that the spirit of the Holy Ghost is ever present in the world. This summary of the poem sketches some of the thematic significance of the lines, but it does not do justice to how they are organized around the use of sound. Hopkins's poem, unlike Southey's "The Cataract of Lodore," employs sounds in a subtle and complex way.

In the opening line Hopkins uses alliteration — a device apparent in almost every line of the poem — to connect "Go*d*" to the "worl*d*," which is "charge*d*" with his "gran*d*eur." These consonants unify the line as well. The alliteration in lines 2–3 suggests a harmony in the creation: the *f*'s in "*f*lame" and "*f*oil," the *sh*'s in "*sh*ining" and "*sh*ook," the *g*'s in "*g*athers" and "*g*reatness," and the visual (not alliterative) similarities of "*ooze of oil*" emphasize a world that is held together by God's will.

That harmony is abruptly interrupted by the speaker's angry question in line 4: "Why do men then now not reck his rod?" The question is as painful to the speaker as it is difficult to pronounce. The arrangement of the alliteration ("*n*ow," "*n*ot"; "*r*eck," "*r*od"), the assonance ("n*o*t," "r*o*d"; "m*e*n," "th*e*n," "r*e*ck"), and the internal rhyme ("m*en*," "th*en*") contribute to the difficulty in saying the line, a difficulty associated with human behavior. That behavior is introduced in line 5 by the repetition of "have trod" to emphasize the repeated mistakes — sins — committed by human beings. The tone is dirgelike because humanity persists in its mistaken path rather than progressing. The speaker's horror at humanity is evident in the cacophonous sounds of lines 6–8. Here the alliteration of "*sm*eared," "*sm*udge," and "*sm*ell" along with the internal rhymes of "s*eared*," "bl*eared*," and "sm*eared*" echo the disgust with which the speaker views human's "toil" with the "soil," an end rhyme that calls attention to our mistaken equation of nature with production rather than with spirituality.

In contrast to this cacophony, the final six lines build toward the joyful recognition of the new possibilities that accompany the rising sun. This recognition leads to the euphonic description of the "H*o*ly Gh*o*st *o*ver" (notice the reassuring consistency of the assonance) the world. Traditionally represented as a dove, the Holy Ghost brings love and peace to the "*w*orld," and "*b*roods *w*ith *w*arm *b*reast and *w*ith ah! *b*right *w*ings." The effect of this alliteration is mellifluous: the sound bespeaks the harmony that prevails at the end of the poem resulting from the speaker's recognition that nature can "never [be] spent" because God loves and protects the world.

The sounds of "God's Grandeur" enhance the poem's theme; more can be said about its sounds, but it is enough to point out here that for this poem the sound strongly echoes the theme in nearly every line. Here are some more poems in which sound plays a significant role.

POEMS FOR FURTHER STUDY

ALICE WALKER (b. 1944)
Revolutionary Petunias   1972

Sammy Lou of Rue
sent to his reward
the exact creature who

murdered her husband,
using a cultivator's hoe   5
with verve and skill;
and laughed fit to kill
in disbelief
at the angry, militant
pictures of herself   10
the Sonneteers quickly drew:
not any of them people that
she knew.
A backwoods woman
her house was papered with   15
funeral home calendars and
faces appropriate for a Mississippi
Sunday School. She raised a George,
a Martha, a Jackie and a Kennedy. Also
a John Wesley° Junior.   20
"Always respect the word of God,"
she said on her way to she didn't
know where, except it would be by
electric chair, and she continued
"Don't yall forgit to *water*   25
my purple petunias."

20 *John Wesley* (1730–1791): The British founder of Methodism.

Considerations for Critical Thinking and Writing

1. Identify the kinds of rhyme that appear in the poem.
2. How do the rhymes contribute to the poem's effect? How would your reading of
   the poem be different if all the rhymed words were replaced by words that did
   not rhyme?
3. Describe what you take to be the themes of the poem. How is the title related to
   the themes?

LEWIS CARROLL
[CHARLES LUTWIDGE DODGSON] (1832–1898)
Jabberwocky   1871

'Twas brillig, and the slithy toves
    Did gyre and gimble in the wabe:
All mimsy were the borogoves,
    And the mome raths outgrabe.

"Beware the Jabberwock, my son!   5
    The jaws that bite, the claws that catch!

Beware the Jubjub bird, and shun
    The frumious Bandersnatch!"

He took his vorpal sword in hand;
    Long time the manxome foe he sought —   10
So rested he by the Tumtum tree,
    And stood awhile in thought.

And, as in uffish thought he stood,
    The Jabberwock, with eyes of flame,
Came whiffling through the tulgey wood,   15
    And burbled as it came!

One, two! One, two! And through and through
    The vorpal blade went snicker-snack!
He left it dead, and with its head
    He went galumphing back.   20

"And hast thou slain the Jabberwock?
    Come to my arms, my beamish boy!
O frabjous day! Callooh, Callay!"
    He chortled in his joy.

'Twas brillig, and the slithy toves   25
    Did gyre and gimble in the wabe:
All mimsy were the borogoves,
    And the mome raths outgrabe.

Considerations for Critical Thinking and Writing

1. What happens in this poem? Does it have any meaning?
2. Not all the words used in this poem appear in dictionaries. In *Through the Looking Glass*, Humpty Dumpty explains to Alice that " 'slithy' means 'lithe and slimy.' 'Lithe' is the same as 'active.' You see it's like a portmanteau — there are two meanings packed up into one word." Are there any other portmanteau words in the poem?
3. Which words in the poem sound especially meaningful, even if they are devoid of any denotative meanings?

Connections to Other Selections

1. Compare Carroll's strategies for creating sound and meaning with those used by May Swenson in "A Nosty Fright" (p. 135).
2. Write an essay comparing what Robert Francis says about the words of a poem in "Glass" (p. 502) with Carroll's use of words. Discuss whether you think the two poets more or less agree or disagree in their respective approaches to writing poetry.

JEAN TOOMER (1894–1967)
Reapers

Black reapers with the sound of steel on stones
Are sharpening scythes. I see them place the hones
In their hip-pockets as a thing that's done,
And start their silent swinging, one by one.
Black horses drive a mower through the weeds,
And there, a field rat, startled, squealing bleeds,
His belly close to ground. I see the blade,
Blood-stained, continue cutting weeds and shade.

Considerations for Critical Thinking and Writing

1. Is this poem primarily about harvesting, or does it suggest something else? Are there any symbols?
2. What is the poem's tone?
3. The reapers' work is described alliteratively as "silent swinging." How are the alliteration and assonance of lines 1–2 and 6 related to their meaning?
4. Why is Toomer's version of line 6 more effective than this one: "And there a startled, squealing field rat bleeds"?

JOHN DONNE (1572–1631)
Song

Go and catch a falling star
    Get with child a mandrake root,°
Tell me where all past years are,
    Or who cleft the Devil's foot,
Teach me to hear mermaids singing,
    Or to keep off envy's stinging,
        And find
        What wind
Serves to advance an honest mind.

If thou be'st borne to strange sights,
    Things invisible to see,
Ride ten thousand days and nights,
    Till age snow white hairs on thee,
Thou, when thou return'st, wilt tell me
    All strange wonders that befell thee,
        And swear
        Nowhere
Lives a woman true, and fair.

2 *mandrake root:* This V-shaped root resembles the lower half of the human body.

If thou findst one, let me know,
    Such a pilgrimage were sweet —   20
Yet do not, I would not go,
    Though at next door we might meet;
Though she were true, when you met her,
    And last, till you write your letter,
        Yet she   25
        Will be
False, ere I come, to two or three.

Considerations for Critical Thinking and Writing

1. What is the speaker's tone in this poem? What is his view of a woman's love? What does the speaker's use of hyperbole reveal about his emotional state?
2. Do you think Donne wants the speaker's argument to be taken seriously? Is there any humor in the poem?
3. Most of these lines end with masculine rhymes. What other kinds of rhymes are used for end rhymes?

JUDY GRAHN (b. 1940)
She Who bears it   1972

She Who bears it
bear down, breathe
bear down, bear down, breathe
bear down, bear down, bear down, breathe

She Who lies down in the darkness and bears it   5
She Who lies down in the lightness and bears it
the labor of She Who carries and bears is the first labor

all over the world
the waters are breaking everywhere
everywhere the waters are breaking   10
the labor of She Who carries and bears
and raises and rears is the first labor,
there is no other first labor.

Considerations for Critical Thinking and Writing

1. How do the sounds of this poem contribute to its sense of urgency?
2. What is the effect of the repeated words and phrases? How is that repetition related to what happens in the poem?
3. What do you think is the meaning of the phrase "the first labor" in line 7? How does the phrase take on additional meanings in lines 12 and 13?

THOMAS HARDY (1840–1928)
The Oxen   1915

Christmas Eve, and twelve of the clock.
    "Now they are all on their knees,"
An elder said as we sat in a flock
    By the embers in hearthside ease.

We pictured the meek mild creatures where   5
    They dwelt in their strawy pen,
Nor did it occur to one of us there
    To doubt they were kneeling then.

So fair a fancy few would weave
    In these years! Yet, I feel,   10
If someone said on Christmas Eve,
    "Come; see the oxen kneel

"In the lonely barton° by yonder coomb°   *farmyard; ravine*
    Our childhood used to know,"
I should go with him in the gloom,   15
    Hoping it might be so.

Considerations for Critical Thinking and Writing

1. Traditionally, European peasants believed that animals worship God on Christmas Eve. How does the speaker feel about this belief? What is the difference between the speaker's attitude as a child and, "In these years," as an adult?
2. The speaker seems to feel nostalgic about his lost childhood. Does he feel the loss of anything more than that?
3. How do the sounds in the final stanza reinforce the tone and theme of the poem?

ALEXANDER POPE (1688–1774)
From *An Essay on Criticism*   1711

    But most by numbers° judge a poet's song;   *versification*
And smooth or rough, with them, is right or wrong;
In the bright muse though thousand charms conspire,
Her voice is all these tuneful fools admire;
Who haunt Parnassus° but to please their ear,   5
Not mend their minds; as some to church repair,
Not for the doctrine, but the music there.
These equal syllables alone require,
Though oft the ear the open vowels tire;

5 *Parnassus:* A Greek mountain sacred to the Muses.

While expletives° their feeble aid do join;   10
And ten low words oft creep in one dull line;
While they ring round the same unvaried chimes,
With sure returns of still expected rhymes;
Where'er you find "the cooling western breeze,"
In the next line, it "whispers through the trees":   15
If crystal streams "with pleasing murmurs creep,"
The reader's threatened (not in vain) with "sleep":
Then, at the last and only couplet fraught
With some unmeaning thing they call a thought,
A needless Alexandrine° ends the song,   20
That, like a wounded snake, drags its slow length along.
Leave such to tune their own dull rhymes, and know
What's roundly smooth, or languishingly slow;
And praise the easy vigor of a line,
Where Denham's strength, and Waller's° sweetness join.   25
True ease in writing comes from art, not chance,
As those move easiest who have learned to dance.
'Tis not enough no harshness gives offense,
The sound must seem an echo to the sense:
Soft is the strain when Zephyr° gently blows,   *the west wind*   30
And the smooth stream in smoother numbers flows;
But when loud surges lash the sounding shore,
The hoarse, rough verse should like the torrent roar:
When Ajax° strives some rock's vast weight to throw,
The line too labors, and the words move slow;   35
Not so, when swift Camilla° scours the plain,
Flies o'er th' unbending corn, and skims along the main.

10 *expletives:* Unnecessary words used to fill a line, as the *do* in this line.   20 *Alexandrine:* A twelve-syllable line, as line 21.   25 *Denham's, Waller's:* Sir John Denham (1615–1669), Edmund Waller (1606–1687) were poets who used heroic couplets.   34 *Ajax:* A Greek warrior famous for his strength in the Trojan War.   36 *Camilla:* A goddess famous for her delicate speed.

Considerations for Critical Thinking and Writing

1. These lines make a case for sound as an important element in poetry. In them Pope describes some faults he finds in poems and illustrates those faults within the lines that describe them. How do lines 4, 9, 10, 11, and 21 illustrate what they describe?
2. What is the objection to the "expected rhymes" in lines 12–17? How do they differ from Pope's end rhymes?
3. Some lines discuss how to write successful poetry. How do lines 23, 24, 32–33, 35, and 36–37 illustrate what they describe?
4. Do you agree that in a good poem "The sound must [always] seem an echo to the sense"?

RICHARD WILBUR (b. 1921)

Year's End   1950

Now winter downs the dying of the year,
And night is all a settlement of snow;
From the soft street the rooms of houses show
A gathered light, a shapen atmosphere,
Like frozen-over lakes whose ice is thin   5
And still allows some stirring down within.

I've known the wind by water banks to shake
The late leaves down, which frozen where they fell
And held in ice as dancers in a spell
Fluttered all winter long into a lake;   10
Graved on the dark in gestures of descent,
They seemed their own most perfect monument.

There was perfection in the death of ferns
Which laid their fragile cheeks against the stone
A million years. Great mammoths overthrown   15
Composedly have made their long sojourns,
Like palaces of patience, in the gray
And changeless lands of ice. And at Pompeii°

The little dog lay curled and did not rise
But slept the deeper as the ashes rose   20
And found the people incomplete, and froze
The random hands, the loose unready eyes
Of men expecting yet another sun
To do the shapely thing they had not done.

These sudden ends of time must give us pause.   25
We fray into the future, rarely wrought
Save in the tapestries of afterthought.
More time, more time. Barrages of applause
Come muffled from a buried radio.
The New-year bells are wrangling with the snow.   30

18 *Pompeii:* A Roman city buried by the eruption of Mount Vesuvius (79 A.D.).

Considerations for Critical Thinking and Writing

1. Identify the internal rhymes in the poem. How do they affect your reading of the
   lines in which they appear?
2. How does Wilbur's use of such rhyme reinforce meaning?
3. Explain why the tone of this poem is appropriate to the subject.
4. How is the speaker's sense of time woven into the poem? How does it compare
   with your own sense of time?

MARIANNE MOORE (1887–1972)
The Fish   1924

wade
through black jade.
   Of the crow-blue mussel shells, one keeps
   adjusting the ash heaps;
      opening and shutting itself like   5

an
injured fan.
   The branches which encrust the side
   of the wave, cannot hide
      there for the submerged shafts of the   10

sun,
split like spun
   glass, move themselves with spotlight swiftness
   into the crevices —
      in and out, illuminating   15

the
torquoise sea
   of bodies. The water drives a wedge
   of iron through the iron edge
      of the cliff; whereupon the stars,   20

pink
rice-grains, ink-
   bespattered jellyfish, crabs like green
   lilies, and submarine
      toadstools, slide each on the other.   25

All
external
   marks of abuse are present on this
   defiant edifice —
      all the physical features of   30

ac-
cident — lack
   of cornice, dynamite grooves, burns, and
   hatchet strokes, these things stand
      out on it; the chasm side is   35

dead.
Repeated
   evidence has proved that it can live
   on what can not revive
      its youth. The sea grows old in it.   40

Considerations for Critical Thinking and Writing

1. This poem is not conventionally shaped the way, for example, Thomas Hardy's "The Oxen" (p. 150) looks on a page. It does, however, have a symmetrical shape. How would you describe that shape?
2. How do the sounds in each stanza help to convey the stanzas' meanings?
3. Describe the poem's tone.
4. Comment on the appropriateness of the title. What alternative titles would suggest the poem's themes?

Connection to Another Selection

1. Write an essay that compares the themes of this poem and Elizabeth Bishop's "The Fish" (p. 19).

PAUL HUMPHREY (b. 1915)
Blow   1983

Her skirt was lofted by the gale;
When I, with gesture deft,
Essayed to stay her frisky sail
She luffed, and laughed, and left.

Considerations for Critical Thinking and Writing

1. Point out instances of alliteration and assonance in this poem, and explain how they contribute to its euphonic effects.
2. What is the poem's controlling metaphor? Why is it especially appropriate?
3. Explain the ambiguity of the title.

ROBERT FRANCIS (1901–1987)
The Pitcher   1953

His art is eccentricity, his aim
How not to hit the mark he seems to aim at,

His passion how to avoid the obvious,
His technique how to vary the avoidance.

The others throw to be comprehended. He   5
Throws to be a moment misunderstood.

Yet not too much. Not errant, arrant, wild,
But every seeming aberration willed.

Not to, yet still, still to communicate
Making the batter understand too late.   10

Considerations for Critical Thinking and Writing

1. Explain how each pair of lines in this poem describes the pitcher's art.
2. Consider how the poem itself works the way a good pitcher does. Which lines illustrate what they describe?
3. Comment on the effects of the poem's rhymes. How are the final two lines different in their rhyme from the previous lines? How does sound echo sense in lines 9–10?
4. Write an essay that considers "The Pitcher" as an extended metaphor for talking about poetry. How well does the poem characterize strategies for writing poetry as well as pitching?
5. Write an essay that develops an extended comparison between writing or reading poetry and playing or watching another sport.

Connections to Other Selections

1. Compare this poem with Robert Wallace's "The Double-Play" (p. 434), another poem that explores the relation of baseball to poetry.
2. Write an essay comparing "The Pitcher" with Francis's "Glass" (p. 502). One poem defines poetry implicitly, the other defines it explicitly. Which poem do you prefer? Why?

HELEN CHASIN (b. 1938)
The Word Plum

1968

The word *plum* is delicious

pout and push, luxury of
self-love, and savoring murmur

full in the mouth and falling
like fruit   5

taut skin
pierced, bitten, provoked into
juice, and tart flesh

question
and reply, lip and tongue   10
of pleasure.

Considerations for Critical Thinking and Writing

1. Underline the alliteration and circle the assonance throughout the poem. What is the effect of these repetitions?
2. Which sounds in the poem are like the sounds one makes while eating a plum?
3. Discuss the title. Explain whether you think this poem is more about the word *plum* or about the plum itself. Consider whether the two can be separated in the poem.

Connection to Another Selection

1. How is Galway Kinnell's "Blackberry Eating" (p. 138) similar in technique to Chasin's poem? Try writing such a poem yourself: choose a food to describe that allows you to evoke its sensuousness in sounds.

RUTH PORRITT (b. 1957)
Read This Poem from the Bottom Up

This simple cathedral of praise.
How you made, from the bottom up,
Is for you to remember
Of Andromeda.° What remains

Until you meet the ancient light   5
With your sight you can keep ascending
Its final transformation into space.
And uphold

The horizon's urge to sculpt the sky
Puts into relief   10
Your family's mountain land
Upon the rising air. In the distance

A windward falcon is open high and steady
Far above the tallest tree
Just beyond your height.   15
You see a young pine lifting its green spire

By raising your eyes
Out onto the roof deck.
You pass through sliding glass doors
And up to where the stairway ends.   20

To the top of the penultimate stanza
Past the second story,
But now you're going the other way,
Line by line, to the bottom of the page.

A force that usually pulls you down,   25
Of moving against the gravity of habit,
While trying not to notice the effort
And feel what it's like to climb stairs

4 *Andromeda*: A constellation named after the daughter of Cepheus and Cassiopeia in Greek mythology who was saved from a sea monster by Perseus, her future husband. After her death, she was placed among the stars.

Considerations for Critical Thinking and Writing

1. Write this poem from the last line to the first — from the bottom up. How do the two versions complement each other? Describe the physical movement in the poems.
2. Read each version aloud. How do they sound different? Explain why.
3. Comment on the purpose and theme of the poem.
4. How important is the title?

7. Patterns of Rhythm

The rhythms of everyday life surround us in regularly recurring movements and sounds. As you read these words, your heart pulsates while somewhere else a clock ticks, a cradle rocks, a drum beats, a dancer sways, a foghorn blasts, a wave recedes, or a child skips. We may tend to overlook rhythm since it is so tightly woven into the fabric of our experience, but it is there nonetheless, one of the conditions of life. Rhythm is also one of the conditions of speech, because the voice alternately rises and falls as words are stressed or unstressed and as the pace quickens or slackens. In poetry *rhythm* refers to the recurrence of stressed and unstressed sounds. Depending upon how the sounds are arranged, this can result in a pace that is fast or slow, choppy or smooth.

SOME PRINCIPLES OF METER

Poets use rhythm to create pleasurable sound patterns and to reinforce meanings. "Rhythm," Edith Sitwell once observed, "might be described as, to the world of sound, what light is to the world of sight. It shapes and gives new meaning." Prose can use rhythm effectively too, but prose that does so tends to be more of an exception. The following exceptional lines are from a speech by Winston Churchill to the House of Commons after Allied forces lost a great battle to German forces at Dunkirk during World War II.

> We shall not flag or fail. We shall go on to the end. We shall fight in France, we shall fight on the seas and oceans, we shall fight with growing confidence and growing strength in the air, we shall defend our island, whatever the cost may be, we shall fight on the beaches, we shall fight on the landing grounds, we shall fight in the fields and in the streets, we shall fight in the hills; we shall never surrender.

The stressed repetition of "we shall" bespeaks the resolute singleness of purpose that Churchill had to convey to the British people if they were to win the war. Repetition is also one of the devices used in poetry to create rhythmic effects. In the following excerpt from "Song of the Open Road," Walt Whitman urges the pleasures of limitless freedom upon his reader.

> Allons!° the road is before us!   *Let's go!*
> It is safe — I have tried it — my own feet have tried it well — be not detain'd!
> Let the paper remain on the desk unwritten, and the book on the shelf unopen'd!
> Let the tools remain in the workshop! Let the money remain unearn'd!
> Let the school stand! mind not the cry of the teacher!   5
> Let the preacher preach in his pulpit! Let the lawyer plead in the court, and the judge expound the law.
>
> Camerado,° I give you my hand!   *friend*
> I give you my love more precious than money,
> I give you myself before preaching or law;
> Will you give me yourself? will you come travel with me?   10
> Shall we stick by each other as long as we live?

These rhythmic lines quickly move away from conventional values to the open road of shared experiences. Their recurring sounds are not created by rhyme or alliteration and assonance (see Chapter 6) but by the repetition of words and phrases.

Although the repetition of words and phrases can be an effective means of creating rhythm in poetry, the more typical method consists of patterns of accented or unaccented syllables. Words contain syllables that are either stressed or unstressed. A **stress** (or **accent**) places more emphasis on one syllable than on another. We say "*syl*lable" not "syl*la*ble," "*em*phasis" not "em*pha*sis." We routinely stress syllables when we speak: "*Is* she con*tent* with the *con*tents of the *yel*low *pack*age?" To distinguish between two people we might say "Is *she* con*tent*. . . ." In this way stress can be used to emphasize a particular word in a sentence. Poets often arrange words so that the desired meaning is suggested by the rhythm; hence, emphasis is controlled by the poet rather than left entirely to the reader.

When a rhythmic pattern of stresses recurs in a poem, the result is **meter.** **Scansion** consists of measuring the stresses in a line to determine its metrical pattern. Several methods can be used to mark lines. One widely used system employs ´ for a stressed syllable and ˘ for an unstressed syllable. In a sense, the stress mark represents the equivalent of tapping one's foot to a beat.

> Híckŏrў, díckŏrў, dóck,
> The móuse răn úp thĕ clóck.
> The clóck strŭck óne,
> Ănd dówn hĕ rún,
> Híckŏrў, díckŏrў, dóck.

In the first two lines and the final line of this familiar nursery rhyme we hear three stressed syllables. In lines 3 and 4, where the meter changes for variety, we hear just two stressed syllables. The combination of stresses provides the pleasure of the rhythm we hear.

To hear the rhythms of "Hickory, dickory, dock" does not require a formal study of meter. Nevertheless, an awareness of the basic kinds of meter that appear in English poetry can enhance your understanding of how a poem achieves its effects. Understanding the sound effects of a poem and having a vocabulary with which to discuss those effects can intensify your pleasure in poetry. Although the study of meter can be extremely technical, the terms used to describe the basic meters of English poetry are relatively easy to comprehend.

The *foot* is the metrical unit by which a line of poetry is measured. A foot usually consists of one stressed and one or two unstressed syllables. A vertical line is used to separate the feet: "The clóck | strŭck óne" consists of two feet. A foot of poetry can be arranged in a variety of patterns; here are five of the chief ones.

Foot	Pattern	Example
iamb	˘ ´	awáy
trochee	´ ˘	Lóvely
anapest	˘ ˘ ´	understánd
dactyl	´ ˘ ˘	désperate
spondee	´ ´	déad sét

The most common lines in English poetry contain meters based on iambic feet. However, even lines that are predominantly iambic will often include variations to create particular effects. Other important patterns include trochaic, anapestic, and dactylic feet. The spondee is not a sustained meter but occurs for variety or emphasis.

Iambic

What képt | his eyés | from gív | ĭng báck | the gáze

Trochaic

Hé wăs | loúder | thán the | preácher

Anapestic

Ĭ am cálled | tŏ the frónt | ŏf the roóm

Dactylic

Síng it all | mérrĭly

These meters have different rhythms and can create different effects. Iambic and anapestic are known as *rising meters* because they move from unstressed to stressed sounds, while trochaic and dactylic are known as *falling meters.* Anapests and dactyls tend to move more lightly and rapidly than iambs or trochees. Although no single kind of meter can be considered always better than another for a given subject, it is possible to determine whether the meter of a specific poem is appropriate for its subject. A serious poem about a tragic death would most likely not be well served by lilting rhythms. Keep in mind too that though one or another of these four basic meters might constitute the predominant rhythm of a poem, variations can occur within lines to change the pace or call attention to a particular word.

A *line* is measured by the number of feet it contains. Here, for example, is an iambic line with three feet: "Ĭf shé | shŏuld wríte | ă nóte." These are the names for line lengths.

monometer: one foot   pentameter: five feet
dimeter: two feet   hexameter: six feet
trimeter: three feet   heptameter: seven feet
tetrameter: four feet   octameter: eight feet

By combining the name of a line length with the name of a foot, we can describe the metrical qualities of a line concisely. Consider, for example, the pattern of feet and length of this line.

I didn't want the boy to hit the dog.

The iambic rhythm of this line falls into five feet; hence it is called *iambic pentameter.* Iambic is the most common pattern in English poetry because its rhythm appears so naturally in English speech and writing. Unrhymed iambic pentameter is called *blank verse;* Shakespeare's plays are built upon such lines.

Less common than the iamb, trochee, anapest, or dactyl is the *spondee,* a two-syllable foot in which both syllables are stressed (´ ´). Note the effect of the spondaic foot at the beginning of this line.

Déad sét | ăgaínst | thĕ plán | hĕ wént | ăway.

Spondees can slow a rhythm and provide variety and emphasis, particularly in iambic and trochaic lines.

The effects of these English meters are easily seen in the following lines by Samuel Taylor Coleridge, in which the rhythm of each line illustrates the meter described in it.

Trochee trips from long to short;
From long to long in solemn sort
Slow Spondee stalks; strong foot yet ill able
Ever to come up with Dactylic trisyllable.
Iambics march from short to long —
With a leap and a bound the swift Anapests throng.

The speed of a line is also affected by the number of pauses in it. A pause within a line is called a *caesura* and is indicated by a double vertical line (||). A caesura can occur anywhere within a line and need not be indicated by punctuation.

> Camerado, || I give you my hand!
> I give you my love || more precious than money.

A slight pause occurs within each of these lines and at its end. Both kinds of pauses contribute to the lines' rhythm.

When a line has a pause at its end, it is called an ***end-stopped line***. Such pauses reflect normal speech patterns and are often marked by punctuation. A line that ends without a pause and continues into the next line for its meaning is called a ***run-on line***. Running over from one line to another is also called ***enjambment***. The first and eighth lines of the following poem are run-on lines; the rest are end-stopped.

WILLIAM WORDSWORTH (1770–1850)
My Heart Leaps Up   1807

My heart leaps up when I behold
    A rainbow in the sky:
So was it when my life began;
So is it now I am a man;
So be it when I shall grow old,
    Or let me die!
The child is father of the Man;
And I could wish my days to be
Bound each to each by natural piety.

Run-on lines have a different rhythm from end-stopped lines. Lines 3–4 and 8–9 are both iambic, but the effect of their rhythms is very different when we read these lines aloud. The enjambment of lines 8 and 9 reinforces their meaning; just as the "days" are bound together, so are the lines.

The rhythm of a poem can be affected by several devices: the kind and number of stresses within lines, the length of lines, and the kinds of pauses that appear within lines or at their ends. In addition, as we saw in Chapter 6, the sound of a poem is affected by alliteration, assonance, rhyme, and consonance. These sounds help to create rhythms by controlling our pronunciations, as in the following lines by Alexander Pope.

> Soft is the strain when Zephyr gently blows,
> And the smooth stream in smoother numbers flows;
> But when loud surges lash the sounding shore,
> The hoarse, rough verse should like the torrent roar.

These lines are effective because their rhythm and sound work with their meaning.

SUGGESTIONS FOR SCANNING A POEM

These suggestions should help you in talking about a poem's meter.

1. After reading the poem through, read it aloud and mark the stressed syllables in each line. Then mark the unstressed syllables.
2. From your markings, identify what kind of foot is dominant (iambic, trochaic, dactylic, or anapestic) and divide the lines into feet, keeping in mind that the vertical line marking a foot may come in the middle of a word as well as at its beginning or end.
3. Determine the number of feet in each line. Remember that there may be variations; some lines may be shorter or longer than the predominant meter. What is important is the overall pattern. Do not assume that variations represent the poet's inability to fulfill the overall pattern. Notice the effects of variations and whether they emphasize words and phrases or disrupt your expectation for some other purpose.
4. Listen for pauses within lines and mark the caesuras; many times there will be no punctuation to indicate them.
5. Recognize that scansion does not always yield a definitive measurement of a line. Even experienced readers may differ over the scansion of a given line. What is important is not a precise description of the line but an awareness of how a poem's rhythms contribute to its effects.

The following poem demonstrates how you can use an understanding of meter and rhythm to gain a greater appreciation for what a poem is saying.

TIMOTHY STEELE (b. 1948)
Waiting for the Storm   1986

Bréeze sént | ă wrínk | lĭng dárk | nĕss
Acróss | thĕ báy. || I knélt
Bĕnéath | ăn úp | turnĕd bóat,
Ănd, mó | mĕnt bў mó | mĕnt, félt

Thĕ sánd | ăt mў féet | grŏw cóld | ĕr,
Thĕ damp | áir chíll | ănd spréad.
Thĕn thĕ | fírst ráin | drŏps sóund | ĕd
Ŏn thĕ húll | ăbóve | mў héad.

The predominant meter of this poem is iambic trimeter, but there is plenty of variation as the storm rapidly approaches and finally begins to pelt the sheltered speaker. The emphatic spondee ("Breeze sent") pushes the darkness quickly across the bay while the caesura at the end of the sentence in line 2 creates a pause that sets up a feeling of suspense and expectation that is measured in the ticking rhythm of line 4, a run-on line that brings us into the chilly sand and air of the second stanza. Perhaps the most impressive sound effect used in the poem appears in the second syllable of "sounded" in line 7. That "*ed*" precedes the sound of the poem's final word "head" just as if it were the first drop of rain hitting the hull above the speaker. The visual, tactile, and auditory images make "Waiting for the Storm" an intense sensory experience.

The next poem also reinforces meanings through its use of meter and rhythm.

WILLIAM BUTLER YEATS (1865–1939)
That the Night Come   1912

She lived | in storm | and strife,
Her soul | had such | desire
For what | proud death | may bring
That it | could not | endure
The com | mon good | of life,   5
But lived | as 'twere | a king
That packed | his mar | riage day
With ban | neret | and pennon,
Trumpet | and kett | ledrum,
And the | outrag | eous cannon,   10
To bun | dle time | away
That the | night come.

Scansion reveals that the predominant meter here is iambic trimeter. Each line contains three stressed and unstressed syllables that form a regular, predictable rhythm through line 7. That rhythm is disrupted, however, when the speaker compares the woman's longing for what death brings to a king's eager anticipation of his wedding night. The king packs the day with noisy fanfares and celebrations to fill up time and distract himself. Unable to accept "The common good of life," the woman fills her days with "storm and strife."

In a determined effort to "bundle time away," she, like the king, impatiently awaits the night.

Lines 8–10 break the regular pattern established in the first seven lines. The extra unstressed syllable in lines 8 and 10 along with the trochaic feet in lines 9 *(trúmpĕt)* and 10 *(Ańd thĕ)* interrupt the basic iambic trimeter and parallel the woman's and the king's frenetic activity. These lines thus echo the inability of the woman and king to "endure" regular or normal time. The last line is the most irregular in the poem. The final two accented syllables sound like the deep resonant beats of a kettledrum or a cannon firing. The words "night come" dramatically remind us that what the woman anticipates is not a lover but the mysterious finality of death. The meter serves, then, in both its regularity and variations to reinforce the poem's meaning and tone.

The following poems are especially rich in their rhythms and sounds. As you read and study them, notice how patterns of rhythm and the sounds of words reinforce meanings and contribute to the poems' effects. And, perhaps most importantly, read the poems aloud so that you can hear them.

POEMS FOR FURTHER STUDY

WALTER SAVAGE LANDOR (1775–1864)
Death of the Day

1858

My pictures blacken in their frames
    As night comes on,
And youthful maids and wrinkled dames
    Are now all one.

Death of the day! a sterner Death
    Did worse before;
The fairest form, the sweetest breath,
    Away he bore.

Considerations for Critical Thinking and Writing

1. What does a scansion of this poem reveal about the rhythm of its lines?
2. Discuss the use of personification in the poem.
3. Describe the effect of the caesura in line 5.

Connection to Another Selection

1. Write an essay comparing the images and tone of "Death of the Day" and Robert Herrick's "To the Virgins, to Make Much of Time" (p. 53).

A. E. HOUSMAN (1859–1936)
When I was one-and-twenty   1896

When I was one-and-twenty
   I heard a wise man say,
"Give crowns and pounds and guineas
   But not your heart away;
Give pearls away and rubies   5
   But keep your fancy free."
But I was one-and-twenty,
   No use to talk to me.

When I was one-and-twenty
   I heard him say again,   10
"The heart out of the bosom
   Was never given in vain;
'Tis paid with sighs a plenty
   And sold for endless rue."
And I am two-and-twenty,   15
   And oh, 'tis true, 'tis true.

Considerations for Critical Thinking and Writing

1. Scan this poem. What is the basic metrical pattern?
2. How do lines 1–8 parallel lines 9–16 in their use of rhyme and metaphor? Are there any significant differences between the stanzas?
3. What do you think has happened to change the speaker's attitude toward love?
4. Explain why you agree or disagree with the advice given by the "wise man."
5. What is the effect of the repetition in line 16?

ROBERT FRANCIS (1901–1987)
Excellence   1941

Excellence is millimeters and not miles.
From poor to good is great. From good to best is small.
From almost best to best sometimes not measurable.
The man who leaps the highest leaps perhaps an inch
Above the runner-up. How glorious that inch
And that split-second longer in the air before the fall.

Considerations for Critical Thinking and Writing

1. How does alliteration help to support the meaning of this poem's first line?
2. Francis does not use iambic pentameter, the most common metrical line in English. What does he use? Why is it a more appropriate choice?

3. What is the effect of the caesura in line 2?
4. Why is Francis's version of line 6 better than this one: "And that split-second in the air before the fall"?

ROBERT HERRICK (1591–1674)
Delight in Disorder   1648

A sweet disorder in the dress
Kindles in clothes a wantonness.
A lawn° about the shoulders thrown   *linen scarf*
Into a fine distraction;
An erring lace, which here and there   5
Enthralls the crimson stomacher,
A cuff neglectful, and thereby
Ribbons to flow confusedly;
A winning wave, deserving note,
In the tempestuous petticoat;   10
A careless shoestring, in whose tie
I see a wild civility;
Do more bewitch me than when art
Is too precise in every part.

Considerations for Critical Thinking and Writing

1. Why does the speaker in this poem value "disorder" so highly?
2. What is the principal rhythmic order of the poem? Is it "precise in every part"? How does the poem's organization relate to its theme?
3. Which words in the poem indicate disorder? Which words indicate the speaker's response to that disorder? What are the connotative meanings of each set of words? Why are they appropriate? What do they suggest about the woman and the speaker?
4. Write a short essay in which you agree or disagree with the speaker's views on dress.

BEN JONSON (1573–1637)
Still to Be Neat   1609

Still° to be neat, still to be dressed,   *continually*
As you were going to a feast;
Still to be powdered, still perfumed;
Lady, it is to be presumed,
Though art's hid causes are not found,   5
All is not sweet, all is not sound.

Give me a look, give me a face
That makes simplicity a grace;
Robes loosely flowing, hair as free;
Such sweet neglect more taketh me   10
Then all th' adulteries of art.
They strike mine eyes, but not my heart.

Considerations for Critical Thinking and Writing

1. What are the speaker's reservations about the lady in the first stanza? What do you think "sweet" means in line 6?
2. What does the speaker want from the lady in the second stanza? How has the meaning of "sweet" shifted from line 6 to line 10? What other words in the poem are especially charged with connotative meanings?
3. How do the rhythms of Jonson's lines help to reinforce meanings? Pay particular attention to lines 6 and 12.

Connections to Another Selection

1. Write an essay comparing the themes of "Still to Be Neat" and Herrick's "Delight in Disorder." How do the speakers make similar points but from different perspectives?
2. How does the rhythm of "Still to Be Neat" compare with that of "Delight in Disorder"? Which do you find more effective? Explain why.

ANNE SEXTON (1928–1974)
Her Kind   1960

I have gone out, a possessed witch,
haunting the black air, braver at night;
dreaming evil, I have done my hitch
over the plain houses, light by light:
lonely thing, twelve-fingered, out of mind.   5
A woman like that is not a woman, quite.
I have been her kind.

I have found the warm caves in the woods,
filled them with skillets, carvings, shelves,
closets, silks, innumerable goods;   10
fixed the suppers for the worms and the elves:
whining, rearranging the disaligned.
A woman like that is misunderstood.
I have been her kind.

I have ridden in your cart, driver,   15
waved my nude arms at villages going by,
learning the last bright routes, survivor
where your flames still bite my thigh

and my ribs crack where your wheels wind.
A woman like that is not ashamed to die.   20
I have been her kind.

Considerations for Critical Thinking and Writing

1. What kind of women does the speaker describe?
2. What is the predominant meter of the poem? Describe its rhythm.
3. How does Sexton use caesura and enjambment to create the poem's rhythm?

WILLIAM BLAKE (1757–1827)
The Lamb   1789

    Little Lamb, who made thee?
    Dost thou know who made thee?
Gave thee life, and bid thee feed
By the stream and o'er the mead;
Gave thee clothing of delight,   5
Softest clothing, wooly, bright;
Gave thee such a tender voice,
Making all the vales rejoice?
    Little Lamb, who made thee?
    Dost thou know who made thee?   10

    Little Lamb, I'll tell thee,
    Little Lamb, I'll tell thee:
He is callèd by thy name,
For he calls himself a Lamb.
He is meek, and he is mild;   15
He became a little child.
I a child, and thou a lamb,
We are callèd by his name.
    Little Lamb, God bless thee!
    Little Lamb, God bless thee!   20

Considerations for Critical Thinking and Writing

1. This poem is from Blake's *Songs of Innocence.* Describe its tone. How do the meter, rhyme, and repetition help to characterize the speaker's voice?
2. Why is it significant that the animal addressed by the speaker is a lamb? What symbolic value would be lost if the animal were, for example, a doe?
3. How does the second stanza answer the question raised in the first? What is the speaker's view of the creation?

WILLIAM BLAKE (1757–1827)
The Tyger   1794

Tyger! Tyger! burning bright
In the forests of the night,
What immortal hand or eye
Could frame thy fearful symmetry?

In what distant deeps or skies   5
Burnt the fire of thine eyes?
On what wings dare he aspire?
What the hand dare seize the fire?

And what shoulder, and what art,
Could twist the sinews of thy heart?   10
And when thy heart began to beat,
What dread hand? and what dread feet?

What the hammer? what the chain?
In what furnace was thy brain?
What the anvil? what dread grasp   15
Dare its deadly terrors clasp?

When the stars threw down their spears,
And watered heaven with their tears,
Did he smile his work to see?
Did he who made the Lamb make thee?   20

Tyger! Tyger! burning bright
In the forests of the night,
What immortal hand or eye
Dare frame thy fearful symmetry?

Considerations for Critical Thinking and Writing

1. This poem is from Blake's *Songs of Experience* and is often paired with "The Lamb." Describe the poem's tone. Is the speaker's voice the same here as in "The Lamb"? Which words are repeated, and how do they contribute to the tone?
2. What is revealed about the nature of the tiger by the words used to describe its creation? What do you think the tiger symbolizes?
3. Unlike in "The Lamb," more than one question is raised in "The Tyger." What are these questions? Are they answered?
4. Compare the rhythms in "The Lamb" and "The Tyger." Each basically uses a seven-syllable line, but the effects are very different. Why?
5. Using these two poems as the basis of your discussion, describe what distinguishes innocence from experience.

DOROTHY PARKER (1893–1967)
One Perfect Rose   1926

A single flow'r he sent me, since we met.
  All tenderly his messenger he chose;
Deep-hearted, pure, with scented dew still wet —
  One perfect rose.

I knew the language of the floweret;   5
  "My fragile leaves," it said, "his heart enclose."
Love long has taken for his amulet
  One perfect rose.

Why is it no one ever sent me yet
  One perfect limousine, do you suppose?   10
Ah no, it's always just my luck to get
  One perfect rose.

Considerations for Critical Thinking and Writing

1. Describe the tone of the first two stanzas. How do rhyme and meter help to establish the tone?
2. How does the meaning of "One perfect rose" in line 12 compare with the way you read it in lines 4 and 8?
3. Describe the speaker. What sort of woman is she? How do you respond to her?

ALFRED, LORD TENNYSON (1809–1892)
Break, Break, Break   1842

Break, break, break,
  On thy cold gray stones, O Sea!
And I would that my tongue could utter
  The thoughts that arise in me.

O, well for the fisherman's boy,   5
  That he shouts with his sister at play!
O, well for the sailor lad,
  That he sings in his boat on the bay!

And the stately ships go on
  To their haven under the hill;   10
But O for the touch of a vanished hand,
  And the sound of a voice that is still!

Break, break, break
   At the foot of thy crags, O Sea!
But the tender grace of a day that is dead   15
   Will never come back to me.

Considerations for Critical Thinking and Writing

1. How do lines 1 and 13 differ from the predominant meter of this poem? How do these two lines control the poem's tone?
2. What is the effect of the repetition? What does "break" refer to in addition to the waves?

THEODORE ROETHKE (1908–1963)
My Papa's Waltz   1948

The whiskey on your breath
Could make a small boy dizzy;
But I hung on like death:
Such waltzing was not easy.

We romped until the pans   5
Slid from the kitchen shelf;
My mother's countenance
Could not unfrown itself.

The hand that held my wrist
Was battered on one knuckle;   10
At every step you missed
My right ear scraped a buckle.

You beat time on my head
With a palm caked hard by dirt,
Then waltzed me off to bed   15
Still clinging to your shirt.

Considerations for Critical Thinking and Writing

1. What details characterize the father in this poem? How does the speaker's choice of words reveal his feeling about his father? Is the remembering speaker still a boy?
2. Characterize the rhythm of the poem. Does it move "like death," or is it more like a waltz? Is the rhythm regular throughout the poem? What is its effect?
3. Comment on the appropriateness of the title. Why do you suppose Roethke didn't use "My Father's Waltz"?

MILLER WILLIAMS (b. 1930)
Ruby Tells All

1985

When I was told, as Delta children were,
that crops don't grow unless you sweat at night,
I thought that it was my own sweat they meant.
I have never felt as important again
as on those early mornings, waking up,   5
my body slick, the moon full on the fields.
That was before air conditioning.
Farm girls sleep cool now and wake up dry,
but still the cotton overflows the fields.
We lose everything that's grand and foolish;   10
it all becomes something else. One by one,
butterflies turn into caterpillars
and we grow up, or more or less we do,
and, Lord, we do lie then. We lie so much
the truth has a false ring and it's hard to tell.   15
I wouldn't take crap off anybody
if I just knew that I was getting crap
in time not to take it. I could have won
a small one now and then if I was smarter,
but I've poured coffee here too many years   20
for men who rolled in in Peterbilts,
and I have gotten into bed with some
if they could talk and seemed to be in pain.
I never asked for anything myself;
giving is more blessed and leaves you free.   25
There was a man, married and fond of whiskey.
Given the limitations of men, he loved me.
Lord, we laid concern upon our bodies
but then he left. Everything has its time.
We used to dance. He made me feel the way   30
a human wants to feel and fears to.
He was a slow man and didn't expect.
I would get off work and find him waiting.
We'd have a drink or two and kiss awhile.
Then a bird-loud morning late one April   35
we woke up naked. We had made a child.
She's grown up now and gone though god knows where.
She ought to write, for I do love her dearly
who raised her carefully and dressed her well.

Everything has its time. For thirty years   40
I never had a thought about time.
Now, turning through newspapers, I pause
to see if anyone who passed away

was younger than I am. If one was
I feel hollow for a little while
but then it passes. Nothing matters enough   45
to stay bent down about. You have to see
that some things matter slightly and some don't.
Dying matters a little. So does pain.
So does being old. Men do not.   50
Men live by negatives, like don't give up,
don't be a coward, don't call me a liar,
don't ever tell me don't. If I could live
two hundred years and had to be a man
I'd take my grave. What's a man but a match,   55
a little stick to start a fire with?
My daughter knows this, if she's alive.
What could I tell her now, to bring her close,
something she doesn't know, if we met somewhere?
Maybe that I think about her father,   60
maybe that my fingers hurt at night,
maybe that against appearances
there is love, constancy, and kindness,
that I have dresses I have never worn.

Considerations for Critical Thinking and Writing

1. What is the predominant meter of this poem? How does it affect the tone of Ruby's monologue?
2. Describe Ruby's attitude toward life. What does she think of men? Of herself?
3. Using the details provided in the poem write an essay that characterizes Ruby's life. Which details are especially revealing?

Connections to Other Selections

1. Write an essay that compares the speakers in "Ruby Tells All" and Katharyn Howd Machan's "Hazel Tells LaVerne" (p. 50).
2. Discuss the attitudes expressed toward men in this poem and in Sharon Olds's "Rite of Passage" (p. 207).

EDWARD HIRSCH (b. 1950)
Fast Break   1985

(In Memory of Dennis Turner, 1946–1984)

A hook shot kisses the rim and
hangs there, helplessly, but doesn't drop

and for once our gangly starting center
boxes out his man and times his jump

perfectly, gathering the orange leather   5
from the air like a cherished possession

and spinning around to throw a strike
to the outlet who is already shoveling

an underhand pass toward the other guard
scissoring past a flat-footed defender   10

who looks stunned and nailed to the floor
in the wrong direction, turning to catch sight

of a high, gliding dribble and a man
letting the play develop in front of him

in slow motion, almost exactly   15
like a coach's drawing on the blackboard,

both forwards racing down the court
the way that forwards should, fanning out

and filling the lanes in tandem, moving
together as brothers passing the ball   20

between them without a dribble, without
a single bounce hitting the hardwood

until the guard finally lunges out
and commits to the wrong man

while the power-forward explodes past them   25
in a fury, taking the ball into the air

by himself now and laying it gently
against the glass for a layup,

but losing his balance in the process,
inexplicably falling, hitting the floor   30

with a wild, headlong motion
for the game he loved like a country

and swiveling back to see an orange blur
floating perfectly through the net.

Considerations for Critical Thinking and Writing

1. Why are run-on lines especially appropriate for this poem? How do they affect its sound and sense? What is the effect of the poem being one long sentence? Do the lines have a regular meter?
2. In addition to describing accurately a fast break, this poem is a tribute to a dead friend. How are the two purposes related in the poem?
3. How might this poem — to borrow a phrase from Robert Frost — represent a "momentary stay against confusion"?

LOUISE BOGAN (1897–1970)
On Formal Poetry
1953

What is formal poetry? It is poetry written in form. And what is *form?* The elements of form, so far as poetry is concerned, are meter and rhyme. Are these elements merely mold and ornaments that have been impressed upon poetry from without? Are they indeed restrictions which blind and fetter language and the thought and emotion behind, under, within language in a repressive way? Are they arbitrary rules which have lost all validity since they have been broken to good purpose by "experimental poets," ancient and modern? Does the breaking up of form, or its total elimination, always result in an increase of power and of effect; and is any return to form a sort of relinquishment of freedom, or retreat to old fogeyism?

From *A Poet's Alphabet*

Considerations for Critical Thinking and Writing

1. Choose one of the questions Bogan raises and write an essay in response to it using two or three poems from this chapter to illustrate your answer.
2. Try writing a poem in meter and rhyme. Does the experience make your writing feel limited or not?

8. Poetic Forms

Poems come in a variety of shapes. Although the best poems always have their own unique qualities, many of them also conform to traditional patterns. Frequently the *form* of a poem — its overall structure or shape — follows an already established design. A poem that can be categorized by the patterns of its lines, meter, rhymes, and stanzas is considered a *fixed form,* because it follows a prescribed model such as a sonnet. However, poems written in a fixed form do not always fit models precisely; writers sometimes work variations on traditional forms to create innovative effects.

Not all poets are content with variations on traditional forms. Some prefer to create their own structures and shapes. Poems that do not conform to established patterns of meter, rhyme, and stanza are called *free verse* or *open form* poetry. (See Chapter 9 for further discussion of open forms.) This kind of poetry creates its own ordering principles through the careful arrangement of words and phrases in line lengths that embody rhythms appropriate to the meaning. Modern and contemporary poets in particular have learned to use the blank space on the page as a significant functional element [for a striking example see e. e. cummings's "l(a," p. 24]. Good poetry of this kind is structured in ways that can be as demanding, interesting, and satisfying as fixed forms. Open and fixed forms represent different poetic styles, but they are identical in the sense that both use language in concentrated ways to convey meanings, experiences, emotions, and effects.

SOME COMMON POETIC FORMS

A familiarity with some of the most frequently used fixed forms of poetry is useful, because it allows for a better understanding of how a poem works. Classifying patterns allows us to talk about the effects of established rhythm and rhyme and recognize how significant variations from them affect the pace and meaning of the lines. An awareness of form also allows us to anticipate how a poem is likely to proceed. As we shall see, a sonnet creates a different set of expectations in a reader from those of, say, a limerick. A reader isn't likely to find in limericks the kind of serious themes that often make their way into sonnets. The discussion that follows identifies some of the important poetic forms frequently encountered in English poetry.

The shape of a fixed form poem is often determined by the way in which the lines are organized into stanzas. A *stanza* consists of a grouping of lines, set off by a space, which usually has a set pattern of meter and rhyme. This pattern is ordinarily repeated in other stanzas throughout the poem. What is usual is not obligatory, however; some poems may use a different pattern for each stanza, somewhat like paragraphs in prose.

Traditionally, though, stanzas do share a common *rhyme scheme*, the pattern of end rhymes. We can map out rhyme schemes by noting patterns of rhyme with small letters: the first rhyme sound is designated *a*, the second becomes *b*, the third *c*, and so on. Using this system, we can describe the rhyme scheme in the following poem this way: *aabb, ccdd, eeff*.

A. E. HOUSMAN (1859–1936)
Loveliest of trees, the cherry now   1896

Loveliest of trees, the cherry now	*a*	
Is hung with bloom along the bough,	*a*	
And stands about the woodland ride	*b*	
Wearing white for Eastertide.	*b*	
Now, of my threescore years and ten,	*c*	5
Twenty will not come again,	*c*	
And take from seventy springs a score,	*d*	
It only leaves me fifty more.	*d*	
And since to look at things in bloom	*e*	
Fifty springs are little room,	*e*	10
About the woodlands I will go	*f*	
To see the cherry hung with snow.	*f*	

Considerations for Critical Thinking and Writing

1. What is the speaker's attitude in this poem toward time and life?
2. Why is spring an appropriate season for the setting rather than, say, winter?
3. Paraphrase each stanza. How do the images in each reinforce the poem's themes?
4. Lines 1 and 12 are not intended to rhyme, but they are close. What is the effect of the near rhyme of "now" and "snow"? How does the rhyme enhance the theme?

Poets often create their own stanzaic patterns; hence there is an infinite number of kinds of stanzas. One way of talking about stanzaic forms is to describe a given stanza by how many lines it contains.

A *couplet* consists of two lines that usually rhyme and have the same meter; couplets are frequently not separated from each other by space on the page. A *heroic couplet* consists of rhymed iambic pentameter. Here is an example from Pope's "An Essay on Criticism."

One science only will one genius fit;	*a*
So vast is art, so narrow human wit:	*a*
Not only bounded to peculiar arts,	*b*
But oft in those confined to single parts.	*b*

A *tercet* is a three-line stanza. When all three lines rhyme they are called a *triplet.* Two triplets make up this captivating poem.

ROBERT HERRICK (1591–1674)
Upon Julia's Clothes 1648

Whenas in silks my Julia goes,	*a*
Then, then, methinks, how sweetly flows	*a*
That liquefaction of her clothes.	*a*
Next, when I cast mine eyes, and see	*b*
That brave vibration, each way free,	*b*
O, how that glittering taketh me!	*b*

Considerations for Critical Thinking and Writing

1. Underline the alliteration in this poem. What purpose does it serve?
2. Comment on the effect of the meter. How is it related to the speaker's description of Julia's clothes?
3. Look up the word *brave* in the *Oxford English Dictionary.* Which of its meanings are appropriate to describe Julia's movement? Some readers interpret lines 4–6 to mean that Julia has no clothes on. What do you think?

Connection to Another Selection

1. Compare the tone of this poem with that of Paul Humphrey's "Blow" (p. 154). Are the situations and speakers similar? Is there any difference in tone between these two poems?

Terza rima consists of an interlocking three-line rhyme scheme: *aba, bcb, cdc, ded,* and so on. Dante's *The Divine Comedy* uses this pattern, as does Robert Frost's "Acquainted with the Night" (p. 109) and Percy Bysshe Shelley's "Ode to the West Wind" (p. 192).

A *quatrain,* or four-line stanza, is the most common stanzaic form in the English language and can have various meters and rhyme schemes (if any). The most common rhyme schemes are *aabb, abba, aaba,* and *abcb.* This last pattern is especially characteristic of the popular **ballad stanza,** which consists of alternating eight- and six-syllable lines. Samuel Taylor

Coleridge adopted this pattern in "The Rime of the Ancient Mariner"; here is one representative stanza.

> All in a hot and copper sky
> The bloody Sun, at noon,
> Right up above the mast did stand,
> No bigger than the Moon.

There are a number of longer stanzaic forms and the list of types of stanzas could be extended considerably, but knowing these three most basic patterns should prove helpful to you in talking about the form of a great many poems. In addition to stanzaic forms, there are fixed forms that characterize entire poems. Lyric poems can be, for example, sonnets, villanelles, sestinas, or epigrams.

Sonnet

The *sonnet* has been a popular literary form in English since the sixteenth century, when it was adopted from the Italian *sonnetto,* meaning "little song." A sonnet consists of fourteen lines, usually written in iambic pentameter. Because the sonnet has been such a favorite form, writers have experimented with many variations on its essential structure. Nevertheless, there are two basic types of sonnets: the Italian and the English.

The *Italian sonnet* (also known as the **Petrarchan sonnet,** from the fourteenth-century Italian poet Petrarch) divides into two parts. The first eight lines (the *octave*) typically rhyme *abbaabba.* The final six lines (the *sestet*) may vary; common patterns are *cdecde, cdcdcd,* and *cdccdc.* Very often the octave presents a situation, attitude, or problem that the sestet comments upon or resolves, as in John Keats's "On First Looking into Chapman's Homer" (p. 215).

This pattern is also used in the next sonnet, but notice that the thematic break between octave and sestet comes within line 9 rather than between lines 8 and 9. This unconventional break helps to reinforce the speaker's impatience with the conventional attitudes he describes.

WILLIAM WORDSWORTH (1770–1850)
The World Is Too Much with Us 1807

The world is too much with us; late and soon,
Getting and spending, we lay waste our powers;
Little we see in Nature that is ours;
We have given our hearts away, a sordid boon!
This Sea that bares her bosom to the moon; 5
The winds that will be howling at all hours,
And are up-gathered now like sleeping flowers;
For this, for everything, we are out of tune;

It moves us not. — Great God! I'd rather be
A Pagan suckled in a creed outworn;   10
So might I, standing on this pleasant lea,
Have glimpses that would make me less forlorn;
Have sight of Proteus rising from the sea;
Or hear old Triton blow his wreathèd horn.

Considerations for Critical Thinking and Writing

1. What is the speaker's complaint in this sonnet? How do the conditions described affect him?
2. Look up "Proteus" and "Triton." What do these mythological allusions contribute to the sonnet's tone?
3. What is the effect of the personification of the sea and wind in the octave?

Connections to Other Selections

1. Compare the theme of this sonnet with that of Gerard Manley Hopkins's "God's Grandeur" (p. 144).
2. Write an essay that explores Amy Clampitt's "Nothing Stays Put" (p. 477) as a modern urban version of Wordsworth's poem.

The *English sonnet,* more commonly known as the *Shakespearean sonnet,* is organized into three quatrains and a couplet, which typically rhyme *abab cdcd efef gg.* This rhyme scheme is more suited to English poetry because English has fewer rhyming words than Italian. English sonnets, because of their four-part organization, also have more flexibility about where thematic breaks can occur. Frequently, however, the most pronounced break or turn comes with the concluding couplet.

In the following Shakespearean sonnet, the three quatrains compare the speaker's loved one to a summer's day and explain why the loved one is even more lovely. The couplet bestows eternal beauty and love upon both the loved one and the sonnet.

WILLIAM SHAKESPEARE (1564–1616)
Shall I compare thee to a summer's day?   1609

Shall I compare thee to a summer's day?
Thou art more lovely and more temperate:
Rough winds do shake the darling buds of May,
And summer's lease hath all too short a date.
Sometime too hot the eye of heaven shines,   5
And often is his gold complexion dimmed;
And every fair from fair sometime declines,
By chance, or nature's changing course, untrimmed.

But thy eternal summer shall not fade,
Nor lose possession of that fair thou ow'st°   *possesses*   10
Nor shall death brag thou wand'rest in his shade,
When in eternal lines to time thou grow'st.
    So long as men can breathe or eyes can see,
    So long lives this, and this gives life to thee.

Considerations for Critical Thinking and Writing

1. Why is the speaker's loved one more lovely than a summer's day? What qualities does he admire in the loved one?
2. Describe the shift in tone and subject matter that begins in line 9.
3. What does the couplet say about the relation between art and love?
4. Which syllables are stressed in the final line? How do these syllables relate to the meaning of the line?

Sonnets have been the vehicles for all kinds of subjects, including love, death, politics, and cosmic questions. Although most sonnets tend to treat their subjects seriously, this fixed form does not mean a fixed expression; humor is also possible in it. Compare this next Shakespearean sonnet with "Shall I compare thee to a summer's day?" They are, finally, both love poems, but their tones are markedly different.

WILLIAM SHAKESPEARE (1564–1616)
My mistress' eyes are nothing like the sun   1609

My mistress' eyes are nothing like the sun;
Coral is far more red than her lips' red;
If snow be white, why then her breasts are dun;
If hairs be wires, black wires grow on her head.
I have seen roses damasked red and white,   5
But no such roses see I in her cheeks;
And in some perfumes is there more delight
Than in the breath that from my mistress reeks.
I love to hear her speak, yet well I know
That music hath a far more pleasing sound;   10
I grant I never saw a goddess go:
My mistress, when she walks, treads on the ground.
    And yet, by heaven, I think my love as rare
    As any she,° belied with false compare.   *lady*

Considerations for Critical Thinking and Writing

1. What does "mistress" mean in this sonnet?
2. Write a description of the mistress based on the images used in the sonnet.
3. What sort of person is the speaker? Does he truly love the woman he describes?
4. In what sense are this sonnet and "Shall I compare thee" about poetry as well as love?

EDNA ST. VINCENT MILLAY (1892–1950)
I will put Chaos into fourteen lines

1954

I will put Chaos into fourteen lines
And keep him there; and let him thence escape
If he be lucky; let him twist, and ape
Flood, fire, and demon — his adroit designs
Will strain to nothing in the strict confines   5
Of this sweet Order, where, in pious rape,
I hold his essence and amorphous shape,
Till he with Order mingles and combines.
Past are the hours, the years, of our duress,
His arrogance, our awful servitude: 10
I have him. He is nothing more nor less
Than something simple not yet understood;
I shall not even force him to confess;
Or answer. I will only make him good.

Considerations for Critical Thinking and Writing

1. What properties of a sonnet does this poem possess? How does the poem contain "Chaos"?
2. What do you think is meant by the phrase "pious rape" in line 6?
3. What is the effect of the personification in the poem?

Connections to Other Selections

1. Compare the theme of this poem with that of Robert Frost's "Design" (p. 311).
2. Write an essay comparing this poem with Donald Justice's "Order in the Streets" (p. 211). In your opinion which poem creates more order out of chaos?

DONALD JUSTICE (b. 1925)
The Snowfall

1959

The classic landscapes of dreams are not
More pathless, though footprints leading nowhere
Would seem to prove that a people once
Survived for a little even here.

Fragments of a pathetic culture   5
Remain, the lost mittens of children,
And a single, bright, detasseled snow-cap,
Evidence of some frantic migration.

The landmarks are gone. Nevertheless
There is something familiar about this country.   10
Slowly now we begin to recall

The terrible whispers of our elders
Falling softly about our ears
In childhood, never believed till now.

Considerations for Critical Thinking and Writing

1. What is dreamlike about what the speaker describes?
2. What does the speaker believe at the end of the poem that the speaker did not believe earlier?
3. How is tone related to theme in this poem?
4. What properties of a sonnet does this poem possess? How does it differ from a sonnet? Pay particular attention to the poem's meter and use of rhyme.

Connections to Other Selections

1. Discuss the snow imagery in "The Snowfall" and Robert Frost's "Stopping by Woods on a Snowy Evening" (p. 308).
2. In an essay compare the themes of "The Snowfall" and Mark Strand's "The Continuous Life" (p. 430).

Villanelle

The *villanelle* is a fixed form consisting of nineteen lines of any length divided into six stanzas: five tercets and a concluding quatrain. The first and third lines of the initial tercet rhyme; these rhymes are repeated in each subsequent tercet *(aba)* and in the final two lines of the quatrain *(abaa)*. Moreover, line 1 appears in its entirety as lines 6, 12, and 18, while line 3 appears as lines 9, 15, and 19. This form may seem to risk monotony, but in competent hands a villanelle can create haunting echoes, as in Dylan Thomas's "Do not go gentle into that good night."

DYLAN THOMAS (1914–1953)
Do not go gentle into that good night

1952

Do not go gentle into that good night,
Old age should burn and rave at close of day;
Rage, rage against the dying of the light.

Though wise men at their end know dark is right,
Because their words had forked no lightning they   5
Do not go gentle into that good night.

Good men, the last wave by, crying how bright
Their frail deeds might have danced in a green bay,
Rage, rage against the dying of the light.

Wild men who caught and sang the sun in flight,   10

And learn, too late, they grieved it on its way,
Do not go gentle into that good night.

Grave men, near death, who see with blinding sight
Blind eyes could blaze like meteors and be gay,
Rage, rage against the dying of the light.   15

And you, my father, there on the sad height,
Curse, bless, me now with your fierce tears, I pray.
Do not go gentle into that good night.
Rage, rage against the dying of the light.

Considerations for Critical Thinking and Writing

1. Thomas's father was close to death when this poem was written. How does the tone contribute to the poem's theme?
2. How is "good" used in line 1?
3. Characterize the men who are "wise" (line 4), "Good" (7), "Wild" (10), and "Grave" (13).
4. What do figures of speech contribute to this poem?
5. Discuss this villanelle's sound effects.

Connections to Other Selections

1. Write an essay comparing Thomas's treatment of death with John Donne's in "Death Be Not Proud" (p. 373).
2. In Thomas's poem we experience "rage against the dying of the light." Contrast this with the rage you find in Sylvia Plath's "Daddy" (p. 410). What produces the emotion in Plath's poem?

Sestina

Although the *sestina* usually does not rhyme, it is perhaps an even more demanding fixed form than the villanelle. A sestina consists of thirty-nine lines of any length divided into six six-line stanzas and a three-line concluding stanza called an *envoy*. The difficulty is in repeating the six words at the ends of the first stanza's lines at the ends of the lines in the other five six-line stanzas as well. Those words must also appear in the final three lines, where they often resonate important themes. The sestina originated in the Middle Ages, but contemporary poets continue to find it a fascinating and challenging form.

ELIZABETH BISHOP (1911–1979)
Sestina   1965

September rain falls on the house.
In the failing light, the old grandmother
sits in the kitchen with the child

beside the Little Marvel Stove,
reading the jokes from the almanac,
laughing and talking to hide her tears.   5

She thinks that her equinoctial tears
and the rain that beats on the roof of the house
were both foretold by the almanac,
but only known to a grandmother.   10
The iron kettle sings on the stove.
She cuts some bread and says to the child,

It's time for tea now; but the child
is watching the teakettle's small hard tears
dance like mad on the hot black stove,   15
the way the rain must dance on the house.
Tidying up, the old grandmother
hangs up the clever almanac

on its string. Birdlike, the almanac
hovers half open above the child,   20
hovers above the old grandmother
and her teacup full of dark brown tears.
She shivers and says she thinks the house
feels chilly, and puts more wood in the stove.

It was to be, says the Marvel Stove.   25
I know what I know, says the almanac.
With crayons the child draws a rigid house
and a winding pathway. Then the child
puts in a man with buttons like tears
and shows it proudly to the grandmother.   30

But secretly, while the grandmother
busies herself about the stove,
the little moons fall down like tears
from between the pages of the almanac
into the flower bed the child   35
has carefully placed in the front of the house.

Time to plant tears, says the almanac.
The grandmother sings to the marvelous stove
and the child draws another inscrutable house.

Considerations for Critical Thinking and Writing

1. Number the end words of the first stanza 1, 2, 3, 4, 5, and 6, and then use those numbers for the corresponding end words in the remaining five stanzas to see how the pattern of the line-end words is worked out in this sestina. Also locate the six end words in the envoy.
2. What happens in this sestina? Why is the grandmother "laughing and talking to hide her tears"?

3. Underline the images that seem especially vivid to you. What effects do they create? What is the tone of the sestina?
4. How are the six end words — "house," "grandmother," "child," "stove," "almanac," and "tears" — central to the sestina's meaning?
5. How is the almanac used symbolically? Does Bishop use any other symbols to convey meanings?
6. Write a brief essay explaining why you think a poet might derive pleasure from writing in a fixed form such as a villanelle or sestina. Can you think of similar activities outside the field of writing in which discipline and restraint give pleasure?

Epigram

An *epigram* is a brief, pointed, and witty poem. Although most rhyme and often are written in couplets, epigrams take no prescribed form. Instead, they are typically polished bits of compressed irony, satire, or paradox. Here is an epigram that defines itself.

SAMUEL TAYLOR COLERIDGE (1772–1834)
What Is an Epigram?   1802

What is an epigram? A dwarfish whole;
Its body brevity, and wit its soul.

These additional examples by A. R. Ammons, David McCord, and Paul Laurence Dunbar satisfy Coleridge's definition.

A. R. AMMONS (b. 1926)
Coward   1975

Bravery runs in my family.

DAVID McCORD (b. 1897)
Epitaph on a Waiter

By and by
God caught his eye.

PAUL LAURENCE DUNBAR (1872–1906)
Theology

1896

There is a heaven, for ever, day by day,
The upward longing of my soul doth tell me so.
There is a hell, I'm quite as sure; for pray,
If there were not, where would my neighbors go?

Considerations for Critical Thinking and Writing

1. In what sense is each of these epigrams, as Coleridge puts it, a "dwarfish whole"?
2. Explain which of these epigrams, in addition to being witty, make a serious point?
3. Try writing a few epigrams that say something memorable about whatever you choose to focus upon.

Limerick

The *limerick* is always light and humorous. Its usual form consists of five predominantly anapestic lines rhyming *aabba;* lines 1, 2, and 5 contain three feet, while lines 3 and 4 contain two. Limericks have delighted everyone from schoolchildren to sophisticated adults, and they range in subject matter from the simply innocent and silly to the satiric or obscene. The sexual humor helps to explain why so many limericks are written anonymously. Here is one that is anonymous but more concerned with physics than physiology.

There was a young lady named Bright,
Who traveled much faster than light,
    She started one day
    In a relative way,
And returned on the previous night.

The next one is a particularly clever definition of a limerick.

LAURENCE PERRINE (b. 1915)
The limerick's never averse

1982

The limerick's never averse
To expressing itself in a terse
    Economical style,
    And yet, all the while,
The limerick's *always* a verse.

Considerations for Critical Thinking and Writing

1. Scan Perrine's limerick. How do the lines measure up to the traditional fixed metrical pattern?
2. Try writing a limerick. Use the following basic pattern.

You might begin with a friend's name or the name of your school or town. Your instructor is, of course, fair game, too, provided your tact matches your wit.

Clerihew

The *clerihew* is another humorous fixed form that, although not as popular as the limerick, has enjoyed a modest reputation ever since Edmund Clerihew Bentley created it. The clerihew usually consists of four irregular lines rhyming *aabb* that comment on a famous person who is named in the first line. Here is an example of the form by the creator himself.

EDMUND CLERIHEW BENTLEY (1875–1956)
John Stuart Mill   date unknown

John Stuart Mill
By a mighty effort of will
Overcame his natural bonhomie
And wrote *Principles of Political Economy.*

Haiku

Another brief fixed poetic form, borrowed from the Japanese, is the *haiku.* A haiku is usually described as consisting of seventeen syllables organized into three unrhymed lines of five, seven, and five syllables. Owing to language difference, however, English translations of haiku are often only approximated, because a Japanese haiku exists in time (Japanese syllables have duration). The number of syllables in our sense is not as significant as the duration. These poems typically present an intense emotion or vivid image of nature, which, in the Japanese, are also designed to lead to a spiritual insight.

MATSUO BASHŌ (1644–1694)
Under cherry trees

date unknown

Under cherry trees
Soup, the salad, fish and all . . .
Seasoned with petals.

The implied metaphor in the next haiku offers a striking comparison between a piece of land jutting out into the water and a bull charging a matador.

RICHARD WILBUR (b. 1921)
Sleepless at Crown Point

1976

All night, this headland
Lunges into the rumpling
Capework of the wind.

ETHERIDGE KNIGHT (b. 1931)
Eastern Guard Tower

1968

Eastern guard tower
glints in sunset; convicts rest
like lizards on rocks.

Considerations for Critical Thinking and Writing

1. What different emotions do these three haiku evoke?
2. What differences and similarities are there between the effects of a haiku and those of an epigram?
3. Compose a haiku; try to make it as allusive and suggestive as possible.

Elegy

An elegy in classical Greek and Roman literature was written in alternating hexameter and pentameter lines. Since the seventeenth century, however, the term *elegy* has been used to describe a lyric poem written to commemorate someone who is dead. The word is also used to refer to a serious meditative poem produced to express the speaker's melancholy thoughts. Elegies no longer conform to a fixed pattern of lines and stanzas, but their characteristic subject is related to death and their tone is mournfully contemplative.

SEAMUS HEANEY (b. 1939)
Mid-term Break 1966

I sat all morning in the college sick bay
Counting bells knelling classes to a close.
At two o'clock our neighbors drove me home.

In the porch I met my father crying —
He had always taken funerals in his stride — 5
And Big Jim Evans saying it was a hard blow.

The baby cooed and laughed and rocked the pram
When I came in, and I was embarrassed
By old men standing up to shake my hand

And tell me they were "sorry for my trouble," 10
Whispers informed strangers I was the eldest,
Away at school, as my mother held my hand

In hers and coughed out angry tearless sighs.
At ten o'clock the ambulance arrived
With the corpse, stanched and bandaged by the nurses. 15

Next morning I went up into the room. Snowdrops
And candles soothed the bedside; I saw him
For the first time in six weeks. Paler now,

Wearing a poppy bruise on his left temple,
He lay in the four foot box as in his cot. 20
No gaudy scars, the bumper knocked him clear.

A four foot box, a foot for every year.

Considerations for Critical Thinking and Writing

1. How do simple details contribute to the effects of this elegy?
2. Does this elegy use any kind of formal pattern for its structure? What is the effect of the last line standing by itself?
3. Another spelling for *stanched* (line 15) is *staunched.* Usage is about evenly divided between the two in the United States. What is the effect of Heaney choosing the former spelling rather than the latter?
4. Comment on the elegy's title.

Connections to Other Selections

1. Compare Heaney's elegy with A. E. Housman's "To an Athlete Dying Young" (p. 391). Which do you find more moving? Explain why.
2. Write an essay comparing this story of a boy's death with John Updike's "Dog's Death" (p. 14). Do you think either of the poems is sentimental? Explain why or why not.

Ode

An *ode* is characterized by a serious topic and formal tone, but no prescribed formal pattern describes all odes. In some odes the pattern of each stanza is repeated throughout, while in others each stanza introduces a new pattern. Odes are lengthy lyrics that often include lofty emotions conveyed by a dignified style. Typical topics include truth, art, freedom, justice, and the meaning of life. Frequently such lyrics tend to be more public than private, and their speakers often employ apostrophe.

PERCY BYSSHE SHELLEY (1792–1822)
Ode to the West Wind   1820

I
O wild West Wind, thou breath of Autumn's being,
Thou, from whose unseen presence the leaves dead
Are driven, like ghosts from an enchanter fleeing,

Yellow, and black, and pale, and hectic red,
Pestilence-stricken multitudes: O thou,   5
Who chariotest to their dark wintry bed

The wingèd seeds, where they lie cold and low,
Each like a corpse within its grave, until
Thine azure sister of the Spring shall blow

Her clarion o'er the dreaming earth, and fill   10
(Driving sweet buds like flocks to feed in air)
With living hues and odors plain and hill:

Wild Spirit, which art moving everywhere;
Destroyer and preserver; hear, oh, hear!

II
Thou on whose stream, mid the steep sky's commotion,   15
Loose clouds like earth's decaying leaves are shed,
Shook from the tangled boughs of Heaven and Ocean,

Angels° of rain and lightning: there are spread   *messengers*
On the blue surface of thine airy surge,
Like the bright hair uplifted from the head   20

Of some fierce Maenad,° even from the dim verge
Of the horizon to the zenith's height,
The locks of the approaching storm. Thou dirge

Of the dying year, to which this closing night

---

21 *Maenad:* In Greek mythology a frenzied worshiper of Dionysus, god of wine and fertility.

Will be the dome of a vast sepulcher,   25
Vaulted with all thy congregated might

Of vapors, from whose solid atmosphere
Black rain, and fire, and hail will burst: oh, hear!

III
Thou who didst waken from his summer dreams
The blue Mediterranean, where he lay,   30
Lulled by the coil of his crystálline streams,

Beside a pumice isle in Baiae's bay,°
And saw in sleep old palaces and towers
Quivering within the wave's intenser day,

All overgrown with azure moss and flowers   35
So sweet, the sense faints picturing them! Thou
For whose path the Atlantic's level powers

Cleave themselves into chasms, while far below
The sea-blooms and the oozy woods which wear
The sapless foliage of the ocean, know   40

Thy voice, and suddenly grow gray with fear,
And tremble and despoil themselves: oh, hear!

IV
If I were a dead leaf thou mightest bear;
If I were a swift cloud to fly with thee;
A wave to pant beneath thy power, and share   45

The impulse of thy strength, only less free
Than thou, O uncontrollable! If even
I were as in my boyhood, and could be

The comrade by thy wanderings over Heaven,
As then, when to outstrip thy skyey speed   50
Scarce seemed a vision; I would ne'er have striven

As thus with thee in prayer in my sore need.
Oh, lift me as a wave, a leaf, a cloud!
I fall upon the thorns of life! I bleed!

A heavy weight of hours has chained and bowed   55
One too like thee: tameless, and swift, and proud.

V
Make me thy lyre,° even as the forest is:
What if my leaves are falling like its own!
The tumult of thy mighty harmonies

Will take from both a deep, autumnal tone,   60
Sweet though in sadness. Be thou, Spirit fierce,

---

32 *Baiae's bay:* A bay in the Mediterranean Sea.   57 *Make me thy lyre:* Sound is produced on an
Aeolian lyre, or wind harp, by wind blowing across its strings.

My spirit! Be thou me, impetuous one!

Drive my dead thoughts over the universe
Like withered leaves to quicken a new birth!
And, by the incantation of this verse,   65

Scatter, as from an unextinguished hearth
Ashes and sparks, my words among mankind!
Be through my lips to unawakened earth

The trumpet of a prophecy! O Wind,
If Winter comes, can Spring be far behind?   70

Considerations for Critical Thinking and Writing

1. Write a summary of each of this ode's five sections.
2. What is the speaker's situation? What is his "sore need"? What does the speaker ask of the wind in lines 57–70?
3. What does the wind signify in this ode? How is it used symbolically?
4. Determine the meter and rhyme of the first five stanzas. How do these elements contribute to the ode's movement? Is this pattern continued in the other four sections?

Picture Poem

By arranging lines into particular shapes, poets can sometimes organize typography into *picture poems* of what they describe. Here is an example.

GEORGE HERBERT (1593–1633)
Easter Wings   1633

Lord, who createdst man in wealth and store,
Though foolishly he lost the same,
Decaying more and more,
Till he became
Most poor:
With thee
O let me rise
As larks, harmoniously,
And sing this day thy victories:
Then shall the fall further the flight in me.

My tender age in sorrow did begin:
And still with sicknesses and shame
Thou didst so punish sin,
That I became
Most thin.
With thee
Let me combine,
And feel this day thy victory;
For, if I imp my wing on thine,
Affliction shall advance the flight in me.

Considerations for Critical Thinking and Writing

1. How is the shape of the poem connected to its theme?
2. How is the content of each line related to its length?
3. Why is the speaker's situation compared to that of larks? How do the poem's images convey the idea of humanity's fall and resurrection?

Words have been arranged into all kinds of shapes, from apples to light bulbs. Notice how the shape of this next contemporary poem embodies its meaning.

MICHAEL McFEE (b. 1954)
In Medias Res°   1985

His waist
like the plot
thickens, wedding
pants now breathtaking,
belt no longer the cinch   5
it once was, belly's cambium
expanding to match each birthday,
his body a wad of anonymous tissue
swung in the same centrifuge of years
that separates a house from its foundation,   10
undermining sidewalks grim with joggers
and loose-filled graves and families
and stars collapsing on themselves,
no preservation society capable
of plugging entropy's dike,   15
under his zipper's sneer
a belly hibernation-
soft, ready for
the kill.

In Medias Res: A Latin term for a story that begins "in the middle of things."

Considerations for Critical Thinking and Writing

1. Explain how the title is related to this poem's shape.
2. Identify the puns. How do they work in the poem?
3. What is "cambium"? Why is the phrase "belly's cambium" especially appropriate?
4. What is the tone of this poem? Is it consistent throughout?

Parody

A *parody* is a humorous imitation of another, usually serious, work. It can take any fixed or open form because parodists imitate the tone, language, and shape of the original. While a parody may be teasingly close to a work's style, it typically deflates the subject matter to make the original seem absurd. Parody can be used as a kind of literary criticism to expose the defects in a work, but it is also very often an affectionate acknowledgment that a well-known work has become both institutionalized in our culture and fair game for some fun. Read Andrew Marvell's "To His Coy Mistress" (p. 55) and then study this parody.

PETER DE VRIES (b. 1910)
To His Importunate Mistress   1986

Andrew Marvell Updated

Had we but world enough, and time,
My coyness, lady, were a crime,
But at my back I always hear
Time's wingèd chariot, striking fear
The hour is nigh when creditors   5
Will prove to be my predators.
As wages of our picaresque,
Bag lunches bolted at my desk
Must stand as fealty to you
For each expensive rendezvous.   10
Obeisance at your marble feet
Deserves the best-appointed suite,
And would have, lacked I not the pelf
To pleasure also thus myself;
But aptly sumptuous amorous scenes   15
Rule out the rake of modest means.

Since mistress presupposes wife,
It means a doubly costly life;
For fools by second passion fired
A second income is required,   20
The earning which consumes the hours
They'd hoped to spend in rented bowers.
To hostelries the worst of fates
That weekly raise their daily rates!
I gather, lady, from your scoffing   25
A bloke more solvent in the offing.
So revels thus to rivals go
For want of monetary flow.

How vexing that inconstant cash
The constant suitor must abash,
Who with excuses vainly pled
Must rue the undisheveled bed,
And that for paltry reasons given
His conscience may remain unriven.

30

Considerations for Critical Thinking and Writing

1. How is De Vries's use of the term *mistress* different from Marvell's (p. 55)? How does the speaker's complaint in this poem differ from that in "To His Coy Mistress"?
2. Explain how "picaresque" is used in line 7.
3. To what extent does this poem duplicate Marvell's style?
4. Choose a poet whose work you know reasonably well or would like to know better and determine what is characteristic about his or her style. Then choose a poem to parody. It's probably best to attempt a short poem or a section of a long work. If you have difficulty selecting an author, you might consider Herrick, Blake, Keats, Dickinson, Whitman, or Frost, since a number of their works are included in this book.

Connection to Another Selection

1. Read Anthony Hecht's "Dover Bitch" (p. 384), a parody of Matthew Arnold's "Dover Beach" (p. 72). Write an essay comparing the effectiveness of Hecht's parody with that of De Vries's "To His Importunate Mistress." Which parody do you prefer? Explain why.

PERSPECTIVE

ROBERT MORGAN (b. 1944)
On the Shape of a Poem

1983

In the body of the poem, lineation is part flesh and part skeleton, as form is the towpath along which the burden of content, floating on the formless, is pulled. All language is both mental and sacramental, is not "real" but is the working of lip and tongue to subvert the "real." Poems empearl irritating facts until they become opalescent spheres of moment, not so much résumés of history as of human faculties working with pain. Every poem is necessarily a fragment empowered by its implicitness. We sing to charm the snake in our spines, to make it sway with the pulse of the world, balancing the weight of consciousness on the topmost vertebra.

From *Epoch,* Fall–Winter 1983

Considerations for Critical Thinking and Writing

1. Explain Morgan's metaphors for describing lineation and form in a poem. Why are these metaphors useful?
2. Choose one of the poems in this chapter that makes use of a particular form and explain how it is "a fragment empowered by its implicitness."

9. Open Form

Many poems, especially those written in the twentieth century, are composed of lines that cannot be scanned for a fixed or predominant meter. Moreover, very often these poems do not rhyme. Known as *free verse* (from the French, *vers libre*), such lines can derive their rhythmic qualities from the repetition of words, phrases, or grammatical structures; the arrangement of words on the printed page; or some other means. In recent years the term *open form* has been used in place of *free verse* to avoid the erroneous suggestion that this kind of poetry lacks all discipline and shape.

Although the following two poems do not use measurable meters, they do have rhythm.

e. e. cummings (1894–1962)
in Just-   1923

in Just-
spring   when the world is mud-
luscious the little
lame balloonman

whistles   far   and wee   5

and eddieandbill come
running from marbles and
piracies and it's
spring

when the world is puddle-wonderful   10

the queer
old balloonman whistles
far   and   wee
and bettyandisbel come dancing

from hop-scotch and jump-rope and 15

it's
spring
and
    the

       goat-footed 20

balloonMan   whistles
far
and
wee

Considerations for Critical Thinking and Writing

1. What is the effect of this poem's arrangement of words and the use of space on the page?
2. What is the effect of cummings combining the names "eddieandbill" and "bettyandisbel"?
3. The allusion in line 20 refers to Pan, a Greek god associated with nature. How does this allusion add to the meaning of the poem?

WALT WHITMAN (1819–1892)
From *I Sing the Body Electric* 1855

O my body! I dare not desert the likes of you in other men and women, nor
    the likes of the parts of you,
I believe the likes of you are to stand or fall with the likes of the soul, (and that
    they are the soul,)
I believe the likes of you shall stand or fall with my poems, and that they are
    my poems.
Man's, woman's, child's, youth's, wife's, husband's, mother's, father's, young
    man's, young woman's poems.
Head, neck, hair, ears, drop and tympan of the ears. 5
Eyes, eye-fringes, iris of the eye, eyebrows, and the waking or sleeping of the
    lids,
Mouth, tongue, lips, teeth, roof of the mouth, jaws, and the jaw-hinges,
Nose, nostrils of the nose, and the partition,
Cheeks, temples, forehead, chin, throat, back of the neck, neck-slue,
Strong shoulders, manly beard, scapula, hind-shoulders, and the ample side-
    round of the chest, 10
Upper-arm, armpit, elbow-socket, lower-arm, arm-sinews, arm-bones,
Wrist and wrist-joints, hand, palm, knuckles, thumb, forefinger, finger-joints, fin-
    ger-nails,
Broad breast-front, curling hair of the breast, breast-bone, breast-side,
Ribs, belly, backbone, joints of the backbone,
Hips, hip-sockets, hip-strength, inward and outward round, man-balls, man-
    root, 15

Strong set of thighs, well carrying the trunk above,
Leg-fibers, knee, knee-pan, upper-leg, under-leg,
Ankles, instep, foot-ball, toes, toe-joints, the heel;
All attitudes, all the shapeliness, all the belongings of my or your body or of any
    one's body, male or female,
The lung-sponges, the stomach-sac, the bowels sweet and clean,   20
The brain in its folds inside the skull-frame,
Sympathies, heart-valves, palate-valves, sexuality, maternity,
Womanhood, and all that is a woman, and the man that comes from woman,
The womb, the teats, nipples, breast-milk, tears, laughter, weeping, love-looks,
    love-perturbations and risings,
The voice, articulation, language, whispering, shouting aloud,   25
Food, drink, pulse, digestion, sweat, sleep, walking, swimming,
Poise on the hips, leaping, reclining, embracing, arm-curving and tightening,
The continual changes of the flex of the mouth, and around the eyes,
The skin, the sunburnt shade, freckles, hair,
The curious sympathy one feels when feeling with the hand the naked meat of
    the body,   30
The circling rivers the breath, and breathing it in and out,
The beauty of the waist, and thence of the hips, and thence downward toward
    the knees,
The thin red jellies within you or within me, the bones and the marrow in the
    bones,
The exquisite realization of health;
O I say these are not the parts and poems of the body only, but of the soul, 35
O I say now these are the soul!

Considerations for Critical Thinking and Writing

1. What informs the speaker's attitude toward the human body in this poem?
2. Read the poem aloud. Is it simply a tedious enumeration of body parts, or do the
   lines achieve some kind of rhythmic cadence?

PERSPECTIVE

WALT WHITMAN (1819–1892)
On Rhyme and Meter   1855

    The poetic quality is not marshaled in rhyme or uniformity or abstract
addresses to things nor in melancholy complaints or good precepts, but is the
life of these and much else and is in the soul. The profit of rhyme is that it drops
seeds of a sweeter and more luxuriant rhyme, and of uniformity that it conveys
itself into its own roots in the ground out of sight. The rhyme and uniformity of
perfect poems show the free growth of metrical laws and bud from them as
unnerringly and loosely as lilacs or roses on a bush, and take shapes as compact
as the shapes of chestnuts and oranges and melons and pears, and shed the

perfume impalpable to form. The fluency and ornaments of the finest poems or music or orations or recitations are not independent but dependent. All beauty comes from beautiful blood and a beautiful brain. If the greatnesses are in conjunction in a man or woman it is enough . . . the fact will prevail through the universe . . . but the gaggery and gilt of a million years will not prevail. Who troubles himself about his ornaments or fluency is lost.

From the preface to the 1855 edition of *Leaves of Grass*

Considerations for Critical Thinking and Writing

1. According to Whitman, what determines the shape of a poem?
2. Why does Whitman prefer open forms over fixed forms such as the sonnet?
3. Is Whitman's poetry devoid of any structure or shape? Choose one of his poems (listed in the index) to illustrate your answer.

Open form poetry is sometimes regarded as formless because it is unlike the strict fixed forms of a sonnet, villanelle, or sestina. But even though open form poems may not employ traditional meters and rhymes, they still rely on an intense use of language to establish rhythms and relations between meaning and form. Open form poems use the arrangement of words and phrases on the printed page, pauses, line lengths, and other means to create unique forms that express their particular meaning and tone.

Cummings's "in Just-" and the excerpt from Whitman's "I Sing the Body Electric" demonstrate how the white space on a page and rhythmic cadences can be aligned with meaning, but there is one kind of open form poetry that doesn't even look like poetry on a page. A *prose poem* is printed as prose and represents, perhaps, the most clear opposite of fixed forms. Here is a brief example.

GEORGE STARBUCK (b. 1931)
Japanese Fish   1985

Have you ever eaten a luchu? It's poisonous like fugu, but it's cheaper and you cook it yourself.

You cut it into little squares as fast as possible but without touching the poison-gland. But first, you get all the thrill you can out of the fact that you're going to do it. You sit around for hours with your closest friends, drinking and telling long nostalgicky stories. You make toasts. You pick up your knives and sing a little song entitled "We who are about to dice a luchu." And then you begin.

1. What is the effect of this prose poem? Does it have a theme?
2. What, if anything, is poetic in this work?
3. Arrange the lines so that they look like poetry on a page. What determines where you break the lines?

Much of the poetry published today is written in open form; however, many poets continue to take pleasure in the requirements imposed by fixed forms. Some write both fixed form and open form poetry. Each kind offers rewards to careful readers as well. Here are several more open form poems that establish their own unique patterns.

WILLIAM CARLOS WILLIAMS (1883–1963)
The Red Wheelbarrow   1923

so much depends
upon

a red wheel
barrow

glazed with rain
water

beside the white
chickens.

Considerations for Critical Thinking and Writing

1. What is the effect of these images? Do they have a particular meaning? What "depends upon" the things mentioned in the poem?
2. Do these lines have any kind of rhythm?
3. How does this poem resemble a haiku? How is it different?

ALLEN GINSBERG (b. 1926)
A Supermarket in California   1956

What thoughts I have of you tonight, Walt Whitman, for I walked down the sidestreets under the trees with a headache self-conscious looking at the full moon.

In my hungry fatigue, and shopping for images, I went into the neon fruit supermarket, dreaming of your enumerations!°

What peaches and what penumbras! Whole families shopping at night! Aisles full of husbands! Wives in the avocados, babies in the tomatoes — and you, Garcia Lorca,° what were you doing down by the watermelons?

I saw you, Walt Whitman, childless, lonely old grubber, poking among the meats in the refrigerator and eyeing the grocery boys.

I heard you asking questions of each: Who killed the pork chops? What price bananas? Are you my Angel?   5

I wandered in and out of the brilliant stacks of cans following you, and followed in my imagination by the store detective.

We strode down the open corridors together in our solitary fancy tasting artichokes, possessing every frozen delicacy, and never passing the cashier.

Where are we going, Walt Whitman? The doors close in an hour. Which way does your beard point tonight?

(I touch your book and dream of our odyssey in the supermarket and feel absurd.)

Will we walk all night through solitary streets? The trees add shade to shade, lights out in the houses, we'll both be lonely.   10

Will we stroll dreaming of the lost America of love past blue automobiles in driveways, home to our silent cottage?

Ah, dear father, graybeard, lonely old courage-teacher, what America did you have when Charon quit poling his ferry and you got out on a smoking bank and stood watching the boat disappear on the black waters of Lethe?°

Berkeley 1955

2 *enumerations:* See the "enumerations" (the catalog of details), a typical poetic device of Whitman's, in "I Sing the Body Electric" (p. 200).   3 *Garcia Lorca:* Federico García Lorca (1898–1936), a Spanish poet whose nonrealistic techniques Ginsberg admired.   12 *When Charon quit poling . . . Lethe:* In Greek mythology Charon ferries the dead into Hades. Lethe is one of the rivers in Hades and is associated with forgetfulness, because a drink from it causes the dead to forget those they have left behind.

Considerations for Critical Thinking and Writing

1. How is the setting used symbolically in this poem?
2. What kinds of thoughts does the speaker have about Whitman?
3. What does the speaker think about America? About himself?

Connections to Other Selections

1. How are Ginsberg's techniques similar to Whitman's in "I Sing the Body Electric" (p. 200)?
2. How is Ginsberg's America different from the description Whitman provides in "Song of the Open Road" (p. 159)? In what sense is Ginsberg "shopping for images"?
3. Write an essay contrasting the tone of this poem with that of "Song of the Open Road."

NAZIK AL-MALA'IKA (b. 1923)
I Am 1949

TRANSLATED BY KAMAL BOULLATA

The night asks me who I am
    Its impenetrable black, its unquiet secret
                    I am
    Its lull rebellious.
    I veil myself with silence 5
    Wrapping my heart with doubt
    Solemnly, I gaze
    While ages ask me
        who I am.

The wind asks me who I am 10
    Its bedevilled spirit I am
    Denied by Time, going nowhere
    I journey on and on
    Passing without a pause
    And when reaching an edge 15
    I think it may be the end
    Of suffering, but then:
        the void.

Time asks me who I am
    A giant enfolding centuries I am 20
    Later to give new births
    I have created the dim past
    From the bliss of unbound hope
    I push it back into its grave
    To make a new yesterday, its tomorrow 25
    is ice.

The self asks me who I am
    Baffled, I stare into the dark
    Nothing brings me peace
    I ask, but the answer 30
    Remains hooded in mirage
    I keep thinking it is near
    Upon reaching it, it dissolves.

Considerations for Critical Thinking and Writing

1. How does the manner in which the lines are spaced on the page structure this poem?
2. What kind of self-identity does the speaker describe? Is this person hopeful or pessimistic about finding a true self?
3. Why do you suppose the poem is titled "I Am" rather than "Who Am I"?

1. Write an essay on conceptions of the self in "I Am" and Emily Dickinson's "I'm Nobody! Who are you?" (p. 264).

DENISE LEVERTOV (b. 1923)
O Taste and See   1962

The world is
not with us enough.
O taste and see

the subway Bible poster said,
meaning The Lord, meaning   5
if anything all that lives
to the imagination's tongue,

grief, mercy, language,
tangerine, weather, to
breathe them, bite,   10
savor, chew, swallow, transform

into our flesh our
deaths, crossing the street, plum, quince,
living in the orchard and being

hungry, and plucking   15
the fruit.

Considerations for Critical Thinking and Writing

1. How does the speaker in this poem want people to respond to the world?
2. Are lines 8–11 simply a list of random words? How do they relate to one another and to the poem's theme?
3. Why are the lines arranged in stanzas? Would the experience of reading the poem be any different if it were all one stanza?

Connection to Another Selection

1. Write a short essay comparing and contrasting this poem in form and content with William Wordsworth's "The World Is Too Much with Us" (p. 180).

CAROLYN FORCHÉ (b. 1950)
The Colonel

May 1978

What you have heard is true. I was in his house. His wife carried
a tray of coffee and sugar. His daughter filed her nails, his son went
out for the night. There were daily papers, pet dogs, a pistol on the
cushion beside him. The moon swung bare on its black cord over
the house. On the television was a cop show. It was in English.　　　5
Broken bottles were embedded in the walls around the house to
scoop the kneecaps from a man's legs or cut his hands to lace. On
the windows there were gratings like those in liquor stores. We had
dinner, rack of lamb, good wine, a gold bell was on the table for
calling the maid. The maid brought green mangoes, salt, a type of　　10
bread. I was asked how I enjoyed the country. There was a brief
commercial in Spanish. His wife took everything away. There was
some talk then of how difficult it had become to govern. The parrot
said hello on the terrace. The colonel told it to shut up, and pushed
himself from the table. My friend said to me with his eyes: say　　　15
nothing. The colonel returned with a sack used to bring groceries
home. He spilled many human ears on the table. They were like
dried peach halves. There is no other way to say this. He took one
of them in his hands, shook it in our faces, dropped it into a water
glass. It came alive there. I am tired of fooling around he said. As　　20
for the rights of anyone, tell your people they can go fuck themselves. He swept the ears to the floor with his arm and held the last
of his wine in the air. Something for your poetry, no? he said. Some
of the ears on the floor caught this scrap of his voice. Some of the
ears on the floor were pressed to the ground.　　　　　　　　　　25

Considerations for Critical Thinking and Writing

1. What kind of horror is described in this prose poem? Characterize the colonel.
2. What makes this prose poem not a typical prose passage? How is it organized
   differently?
3. What poetic elements can you find in it?
4. What is the tone of the final two sentences?

SHARON OLDS (b. 1942)
Rite of Passage

1983

As the guests arrive at my son's party
they gather in the living room —
short men, men in first grade
with smooth jaws and chins.
Hands in pockets, they stand around　　　　　　　5
jostling, jockeying for place, small fights

breaking out and calming. One says to another
How old are you? Six. I'm seven. So?
They eye each other, seeing themselves
tiny in the other's pupils. They clear their   10
throats a lot, a room of small bankers,
they fold their arms and frown. *I could beat you
up,* a seven says to a six,
the dark cake, round and heavy as a
turret, behind them on the table. My son,   15
freckles like specks of nutmeg on his cheeks,
chest narrow as the balsa keel of a
model boat, long hands
cool and thin as the day they guided him
out of me, speaks up as a host   20
for the sake of the group.
We could easily kill a two-year-old,
he says in his clear voice. The other
men agree, they clear their throats
like Generals, they relax and get down to   25
playing war, celebrating my son's life.

Considerations for Critical Thinking and Writing

1. In what sense is this birthday party a "Rite of Passage"?
2. How does the speaker transform these six- and seven-year-old boys into men? What is the point of doing so?
3. Comment on the appropriateness of the image of the cake in lines 14–15.
4. Why does the son's claim that "We could easily kill a two-year-old" come as such a shock at that point in the poem?

Connections to Other Selections

1. In an essay discuss the treatment of violence in "Rite of Passage" and Carolyn Forché's "The Colonel" (p. 207). To what extent might the colonel be regarded as an adult version of the generals in Olds's' poem?
2. Discuss the use of irony in "Rite of Passage" and Wilfred Owen's "Dulce et Decorum Est" (p. 76). Which do you think is a more effective antiwar poem? Explain why.

ANONYMOUS
The Frog   date unknown

What a wonderful bird the frog are!
When he stand he sit almost;
When he hop he fly almost.
He ain't got no sense hardly;
He ain't got no tail hardly either.
When he sit, he sit on what he ain't got almost.

Considerations for Critical Thinking and Writing

1. Though this poem is ungrammatical, it does have a patterned structure. How does the pattern of sentences create a formal structure?
2. How is the poem a description of the speaker as well as of a frog?

TATO LAVIERA (b. 1951)
AmeRícan   1985

we gave birth to a new generation,
AmeRícan, broader than lost gold
never touched, hidden inside the
puerto rican mountains.

we gave birth to a new generation,   5
AmeRícan, it includes everything
imaginable you-name-it-we-got-it
society.

we gave birth to a new generation,
AmeRícan salutes all folklores,   10
european, indian, black, spanish,
and anything else compatible:

AmeRícan,   singing to composer pedro flores'° palm
             trees high up in the universal sky!

AmeRícan,   sweet soft spanish danzas gypsies   15
             moving lyrics la *española*° cascabelling   *Spanish*
             presence always singing at our side!

AmeRícan,   beating jíbaro° modern troubadours
             crying guitars romantic continental
             bolero love songs!   20

AmeRícan,   across forth and across back
             back across and forth back
             forth across and back and forth
             our trips are walking bridges!

             it all dissolved into itself, the attempt   25
             was truly made, the attempt was truly
             absorbed, digested, we spit out
             the poison, we spit out the malice,
             we stand, affirmative in action,
             to reproduce a broader answer to the   30
             marginality that gobbled us up abruptly!

---

13 *Pedro Flores:* Puerto Rican composer of popular romantic songs.   18 *jíbaro:* A particular style of music played by Puerto Rican mountain farmers.

AmeRícan,	walking plena- rhythms° in new york,	
	strutting beautifully alert, alive,	
	many turning eyes wondering,	
	admiring!	35

AmeRícan,	defining myself my own way any way many
	ways Am e Rícan, with the big R and the
	accent on the í!

AmeRícan,   like the soul gliding talk of gospel
boogie music!   40

AmeRícan,   speaking new words in spanglish tenements,
fast tongue moving street corner *"que
corta"*° talk being invented at the insistence   *that cuts*
of a smile!

AmeRícan,   abounding inside so many ethnic english   45
people, and out of humanity, we blend
and mix all that is good!

AmeRícan,   integrating in new york and defining our
own *destino,*° our own way of life,   *destiny*

AmeRícan,   defining the new america, humane america,   50
admired america, loved america, harmonious
america, the world in peace, our energies
collectively invested to find other civili-
zations, to touch God, further and further,
to dwell in the spirit of divinity!   55

AmeRícan,   yes, for now, for i love this, my second
land, and i dream to take the accent from
the altercation, and be proud to call
myself american, in the u.s. sense of the
word, AmeRícan, America!   60

32 *plena- rhythms:* African–Puerto Rican folklore, music, and dance.

Considerations for Critical Thinking and Writing

1. How does the arrangement of lines communicate a sense of energy and vitality?
2. How does the speaker portray Puerto Ricans living in the United States?
3. How does the poet describe the United States?

Connection to Another Selection

1. In an essay consider the themes, styles, and tones of "AmeRícan" and Allen Ginsberg's "America" (p. 376).

Found Poem

The next poem is a *found poem,* an unintentional poem discovered in a nonpoetic context, such as a conversation, news story, or advertisement. Found poems are playful reminders that the words in poems are very often the language we use every day. Whether such found language should be regarded as a poem is an issue left for you to consider.

DONALD JUSTICE (b. 1925)
Order in the Streets 1969

(From instructions printed on a child's toy, Christmas 1968, as reported in the New York Times*)*

1. 2. 3.
Switch on.

Jeep rushes
to the scene
of riot   5

Jeep goes
in all directions
by mystery action.

Jeep stops periodically
to turn hood over   10

machine gun appears
with realistic
shooting noise.

After putting down riot,
jeep goes   15
back to the headquarters.

Considerations for Critical Thinking and Writing

1. What is the effect of arranging these instructions in lines? How are the language and meaning enhanced by this arrangement?
2. Look for phrases or sentences in ads, textbooks, labels, or directions — in anything that might inadvertently contain provocative material that would be revealed by arranging the words in lines. You may even discover some patterns of rhyme and rhythm. After arranging the lines, explain why you organized them as you did.

10. A Study of Three Poets: John Keats, Emily Dickinson, and Robert Frost

This chapter includes a number of poems by John Keats, Emily Dickinson, and Robert Frost in order to provide an opportunity to study three major poets in some depth. None of the collections is wholly representative of the poet's work, but each offers enough poems to suggest some of the techniques and concerns that characterize the poet's writings. The poems within each group speak not only to readers but to one another. That's natural enough: the more familiar you are with a writer's work, the easier it is to perceive and enjoy the strategies and themes he or she employs.

JOHN KEATS (1795–1821)

The stone marking the grave of John Keats bears an epitaph composed by him shortly before his death: "Here lies one whose name was writ in water." This assessment of his own achievement and fame is informed by the disappointment and anguish that characterized much of his life, but the inscription does not — because it could not — take into account the remarkable reputation that posterity has bestowed on Keats's poetry. His name, as it turns out, is written not only in stone rather than water but also in the minds of readers who have come to appreciate his literary art.

Keats's literary career had barely started when he died at the age of twenty-five. He did not begin writing poetry until he was eighteen, and critics generally agree that this early verse was not very promising. In 1816, however, he wrote the first of his greatest poems, a sonnet entitled "On First Looking into Chapman's Homer"; as he turned twenty-one he was also turning into a genuine poet.

His first volume, *Poems,* appeared in 1817 and was largely ignored; it was followed the next year by *Endymion,* a single poem of more than 4,000 lines about a quest for ideal beauty and happiness. Keats's most productive year was 1819, when he wrote nearly all the poems that have earned him a reputation as a major poet. His third and final volume of poetry, *Lamia, Isabella, The Eve of St. Agnes, and Other Poems,* was published in 1820.

During the final year of his life Keats could not write poetry because of the tuberculosis that was overtaking him. He traveled to Rome with the hope of regaining his health but wrote to a friend that he had "an habitual feeling of my life having past, and that I am leading a posthumous existence." He knew his illness was fatal and died three months later, in February of 1821. Almost incredibly, Keats's life as a writer spanned little more than the time required by most undergraduates to earn a bachelor's degree; and, more important, within those few years he outgrew his early sentimental and derivative verse to emerge as a powerful poet.

Keats's literary life moved toward greatness as he matured, but his personal life presented a series of abrupt dislocations and unfulfilled expectations. As a young boy he was exposed to the frailty and unpredictability of life. His father, manager of a livery stable in London, was killed by falling off a horse when Keats was only eight years old, and when the poet was fourteen his mother died of tuberculosis. The next year Keats's guardian withdrew him from school and apprenticed him to a five-year course in medicine at a London hospital.

While he studied medicine, Keats pursued his interest in literary studies, and upon completion of his surgical training he gave up medicine for poetry, a decision influenced by several literary friends who encouraged his efforts to become a writer. In 1818, however, this decision was severely tested by two reviews of *Endymion* that were so brutal as to foster the legend that they were the cause of Keats's early death.

But it was tuberculosis that killed Keats and that had caused his brother's death in 1818. Keats faithfully nursed his brother and therefore had a long hard look at the disease of which he was beginning to show symptoms. During this year Keats also lost another brother, who emigrated to America. But despite all these blows, Keats's spirits were high when he fell in love with Fanny Brawne. Unfortunately, his commitment to poetry as well as his financial situation and health prohibited their marriage and made his passionate love agonizing until his death. Keats's brief life seems hopelessly sad — his letters especially convey the sense of a remarkable sensibility overcome by a "world of circumstances."

Keats took a great risk by rejecting a medical career, but his interests were elsewhere. Perhaps his choice of profession was foreshadowed by the flowers that he sketched in the margins of his anatomy notes. Keats seems always to have been more concerned with beauty in life. In a sense, beauty was life to him. In life's transient materiality he found a constant that transcends space, time, and matter. He described this perception in these famous euphonic lines from *Endymion.*

A thing of beauty is a joy for ever:
Its loveliness increases; it will never
Pass into nothingness; but still will keep
A bower quiet for us, and a sleep
Full of sweet dreams, and health, and quiet breathing.
Therefore, on every morrow, are we wreathing
A flowery band to bind us to the earth,
Spite of despondence, of the inhuman dearth
Of noble natures, of the gloomy days,
Of all the unhealthy and o'er-darkened ways
Made for our searching: yes, in spite of all,
Some shape of beauty moves away the pall
From our dark spirits.

Keats preferred a direct, spontaneous response to life over the logical, rational abstractions that informed the intellectual tenor of his times. Putting his faith in an imaginative rather than a scientific approach to existence, he believed that literary imagination requires what he called a "Negative Capability," the ability to be "in uncertainties, mysteries, doubts, without any irritable reaching after fact and reason." Keats believed that the poetic imagination can tolerate ambiguities, and though it might not have all the answers, it has a greater capacity for asking questions than the sort of mind that demands "fact and reason." Truth was infinitely complex and problematic for Keats, and he found that he could not create beauty without being alert to the ugliness of evil. His ideal of "Negative Capability" represented, however, a positive creative power for the poet, because it demanded an openness to and sympathy with the possibilities of life and thought.

Although Keats created an imaginative world in his poems, he did not abandon "fact." Indeed, one of the major characteristics of his poetry is his use of detailed sensuous description. He builds a world by invoking the reader's senses of touch, smell, taste, hearing, and seeing so that experience is richly savored. His imagery is detailed and strong. Using diction that is both precise and opulent, Keats creates images that are not unlike a holograph. His melodic lines give us more of experience than a flat objective description could possibly offer.

Sonnets, odes, and narrative poems are the three poetic forms on which Keats's reputation rests. The typical subjects of his poems are familiar ones; he writes about love, death, fame, failure, poetry, art, and nature. The common thread running through these subjects is his keen awareness that everything is subject to change. Sometimes Keats attempts to transcend this changing world by pursuing a visionary imagination, but at other points he comes to understand that an acceptance of the transient nature of existence can be a way to appreciate its beauty. This conflict leads him into a series of tensions in which he celebrates sensations but simultaneously expresses a sadness that they cannot last. For Keats, pleasure and pain, love and death, dream and reality are the breathing out and breathing in of poetic imagination. He does not resolve these conflicts so much as articulate them.

"On First Looking into Chapman's Homer" is a fitting introduction to Keats's poetry, because it is about his own sense of discovery. At the age of twenty-one, Keats was introduced by a friend to George Chapman's poetic Elizabethan translation of Homer's *Iliad* and *Odyssey*. Before his reading in Chapman, Keats had known only eighteenth-century translations, which were stilted and pedestrian, but with Chapman's version he suddenly realized the power and energy of Homer's poetry. Immediately after reading Chapman, Keats spent the night writing the following sonnet.

On First Looking into Chapman's Homer   1816

Much have I traveled in the realms of gold,
    And many goodly states and kingdoms seen;
    Round many western islands have I been
Which bards in fealty to Apollo° hold.
Oft of one wide expanse had I been told   5
    That deep-browed Homer ruled as his demesne;
    Yet did I never breathe its pure serene°   *atmosphere*
Till I heard Chapman speak out loud and bold:
Then felt I like some watcher of the skies
    When a new planet swims into his ken;   10
Or like stout Cortez° when with eagle eyes
    He stared at the Pacific — and all his men
Looked at each other with a wild surmise —
    Silent, upon a peak in Darien.

4 *Apollo:* Greek god of poetry.   11 *Cortez:* Vasco Núñez de Balboa, not Hernando Cortés, was the first European to sight the Pacific from Darien, a peak in Panama.

This is one of those rare poems in which we can accurately identify the speaker with the poet. Even so, it is less a fragment of autobiography than an evocation of excitement and wonder. This sonnet is not only about Keats's discovery of Chapman's Homer, because that personal experience serves as a symbol for any discovery. One way to state the theme is to say that reading can be a source of imaginative discovery as significant as the discovery of a planet or ocean. To express this theme, Keats uses a controlling metaphor built around a comparison of reading with traveling and exploration, an especially apt metaphor given the many journeys that appear in Homer. Keats shapes this metaphor into an Italian sonnet, which is often enough a traditional form for love poetry to suggest Keats's own passion for poetry.

In the octave, the speaker tells us that he has "traveled in the realms of gold" and seen many "goodly states and kingdoms." Given the context of the rest of the poem, we know that the speaker is referring to his wide reading in the literature of Western civilization ("western islands"). The diction of the octave is formal and dignified ("goodly states," "bards in fealty," "demesne," "serene"), fitting the respectful, if dispassionate, assessment of what the speaker has experienced in his reading. A shift occurs, however, between the octave and sestet, when the speaker moves to the impact that reading Chapman's Homer has had on him. Images of exploration give way to images of discovery, and the tone changes from elevated description to intense feelings of wonder.

Two similes in the sestet convey the speaker's wonder. First, he compares his excitement to that of an astronomer, a purposeful "watcher of the skies" who suddenly sees a new planet through a telescope. That discovery of a new world is brought down to earth in the second simile, when the speaker likens himself to Cortés, who (Keats mistakenly believed) inadvertently discovered the Pacific Ocean. Although the second simile brings us down to earth, it soars even higher than the first in its effect. The discovery of the ocean is more startling because it comes as a complete surprise. Cortés had no idea that the Pacific Ocean would be on the other side of the mountains.

The speaker's excitement is also evident in the change of rhythm in the sestet. A calm and measured movement can be heard in the octave, but the sestet's lines are less regular. This deviation from the predominant iambic pentameter is accompanied by run-on lines and dashes that convey the speaker's heightened emotions, which reach a climax in the final line. Here the trochaic "Silent," along with the comma that follows it, slows down the line, preparing us for the concluding image of awe.

The final allusive image of "stout Cortez" (notice how the heavy accents on these syllables emphasize the explorer's power) is a visual representation of the emotional intensity experienced by the speaker. This also completes the speaker's imagining himself as an explorer. We leave both the speaker and the explorer contemplating the beginning of further explorations and discoveries in worlds previously not even imagined. The sense of awe and expectation created in this poem serves as an appropriate first encounter with Keats's poetry, because it evokes some of the remarkable discoveries that readers have made in these poems.

Chronology

1795   Born on October 31 in London.

1803   Enters Clarke School.

1804   Father dies unexpectedly.

1810   Mother dies from tuberculosis.

1811	Leaves school to be apprenticed to an apothecary-surgeon; completes a prose translation of the *Aeneid*.
1814	Actively writing poetry.
1815	Continues medical education at Guy's Hospital, London.
1816	"To Solitude," a sonnet, becomes his first publication; earns his Apothecaries' Certificate but abandons further interest in medicine.
1817	*Poems,* his first book, is published.
1818	*Endymion* is published; takes a walking tour of northern England, Scotland, and Ireland; declares his love for Fanny Brawne.
1819	Writes many of his major odes as well as *Lamia* and *The Fall of Hyperion*; dogged by ill health, poverty, and frustration over not being able to marry Fanny Brawne.
1820	*Lamia; Isabella; The Eve of St. Agnes, and Other Poems* is published. Travels to Naples, Italy, in an attempt to restore his declining health.
1821	Dies on February 23 in Rome.

On the Grasshopper and the Cricket   1816

The poetry of earth is never dead:
When all the birds are faint with the hot sun,
And hide in cooling trees, a voice will run
From hedge to hedge about the new-mown mead;°   *meadow*
That is the grasshopper's — he takes the lead   5
In summer luxury — he has never done
With his delights; for when tired out with fun
He rests at ease beneath some pleasant weed.
The poetry of earth is ceasing never:
On a lone winter evening, when the frost   10
Has wrought a silence, from the stove there shrills
The cricket's song, in warmth increasing ever,
And seems to one in drowsiness half lost,
The grasshopper's among some grassy hills.

Considerations for Critical Thinking and Writing

1. How are two seasons contrasted in the octave and sestet of this sonnet?
2. What does the speaker mean by "The poetry of earth"? What is the view of nature in the sonnet?
3. How does the imagery contribute to the sonnet's effect?

To One Who Has Been Long in City Pent   1816

To one who has been long in city pent,
    'Tis very sweet to look into the fair
    And open face of heaven, — to breathe a prayer
Full in the smile of the blue firmament.
Who is more happy, when, with heart's content,   5
    Fatigued he sinks into some pleasant lair
    Of wavy grass, and reads a debonair
And gentle tale of love and languishment?

Returning home at evening, with an ear
    Catching the notes of Philomel,° — an eye   10
Watching the sailing cloudlet's bright career,
    He mourns that day so soon has glided by:
E'en like the passage of an angel's tear
    That falls through the clear ether silently.

10 *Philomel:* A nightingale.

Considerations for Critical Thinking and Writing

1. Although the city is not described in the sonnet, how does Keats make you feel about it?
2. What values is the countryside associated with here? How does this sonnet's evocation of nature compare with that of "On the Grasshopper and the Cricket"?
3. Do you think this sonnet is more about a sense of loss or a celebration of nature?

Written in Disgust of Vulgar Superstition   1816

The church bells toll a melancholy round,
    Calling the people to some other prayers,
    Some other gloominess, more dreadful cares,
More hearkening to the sermon's horrid sound.
Surely the mind of man is closely bound   5
    In some black spell; seeing that each one tears
    Himself from fireside joys, and Lydian airs,
And converse high of those with glory crown'd.
Still, still they toll, and I should feel a damp —
    A chill as from a tomb, did I not know   10
That they are going like an outburnt lamp;
    That 'tis their sighing, wailing ere they go
    Into oblivion; — that fresh flowers will grow,
And many glories of immortal stamp.

Considerations for Critical Thinking and Writing

1. What is Keats's view of religion in this poem?
2. Use the library to explain the allusion to "Lydian airs." What does it add to the poem?
3. Discuss the bells and flowers as opposing symbols.

Connection to Another Selection

1. In an essay compare attitudes toward religion in this poem and in Emily Dickinson's "Some keep the Sabbath going to Church — " (p. 261).

On Seeing the Elgin Marbles°   1817

My spirit is too weak; mortality
　　Weighs heavily on me like unwilling sleep,
　　And each imagined pinnacle and steep
Of godlike hardship tells me I must die
Like a sick eagle looking at the sky.   5
　　Yet 'tis a gentle luxury to weep,
　　That I have not the cloudy winds to keep
Fresh for the opening of the morning's eye.
Such dim-conceived glories of the brain
　　Bring round the heart an indescribable feud;   10
So do these wonders a most dizzy pain,
　　That mingles Grecian grandeur with the rude
Wasting of old Time — with a billowy main,
　　A sun, a shadow of a magnitude.

Elgin Marbles: The remains of ancient figures and friezes from the Athenian Parthenon, acquired by Lord Elgin for the British Museum.

Considerations for Critical Thinking and Writing

1. Why is the speaker in this sonnet "weak"? What causes the "dizzy pain" he feels in line 11?
2. What is the relationship between time and art in this sonnet?

When I have fears that I may cease to be   1818

When I have fears that I may cease to be
　　Before my pen has gleaned my teeming brain,
Before high-piled books, in charactery,°   *print*
　　Hold like rich garners the full ripened grain;

When I behold, upon the night's starred face,   5
    Huge cloudy symbols of a high romance,
And think that I may never live to trace
    Their shadows, with the magic hand of chance;
And when I feel, fair creature of an hour,
    That I shall never look upon thee more,   10
Never have relish in the faery° power   *magic*
    Of unreflecting love; — then on the shore
Of the wide world I stand alone, and think
Till love and fame to nothingness do sink.

Considerations for Critical Thinking and Writing

1. Describe the speaker's fear in each of the three quatrains of this sonnet. Is there any kind of progression?
2. What impact does the fear of death have on "love and fame" in the concluding couplet?

Connection to Another Selection

1. Compare the view of death in this poem with the attitude expressed in Robert Frost's "Provide, Provide" (p. 312).

The Eve of St. Agnes°   1819

I

St. Agnes' Eve — Ah, bitter chill it was!
The owl, for all his feathers, was a-cold;
The hare limped trembling through the frozen grass,
And silent was the flock in woolly fold:
Numb were the Beadsman's° fingers, while he told   5
His rosary, and while his frosted breath,
Like pious incense from a censer old,
Seemed taking flight for heaven, without a death,
Past the sweet Virgin's picture, while his prayer he saith.

II

His prayer he saith, this patient, holy man;   10
Then takes his lamp, and riseth from his knees,
And back returneth, meager, barefoot, wan,
Along the chapel aisle by slow degrees:
The sculptured dead, on each side, seem to freeze,

Eve of St. Agnes: January 20, supposed to be the coldest night of the year. St. Agnes, martyred in the fourth century, is the patroness of virgins. According to folk legend, a girl who performed certain rituals on St. Agnes's Eve would have a vision of her future husband.   5 *Beadsman:* A person hired to pray for someone.

Imprisoned in black, purgatorial rails: 15
Knights, ladies, praying in dumb orat'ries,°   *chapels*
He passeth by; and his weak spirit fails
To think how they may ache in icy hoods and mails.

III

Northward he turneth through a little door,
And scarce three steps, ere Music's golden tongue   20
Flattered to tears this aged man and poor;
But no — already had his deathbell rung:
The joys of all his life were said and sung:
His was harsh penance on St. Agnes' eve:
Another way he went, and soon among   25
Rough ashes sat he for his soul's reprieve,
And all night kept awake, for sinner's sake to grieve.

IV

That ancient Beadsman heard the prelude soft;
And so it chanced, for many a door was wide,
From hurry to and fro. Soon, up aloft,   30
The silver, snarling trumpets 'gan to chide:
The level chambers, ready with their pride,
Were glowing to receive a thousand guests:
The carvèd angels, ever eager-eyed,
Stared, where upon their heads the cornice rests,   35
With hair blown back, and wings put crosswise on their breasts.

V

At length burst in the argent revelry,
With plume, tiara, and all rich array,
Numerous as shadows haunting faerily°   *magically*
The brain, new stuffed, in youth, with triumphs gay   40
Of old romance. These let us wish away,
And turn, sole-thoughted, to one Lady there,
Whose heart had brooded, all that wintry day,
On love, and winged St. Agnes' saintly care,
As she had heard old dames full many times declare.   45

VI

They told her how, upon St. Agnes' Eve,
Young virgins might have visions of delight,
And soft adorings from their loves receive
Upon the honeyed middle of the night,
If ceremonies due they did aright;   50
As, supperless to bed they must retire,
And couch supine their beauties, lily white;
Nor look behind, nor sideways, but require
Of heaven with upward eyes for all that they desire.

VII

Full of this whim was thoughtful Madeline: 55
The music, yearning like a God in pain,

She scarcely heard: her maiden eyes divine,
Fixed on the floor, saw many a sweeping train
Pass by — she heeded not at all: in vain
Came many a tiptoe, amorous cavalier,   60
And back retired; not cooled by high disdain;
But she saw not: her heart was otherwhere:
She sighed for Agnes' dreams, the sweetest of the year.

VIII

She danced along with vague, regardless eyes,
Anxious her lips, her breathing quick and short: 65
The hallowed hour was near at hand: she sighs
Amid the timbrels, and the thronged resort
Of whisperers in anger, or in sport;
'Mid looks of love, defiance, hate, and scorn,
Hoodwinked with faery fancy: all amort,°   *as if dead*   70
Save to St. Agnes and her lambs unshorn,
And all the bliss to be before tomorrow morn.

IX

So, purposing each moment to retire,
She lingered still. Meantime, across the moors,
Had come young Porphyro, with heart on fire   75
For Madeline. Beside the portal doors,
Buttressed from moonlight,° stands he, and implores   *in shadows*
All saints to give him sight of Madeline,
But for one moment in the tedious hours,
That he might gaze and worship all unseen;   80
Perchance speak, kneel, touch, kiss — in sooth such things have been.

X

He ventures in: let no buzzed whisper tell:
All eyes be muffled, or a hundred swords
Will storm his heart, Love's fev'rous citadel:
For him, those chambers held barbarian hordes,   85
Hyena foeman, and hot-blooded lords,
Whose very dogs would execrations howl
Against his lineage: not one breast affords
Him any mercy, in that mansion foul,
Save one old beldame, weak in body and in soul.   90

XI

Ah, happy chance! the aged creature came,
Shuffling along with ivory-headed wand,
To where he stood, hid from the torch's flame,
Behind a broad hall-pillar, far beyond
The sound of merriment and chorus bland:°   *soft*   95
He startled her; but soon she knew his face,
And grasped his fingers in her palsied hand,
Saying, "Mercy, Porphyro! hie thee from this place;
They are all here tonight, the whole bloodthirsty race!

XII

"Get hence! get hence! there's dwarfish Hildebrand;   100
He had a fever late, and in the fit
He cursed thee and thine, both house and land:
Then there's that old Lord Maurice, not a whit
More tame for his gray hairs — Alas me! flit!
Flit like a ghost away." — "Ah, Gossip° dear,   *friend*   105
We're safe enough; here in this armchair sit,
And tell me how" — "Good Saints! not here, not here;
Follow me, child, or else these stones will be thy bier."

XIII

He followed through a lowly archèd way,
Brushing the cobwebs with his lofty plume,   110
And as she muttered "Well-a — well-a-day!"
He found him in a little moonlight room,
Pale, latticed, chill, and silent as a tomb.
"Now tell me where is Madeline," said he,
"O tell me, Angela, by the holy loom   115
Which none but secret sisterhood may see,
When they St. Agnes' wool are weaving piously."

XIV

"St. Agnes! Ah! it is St. Agnes' Eve —
Yet men will murder upon holy days:
Thou must hold water in a witch's sieve,   120
And be liege-lord of all the Elves and Fays,
To venture so: it fills me with amaze
To see thee, Porphyro! — St. Agnes' Eve!
God's help! my lady fair the conjuror plays
This very night: good angels her deceive!   125
But let me laugh awhile, I've mickle° time to grieve."   *much*

XV

Feebly she laugheth in the languid moon,
While Porphyro upon her face doth look,
Like puzzled urchin on an aged crone
Who keepeth closed a wondrous riddle-book,   130
As spectacled she sits in chimney nook.
But soon his eyes grew brilliant, when she told
His lady's purpose; and he scarce could brook°   *hold back*
Tears, at the thought of those enchantments cold,
And Madeline asleep in lap of legends old.   135

XVI

Sudden a thought came like a full-blown rose,
Flushing his brow, and in his pained heart
Made purple riot: then doth he propose
A stratagem, that makes the beldame start:
"A cruel man and impious thou art: 140
Sweet lady, let her pray, and sleep, and dream

Alone with her good angels, far apart
From wicked men like thee. Go, go! — I deem
Thou canst not surely be the same that thou didst seem."

XVII

"I will not harm her, by all saints I swear,"   145
Quoth Porphyro: "O may I ne'er find grace
When my weak voice shall whisper its last prayer,
If one of her soft ringlets I displace,
Or look with ruffian passion in her face:
Good Angela, believe me by these tears;   150
Or I will, even in a moment's space,
Awake, with horrid shout, my foemen's ears,
And beard them, though they be more fanged than wolves and bears."

XVIII

"Ah! why wilt thou affright a feeble soul?
A poor, weak, palsy-stricken, churchyard thing,   155
Whose passing bell° may ere the midnight toll;   *death knell*
Whose prayers for thee, each morn and evening,
Were never missed" — Thus plaining,° doth she bring   *complaining*
A gentler speech from burning Porphyro;
So woeful, and of such deep sorrowing,   160
That Angela gives promise she will do
Whatever he shall wish, betide her weal or woe.

XIX

Which was, to lead him, in close secrecy,
Even to Madeline's chamber, and there hide
Him in a closet, of such privacy   165
That he might see her beauty unespied,
And win perhaps that night a peerless bride,
While legioned faeries paced the coverlet,
And pale enchantment held her sleepy-eyed.
Never on such a night have lovers met,   170
Since Merlin paid his Demon all the monstrous debt.°

XX

"It shall be as thou wishest," said the Dame:
"All cates° and dainties shall be stored there   *delicacies*
Quickly on this feast night: by the tambour frame
Her own lute thou wilt see: no time to spare,   175
For I am slow and feeble, and scarce dare
On such a catering trust my dizzy head.
Wait here, my child, with patience; kneel in prayer
The while: Ah! thou must needs the lady wed,
Or may I never leave my grave among the dead."   180

---

171 *Since Merlin paid . . . debt:* Merlin, the great magician of Arthurian legend, was duped by a crafty
woman who turned one of his spells against him, causing his death.

XXI

So saying, she hobbled off with busy fear.
The lover's endless minutes slowly passed;
The dame returned, and whispered in his ear
To follow her; with aged eyes aghast
From fright of dim espial. Safe at last,   185
Through many a dusky gallery, they gain
The maiden's chamber, silken, hushed, and chaste;
Where Porphyro took covert, pleased amain.°   *greatly*
His poor guide hurried back with agues in her brain.

XXII

Her falt'ring hand upon the balustrade,   190
Old Angela was feeling for the stair,
When Madeline, St. Agnes' charmed maid,
Rose, like a missioned spirit, unaware:
With silver taper's light, and pious care,
She turned, and down the aged gossip led   195
To a safe level matting. Now prepare,
Young Porphyro, for gazing on that bed;
She comes, she comes again, like ring-dove frayed° and fled.   *frightened*

XXIII

Out went the taper as she hurried in;
Its little smoke, in pallid moonshine, died: 200
She closed the door, she panted, all akin
To spirits of the air, and visions wide:
No uttered syllable, or, woe betide!
But to her heart, her heart was voluble,
Paining with eloquence her balmy side;   205
As though a tongueless nightingale should swell
Her throat in vain, and die, heart-stifled, in her dell.

XXIV

A casement high and triple-arched there was,
All garlanded with carven imag'ries
Of fruits, and flowers and bunches of knotgrass,   210
And diamonded with panes of quaint device,
Innumerable of stains and splendid dyes,
As are the tiger-moth's deep-damasked wings;
And in the midst, 'mong thousand heraldries,
And twilight saints, and dim emblazonings,   215
A shielded scutcheon° blushed with blood of queens and kings.   *coat of arms*

XXV

Full on this casement shone the wintry moon,
And threw warm gules on Madeline's fair breast,
As down she knelt for heaven's grace and boon;
Rose-bloom fell on her hands, together pressed,   220
And on her silver cross soft amethyst,
And on her hair a glory, like a saint:

She seemed a splendid angel, newly dressed,
Save wings, for heaven: — Porphyro grew faint:
She knelt, so pure a thing, so free from mortal taint.   225

XXVI

Anon his heart revives: her vespers done,
Of all its wreathed pearls her hair she frees;
Unclasps her warmed jewels one by one;
Loosens her fragrant bodice; by degrees
Her rich attire creeps rustling to her knees: 230
Half-hidden, like a mermaid in sea-weed,
Pensive awhile she dreams awake, and sees,
In fancy, fair St. Agnes in her bed,
But dares not look behind, or all the charm is fled.

XXVII

Soon, trembling in her soft and chilly nest,   235
In sort of wakeful swoon, perplexed she lay,
Until the poppied warmth of sleep oppressed
Her soothed limbs, and soul fatigued away;
Flown, like a thought, until the morrow-day;
Blissfully havened both from joy and pain;   240
Clasped like a missal where swart Paynims° pray;   *dark-skinned pagans*
Blinded alike from sunshine and from rain,
As though a rose should shut, and be a bud again.

XXVIII

Stolen to this paradise, and so entranced,
Porphyro gazed upon her empty dress,   245
And listened to her breathing, if it chanced
To wake into a slumberous tenderness;
Which when he heard, that minute did he bless,
And breathed himself: then from the closet crept,
Noiseless as fear in a wide wilderness,   250
And over the hushed carpet, silent, stepped,
And tween the curtains peeped, where, lo! — how fast she slept.

XXIX

Then by the bedside, where the faded moon
Made a dim, silver twilight, soft he set
A table, and, half anguished, threw thereon   255
A cloth of woven crimson, gold, and jet —
O for some drowsy Morphean amulet!°
The boisterous, midnight, festive clarion,
The kettledrum, and far-heard clarinet,
Affray his ears, though but in dying tone —   260
The hall door shuts again, and all the noise is gone.

257 *Morphean amulet:* A charm used to induce sleep.

XXX

And still she slept an azure-lidded sleep,
In blanchèd linen, smooth, and lavendered,
While he from forth the closet brought a heap
Of candied apple, quince, and plum, and gourd;   265
With jellies soother° than the creamy curd,   *sweeter*
And lucent syrups, tinct with cinnamon;
Manna and dates, in argosy transferred
From Fez; and spiced dainties, every one,
From silken Samarcand to cedared Lebanon.   270

XXXI

These delicates he heaped with glowing hand
On golden dishes and in baskets bright
Of wreathed silver: sumptuous they stand
In the retired quiet of the night,
Filling the chilly room with perfume light. —   275
"And now, my love, my seraph fair, awake!
Thou art my heaven, and I thine eremite:°   *hermit*
Open thine eyes, for meek St. Agnes' sake,
Or I shall drowse beside thee, so my soul doth ache."

XXXII

Thus whispering, his warm, unnerved arm   280
Sank in her pillow. Shaded was her dream
By the dusk curtains: 'twas a midnight charm
Impossible to melt as icèd stream:
The lustrous salvers in the moonlight gleam;
Broad golden fringe upon the carpet lies: 285
It seemed he never, never could redeem
From such a stedfast spell his lady's eyes;
So mused awhile, entoiled in woofèd° phantasies.   *woven*

XXXIII

Awakening up, he took her hollow lute —
Tumultuous — and, in chords that tenderest be,   290
He played an ancient ditty, long since mute,
In Provence called, "La belle dame sans merci":
Close to her ear touching the melody; —
Wherewith disturbed, she uttered a soft moan:
He ceased — she panted quick — and suddenly   295
Her blue affrayed eyes wide open shone:
Upon his knees he sank, pale as smooth-sculptured stone.

XXXIV

Her eyes were open, but she still beheld,
Now wide awake, the vision of her sleep:
There was a painful change, that nigh expelled   300
The blisses of her dream so pure and deep,
At which fair Madeline began to weep,
And moan forth witless words with many a sigh;

While still her gaze on Porphyro would keep,
Who knelt, with joined hands and piteous eye,   305
Fearing to move or speak, she looked so dreamingly.

XXXV

"Ah, Porphyro!" said she, "but even now
Thy voice was at sweet tremble in mine ear,
Made tunable with every sweetest vow;
And those sad eyes were spiritual and clear: 310
How changed thou art! how pallid, chill, and drear!
Give me that voice again, my Porphyro,
Those looks immortal, those complainings dear!
Oh leave me not in this eternal woe,
For if thou diest, my Love, I know not where to go."   315

XXXVI

Beyond a mortal man impassioned far
At these voluptuous accents, he arose,
Ethereal, flushed, and like a throbbing star
Seen mid the sapphire heaven's deep repose;
Into her dream he melted, as the rose   320
Blendeth its odor with the violet —
Solution sweet: meantime the frost-wind blows
Like Love's alarum pattering the sharp sleet
Against the windowpanes; St. Agnes' moon hath set.

XXXVII

'Tis dark: quick pattereth the flaw-blown° sleet: *gusting*   325
"This is no dream, my bride, my Madeline!"
'Tis dark: the iced gusts still rave and beat:
"No dream, alas! alas! and woe is mine!
Porphyro will leave me here to fade and pine. —
Cruel! what traitor could thee hither bring?   330
I curse not, for my heart is lost in thine,
Though thou forsakest a deceivèd thing; —
A dove forlorn and lost with sick unprunèd wing."

XXXVIII

"My Madeline! sweet dreamer! lovely bride!
Say, may I be for aye° thy vassal blest?   *forever*   335
Thy beauty's shield, heart-shaped and vermeil dyed?
Ah, silver shrine, here will I take my rest
After so many hours of toil and quest,
A famished pilgrim — saved by miracle.
Though I have found, I will not rob thy nest   340
Saving of thy sweet self; if thou think'st well
To trust, fair Madeline, to no rude infidel.

XXXIX

"Hark! 'tis an elfin-storm from faery land,
Of haggard° seeming, but a boon indeed: *wild*
Arise — arise! the morning is at hand; —   345

The bloated wassailers will never heed: —
Let us away, my love, with happy speed;
There are no ears to hear, or eyes to see —
Drowned all in Rhenish and the sleepy mead:°
Awake! arise! my love, and fearless be,   350
For o'er the southern moors I have a home for thee."

XL

She hurried at his words, beset with fears,
For there were sleeping dragons all around,
At glaring watch, perhaps, with ready spears —
Down the wide stairs a darkling way they found. —   355
In all the house was heard no human sound.
A chain-drooped lamp was flickering by each door;
The arras, rich with horseman, hawk, and hound,
Fluttered in the besieging wind's uproar;
And the long carpets rose along the gusty floor.   360

XLI

They glide, like phantoms, into the wide hall;
Like phantoms, to the iron porch, they glide;
Where lay the Porter, in uneasy sprawl,
With a huge empty flagon by his side:
The wakeful bloodhound rose, and shook his hide,   365
But his sagacious eye an inmate owns:
By one, and one, the bolts full easy slide: —
The chains lie silent on the footworn stones; —
The key turns, and the door upon its hinges groans.

XLII

And they are gone: ay, ages long ago   370
These lovers fled away into the storm.
That night the Baron dreamt of many a woe,
And all his warrior-guests, with shade and form
Of witch, and demon, and large coffin-worm,
Were long be-nightmared. Angela the old   375
Died palsy-twitched, with meager face deform;
The Beadsman, after thousand aves° told,   *prayers*
For aye unsought for slept among his ashes cold.

349 *Rhenish:* Rhine wine; *mead:* A fermented drink made with honey.

Considerations for Critical Thinking and Writing

1. Summarize the story told in this poem.
2. What is the setting? Contrast the interior and exterior settings. How do the descriptions of the setting help establish the poem's mood?
3. What roles do the Beadsman, Angela, and the revelers play in the story?
4. Are Madeline and Porphyro individualized characters as well as recognizable types? How are they individuals, and how are they types?
5. What do the contrasting images of sensuality and spirituality contribute to the

poem's meaning? How does Keats build on contrasts of youth and age, love and hate, opulence and austerity, life and death, and heaven and hell? Use specific examples to explain how these contrasts relate to one another and to the poem's theme.

6. What sound effects in the poem seem especially effective? Why?
7. Select a stanza and analyze it in terms of sound and meter.

Bright star! would I were steadfast as thou art —   1819

Bright star, would I were steadfast as thou art —
    Not in lone splendor hung aloft the night
And watching, with eternal lids apart,
    Like nature's patient, sleepless Eremite,
The moving waters at their priestlike task   5
    Of pure ablution round earth's human shores,
Or gazing on the new soft fallen mask
    Of snow upon the mountains and the moors —
No — yet still steadfast, still unchangeable,
    Pillowed upon my fair love's ripening breast,   10
To feel forever its soft fall and swell,
    Awake forever in a sweet unrest,
Still, still to hear her tender-taken breath,
And so live ever — or else swoon to death.

Considerations for Critical Thinking and Writing

1. What does the speaker in this sonnet admire about the star? What qualities of the star does he reject?
2. What kind of sonnet is this? How does its structure help to shape its meaning?
3. How do the sound effects, particularly assonance and consonance, contribute to the meaning?
4. How does Keats vary the iambic pentameter here? What is the effect of these variations?
5. Is the theme of this sonnet similar to or different from that of "To Autumn" (p. 240)?

Why did I laugh to-night?   1819

Why did I laugh to-night? No voice will tell:
    No God, no Demon of severe response,
Deigns to reply from Heaven or from Hell.
    Then to my human heart I turn at once.
Heart! Thou and I are here sad and alone;   5
    I say, why did I laugh? O mortal pain!

O Darkness! Darkness! ever must I moan,
    To question Heaven and Hell and Heart in vain.
Why did I laugh? I know this Being's lease,
    My fancy to its utmost blisses spreads;   10
Yet would I on this very midnight cease,
    And the world's gaudy ensigns see in shreds;
Verse, Fame, and Beauty are intense indeed,
But Death intenser — Death is Life's high meed.°   *reward*

Considerations for Critical Thinking and Writing

1. What is the speaker's answer to the question posed in this sonnet?
2. Describe the sonnet's tone.
3. Write an essay considering the idea that "Death is Life's high meed" is a characteristic Keatsian sentiment.

La Belle Dame sans Merci°   1819

O what can ail thee, knight-at-arms,
    Alone and palely loitering?
The sedge has withered from the lake,
    And no birds sing.

O what can ail thee, knight-at-arms,   5
    So haggard and so woe-begone?
The squirrel's granary is full,
    And the harvest's done.

I see a lily on thy brow,
    With anguish moist and fever dew,   10
And on thy cheeks a fading rose
    Fast withereth too.

I met a lady in the meads,°   *meadows*
Full beautiful — a faery's child,
Her hair was long, her foot was light,   15
    And her eyes were wild.

I made a garland for her head,
    And bracelets too, and fragrant zone;°   *belt*
She looked at me as she did love,
    And made sweet moan.   20

I set her on my pacing steed,
    And nothing else saw all day long,
For sidelong would she bend, and sing
    A faery's song.

La Belle Dame sans Merci: This title is borrowed from a medieval poem and means "The Beautiful Lady without Mercy."

She found me roots of relish sweet,   25
    And honey wild, and manna dew,
And sure in language strange she said,
    "I love thee true."

She took me to her elfin grot,°   *grotto*
    And there she wept, and sighed full sore,   30
And there I shut her wild wild eyes
    With kisses four.

And there she lullèd me asleep,
    And there I dreamed — Ah! woe betide!
The latest° dream I ever dreamed   *last*   35
    On the cold hill side.

I saw pale kings and princes too,
    Pale warriors, death-pale were they all;
They cried — "La Belle Dame sans Merci
    Hath thee in thrall!"   40

I saw their starved lips in the gloam,
    With horrid warning gapèd wide,
And I awoke and found me here,
    On the cold hill's side.

And this is why I sojourn here,   45
    Alone and palely loitering,
Though the sedge has withered from the lake,
    And no birds sing.

Considerations for Critical Thinking and Writing

1. How do the first three stanzas of this ballad serve to characterize the knight who describes his experience with the lady?
2. The lady is a familiar character in literature, a "femme fatale." Characterize her. Have you encountered other versions of her in literature or film?
3. What is the effect of the shortened final line in each stanza of this ballad?

Ode to Psyche°   1819

O Goddess! hear these tuneless numbers, wrung
    By sweet enforcement and remembrance dear,
And pardon that thy secrets should be sung
    Even into thine own soft-conchèd° ear;   *soft like a shell*

Psyche: In Greek, *psyche* means soul or mind, but Psyche was not one of the original Greek gods. Apuleius, a second-century Latin author, told the story of Cupid's love for Psyche and their eventual immortality together.

Surely I dreamt today, or did I see
    The winged Psyche with awakened eyes?   5
I wandered in a forest thoughtlessly,
    And, on the sudden, fainting with surprise,
Saw two fair creatures, couchèd side by side
    In deepest grass, beneath the whisp'ring roof   10
    Of leaves and trembled blossoms, where there ran
        A brooklet, scarce espied:

'Mid hushed, cool-rooted flowers, fragrant-eyed,
    Blue, silver-white, and budded Tyrian,°
They lay calm-breathing on the bedded grass;   15
    Their arms embraced, and their pinions° too;   *wings*
    Their lips touched not, but had not bade adieu,
As if disjoined by soft-handed slumber,
And ready still past kisses to outnumber
    At tender eye-dawn of aurorean love: 20
        The wingèd boy I knew;
    But who wast thou, O happy, happy dove?
        His Psyche true!

O latest born and loveliest vision far
    Of all Olympus' faded hierarchy!°   25
Fairer than Phoebe's° sapphire-regioned star,   *Diana, the moon*
    Or Vesper;° amorous glowworm of the sky;   *evening star*
Fairer than these, though temple thou hast none,
    Nor altar heaped with flowers;
Nor virgin choir to make delicious moan   30
    Upon the midnight hours;
    No voice, no lute, no pipe, no incense sweet
    From chain-swung censer teeming;
    No shrine, no grove, no oracle, no heat
    Of pale mouthed prophet dreaming.   35

O brightest! though too late for antique vows,
    Too, too late for the fond believing lyre,
When holy were the haunted forest boughs,
    Holy the air, the water, and the fire;
Yet even in these days so far retired   40
    From happy pieties, thy lucent fans,°   *translucent wings*
    Fluttering among the faint Olympians,
I see, and sing, by my own eyes inspired.
So let me be thy choir, and make a moan
    Upon the midnight hours;   45
Thy voice, thy lute, thy pipe, thy incense sweet
    From swinged censer teeming;
Thy shrine, thy grove, thy oracle, thy heat
    Of pale-mouthed prophet dreaming.

14 *budded Tyrian:* Purple dye produced in ancient Tyre.   25 *Of all Olympus' . . . hierarchy:* Psyche
was not regarded as a goddess before Apuleius wrote of her.

Yes, I will be thy priest, and build a fane   50
    In some untrodden region of my mind,
Where branched thoughts, new grown with pleasant pain,
    Instead of pines shall murmur in the wind:
Far, far around shall those dark-clustered trees
    Fledge the wild-ridged mountains steep by steep;   55
And there by zephyrs, streams, and birds, and bees,
    The moss-lain Dryads° shall be lulled to sleep;   *wood nymphs*
And in the midst of this wide quietness
A rosy sanctuary will I dress
With the wreathed trellis of a working brain,   60
    With buds, and bells, and stars without a name,
With all the gardener Fancy e'er could feign,
    Who breeding flowers, will never breed the same:
And there shall be for thee all soft delight
    That shadowy thought can win,   65
A bright torch, and a casement ope at night,
    To let the warm Love° in!   *Cupid*

Considerations for Critical Thinking and Writing

1. What does the ideal love of Psyche and Cupid represent to the speaker in this ode?
2. What does the speaker lament in lines 36–39? What kind of loss is experienced here?
3. How will the speaker be a "priest, and build a fane / In some untrodden region of my mind" (lines 50–51)?
4. In what sense might it be said that this ode is about poetic imagination?

To Sleep   1819

O soft embalmer of the still midnight,
    Shutting, with careful fingers and benign,
Our gloom-pleased eyes, embowered from the light,
    Enshaded in forgetfulness divine:
O soothest Sleep! if so it please thee, close,   5
    In midst of this thine hymn, my willing eyes,
Or wait the Amen, ere thy poppy throws
    Around my bed its lulling charities.
Then save me, or the passed day will shine
    Upon my pillow, breeding many woes: 10
Save me from curious conscience, that still hoards
    Its strength for darkness, burrowing like the mole;
Turn the key deftly in the oiled wards,
    And seal the hushed casket of my soul.

Considerations for Critical Thinking and Writing

1. How is sleep personified? What sort of "person" is it?
2. What does the speaker want to be saved from?
3. What extended metaphor is used? What purpose does it serve?

Connection to Another Selection

1. In an essay compare Keats's treatment of sleep with Robert Bly's "Waking from Sleep" (p. 361).

Ode to a Nightingale   1819

I

My heart aches, and a drowsy numbness pains
    My sense, as though of hemlock° I had drunk,   *a poison*
Or emptied some dull opiate to the drains
    One minute past, and Lethe-wards° had sunk:
'Tis not through envy of thy happy lot,   5
    But being too happy in thine happiness —
        That thou, light-wingèd Dryad° of the trees,   *wood nymph*
           In some melodious plot
    Of beechen green, and shadows numberless,
        Singest of summer in full-throated ease.   10

II

O, for a draught of vintage! that hath been
    Cooled a long age in the deep-delved earth,
Tasting of Flora° and the country green,   *goddess of flowers*
    Dance, and Provençal song,° and sunburnt mirth!
O for a beaker full of the warm South,   15
    Full of the true, the blushful Hippocrene,°
        With beaded bubbles winking at the brim,
           And purple-stainèd mouth;
That I might drink, and leave the world unseen,
    And with thee fade away into the forest dim: 20

III

Fade far away, dissolve, and quite forget
    What thou among the leaves hast never known,
The weariness, the fever, and the fret
    Here, where men sit and hear each other groan;
Where palsy shakes a few, sad, last gray hairs,   25
    Where youth grows pale, and specter-thin, and dies,

4 *Lethe-wards:* Toward Lethe, the river of forgetfulness in the Hades of Greek mythology.
14 *Provençal song:* The medieval troubadours of Provence, France, were known for their singing.
16 *Hippocrene:* The fountain of the Muses in Greek mythology.

John Keats **235**

Where but to think is to be full of sorrow
    And leaden-eyed despairs,
Where Beauty cannot keep her lustrous eyes;
    Or new Love pine at them beyond tomorrow.   30

IV

Away! away! for I will fly to thee,
    Not charioted by Bacchus and his pards,°
But on the viewless wings of Poesy,
    Though the dull brain perplexes and retards:
Already with thee! tender is the night,   35
    And haply the Queen-Moon is on her throne,
        Clustered around by all her starry Fays;
     · But here there is no light,
Save what from heaven is with the breezes blown
        Through verdurous glooms and winding mossy ways.   40

V

I cannot see what flowers are at my feet,
    Nor what soft incense hangs upon the boughs,
But, in embalmèd° darkness, guess each sweet   *perfumed*
    Wherewith the seasonable month endows
The grass, the thicket, and the fruit-tree wild;   45
    White hawthorn, and the pastoral eglantine;
        Fast fading violets covered up in leaves;
          And mid-May's eldest child,
The coming musk-rose, full of dewy wine,
        The murmurous haunt of flies on summer eves.   50

VI

Darkling° I listen; and for many a time   *in the dark*
    I have been half in love with easeful Death,
Called him soft names in many a musèd rhyme,
    To take into the air my quiet breath;
Now more than ever seems it rich to die,   55
    To cease upon the midnight with no pain,
        While thou art pouring forth thy soul abroad
          In such an ecstasy!
    Still wouldst thou sing, and I have ears in vain —
        To thy high requiem become a sod.   60

VII

Thou wast not born for death, immortal Bird!
    No hungry generations tread thee down;
The voice I hear this passing night was heard
    In ancient days by emperor and clown:
Perhaps the selfsame song that found a path   65

---

32 *Bacchus and his pards:* The Greek god of wine traveled in a chariot drawn by leopards.

Through the sad heart of Ruth,° when, sick for home,
    She stood in tears amid the alien corn:
        The same that oft-times hath
    Charmed magic casements, opening on the foam
        Of perilous seas, in faery lands forlorn.   70

VIII

Forlorn! the very word is like a bell
    To toll me back from thee to my sole self!
Adieu! the fancy cannot cheat so well
    As she is famed to do, deceiving elf.
Adieu! adieu! thy plaintive anthem fades   75
    Past the near meadows, over the still stream,
        Up the hill side; and now 'tis buried deep
            In the next valley-glades:
    Was it a vision, or a waking dream?
        Fled is that music: — Do I wake or sleep?   80

66 *Ruth:* A young widow in the Bible (see the Book of Ruth).

Considerations for Critical Thinking and Writing

1. Why does the speaker in this ode want to leave his world for the nightingale's? What does the nightingale symbolize?
2. How does the speaker attempt to escape his world? Is he successful?
3. What changes the speaker's view of death at the end of stanza VI?
4. What does the allusion to Ruth (line 66) contribute to the ode's meaning?
5. In which lines is the imagery especially sensuous? How does this effect add to the conflict presented?
6. What calls the speaker back to himself at the end of stanza VII and the beginning of stanza VIII?
7. Choose a stanza and explain how sound is related to its meaning.
8. How regular is the stanza form of this ode?

Ode on a Grecian Urn   1819

I

Thou still unravished bride of quietness,
    Thou foster-child of silence and slow time,
Sylvan° historian, who canst thus express
    A flowery tale more sweetly than our rhyme:
What leaf-fringed legend haunts about thy shape   5
    Of deities or mortals, or of both,
        In Tempe or the dales of Arcady?°

3 *Sylvan:* Rustic. The urn is decorated with a forest scene.   7 *Tempe, Arcady:* Beautiful rural valleys in Greece.

What men or gods are these? What maidens loath?
    What mad pursuit? What struggle to escape?
        What pipes and timbrels? What wild ecstasy?   10

II

Heard melodies are sweet, but those unheard
    Are sweeter; therefore, ye soft pipes, play on;
Not to the sensual ear, but, more endeared,
    Pipe to the spirit ditties of no tone:
Fair youth, beneath the trees, thou canst not leave   15
    Thy song, nor ever can those trees be bare;
        Bold Lover, never, never canst thou kiss,
Though winning near the goal — yet, do not grieve;
    She cannot fade, though thou hast not thy bliss,
        For ever wilt thou love, and she be fair!   20

III

Ah, happy, happy boughs! that cannot shed
    Your leaves, nor ever bid the Spring adieu;
And, happy melodist, unwearièd,
    For ever piping songs for ever new;
More happy love! more happy, happy love!   25
    For ever warm and still to be enjoyed,
        For ever panting, and for ever young;
All breathing human passion far above,
    That leaves a heart high-sorrowful and cloyed,
        A burning forehead, and a parching tongue.   30

IV

Who are these coming to the sacrifice?
    To what green altar, O mysterious priest,
Lead'st thou that heifer lowing at the skies,
    And all her silken flanks with garlands drest?
What little town by river or sea shore,   35
    Or mountain-built with peaceful citadel,
        Is emptied of this folk, this pious morn?
And, little town, thy streets for evermore
    Will silent be; and not a soul to tell
        Why thou art desolate, can e'er return.   40

V

O Attic° shape! Fair attitude! with brede°
    Of marble men and maidens overwrought,
With forest branches and the trodden weed;
    Thou, silent form, dost tease us out of thought
As doth eternity: Cold Pastoral!   45
    When old age shall this generation waste,
        Thou shalt remain, in midst of other woe

41 *Attic:* Possessing classic Athenian simplicity; *brede:* Design.

Than ours, a friend to man, to whom thou say'st,
    Beauty is truth, truth beauty — that is all
        Ye know on earth, and all ye need to know.   50

Considerations for Critical Thinking and Writing

1. What is the speaker's attitude toward the urn in this ode? Does his view develop or change?
2. How is the happiness in stanza III related to the assertion in lines 11–12 that "Heard melodies are sweet, but those unheard / Are sweeter"?
3. What is the difference between the world depicted on the urn and the speaker's world?
4. What do lines 49–50 suggest about the relation of art to life? Why is the urn described as a "Cold Pastoral" (line 45)?
5. Which world does the speaker seem to prefer, the urn's or his own?

Connections to Other Selections

1. Write an essay comparing the view of time in this ode with that in Andrew Marvell's "To His Coy Mistress" (p. 55).
2. Discuss the treatment and meaning of love in this ode and in Richard Wilbur's "Love Calls Us to the Things of This World" (p. 437).
3. Compare the tone and attitude toward life in this ode with those in Keats's "To Autumn" (p. 240).

Ode on Melancholy   1819

I

No, no! go not to Lethe,° neither twist
    Wolfsbane,° tight-rooted, for its poisonous wine;
Nor suffer thy pale forehead to be kissed
    By nightshade,° ruby grape of Proserpine;°   *Queen of Hades*
Make not your rosary of yew-berries,°   5
    Nor let the beetle, nor the death-moth be
        Your mournful Psyche,° nor the downy owl
A partner in your sorrow's mysteries;
    For shade to shade will come too drowsily,
        And drown the wakeful anguish of the soul.   10

II

But when the melancholy fit shall fall
    Sudden from heaven like a weeping cloud,

---

1 *Lethe:* In Greek mythology, the river of forgetfulness, which the dead cross to enter Hades.
2 *Wolfsbane:* A poisonous plant.   4 *nightshade:* Also a poisonous plant.   5 *yew-berries:* Associated with death, as are the beetle, moth, and owl in this stanza.   6–7 *nor let the death-moth be. . . Psyche:* The soul was depicted as a butterfly in Greek mythology. *Psyche* means soul or mind in Greek.

That fosters the droop-headed flowers all,
And hides the green hill in an April shroud;
Then glut thy sorrow on a morning rose, 15
Or on the rainbow of the salt sand-wave,
Or on the wealth of globed peonies;
Or if thy mistress some rich anger shows,
Imprison her soft hand, and let her rave,
And feed deep, deep upon her peerless eyes. 20

III
She dwells with Beauty — Beauty that must die;
And Joy, whose hand is ever at his lips
Bidding adieu; and aching Pleasure nigh,
Turning to Poison while the bee-mouth sips:
Aye, in the very temple of Delight 25
Veiled Melancholy has her sovereign shrine,
Though seen of none save him whose strenuous tongue
Can burst Joy's grape against his palate fine;
His soul shall taste the sadness of her might,
And be among her cloudy trophies hung. 30

Considerations for Critical Thinking and Writing

1. What is melancholy? According to the speaker of this ode (lines 27–30), what produces the most intense melancholy? Is it good or bad, a strength or a weakness, to suffer from melancholy?
2. What do the images in this ode reveal about the relation between beauty and time? Between pleasure and pain?
3. Is this a sentimental poem? Explain why or why not.

To Autumn 1819

I
Season of mists and mellow fruitfulness,
Close bosom-friend of the maturing sun;
Conspiring with him how to load and bless
With fruit the vines that round the thatch-eves run;
To bend with apples the mossed cottage-trees, 5
And fill all fruit with ripeness to the core;
To swell the gourd, and plump the hazel shells
With a sweet kernel; to set budding more,
And still more, later flowers for the bees,
Until they think warm days will never cease, 10
For summer has o'er-brimmed their clammy cells.

II
Who hath not seen thee oft amid thy store?
Sometimes whoever seeks abroad may find

Thee sitting careless on a granary floor,
    Thy hair soft-lifted by the winnowing wind;   15
Or on a half-reaped furrow sound asleep,
    Drowsed with the fume of poppies, while thy hook°   *scythe*
        Spares the next swath and all its twinèd flowers:
And sometimes like a gleaner thou dost keep
    Steady thy laden head across a brook;   20
    Or by a cider-press, with patient look,
        Thou watchest the last oozings hours by hours.

III
Where are the songs of spring? Ay, where are they?
    Think not of them, thou hast thy music too, —
While barred clouds bloom the soft-dying day,   25
    And touch the stubble-plains with rosy hue;
Then in a wailful choir the small gnats mourn
    Among the river sallows,° borne aloft   *willows*
        Or sinking as the light wind lives or dies;
And full-grown lambs loud bleat from hilly bourn;°   *territory* 30
    Hedge-crickets sing; and now with treble soft
    The redbreast whistles from a garden-croft,
        And gathering swallows twitter in the skies.

Considerations for Critical Thinking and Writing

1. How is autumn personified in each stanza of this ode?
2. Which senses are most emphasized in each stanza?
3. How is the progression of time expressed in the ode?
4. How does the imagery convey tone? Which words have particularly strong connotative values?
5. What is the speaker's view of death?

Connections to Other Selections

1. Compare this poem's tone and its perspective on death with those of Robert Frost's "After Apple-Picking" (p. 303).
2. Write an essay comparing the significance of the images of "mellow fruitfulness" in "To Autumn" with that of the images of ripeness in Theodore Roethke's "Root Cellar" (p. 72). Explain how the images in each poem lead to very different feelings about the same phenomenon.

PERSPECTIVES ON KEATS

Keats on the Truth of the Imagination   1817

I am certain of nothing but of the holiness of the Heart's affections and the truth of Imagination — What the imagination seizes as Beauty must be truth — whether it existed before or not — for I have the same Idea of all our Passions as of Love they are all in their sublime, creative of essential Beauty. . . . The

Imagination may be compared to Adam's dream° — he awoke and found it truth. I am the more zealous in this affair, because I have never yet been able to perceive how any thing can be known for truth by consequitive reasoning — and yet it must be — Can it be that even the greatest Philosopher ever ~~when~~° arrived at his goal without putting aside numerous objections — However it may be, O for a Life of Sensations rather than of Thoughts! It is "a Vision in the form of Youth" a Shadow of reality to come — and this consideration has further conv[i]nced me for it has come as auxiliary to another favorite Speculation of mine, that we shall enjoy ourselves here after by having what we called happiness on Earth repeated in a finer tone and so repeated — And yet such a fate can only befall those who delight in sensation rather than hunger as you do after Truth — Adam's dream will do here and seems to be a conviction that Imagination and its empyreal reflection is the same as human Life and its spiritual repetition. But as I was saying — The simple imaginative Mind may have its rewards in the repeti[ti]on of its own silent Working coming continually on the spirit with a fine suddenness — to compare great things with small — have you never by being surprised with an old Melody — in a delicious place — by a delicious voice, fe[l]t over again your very speculations and surmises at the time it first operated on your soul — do you not remember forming to yourself the singer's face more beautiful that [*for* than] it was possible and yet with the elevation of the Moment you did not think so — even then you were mounted on the Wings of Imagination so high — that the Prototype must be here after — that delicious face you will see — What a time! I am continually running away from the subject — sure this cannot be exactly the case with a complex Mind — one that is imaginative and at the same time careful of its fruits — who would exist partly on sensation partly on thought — to whom it is necessary that years should bring the philosophic Mind — such an one I consider your's and therefore it is necessary to your eternal Happiness that you not only ~~have~~ drink this old Wine of Heaven which I shall call the redigestion of our most ethereal Musings on Earth; but also increase in knowledge and know all things.

From a letter to Benjamin Bailey, November 22, 1817

Considerations for Critical Thinking and Writing

1. "O for a life of Sensations rather than of Thoughts!" What do you think Keats means by this? Is this an antiintellectual statement?
2. Consider this passage from a letter to a friend, C. W. Dilke (September 22, 1819), in which Keats "Talking of pleasure" writes, "this moment I was writing with one hand, and with the other holding to my mouth a Nectarine — good God how fine. It went down soft, slushy, oozy — all its delicious embonpoint [plumpness] melted down my throat like a beatified Strawberry." Why is "delight in sensation," as Keats puts it in his letter to Bailey, so important to Keats's view of life and poetry?
3. How does Keats's description of the relation between beauty and truth in this letter compare with what he says in "Ode on a Grecian Urn" (p. 237)?

Adam's dream: In John Milton's *Paradise Lost* (Book VIII, 460–90), Adam dreams of Eve's creation and wakes up to find that she exists.   ~~*when:*~~ Excerpts from Keats's letters in this section are reprinted from Hyder E. Rollins's edition of *The Letters of John Keats* (Cambridge, Mass.: Harvard University Press, 1970), which reproduces the letters as Keats wrote them, including the crossed-out words. Rollins's comments are in brackets.

We hate poetry that has a palpable design upon us — and if we do not agree, seems to put its hand in its breeches pocket. Poetry should be great & unobtrusive, a thing which enters into one's soul, and does not startle it or amaze it with itself but with its subject. — How beautiful are the retired flowers! how would they lose their beauty were they to throng into the highway crying out, "admire me I am a violet! dote upon me I am a primrose!"

From a letter to J. H. Reynolds, February 3, 1818

Considerations for Critical Thinking and Writing

1. Does Keats's poetry have a "palpable design" upon the reader? How do you think Keats would regard didactic poetry such as the excerpt from Alexander Pope's "An Essay on Criticism" (p. 150)?
2. In another letter to Reynolds (on April 9, 1819), Keats wrote, "I never wrote one single Line of Poetry with the least Shadow of public thought." With reference to specific poems, explain why Keats's poetry is more personal than public and more concerned with feelings than teachings.

Keats on His Poetic Principles   1818

In Poetry I have a few Axioms, and you will see how far I am from their Centre. 1st I think Poetry should surprise by a fine excess and not by Singularity — it should strike the Reader as a wording of his own highest thoughts, and appear almost a Remembrance — 2nd Its touches of Beauty should never be half way therby making the reader breathless instead of content: the rise, the progress, the setting of imagery should like the Sun come natural natural too him — shine over him and set soberly although in magnificence leaving him in the Luxury of twilight — but it is easier to think what Poetry should be than to write it — and this leads me on to another axiom. That if Poetry comes not as naturally as the Leaves to a tree it had better not come at all.

From a Letter to John Taylor, February 27, 1818

Considerations for Critical Thinking and Writing

1. The phrase *fine excess* appears to be a contradiction in terms. How does Keats's poetry resolve this seeming contradiction?
2. Given that Keats wrote in fixed poetic forms, such as the sonnet and ode, in what sense can his poetry be regarded as coming "naturally as the Leaves to a tree"?
3. Based on your reading of Keats's poems, create another axiom that serves as a useful generalization about his poetry.

The common cognomen of this world among the misguided and superstitious is "a vale of tears" from which we are to be redeemed by a certain arbitrary interposition of God and taken to Heaven — What a little circumscribe[d] straightened notion! Call the world if you Please "The vale of Soul-making" Then you will find out the use of the world (I am speaking now in the highest terms for human nature admitting it to be immortal which I will here take for granted for the purpose of showing a thought which has struck me concerning it) I say *"Soul making"* Soul as distinguished from an Intelligence — There may be intelligences or sparks of the divinity in millions — but they are not Souls the till they acquire identities, till each one is personally itself. I[n]telligences are atoms of perception — they know and they see and they are pure, in short they are God — how then are Souls to be made? How then are these sparks which are God to have identity given them — so as ever to possess a bliss peculiar to each ones individual existence? How, but by the medium of a world like this? This point I sincerely wish to consider because I think it a grander system of salvation than the chrysteain religion — or rather it is a system of Spirit-creation — This is effected by three grand materials acting the one upon the other for a series of years — These three Materials are the *Intelligence* — the *human heart* (as distinguished from intelligence or Mind) and the *World* or *Elemental space* suited for the proper action of *Mind and Heart* on each other for the purpose of forming the *Soul* or *Intelligence destined to possess the sense of Identity*. I can scarcely express what I but dimly perceive — and yet I think I perceive it — that you may judge the more clearly I will put it in the most homely form possible — I will call the *world* a School instituted for the purpose of teaching little children to read — I will call the *human heart* the *horn Book* used in that School — and I will call the *Child able to read, the Soul* made from that *school* and its *hornbook*. Do you not see how necessary a World of Pains and troubles is to school an Intelligence and make it a soul? A Place where the heart must feel and suffer in a thousand diverse ways! Not merely is the Heart a Hornbook, It is the Minds Bible, it is the Minds experience, it is the teat from which the Mind or intelligence sucks its identity — As various as the Lives of Men are — so various become their souls, and thus does God make individual beings, Souls, identical Souls of the sparks of his own essence — This appears to me a faint sketch of a system of Salvation which does not affront our reason and humanity.

From a letter to George and Georgiana Keats, February 14–May 3, 1819

Considerations for Critical Thinking and Writing

1. How does Keats's perception of pain and suffering contrast with what he takes to be the traditional Christian view that life is "a vale of tears" that tests the soul? How are "Souls to be made"?
2. How is Keats's emphasis on a "World of Pains and troubles . . . to school an Intelligence and make it a soul" demonstrated in his poetry? What is the function of pain and suffering in his poetry? How are they related to the process of *"Soul Making"*?

3. Research Keats's personal life, particularly his illness. How does the biographical information you have found shed light on the characteristic tone and subject matter of his poetry?

F. SCOTT FITZGERALD (1896–1940)
On the "Extraordinary Genius" of Keats   1940

Poetry is either something that lives like fire inside you — like music to the musician or Marxism to the Communist — or else it is nothing, an empty, formalized bore, around which pedants can endlessly drone their notes and explanations. *The Grecian Urn* is unbearably beautiful, with every syllable as inevitable as the notes in Beethoven's *Ninth Symphony,* or it's just something you don't understand. It is what it is because an extraordinary genius paused at that point in history and touched it. I suppose I've read it a hundred times. About the tenth time I began to know what it was about, and caught the chime in it and the exquisite inner mechanics. Likewise with the *Nightingale,* which I can never read through without tears in my eyes; . . . and *The Eve of Saint Agnes,* which has the richest, most sensuous imagery in English, not excepting Shakespeare. And finally his three or four great sonnets: *Bright Star* and the others. . . .

Knowing those things very young and granted an ear, one could scarcely ever afterwards be unable to distinguish between gold and dross in what one read. In themselves those eight poems are a scale of workmanship for anybody who wants to know truly about words, their most utter value for evocation, persuasion, or charm. For awhile after you quit Keats all other poetry seems to be only whistling or humming.

From *The Crack-Up*

Considerations for Critical Thinking and Writing

1. What qualities does Fitzgerald particularly value in Keats's poetry?
2. Which of his comments about the poems he cites is the most specific? Explain whether you agree with it, and why.
3. Perhaps you have already read Fitzgerald's *The Great Gatsby.* Based on that novel or other information you can find in the library about his life, why do you think Fitzgerald was especially attracted to Keats's poetry?

HAROLD BLOOM (b. 1930)
On "Bright star! would I were steadfast as thou art — " 1961

Bright star, the best of Keats's sonnets, left by him unpublished, written on a blank page in Shakespeare's *Poems,* facing *A Lover's Complaint,* is a direct analogue to the ode *To Autumn,* for it also is a poem beyond argument, though not also calm in mind, for passion informs it throughout. The octet is one of the major expressions of Keats's humanism; the sestet one of the most piercing of his longings after the world of Beulah land, the breathing garden of repose beyond bounds. The unity of the poem is constituted by its total freedom from Keats's characteristic conflicts. The octet shares in the resolution of *To Autumn,* giving us an anagoge of poetic eternity, without contraries. The sestet, as a Beulah poem, is set in that state of being where, according to Blake, "all contraries are equally true."

The initial line is a prayer. The next seven lines *describe* the steadfastness of the star, after making it clear that Keats wants to be as steadfast as the star, but not in the star's way of steadfastness. The sestet describes Keats's mode of desired being, and finally declares for an eternity of this being, or an immediate swoon to death. This tight structure confines a remarkable contrast, between the state of Eden and the state of Beulah, Blake would have said, but Keats, by his own choice, clearly opts for the lower paradise as his own.

The Miltonic bright star is not God's hermit but nature's patient, sleepless eremite. Never sleeping, its "eternal lids apart," like Milton's Eyelids of the Morning, it watches:

> The moving waters at their priestlike task
> Of pure ablution round earth's human shores

"Human shores" is powerfully Blakean; the contrast here is between the star as motionless, solitary hermit, and the waters as moving, companionable priest, the one watching, the other cleansing man. We miss the force of this if we do not see it as humanistic, not Christian, in its religious emphasis. The oceans themselves, as a part of unfallen nature, perform their task of *pure* ablution, and the shores of earth are themselves *human.* That last is more than similitude, i.e., metaphor; it is identity, anagogical typology. As Blake saw the physical universe as having itself an ultimately human form, so here also Keats sees the shores of earth as being "men seen afar." As in *To Autumn,* nature alone is sufficient for purifying herself and ourselves, insofar as we can still be hers. Nature's own grace, akin to Keats's poetry, reveals the human countenance of earth:

> Or gazing on the new soft fallen mask
> Of snow upon the mountains and the moors —

The snow is a mask because it covers the human features of earth — that is, mountains and moors. Keats does not ask for himself the priestlike work of the moving waters. . . . Here, at the furthest reach of his poetry, he prays instead for the hermit star's eminence and function, to watch, benevolently, nature's work of humanizing herself. But in his own place; "not in lone splendour hung aloft the night," but in his own Gardens of Adonis, where, still steadfast, still unchangeable (though how, there, can he expect that?) he will be able:

> Pillow'd upon my fair love's ripening breast,
> To feel for ever its soft fall and swell,
> Awake for ever in a sweet unrest,
> Still, still to hear her tender-taken breath
> And so live ever —

Her breast would be forever ripening, never ripe; keeping its sleeping rhythm forever while Keats, awake forever in his sweet unrest, could hear always that recurrence of her breath. This poem can help explain Keats's life; his life cannot explain the poem. Alternatively, the poem can help explain certain contemporary psychological reductions of human desire, but *they* cannot explain *it*.

From *The Visionary Company: A Reading of English Romantic Poetry*

Considerations for Critical Thinking and Writing

1. Explain how Bloom distinguishes between the poem's octet and sestet.
2. How do Bloom's allusions to Blake and Milton help explain his points?
3. What attitudes concerning psychological criticism does Bloom reveal in his final comments? Explain whether you agree or not.

JACK STILLINGER (b. 1931)
On "The Eve of St. Agnes"   1961

The commonest response to *The Eve of St. Agnes* has been the celebration of its "heady and perfumed loveliness." The poem has been called "a monody of dreamy richness," "one long sensuous utterance," "an expression of lyrical emotion," "a great affirmation of love," "a great choral hymn," an expression of "unquestioning rapture," and many things else. Remarks like these tend to confirm one's uneasy feeling that what is sometimes called "the most perfect" of Keats's longer poems is a mere fairy-tale romance, unhappily short on meaning. For many readers, as for Douglas Bush, the poem is "no more than a romantic tapestry of unique richness of color"; one is "moved less by the experience of the characters than . . . by the incidental and innumerable beauties of descriptive phrase and rhythm."

To be sure, not all critics have merely praised Keats's pictures. After all, the poem opens on a note of "bitter chill," and progresses through images of cold and death before the action gets under way. When young Porphyro comes from across the moors to claim his bride, he enters a hostile castle, where Madeline's kinsmen will murder even upon holy days; and in the face of this danger he proceeds to Madeline's bedchamber. With the sexual consummation of their love, a storm comes up, and they must escape the castle, past "sleeping dragons," porter, and bloodhound, out into the night. The ending reverts to the opening notes of bitter chill and death: Madeline's kinsmen are benightmared, the old Beadsman and Madeline's nurse Angela are grotesquely dispatched into the next world. Some obvious contrasts are made in the poem: the lovers' youth and vitality are set against the old age and death associated with Angela and the Beadsman; the warmth and security of Madeline's chamber are contrasted with the coldness and hostility of the rest of the castle and the icy storm outside; the innocence and purity of young love are played off against the sensuousness of the revelers elsewhere in the castle; and so on. Through these contrasts, says one critic [R. H. Fogle], Keats created a tale of young love "not by forgetting what everyday existence is like, but by using the mean, sordid, and commonplace as a foundation upon which to build a high romance"; the result is no mere fairy tale, but a poem that "has a rounded fulness, a complexity and seriousness, a balance which remove it from the realm of mere magnificent tour de force."

From "The Hoodwinking of Madeline: Skepticism in 'The Eve of St. Agnes,'" *Studies in Philology,* 1961.

Considerations for Critical Thinking and Writing

1. What is it about "The Eve of St. Agnes" that has drawn praise for "Keats's pictures"? Identify and discuss several passages that seem especially beautiful in their "descriptive phrase and rhythm."
2. What other contrasts do you find paired in the poem besides the "obvious" one cited by Stillinger?
3. Discuss whether you agree or disagree with the claim that "The Eve of St. Agnes" is "a mere fairy-tale romance, unhappily short on meaning."

TWO COMPLEMENTARY CRITICAL READINGS

CLEANTH BROOKS (1906–1994)
History in "Ode on a Grecian Urn"   1944

The marble men and maidens of the urn will not age as flesh-and-blood men and women will: "When old age shall this generation waste." (The word "generation," by the way, is very rich. It means on one level "that which is generated"—that which springs from human loins—Adam's breed; and yet, so intimately is death wedded to men, the word "generation" itself has become, as here, a measure of time.) The marble men and women lie outside time. The urn which they adorn will remain. The "Sylvan historian" will recite its history to other generations.

What will it say to them? Presumably, what it says to the poet now: that "formed experience," imaginative insight, embodies the basic and fundamental perception of man and nature. The urn is beautiful, and yet its beauty is based — what else is the poem concerned with? — on an imaginative perception of essentials. Such a vision is beautiful but it is also true. The sylvan historian presents us with beautiful histories, but they are true histories, and it is a good historian.

Moreover, the "truth" which the sylvan historian gives is the only kind of truth which we are likely to get on this earth, and, furthermore, it is the only kind that we *have* to have. The names, dates, and special circumstances, the wealth of data — these the sylvan historian quietly ignores. But we shall never get all the facts anyway — there is no end to the accumulation of facts. Moreover, mere accumulations of facts — a point our own generation is only beginning to realize — are meaningless. The sylvan historian does better than that: it takes a few details and so orders them that we have not only beauty but insight into essential truth. Its "history," in short, is a history without footnotes. It has the validity of myth — not myth as a pretty but irrelevant make-belief, an idle fancy, but myth as a valid perception into reality. . . .

And now, what of the objection that the final lines break the tone of the poem with a display of misplaced sententiousness? One can summarize the answer already implied thus: throughout the poem the poet has stressed the paradox of the speaking urn. First, the urn itself can tell a story, can give a history. Then, the various figures depicted upon the urn play music, or speak or sing. If we have been alive to these items, we shall not, perhaps, be too much surprised to have the urn speak once more, not in the sense in which it tells a story — a metaphor which is rather easy to accept — but, to have it speak on a higher level, to have it make a commentary on its own nature. If the urn has been properly dramatized, if we have followed the development of the meta-phors, if we have been alive to the paradoxes which work throughout the poem, perhaps then, we shall be prepared for the enigmatic, final paradox which the "silent form" utters. But in that case, we shall not feel that the generalization, unqualified and to be taken literally, is meant to march out of its context to compete with the scientific and philosophical generalizations which dominate our world. . . .

To conclude thus may seem to weight the principle of dramatic propriety with more than it can bear. This would not be fair to the complexity of the problem of truth in art nor fair to Keats's little parable. Granted; and yet the principle of dramatic propriety may take us further than would first appear. Respect for it may at least insure our dealing with the problem of truth at the level on which it is really relevant to literature. If we can see that the assertions made in a poem are to be taken as part of an organic context, if we can resist the temptation to deal with them in isolation, then we may be willing to go on to deal with the world-view, or "philosophy," or "truth" of the *poem as a whole* in terms of its dramatic wholeness: that is, we shall not neglect the maturity of attitude, the dramatic tension, the emotional *and* intellectual coherence in favor of some statement of theme abstracted from it by paraphrase. Perhaps, best of all, we might learn to distrust our ability to represent any poem adequately by paraphrase. Such a distrust is healthy. Keats's sylvan historian, who is not above "teasing" us, exhibits such a distrust, and perhaps the point of what the sylvan historian "says" is to confirm us in our distrust.

From *The Sewanee Review* 52 (1944)

Considerations for Critical Thinking and Writing

1. According to Brooks, what sort of "history" does the urn present us with in the poem?
2. How does Brooks defend the final lines from the charge of "sententiousness"?
3. What does Brooks see as one of the dangers of paraphrase?

M. H. ABRAMS (b. 1912)
The Speakers in "Ode on a Grecian Urn"   1958

"Beauty is truth, truth beauty" is not asserted by Keats, either as a statement or as a pseudo statement. The Grecian Urn, after remaining obdurately mute under a hail of questions, unexpectedly gives voice to this proposition near the end of the poem. . . .

There is also a second and more important speaker in the poem. The whole of the "Ode on a Grecian Urn," in fact, consists of the utterance of this unnamed character, whose situation and actions we follow as he attends first to the whole, then to the sculptured parts, and again to the whole of the Urn; and who expresses in the process not only his perceptions, but his thoughts and feelings, and thereby discovers to us a determinate temperament. By a standard poetic device we accept without disbelief, he attributes to the Urn a statement about beauty and truth which is actually a thought that the Urn evokes in him. How we are to take the statement, therefore, depends not only on its status as an utterance, in that place, by the particular Urn, but beyond that as the penultimate stage, dramatically rendered, in the meditation of the lyric speaker himself. Obviously the earlier part of the "Ode" by no means gives the Urn a character that would warrant either its profundity or its reliability as a moral philosopher. In the mixed attitudes of the lyric speaker toward the Urn the playfulness and the pity, which are no less evident than the envy and the admiration, imply a position of superior understanding:

> Bold lover, never, never canst thou kiss,
> Though winning near the goal — yet, do not grieve;
> She cannot fade, though thou hast not thy bliss. . . .

The perfection represented on the Urn is the perdurability of the specious present, which escapes the "woe" of our mutable world only by surrendering any possibility of consummation and by trading grieving flesh for marble. The Urn, then, speaks from the limited perspective of a work in Grecian art; and it is from the larger viewpoint of this life, with its possibilities and its sorrows, that the lyric speaker has the last word, addressed to the figures on the Urn:

> That is all
> Ye know on earth, and all ye need to know.

The Urn has said, "Only the beautiful exists, and all that exists is beautiful" — but not, the speaker replies, in life, only in that sculptured Grecian world of noble simplicity where much that humanly matters is sacrificed for an enduring Now.

I entirely agree, then, with Professor Brooks in his explication of the "Ode," that "Beauty is truth" is not meant "to compete with . . . scientific and philosophical generalizations," but is to be considered as a speech "in character" and "dramatically appropriate" to the Urn. I am uneasy, however, about his final reference to "the world-view, or 'philosophy,' or 'truth' of the poem as a whole." For the poem as a whole is equally an utterance by a dramatically presented speaker, and none of its statements is proffered for our endorsement as a philosophical generalization of unlimited scope. They are all, therefore, to be apprehended as histrionic elements which are "in character" and "dramatically appropriate," for their inherent interest as stages in the evolution of an artistically ordered, hence all the more emotionally effective, experience of a credible human being.

From Literature and Belief: English Institute Essays

Considerations for Critical Thinking and Writing

1. Who is the second speaker in the poem, according to Abrams?
2. What distinction does Abrams make between the sculptured Grecian world and the speaker's world?
3. Explain how Abrams's view of the poem compares with Brooks's.

EMILY DICKINSON (1830–1886)

Emily Dickinson grew up in a prominent and prosperous household in Amherst, Massachusetts. Along with her younger sister Lavinia and older brother Austin, she experienced a quiet and reserved family life headed by her father Edward Dickinson. In a letter to Austin at law school, she once described the atmosphere in her father's house as "pretty much all sobriety." Her mother, Emily Norcross Dickinson, was not as powerful a presence in her life; she seems not to have been as emotionally accessible as Dickinson would have liked. Her daughter is said to have characterized her as not the sort of mother "to whom you hurry when you are troubled." Both parents raised Dickinson to be a cultured Christian woman who would one day be responsible for a family of her own. Her father attempted to protect her from reading books that might "joggle" her mind, particularly her religious faith, but Dickinson's individualistic instincts and irreverent sensibilities created conflicts that did not allow her to fall into step with the conventional piety, domesticity, and social duty prescribed by her father and the orthodox Congregationalism of Amherst.

The Dickinsons were well known in Massachusetts. Her father was a lawyer and served as the treasurer of Amherst College (a position Austin eventually took up as well), and her grandfather was one of the college's founders. Although nineteenth-century politics, economics, and social issues do not appear in the foreground of her poetry, Dickinson lived in a family environment that was steeped in them: her father was an active town official and served in the General Court of Massachusetts, the State Senate, and the United States House of Representatives.

Dickinson, however, withdrew not only from her father's public world but also from almost all social life in Amherst. She refused to see most people, and aside from a single year at South Hadley Female Seminary (now

Mount Holyoke College), one excursion to Philadelphia and Washington, and several brief trips to Boston to see a doctor about eye problems, she lived all her life in her father's house. She dressed only in white and developed a reputation as a reclusive eccentric. Dickinson selected her own society carefully and frugally. Like her poetry, her relationship to the world was intensely reticent. Indeed, during the last twenty years of her life she rarely left the house.

Though Dickinson never married, she had significant relationships with several men who were friends, confidantes, and mentors. She also enjoyed an intimate relationship with her friend Susan Huntington Gilbert, who became her sister-in-law by marrying Austin. Susan and her husband lived next door and were extremely close with Dickinson. Biographers have attempted to find in a number of her relationships the source for the passion of some of her love poems and letters. Several possibilities have been put forward as the person she addressed in three letters as "Dear Master": Benjamin Newton, a clerk in her father's office who talked about books with her; Samuel Bowles, editor of the *Springfield Republican* and friend of the family; the Reverend Charles Wadsworth, a Presbyterian preacher with a reputation for powerful sermons; and an old friend and widower, Judge Otis P. Lord. Despite these speculations, no biographer has been able to identify definitively the object of Dickinson's love. What matters, of course, is not with whom she was in love — if, in fact, there was any single person — but that she wrote about such passions so intensely and convincingly in her poetry.

Choosing to live life internally within the confines of her home, Dickinson brought her life into sharp focus. For she also chose to live within the limitless expanses of her imagination, a choice she was keenly aware of and which she described in one of her poems this way: "I dwell in Possibility" (p. 268). Her small circle of domestic life did not impinge upon her creative sensibilities. Like Henry David Thoreau, she simplified her life so that doing without was a means of being within. In a sense she redefined the meaning of deprivation because being denied something — whether it was faith, love, literary recognition, or some other desire — provided a sharper, more intense understanding than she would have experienced had she achieved what she wanted: "'Heaven,'" she wrote, "is what I cannot reach!" This poem (p. 262), along with many others, such as "Water, is taught by thirst" (p. 258) and "Success is counted sweetest / By those who ne'er succeed" (p. 257), suggest just how persistently she saw deprivation as a way of sensitizing herself to the value of what she was missing. For Dickinson hopeful expectation was always more satisfying than achieving a golden moment. Perhaps that's one reason she was so attracted to John Keats's poetry (see, for example, his "Ode on a Grecian Urn," p. 237).

Dickinson enjoyed reading Keats as well as Emily and Charlotte Brönte; Robert and Elizabeth Barrett Browning; Alfred, Lord Tennyson; and George Eliot. Even so, these writers had little or no effect upon the style of her writing. In her own work she was original and innovative, but she did draw upon her knowledge of the Bible, classical myths, and Shakespeare for allusions and references in her poetry. She also used contemporary popular church hymns, transforming their standard rhythms into free-form hymn meters. Among American writers she appreciated Ralph Waldo Emerson and Thoreau, but she apparently felt Walt Whitman was better left unread. She once mentioned to Thomas Wentworth Higginson, a leading critic with whom she corresponded about her poetry, that as for Whitman "I never read his Book — but was told that he was disgraceful" (for the kind of Whitman poetry she had been warned against see his "I Sing the Body Electric," p. 200). Nathaniel Hawthorne, however, intrigued her with his faith in the imagination and his dark themes: "Hawthorne appals — entices," a remark that might be used to describe her own themes and techniques.

Today, Dickinson is regarded as one of America's greatest poets, but when she died at the age of fifty-six after devoting most of her life to writing poetry, her nearly 2,000 poems — only a dozen of which were published anonymously during her lifetime — were unknown except to a small number of friends and relatives. Dickinson was not recognized as a major poet until the twentieth century, when modern readers ranked her as a major new voice whose literary innovations were unmatched by any other nineteenth-century poet in the United States.

Dickinson neither completed many poems nor prepared them for publication. She wrote her drafts on scraps of paper, grocery lists, and the backs of recipes and used envelopes. Early editors of her poems took the liberty of making them more accessible to nineteenth-century readers when several volumes of selected poems were published in the 1890s. The poems were made to appear like traditional nineteenth-century verse by assigning them titles, rearranging their syntax, normalizing their grammar, and regularizing their capitalizations. Instead of dashes editors used standard punctuation; instead of the highly elliptical telegraphic lines so characteristic of her poems editors added articles, conjunctions, and prepositions to make them more readable and in line with conventional expectations. In addition, the poems were made more predictable by organizing them into categories such as friendship, nature, love, and death. Not until 1955, when Thomas Johnson published Dickinson's complete works in a form that attempted to be true to her manuscript versions, did readers have an opportunity to see the full range of her style and themes.

Like that of Robert Frost, Dickinson's popular reputation has sometimes relegated her to the role of a New England regionalist who writes quaint uplifting verses that touch the heart. In 1971 that image was mailed first class all over the country by the United States Postal Service. In addition to issuing a commemorative stamp featuring a portrait of Dickinson, the Postal Service affixed the stamp to a first-day-of-issue envelope that included an engraved rose and one of her poems. Here's the poem chosen from among the nearly 2,000 she wrote:

If I can stop one Heart from breaking

c. 1864

If I can stop one Heart from breaking
I shall not live in vain
If I can ease one Life the Aching
or cool one Pain

Or help one fainting Robin
Unto his Nest again
I shall not live in Vain.

This is typical not only of many nineteenth-century popular poems, but of the kind of verse that can be found in contemporary greeting cards. The speaker tells us what we imagine we should think about and makes the point simply with a sentimental image of a "fainting Robin." To point out that robins don't faint or that altruism isn't necessarily the only rule of conduct by which one should live one's life is to make trouble for this poem. Moreover, its use of language is unexceptional; the metaphors used, like that Robin, are a bit weary. If this poem were characteristic of Dickinson's poetry, the Postal Service probably would not have been urged to issue a stamp in her honor nor would you be reading her poems in this anthology or many others. Here's another poem by Dickinson that is more typical of her writing:

If I shouldn't be alive

c. 1860

If I shouldn't be alive
When the Robins come,
Give the one in Red Cravat,
A Memorial crumb.

If I couldn't thank you,
Being fast asleep,
You will know I'm trying
With my Granite lip!

This poem is more representative of Dickinson's sensibilities and techniques. Although the first stanza sets up a rather mild concern that the speaker might not survive the winter (a not uncommon fear for those who fell prey to pneumonia, for example, during Dickinson's time), the concern can't be taken too seriously — a gentle humor lightens the poem when we realize that all robins have red cravats and are therefore the speaker's favorite. Furthermore, the euphemism that describes the speaker "Being fast asleep" in line 6 makes death seem not so threatening after all. But the sentimental expectations of the first six lines — lines that could have been written by any number of popular nineteenth-century writers — are dashed by the penultimate word of the last line. "Granite" is the perfect word here because it forces us to reread the poem and to recognize that it's not about feeding robins or offering a cosmetic treatment of death; rather it's a bone-chilling description of a corpse's lip that evokes the cold, hard texture and grayish color of tombstones. These lips will never say "Thank you" or anything else.

Instead of the predictable rhymes and sentiments of "If I can stop one Heart from breaking," this poem is unnervingly precise in its use of language and tidily points out how much emphasis Dickinson places on an individual word. Her use of near rhyme with "asleep" and "lip" brilliantly mocks a euphemistic approach to death by its jarring dissonance. This is a better poem, not because it's grim or about death, but because it demonstrates Dickinson's skillful use of language to produce a shocking irony.

Dickinson found irony, ambiguity, and paradox lurking in the simplest and commonest experiences. The materials and subject matter of her poetry are quite conventional. Her poems are filled with robins, bees, winter light, household items, and domestic duties. These materials represent the range of what she experienced in and around her father's house. She used them because they constituted so much of her life and, more importantly, because she found meanings latent in them. Though her world was simple, it was also complex in its beauties and its terrors. Her lyric poems capture impressions of particular moments, scenes, or moods, and she characteristically focuses upon topics such as nature, love, immorality, death, faith, doubt, pain, and the self.

Though her materials were conventional, her treatment of them was innovative, because she was willing to break whatever poetic conventions stood in the way of the intensity of her thought and images. Her conciseness, brevity, and wit are tightly packed. Typically she offers her observations via one or two images that reveal her thought in a powerful manner. She once characterized her literary art by writing "My business is circumference." Her method is to reveal the inadequacy of declarative statements by evoking qualifications and questions with images that complicate firm assertions and affirmations. In one of her poems she describes her strategies this way: "Tell all the Truth but tell it slant — / Success in Circuit lies." This might well stand as a working definition of Dickinson's aesthetics and is embodied in the following poem:

The Thought beneath so slight a film —   c. 1860

The Thought beneath so slight a film —
Is more distinctly seen —
As laces just reveal the surge —
Or Mists — the Apennine°   *Italian mountain range*

Paradoxically, "thought" is more clearly understood precisely because a slight "film" — in this case language — covers it. Language, like lace, enhances what it covers and reveals it all the more — just as a mountain range is more engaging to the imagination if it is covered in mists rather than starkly presenting itself. Poetry for Dickinson intensifies, clarifies, and organizes experience.

Dickinson's poetry is challenging because it is radical and original in its rejection of most traditional nineteenth-century themes and techniques. Her poems require active engagement from the reader, because she seems to leave out so much with her elliptical style and remarkable contracting metaphors. But these apparent gaps are filled with meaning if we are sensitive to her use of devices such as personification, allusion, symbolism, and startling syntax and grammar. Since her use of dashes is sometimes puzzling, it helps to read her poems aloud to hear how carefully the words are arranged. What might initially seem intimidating on a silent page can surprise the reader with meaning when heard. It's also worth keeping in mind that Dickinson was not always consistent in her views and that they can change from poem to poem, depending upon how she felt at a given moment. For example, her definition of religious belief in "'Faith' is a fine invention" (p. 260) reflects an ironically detached wariness in contrast to the faith embraced in "I never saw a Moor —" (p. 276). Dickinson was less interested in absolute answers to questions than she was in examining and exploring their "circumference."

Because Dickinson's poems are all relatively brief (none is longer than fifty lines), they invite browsing and sampling, but perhaps a useful way into their highly metaphoric and witty world is this "how to" poem that reads almost like a recipe:

To make a prairie
it takes a clover and one bee   date unknown

To make a prairie it takes a clover and one bee,
One clover, and a bee,
And revery.
The revery alone will do,
If bees are few.

This quiet but infinite claim for a writer's imagination brings together the range of ingredients in Dickinson's world of domestic and ordinary natural details. Not surprisingly, she deletes rather than adds to the recipe, because the one essential ingredient is the writer's creative imagination. *Bon appétit.*

Chronology

Success is counted sweetest   c. 1859

Success is counted sweetest
By those who ne'er succeed.
To comprehend a nectar
Requires sorest need.

Not one of all the purple Host   5
Who took the Flag today
Can tell the definition
So clear of Victory

As he defeated — dying —
On whose forbidden ear   10
The distant strains of triumph
Burst agonized and clear!

Considerations for Critical Thinking and Writing

1. How is success defined in this poem? To what extent does that definition agree with your own understanding of the word?
2. What do you think is meant by the use of "comprehend" in line 3? How can a nectar be comprehended?
3. Why do the defeated understand victory better than the victorious?
4. Discuss the effect of the poem's final line.

Connections to Other Selections

1. In an essay compare the themes of this poem with those of John Keats's "Ode on a Grecian Urn" (p. 237).
2. How might this poem be used as a commentary on Edwin Arlington Robinson's "Richard Cory" (p. 113)?

Water, is taught by thirst

c. 1859

Water, is taught by thirst.
Land — by the Oceans passed.
Transport — by throe —
Peace — by its battles told —
Love, by Memorial Mold —
Birds, by the Snow.

Considerations for Critical Thinking and Writing

1. How is the paradox of each line of the poem resolved? How is the first word of each line "taught" by the phrase that follows it?
2. Which image do you find most powerful? Explain why.
3. Try your hand at writing similar lines in which something is "taught."

Connections to Other Selections

1. What does this poem have in common with the preceding poem, "Success is counted sweetest"? Which poem do you think is more effective? Explain why.
2. How is the crucial point of this poem related to "I like a look of Agony" (p. 263)?

Safe in their Alabaster Chambers —

1859 version

Safe in their Alabaster Chambers —
Untouched by Morning
And untouched by Noon —
Sleep the meek members of the Resurrection —
Rafter of satin,   5
And Roof of stone.

Light laughs the breeze
In her Castle above them —
Babbles the Bee in a stolid Ear,
Pipe the Sweet Birds in ignorant cadence —   10
Ah, what sagacity perished here!

Safe in their Alabaster Chambers —   1861 version

Safe in their Alabaster Chambers —
Untouched by Morning —
And untouched by Noon —
Lie the meek members of the Resurrection —
Rafter of Satin — and Roof of Stone!   5

Grand go the Years — in the Crescent — above them —
Worlds scoop their Arcs —
And Firmaments — row —
Diadems — drop — and Doges° — surrender —
Soundless as dots — on a Disc of Snow —   10

9 *Doges:* Chief magistrates of Venice from the twelfth to the sixteenth centuries.

Considerations for Critical Thinking and Writing

1. Dickinson permitted the 1859 version of this poem, entitled "The Sleeping," to be printed in the *Springfield Republican.* The second version she sent privately to Thomas W. Higginson. Why do you suppose she would agree to publish the first but not the second version?
2. Are there any significant changes in the first stanzas of the two versions? If you answered yes, explain the significance of the changes.
3. Describe the different kinds of images used in the two second stanzas. How do those images affect the tones and meanings of those stanzas?
4. Discuss why you prefer one version of the poem over the other.

Connections to Other Selections

1. Compare the theme in the 1861 version with the theme of Robert Frost's "Design" (p. 311).
2. In an essay discuss the attitude toward death in the version of 1859 and in "Apparently with no surprise" (p. 278).

"Faith" is a fine invention

c. 1860

"Faith" is a fine invention
When Gentlemen can *see* —
But *Microscopes* are prudent
In an Emergency.

Considerations for Critical Thinking and Writing

1. What affects the speaker's attitude toward faith?
2. Describe the tone. Why can't this poem be accurately described as reverent?
3. Discuss the use of diction and its effects.

Connections to Other Selections

1. Write an essay comparing the view of faith in this poem with that expressed in "I never saw a Moor — " (p. 276).
2. Consider "I know that He exists" (p. 270) as an "Emergency" of the kind cited in this poem. How are the two poems related?
3. Compare the use of the word "fine" here with its use in the next poem, "Portraits are to daily faces."

Portraits are to daily faces

c. 1860

Portraits are to daily faces
As an Evening West,
To a fine, pedantic sunshine —
In a satin Vest!

Considerations for Critical Thinking and Writing

1. How is the basic strategy of this poem similar to the following statement: "Doorknob is to door as button is to sweater"?
2. Identify the four metonymies in the poem. Pay close attention to their connotative meanings.
3. If you don't know the meaning of *pedantic,* look it up in a dictionary. How does its meaning affect your reading of the word *fine?*
4. Dickinson once described herself as a literary artist this way: "My business is circumference." Discuss how this poem explains and expresses this characterization of her poetry.

Connections to Other Selections

1. Compare Dickinson's view of poetry in this poem with Robert Francis's perspective in "Catch" (p. 17). What important similarities and differences do you find?
2. Write an essay describing Robert Frost's strategy in "Mending Wall" (p. 298) or "Birches" (p. 304) as the business of circumference.
3. How is the theme of this poem related to the central idea in "The Thought beneath so slight a film — " (p. 255)?

Some keep the Sabbath going to Church —

Some keep the Sabbath going to Church —
I keep it, staying at Home —
With a Bobolink for a Chorister —
And an Orchard, for a Dome —

Some keep the Sabbath in Surplice° —   *holy robes*   5
I just wear my Wings —
And instead of tolling the Bell, for Church,
Our little Sexton — sings.

God preaches, a noted Clergyman —
And the sermon is never long,   10
So instead of getting to Heaven, at last —
I'm going, all along.

Considerations for Critical Thinking and Writing

1. What is the effect of referring to "Some" people?
2. Characterize the speaker's tone.
3. How does the speaker distinguish himself or herself from those who go to church?
4. How might "Surplice" be read as a pun?
5. According to the speaker, how should the Sabbath be observed?

Connections to Other Selections

1. Discuss the attitude toward formal religion in this poem and in John Keats's "Written in Disgust of Vulgar Superstition" (p. 218).
2. Write an essay that discusses nature in this poem and in Walt Whitman's "When I Heard the Learn'd Astronomer" (p. 499).

I taste a liquor never brewed —

1861

I taste a liquor never brewed —
From Tankards scooped in Pearl —
Not all the Vats upon the Rhine
Yield such an Alcohol!

Inebriate of Air — am I —   5
And Debauchee of Dew —
Reeling — thro endless summer days —
From inns of Molten Blue —

When "Landlords" turn the drunken Bee
Out of the Foxglove's door —   10
When Butterflies — renounce their "drams" —
I shall but drink the more!

Till Seraphs° swing their snowy Hats —   *angels*
And Saints — to windows run —
To see the little Tippler   15
Leaning against the — Sun —

Considerations for Critical Thinking and Writing

1. What is the poem's central metaphor? How is it developed in each stanza?
2. Which images suggest the causes of the speaker's intoxication?
3. Characterize the speaker's relationship to nature.

Connections to Other Selections

1. In an essay compare this speaker's relationship with nature to that of "A narrow Fellow in the Grass" (p. 4).
2. Discuss the tone created by the images in this poem and in Galway Kinnell's "Blackberry Eating" (p. 138).

"Heaven" — is what I cannot reach!   c. 1861

"Heaven" — is what I cannot reach!
The Apple on the Tree —
Provided it do hopeless — hang —
That — "Heaven" is — to Me!

The Color, on the Cruising Cloud —   5
The interdicted Land —
Behind the Hill — the House behind —
There — Paradise — is found!

Her teasing Purples — Afternoons —
The credulous — decoy —   10
Enamored — of the Conjuror —
That spurned us — Yesterday!

Considerations for Critical Thinking and Writing

1. Look up the myth of Tantalus and explain the allusion in line 3.
2. How does the speaker define heaven? How does that definition compare with conventional views of heaven?
3. Given the speaker's definition of heaven, how do you think the speaker would describe hell?

Connections to Other Selections

1. Write an essay that discusses desire in this poem and in "Water, is taught by thirst" (p. 258).
2. Discuss the speakers' attitudes toward pleasure in this poem and in Diane Ackerman's "A Fine, A Private Place" (p. 65).

"Hope" is the thing with feathers —

"Hope" is the thing with feathers —
That perches in the soul —
And sings the tune without the words —
And never stops — at all —

And sweetest — in the Gale — is heard —　　　　　　　　　5
And sore must be the storm —
That could abash the little Bird
That kept so many warm —

I've heard it in the chillest land —
And on the strangest Sea —　　　　　　　　　　　　　　10
Yet, never, in Extremity,
It asked a crumb — of Me.

Considerations for Critical Thinking and Writing

1. Why do you think the speaker defines hope in terms of a bird? Why is this metaphor more appropriate than, say, a dog?
2. Discuss the effects of the rhymes in each stanza.
3. What is the central point of the poem?

Connections to Other Selections

1. Compare the tone of this definition of hope with that of "'Faith' is a fine invention" (p. 260). How is "Extremity" handled differently from the "Emergency" in the latter poem?
2. Compare the strategies used to define hope in this poem and heaven in the preceding poem, "'Heaven' — is what I cannot reach!" Which poem, in your opinion, creates a more successful definition? In an essay explain why.

I like a look of Agony

I like a look of Agony,
Because I know it's true —
Men do not sham Convulsion,
Nor simulate, a Throe —

The Eyes glaze once — and that is Death —
Impossible to feign
The Beads upon the Forehead
By homely Anguish strung.

Considerations for Critical Thinking and Writing

1. Why does the speaker "like a look of Agony"?
2. Discuss the image of "The Eyes glaze once — ." Why is that a particularly effective metaphor for death?
3. Characterize the speaker. One critic once described the voice in this poem as "almost a hysterical shriek." Explain why you agree or disagree.

Connections to Other Selections

1. Write an essay on Dickinson's attitudes toward pain and deprivation, using this poem, "'Heaven' — is what I cannot reach!" (p. 262), and "Success is counted sweetest" (p. 257) as the basis for your discussion.
2. Consider how death is treated here and in "I've seen a Dying Eye" (p. 269).

I'm Nobody! Who are you?

c. 1861

I'm Nobody! Who are you?
Are you — Nobody — too?
Then there's a pair of us!
Don't tell! they'd advertise — you know!

How dreary — to be — Somebody!
How public — like a Frog —
To tell your name — the livelong June —
To an admiring Bog!

Considerations for Critical Thinking and Writing

1. What does the speaker wish to have in common with the reader? Explain whether you feel it is better to be "Nobody" or "Somebody."
2. Explain why it is "dreary — to be — Somebody!"
3. Discuss the simile in line 6. Why does it work so well?
4. What does the speaker think of most people?

Connections to Other Selections

1. What significant similarities in theme and technique does this poem share with e. e. cummings's "anyone lived in a pretty how town" (p. 370)?
2. Contrast the sense of self in this poem and Walt Whitman's "One's-Self I Sing" (p. 436).

The Robin's my Criterion for Tune

c. 1861

The Robin's my Criterion for Tune —
Because I grow — where Robins do —
But, were I Cuckoo born —

I'd swear by him —
The ode familiar — rules the Noon —   5
The Buttercup's, my Whim for Bloom —
Because, we're Orchard sprung —
But, were I Britain born,
I'd Daisies spurn —
None but the Nut — October fit —   10
Because, through dropping it,
The Seasons flit — I'm taught —
Without the Snow's Tableau
Winter, were lie — to me —
Because I see — New Englandly —   15
The Queen, discerns like me —
Provincially —

Considerations for Critical Thinking and Writing

1. Why are robins crucial to the speaker?
2. How would the speaker's "Tune" be affected if she were "Britain born"?
3. How does the speaker "see — New Englandly" in this poem? Why do you suppose
   she transforms New England into an adverb?

Connections to Other Selections

1. Discuss Dickinson's use of robins here and in "If I can stop one Heart from
   breaking" and "If I shouldn't be alive" (p. 254). How are robins used in each
   poem to convey meanings?
2. Choose a poem by Robert Frost and explain in an essay how he too sees "New
   Englandly."

Wild Nights — Wild Nights!   c. 1861

Wild Nights — Wild Nights!
Were I with thee
Wild Nights should be
Our luxury!

Futile — the Winds —   5
To a Heart in port —
Done with the Compass —
Done with the Chart!

Rowing in Eden —
Ah, the Sea!
Might I but moor — Tonight —   10
In Thee!

Considerations for Critical Thinking and Writing

1. Look up the meaning of "luxury" in a dictionary. Why does this word work especially well here?
2. Given the imagery of the final stanza, do you think the speaker is a man or woman? Explain why.
3. T. W. Higginson, Dickinson's mentor, once said he was afraid that some "malignant" readers might "read into [a poem like this] more than that virgin recluse ever dreamed of putting there." What do you think?

Connections to Other Selections

1. Write an essay that compares the voice, figures of speech, and theme of this poem with those of Margaret Atwood's "you fit into me" (p. 90).
2. Discuss the treatment of passion in this poem and in Sappho's "With his venom" (p. 86).

What Soft — Cherubic Creatures —   1862

What Soft — Cherubic Creatures —
These Gentlewomen are —
One would as soon assault a Plush —
Or violate a Star —

Such Dimity° Convictions —   *sheer cotton fabric*   5
A Horror so refined
Of freckled Human Nature —
Of Deity — ashamed —

It's such a common — Glory —
A Fisherman's — Degree —   10
Redemption — Brittle Lady —
Be so — ashamed of Thee —

Considerations for Critical Thinking and Writing

1. Characterize the "Gentlewomen" in this poem.
2. How do the sounds produced in the first line help to reinforce their meaning?
3. What are "Dimity convictions," and what do they make of "freckled Human Nature"?
4. Discuss the irony in the final stanza.

Connection to Another Selection

1. How are the "Gentlewomen" in this poem similar to the "Gentlemen" in "'Faith' is a fine invention" (p. 260)?

The Soul selects her own Society —

c. 1862

The Soul selects her own Society —
Then — shuts the Door —
To her divine Majority —
Present no more —

Unmoved — she notes the Chariots — pausing —   5
At her low Gate —
Unmoved — an Emperor be kneeling
Upon her Mat —

I've known her — from an ample nation —
Choose One —   10
Then — close the Valves of her attention —
Like Stone —

Considerations for Critical Thinking and Writing

1. What images reveal the speaker to be self-reliant and self-sufficient?
2. Why do you suppose the "Soul" in this poem is female? Would it make any difference if it were male?
3. Discuss the effect of the images in the final two lines. Pay particular attention to the meanings of "Valves" in line 11.

Connection to Another Selection

1. Though this poem takes up a different subject matter from "Shall I take thee, the Poet said" (p. 277), consider the process of selection in each poem and what it reveals about the speakers' sensibilities.

Much Madness is divinest Sense —

c. 1862

Much Madness is divinest Sense —
To a discerning Eye —
Much Sense — the starkest Madness —
'Tis the Majority
In this, as All, prevail —
Assent — and you are sane —
Demur — you're straightway dangerous —
And handled with a Chain —

Considerations for Critical Thinking and Writing

1. Discuss the conflict between the individual and society in this poem. Which images are used to describe each? How do these images affect your attitudes about them?
2. Comment on the effectiveness of the poem's final line.

3. T. W. Higginson's wife once referred to Dickinson as the "partially cracked poetess of Amherst." Assuming that Dickinson had some idea of how she was regarded by the "Majority," how might this poem be seen as an insight into her life?

Connections to Other Selections

1. How does Elisabeth Eybers's "Emily Dickinson" (p. 453) serve as a commentary on this poem?
2. Discuss the theme of self-reliance in this poem and the preceding one, "The Soul selects her own Society."

I dwell in Possibility —

c. 1862

I dwell in Possibility —
A fairer House than Prose —
More numerous of Windows —
Superior — for Doors —

Of Chambers as the Cedars —   5
Impregnable of Eye —
And for an Everlasting Roof
The Gambrels° of the Sky —   *angled roofs*

Of Visiters — the fairest —
For Occupation — This —   10
The spreading wide my narrow Hands
To gather Paradise —

Considerations for Critical Thinking and Writing

1. What distinction is made between poetry and prose in this poem? Explain why you agree or disagree with the speaker's distinctions.
2. What is the poem's central metaphor in the second and third stanzas?
3. How does the use of metaphor in this poem become a means for the speaker to envision and create a world beyond the circumstances of the speaker's actual life?

Connections to Other Selections

1. Compare what this poem says about poetry and prose with T. E. Hulme's comments in the perspective "On the Differences between Poetry and Prose" (p. 87).
2. How can the speaker's sense of expansiveness in this poem be reconciled with the speaker's insistence upon contraction in "The Soul selects her own Society —" (p. 267). Are these poems contradictory? Explain why or why not.

I've seen a Dying Eye

c. 1862

I've seen a Dying Eye
Run round and round a Room —
In search of Something — as it seemed —
Then Cloudier become —
And then — obscure with Fog —
And then — be soldered down
Without disclosing what it be
'Twere blessed to have seen —

Considerations for Critical Thinking and Writing

1. Characterize the emotional state of the person dying.
2. What is the "Something" the eye searches for?
3. Discuss the progression described in lines 4–6.
4. Discuss the wordplay at work in the speaker's use of "soldered" and "disclosing."

Connections to Other Selections

1. Discuss the similarities in theme in this poem and "If I shouldn't be alive" (p. 254).
2. In an essay explain how the images in this poem and in "I heard a Fly buzz — when I died — " (p. 271) constitute a visual and auditory evocation of death.

The Brain — is wider than the Sky —

c. 1862

The Brain — is wider than the Sky —
For — put them side by side —
The one the other will contain
With ease — and You — beside —

The Brain is deeper than the sea —   5
For — hold them — Blue to Blue —
The one the other will absorb —
As Sponges — Buckets — do —

The Brain is just the weight of God —
For — Heft them — Pound for Pound —   10
And they will differ — if they do —
As Syllable from Sound —

Considerations for Critical Thinking and Writing

1. What does the speaker say is the relationship between one's "Brain" and physical reality?
2. In the final stanza how do "Brain" and "God," "Syllable" and "Sound" "differ"?
3. How does this poem validate Dickinson's claim that "My business is circumference"?

1. Discuss the treatment of imagination in this poem and in "To make a prairie it takes a clover and one bee" (p. 256).
2. In an essay compare the sense of human possibility here with that found in "I dwell in Possibility — " (p. 268).

I know that He exists

c. 1862

I know that He exists.
Somewhere — in Silence —
He has hid his rare life
From our gross eyes.

'Tis an instant's play.   5
'Tis a fond Ambush —
Just to make Bliss
Earn her own surprise!

But — should the play
Prove piercing earnest —   10
Should the glee-glaze —
In Death's — stiff — stare —

Would not the fun
Look too expensive!
Would not the jest —   15
Have crawled too far!

Considerations for Critical Thinking and Writing

1. Identify the "He" in the first line of this poem.
2. What is the poem's controlling metaphor?
3. What does the speaker contemplate in lines 9–12?
4. How does the speaker's tone change from beginning to end? Where does it start to change?
5. Comment on the appropriateness of "crawled" (line 16). Is there an allusion here?

Connections to Other Selections

1. Discuss the theme of this poem and Robert Frost's "Provide, Provide" (p. 312).
2. Write an essay on attitudes about God in "I know that He exists" and Gerard Manley Hopkins's "God's Grandeur" (p. 144).

After great pain, a formal feeling comes —
c. 1862

After great pain, a formal feeling comes —
The Nerves sit ceremonious, like Tombs —
The stiff Heart questions was it He, that bore,
And Yesterday, or Centuries before?

The Feet, mechanical, go round —   5
Of Ground, or Air, or Ought —
A Wooden way
Regardless grown,
A Quartz contentment, like a stone —

This is the Hour of Lead —   10
Remembered, if outlived,
As Freezing persons, recollect the Snow —
First — Chill — then Stupor — then the letting go —

Considerations for Critical Thinking and Writing

1. What is the cause of the speaker's pain?
2. How does the rhythm of the lines create a slow, somber pace?
3. Discuss why "the Hour of Lead" (line 10) could serve as a useful title for this poem.

Connections to Other Selections

1. How might this poem be read as a kind of sequel to "I've seen a Dying Eye" (p. 269)?
2. Write an essay that discusses this poem in relation to Robert Frost's "Home Burial" (p. 300).

I heard a Fly buzz — when I died —
c. 1862

I heard a Fly buzz — when I died —
The Stillness in the Room
Was like the Stillness in the Air —
Between the Heaves of Storm —

The Eyes around — had wrung them dry —   5
And Breaths were gathering firm
For that last Onset — when the King
Be witnessed — in the Room —

I willed my Keepsakes — Signed away
What portion of me be   10
Assignable — and then it was
There interposed a Fly —

With Blue — uncertain stumbling Buzz —
Between the light — and me —
And then the Windows failed — and then
I could not see to see —

15

Considerations for Critical Thinking and Writing

1. What was expected to happen "when the King" was "witnessed"? What happened instead?
2. Why do you think Dickinson chooses a fly rather than perhaps a bee or gnat?
3. What is the effect of the last line? Why not end the poem with "I could not see" instead of the additional "to see"?
4. Discuss the sounds in the poem. Are there any instances of onomatopoeia?

Connections to Other Selections

1. Discuss the final lines of this poem and "I've seen a Dying Eye" (p. 269). Are the themes similar or are there significant differences?
2. Contrast the symbolic significance of the fly with the spider in Walt Whitman's "A Noiseless Patient Spider" (p. 100).
3. Consider the meaning of "light" in this poem and in "There's a certain Slant of light," (p. 573).

It dropped so low — in my Regard —

c. 1863

It dropped so low — in my Regard —
I heard it hit the Ground —
And go to pieces on the Stones
At bottom of my Mind —

Yet blamed the Fate that flung it — *less*
Than I denounced Myself,
For entertaining Plated Wares
Upon My Silver Shelf —

Considerations for Critical Thinking and Writing

1. What does "It" refer to? Is it possible to be specific? What in the first stanza limits the meaning of "It"?
2. Why does the speaker denounce himself or herself?
3. What is the difference between "Plated Wares" and silver? Why is this crucial to an understanding of the poem?

Connections to Other Selections

1. Describe the difference in sensibility between this speaker and the "Gentlewomen" in "What Soft — Cherubic Creatures — " (p. 266).
2. In an essay compare how the mind is presented in this poem with how it is presented in "The Brain — is wider than the Sky — " (p. 269).

Because I could not stop for Death —

Because I could not stop for Death —
He kindly stopped for me —
The Carriage held but just Ourselves —
And Immortality.

We slowly drove — He knew no haste   5
And I had put away
My labor and my leisure too,
For His Civility —

We passed the School, where Children strove
At Recess — in the Ring —   10
We passed the Fields of Gazing Grain —
We passed the Setting Sun —

Or rather — He passed Us —
The Dews drew quivering and chill —
For only Gossamer, my Gown —   15
My Tippet° — only Tulle —   *shawl*

We paused before a House that seemed
A Swelling of the Ground —
The Roof was scarcely visible —
The Cornice — in the Ground —   20

Since then — 'tis Centuries — and yet
Feels shorter than the Day
I first surmised the Horses' Heads
Were toward Eternity —

Considerations for Critical Thinking and Writing

1. Why couldn't the speaker stop for death?
2. How is Death personified in this poem? How does the speaker respond to him? Why are they accompanied by Immortality?
3. What is the significance of the things they "passed" in the third stanza?
4. What is the "House" in lines 17–20?
5. Discuss the rhythm of the lines. How, for example, is the rhythm of line 14 related to its meaning?

Connections to Other Selections

1. Compare the tone of this poem with that of Dickinson's "I heard a Fly buzz — when I died — " (p. 271).
2. Write an essay comparing Dickinson's view of death in this poem and in "If I shouldn't be alive" (p. 254). Which poem is more powerful for you? Explain why.

My Life had stood — a Loaded Gun —

c. 1863

My Life had stood — a Loaded Gun —
In Corners — till a Day
The Owner passed — identified —
And carried Me away —

And now We roam in Sovereign Woods —   5
And now We hunt the Doe —
And every time I speak for Him —
The Mountains straight reply —

And do I smile, such cordial light
Upon the Valley glow —   10
It is as a Vesuvian face°
Had let its pleasure through —

And when at Night — Our good Day done —
I guard My Master's Head —
'Tis better than the Eider-Duck's   15
Deep Pillow — to have shared —

To foe of His — I'm deadly foe —
None stir the second time —
On whom I lay a Yellow Eye —
Or an emphatic Thumb —   20

Though I than He — may longer live
He longer must — than I —
For I have but the power to kill,
Without — the power to die —

11 *Vesuvian face:* A face that could erupt like the volcano Mt. Vesuvius.

Considerations for Critical Thinking and Writing

1. What metaphor does the speaker use to characterize herself? Why is this a surprising but appropriate metaphor?
2. What is the relationship between the speaker and the hunter?
3. To what extent can this poem be regarded as a ballad?

Connections to Other Selections

1. Compare the emotional tension in this poem with that in "Wild Nights — Wild Nights!" (p. 265).
2. Compare the theme here with the theme in "'Heaven' — is what I cannot reach!" (p. 262).

The Bustle in a House

The Bustle in a House
The Morning after Death
Is solemnest of industries
Enacted upon Earth —

The Sweeping up the Heart
And putting Love away
We shall not want to use again
Until Eternity.

Considerations for Critical Thinking and Writing

1. What is the relationship between love and death in this poem?
2. Why do you think mourning (notice the pun in line 2) is described as an industry?
3. Discuss the tone of the ending of the poem. Consider whether you think it is hopeful, sad, resigned, or some other mood.

Connections to Other Selections

1. Compare this poem with "After great pain, a formal feeling comes — " (p. 271). Which poem is, for you, a more powerful treatment of mourning?
2. How does this poem qualify "I like a look of Agony" (p. 263)? Does it contradict the latter poem? Explain why or why not.

Tell all the Truth but tell it slant —

Tell all the Truth but tell it slant —
Success in Circuit lies
Too bright for our infirm Delight
The Truth's superb surprise

As Lightning to the Children eased
With explanation kind
The Truth must dazzle gradually
Or every man be blind —

Considerations for Critical Thinking and Writing

1. Why should truth be told "slant" and circuitously?
2. How does the second stanza explain the first?
3. How is this poem an example of its own theme?

Connections to Other Selections

1. How does the first stanza of "I know that He exists" (p. 270) suggest a similar idea to this poem? Why do you think the last eight lines of the former aren't similar in theme to this poem?

2. Write an essay on Dickinson's attitudes about the purpose and strategies of poetry by considering this poem as well as "The Thought beneath so slight a film —" (p. 255) and "Portraits are to daily faces" (p. 260).

From all the Jails the Boys and Girls

c. 1881

From all the Jails the Boys and Girls
Ecstatically leap —
Beloved only Afternoon
That Prison doesn't keep

They storm the Earth and stun the Air,
A Mob of solid Bliss —
Alas — that Frowns should lie in wait
For such a Foe as this —

Considerations for Critical Thinking and Writing

1. What are the "jails"?
2. Comment on the effectiveness of the description in lines 5 and 6.
3. How might "Frowns" be read symbolically?

Connections to Other Selections

1. Compare the theme of this poem with that of William Blake's "The Garden of Love" (p. 359).
2. In an essay discuss the treatment of childhood in this poem and in Robert Frost's "Out, Out —" (p. 307).

I never saw a Moor —

c. 1865

I never saw a Moor —
I never saw the Sea —
Yet know I how the Heather looks
And what a Billow be.

I never spoke with God
Nor visited in Heaven —
Yet certain am I of the spot
As if the Checks were given —

Considerations for Critical Thinking and Writing

1. How does the first stanza serve as a premise for the second stanza?
2. Comment on the poem's images. Are they effective, in your opinion?

1. In an essay compare this poem with Paul Laurence Dunbar's "Theology" (p. 188). How might each poem be read as a statement of faith? How are the poems different in tone?
2. Compare the themes of this poem and "I know that He exists" (p. 270).

Lightly stepped a yellow star — date unknown

Lightly stepped a yellow star
To its lofty place —
Loosed the moon her silver hat
From her lustral Face —
All of Evening softly lit
As an Astral Hall —
Father, I observed to Heaven,
You are punctual.

Considerations for Critical Thinking and Writing

1. Given the description in lines 1–7, why does the last line of this poem come as a surprise? What sort of sentiment did you expect? How does the speaker disrupt that expectation?
2. Describe the speaker's relationship to the "Father." What tone does the speaker adopt? How does the personification of the star contribute to the tone?

Connections to Other Selections

1. Write an essay comparing the theme and techniques of Dickinson's poem with those of Gerard Manley Hopkins's "God's Grandeur" (p. 144).
2. Discuss the views of God offered by Dickinson in this poem and in "I know that He exists" (p. 270). How does the tone contribute to the ways God is presented in each poem?

Shall I take thee, the Poet said — c. 1868

Shall I take thee, the Poet said
To the propounded word?
Be stationed with the Candidates
Till I have finer tried —

The Poet searched Philology   5
And when about to ring
For the suspended Candidate
There came unsummoned in —

That portion of the Vision
The World applied to fill
Not unto nomination   10
The Cherubim reveal —

Considerations for Critical Thinking and Writing

1. What metaphor is used to describe the poet?
2. What does it mean to search philology?
3. How does the poet wind up getting the right word?

Connection to Another Selection

1. Choose a Dickinson poem that you think is especially rich in its word choice, and discuss how substitutes wouldn't (or would) do for the "propounded word."

Apparently with no surprise   c. 1884

Apparently with no surprise
To any happy Flower
The Frost beheads it at its play —
In accidental power —
The blond Assassin passes on —
The Sun proceeds unmoved
To measure off another Day
For an Approving God.

Considerations for Critical Thinking and Writing

1. Describe the speaker's tone.
2. How is nature presented in this poem?
3. Who is the "blonde Assassin?" Explain this metaphor.
4. What does the final line suggest about the nature of God?

Connections to Other Selections

1. Compare this glimpse of nature with "A Bird came down the Walk — " (p. 136). In an essay discuss the significant differences you see in each poem's treatment of nature.
2. Discuss the theme of this poem along with that of Stephen Crane's "A Man Said to the Universe" (p. 116).

Dickinson's Description of Herself   1862

Mr Higginson,

Your kindness claimed earlier gratitude — but I was ill — and write today, from my pillow.

Thank you for the surgery — it was not so painful as I supposed. I bring you others° — as you ask — though they might not differ —

While my thought is undressed — I can make the distinction, but when I put them in the Gown — they look alike, and numb.

You asked how old I was? I made no verse — but one or two° — until this winter — Sir —

I had a terror — since September — I could tell to none — and so I sing, as the Boy does by the Burying Ground — because I am afraid — You inquire my Books — For Poets — I have Keats — and Mr and Mrs Browning. For Prose — Mr Ruskin — Sir Thomas Browne — and the Revelations. I went to school — but in your manner of the phrase — had no education. When a little Girl, I had a friend, who taught me Immortality — but venturing too near, himself — he never returned — Soon after, my Tutor, died — and for several years, my Lexicon — was my only companion — Then I found one more — but he was not contented I be his scholar — so he left the Land.

You ask of my Companions Hills — Sir — and the Sundown — and a Dog — large as myself, that my Father bought me — They are better than Beings — because they know — but do not tell — and the noise in the Pool, at Noon — excels my Piano. I have a Brother and Sister — My Mother does not care for thought — and Father, too busy with his Briefs — to notice what we do — He buys me many Books — but begs me not to read them — because he fears they joggle the Mind. They are religious — except me — and address an Eclipse, every morning — whom they call their "Father." But I fear my story fatigues you — I would like to learn — Could you tell me how to grow — or is it unconveyed — like Melody — or Witchcraft?

From a letter to Thomas Wentworth Higginson, April 25, 1862

Others: Dickinson had sent poems to Higginson for his opinions and enclosed more with this letter.
one or two: Actually she had written almost 300 poems.

Considerations for Critical Thinking and Writing

1. What impressions does this letter give you of Dickinson?
2. What kinds of thoughts are in the foreground of her thinking?
3. To what extent is the style of her letter writing like her poetry?

THOMAS WENTWORTH HIGGINSON (1823–1911)
On Meeting Dickinson for the First Time 1870

A large county lawyer's house, brown brick, with great trees & a garden — I sent up my card. A parlor dark & cool & stiffish, a few books & engravings & an open piano. . . .

A step like a pattering child's in entry & in glided a little plain woman with two smooth bands of reddish hair & a face a little like Belle Dove's; not plainer — with no good feature — in a very plain & exquisitely clean white pique & a blue net worsted shawl. She came to me with two day lilies which she put in a sort of childlike way into my hand & said "These are my introduction" in a soft frightened breathless childlike voice — & added under her breath Forgive me if I am frightened; I never see strangers & hardly know what I say — but she talked soon & thenceforward continuously — & deferentially — sometimes stopping to ask me to talk instead of her — but readily recommencing . . . thoroughly ingenuous & simple . . . & saying many things which you would have thought foolish & I wise — & some things you wd. hv. liked. I add a few over the page. . . .

"Women talk; men are silent; that is why I dread women.

"My father only reads on Sunday — he reads *lonely* & *rigorous* books."

"If I read a book [and] it makes my whole body so cold no fire ever can warm me I know *that* is poetry. If I feel physically as if the top of my head were taken off, I know *that* is poetry. These are the only way I know it. Is there any other way."

"How do most people live without any thoughts. There are many people in the world (you must have noticed them in the street) How do they live. How do they get strength to put on their clothes in the morning"

"When I lost the use of my Eyes it was a comfort to think there were so few real *books* that I could easily find some one to read me all of them"

"Truth is such a *rare* thing it is delightful to tell it."

"I find ecstasy in living — the mere sense of living is joy enough"

I asked if she never felt want of employment, never going off the place & never seeing any visitor "I never thought of conceiving that I could ever have the slightest approach to such a want in all future time" (& added) "I feel that I have not expressed myself strongly enough."

From a letter for his wife, August 16, 1870

Considerations for Critical Thinking and Writing

1. How old is Dickinson when Higginson meets her? Does this description seem commensurate with her age? Explain why or why not.
2. Choose one of the quotations from Dickinson that Higginson includes and write an essay about what it reveals about her.

MABEL LOOMIS TODD (1856–1932)
The Character *of Amherst*   1881

I must tell you about the *character* of Amherst. It is a lady whom the people call the *Myth*. She is a sister of Mr. Dickinson, & seems to be the climax of all the family oddity. She has not been outside of her own house in fifteen years, except once to see a new church, when she crept out at night, & viewed it by moonlight. No one who calls upon her mother & sister ever see her, but she allows little children once in a great while, & one at a time, to come in, when she gives them cake or candy, or some nicety, for she is very fond of little ones. But more often she lets down the sweetmeat by a string, out of a window, to them. She dresses wholly in white, & her mind is said to be perfectly wonderful. She writes finely, but no one *ever* sees her. Her sister, who was at Mrs. Dickinson's party, invited me to come & sing to her mother sometime. . . . People tell me the *myth* will hear every note — she will be near, but unseen. . . . Isn't that like a book? So interesting.

                                   From a letter to her parents, November 6, 1881

Considerations for Critical Thinking and Writing

1. Todd, who in the 1890s would edit Dickinson's poems and letters, had known her for only two months when she wrote this letter. How does Todd characterize Dickinson?
2. Does this description seem positive or negative to you? Explain your answer.
3. A few of Dickinson's poems, such as "Much Madness is divinest Sense — ," suggest that she was aware of this perception of her. Refer to her poems in discussing Dickinson's response to this perception.

RICHARD WILBUR (b. 1921)
On Dickinson's Sense of Privation   1960

What did Emily Dickinson do, as a poet, with her sense of privation? One thing she quite often did was to pose as the laureate and attorney of the empty-handed, and question God about the economy of His creation. Why, she asked, is a fatherly God so sparing of His presence? Why is there never a sign that prayers are heard? Why does Nature tell us no comforting news of its Maker? Why do some receive a whole loaf, while others must starve on a crumb? Where is the benevolence in shipwreck and earthquake? By asking such questions as these, she turned complaint into critique, and used her own sufferings as experiential evidence about the nature of the deity. The God who emerges from these poems is a God who does not answer, an unrevealed God whom one cannot confidently approach through Nature or through doctrine.

But there was another way in which Emily Dickinson dealt with her sentiment of lack — another emotional strategy which was both more frequent and
more fruitful. I refer to her repeated assertion of the paradox that privation is
more plentiful than plenty; that to renounce is to possess the more; that "The
Banquet of abstemiousness / Defaces that of wine." We all know how the poet
illustrated this ascetic paradox in her behavior — how in her latter years she
chose to live in relative retirement, keeping the world, even in its dearest aspects,
at a physical remove. She would write her friends, telling them how she missed
them, then flee upstairs when they came to see her; afterward, she might send
a note of apology, offering the odd explanation that "We shun because we prize."
Any reader of Dickinson biographies can furnish other examples, dramatic or
homely, of this prizing and shunning, this yearning and renouncing: in my own
mind's eye is a picture of Emily Dickinson watching a gay circus caravan from
the distance of her chamber window.

From "Sumptuous Destination" in *Emily Dickinson: Three Views,*
by Richard Wilbur, Louise Bogan, and Archibald MacLeish

Considerations for Critical Thinking and Writing

1. Which poems by Dickinson reprinted in this anthology suggest that she was "the
   laureate and attorney of the empty-handed"?
2. Which poems suggest that "privation is more plentiful"?
3. Of these two types of poems, which do you prefer? Write an essay that explains
   your preference.

JOHN B. PICKARD (b. 1928)
On "I heard a Fly buzz — when I died — "   1967

Some of her best lyrics on death considered the sensations of the dying
person, the physical experiences as the soul leaves the body. In all these poems
tension is established by contrasting the inertness of the dead person with the
movement of the living and the external growth of nature. "I heard a Fly buzz —
when I died — " contrasts the expectations of death with its realistic occurrence.
The traditional Christian belief that death leads to eternal happiness is undercut
by the appearance of an insignificant, distracting fly. . . .

. . . The opening lines jolt as the buzz of a fly ludicrously interrupts the
awesome approach of death. After this initial shock the poet describes the
atmosphere of the sick room. The moment is tense; the soul is poised, ready to
depart; and the stillness in the room is like the deceptively calm center of a
hurricane. The second stanza considers the dry-eyed and expectant onlookers,
as they crowd closer to view the last dying movements. The scene appears
morbid to modern readers; yet it was common practice in Emily Dickinson's
time to observe the dying. For those with a religious faith, the moment of death
meant that a soul left its body to enter paradise. Thus the dying person's final
actions were carefully scrutinized for an indication of immortality's approach.

Even Emily Dickinson avidly hoped that the last words or gestures before death would ease some of her own doubts about immortality. The final death struggle of soul and body is termed an "Onset," as the king sweeps majestically in with the treasures of paradise. Like disciples giving testimony to the grandeur of God, the onlookers expect to witness this sublime ceremony.

The last two stanzas [see pp. 271–272] bring the climax. . . . The final acts of the dying person are presented with a crisp detachment. In its careful preparation for Death's entrance, the soul rigidly controls the final moments. The pun in "Signed" and "Assignable" ironically illustrates death's supreme power, for only worthless documents, empty phrases, curious mementos, and a corrupting body can be left behind. The irony increases as the soul precisely arranges everything and waits confidently for death. Now the grand moment is at hand, but unfortunately a fly interrupts the ceremony.

Like so much of life's experience the fly comes at the wrong time, as a petty irritant which distracts from the magnificent approach of death. What the dying person fails to realize is that the fly signals death's presence. Its stumbling blue buzz, an apt synesthetic image that conveys the confusion of the dying mind, imitates the pattern of life, where moments of beauty and confidence are juxtaposed with ugliness and uncertainty. The fly comes between the light and the dying person, not just blocking physical sight but obscuring the radiance of immortality as well. The final line captures the desperate intensity of the person's struggle for life. Instead of the calm assurance of the earlier stanzas, the person now fails to recognize death's arrival and fights to prevent subjection. Pathetically the person claims that the windows fail, not his eyesight. "I could not see to see" is the last effort at self-control. In these few seconds the soul says that it could not will its eyes open for a final view. One of the deepest ironies here is the soul's confidence that it still controls the body. Only the reader knows the hopelessness of these attempts and how aptly the fly symbolizes life and death, since its buzz is associated with daily household activities, while its food often consists of carrion. The whole poem satirizes the traditional view of death as a peaceful release from life's pressures and a glorious entrance into immortality. Emily Dickinson sees only disappointment, a buzzing fly, and the terrible attempts of a soul to prolong life.

From *Emily Dickinson: An Introduction and Interpretation*

Considerations for Critical Thinking and Writing

1. According to Pickard what is the symbolic value of the fly? How does this symbol work with the rest of the poem?
2. Does Pickard leave out any significant elements of the poem in his analysis? Explain why or why not.
3. Choose a Dickinson poem and write a detailed analysis that attempts to account for all its major elements.

ROBERT WEISBUCH (b. 1946)
On Dickinson's Use of Analogy   1975

Dickinson is a difficult poet but she becomes incomprehensible only when we neglect to raise the questions necessary for an understanding of any poet. In what ways does this poetry create meaning from language? For what kinds of meaning should we look?

We can begin to answer these questions by considering the kind of obscurity which worried Dickinson herself. "While my thought is undressed — I can make the distinction, but when I put them in the Gown — they look alike, and numb," she complains in [a] letter to Higginson. She fears that the demands of poetic composition — rhyme, meter, all the elements of decorum, and especially, perhaps, the popular idea of poetry as a comment on a particular aspect of life, a footnote to existence — will limit the scope and obscure the outline of an individual thought. But the apparently humble note to Higginson, which takes up the clothing imagery he himself had employed in an advisory article to young writers, may have been written more as a hint toward proper appreciation than as self-criticism. For by the time she wrote the letter in 1862, Dickinson had discovered a poetic method which does not dress but illustrates, thus *is,* the pattern of her thought.

The essence of the method is analogy, and analogy becomes a way of poetic life. As "I dwell in Possibility — " develops, Dickinson reveals, with characteristic wit, that her House of Possibility is a non-house: it is all of phenomenal nature, with "The Gambrels of the Sky" affording "an Everlasting Roof." She concludes by defining more precisely her activity within that "house":

> For Occupation — This —
> The spreading wide my narrow Hands
> To gather Paradise —

Translated into the language of logic, this hand-spreading becomes a method for expanding analogical relations into inclusive visions. Dickinson's typical poem enacts a hypothesis about the world by patterning a parallel, analogical world. This is the linguistic basis for Dickinson's revolt against a mentality unwilling to look deeply into things: to make words mean as much as they can, to take them out of the dull round of cliché, to renew them by realizing their connotative and etymological potential, and to reorbit them in analogical combination. At each stage of this process in Dickinson's best poems, the persona serves to make the word flesh, to register the human consequences of the transformed meanings. Thus the very creator of a poetic world will respond to it, often with Frankenstein-like shock and always with surprise. Dickinson's visionary and confessional strains merge perfectly in the rhetorical grain of such poems.

From Emily Dickinson's Poetry

Considerations for Critical Thinking and Writing

1. According to Weisbuch why is analogy essential to Dickinson's poetry?
2. How does her use of analogy "make words mean as much as they can"?
3. Choose a Dickinson poem and explain how her use of analogy unravels what is otherwise seemingly obscure or incomprehensible.

SANDRA M. GILBERT (b. 1936) AND
SUSAN GUBAR (b. 1944)
On Dickinson's White Dress   1979

Today a dress that the Amherst Historical Society assures us is *the* white dress Dickinson wore — or at least one of her "Uniforms of Snow" — hangs in a drycleaner's plastic bag in the closet of the Dickinson homestead. Perfectly preserved, beautifully flounced and tucked, it is larger than most readers would have expected this self-consciously small poet's dress to be, and thus reminds visiting scholars of the enduring enigma of Dickinson's central metaphor, even while it draws gasps from more practical visitors, who reflect with awe upon the difficulties of maintaining such a costume. But what exactly did the literal and figurative whiteness of this costume represent? What rewards did it offer that would cause an intelligent woman to overlook those practical difficulties? Comparing Dickinson's obsession with whiteness to Melville's, William R. Sherwood suggests that "it reflected in her case the Christian mystery and not a Christian enigma . . . a decision to announce . . . the assumption of a worldly death that paradoxically involved regeneration." This, he adds, her gown — "a typically slant demonstration of truth" — should have revealed "to anyone with the wit to catch on."[1]

We might reasonably wonder, however, if Dickinson herself consciously intended her wardrobe to convey any one message. The range of associations her white poems imply suggests, on the contrary, that for her, as for Melville, white is the ultimate symbol of enigma, paradox, and irony, "not so much a color as the visible absence of color, and at the same time the concrete of all colors." Melville's question [in *Moby-Dick*] might, therefore, also be hers: "is it for these reasons that there is such a dumb blankness, full of meaning, in a wide landscape of snows — a colorless, all-color of atheism from which we shrink?" And his concluding speculation might be hers too, his remark "that the mystical cosmetic which produces every one of [Nature's] hues, the great principle of light, for ever remains white or colorless in itself, and if operating without medium upon matter, would touch all objects . . . with its own blank tinge." For white, in Dickinson's poetry, frequently represents both the energy (the white heat) of Romantic creativity, and the loneliness (the polar cold) of the renuncia-

---

[1] *Circumference and Circumstance: Stages in the Mind and Art of Emily Dickinson* (New York: Columbia UP, 1968) 152, 231.

tion or tribulation Romantic creativity may demand, both the white radiance of eternity — or Revelation — and the white terror of a shroud.

From *The Madwoman in the Attic: The Woman Writer*
and the Nineteenth-Century Literary Imagination

Considerations for Critical Thinking and Writing

1. What meanings do Gilbert and Gubar attribute to Dickinson's white dress?
2. Discuss the meaning of the implicit whiteness in "Safe in their Alabaster Chambers — " (pp. 258–259) and "After great pain, a formal feeling comes — " (p. 271). To what extent do these poems incorporate the meanings of whiteness that Gilbert and Gubar suggest?
3. What other possible reasons can you think of that would account for Dickinson's wearing only white?

KARL KELLER (b. 1933)
Robert Frost on Dickinson   1979

Frost lived in Amherst for quite a number of years — 1917–20, 1923–25, 1926–38, and then intermittently in the late 1940s and throughout the 1950s when he taught regularly at Amherst College. He often recited her poems from memory, and he conversed with students, friends, and townspeople about her poetry; his concern was almost always over her ability to contain/limit an open-ended universe. He felt this was "what Emily Dickinson surely intends," as he put it, "when she contends: 'In insecurity to lie / Is Joy's insuring quality.'"

It appears that Frost had a one-track mind about Emily Dickinson — her doggedness. For him she was an example of the poet "whose 'state,'" as he put it himself, "never gets sidetracked."

> Since she wrote without thought of publication and was not under the necessity of revamping and polishing, it was easy for her to go right to the point and say precisely what she thought and felt. Her technical irregularities give her poems strength as if she were saying, "Look out, Rhyme and Meter, here I come."

Frost apparently liked this willfulness, this unmanageability of the thought by the poetic form, and yet he thought she arrived at it a little too easily and that it was therefore sometimes indistinguishable from carelessness. He felt she had given up the technical struggle too easily. For Frost, to use a general statement of his about poetic rhythm, she was a little too "easy in [her] harness."[1]

Emily Dickinson succeeded, Frost was forced to admit, by flouting poetic systems, by playing freely with the form.

> I try to make good sentences fit the meter. That is important. Good grammar. I don't like to twist the order around in order to fit a form. I try to keep to regular structure and good rhymes. Though I admit that Emily Dickinson, for

---

[1]Robert Francis, *Frost: A Time to Talk* (Amherst, 1972) 53–54.

one, didn't do this always. When she started a poem, it was "Here I come!" and she came plunging through. The meter and rhyme often had to take care of itself.[2]

Though envious of this carefree energy, Frost was also critical of her when she did not achieve regular forms.

> Emily Dickinson didn't study technique. But she should have been more careful. She was more interested in getting the poem down and writing a new one. I feel that she left some to be revised later, and she never revised them. And those two ladies at Amherst printed a lot of her slipshod work which she might not have liked to see printed. She has all kinds of off rhymes. Some that do not rhyme. Her meter does not always go together.[3]

She was therefore substantially different from him; her ability to be conscious of poetic conventions and yet to rise above them surprised him. He generously yielded her his highest admiration for the heresy.

> One of the great things in life is being true within the conventions. I deny in a good poem or a good life that there is compromise. When there is, it is an attempt to so flex the lines that no suspicion can be cast upon what the poet does. Emily Dickinson's poems are examples of this. When the rhyme begins to bother, she says, "Here I come with my truth. Let the rhyme take care of itself." This makes me feel her strength.[4]

For him the large strain of poetry was "a little shifted from the straight-out, a little curved from the straight." Emily Dickinson's poems were, for him, the best examples of this liberty, this flawing. "Can you imagine some people taking that? Can't you imagine some people not accepting that kind of play at all?"[5]

It was this factor of play in Emily Dickinson's poetry that consistently attracted Frost. "Rime reminds you that poetry is play," he said on one occasion, after reciting a Dickinson poem ("The Mountains — grow unnoticed") and calling it "particularly fine," "and that is one of its chief importances. You shouldn't be too sincere to play or you'll be a fraud."[6] Her mischief with poetic form was an indication to him that she was serious about what she was saying and would bend conventions to get it said, and also that she was having a good time trying to say it, but more important than that, that with her poetry (and her ideas) she was *at play*. He appears to have marveled at that in her. "Poetry," Frost used to exclaim to his friends, "is fooling."[7]

From *The Only Kangaroo among the Beauty: Emily Dickinson in America*

Considerations for Critical Thinking and Writing

1. According to Keller, how did Frost respond to Dickinson's "poetic systems" of rhyme and meter?
2. Explain why you agree or disagree with Frost's assessment of Dickinson's poetry being "slipshod."
3. Choose a poem from each poet and demonstrate how both are versions of "play."

[2]Daniel Smythe, *Robert Frost Speaks* (New York, np, 1964) 140.
[3]Smythe, 140.
[4]Reginald Lansing Cook, *The Dimensions of Robert Frost* (New York: Barnes and Noble, 1968) 57–58.
[5]Cook, 99.
[6]Cook, 180.
[7]Cook, 181.

JANE DONAHUE EBERWEIN (b. 1943)
On Making Do with Dickinson   1984

Like any Yankee girl trained from childhood in habits of thrift, Dickinson instinctively conserved her resources rather than trying to extend them, and she applied to sisterhood the same practical prudence with which she learned to "Use it up, wear it out, / Make it do, or do without." In a family whose prosperous and socially prominent mother devoted herself to mending her student son's shirts, Emily Dickinson cultivated a pride in thrift which would have extraordinary influence on the poetry she wrote and the attitude she took toward herself as a writer. She would be resourceful, careful, shrewd. She would make do with what she had or do without whatever she lacked.

This Yankee parsimony distances Dickinson from many modern admirers who wish she had been a more assertive woman and a more conscious representative of her sex. We who live in a twentieth-century middle-class economy of abundance unconsciously apply our own fiscal metaphors to social and artistic issues, and we raise questions about Dickinson's strategies in accordance with cultural assumptions which she never shared. For us, who imagined until recently that the world's resources might be infinite, it makes no sense to make do with little or do without; those who find themselves deprived should demand more. Improvement, for us, tends to be associated with expansion. Success is measured in terms of profit and celebrity. Responsibility involves identification with other people, especially those who share similar deprivations, and it requires social solidarity for the common good. Given such assumptions it is no wonder that we find Emily Dickinson so mysterious, even at times so alienating. That she, the greatest woman poet in nineteenth-century America and quite possibly the most brilliant female artist this country has yet produced, should never have earned money for her poems, never have seen her name in print except for winning a baking prize, never exerted her influence to assist her artistically deprived sisters seems to us a waste of ability. Assuming that she wanted the opportunities modern women have learned to demand, we tend to think of Emily Dickinson as a victim of cultural limitations, especially of those restrictions her society placed on gently-bred young women. We regard her as a silent and generally ineffective rebel against social conventions, writing secretly like some Soviet dissident with no assurance of ever reaching an audience. We take it for granted that she needed to break out of the limitations her culture placed around her and that she, and we, would have benefited from greater freedom.

From "Doing Without: Dickinson as Yankee Woman Poet"
in *Critical Essays on Emily Dickinson,* ed. Paul J. Ferlazzo

Considerations for Critical Thinking and Writing

1. How do you think Dickinson's "pride in thrift" is related to her style?
2. According to Eberwein, why do some readers find Dickinson "alienating"? Explain why you agree or disagree.

3. In an essay consider whether or not Dickinson's poetry "would have benefited from [her having] greater freedom."

CYNTHIA GRIFFIN WOLFF (b. 1935)
On the Many Voices in Dickinson's Poetry   1986

There were many "Voices." This fact has sometimes puzzled Dickinson's readers. One poem may be delivered in a child's Voice; another in the Voice of a young woman scrutinizing nature and the society in which she makes her place. Sometimes the Voice is that of a woman self-confidently addressing her lover in a language of passion and sexual desire. At still other times, the Voice of the verse seems so precariously balanced at the edge of hysteria that even its calmest observations grate like the shriek of dementia. There is the Voice of the housewife and the Voice that has recourse to the occasionally agonizing, occasionally regal language of the conversion experience of latter-day New England Puritanism. In some poems the Voice is distinctive principally because it speaks in the aftermath of wounding and can comprehend extremities of pain. Moreover, these Voices are not always entirely distinct from one another: the child's Voice that opens a poem may yield to the Voice of a young woman speaking the idiom of ardent love; in a different poem, the speaker may fall into a mood of almost religious contemplation in an attempt to analyze or define such abstract entities as loneliness or madness or eternity; the diction of the housewife may be conflated with the sovereign language of the New Jerusalem, and taken together, they may render some aspect of the wordsmith's labor. No manageable set of discrete categories suffices to capture the diversity of discourse, and any attempt to simplify Dickinson's methods does violence to the verse.

Yet there is a paradox here. This is, by no stretch of the imagination, a body of poetry that might be construed as a series of lyrics spoken by many different people. Disparate as these many Voices are, somehow they all appear to issue from the same "self." . . . It is the enigmatic "Emily Dickinson" readers suppose themselves to have found in this poetry, even in the extreme case when Dickinson's supposed speaker is male. One explanation for this sense of intrinsic unity in the midst of diversity is the persistence with which Dickinson addresses the same set of problems, using a remarkably durable repertoire of linguistic modes. Evocations of injury and wounding — threats to the coherence of the self — appear in the earliest poems and continue until the end; ways of rendering face-to-face encounters change, but this preoccupation with "interview" is sustained by metaphors of "confrontation" that weave throughout. The summoning of one or another Voice in a given poem, then, is not an unselfconscious emotive reflection of Emily Dickinson's mood at the moment of creation. Rather, each different Voice is a calculated tactic, an attempt to touch her readers and engage them intimately with the poetry. Each Voice had its unique advantages; each its limitations. A poet self-conscious in her craft, she calculated this element as carefully as every other.

From *Emily Dickinson*

Considerations for Critical Thinking and Writing

1. Try adding to the list of voices Wolff cites from the poems in this anthology.
2. Despite the many voices in Dickinson's poetry, why, according to Wolff, is there still a "sense of intrinsic unity" in her poetry?
3. Choose a Dickinson poem and describe how the choice of voice is a "calculated tactic."

TWO COMPLEMENTARY CRITICAL READINGS

CHARLES R. ANDERSON (b. 1902)
Eroticism in "Wild Nights — Wild Nights!"   1960

The frank eroticism of this poem might puzzle the biographer of a spinster, but the critic can only be concerned with its effectiveness as a poem. Unless one insists on taking the "I" to mean Emily Dickinson, there is not even any reversal of the lovers' roles (which has been charged, curiously enough, as a fault in this poem). The opening declaration — "Wild Nights should be / Our Luxury!" — sets the key of her song, for *luxuria* included the meaning of lust as well as lavishness of sensuous enjoyment, as she was Latinist enough to know. This is echoed at the end in "Eden," her recurring image, in letters and poems, for the paradise of earthly love. The theme here is that of sexual passion which is lawless, outside the rule of "Chart" and "Compass." But it lives by a law of its own, the law of Eden, which protects it from mundane wind and wave.

This is what gives the magic to her climactic vision, "Rowing in Eden," sheltered luxuriously in those paradisiac waters while the wild storms of this world break about them. Such love was only possible before the Fall. Since then the bower of bliss is frugal of her leases, limiting each occupant to "an instant" she says in another poem, for "Adam taught her Thrift / Bankrupt once through his excesses." In the present poem she limits her yearning to the mortal term, just "Tonight." But this echoes the surge of ecstasy that initiated her song and gives the reiterated "Wild Nights!" a double reference, to the passionate experience in Eden as well as to the tumult of the world shut out by it. So she avoids the chief pitfall of the love lyric, the tendency to exploit emotion for its own sake. Instead she generates out of the conflicting aspects of love, its ecstasy and its brevity, the symbol that contains the poem's meaning.

From Emily Dickinson's Poetry: Stairway of Surprise

Considerations for Critical Thinking and Writing

1. According to Anderson what is the theme of "Wild Nights — Wild Nights!"?
2. How does Anderson discuss the "frank eroticism" of the poem? How detailed is his discussion?
3. If there is a "reversal of the lovers' roles" in this poem, do you think it represents, as some critics have charged, "a fault in this poem"? Explain why or why not.

4. Compare Anderson's treatment of this poem with David S. Reynolds's reading below. Discuss which one you find more useful, and explain why.

DAVID S. REYNOLDS (b. 1949)
Popular Literature and "Wild Nights — Wild Nights!"   1988

It is not known whether Dickinson had read any of the erotic literature of the day or if she knew of the stereotype of the sensual woman. Given her fascination with sensational journalism and with popular literature in general, it is hard to believe she would not have had at least some exposure to erotic literature. At any rate, her treatment of the daring theme of woman's sexual fantasy in this deservedly famous poem bears comparison with erotic themes as they appeared in popular sensational writings. The first stanza of the poem provides an uplifting or purification of sexual fantasy not distant from the effect of Whitman's cleansing rhetoric, which, as we have seen, was consciously designed to counteract the prurience of the popular "love plot." Dickinson's repeated phrase "Wild Nights" is a simple but dazzling metaphor that communicates wild passion — even lust — but simultaneously lifts sexual desire out of the scabrous by fusing it with the natural image of the night. The second verse introduces a second nature image, the turbulent sea and the contrasting quiet port, which at once universalizes the passion and purifies it further by distancing it through a more abstract metaphor. Also, the second verse makes clear that this is not a poem of sexual consummation but rather of pure fantasy and sexual impossibility. Unlike popular erotic literature, the poem portrays neither a consummated seduction nor the heartless deception that it involves. There is instead a pure, fervent fantasy whose frustration is figured forth in the contrasting images of the ocean (the longed-for-but-never-achieved consummation) and the port (the reality of the poet's isolation). The third verse begins with an image, "Rowing in Eden," that further uplifts sexual passion by yoking it with a religious archetype. Here as elsewhere, Dickinson capitalizes nicely on the new religious style, which made possible such fusions of the divine and the earthly. The persona's concluding wish to "moor" in the sea expresses the sustained intense sexual longing and the simultaneous frustration of that longing. In the course of the poem, Dickinson has communicated great erotic passion, and yet, by effectively projecting this passion through unusual nature and religious images, has rid it of even the tiniest residue of sensationalism.

From *Beneath the American Renaissance:*
The Subversive Imagination in the Age of Emerson and Melville

Considerations for Critical Thinking and Writing

1. According to Reynolds, how do Dickinson's images provide a "cleansing" effect in the poem?
2. Explain whether you agree that the poem portrays a "pure, fervent fantasy" or something else.

3. Does Reynolds's reading of the poem compete with Anderson's, or complement it? Explain your answer.
4. Given the types of critical strategies described in Chapter 14, how would you characterize Anderson's and Reynolds's approaches?

ROBERT FROST (1874–1963)

Few poets have enjoyed the popular success that Robert Frost achieved during his lifetime, and no twentieth-century American poet has had his or her work as widely read and honored. Frost is as much associated with New England as the stone walls that help define its landscape; his reputation, however, transcends regional boundaries. Although he was named poet laureate of Vermont only two years before his death, he was for many years the nation's unofficial poet laureate. Frost collected honors the way some people pick up burrs on country walks. Among his awards were four Pulitzer Prizes, the Bollingen Prize, a Congressional Medal, and dozens of honorary degrees. Perhaps his most moving appearance was his recitation of "The Gift Outright" for millions of Americans at the inauguration of John F. Kennedy in 1961.

Frost's recognition as a poet is especially remarkable because his career as a writer did not attract any significant attention until he was nearly forty years old. He taught himself to write while he labored at odd jobs, taught school, or farmed.

Frost's early identity seems very remote from the New England soil. Although his parents were descended from generations of New Englanders, he was born in San Francisco and was named Robert Lee Frost after the Confederate general. After his father died in 1885, his mother moved the family back to Massachusetts to live with relatives. Frost graduated from high school sharing valedictorian honors with the classmate who would become his wife three years later. Between high school and marriage, he attended Dartmouth College for a few months and then taught. His teaching prompted him to enroll in Harvard in 1897, but after less than two years he withdrew without a degree (though Harvard would eventually award him an honorary doctorate in 1937, four years after Dartmouth conferred its honorary degree upon him). For the next decade, Frost read and wrote poems when he was not chicken farming or teaching. In 1912, he sold his farm and moved his family to England, where he hoped to find the audience that his poetry did not have in America.

Three years in England made it possible for Frost to return home as a poet. His first two volumes of poetry, *A Boy's Will* (1913) and *North of Boston* (1914), were published in England. During the next twenty years, honors and awards were conferred on collections such as *Mountain Interval* (1916),

New Hampshire (1923), *West-Running Brook* (1928), and *A Further Range* (1936). These are the volumes on which most of Frost's popular and critical reputation rests. Later collections include *A Witness Tree* (1942), *A Masque of Reason* (1945), *Steeple Bush* (1947), *A Masque of Mercy* (1947), *Complete Poems* (1949), and *In the Clearing* (1962). In addition to publishing his works, Frost endeared himself to audiences throughout the country by presenting his poetry almost as conversations. He also taught at a number of schools, including Amherst College, the University of Michigan, Harvard University, Dartmouth College, and Middlebury College.

Frost's countless poetry readings generated wide audiences eager to claim him as their poet. The image he cultivated resembled closely what the public likes to think a poet should be. Frost was seen as a lovable, wise old man; his simple wisdom and cracker-barrel sayings appeared comforting and homey. From this Yankee rustic, audiences learned that "There's a lot yet that isn't understood" or "We love the things we love for what they are" or "Good fences make good neighbors."

In a sense, Frost packaged himself for public consumption. "I am . . . my own salesman," he said. When asked direct questions about the meanings of his poems, he often winked or scratched his head to give the impression that the customer was always right. To be sure, there is a simplicity in Frost's language, but that simplicity does not fully reflect the depth of the man, the complexity of his themes, or the richness of his art.

The folksy optimist behind the public lectern did not reveal his private troubles to his audiences, although he did address those problems at his writing desk. Frost suffered from professional jealousies, anger, and depression. His family life was especially painful. Three of his four children died: a son at the age of four, a daughter in her late twenties from tuberculosis, and another son who was a suicide. His marriage was filled with tension. Although Frost's work is landscaped with sunlight, snow, birches, birds, blueberries, and squirrels, it is important to recognize that he was also intimately "acquainted with the night," a phrase that serves as the haunting title of one of his poems (see p. 109).

As a corrective to Frost's popular reputation, one critic, Lionel Trilling, described the world Frost creates in his poems as a "terrifying universe," characterized by loneliness, anguish, frustration, doubts, disappointment, and despair (see p. 320 for an excerpt from this essay). To point this out is not to annihilate the pleasantness and even good-natured cheerfulness that can be enjoyed in Frost's poetry, but it is to say that Frost is not so one-dimensional as he is sometimes assumed to be. Frost's poetry requires readers who are alert and willing to penetrate the simplicity of its language to see the elusive and ambiguous meanings that lie below the surface.

Frost's treatment of nature helps to explain the various levels of meaning in his poetry. The familiar natural world his poems evoke is sharply detailed. We hear icy branches clicking against themselves, we see the snow-white trunks of birches, we feel the smarting pain of a twig lashing across a face. The aspects of the natural world Frost describes are designed to give pleasure, but they are also frequently calculated to provoke thought. His use of nature tends to be symbolic. Complex meanings are derived from simple facts, such as a spider killing a moth or a tiny mite on a sheet of paper (see "Design," p. 311, and "A Considerable Speck," p. 313). Although Frost's strategy is to talk about particular events and individual experiences, his poems evoke universal issues.

Frost's poetry has strong regional roots and is "versed in country things," but it flourishes in any receptive imagination because, in the final analysis, it is concerned with human beings. Frost's New England landscapes are the occasion rather than the ultimate focus of his poems. Like the rural voices he creates in his poems, Frost typically approaches his themes indirectly. He explained the reason for this in a talk titled "Education by Poetry."

> Poetry provides the one permissible way of saying one thing and meaning another. People say, "why don't you say what you mean?" We never do that, do we, being all of us too much poets. We like to talk in parables and in hints and in indirections — whether from diffidence or some other instinct.

The result is that the settings, characters, and situations that make up the subject matter of Frost's poems are vehicles for his perceptions about life.

In "Stopping by Woods on a Snowy Evening" (p. 308), for example, Frost uses the kind of familiar New England details that constitute his poetry for more than descriptive purposes. He shapes them into a meditation on the tension we sometimes feel between life's responsibilities and the "lovely, dark, and deep" attraction that death offers. When the speaker's horse "gives his harness bells a shake," we are reminded that we are confronting a universal theme as well as a quiet moment of natural beauty.

Among the major concerns that appear in Frost's poetry are the fragility of life, the consequences of rejecting or accepting the conditions of one's life, the passion of inconsolable grief, the difficulty of sustaining intimacy, the fear of loneliness and isolation, the inevitability of change, the tensions between the individual and society, and the place of tradition and custom.

Whatever theme is encountered in a poem by Frost, a reader is likely to agree with him that "the initial delight is in the surprise of remembering something I didn't know." To achieve that fresh sense of discovery, Frost allowed himself to follow his instincts; his poetry

> inclines to the impulse, it assumes direction with the first line laid down, it runs a course of lucky events, and ends in a clarification of life — not necessarily a great clarification, such as sects and cults are founded on, but in a momentary stay against confusion.

This description from "The Figure a Poem Makes" (see p. 317 for the complete essay), Frost's brief introduction to *Complete Poems,* may sound as if his poetry is formless and merely "lucky," but his poems tend to be more conventional than experimental: "The artist in me," as he put the matter in one of his poems, "cries out for design."

From Frost's perspective, "free verse is like playing tennis with the net down." He exercised his own freedom in meeting the challenges of rhyme and meter. His use of fixed forms such as couplets, tercets, quatrains, blank verse, and sonnets was not slavish, because he enjoyed working them into the natural English speech patterns — especially the rhythms, idioms, and tones of speakers living north of Boston — that give voice to his themes. Frost often liked to use "Stopping by Woods on a Snowy Evening" as an example of his graceful way of making conventions appear natural and inevitable. He explored "the old ways to be new."

Frost's eye for strong, telling details was matched by his ear for natural speech rhythms. His flexible use of what he called "iambic and loose iambic" enabled him to create moving lyric poems that reveal the personal thoughts of a speaker and dramatic poems that convincingly characterize people caught in intense emotional situations. The language in his poems appears to be little more than a transcription of casual and even rambling speech, but it is in actuality Frost's poetic creation, carefully crafted to reveal the joys and sorrows that are woven into people's daily lives. What is missing from Frost's poems is artificiality, not art. Consider this poem.

The Road Not Taken   1916

Two roads diverged in a yellow wood,
And sorry I could not travel both
And be one traveler, long I stood
And looked down one as far as I could
To where it bent in the undergrowth;   5

Then took the other, as just as fair,
And having perhaps the better claim,
Because it was grassy and wanted wear;
Though as for that the passing there
Had worn them really about the same,   10

And both that morning equally lay
In leaves no step had trodden black.
Oh, I kept the first for another day!
Yet knowing how way leads on to way,
I doubted if I should ever come back.   15

I shall be telling this with a sigh
Somewhere ages and ages hence:

Two roads diverged in a wood, and I—
I took the one less traveled by,
And that has made all the difference.   20

This poem intrigues readers because it is at once so simple and so deeply resonant. Recalling a walk in the woods, the speaker describes how he came upon a fork in the road, which forced him to choose one path over another. Though "sorry" that he "could not travel both," he made a choice after carefully weighing his two options. This, essentially, is what happens in the poem; there is no other action. However, the incident is charged with symbolic significance by the speaker's reflections on the necessity and consequences of his decision.

The final stanza indicates that the choice concerns more than simply walking down a road, for the speaker says that his chosen path has affected his entire life—"that [it] has made all the difference." Frost draws on a familiar enough metaphor when he compares life to a journey, but he is also calling attention to a less commonly noted problem: despite our expectations, aspirations, appetites, hopes, and desires, we can't have it all. Making one choice precludes another. It is impossible to determine what particular decision the speaker refers to: perhaps he had to choose a college, a career, a spouse; perhaps he was confronted with mutually exclusive ideas, beliefs, or values. There is no way to know, because Frost wisely creates a symbolic choice and implicitly invites us to supply our own circumstances.

The speaker's reflections about his choice are as central to an understanding of the poem as the choice itself; indeed, they may be more central. He describes the road taken as "having perhaps the better claim, / Because it was grassy and wanted wear"; he prefers the "less traveled" path. This seems to be an expression of individualism, which would account for "the difference" his choice made in his life. But Frost complicates matters by having the speaker also acknowledge that there was no significant difference between the two roads: one was "just as fair" as the other; each was "worn . . . really about the same"; and "both that morning equally lay / In leaves no step had trodden black."

The speaker imagines that in the future, "ages and ages hence," he will recount his choice with "a sigh" that will satisfactorily explain the course of his life, but Frost seems to be having a little fun here by showing us how the speaker will embellish his past decision to make it appear more dramatic. What we hear is someone trying to convince himself that the choice he made significantly changed his life. When he recalls what happened in the "yellow wood," a color that gives a glow to that irretrievable moment when his life seemed to be on verge of a momentous change, he appears more concerned with the path he did not choose than with the one he took. Frost shrewdly titles the poem to suggest the speaker's sense of loss at not being able to "travel both" roads. When the speaker's reflections about his choice are examined, the poem reveals his nostalgia instead of affirming his decision to travel a self-reliant path in life.

The rhymed stanzas of "The Road Not Taken" follow a pattern established in the first five lines *(abaab)*. This rhyme scheme reflects, perhaps, the speaker's efforts to shape his life into a pleasing and coherent form. The natural speech rhythms Frost uses allow him to integrate the rhymes unobtrusively, but there is a slight shift in lines 19–20, when the speaker asserts self-consciously that the "less traveled" road — which we already know to be basically the same as the other road — "made all the difference." Unlike all the other rhymes in the poem, "difference" does not rhyme precisely with "hence." The emphasis that must be placed on "differ*ence*" to make it rhyme perfectly with "hence" may suggest that the speaker is trying just a little too hard to pattern his life on his earlier choice in the woods.

Perhaps the best way to begin reading Frost's poetry is to accept the invitation he placed at the beginning of many volumes of his poems. "The Pasture" means what it says of course; it is about taking care of some farm chores, but it is also a means of "saying one thing in terms of another."

The Pasture   1913

I'm going out to clean the pasture spring;
I'll only stop to rake the leaves away
(And wait to watch the water clear, I may):
I shan't be gone long. — You come too.

I'm going out to fetch the little calf
That's standing by the mother. It's so young
It totters when she licks it with her tongue.
I shan't be gone long. — You come too.

"The Pasture" is a simple but irresistible songlike invitation to the pleasure of looking at the world through the eyes of a poet.

Chronology

1874   Born on March 26 in San Francisco, California.

1885   Father dies and family moves to Lawrence, Massachusetts.

1892   Graduates from Lawrence High School.

1893–94 Studies at Dartmouth College.

1895   Marries his high school sweetheart, Elinor White.

1897–99 Studies at Harvard College.

1900	Moves to a farm in West Derry, New Hampshire.
1912	Moves to England where he farms and writes.
1913	*A Boy's Will* is published in London.
1914	*North of Boston* is published in London.
1915	Moves to a farm near Franconia, New Hampshire.
1916	Elected to National Institute of Letters.
1917–20	Teaches at Amherst College.
1919	Moves to South Shaftsbury, Vermont.
1921–23	Teaches at University of Michigan.
1923	*Selected Poems* and *New Hampshire* are published; the latter is awarded a Pulitzer Prize.
1928	*West-Running Brook* is published.
1930	*Collected Poems* is published.
1936	*A Further Range* is published; teaches at Harvard.
1938	Wife dies.
1939–42	Teaches at Harvard.
1942	*A Witness Tree* is published, which is awarded a Pulitzer Prize.
1943–49	Teaches at Dartmouth.
1945	*A Masque of Reason* is published.
1947	*Steeple Bush* and *A Masque of Mercy* are published.
1949	*Complete Poems* (enlarged) is published.
1961	Reads "The Gift Outright" at President John F. Kennedy's inauguration.
1963	Dies on January 29 in Boston.

Mending Wall   1914

Something there is that doesn't love a wall,
That sends the frozen-ground-swell under it,
And spills the upper boulders in the sun;
And makes gaps even two can pass abreast.
The work of hunters is another thing: 5
I have come after them and made repair

Where they have left not one stone on a stone,
But they would have the rabbit out of hiding,
To please the yelping dogs. The gaps I mean,
No one has seen them made or heard them made,   10
But at spring mending-time we find them there.
I let my neighbor know beyond the hill;
And on a day we meet to walk the line
And set the wall between us once again.
We keep the wall between us as we go.   15
To each the boulders that have fallen to each.
And some are loaves and some so nearly balls
We have to use a spell to make them balance:
"Stay where you are until our backs are turned!"
We wear our fingers rough with handling them.   20
Oh, just another kind of outdoor game,
One on a side. It comes to little more:
There where it is we do not need the wall:
He is all pine and I am apple orchard.
My apple trees will never get across   25
And eat the cones under his pines, I tell him.
He only says, "Good fences make good neighbors."
Spring is the mischief in me, and I wonder
If I could put a notion in his head:
"*Why* do they make good neighbors? Isn't it   30
Where there are cows? But here there are no cows.
Before I built a wall I'd ask to know
What I was walling in or walling out,
And to whom I was like to give offense.
Something there is that doesn't love a wall,   35
That wants it down." I could say "Elves" to him,
But it's not elves exactly, and I'd rather
He said it for himself. I see him there
Bringing a stone grasped firmly by the top
In each hand, like an old-stone savage armed.   40
He moves in darkness as it seems to me,
Not of woods only and the shade of trees.
He will not go behind his father's saying,
And he likes having thought of it so well
He says again, "Good fences make good neighbors."   45

Considerations for Critical Thinking and Writing

1. How do the speaker and his neighbor in this poem differ in sensibilities? What is
   suggested about the neighbor in lines 41–42?
2. What might the "Something" be that "doesn't love a wall"? Why does the speaker
   remind his neighbor each spring that the wall needs to be repaired? Is it ironic
   that the *speaker* initiates the mending? Is there anything good about the wall?
3. The neighbor likes the saying "Good fences make good neighbors" so well that
   he repeats it. Does the speaker also say something twice? What else suggests that
   the speaker's attitude toward the wall is not necessarily Frost's?

4. Although the speaker's language is colloquial, what is poetic about the sounds and rhythms he uses?
5. This poem was first published in 1914; Frost read it to an audience when he visited Russia in 1962. What do these facts suggest about the symbolic value of "Mending Wall"?

Connections to Other Selections

1. How is the speaker's perspective on tradition and custom in this poem similar to that in Robert Frost's "Mending Wall" (p. 298)?
2. The final line of this poem is startling. Why? How is it similar in its strategy to James Merrill's "Casual Wear" (p. 123)?
3. Compare the view of change in this poem with that in Amy Clampitt's "Nothing Stays Put" (p. 477).

Home Burial   1914

He saw her from the bottom of the stairs
Before she saw him. She was starting down,
Looking back over her shoulder at some fear.
She took a doubtful step and then undid it
To raise herself and look again. He spoke   5
Advancing toward her: "What is it you see
From up there always — for I want to know."
She turned and sank upon her skirts at that,
And her face changed from terrified to dull.
He said to gain time: "What is it you see,"   10
Mounting until she cowered under him.
"I will find out now — you must tell me, dear."
She, in her place, refused him any help
With the least stiffening of her neck and silence.
She let him look, sure that he wouldn't see,   15
Blind creature; and awhile he didn't see.
But at last he murmured, "Oh," and again, "Oh."

"What is it — what?" she said.

                    "Just that I see."

"You don't," she challenged. "Tell me what it is."   20

"The wonder is I didn't see at once.
I never noticed it from here before.
I must be wonted to it — that's the reason.
The little graveyard where my people are!
So small the window frames the whole of it.   25
Not so much larger than a bedroom, is it?
There are three stones of slate and one of marble,
Broad-shouldered little slabs there in the sunlight
On the sidehill. We haven't to mind *those*.

But I understand: it is not the stones,   30
But the child's mound —"

       "Don't, don't, don't, don't," she cried.

She withdrew, shrinking from beneath his arm
That rested on the banister, and slid downstairs;
And turned on him with such a daunting look,   35
He said twice over before he knew himself:
"Can't a man speak of his own child he's lost?"

"Not you! — Oh, where's my hat? Oh, I don't need it!
I must get out of here. I must get air.
I don't know rightly whether any man can."   40

"Amy! Don't go to someone else this time.
Listen to me. I won't come down the stairs."
He sat and fixed his chin between his fists.
"There's something I should like to ask you, dear."

"You don't know how to ask it."   45

       "Help me, then."
Her fingers moved the latch for all reply.

"My words are nearly always an offense.
I don't know how to speak of anything
So as to please you. But I might be taught,   50
I should suppose. I can't say I see how.
A man must partly give up being a man
With women-folk. We could have some arrangement
By which I'd bind myself to keep hands off
Anything special you're a-mind to name.   55
Though I don't like such things 'twixt those that love.
Two that don't love can't live together without them.
But two that do can't live together with them."
She moved the latch a little. "Don't — don't go.
Don't carry it to someone else this time.   60
Tell me about it if it's something human.
Let me into your grief. I'm not so much
Unlike other folks as your standing there
Apart would make me out. Give me my chance.
I do think, though, you overdo it a little.   65
What was it brought you up to think it the thing
To take your mother-loss of a first child
So inconsolably — in the face of love.
You'd think his memory might be satisfied —"

"There you go sneering now!"   70

       "I'm not, I'm not!
You make me angry. I'll come down to you.
God, what a woman! And it's come to this,
A man can't speak of his own child that's dead."

"You can't because you don't know how to speak.   75
If you had any feelings, you that dug
With your own hand — how could you? — his little grave;
I saw you from that very window there,
Making the gravel leap and leap in air,
Leap up, like that, like that, and land so lightly   80
And roll back down the mound beside the hole.
I thought, Who is that man? I didn't know you.
And I crept down the stairs and up the stairs
To look again, and still your spade kept lifting.
Then you came in. I heard your rumbling voice   85
Out in the kitchen, and I don't know why,
But I went near to see with my own eyes.
You could sit there with the stains on your shoes
Of the fresh earth from your own baby's grave
And talk about your everyday concerns.   90
You had stood the spade up against the wall
Outside there in the entry, for I saw it."

"I shall laugh the worst laugh I ever laughed.
I'm cursed. God, if I don't believe I'm cursed."

"I can repeat the very words you were saying.   95
'Three foggy mornings and one rainy day
Will rot the best birch fence a man can build.'
Think of it, talk like that at such a time!
What had how long it takes a birch to rot
To do with what was in the darkened parlor.   100
You *couldn't* care! The nearest friends can go
With anyone to death, comes so far short
They might as well not try to go at all.
No, from the time when one is sick to death,
One is alone, and he dies more alone.   105
Friends make pretense of following to the grave.
But before one is in it, their minds are turned
And making the best of their way back to life
And living people, and things they understand.
But the world's evil. I won't have grief so   110
If I can change it. Oh, I won't, I won't!"

"There, you have said it all and you feel better.
You won't go now. You're crying. Close the door.
The heart's gone out of it: why keep it up.
Amy! There's someone coming down the road!"   115

"*You* — oh, you think the talk is all. I must go —
Somewhere out of this house. How can I make you — "

"If — you — do!" She was opening the door wider.
"Where do you mean to go? First tell me that.
I'll follow and bring you back by force. I *will!* — "   120

Considerations for Critical Thinking and Writing

1. How has the burial of the child within sight of the stairway window affected the relationship of the couple in this poem? Is the child's grave a symptom or a cause of the conflict between them?
2. Is the husband insensitive and indifferent to his wife's grief? Characterize the wife. Has Frost invited us to sympathize with one character more than with the other?
3. What is the effect of splitting the iambic pentameter pattern in lines 18–19, 31–32, 45–46, and 70–71?
4. Is the conflict resolved at the conclusion of the poem? Do you think the husband and wife will overcome their differences?

After Apple-Picking   1914

My long two-pointed ladder's sticking through a tree
Toward heaven still,
And there's a barrel that I didn't fill
Beside it, and there may be two or three
Apples I didn't pick upon some bough.   5
But I am done with apple-picking now.
Essence of winter sleep is on the night,
The scent of apples: I am drowsing off.
I cannot rub the strangeness from my sight
I got from looking through a pane of glass   10
I skimmed this morning from the drinking trough
And held against the world of hoary grass.
It melted, and I let it fall and break.
But I was well
Upon my way to sleep before it fell,   15
And I could tell
What form my dreaming was about to take.
Magnified apples appear and disappear,
Stem end and blossom end,
And every fleck of russet showing clear.   20
My instep arch not only keeps the ache,
It keeps the pressure of a ladder-round.
I feel the ladder sway as the boughs bend.
And I keep hearing from the cellar bin
The rumbling sound   25
Of load on load of apples coming in.
For I have had too much
Of apple-picking: I am overtired
Of the great harvest I myself desired.
There were ten thousand thousand fruit to touch,   30
Cherish in hand, lift down, and not let fall.
For all
That struck the earth,

No matter if not bruised or spiked with stubble,
Went surely to the cider-apple heap   35
As of no worth.
One can see what will trouble
This sleep of mine, whatever sleep it is.
Were he not gone,
The woodchuck could say whether it's like his   40
Long sleep, as I describe its coming on,
Or just some human sleep.

Considerations for Critical Thinking and Writing

1. How does this poem illustrate Frost's view that "Poetry provides the one permissible way of saying one thing and meaning another"? When do you first sense that the detailed description of apple picking is being used that way?
2. What comes after apple picking? What does the speaker worry about in the dream beginning in line 18?
3. Why do you suppose Frost uses apples rather than, say, pears or squash?

Birches   1916

When I see birches bend to left and right
Across the lines of straighter darker trees,
I like to think some boy's been swinging them.
But swinging doesn't bend them down to stay
As ice-storms do. Often you must have seen them   5
Loaded with ice a sunny winter morning
After a rain. They click upon themselves
As the breeze rises, and turn many-colored
As the stir cracks and crazes their enamel.
Soon the sun's warmth makes them shed crystal shells   10
Shattering and avalanching on the snow-crust —
Such heaps of broken glass to sweep away
You'd think the inner dome of heaven had fallen.
They are dragged to the withered bracken by the load,
And they seem not to break; though once they are bowed   15
So low for long, they never right themselves:
You may see their trunks arching in the woods
Years afterwards, trailing their leaves on the ground
Like girls on hands and knees that throw their hair
Before them over their heads to dry in the sun.   20
But I was going to say when Truth broke in
With all her matter-of-fact about the ice-storm,
I should prefer to have some boy bend them
As he went out and in to fetch the cows —
Some boy too far from town to learn baseball,   25
Whose only play was what he found himself,

Summer or winter, and could play alone.
One by one he subdued his father's trees
By riding them down over and over again
Until he took the stiffness out of them,   30
And not one but hung limp, not one was left
For him to conquer. He learned all there was
To learn about not launching out too soon
And so not carrying the tree away
Clear to the ground. He always kept his poise   35
To the top branches, climbing carefully
With the same pains you use to fill a cup
Up to the brim, and even above the brim.
Then he flung outward, feet first, with a swish,
Kicking his way down through the air to the ground.   40
So was I once myself a swinger of birches.
And so I dream of going back to be.
It's when I'm weary of considerations,
And life is too much like a pathless wood
Where your face burns and tickles with the cobwebs   45
Broken across it, and one eye is weeping
From a twig's having lashed across it open.
I'd like to get away from earth awhile
And then come back to it and begin over.
May no fate willfully misunderstand me   50
And half grant what I wish and snatch me away
Not to return. Earth's the right place for love:
I don't know where it's likely to go better.
I'd like to go by climbing a birch tree,
And climb black branches up a snow-white trunk,   55
Toward heaven, till the tree could bear no more,
But dipped its top and set me down again.
That would be good both going and coming back.
One could do worse than be a swinger of birches.

Considerations for Critical Thinking and Writing

1. Why does the speaker in this poem prefer the birches to have been bent by boys instead of ice storms?
2. What does the swinging of birches symbolize?
3. How is "earth" described in the poem? Why does the speaker choose it over "heaven"?
4. How might the effect of this poem be changed if it were written in heroic couplets instead of blank verse?

An Old Man's Winter Night

1916

All out-of-doors looked darkly in at him
Through the thin frost, almost in separate stars,
That gathers on the pane in empty rooms.
What kept his eyes from giving back the gaze
Was the lamp tilted near them in his hand.   5
What kept him from remembering what it was
That brought him to that creaking room was age.
He stood with barrels round him — at a loss.
And having scared the cellar under him
In clomping here, he scared it once again   10
In clomping off — and scared the outer night,
Which has its sounds, familiar, like the roar
Of trees and crack of branches, common things,
But nothing so like beating on a box.
A light he was to no one but himself   15
Where now he sat, concerned with he knew what,
A quiet light, and then not even that.
He consigned to the moon, such as she was,
So late-arising, to the broken moon
As better than the sun in any case   20
For such a charge, his snow upon the roof,
His icicles along the wall to keep;
And slept. The log that shifted with a jolt
Once in the stove, disturbed him and he shifted,
And eased his heavy breathing, but still slept.   25
One aged man — one man — can't keep a house,
A farm, a countryside, or if he can,
It's thus he does it of a winter night.

Considerations for Critical Thinking and Writing

1. Describe the tone of this poem. Which images are especially effective in evoking the old man, the winter, and night?
2. What emotions do you feel for the old man? Is this a sentimental poem?
3. Comment on the sounds described in the poem. What effects do they create?

Connections to Other Selections

1. Compare the speaker in "The Road Not Taken" (p. 295) with the old man in this poem. Are they essentially similar or different? Explain your response in an essay.
2. Discuss images of winter and night in "An Old Man's Winter Night" and "Stopping by Woods on a Snowy Evening" (p. 308).

"Out, Out — "°   1916

The buzz-saw snarled and rattled in the yard
And made dust and dropped stove-length sticks of wood,
Sweet-scented stuff when the breeze drew across it.
And from there those that lifted eyes could count
Five mountain ranges one behind the other   5
Under the sunset far into Vermont.
And the saw snarled and rattled, snarled and rattled,
As it ran light, or had to bear a load.
And nothing happened: day was all but done.
Call it a day, I wish they might have said   10
To please the boy by giving him the half hour
That a boy counts so much when saved from work.
His sister stood beside them in her apron
To tell them "Supper." At the word, the saw,
As if to prove saws knew what supper meant,   15
Leaped out at the boy's hand, or seemed to leap —
He must have given the hand. However it was,
Neither refused the meeting. But the hand!
The boy's first outcry was a rueful laugh,
As he swung toward them holding up the hand   20
Half in appeal, but half as if to keep
The life from spilling. Then the boy saw all —
Since he was old enough to know, big boy
Doing a man's work, though a child at heart —
He saw all spoiled. "Don't let him cut my hand off —   25
The doctor, when he comes. Don't let him, sister!"
So. But the hand was gone already.
The doctor put him in the dark of ether.
He lay and puffed his lips out with his breath.
And then — the watcher at his pulse took fright.   30
No one believed. They listened at his heart.
Little — less — nothing! — and that ended it.
No more to build on there. And they, since they
Were not the one dead, turned to their affairs.

"*Out, Out — *": From Act V, Scene v, of Shakespeare's *Macbeth*. The passage appears on page 89.

Considerations for Critical Thinking and Writing

1. How does Frost's allusion to *Macbeth* contribute to the meaning of this poem?
   Does the speaker seem to agree with the view of life expressed in Macbeth's lines?
2. This narrative poem is about the accidental death of a Vermont boy. What is the
   purpose of the story? Some readers have argued that the final lines reveal the
   speaker's callousness and indifference. What do you think?

Connections to Other Selections

1. What are the similarities and differences in theme between this poem and Frost's "Nothing Gold Can Stay" (p. 309)?
2. Write an essay comparing how grief is handled by the boy's family in this poem and the couple in "Home Burial" (p. 300).
3. Compare the tone and theme of "Out, Out —" and those of Stephen Crane's "A Man Said to the Universe" (p. 116).

Fire and Ice   1923

Some say the world will end in fire,
Some say in ice.
From what I've tasted of desire
I hold with those who favor fire.
But if it had to perish twice,
I think I know enough of hate
To say that for destruction ice
Is also great
And would suffice.

Considerations for Critical Thinking and Writing

1. What theories about the end of the world are alluded to in lines 1 and 2?
2. What characteristics of human behavior does the speaker associate with fire and ice?
3. How does the speaker's use of understatement and rhyme affect the tone of this poem?

Stopping by Woods on a Snowy Evening   1923

Whose woods these are I think I know.
His house is in the village, though;
He will not see me stopping here
To watch his woods fill up with snow.

My little horse must think it queer   5
To stop without a farmhouse near
Between the woods and frozen lake
The darkest evening of the year.

He gives his harness bells a shake
To ask if there is some mistake.   10
The only other sound's the sweep
Of easy wind and downy flake.

The woods are lovely, dark and deep,

But I have promises to keep,
And miles to go before I sleep,   15
And miles to go before I sleep.

Considerations for Critical Thinking and Writing

1. What is the significance of the setting in this poem? How is tone conveyed by the images?
2. What does the speaker find appealing about the woods? What is the purpose of the horse in the poem?
3. Although the last two lines are identical, they are not read at the same speed. Why the difference? What is achieved by the repetition?
4. What is the rhyme scheme of this poem? What is the effect of the rhyme in the final stanza?

Nothing Gold Can Stay   1923

Nature's first green is gold,
Her hardest hue to hold.
Her early leaf's a flower;
But only so an hour.
Then leaf subsides to leaf.
So Eden sank to grief.
So dawn goes down to day.
Nothing gold can stay.

Considerations for Critical Thinking and Writing

1. What is meant by "gold" in the poem? Why can't it "stay"?
2. What do the leaf, humanity, and a day have in common?

Connection to Another Selection

1. Write an essay comparing the tone and theme of "Nothing Gold Can Stay" with Robert Herrick's "To the Virgins, to Make Much of Time" (p. 53).

For Once, Then, Something   1923

Others taunt me with having knelt at well-curbs
Always wrong to the light, so never seeing
Deeper down in the well than where the water
Gives me back in a shining surface picture
Me myself in the summer heaven, godlike,   5
Looking out of a wreath of fern and cloud puffs.
Once, when trying with chin against a well-curb,
I discerned, as I thought, beyond the picture,

Through the picture, a something white, uncertain,
Something more of the depths — and then I lost it. 10
Water came to rebuke the too clear water.
One drop fell from a fern, and lo, a ripple
Shook whatever it was lay there at bottom,
Blurred it, blotted it out. What was that whiteness?
Truth? A pebble of quartz? For once, then, something. 15

Considerations for Critical Thinking and Writing

1. How does this poem play on the Greek proverb that "truth lies at the bottom of wells"?
2. How do others view the speaker's way of looking in wells?
3. What is the symbolic value of the "something white" in line 9?
4. What does the poem suggest to you about humanity's search for ultimate truths?

Connections to Other Selections

1. Compare this speaker's search for truth with that of the people described in "Neither Out Far nor In Deep" (p. 311).
2. In an essay discuss "whiteness" in this poem and in "Design" (p. 311).

Desert Places 1936

Snow falling and night falling fast, oh, fast
In a field I looked into going past,
And the ground almost covered smooth in snow,
But a few weeds and stubble showing last.

The woods around it have it — it is theirs. 5
All animals are smothered in their lairs.
I am too absent-spirited to count;
The loneliness includes me unawares.

And lonely as it is, that loneliness
Will be more lonely ere it will be less — 10
A blanker whiteness of benighted snow
With no expression, nothing to express.

They cannot scare me with their empty spaces
Between stars — on stars where no human race is.
I have it in me so much nearer home 15
To scare myself with my own desert places.

Considerations for Critical Thinking and Writing

1. What kind of desert places does the speaker in this poem describe?
2. How does the speaker view the snow? Is this the same perspective as the one in "Stopping by Woods on a Snowy Evening" (p. 308)?
3. Who are "They" in line 13? Why is it that the speaker cannot be scared by them?

Design   1936

I found a dimpled spider, fat and white,
On a white heal-all,° holding up a moth
Like a white piece of rigid satin cloth —
Assorted characters of death and blight
Mixed ready to begin the morning right,   5
Like the ingredients of a witches' broth —
A snow-drop spider, a flower like a froth,
And dead wings carried like a paper kite.

What had the flower to do with being white,
The wayside blue and innocent heal-all?   10
What brought the kindred spider to that height,
Then steered the white moth thither in the night?
What but design of darkness to appall? —
If design govern in a thing so small.

2 *heal-all:* A common flower, usually blue, once used for medicinal purposes.

Considerations for Critical Thinking and Writing

1. How does the division of the octave and sestet in this sonnet serve to organize
   the speaker's thoughts and feelings? What is the predominant rhyme? How does
   that rhyme relate to the poem's meaning?
2. Which words seem especially rich in connotative meanings? Explain how they
   function in the sonnet.
3. What kinds of speculations are raised in the final two lines? Consider the meaning
   of the title. Is there more than one way to read it?

Connections to Other Selections

1. Compare the ironic tone of "Design" with the tone of William Hathaway's "Oh, Oh"
   (p. 16). What would you have to change in Hathaway's poem to make it more like
   Frost's?
2. In an essay discuss Frost's view of God in this poem and Dickinson's perspective
   in "I know that He exists" (p. 270).
3. Compare "Design" with "In White," Frost's early version of it (p. 315).

Neither Out Far nor In Deep   1936

The people along the sand
All turn and look one way.
They turn their back on the land.
They look at the sea all day.

As long as it takes to pass   5
A ship keeps raising its hull;
The wetter ground like glass
Reflects a standing gull.

The land may vary more;
But wherever the truth may be —   10
The water comes ashore,
And the people look at the sea.

They cannot look out far.
They cannot look in deep.
But when was that ever a bar   15
To any watch they keep?

Considerations for Critical Thinking and Writing

1. Frost built this poem around a simple observation that raises some questions. Why do people at the beach almost always face the ocean? What feelings and thoughts are evoked by looking at the ocean?
2. Notice how the verb *look* takes on added meaning as the poem progresses. What are the people looking for?
3. How does the final stanza extend the poem's significance?
4. Does the speaker identify with the people described, or does he ironically distance himself from them?

Provide, Provide   1936

The witch that came (the withered hag)
To wash the steps with pail and rag,
Was once the beauty Abishag,°

The picture pride of Hollywood.
Too many fall from great and good   5
For you to doubt the likelihood.

Die early and avoid the fate.
Or if predestined to die late,
Make up your mind to die in state.

Make the whole stock exchange your own!   10
If need be occupy a throne,
Where nobody can call *you* crone.

Some have relied on what they knew;
Others on being simply true.
What worked for them might work for you.   15

3 *Abishag:* A beautiful young woman who comforted King David in his old age (1 Kings 1:1–4).

No memory of having starred
Atones for later disregard,
Or keeps the end from being hard.

Better to go down dignified
With boughten friendship at your side   20
Than none at all. Provide, provide!

Considerations for Critical Thinking and Writing

1. Do you agree or disagree with the sentiments expressed in lines 19–21 of this poem?
2. Does the speaker offer serious advice or satirize the values described here? Is this poem didactic or ironic?
3. What is the effect of the rhymes? Is this much rhyme characteristic of Frost's work?

The Silken Tent   1942

She is as in a field a silken tent
At midday when a sunny summer breeze
Has dried the dew and all its ropes relent,
So that in guys° it gently sways at ease,   *ropes that steady a tent*
And its supporting central cedar pole,   5
That is its pinnacle to heavenward
And signifies the sureness of the soul,
Seems to owe naught to any single cord,
But strictly held by none, is loosely bound
By countless silken ties of love and thought   10
To everything on earth the compass round,
And only by one's going slightly taut
In the capriciousness of summer air
Is of the slightest bondage made aware.

Considerations for Critical Thinking and Writing

1. What is being compared in this sonnet? How does the detail accurately describe both elements of the comparison?
2. How does the form of this one-sentence sonnet help to express its theme? Pay particular attention to the final three lines.
3. How do the sonnet's sounds contribute to its meaning?

A Considerable Speck   1942

(Microscopic)

A speck that would have been beneath my sight
On any but a paper sheet so white
Set off across what I had written there.

And I had idly poised my pen in air
To stop it with a period of ink   5
When something strange about it made me think.
This was no dust speck by my breathing blown,
But unmistakably a living mite
With inclinations it could call its own.
It paused as with suspicion of my pen,   10
And then came racing wildly on again
To where my manuscript was not yet dry;
Then paused again and either drank or smelt —
With loathing, for again it turned to fly.
Plainly with an intelligence I dealt.   15
It seemed too tiny to have room for feet,
Yet must have had a set of them complete
To express how much it didn't want to die.
It ran with terror and with cunning crept.
It faltered: I could see it hesitate;   20
Then in the middle of the open sheet
Cower down in desperation to accept
Whatever I accorded it of fate.
I have none of the tenderer-than-thou
Collectivistic regimenting love   25
With which the modern world is being swept
But this poor microscopic item now!
Since it was nothing I knew evil of
I let it lie there till I hope it slept.
I have a mind myself and recognize   30
Mind when I meet with it in any guise.
No one can know how glad I am to find
On any sheet the least display of mind.

Considerations for Critical Thinking and Writing

1. Describe the speaker's sense of humor. How does it help to characterize the speaker?
2. Given lines 24–26, why does the speaker spare the mite?
3. How do the final two lines sum up the point of this observation on a speck?
4. How is the tone of the speaker's voice created through rhyme, meter, and diction?

The Gift Outright   1942

The land was ours before we were the land's.
She was our land more than a hundred years
Before we were her people. She was ours
In Massachusetts, in Virginia,
But we were England's, still colonials,   5
Possessing what we still were unpossessed by,

Possessed by what we now no more possessed.
Something we were withholding made us weak
Until we found out that it was ourselves
We were withholding from our land of living,   10
And forthwith found salvation in surrender.
Such as we were we gave ourselves outright
(The deed of gift was many deeds of war)
To the land vaguely realizing westward,
But still unstoried, artless, unenhanced,   15
Such as she was, such as she would become.

Considerations for Critical Thinking and Writing

1. Frost once described this poem as "a history of the United States in sixteen lines."
   Is it? What events in American history does the poem focus on? What does it leave
   out?
2. This poem is built on several paradoxes. How are the paradoxes in lines 1, 6, 7,
   and 11 resolved?

Connections to Other Selections

1. Compare and contrast the theme and tone of this poem with those of e. e.
   cummings's "next to of course god america i" (p. 115).
2. Write an essay comparing Frost's view of America with the view offered by Allen
   Ginsberg in "America" (p. 376).

PERSPECTIVES ON FROST

In White: Frost's Early Version of *Design*   1912

A dented spider like a snow drop white
On a white Heal-all, holding up a moth
Like a white piece of lifeless satin cloth —
Saw ever curious eye so strange a sight? —
Portent in little, assorted death and blight   5
Like the ingredients of a witches' broth? —
The beady spider, the flower like a froth,
And the moth carried like a paper kite.

What had that flower to do with being white,
The blue prunella every child's delight.   10
What brought the kindred spider to that height?
(Make we no thesis of the miller's° plight.)   *miller moth*
What but design of darkness and of night?
Design, design! Do I use the word aright?

Considerations for Critical Thinking and Writing

1. Read "In White" and "Design" (p. 311) aloud. Which version sounds better to you? Why?
2. Compare these versions line for line, paying attention to word choice. List the differences, and try to explain why you think Frost revised the lines.
3. How does the change in titles reflect a shift in emphasis in the poem?

Frost on the Living Part of a Poem   1914

The living part of a poem is the intonation entangled somehow in the syntax, idiom, and meaning of a sentence. It is only there for those who have heard it previously in conversation. . . . It is the most volatile and at the same time important part of poetry. It goes and the language becomes dead language, the poetry dead poetry. With it go the accents, the stresses, the delays that are not the property of vowels and syllables but that are shifted at will with the sense. Vowels have length there is no denying. But the accent of sense supersedes all other accent, overrides it and sweeps it away. I will find you the word *come* variously used in various passages, a whole, half, third, fourth, fifth, and sixth note. It is as long as the sense makes it. When men no longer know the intonations on which we string our words they will fall back on what I may call the absolute length of our syllables, which is the length we would give them in passages that meant nothing. . . . I say you can't read a single good sentence with the salt in it unless you have previously heard it spoken. Neither can you with the help of all the characters and diacritical marks pronounce a single word unless you have previously heard it actually pronounced. Words exist in the mouth not books.

From a letter to Sidney Cox in *A Swinger of Birches: A Portrait of Robert Frost*

Considerations for Critical Thinking and Writing

1. Why does Frost place so much emphasis on hearing poetry spoken?
2. Choose a passage from "Home Burial" (p. 300) or "After Apple-Picking" (p. 303) and read it aloud. How does Frost's description of his emphasis on intonation help explain the effects he achieves in the passage you have selected?
3. Do you think it is true that all poetry must be heard? Do "Words exist in the mouth not books"?

AMY LOWELL (1874–1925)
On Frost's Realistic Technique   1915

I have said that Mr. Frost's work is almost photographic. The qualification was unnecessary, it is photographic. The pictures, the characters, are reproduced directly from life, they are burnt into his mind as though it were a sensitive plate. He gives out what has been put in unchanged by any personal mental process. His imagination is bounded by what he has seen, he is confined within the limits of his experience (or at least what might have been his experience) and bent all one way like the windblown trees of New England hillsides.

From a review of *North of Boston, The New Republic,* February 20, 1915

Considerations for Critical Thinking and Writing

1. Consider the "photographic" qualities of Frost's poetry by discussing particular passages that strike you as having been "reproduced directly from life."
2. Write an essay that supports or refutes Lowell's assertion that "He gives out what has been put in unchanged by any personal mental process."

Frost on the Figure a Poem Makes   1939

Abstraction is an old story with the philosophers, but it has been like a new toy in the hands of the artists of our day. Why can't we have any one quality of poetry we choose by itself? We can have in thought. Then it will go hard if we can't in practice. Our lives for it.

Granted no one but a humanist much cares how sound a poem is if it is only *a* sound. The sound is the gold in the ore. Then we will have the sound out alone and dispense with the inessential. We do till we make the discovery that the object in writing poetry is to make all poems sound as different as possible from each other, and the resources for that of vowels, consonants, punctuation, syntax, words, sentences, meter are not enough. We need the help of context — meaning — subject matter. That is the greatest help towards variety. All that can be done with words is soon told. So also with meters — particularly in our language where there are virtually but two, strict iambic and loose iambic. The ancients with many were still poor if they depended on meters for all tune. It is painful to watch our sprung-rhythmists straining at the point of omitting one short from a foot for relief from monotony. The possibilities for tune from the dramatic tones of meaning struck across the rigidity of a limited meter are endless. And we are back in poetry as merely one more art of having something to say, sound or unsound. Probably better if sound, because deeper and from wider experience.

Then there is this wildness whereof it is spoken. Granted again that it has an equal claim with sound to being a poem's better half. If it is a wild tune, it is a poem. Our problem then is, as modern abstractionists, to have the wildness pure; to be wild with nothing to be wild about. We bring up as aberrationists, giving way to undirected associations and kicking ourselves from one chance suggestion to another in all directions as of a hot afternoon in the life of a grasshopper. Theme alone can steady us down. Just as the first mystery was how a poem could have a tune in such a straightness as meter, so the second mystery is how a poem can have wildness and at the same time a subject that shall be fulfilled.

It should be of the pleasure of a poem itself to tell how it can. The figure a poem makes. It begins in delight and ends in wisdom. The figure is the same as for love. No one can really hold that the ecstasy should be static and stand still in one place. It begins in delight, it inclines to the impulse, it assumes direction with the first line laid down, it runs a course of lucky events, and ends in a clarification of life — not necessarily a great clarification, such as sects and cults are founded on, but in a momentary stay against confusion. It has denouement. It has an outcome that though unforeseen was predestined from the first image of the original mood — and indeed from the very mood. It is but a trick poem and no poem at all if the best of it was thought of first and saved for the last. It finds its own name as it goes and discovers the best waiting for it in some final phrase at once wise and sad — the happy-sad blend of the drinking song.

No tears in the writer, no tears in the reader. No surprise for the writer, no surprise for the reader. For me the initial delight is in the surprise of remembering something I didn't know I knew. I am in a place, in a situation, as if I had materialized from cloud or risen out of the ground. There is a glad recognition of the long lost and the rest follows. Step by step the wonder of unexpected supply keeps growing. The impressions most useful to my purpose seem always those I was unaware of and so made no note of at the time when taken, and the conclusion is come to that like giants we are always hurling experience ahead of us to pave the future with against the day when we may want to strike a line of purpose across it for somewhere. The line will have the more charm for not being mechanically straight. We enjoy the straight crookedness of a good walking stick. Modern instruments of precision are being used to make things crooked as if by eye and hand in the old days.

I tell how there may be a better wildness of logic than of inconsequence. But the logic is backward, in retrospect, after the act. It must be more felt than seen ahead like prophecy. It must be a revelation, or a series of revelations, as much for the poet as for the reader. For it to be that there must have been the greatest freedom of the material to move about in it and to establish relations in it regardless of time and space, previous relation, and everything but affinity. We prate of freedom. We call our schools free because we are not free to stay away from them till we are sixteen years of age. I have given up my democratic prejudices and now willingly set the lower classes free to be completely taken care of by the upper classes. Political freedom is nothing to me. I bestow it right and left. All I would keep for myself is the freedom of my material — the condition of body and mind now and then to summon aptly from the vast chaos of all I have lived through.

Scholars and artists thrown together are often annoyed at the puzzle of where they differ. Both work for knowledge; but I suspect they differ most importantly in the way their knowledge is come by. Scholars get theirs with conscientious thoroughness along projected lines of logic; poets theirs cavalierly and as it happens in and out of books. They stick to nothing deliberately, but let what will stick to them like burrs where they walk in the fields. No acquirement is on assignment, or even self-assignment. Knowledge of the second kind is much more available in the wild free ways of wit and art. A school boy may be defined as one who can tell you what he knows in the order in which he learned it. The artist must value himself as he snatches a thing from some previous order in time and space into a new order with not so much as a ligature clinging to it of the old place where it was organic.

More than once I should have lost my soul to radicalism if it had been the originality it was mistaken for by its young converts. Originality and initiative are what I ask for my country. For myself the originality need be no more than the freshness of a poem run in the way I have described: from delight to wisdom. The figure is the same as for love. Like a piece of ice on a hot stove the poem must ride on its own melting. A poem may be worked over once it is in being, but may not be worried into being. Its most precious quality will remain its having run itself and carried away the poet with it. Read it a hundred times: it will forever keep its freshness as a metal keeps its fragrance. It can never lose its sense of a meaning that once unfolded by surprise as it went.

From *Complete Poems of Robert Frost*

Considerations for Critical Thinking and Writing

1. Frost places a high premium on sound in his poetry, because it "is the gold in the ore." Choose one of Frost's poems in this book and explain the effects of its sounds and how they contribute to its meaning.
2. Discuss Frost's explanation of how his poems are written. In what sense is the process both spontaneous and "predestined"?
3. What do you think Frost means when he says he's given up his "democratic prejudices"? Why is "political freedom" nothing to him?
4. Write an essay that examines in more detail the ways scholars and artists "come by" knowledge.
5. Explain what you think Frost means when he writes that "Like a piece of ice on a hot stove the poem must ride on its own melting."

Frost on the Way to Read a Poem   1951

The way to read a poem in prose or verse is in the light of all the other poems ever written. We may begin anywhere. We *duff* into our first. We read that imperfectly (thoroughness with it would be fatal), but the better to read the second. We read the second the better to read the third, the third the better to read the fourth, the fourth the better to read the fifth, the fifth the better to read the first again, or the second if it so happens. For poems are not meant to be read in course any more than they are to be made a study of. I once made a resolve never to put any book to any use it wasn't intended for by its author. Improvement will not be a progression but a widening circulation. Our instinct is to settle down like a revolving dog and make ourselves at home among the poems, completely at our ease as to how they should be taken. The same people will be apt to take poems right as know how to take a hint when there is one and not to take a hint when none is intended. Theirs is the ultimate refinement.

From "Poetry and School," *Atlantic Monthly,* June 1951

Considerations for Critical Thinking and Writing

1. Given your own experience, how good is Frost's advice about reading in general and his poems in particular?
2. In what sense is a good reader like a "revolving dog" and a person who knows "how to take a hint"?
3. Frost elsewhere in this piece writes that "One of the dangers of college to anyone who wants to stay a human reader (that is to say a humanist) is that he will become a specialist and lose his sensitive fear of landing on the lovely too hard. (With beak and talon.)" Write an essay in response to this concern. Do you agree with Frost's distinction between a "human reader" and a "specialist"?

LIONEL TRILLING (1905–1975)
On Frost as a Terrifying Poet   1959

I have to say that my Frost — *my Frost:* what airs we give ourselves when once we believe that we have come into possession of a poet! — I have to say that my Frost is not the Frost I seem to perceive existing in the minds of so many of his admirers. He is not the Frost who confounds the characteristically modern practice of poetry by his notable democratic simplicity of utterance: on the contrary. He is not the Frost who controverts the bitter modern astonishment at the nature of human life: the opposite is so. He is not the Frost who reassures us by his affirmation of old virtues, simplicities, pieties, and ways of feeling: anything but. I will not go so far as to say that my Frost is not essentially an American poet at all: I believe that he is quite as American as everyone thinks he is, but not in the way that everyone thinks he is.

In the matter of the Americanism of American literature one of my chief guides is that very remarkable critic, D. H. Lawrence. Here are the opening sentences of Lawrence's great outrageous book about classic American literature. "We like to think of the old fashioned American classics as children's books. Just childishness on our part. The old American art speech contains an alien quality which belongs to the American continent and to nowhere else." And this unique alien quality, Lawrence goes on to say, the world has missed. "It is hard to hear a new voice," he says, "as hard as to listen to an unknown language. . . . Why? Out of fear. The world fears a new experience more than it fears anything. It can pigeonhole any idea. But it can't pigeonhole a real new experience. It can only dodge. The world is a great dodger, and the Americans the greatest. Because they dodge their own very selves." I should like to pick up a few more of Lawrence's sentences, feeling the freer to do so because they have an affinity to Mr. Frost's prose manner and substance: "An artist is usually a damned liar, but his art, if it be art, will tell you the truth of his day. And that is all that matters. Away with eternal truth. Truth lives from day to day. . . . The old American artists were hopeless liars. . . . Never trust the artist. Trust the tale. The proper function of the critic is to save the tale from the artist who created it. . . . Now listen to me, don't listen to him. He'll tell you the lie you expect, which is partly your fault for expecting it."

Now in point of fact Robert Frost is *not* a liar. I would not hesitate to say that he was if I thought he was. But no, he is not. In certain of his poems — I shall mention one or two in a moment — he makes it perfectly plain what he is doing; and if we are not aware of what he is doing in other of his poems, where he is not quite so plain, that is not his fault but our own. It is not from him that the tale needs to be saved.

I conceive that Robert Frost is doing in his poems what Lawrence says the great writers of the classic American tradition did. That enterprise of theirs was of an ultimate radicalism. It consisted, Lawrence says, of two things: a disintegration and sloughing off of the old consciousness, by which Lawrence means the old European consciousness, and the forming of a new consciousness underneath.

So radical a work, I need scarcely say, is not carried out by reassurance, nor by the affirmation of old virtues and pieties. It is carried out by the representation of the terrible actualities of life in a new way. I think of Robert Frost as a terrifying poet. Call him, if it makes things any easier, a tragic poet, but it might be useful every now and then to come out from under the shelter of that literary word. The universe that he conceives is a terrifying universe. Read the poem called "Design" and see if you sleep the better for it. Read "Neither Out Far nor In Deep," which often seems to me the most perfect poem of our time, and see if you are warmed by anything in it except the energy with which emptiness is perceived.

But the *people,* it will be objected, the *people* who inhabit this possibly terrifying universe! About them there is nothing that can terrify; surely the people in Mr. Frost's poems can only reassure us by their integrity and solidity. Perhaps so. But I cannot make the disjunction. It may well be that ultimately they reassure us in some sense, but first they terrify us, or should. We must not be misled about them by the curious tenderness with which they are represented, a tenderness which extends to a recognition of the tenderness which they themselves can often give. But when ever have people been so isolated, so lightning-blasted, so tried down and calcined by life, so reduced, each in his own way, to some last irreducible core of being. Talk of the disintegration and sloughing off of the old consciousness! The people of Robert Frost's poems have done that with a vengeance. Lawrence says that what the Americans refused to accept was "the post-Renaissance humanism of Europe," "the old European spontaneity," "the flowing easy humor of Europe" and that seems to me a good way to describe the people who inhabit Robert Frost's America. In the interests of what great other thing these people have made this rejection we cannot know for certain. But we can guess that it was in the interest of truth, of some truth of the self. This is what they all affirm by their humor (which is so *not* "the easy flowing humor of Europe"), by their irony, by their separateness and isolateness. They affirm *this* of themselves: that they are what they are, that this is their truth, and that if the truth be bare, as truth often is, it is far better than a lie. For me the process by which they arrive at that truth is always terrifying. The manifest America of Mr. Frost's poems may be pastoral; the actual America is tragic.

From "A Speech on Robert Frost: A Cultural Episode,"
Partisan Review, Summer 1959

Considerations for Critical Thinking and Writing

1. How does Trilling distinguish *"my Frost"* from other readers'?
2. Read the section on biographical criticism in Chapter 14 (p. 524) and familiarize yourself with Frost's life. How does a knowledge of Frost's biography influence your reading of his poems?
3. Write an essay indicating whether you agree or disagree with Trilling's assessment of Frost "as a terrifying poet." Use evidence from the poems to support your view.

GALWAY KINNELL (b. 1927)
From *For Robert Frost°*   1965

    I saw you once on the TV,
Unsteady at the lectern,
The flimsy white leaf
Of hair standing straight up
In the wind, among top hats,   5
Old farmer and son
Of worse winters than this,
Stopped in the first dazzle

Of the District of Columbia,
Suddenly having to pay   10
For the cheap onionskin,
The worn-out ribbon, the eyes
Wrecked from writing poems
For us — stopped,
Lonely before millions,   15
The paper jumping in your grip,

And as the Presidents
Also on the platform
Began flashing nervously

Their Presidential smiles   20
For the harmless old guy,
And poets watching on the TV
Started thinking, Well that's
The end of *that* tradition,

And the managers of the event   25
Said, Boys this is it,
This sonofabitch poet
Is gonna croak,
Putting the paper aside

This tribute to Frost recalls his reciting "The Gift Outright" (p. 314) at the inauguration of John F. Kennedy in 1961. Frost originally planned to read the poem but was prevented from doing so by the glaring sun.

You drew forth   30
From your great faithful heart
The poem.

Considerations for Critical Thinking and Writing

1. Describe the difference in attitude expressed by the "Presidents" (line 16), the "poets" (22), and the "managers" (25) and that expressed by Kinnell in this excerpt. Why does Kinnell include the others in the poem?
2. Frost is said here to represent "The end of *that* tradition." What kind of tradition does he represent?
3. Research Frost's reputation. Why was he so popular with the American public?

HERBERT R. COURSEN, JR. (b. 1932)
A Reading of "Stopping by Woods on a Snowy Evening"   1962

Much ink has spilled on many pages in exegesis of this little poem. Actually, critical jottings have only obscured what has lain beneath critical noses all these years. To say that the poem means merely that a man stops one night to observe a snowfall, or that the poem contrasts the mundane desire for creature comfort with the sweep of aesthetic appreciation, or that it renders worldly responsibilities paramount, or that it reveals the speaker's latent death-wish is to miss the point rather badly. Lacking has been that mind simple enough to see what is *really* there. . . .

The "darkest evening of the year" in New England is December 21st, a date near that on which the western world celebrates Christmas. It may be that December 21st *is* the date of the poem, or (and with poets this seems more likely) that this is the closest the poet can come to Christmas without giving it all away. Who has "promises to keep" at or near this date, and who must traverse much territory to fulfill these promises? Yes, and who but St. Nick would know the location of *each* home? Only he would know who had "just settled down for a long winter's nap" (the poem's third line — "He will not see me stopping here" — is clearly a veiled allusion) and would not be out inspecting his acreage this night. The unusual phrase "fill up with snow," in the poem's fourth line, is a transfer of Santa's occupational preoccupation to the countryside; he is mulling the filling of countless stockings hung above countless fireplaces by countless careful children. "Harness bells," of course, allude to "Sleighing Song," a popular Christmas tune of the time the poem was written in which the refrain "Jingle Bells! Jingle Bells!" appears; thus again are we put on the Christmas track. The "little horse," like the date is another attempt at poetic obfuscation. Although the "rein-reindeer" ambiguity has been eliminated from the poem's final version,[1]

---

[1] The original draft contained the following line: "That bid me give the reins a shake" (Stageberg-Anderson, *Poetry as Experience* [New York, 1952], p. 457). [Coursen's note]

probably because too obvious, we may speculate that the animal is really a reindeer disguised as a horse by the poet's desire for obscurity, a desire which we must concede has been fulfilled up to now.

The animal is clearly concerned, like the faithful Rudolph — another possible allusion (post facto, hence unconscious) — lest his master fail to complete his mission. Seeing no farmhouse in the second quatrain, but pulling a load of presents, no wonder the little beast wonders! It takes him a full two quatrains to rouse his driver to remember all the empty stockings which hang ahead. And Santa does so reluctantly at that, poor soul, as he ponders the myriad farmhouses and villages which spread between him and his own "winter's nap." The modern St. Nick, lonely and overworked, tosses no "Happy Christmas to all and to all a good night!" into the precipitation. He merely shrugs his shoulders and resignedly plods away.

From "The Ghost of Christmas Past: 'Stopping by Woods on a Snowy Evening,'"
College English, December 1962

Considerations for Critical Thinking and Writing

1. Is this critical spoof at all credible? Does the interpretation hold any water? Is the evidence reasonable? Why or why not? Which of the poem's details are accounted for and which are ignored?
2. Choose a Frost poem and try writing a parodic interpretation of it.
3. What criteria do you use to distinguish between a sensible interpretation of a poem and an absurd one?

ROBERT H. SWENNES
Fear in "Home Burial"   1970

In "Home Burial" the decay of the marriage unit is placed in a setting which is harshly realistic and material. The conversations between husband and wife and their actions are filled with overtones of sexual aggression and withdrawal. For instance, the wife first appears poised near the top of the stairs, an emblem of womanhood to her husband who stands below. Yet this portrait is at once crushed as the husband ascends the stairs, demanding to know what his wife has been watching. Her face registers terror and then dullness as he continues "mounting until she cowered under him." The reader senses the antipathy which she feels toward her husband, even before she explains what he has done that so offended her. She is sickened by reality and is sure that "the world's evil." Her husband is a workaday farmer who cannot understand her growing morbidity since the death of their child. He tries to speak to her, to force the problem out into the open, but he overplays his hand. He reveals his own deep-seated sense of male superiority. He regrets, "A man must partly give up being a man / With women-folk." She interprets this as his regret of their courtship and marriage. The wife does not believe that any man can understand a woman's loss of her child. She shuns every hesitant attempt he makes to reach her. Her only comfort lies in self-pity.

The controlling emotion in the dramatic dialogue is fear. Since the awful sight of her husband burying her child behind the house, the wife has regarded him as a stranger, someone she really never knew before. She would rather leave the house than talk to this man who, together with all the world, now seems so brutal and evil to her. . . . The farmer no less than his wife is moved by fear, though it outwardly appears in both of them as anger. She threatens his personal dignity with her wild charges against him, and he reacts toward her in kind. Frost, as his biographer Lawrance Thompson explains, was himself a man who masked his fears with outward displays of anger. . . . "Home Burial" illustrates the existential fear, and sometimes even madness, which comes from the breakup of a once happy marital relationship. The farmer and his wife are being dragged down by the barriers she has raised between them. He is not adept and patient enough to minimize the conflict. The woman no longer conceives of herself as a wife, her husband's lover, or the mother of his future family. Not only has her domestic personality collapsed, but her psychological identity as well. She can relate to no one about her. With rare perception she recognizes, "from the time when one is sick to death, / One is alone." Isolated by her own hypersensitivity and refusal to talk, she wants nothing more to do with life. She waits to follow her child to the grave.

In "Home Burial" . . . the weakening of personal identity and self-assurance, the breakdown of person-to-person communication, and the death of the spiritual will to struggle and survive work to draw apart those who love. Once cast adrift, they find life to be a chaotic void.

From "Man and Wife: The Dialogue of Contraries in Robert Frost's Poetry," *American Literature,* November 1970

Considerations for Critical Thinking and Writing

1. Explain why you agree or disagree that the "controlling emotion" in the poem "is fear." What are the wife and husband afraid of and why can't they communicate adequately?
2. Discuss whether Swennes sympathizes more with the wife or husband.
3. Which character do you feel more sympathetic toward? Do you think Frost sides with one or the other? Explain your responses.

BLANCHE FARLEY (b. 1937)
The Lover Not Taken   1984

Committed to one, she wanted both
And, mulling it over, long she stood,
Alone on the road, loath
To leave, wanting to hide in the undergrowth.
This new guy, smooth as a yellow wood   5

Really turned her on. She liked his hair,
His smile. But the other, Jack, had a claim
On her already and she had to admit, he did wear

Well. In fact, to be perfectly fair,
He understood her. His long, lithe frame   10

Beside hers in the evening tenderly lay.
Still, if this blond guy dropped by someday,
Couldn't way just lead on to way?
No. For if way led on and Jack
Found out, she doubted if he would ever come back.   15

Oh, she turned with a sigh.
Somewhere ages and ages hence,
She might be telling this. "And I — "
She would say, "stood faithfully by."
But by then who would know the difference?   20

With that in mind, she took the fast way home,
The road by the pond, and phoned the blond.

Considerations for Critical Thinking and Writing

1. Which Frost poem is the object of this parody?
2. Describe how the stylistic elements mirror Frost's poem.
3. Does this parody seem successful to you? Explain what makes a successful parody.
4. Choose a Frost poem — or a portion of one if it is long — and try writing a parody of it.

TWO COMPLEMENTARY CRITICAL READINGS

REUBEN A. BROWER (1908–1975)
On the "Essence of Winter Sleep"
in "After Apple-Picking"   1963

Everything said throughout the poem comes to the reader through sentences filled with incantatory repetitions and rhymes and in waves of sound linked by likeness of pattern. From the opening lines, apparently matter-of-fact talk falls into curious chainlike sentences, rich in end-rhymes and echoes of many sorts. . . .

The meaning implied by the self-hypnosis and dreamy confusion of rhythm is finely suggested in the image of "the world of hoary grass," the blurred seeing of morning that anticipates the night vision. This blurring of experience focuses in the central metaphor of the poem, "essence of winter sleep." "Essence" is both the abstract "ultimate nature" of sleep and the physical smell, "the scent of apples" — a metaphysical image in T. S. Eliot's sense of the term. Fragrance and sleep blend, as sight and touch merge in "I cannot rub the strangeness from my sight . . ." The metaphor is renewed in many other expressions, for example, in "Magnified apples," which are apples seen against the sky with daylight accuracy, and also great dreamlike spheres. Other similarly precise details are blurred through the over-and-over way of recalling and describing them: "stem end and blossom end," "load on load," "ten thousand thousand." The closing metaphor of the poem, the woodchuck's "long sleep," adds to the strangeness of "winter sleep" by bringing in the nonhuman deathlike sleep of hibernation. We are finally quite uncertain of what *is* happening, and that is what the poem is about:

One can see what will trouble
This sleep of mine, whatever sleep it is.

In these two lines tone and rhythm work together beautifully, implying a great deal in relation to Frost's metaphor. The slight elevation of "One can see" recalls the more mysterious seeing of the morning, just as the almost banal lyricism of "This sleep of mine" sustains the rhythm of dream-confusion. The rest of the second line, barely iambic, barely rhyming, casual and rough, assures us that the speaker has at least one toe in reality. The contrasts of tone and rhythm, fitting the puzzlement of the sleeper's state, look ahead to the woodchuck's sleep and back to the initial balance of tones in "*sticking* through a tree / *Toward heaven* still." The poem is absorbed with "states-between," not only of winter sleep, but of all similar areas where real and unreal appear and disappear.

From *The Poetry of Robert Frost: Constellations of Intention*

Considerations for Critical Thinking and Writing

1. Discuss the sounds and images that contribute to what Brower describes as the speaker's "self-hypnosis and dreamy confusion."
2. Brower suggests that the central metaphor of the poem is "essence of winter sleep." Aside from the examples he provides, can you find other instances of this metaphor at work?
3. Write an essay that explores the idea that this poem is "absorbed with 'states-between.'"
4. Compare Brower's reading of "After Apple-Picking" with Greiner's below. Which reading do you think offers the more interesting interpretation of the poem? In your response be sure to define "interesting."

DONALD J. GREINER (b. 1940)
On What Comes "After Apple-Picking" 1982

"After Apple-Picking" was first published in *North of Boston* (1914), and it is my nomination for Frost's greatest poem. In the letter to John Cournos (27 July 1914), Frost explains that "After Apple-Picking" is the only poem in his second book that "will intone." Although he does not elaborate, he means that the rest of the poems sound like human speech whereas "After Apple-Picking" is a lyrical meditation on the tension between a job well done and the uncertainties accompanying the end of something significant. Note that the first word in the title is "After." Frost's refusal to specify what has ended, other than apple picking, is one of the glories of the poem.

The other glories are the examples of technical brilliance. The rhymes alone are worth the reading. Every one of the forty-two lines is rhymed, but Frost eschews the tradition of rhyme scheme altogether. The result is a beautiful, even haunting, rendering of the natural progression of a person's meditation as he uneasily ponders the ambiguities which suddenly well up before him now that his job is done. Similarly, the brilliant use of irregular iambic pentameter . . . to suggest the uncertain balance between the poet figure's need to maintain form in the face of confusion and the threat to his effort cast in the form of truncated lines illustrates the union of technique and theme when Frost is at his best. Although the poem begins with its longest line, the iambic heptameter "My long two-pointed ladder's sticking through a tree," and includes a line as short as "For all," the meter invariably returns to the predominant rhythm of iambic pentameter as the meditator struggles to keep his balance in uncertainty as he has kept it on the ladder of his life.

Nuances of aspiration, satisfaction, completion, rest, and death echo throughout "After Apple-Picking" beginning with the title. Like the speaker, the reader never knows how far to pursue the mythical associations between apples and man's expulsion from Eden. If such associations are to be dismissed, then the speaker has safely and satisfactorily completed his task — whatever it literally is — of harvesting the "ten thousand thousand fruit." The phrase "after apple-picking" thus suggests rest. But the genius of the poem is that the speaker is never sure. If the associations between apples and Eden are not to be dismissed, then the poet figure has finished his life's work only to be confronted with an overwhelming uncertainty about what awaits him now. "After Apple-Picking" thus suggests death.

The imagery of hazy speculation is precise. The phrase "toward heaven" indicates the speaker's ultimate aspiration, and the line "Essence of winter sleep is on the night" reverberates with suggestions of termination and the question of rebirth. The point is that the poet figure needs answers to questions he will not pose, and he can only see as through a glass darkly:

> I cannot rub the strangeness from my sight
> I got from looking through a pane of glass
> I skimmed this morning from the drinking trough. . . .

The woodchuck, so unthinkingly confident of rebirth from its winter hibernation, cannot help him. "After Apple-Picking" is a poem of encroaching fear because it is a poem of uncertainty. Although the religious connotations are never obtrusive, this great poem is another of Frost's explorations of what he considered to be man's greatest terror: that our best may not be good enough in Heaven's sight.

From "The Indispensable Robert Frost," in *Critical Essays on Robert Frost,* edited by Philip L. Gerber

Considerations for Critical Thinking and Writing

1. How far do you think "the mythical associations between apples and man's expulsion from Eden" should be pursued by readers of this poem?
2. Greiner cites several examples of the poem's "technical brilliance." What other examples can you find?
3. Write an essay that explores as the theme of the poem Greiner's idea "that our best may not be good enough in Heaven's sight."

11. Critical Case Study: T. S. Eliot's "The Love Song of J. Alfred Prufrock"

This chapter provides several critical approaches to a challenging but highly rewarding poem by T. S. Eliot. After studying this poem, you're likely to find yourself quoting bits of its striking imagery. At the very least, you'll recognize the lines when you hear other people fold them into their own conversations. There have been numerous critical approaches to this poem because it raises so many issues relating to matters such as history and biography as well as imagery, symbolism, irony, and myth. The following critical excerpts offer a small and partial sample of the possible formalist, biographical, historical, mythological, psychological, sociological, and other perspectives that have attempted to shed light on the poem (see Chapter 14, "Critical Strategies for Reading," for a discussion of a variety of critical methods). They should help you to enjoy the poem more by raising questions, providing insights, and inviting you further into the text.

T. S. ELIOT (1888–1965)

Born into a prominent New England family that had moved to St. Louis, Missouri, Thomas Stearns Eliot was a major voice in English Literature between the two world wars. He studied literature and philosophy at Harvard and on the Continent, subsequently choosing to live in England for most of his life and becoming a citizen there in 1927. His allusive and challenging poetry had a powerful influence on other writers, particularly his treatment of postwar life in *The Waste Land* (1922) and his exploration of religious questions in *The Four Quartets* (1943). In addition, he wrote plays, including *Murder in the Cathedral* (1935) and *The Cocktail Party* (1950). He was awarded the Nobel Prize for Literature in 1948. In "The Love Song of J. Alfred Prufrock," Eliot presents a comic but serious figure who expresses through a series of fragmented images the futility, boredom, and meaninglessness associated with much of modern life.

The Love Song of J. Alfred Prufrock 1917

S'io credesse che mia risposta fosse
A persona che mai tornasse al mondo,
Questa fiamma staria senza più scosse.
Ma perciocchè giammai di questo fondo
Non tornò vivo alcun, s'i'odo il vero,
Senza tema d'infamia ti rispondo.°

Let us go then, you and I,
When the evening is spread out against the sky
Like a patient etherized upon a table;
Let us go, through certain half-deserted streets,
The muttering retreats   5
Of restless nights in one-night cheap hotels
And sawdust restaurants with oyster-shells:
Streets that follow like a tedious argument
Of insidious intent
To lead you to an overwhelming question . . .   10
Oh, do not ask, "What is it?"
Let us go and make our visit.

    In the room the women come and go
Talking of Michelangelo.

    The yellow fog that rubs its back upon the window panes,   15
The yellow smoke that rubs its muzzle on the window panes
Licked its tongue into the corners of the evening,
Lingered upon the pools that stand in drains,
Let fall upon its back the soot that falls from chimneys,
Slipped by the terrace, made a sudden leap,   20
And seeing that it was a soft October night,
Curled once about the house, and fell asleep.

    And indeed there will be time°
For the yellow smoke that slides along the street,
Rubbing its back upon the window panes;   25

Epigraph: *S'io credesse . . . rispondo:* Dante's *Inferno,* XXVII, 58–63. In the Eighth Chasm of the Inferno, Dante and Virgil meet Guido da Montefeltro, one of the False Counselors, who is punished by being enveloped in an eternal flame. When Dante asks Guido to tell his life story, the spirit replies: "If I thought that my answer were to one who might ever return to the world, this flame would shake no more; but since from this depth none ever returned alive, if what I hear is true, I answer you without fear of infamy."   23 *there will be time:* An allusion to Ecclesiastes 3:1–8: "To everything there is a season, and a time to every purpose under heaven. . . ."

There will be time, there will be time
To prepare a face to meet the faces that you meet;
There will be time to murder and create,
And time for all the works and days° of hands
That lift and drop a question on your plate;   30
Time for you and time for me,
And time yet for a hundred indecisions,
And for a hundred visions and revisions,
Before the taking of a toast and tea.

    In the room the women come and go   35
Talking of Michelangelo.

    And indeed there will be time
To wonder, "Do I dare?" and, "Do I dare?"
Time to turn back and descend the stair,
With a bald spot in the middle of my hair —   40
(They will say: "How his hair is growing thin!")
My morning coat, my collar mounting firmly to the chin,
My necktie rich and modest, but asserted by a simple pin —
(They will say: "But how his arms and legs are thin!")
Do I dare   45
Disturb the universe?
In a minute there is time
For decisions and revisions which a minute will reverse.

    For I have known them already, known them all: —
Have known the evenings, mornings, afternoons,
I have measured out my life with coffee spoons;   50
I know the voices dying with a dying fall
Beneath the music from a farther room.
    So how should I presume?

    And I have known the eyes already, known them all —   55
The eyes that fix you in a formulated phrase,
And when I am formulated, sprawling on a pin,
When I am pinned and wriggling on the wall,
Then how should I begin
To spit out all the butt-ends of my days and ways?   60
    And how should I presume?

    And I have known the arms already, known them all —
Arms that are braceleted and white and bare
(But in the lamplight, downed with light brown hair!)
Is it perfume from a dress   65
That makes me so digress?
Arms that lie along a table, or wrap about a shawl.
    And should I then presume?
    And how should I begin?

     . . . . .

29 *works and days:* Hesiod's eighth century B.C. poem *Works and Days* gave practical advice on how
to conduct one's life in accordance with the seasons.

Shall I say, I have gone at dusk through narrow streets, 70
And watched the smoke that rises from the pipes
Of lonely men in shirtsleeves, leaning out of windows? . . .

　　　I should have been a pair of ragged claws
Scuttling across the floors of silent seas.

　　　　　　. . . . .

And the afternoon, the evening, sleeps so peacefully! 75
Smoothed by long fingers,
Asleep . . . tired . . . or it malingers,
Stretched on the floor, here beside you and me.
Should I, after tea and cakes and ices,
Have the strength to force the moment to its crisis? 80
But though I have wept and fasted, wept and prayed,
Though I have seen my head (grown slightly bald) brought in upon a platter,°
I am no prophet — and here's no great matter;
I have seen the moment of my greatness flicker,
And I have seen the eternal Footman hold my coat, and snicker, 85
And in short, I was afraid.

　　　And would it have been worth it, after all,
After the cups, the marmalade, the tea,
Among the porcelain, among some talk of you and me,
Would it have been worth while 90
To have bitten off the matter with a smile,
To have squeezed the universe into a ball°
To roll it toward some overwhelming question,
To say: "I am Lazarus,° come from the dead,
Come back to tell you all, I shall tell you all" — 95
If one, settling a pillow by her head,
　　　Should say: "That is not what I meant at all;
　　　That is not it, at all."

　　　And would it have been worth it, after all,
Would it have been worth while, 100
After the sunsets and the dooryards and the sprinkled streets,
After the novels, after the teacups, after the skirts that trail along the floor —
And this, and so much more? —
It is impossible to say just what I mean!
But as if a magic lantern threw the nerves in patterns on a screen: 105
Would it have been worth while
If one, settling a pillow or throwing off a shawl,

---

82 *head . . . upon a platter:* At Salome's request, Herod had John the Baptist decapitated and had the severed head delivered to her on a platter (see Matt. 14:1–12 and Mark 6:17–29).　92 *squeezed the universe into a ball:* See Marvell's "To His Coy Mistress" (p. 55), lines 41–42: "Let us roll all our strength and all / Our sweetness up into one ball."　94 *Lazarus:* The brother of Mary and Martha who was raised from the dead by Jesus (John 11:1–44). In Luke 16:19–31, a rich man asks that another Lazarus return from the dead to warn the living about their treatment of the poor.

And turning toward the window, should say:
    "That is not it at all,
    That is not what I meant, at all."   110
             . . . . .

    No! I am not Prince Hamlet, nor was meant to be;
Am an attendant lord,° one that will do
To swell a progress,° start a scene or two   *state procession*
Advise the prince: withal, an easy tool,
Deferential, glad to be of use,   115
Politic, cautious, and meticulous;
Full of high sentence, but a bit obtuse;
At times, indeed, almost ridiculous —
Almost, at times, the Fool.

I grow old . . . I grow old . . .   120
I shall wear the bottoms of my trousers rolled.

    Shall I part my hair behind? Do I dare to eat a peach?
I shall wear white flannel trowsers, and walk upon the beach.
I have heard the mermaids singing, each to each.
I do not think that they will sing to me.   125

I have seen them riding seaward on the waves,
Combing the white hair of the waves blown back
When the wind blows the water white and black.

We have lingered in the chambers of the sea
By seagirls wreathed with seaweed red and brown,   130
Till human voices wake us, and we drown.

112 *attendant lord:* Like Polonius in Shakespeare's *Hamlet.*

Considerations for Critical Thinking and Writing

1. What does J. Alfred Prufrock's name connote? How would you characterize him?
2. What do you think is the purpose of the epigraph from Dante's *Inferno?*
3. What is it that Prufrock wants to do? How does he behave? What does he think of himself? Which parts of the poem answer these questions?
4. Who is the "you" of line 1 and the "we" in the final lines?
5. Discuss the imagery in the poem. How does the imagery reveal Prufrock's character? Which images seem especially striking to you?

Connections to Other Selections

1. "No! I am not Prince Hamlet" says Prufrock. Despite this disclaimer, do you think it is possible to see some significant similarities between them? In an essay, acknowledge the differences between Prufrock and Hamlet, and then explore what they have in common.
2. For a different side of Eliot's poetry read "Macavity: The Mystery Cat" (p. 375). How does Macavity's character serve to highlight everything that Prufrock is not? Write an essay that discusses them as character foils.

ELISABETH SCHNEIDER (1897–1984)

Schneider uses a biographical approach to the poem to suggest that part of what went into the characterization of Prufrock were some of Eliot's own sensibilities.

Hints of Eliot in Prufrock 1952

Perhaps never again did Eliot find an epigraph quite so happily suited to his use as the passage from the *Inferno* which sets the underlying serious tone for *Prufrock* and conveys more than one level of its meaning: "S'io credesse che mia risposta . . . ," lines in which Guido da Montefeltro consents to tell his story to Dante only because he believes that none ever returns to the world of the living from his depth. One in Hell can bear to expose his shame only to another of the damned; Prufrock speaks to, will be understood only by, other Prufrocks (the "you and I" of the opening, perhaps), and, I imagine the epigraph also hints, Eliot himself is speaking to those who know this kind of hell. The poem, I need hardly say, is not in a literal sense autobiographical: for one thing, though it is clear that Prufrock will never marry, the poem was published in the year of Eliot's own first marriage. Nevertheless, friends who knew the young Eliot almost all describe him, retrospectively but convincingly, in Prufrockian terms; and Eliot himself once said of dramatic monologue in general that what we normally hear in it "is the voice of the poet, who has put on the costume and make-up either of some historical character, or of one out of fiction." . . . I suppose it to be one of the many indirect clues to his own poetry planted with evident deliberation throughout his prose. "What every poet starts from," he also once said, "is his own emotions," and, writing of Dante, he asserted that the *Vita nuova* "could only have been written around a personal experience," a statement that, under the circumstances, must be equally applicable to Prufrock; Prufrock was Eliot, though Eliot was much more than Prufrock. We miss the whole tone of the poem, however, if we read it as social satire only. Eliot was not either the dedicated apostle in theory, or the great exemplar in practice, of complete "depersonalization" in poetry that one influential early essay of his for a time led readers to suppose.

From "Prufrock and After: The Theme of Change," *PMLA*, October 1952

Considerations for Critical Thinking and Writing

1. Though Schneider concedes that the poem is not literally autobiographical, she does assert that "Prufrock was Eliot." How does she argue this point? Explain why you find her argument convincing or unconvincing.
2. Find information in the library about Eliot's early career when he was writing this poem. To what extent does the poem reveal his circumstances and concerns at that point in his life?

ROBERT G. COOK (b. 1932)

This source study makes a case for Eliot's indebtedness to Ralph Waldo Emerson's 1841 essay, "Self-Reliance," as a historical influence on his characterization of Prufrock.

The Influence of Emerson's "Self-Reliance" on Prufrock   1970

It is likely that Prufrock . . . was affected by Eliot's reading of "Self-Reliance," for in that essay there are a striking number of passages that virtually define Prufrock's character . . . For example, we read:

> Let a man then know his worth, and keep things under his feet. Let him not peep or steal, or skulk up and down with the air of a charity-boy, a bastard, or an interloper in the world which exists for him. But the man in the street, finding no worth in himself which corresponds to the force which built a tower or sculptured a marble god, feels poor when he looks on these. To him a palace, a statue, or a costly book have an alien and forbidding air, much like a gay equipage, and seem to say like that, "Who are you, Sir?"

One of the main purposes of Emerson's essay is to overcome, in this fashion, the intimidations of "the man in the street." Eliot's Prufrock may be seen as a caricature of this man, an antitype to Emerson's self-reliant man, a totally un-self-reliant man. Prufrock constantly feels that he is being asked: "Who are you, Sir?"

Early in the essay Emerson points to the "nonchalance of boys who are sure of a dinner" as an example of natural self-trust and lack of self-consciousness. In contrast,

> the man is as it were clapped into jail by his consciousness. As soon as he has once acted or spoken with *éclat* he is a committed person, watched by the sympathy or the hatred of hundreds, whose affections must now enter into his account. There is no Lethe for this. Ah, that he could pass again into his neutrality! Who can thus avoid all pledges and, having observed, observe again from the same unaffected, unbiased, unbribable unaffrighted innocence, — must always be formidable. He would utter opinions on all passing affairs, which being seen to be not private but necessary, would sink like darts into the ear of men and put them in fear.

Prufrock, clapped into jail by his consciousness, has an *excessive* fear of expressing himself ("Shall I say, I have gone at dusk through narrow streets . . . ?"). For him there is no Lethe which would free him from abnormal concern for the opinions of others; he desires an even stronger Lethe, total inconspicuousness and oblivion ("I should have been a pair of ragged claws / Scuttling across the floors of silent seas"). At the same time, he longs, like a self-reliant man, to utter opinions which would sink like darts into the ear of men and put them in fear ("I am Lazarus, come from the dead . . .").

Where Emerson teaches "What I must do is all that concerns me, not what the people think," Prufrock is paralyzed by his fears of what people think. Where Emerson teaches that "the great man is he who in the midst of the crowd keeps with perfect sweetness the independence of solitude," Prufrock is "pinned and wriggling on the wall." Prufrock is incapable of regarding the faces he has known with Emerson's equanimity: "the sour faces of the multitude, like their sweet faces, have no deep cause, but are put on and off as the wind blows and a newspaper directs."

One reason Prufrock does not speak out is his fear of being misunderstood: "Would it have been worthwhile . . ." In this too, Prufrock has not profited from the teaching of Emerson: "Is it so bad then to be misunderstood? Pythagoras was misunderstood, and Socrates, and Jesus, and Luther, and Copernicus, and Galileo, and Newton, and every pure and wise spirit that ever took flesh. To be great is to be misunderstood."

One of the symptoms of Prufrock's paranoia is his lack of a sense of proportion, his inability to distinguish between great and small, with the result that everything takes on exaggerated importance. In the timorous formula "Do I dare?" eating a peach becomes tantamount to disturbing the universe. The phrase "eternal Footman" expresses his undifferentiated fear of an ordinary servant and the eternal God. Emerson's self-reliant man goes to the opposite extreme and fears nobody, not even the great: "Let us never bow and apologize more. A great man is coming to eat at my house. I do not wish to please him; I wish that he should wish to please me." As far as God is concerned, the self-reliant man need not fear Him, for in fact He is present within the self-reliant man:

> Let us affront and reprimand the smooth mediocrity and squalid contentment of the times, and hurl in the face of custom and trade and office, the fact which is the upshot of all history, that there is a great responsible Thinker and Actor working wherever a man works; that a true man belongs to no other time or place, but is the centre of things. Where he is, there is nature. He measures you and all men and all events.

On all these counts, basic both to Emerson's essay and to Eliot's portrayal, it is clear that Prufrock is the very opposite of the man Emerson envisions. In fact, he is remarkably like the man Emerson is preaching against: "The sinew and heart of man seem to be drawn out, and we are become timorous, desponding whimperers. We are afraid of truth, afraid of fortune, afraid of death, and afraid of each other." "Fear" is also the key word for Prufrock: "And in short, I was afraid."

From "Emerson's 'Self-Reliance,' Sweeney, and Prufrock,"
American Literature, May 1970

Considerations for Critical Thinking and Writing

1. Describe how "Self-Reliance" "virtually define[s] Prufrock's character."
2. How does this negative definition shed light on Prufrock for you? How does knowing about Emerson's essay produce better understanding of Prufrock?
3. Cook concludes his essay by noting that Prufrock's character flaws are "Eliot's realistic responses to Emerson's idealistic proposals." How does Prufrock serve to measure the distance between nineteenth- and twentieth-century views of the self?

MICHAEL L. BAUMANN (b. 1926)

Baumann takes a close look at the poem's images in his formalist efforts to make a point about Prufrock's character.

The "Overwhelming Question" for Prufrock   1981

Most critics . . . have seen the overwhelming question related to sex. . . . They have implicitly assumed — and given their readers to understand — that Prufrock's is the male's basic question: Can I?

Delmore Schwartz once said that "J. Alfred Prufrock is unable to make love to women of his own class and kind because of shyness, self-consciousness, and fear of rejection."[1] This is undoubtedly true, but Prufrock's inability to *feel* love has something to do with his inability to *make* love, too. . . . A simple desire, lust, is more than honest Prufrock can cope with as he mounts the stairs.

But Prufrock is coping with another, less simple desire as well. . . . If birth, copulation, and death is all there is, then, once we are born, once we have copulated, only death remains (for the male of the species, at least). Prufrock, having "known them all already, known them all," having "known the evenings, mornings, afternoons," having "measured out" his life "with coffee spoons," desires death. The "overwhelming question" that assails him would no longer be the romantic's rhetorical "Is life worth living?" (to which the answer is obviously No), but the more immediate shocker: "Should one commit suicide?" which is to say: "Should I?" . . .

. . . The poem makes clear that Prufrock wants more than the "entire destruction of consciousness as we understand it," a notion Prufrock expresses by wishing he were "a pair of ragged claws, / Scuttling across the floors of silent seas." Prufrock wants death itself, physical death, and the poem, I believe, is explicit about this desire.

Not only does Prufrock seem to be tired of time — "time yet for a hundred indecisions" — a tiredness that goes far beyond the acedia Prufrock is generally credited with feeling, if only because "there will be time to murder and create," time, in other words (in one sense at least) to copulate, but Prufrock is also tired of his own endless vanities, from feeling he must "prepare a face to meet the faces that you meet," to having to summon up those ironies with which to contemplate his own thin arms and legs, and, indeed, to asking if, in the rather tedious enterprise of preparing for copulation, the moment is worth "forcing to its crisis." No wonder Prufrock compares himself to John the Baptist and, in conjuring up this first concrete image of his own death, sees his head brought in upon a platter. That would be the easy way out. He had, after all, "wept and

---

[1]"T. S. Eliot as the International Hero," *Partisan Review*, 12 (1945), 202; rpt. in *T. S. Eliot: A Selected Critique*, ed. Leonard Unger (New York: Rinehart & Company, Inc., 1948), 46.

fasted, wept and prayed," but he realizes he is no prophet — and no Salome will burst into passion, will ignite for him. When the eternal Footman, Death, who holds his coat, snickers, he does so because Prufrock has let "the moment" of his "greatness" flicker, because Prufrock was unable to comply with the one imperative greatness would have thrust upon him: to kill himself. Prufrock explains: "I was afraid." Yet the achievement of his vision at the end of the poem, his being able to linger "in the chambers of the sea / By sea-girls wreathed with seaweed red and brown," is an act of the imagination that only physical death can complete, unless Prufrock wants human voices to wake him, and drown him. His romantic vision demands the voluntary act: suicide. It is to be expected that he will fail in this too, as he has failed in everything else.

From "Let Us Ask 'What Is It,' " *Arizona Quarterly*, Spring 1981

Considerations for Critical Thinking and Writing

1. Describe the evidence used by Baumann to argue that Prufrock contemplates suicide.
2. Explain in an essay why you do or do not find Baumann's argument convincing.
3. Later in his essay Baumann connects Prufrock's insistence that "No, I am not Prince Hamlet" with Hamlet's "To be or not to be" speech. How do you think this reference might be used to support Baumann's argument?

FREDERIK L. RUSCH (b. 1938)

Rusch makes use of the insights developed by Erich Fromm, a social psychologist who believed "psychic forces [are] a process of constant inter-action between man's needs and the social and historical reality in which he participates."

Society and Character in "The Love Song of J. Alfred Prufrock" 1984

In looking at fiction, drama, and poetry from the Frommian point of view, the critic understands literature to be social portrayal as well as character portrayal or personal statement. Society and character are inextricably joined. The Frommian approach opens up the study of literary work, giving a social context to its characters, which suggests why those characters behave as they do. The Frommian approach recognizes human beings for what they are — basically gregarious individuals who are interdependent upon each other, in need of each other, and thus, to a certain degree, products of their social environments, although those environments may be inimical to their mental well-being. That is, as stated earlier, the individual's needs and drives have a social component and are not purely biological. The Frommian approach to literature assumes that a writer is — at least by implication — analyzing society and its setting as well as character. . . .

In T. S. Eliot's "The Love Song of J. Alfred Prufrock," Prufrock is talking to himself, expressing a fantasy or daydream. In his monologue, Prufrock, as noted by Grover Smith, "is addressing, as if looking into a mirror, his whole public personality."[1] Throughout the poem, Prufrock is extremely self-conscious, believing that the people in his imaginary drawing room will examine him as a specimen insect, "sprawling on a pin, / . . . pinned and wriggling on the wall. . . ." Of course, self-consciousness — being conscious of one's self — is not necessarily neurotic. Indeed, it is part of being a human being. It is only when self-consciousness, which has always led man to feel a separation from nature, becomes obsessive that we have a problem. Prufrock is certainly obsessed with his self-consciousness, convinced that everyone notices his balding head, his clothes (his prudent frocks), his thin arms and legs.

On one level, however, Prufrock is merely expressing the pain that all human beings must feel. Although his problem is extreme, he is quite representative of the human race:

> Self-awareness, reason, and imagination have disrupted the "harmony" that characterizes animal existence. Their emergence has made man into an anomaly, the freak of the universe. He is part of nature, subject to her physical laws and unable to change them, yet he transcends nature. He is set apart while being a part; he is homeless, yet chained to the home he shares with all creatures. . . . Being aware of himself, he realizes his powerlessness and the limitations of his existence. He is never free from the dichotomy of his existence: he cannot rid himself of his mind, even if he would want to; he cannot rid himself of his body as long as he is alive — and his body makes him want to be alive.[2]

This is the predicament of the human being. His self-awareness has made him feel separate from nature. This causes pain and sorrow. What, then, is the solution to the predicament? Fromm believed that mankind filled the void of alienation from nature with the creation of a culture, a society: "Man's existential, and hence unavoidable disequilibrium can be relatively stable when he has found, with the support of his culture, a more or less adequate way of coping with his existential problems" (*Destructiveness*, 225). But, unfortunately for Prufrock, his culture and society do not allow him to overcome his existential predicament. The fact is, he is bored by his modern, urban society.

In image after image, Prufrock's mind projects boredom:

> For I have known them all already, known them all:
> Have known the evenings, mornings, afternoons,
> I have measured out my life with coffee spoons. . . .

[1]Grover Smith, *T. S. Eliot's Poetry and Plays: A Study in Sources and Meaning* (Chicago: U of Chicago P, 1962), 16.
[2]Erich Fromm, *The Anatomy of Human Destructiveness* (New York: Holt, Rinehart & Winston, 1973), 225.

And I have known the eyes already, known them all —. . .
Then how should I begin
To spit out all the butt-ends of my days and ways?

. . . .

And I have known the arms already, known them all —. . . .

Prufrock is completely unstimulated by his social environment, to the point of near death. The evening in which he proposes to himself to make a social visit is "etherised upon a table." The fog, as a cat, falls asleep; it is "tired . . . or it malingers, / Stretched on the floor. . . ."

Prufrock, living in a city of "half-deserted streets, / . . . one-night cheap hotels / And sawdust restaurants with oyster-shells," gets no comfort, no nurturing from his environment. He is, in the words of Erich Fromm, a "modern mass man . . . isolated and lonely" (*Destructiveness*, 107). He lives in a destructive environment. Instead of providing communion with fellow human beings, it alienates him through boredom. Such boredom leads to "a state of chronic depression" that can cause the pathology of "insufficient inner productivity" in the individual (*Destructiveness*, 243). Such a lack of productivity is voiced by Prufrock when he confesses that he is neither Hamlet nor John the Baptist.

An interesting tension in "The Love Song of J. Alfred Prufrock" is caused by the reader's knowledge that Prufrock understands his own predicament quite well. Although he calls himself a fool, he has wisdom about himself and his predicament. This, however, only reinforces his depression and frustration. In his daydream, he is able to reveal truths about himself that, while they lead to self-understanding, apparently cannot alleviate his problems in his waking life. The poem suggests no positive movement out of the predicament. Prufrock is like a patient cited by Fromm, who under hypnosis envisioned "a black barren place with many masks," and when asked what the vision meant said "that everything was dull, dull, dull; that the masks represent the different roles he takes to fool people into thinking he is feeling well" (*Destructiveness*, 246). Likewise, Prufrock understands that "There will be time, there will be time / To prepare a face to meet the faces that you meet. . . ." But despite his understanding of the nature of his existence, he cannot attain a more productive life.

It was Fromm's belief that with boredom "the decisive conditions are to be found in the overall environmental situation. . . . It is highly probable that even cases of severe depression-boredom would be less frequent and less intense . . . in a society where a mood of hope and love of life predominated. But in recent decades the opposite is increasingly the case, and thus a fertile soil for the development of individual depressive states is provided" (*Destructiveness*, 251). There is no "mood of hope and love of life" in Prufrock's society. Prufrock is a lonely man, as lonely as "the lonely men in shirt-sleeves, leaning out of windows" of his fantasy. His only solution is to return to the animal state that his race was in before evolving into human beings.

Animals are one with nature, not alienated from their environments. They *are* nature, unselfconscious. Prufrock would return to a preconscious existence in the extreme: "I should have been a pair of ragged claws / Scuttling across the floors of silent seas." Claws *without a head* surely would not be alienated, bored, or depressed. They would seek and would need no psychological nurturing from their environment. And in the end Prufrock's fantasy of becoming claws is definitely more positive for him than his life as a human being. He completes his monologue with depressing irony, to say the least: it is with human voices waking us, bringing us back to human society, that we drown.

From "Approaching Literature Through the Social Psychology of Erich Fromm," in *Psychological Perspectives on Literature: Freudian Dissidents and Non-Freudians*, ed. Joseph Natoli

Considerations for Critical Thinking and Writing

1. According to Rusch, why is Fromm's approach useful for understanding Prufrock's character as well as his social context?
2. In what ways is Prufrock "representative of the human race"? Is he like any other characters you have read about in this anthology? Explain your response.
3. In an essay consider how Rusch's analysis of Prufrock might be used to support Baumann's argument that Prufrock's "overwhelming question" is whether or not he should kill himself (p. 337).
4. Discuss the difference between Fromm's description of humanity's self-awareness and Emerson's insistence upon self-reliance (p. 335) for humanity. How do both perspectives help to account for Prufrock's characterization?

12. A Collection of Poems

QUESTIONS FOR RESPONSIVE READING

The following questions can help you respond to important elements that reveal a poem's effects and meanings. The questions are general, so not all of them will necessarily be relevant to a particular poem. Many, however, should prove useful for thinking, talking, and writing about each poem in this collection. If you are uncertain about the meaning of a term used in a question, consult the Index of Terms, which lists pages that discuss the terms and is located on the inside back cover.

Before addressing these questions, read the poem you are studying in its entirety. Don't worry about interpretation on a first reading; allow yourself the pleasure of enjoying whatever makes itself apparent to you. Then on subsequent readings, use the questions to understand and appreciate how the poem works.

1. Who is the speaker? Is it possible to determine the speaker's age, sex, sensibilities, level of awareness, and values?
2. Is the speaker addressing anyone in particular?
3. How do you respond to the speaker? favorably? negatively? What is the situation? Are there any special circumstances that inform what the speaker says?
4. Is there a specific setting of time and place?
5. Does reading the poem aloud help you to understand it?
6. Does a paraphrase reveal the basic purpose of the poem?
7. What does the title emphasize?
8. Is the theme presented directly or indirectly?
9. Do any allusions enrich the poem's meaning?
10. How does the diction reveal meaning? Are any words repeated? Do any carry evocative connotative meanings? Are there any puns or other forms of verbal wit?

11. Are figures of speech used? How does the figurative language contribute to the poem's vividness and meaning?

12. Do any objects, persons, places, events, or actions have allegorical or symbolic meanings? What other details in the poem support your interpretation?

13. Is irony used? Are there any examples of situational irony, verbal irony, or dramatic irony? Is understatement or paradox used?

14. What is the tone of the poem? Is the tone consistent?

15. Does the poem use onomatopoeia, assonance, consonance, or alliteration? How do these sounds affect you?

16. What sounds are repeated? If there are rhymes, what is their effect? Do they seem forced or natural? Is there a rhyme scheme? Do the rhymes contribute to the poem's meaning?

17. Do the lines have a regular meter? What is the predominant meter? Are there significant variations? Does the rhythm seem appropriate for the tone of the poem?

18. Does the poem's form — its overall structure — follow an established pattern? Do you think the form is a suitable vehicle for the poem's meaning and effects?

19. Is the language of the poem intense and concentrated? Do you think it warrants more than one or two close readings?

20. Did you enjoy the poem? What, specifically, pleased or displeased you about what was expressed and how it was expressed?

21. Is there a particular critical approach that seems especially appropriate for this poem? (See the discussion of "Critical Strategies for Reading" beginning on page 517.)

22. How might biographical information about the author help to determine the central concerns of the poem?

23. How might historical information about the poem provide a useful context for interpretation?

24. To what extent do your own experiences, values, beliefs, and assumptions inform your interpretation?

25. What kinds of evidence from the poem are you focusing on to support your interpretation? Does your interpretation leave out any important elements that might undercut or qualify your interpretation?

26. Given that there are a variety of ways to interpret the poem, which one seems the most useful to you?

PAULA GUNN ALLEN (b. 1939)
Pocahontas to Her English Husband,
John Rolfe°

1988

> *In a way, then, Pocahontas was a kind of traitor to her people. . . . Perhaps I am being a little too hard on her. The crucial point, it seems to me, is to remember that Pocahontas was a hostage. Would she have converted freely to Christianity if she had not been in captivity? There is no easy answer to this question other than to note that once she was free to do what she wanted, she avoided her own people like the plague. . . .*
> *Pocahontas was a white dream — a dream of cultural superiority.*
> –Charles Larson, *American Indian Fiction*

Had I not cradled you in my arms
oh beloved perfidious one,
you would have died.
And how many times did I pluck you
from certain death in the wilderness —   5
my world through which you stumbled
as though blind?
Had I not set you tasks
your masters far across the sea
would have abandoned you —   10
did abandon you, as many times
they left you
to reap the harvest of their lies.
Still you survived, oh my fair husband,
and brought them gold   15
wrung from a harvest I taught you
to plant. Tobacco.
It is not without irony that by this crop
your descendants die, for other
powers than you know   20
take part in this and all things.
And indeed I did rescue you —
not once but a thousand thousand times
and in my arms you slept, a foolish child,
and under my protecting gaze you played,   25
chattering nonsense about a God
you had not wit to name. I'm sure

Pocahontas . . . Rolfe: In 1614 Pocahontas (1595?–1617), a princess of the Wampanoag Indians, married Rolfe (1585–1622), an English colonist and founder of Jamestown, Virginia. Legend has it that she saved the life of Captain John Smith (1580–1631), another English colonist, by holding his head in her arms so that Wampanoag warriors could not club him to death.

you wondered at my silence, saying I was
a simple wanton, a savage maid,
dusky daughter of heathen sires   30
who cartwheeled naked through the muddy towns
who would learn the ways of grace only
by your firm guidance, through
your husbandly rule:
no doubt, no doubt.   35
I spoke little, you said.
And you listened less,
but played with your gaudy dreams
and sent ponderous missives to the throne
striving thereby to curry favor   40
with your king.
I saw you well. I
understood your ploys and still
protected you, going so far as to die
in your keeping — a wasting,   45
putrefying Christian death° — and you,
deceiver, whiteman, father of my son,
survived, reaping wealth greater
than any you had ever dreamed
from what I taught you and   50
from the wasting of my bones.

46 *death:* Pocahontas is supposed to have died from tuberculosis.

MAYA ANGELOU (b. 1928)
My Arkansas   1978

There is a deep brooding
in Arkansas.
Old crimes like moss pend
from poplar trees.
The sullen earth   5
is much too
red for comfort.

Sunrise seems to hesitate
and in that second
lose its   10
incandescent aim, and
dusk no more shadows
than the noon.
The past is brighter yet.

Old hates and
ante-bellum° lace, are rent
but not discarded.
Today is yet to come
in Arkansas.
It writhes. It writhes in awful
waves of brooding.

15

20

16 *ante-bellum:* Before the Civil War.

ANONYMOUS (traditional Scottish ballad)
Bonny Barbara Allan   date unknown

It was in and about the Martinmas° time,
    When the green leaves were afalling,
That Sir John Graeme, in the West Country,
    Fell in love with Barbara Allan.

He sent his men down through the town,   5
    To the place where she was dwelling:
"O haste and come to my master dear,
    Gin° ye be Barbara Allan."   *if*

O hooly,° hooly rose she up,   *slowly*
    To the place where he was lying,   10
And when she drew the curtain by:
    "Young man, I think you're dying."

"O it's I'm sick, and very, very sick,
    And 'tis a' for Barbara Allan." —
"O the better for me ye's never be,   15
    Tho your heart's blood were aspilling.

"O dinna ye mind,° young man," said she,   *don't you remember*
    "When ye was in the tavern adrinking,
That ye made the health° gae round and round,   *toasts*
    And slighted Barbara Allan?"   20

He turned his face unto the wall,
    And death was with him dealing:
"Adieu, adieu, my dear friends all,
    And be kind to Barbara Allan."

And slowly, slowly raise she up,   25
    And slowly, slowly left him,
And sighing said she could not stay,
    Since death of life had reft him.

1 *Martinmas:* St. Martin's Day, November 11.

She had not gane a mile but twa,
    When she heard the dead-bell ringing,   30
And every jow° that the dead-bell geid,   *stroke*
    It cried, "Woe to Barbara Allan!"

"O mother, mother, make my bed!
    O make it saft and narrow!
Since my love died for me today,   35
    I'll die for him tomorrow."

ANONYMOUS

Lord Randal   1500s

"Oh, where have you been, Lord Randal, my son?
Oh, where have you been, my handsome young man?"
"Oh, I've been to the wildwood; mother, make my bed soon,
I'm weary of hunting and I fain° would lie down."   *gladly*

"And whom did you meet there, Lord Randal, my son?   5
And whom did you meet there, my handsome young man?"
"Oh, I met with my true love; mother, make my bed soon,
I'm weary of hunting and I fain would lie down."

"What got you for supper, Lord Randal, my son?
What got you for supper, my handsome young man?"   10
"I got eels boiled in broth; mother, make my bed soon,
I'm weary of hunting and I fain would lie down."

"And who got your leavings, Lord Randal, my son?
And who got your leavings, my handsome young man?"
"I gave them to my dogs; mother, make my bed soon,   15
I'm weary of hunting and I fain would lie down."

"And what did your dogs do, Lord Randal, my son?
And what did your dogs do, my handsome young man?"
"Oh, they stretched out and died; mother, make my bed soon,
I'm weary of hunting and I fain would lie down."   20

"Oh, I fear you are poisoned, Lord Randal, my son,
Oh, I fear you are poisoned, my handsome young man."
"Oh, yes, I am poisoned; mother, make my bed soon,
For I'm sick at my heart and I fain would lie down."

"What will you leave your mother, Lord Randal, my son?   25
What will you leave your mother, my handsome young man?"
"My house and my lands; mother, make my bed soon,
For I'm sick at my heart and I fain would lie down."

"What will you leave your sister, Lord Randal, my son?
What will you leave your sister, my handsome young man?"   30
"My gold and my silver; mother, make my bed soon,
For I'm sick at my heart and I fain would lie down."

"What will you leave your brother, Lord Randal, my son?
What will you leave your brother, my handsome young man?"
"My horse and my saddle; mother, make my bed soon,   35
For I'm sick at my heart and I fain would lie down."

"What will you leave your true-love, Lord Randal, my son?
What will you leave your true-love, my handsome young man?"
"A halter to hang her; mother, make my bed soon,
For I'm sick at my heart and I want to lie down."   40

ANONYMOUS

Frankie and Johnny   date unknown

Frankie and Johnny were lovers,
    Lordy, how they could love,
Swore to be true to each other,
    True as the stars up above,
        He was her man, but he done her wrong.   5

Frankie went down to the corner,
    To buy her a bucket of beer,
Frankie says "Mister Bartender,
    Has my lovin' Johnny been here?
        He is my man, but he's doing me wrong."   10

"I don't want to cause you no trouble
    Don't want to tell you no lie,
I saw your Johnny half-an-hour ago
    Making love to Nelly Bly.
        He is your man, but he's doing you wrong."   15

Frankie went down to the hotel
    Looked over the transom so high,
There she saw her lovin' Johnny
    Making love to Nelly Bly.
        He was her man; he was doing her wrong.   20

Frankie threw back her kimono,
    Pulled out her big forty-four;
Rooty-toot-toot: three times she shot
    Right through that hotel door,
        She shot her man, who was doing her wrong.   25

"Roll me over gently,
    Roll me over slow,
Roll me over on my right side,
    'Cause these bullets hurt me so,
        I was your man, but I done you wrong."   30

Bring all your rubber-tired hearses
    Bring all your rubber-tired hacks,
They're carrying poor Johnny to the burying ground
    And they ain't gonna bring him back,
        He was her man, but he done her wrong.   35

Frankie says to the sheriff,
    "What are they going to do?"
The sheriff he said to Frankie,
    "It's the 'lectric chair for you.
        He was your man, and he done you wrong."   40

"Put me in that dungeon,
    Put me in that cell,
Put me where the northeast wind
    Blows from the southeast corner of hell,
        I shot my man, 'cause he done me wrong."   45

ANONYMOUS

Scarborough Fair   date unknown

Where are you going? To Scarborough Fair?
Parsley, sage, rosemary, and thyme,
Remember me to a bonny lass there,
For once she was a true lover of mine.

Tell her to make me a cambric shirt,   5
Parsley, sage, rosemary, and thyme,
Without any needle or thread work'd in it,
And she shall be a true lover of mine.

Tell her to wash it in yonder well,
Parsley, sage, rosemary, and thyme,   10
Where water ne'er sprung nor a drop of rain fell,
And she shall be a true lover of mine.

Tell her to plough me an acre of land,
Parsley, sage, rosemary, and thyme,
Between the sea and the salt sea strand,   15
And she shall be a true lover of mine.

Tell her to plough it with one ram's horn,
Parsley, sage, rosemary, and thyme,
And sow it all over with one peppercorn,
And she shall be a true lover of mine.   20

Tell her to reap it with a sickle of leather,
Parsley, sage, rosemary, and thyme,

And tie it all up with a tom tit's feather,
And she shall be a true lover of mine.

Tell her to gather it all in a sack,   25
Parsley, sage, rosemary, and thyme,
And carry it home on a butterfly's back,
And then she shall be a true lover of mine.

ANONYMOUS
Scottsboro°   1936

Paper come out — done strewed de news
Seven po' chillun moan deat' house blues,
Seven po' chillun moanin' deat' house blues.
Seven nappy heads wit' big shiny eye
All boun' in jail and framed to die,   5
All boun' in jail and framed to die.

Messin' white woman — snake lyin' tale
Hang and burn and jail wit' no bail.
Dat hang and burn and jail wit' no bail.
Worse ol' crime in white folks' lan'   10
Black skin coverin' po' workin' man,
Black skin coverin' po' workin' man.

Judge and jury — all in de stan'
Lawd, biggety name for same lynchin' ban'
Lawd, biggety name for same lynchin' ban'.   15
White folks and nigger in great co't house
Like cat down cellar wit' nohole mouse.
Like cat down cellar wit' nohole mouse.

Scottsboro: This blues song refers to the 1931 arrest of nine black youths in Scottsboro, Alabama, who were charged with raping two white women. All nine were acquitted after several trials, but a few of them had already been sentenced to death when this song was written.

ANONYMOUS (traditional Scottish ballad)
The Twa Corbies°   date unknown

As I was walking all alane,
I heard twa corbies making a mane;°   *lament*

The Twa Corbies: The two ravens.

The tane° unto the t' other say,   *one*
"Where sall we gang° and dine to-day?"   *shall we go*

"In behint yon auld fail dyke,°   *old turf wall* 5
I wot° there lies a new-slain knight;   *know*
And naebody kens that he lies there,
But his hawk, his hound, and lady fair.

"His hound is to the hunting gane,
His hawk, to fetch the wild-fowl hame,   10
His lady's ta'en another mate,
So we may mak our dinner sweet.

"Ye'll sit on his white hause-bane,°   *neck bone*
And I'll pike out his bonny blue een.°   *eyes*
Wi' ae° lock o' his gowden° hair   *with one; golden* 15
We'll theek° our nest when it grows bare.   *thatch*

"Mony a one for him makes mane,
But nane sall ken whare he is gane;
O'er his white banes, when they are bare,
The wind sall blaw for evermair."   20

JOHN ASHBERY (b. 1927)
Paradoxes and Oxymorons   1981

This poem is concerned with language on a very plain level.
Look at it talking to you. You look out a window
Or pretend to fidget. You have it but you don't have it.
You miss it, it misses you. You miss each other.

The poem is sad because it wants to be yours, and cannot.   5
What's a plain level? It is that and other things,
Bringing a system of them into play. Play?
Well, actually, yes, but I consider play to be

A deeper outside thing, a dreamed role-pattern,
As in the division of grace these long August days   10
Without proof. Open-ended. And before you know
It gets lost in the steam and chatter of typewriters.

It has been played once more. I think you exist only
To tease me into doing it, on your level, and then you aren't there
Or have adopted a different attitude. And the poem   15
Has set me softly down beside you. The poem is you.

W. H. AUDEN (1907–1973)
As I Walked Out One Evening   1940

As I walked out one evening,
    Walking down Bristol Street,
The crowds upon the pavement
    Were fields of harvest wheat.

And down by the brimming river   5
    I heard a lover sing
Under an arch of the railway:
    "Love has no ending.

"I'll love you, dear, I'll love you
    Till China and Africa meet,   10
And the river jumps over the mountain
    And the salmon sing in the street,

"I'll love you till the ocean
    Is folded and hung up to dry
And the seven stars go squawking   15
    Like geese about the sky.

"The years shall run like rabbits,
    For in my arms I hold
The Flower of the Ages,
    And the first love of the world."   20

But all the clocks in the city
    Began to whirr and chime:
"O let not Time deceive you,
    You cannot conquer Time.

"In the burrows of the Nightmare   25
    Where Justice naked is,
Time watches from the shadow
    And coughs when you would kiss.

"In headaches and in worry
    Vaguely life leaks away,   30
And Time will have his fancy
    Tomorrow or today.

"Into many a green valley
    Drifts the appalling snow;
Time breaks the threaded dances   35
    And the diver's brilliant bow.

"O plunge your hands in water,
    Plunge them in up to the wrist;
Stare, stare in the basin
    And wonder what you've missed.   40

"The glacier knocks in the cupboard,
   The desert sighs in the bed,
And the crack in the teacup opens
   A lane to the land of the dead.

"Where the beggars raffle the banknotes   45
   And the Giant is enchanting to Jack,
And the Lily-white Boy is a Roarer,
   And Jill goes down on her back.

"O look, look in the mirror,
   O look in your distress;   50
Life remains a blessing
   Although you cannot bless.

"O stand, stand at the window
   As the tears scald and start;
You shall love your crooked neighbor   55
   With your crooked heart."

It was late, late in the evening,
   The lovers they were gone;
The clocks had ceased their chiming,
   And the deep river ran on.   60

W. H. AUDEN (1907–1973)
Lay Your Sleeping Head, My Love   1940

Lay your sleeping head, my love,
Human on my faithless arm;
Time and fevers burn away
Individual beauty from

Thoughtful children, and the grave   5
Proves the child ephemeral:
But in my arms till break of day
Let the living creature lie,
Mortal, guilty, but to me
The entirely beautiful.   10

Soul and body have no bounds:
To lovers as they lie upon
Her tolerant enchanted slope
In their ordinary swoon,
Grave the vision Venus sends   15
Of supernatural sympathy,
Universal love and hope;
While an abstract insight wakes
Among the glaciers and the rocks
The hermit's sensual ecstasy.   20

Certainty, fidelity
On the stroke of midnight pass
Like vibrations of a bell,
And fashionable madmen raise
Their pedantic boring cry: 25
Every farthing of the cost,
All the dreaded cards foretell,
Shall be paid, but from this night
Not a whisper, not a thought,
Not a kiss nor look be lost.   30

Beauty, midnight, vision dies:
Let the winds of dawn that blow
Softly round your dreaming head
Such a day of sweetness show
Eye and knocking heart may bless,   35
Find the mortal world enough;
Noons of dryness see you fed
By the involuntary powers,
Nights of insult let you pass
Watched by every human love.   40

W. H. AUDEN (1907–1973)
Musée des Beaux Arts°   1938

About suffering they were never wrong,
The Old Masters: how well they understood
Its human position; how it takes place
While someone else is eating or opening a window or just walking dully
    along;
How, when the aged are reverently, passionately waiting   5
For the miraculous birth, there always must be
Children who did not specially want it to happen, skating
On a pond at the edge of the wood:
They never forgot
That even the dreadful martyrdom must run its course   10
Anyhow in a corner, some untidy spot
Where the dogs go on with their doggy life and the torturer's horse
Scratches its innocent behind on a tree.

In Brueghel's *Icarus,°* for instance: how everything turns away
Quite leisurely from the disaster; the plowman may   15
Have heard the splash, the forsaken cry,

Musée des Beaux Arts: Museum of Fine Arts, in Brussels.   14 *Brueghel's* Icarus: *Landscape with the Fall of Icarus,* painting by Pieter Brueghel the Elder (c. 1525–1569), in the Brussels Museum.

But for him it was not an important failure; the sun shone
As it had to on the white legs disappearing into the green
Water; and the expensive delicate ship that must have seen
Something amazing, a boy falling out of the sky,   20
Had somewhere to get to and sailed calmly on.

W. H. AUDEN (1907–1973)
The Unknown Citizen   1940

(To JS/07/M/378
This Marble Monument
Is Erected by the State)

He was found by the Bureau of Statistics to be
One against whom there was no official complaint,
And all the reports on his conduct agree
That, in the modern sense of an old-fashioned word, he was a saint,
For in everything he did he served the Greater Community.   5
Except for the War till the day he retired
He worked in a factory and never got fired,
But satisfied his employers, Fudge Motors Inc.
Yet he wasn't a scab or odd in his views,
For his Union reports that he paid his dues,   10
(Our report on his Union shows it was sound)
And our Social Psychology workers found
That he was popular with his mates and liked a drink.
The Press are convinced that he bought a paper every day
And that his reactions to advertisements were normal in every way.   15
Policies taken out in his name prove that he was fully insured,
And his Health-card shows he was once in hospital but left it cured.
Both Producers Research and High-Grade Living declare
He was fully sensible to the advantages of the Installment Plan
And had everything necessary to the Modern Man,   20
A phonograph, radio, a car and a frigidaire.
Our researchers into Public Opinion are content
That he held the proper opinions for the time of year;
When there was peace, he was for peace; when there was war, he went.
He was married and added five children to the population,   25
Which our Eugenist says was the right number for a parent of his
      generation,
And our teachers report that he never interfered with their education.
Was he free? Was he happy? The question is absurd:
Had anything been wrong, we should certainly have heard.

APHRA BEHN (1640–1689)
Love Armed
1665

Love in Fantastic Triumph sat,
Whilst Bleeding Hearts around him flowed,
For whom Fresh pains he did Create,
And strange Tyrannic power he showed;
From thy Bright Eyes he took his fire,   5
Which round about, in sport he hurled;
But 'twas from mine he took desire,
Enough to undo the Amorous World

From me he took his sighs and tears,
From thee his Pride and Cruelty;   10
From me his Languishments and Fears,
And every Killing Dart from thee;
Thus thou and I, the God° have armed,   *Cupid, god of love*
And set him up a Deity;
But my poor Heart alone is harmed,   15
Whilst thine the Victor is, and free.

JOHN BERRYMAN (1914–1972)
Dream Song 14
1964

Life, friends, is boring. We must not say so.
After all, the sky flashes, the great sea yearns,
we ourselves flash and yearn,
and moreover my mother told me as a boy
(repeatedly) "Ever to confess you're bored   5
means you have no

Inner Resources." I conclude now I have no
inner resources, because I am heavy bored.
Peoples bore me,
literature bores me, especially great literature,   10
Henry bores me, with his plights & gripes
as bad as achilles,°

Who loves people and valiant art, which bores me.
And the tranquil hills, & gin, look like a drag
and somehow a dog   15
has taken itself & its tail considerably away
into mountains or sea or sky, leaving
behind: me, wag.

12 *Achilles:* Greek hero who fought in the Trojan War.

MEI-MEI BERSSENBRUGGE (b. 1947)

Jealousy   1989

Attention was commanded through a simple, unadorned,
    unexplained, often decentered presence,
up to now, a margin of empty space like water, its surface
    contracting, then melting
along buried pipelines, where gulls gather in euphoric buoyancy.   5
    Now,
the growth of size is vital, the significance of contraction by a moat,
    a flowerbed, or
a fenced path around the reservoir, its ability to induce the mind's
    growing experience of the breadth   10
and depth of physical association, which turns out to be both vital
    and insufficient, because
nature never provides a border for us, of infinite elements irregularly
    but flexibly integrated,
like the rhythm between fatigue and relief of accommodation, or   15
    like a large apartment. Now,
the construction is not the structure of your making love to me.
    The size of your body on mine
does not equal your weight or buoyancy, like fireworks on a tele-
    vision screen, or the way   20
an absent double expresses inaccuracy between what exists and does
    not exist in the room,
of particular shape, volume, etc., minute areas and inferred lines we
    are talking about.
You have made a vow to a woman not to sleep with me. For me,   25
    it seemed enough
that love was a spiritual exercise in physical form and what was
    seen is what it was,
looking down from the twelfth floor, our arms resting on pillows
    on the windowsill. It is midnight.   30
Fireworks reflected in the reservoir burst simultaneously on the
    south and the north shores,
so we keep turning our heads quickly for both of the starry spheres,
instead of a tangible, and an intangible event that does not reflect.
    Certain   35
definite brightness contains spaciousness. A starry night, like a fully
    reflecting surface,
claims no particular status in space, or being of its own.

ELIZABETH BISHOP (1911–1979)
Manners

1965

for a Child of 1918

My grandfather said to me
as we sat on the wagon seat,
"Be sure to remember to always
speak to everyone you meet."

We met a stranger on foot.   5
My grandfather's whip tapped his hat.
"Good day, sir. Good day. A fine day."
And I said it and bowed where I sat.

Then we overtook a boy we knew
with his big pet crow on his shoulder.   10
"Always offer everyone a ride;
don't forget that when you get older,"

my grandfather said. So Willy
climbed up with us, but the crow
gave a "Caw!" and flew off. I was worried.   15
How would he know where to go?

But he flew a little way at a time
from fence post to fence post, ahead;
and when Willy whistled he answered.
"A fine bird," my grandfather said,   20

"and he's well brought up. See, he answers
nicely when he's spoken to.
Man or beast, that's good manners.
Be sure that you both always do."

When automobiles went by,   25
the dust hid the people's faces,
but we shouted "Good day! Good day!
Fine day!" at the top of our voices.

When we came to Hustler Hill,
he said that the mare was tired,   30
so we all got down and walked,
as our good manners required.

ELIZABETH BISHOP (1911–1979)
The Shampoo   1955

The still explosions on the rocks,
the lichens, grow
by spreading, gray, concentric shocks.
They have arranged
to meet the rings around the moon, although   5
within our memories they have not changed.

And since the heavens will attend
as long on us,
you've been, dear friend,
precipitate and pragmatical;   10
and look what happens. For Time is
nothing if not amenable.

The shooting stars in your black hair
in bright formation
are flocking where,   15
so straight, so soon?
—Come, let me wash it in this big tin basin,
battered and shiny like the moon.

WILLIAM BLAKE (1757–1827)
The Garden of Love   1794

I went to the Garden of Love,
And saw what I never had seen:
A Chapel was built in the midst,
Where I used to play on the green.

And the gates of this Chapel were shut,   5
And "Thou shalt not" writ over the door;
So I turned to the Garden of Love
That so many sweet flowers bore;

And I saw it was filled with graves,
And tomb-stones where flowers should be;   10
And Priests in black gowns were walking their rounds,
And binding with briars my joys and desires.

WILLIAM BLAKE (1757–1827)
The Little Black Boy

1789

Illuminated printing: Blake etched his poems and designs in relief, with acid on copper. Each printed page was then colored by hand. The design and the text work together to express Blake's vision.

WILLIAM BLAKE (1757–1827)
A Poison Tree

1794

I was angry with my friend:
I told my wrath, my wrath did end.
I was angry with my foe:
I told it not, my wrath did grow.

And I water'd it in fears,
Night & morning with my tears;
And I sunnèd it with smiles,
And with soft deceitful wiles.

5

And it grew both day and night,
Till it bore an apple bright.   10
And my foe beheld it shine,
And he knew that it was mine,

And into my garden stole,
When the night had veild the pole;
In the morning glad I see   15
My foe outstretched beneath the tree.

ROBERT BLY (b. 1926)
Waking from Sleep   1962

Inside the veins there are navies setting forth,
Tiny explosions at the water lines,
And seagulls weaving in the wind of the salty blood.

It is the morning. The country has slept the whole winter.
Window seats were covered with fur skins, the yard was full   5
Of stiff dogs, and hands that clumsily held heavy books.

Now we wake, and rise from bed, and eat breakfast! —
Shouts rise from the harbor of the blood,
Mist, and masts rising, the knock of wooden tackle in the sunlight.

Now we sing, and do tiny dances on the kitchen floor.   10
Our whole body is like a harbor at dawn;
We know that our master has left us for the day.

LOUISE BOGAN (1897–1970)
Single Sonnet   1930

Now, you great stanza, you heroic mould,
Bend to my will, for I must give you love:
The weight in the heart that breathes, but cannot move,
Which to endure flesh only makes so bold.

Take up, take up, as it were lead or gold   5
The burden; test the dreadful mass thereof.
No stone, slate, metal under or above
Earth, is so ponderous, so dull, so cold.

Too long as ocean bed bears up the ocean,
As earth's core bears the earth, have I borne this;   10

Too long have lovers, bending for their kiss,
Felt bitter force cohering without motion.

Staunch meter, great song, it is yours, at length,
To prove how stronger you are than my strength.

ANNE BRADSTREET (c. 1612–1672)
Before the Birth of One of Her Children   1678

All things within this fading world hath end,
Adversity doth still our joys attend;
No ties so strong, no friends so dear and sweet,
But with death's parting blow is sure to meet.
The sentence past is most irrevocable,   5
A common thing, yet oh, inevitable.
How soon, my Dear, death may my steps attend,
How soon't may be thy lot to lose thy friend,
We both are ignorant, yet love bids me
These farewell lines to recommend to thee,   10
That when that knot's untied that made us one,
I may seem thine, who in effect am none.
And if I see not half my days that's due,
What nature would, God grant to yours and you;
The many faults that well you know I have   15
Let be interred in my oblivious grave;
If any worth or virtue were in me,
Let that live freshly in thy memory
And when thou feel'st no grief, as I no harms,
Yet love thy dead, who long lay in thine arms,   20
And when thy loss shall be repaid with gains
Look to my little babes, my dear remains.
And if thou love thyself, or loved'st me,
These O protect from stepdame's° injury.   *stepmother's*
And if chance to thine eyes shall bring this verse,   25
With some sad sighs honor my absent hearse;
And kiss this paper for thy love's dear sake,
Who with salt tears this last farewell did take.

RUPERT BROOKE (1887–1915)
The Soldier

If I should die, think only this of me:
    That there's some corner of a foreign field
That is for ever England. There shall be
    In that rich earth a richer dust concealed;
A dust whom England bore, shaped, made aware,   5
    Gave, once, her flowers to love, her ways to roam,
A body of England's, breathing English air,
    Washed by the rivers, blest by suns of home.

And think, this heart, all evil shed away,
    A pulse in the eternal mind, no less   10
        Gives somewhere back the thoughts by England given;
Her sights and sounds; dreams happy as her day;
    And laughter, learnt of friends; and gentleness,
        In hearts at peace, under an English heaven.

GWENDOLYN BROOKS (b. 1917)
The Bean Eaters

1959

They eat beans mostly, this old yellow pair.
Dinner is a casual affair.
Plain chipware on a plain and creaking wood,
Tin flatware.

Two who are Mostly Good.   5
Two who have lived their day,
But keep on putting on their clothes
And putting things away.

And remembering . . .
Remembering, with twinklings and twinges,   10
As they lean over the beans in their rented back room
    that is full of beads and receipts and dolls and cloths,
    tobacco crumbs, vases and fringes.

GWENDOLYN BROOKS (b. 1917)

The Mother

1945

Abortions will not let you forget.
You remember the children you got that you did not get,
The damp small pulps with a little or with no hair,
The singers and workers that never handled the air.
You will never neglect or beat   5
Them, or silence or buy with a sweet.
You will never wind up the sucking-thumb
Or scuttle off ghosts that come.
You will never leave them, controlling your luscious sigh,
Return for a snack of them, with gobbling mother-eye.   10

I have heard in the voices of the wind the voices of my dim
    killed children.
I have contracted. I have eased
My dim dears at the breasts they could never suck.
I have said, Sweets, if I sinned, if I seized
Your luck   15
And your lives from your unfinished reach,
If I stole your births and your names,
Your straight baby tears and your games,
Your stilted or lovely loves, your tumults, your marriages, aches,
    and your deaths,
If I poisoned the beginnings of your breaths,   20
Believe that even in my deliberateness I was not deliberate.
Though why should I whine,
Whine that the crime was other than mine? —
Since anyhow you are dead.
Or rather, or instead,   25
You were never made.

But that too, I am afraid,
Is faulty: oh, what shall I say, how is the truth to be said?
You were born, you had body, you died.
It is just that you never giggled or planned or cried.   30

Believe me, I loved you all.
Believe me, I knew you, though faintly, and I loved, I loved you
All.

ROBERT BROWNING (1812–1889)
Meeting at Night

1845

The gray sea and the long black land;
And the yellow half-moon large and low;
And the startled little waves that leap
In fiery ringlets from their sleep,
As I gain the cove with pushing prow,   5
And quench its speed i' the slushy sand.

Then a mile of warm sea-scented beach;
Three fields to cross till a farm appears;
A tap at the pane, the quick sharp scratch
And blue spurt of a lighted match,   10
And a voice less loud, through its joys and fears,
Than the two hearts beating each to each!

ROBERT BROWNING (1812–1889)
Parting at Morning

1845

Round the cape of a sudden came the sea,
And the sun looked over the mountain's rim:
And straight was a path of gold for him,
And the need of a world of men for me.

ROBERT BURNS (1759–1796)
John Anderson My Jo

1790

John Anderson my jo,° John,   *dear*
    When we were first acquent,
Your locks were like the raven,
    Your bonnie brow was brent;°   *smooth*
But now your brow is beld, John,   5
    Your locks are like the snaw,
But blessings on your frosty pow,°   *head*
    John Anderson my jo!

John Anderson my jo, John,
    We clamb the hill thegither,   10
And monie a cantie° day, John   *happy*
    We've had wi' ane anither:
Now we maun° totter down, John,   *must*

And hand in hand we'll go,
And sleep thegither at the foot,   15
    John Anderson my jo!

GEORGE GORDON, LORD BYRON (1788–1824)
She Walks in Beauty   1814

FROM HEBREW MELODIES

I
She walks in Beauty, like the night
    Of cloudless climes and starry skies;
And all that's best of dark and bright
    Meet in her aspect and her eyes:
Thus mellowed to that tender light   5
    Which Heaven to gaudy day denies.

II
One shade the more, one ray the less,
    Had half impaired the nameless grace
Which waves in every raven tress,
    Or softly lightens o'er her face;   10
Where thoughts serenely sweet express,
    How pure, how dear their dwelling-place.

III
And on that cheek, and o'er that brow,
    So soft, so calm, yet eloquent,
The smiles that win, the tints that glow,   15
    But tell of days in goodness spent,
A mind at peace with all below,
    A heart whose love is innocent!

THOMAS CAMPION (1567–1620)
There is a garden in her face   1617

    There is a garden in her face
Where roses and white lilies grow;
    A heav'nly paradise is that place
Wherein all pleasant fruits do flow.
    There cherries grow which none may buy   5
    Till "Cherry-ripe"° themselves do cry.

    Those cherries fairly do enclose

6 *"Cherry-ripe"*: Street cry of London fruit peddlers.

Of orient pearl a double row,
    Which when her lovely laughter shows,
They look like rose-buds filled with snow;   10
      Yet them nor° peer nor prince can buy,   *neither*
      Till "Cherry-ripe" themselves do cry.

      Her eyes like angels watch them still;
Her brows like bended bows do stand,
      Threat'ning with piercing frowns to kill   15
All that attempt, with eye or hand
      Those sacred cherries to come nigh
      Till "Cherry-ripe" themselves do cry.

LUCILLE CLIFTON (b. 1936)
for deLawd   1969

people say they have a hard time
understanding how I
go on about my business
playing my Ray Charles
hollering at the kids —   5
seem like my Afro
cut off in some old image
would show I got a long memory
and I come from a line
of black and going on women   10
who got used to making it through murdered sons
and who grief kept on pushing
who fried chicken
ironed
swept off the back steps   15
who grief kept
for their still alive sons
for their sons coming
just pushing   20

LUCILLE CLIFTON (b. 1936)
the poet   1974

i beg my bones to be good but
they keep clicking music and
i spin in the center of myself

a foolish frightful woman
moving my skin against the wind and
tap dancing for my life.

SAMUEL TAYLOR COLERIDGE (1772–1834)
Kubla Khan: or, a Vision in a Dream°

1798

In Xanadu did Kubla Khan°
    A stately pleasure-dome decree:
Where Alph, the sacred river, ran
Through caverns measureless to man
    Down to a sunless sea.   5
So twice five miles of fertile ground
With walls and towers were girdled round:
And here were gardens bright with sinuous rills
Where blossomed many an incense-bearing tree;
And there were forests ancient as the hills,   10
Enfolding sunny spots of greenery.

But oh! that deep romantic chasm which slanted
Down the green hill athwart a cedarn cover!°
A savage place! as holy and enchanted
As e'er beneath a waning moon was haunted   15
By woman wailing for her demon-lover!
And from this chasm, with ceaseless turmoil seething,
As if this earth in fast thick pants were breathing,
A mighty fountain momently was forced,
Amid whose swift half-intermitted burst   20
Huge fragments vaulted like rebounding hail,
Or chaffy grain beneath the thresher's flail:
And 'mid these dancing rocks at once and ever
It flung up momently the sacred river.
Five miles meandering with a mazy motion   25
Through wood and dale the sacred river ran,
Then reached the caverns measureless to man,
And sank in tumult to a lifeless ocean:
And 'mid this tumult Kubla heard from far
Ancestral voices prophesying war!   30

Vision in a Dream: This poem came to Coleridge in an opium-induced dream, but he was interrupted while writing it down by a visitor. He was later unable to remember the rest of the poem.   1 *Kubla Khan:* The historical Kublai Khan (1216–1294, grandson of Genghis Khan) was the founder of the Mongol dynasty in China.   13 *athwart . . . cover:* Spanning a grove of cedar trees.

The shadow of the dome of pleasure
Floated midway on the waves;
Where was heard the mingled measure
From the fountain and the caves.
It was a miracle of rare device,   35
A sunny pleasure-dome with caves of ice!

A damsel with a dulcimer
In a vision once I saw:
It was an Abyssinian maid,
And on her dulcimer she played,   40
Singing of Mount Abora.
Could I revive within me
Her symphony and song,
To such a deep delight 'twould win me,
That with music loud and long,   45
I would build that dome in air,
That sunny dome! those caves of ice!
And all who heard should see them there,
And all should cry, Beware! Beware!
His flashing eyes, his floating hair!   50
Weave a circle round him thrice,
And close your eyes with holy dread,
For he on honey-dew hath fed,
And drunk the milk of Paradise.

COUNTEE CULLEN (1903–1946)
For a Lady I Know   1925

She even thinks that up in heaven
Her class lies late and snores,
While poor black cherubs rise at seven
To do celestial chores.

COUNTEE CULLEN (1903–1946)
Saturday's Child°   1925

Some are teethed on a silver spoon,
With the stars strung for a rattle;
I cut my teeth as the black raccoon ——
For implements of battle.

Saturday's Child: Reference to the nursery rhyme: Monday's child is fair of face . . . / Saturday's child
must work hard for a living. . . .

Some are swaddled in silk and down,   5
And heralded by a star;
They swathed my limbs in a sackcloth gown
On a night that was black as tar.

For some, godfather and goddame
The opulent fairies be;   10
Dame Poverty gave me my name,
And Pain godfathered me.

For I was born on Saturday ——
"Bad time for planting a seed,"
Was all my father had to say,   15
And, "One mouth more to feed."

Death cut the strings that gave me life,
And handed me to Sorrow,
The only kind of middle wife
My folks could beg or borrow.   20

e. e. cummings (1894–1962)
anyone lived in a pretty how town   1940

anyone lived in a pretty how town
(with up so floating many bells down)
spring summer autumn winter
he sang his didn't he danced his did.

Women and men (both little and small)   5
cared for anyone not at all
they sowed their isn't they reaped their same
sun moon stars rain

children guessed (but only a few
and down they forgot as up they grew   10
autumn winter spring summer)
that noone loved him more by more

when by now and tree by leaf
she laughed his joy she cried his grief
bird by snow and stir by still   15
anyone's any was all to her

someones married their everyones
laughed their cryings and did their dance
(sleep wake hope and then) they
said their nevers they slept their dream   20

stars rain sun moon
(and only the snow can begin to explain

how children are apt to forget to remember
with up so floating many bells down)

one day anyone died i guess   25
(and noone stooped to kiss his face)
busy folk buried them side by side
little by little and was by was

all by all and deep by deep
and more by more they dream their sleep   30
noone and anyone earth by april
wish by spirit and if by yes.

Women and men (both dong and ding)
summer autumn winter spring
reaped their sowing and went their came   35
sun moon stars rain

e. e. cummings (1894–1962)
Buffalo Bill 's°   1923

Buffalo Bill 's
defunct
        who used to
        ride a watersmooth-silver
                        stallion   5
and break onetwothreefourfive pigeonsjustlikethat
                        Jesus

he was a handsome man
                and what i want to know is
how do you like your blueeyed boy   10
Mister Death

Buffalo Bill: William Frederick Cody (1846–1917). An American frontier scout and Indian killer turned
international circus showman with his Wild West show, which employed Sitting Bull and Annie
Oakley.

e. e. cummings (1894–1962)
since feeling is first   1926

since feeling is first
who pays any attention
to the syntax of things
will never wholly kiss you;

wholly to be a fool
while Spring is in the world

my blood approves,
and kisses are a better fate
than wisdom
lady i swear by all flowers. Don't cry
— the best gesture of my brain is less than
your eyelids' flutter which says

we are for each other: then
laugh, leaning back in my arms
for life's not a paragraph

And death i think is no parenthesis

JOHN DONNE (1572–1631)
The Apparition

c. 1600

When by thy scorn, O murderess, I am dead,
      And that thou thinkst thee free
From all solicitation from me,
Then shall my ghost come to thy bed,
And thee, feigned vestal, in worse arms shall see;
Then thy sick taper° will begin to wink,   *candle*
And he, whose thou art then, being tired before,
Will, if thou stir, or pinch to wake him, think
      Thou call'st for more,
And in false sleep will from thee shrink.
And then, poor aspen wretch, neglected, thou,
Bathed in a cold quicksilver sweat, wilt lie
      A verier° ghost than I.   *truer*
What I will say, I will not tell thee now,
Lest that preserve thee; and since my love is spent,
I had rather thou shouldst painfully repent,
Than by my threatenings rest still innocent.

JOHN DONNE (1572–1631)
Batter My Heart

1610

Batter my heart, three-personed God; for You
As yet but knock, breathe, shine, and seek to mend;
That I may rise and stand, o'erthrow me, and bend
Your force, to break, blow, burn, and make me new.
I, like an usurped town, to another due,

Labor to admit You, but Oh, to no end!
Reason, Your viceroy in me, me should defend,
But is captived, and proves weak or untrue.
Yet dearly I love You, and would be loved fain.
But am betrothed unto Your enemy: 10
Divorce me, untie, or break that knot again,
Take me to You, imprison me, for I,
Except You enthrall me, never shall be free,
Nor ever chaste, except You ravish me.

JOHN DONNE (1572–1631)
Death Be Not Proud   1611

Death be not proud, though some have called thee
Mighty and dreadful, for thou art not so;
For those whom thou think'st thou dost overthrow
Die not, poor Death, nor yet canst thou kill me.
From rest and sleep, which but thy pictures° be,   *images* 5
Much pleasure; then from thee much more must flow,
And soonest our best men with thee do go,
Rest of their bones, and soul's delivery.°   *deliverance*
Thou art slave to Fate, Chance, kings, and desperate men,
And dost with Poison, War, and Sickness dwell;   10
And poppy or charms can make us sleep as well,
And better than thy stroke; why swell'st° thou then?   *swell with pride*
One short sleep past, we wake eternally
And death shall be no more; Death, thou shalt die.

JOHN DONNE (1572–1631)
The Flea   1633

Mark but this flea, and mark in this°
How little that which thou deny'st me is;
It sucked me first, and now sucks thee,
And in this flea our two bloods mingled be;
Thou know'st that this cannot be said   5
A sin, nor shame, nor loss of maidenhead,
    Yet this enjoys before it woo,
    And pampered swells with one blood made of two,
    And this, alas, is more than we would do.°

1 *mark in this:* Take note of the moral lesson in this object.   9 *more than we would do:* I.e., if we
do not join our blood in conceiving a child.

Oh stay, three lives in one flea spare,   10
Where we almost, yea more than, married are.
This flea is you and I, and this
Our marriage bed, and marriage temple is;
Though parents grudge, and you, we're met
And cloistered in these living walls of jet.   15
    Though use° make you apt to kill me,   *habit*
    Let not to that, self-murder added be,
    And sacrilege, three sins in killing three.

Cruel and sudden, hast thou since
Purpled thy nail in blood of innocence?   20
Wherein could this flea guilty be,
Except in that drop which it sucked from thee?
Yet thou triumph'st, and say'st that thou
Find'st not thyself, nor me, the weaker now;
    'Tis true; then learn how false, fears be;   25
    Just so much honor, when thou yield'st to me,
    Will waste, as this flea's death took life from thee.

JOHN DONNE (1572–1631)
Hymn to God, My God, in My Sickness   1635

Since I am coming to that holy room
    Where, with thy choir of saints for evermore,
I shall be made thy music, as I come
    I tune the instrument here at the door,
    And what I must do then, think now before.   5

Whilst my physicians by their love are grown
    Cosmographers, and I their map, who lie
Flat on this bed, that by them may be shown
    That this is my southwest discovery,
    Per fretum febris,° by these straits to die,   *through the* 10
                                                strait of fever

I joy that in these straits I see my west;
    For though those currents yield return to none,
What shall my west hurt me? As west and east
    In all flat maps (and I am one) are one,
    So death doth touch the resurrectïon.   15

Is the Pacific Sea my home? Or are
    The eastern riches? Is Jerusalem?
Anyan° and Magellan and Gibraltar,   *Bering Strait*
    All straits, and none but straits, are ways to them,
    Whether where Japhet dwelt, or Cham, or Shem.°   20

20 *Japhet . . . Cham . . . Shem:* The three sons of Noah, who after the flood became the progenitors of the northern, southern, and Semitic peoples respectively (see Gen. 9:18–27).

We think that Paradise and Calvary,
    Christ's cross and Adam's tree, stood in one place;
Look, Lord, and find both Adams met in me;
    As the first Adam's sweat surrounds my face,
    May the last Adam's blood my soul embrace.   25

So, in his purple wrapped receive me, Lord;
    By these his thorns give me his other crown;
And as to others' souls I preached thy word,
    Be this my text, my sermon to mine own:
    Therefore that he may raise, the Lord throws down.   30

MICHAEL DRAYTON (1563–1631)
Since There's No Help   1619

Since there's no help, come let us kiss and part;
Nay, I have done, you get no more of me,
And I am glad, yea glad with all my heart
That thus so cleanly I myself can free;
Shake hands for ever, cancel all our vows,   5
And when we meet at any time again,
Be it not seen in either of our brows
That we one jot of former love retain.
Now at the last gasp of Love's latest breath,
When, his pulse failing, Passion speechless lies,   10
When Faith is kneeling by his bed of death,
And Innocence is closing up his eyes,
    Now if thou wouldst, when all have given him over,
    From death to life thou mightst him yet recover.

T. S. ELIOT (1888–1965)
Macavity: The Mystery Cat   1939

Macavity's a Mystery Cat: he's called the Hidden Paw —
For he's the master criminal who can defy the Law.
He's the bafflement of Scotland Yard, the Flying Squad's despair:
For when they reach the scene of the crime — *Macavity's not there!*

  Macavity, Macavity, there's no one like Macavity,   5
He's broken every human law, he breaks the law of gravity.
His powers of levitation would make a fakir stare,
And when you reach the scene of crime — *Macavity's not there!*
You may seek him in the basement, you may look up in the air —
But I tell you once and once again, *Macavity's not there!*   10

Macavity's a ginger cat, he's very tall and thin;
You would know him if you saw him, for his eyes are sunken in.
His brow is deeply lined with thought, his head is highly domed;
His coat is dusty from neglect, his whiskers are uncombed.
He sways his head from side to side, with movements like a snake;   15
And when you think he's half asleep, he's always wide awake.

Macavity, Macavity, there's no one like Macavity,
For he's a fiend in feline shape, a monster of depravity.
You may meet him in a by-street, you may see him in the square —
But when a crime's discovered, then *Macavity's not there!*   20

He's outwardly respectable. (They say he cheats at cards.)
And his footprints are not found in any file of Scotland Yard's.
And when the larder's looted, or the jewel-case is rifled,
Or when the milk is missing, or another Peke's been stifled,°
Or the greenhouse glass is broken, and the trellis past repair —   25
Ay, there's the wonder of the thing! *Macavity's not there!*

And when the Foreign Office find a Treaty's gone astray,
Or the Admiralty lose some plans and drawings by the way,
There may be a scrap of paper in the hall or on the stair —
But it's useless to investigate — *Macavity's not there!*   30
And when the loss has been disclosed, the Secret Service say:
"It *must* have been Macavity!" — but he's a mile away.
You'll be sure to find him resting, or a-licking of his thumbs,
Or engaging in doing complicated long division sums.

Macavity, Macavity, there's no one like Macavity,   35
There never was a Cat of such deceitfulness and suavity.
He always has an alibi, and one or two to spare:
At whatever time the deed took place — MACAVITY WASN'T THERE!
And they say that all the Cats whose wicked deeds are widely known
(I might mention Mungojerrie, I might mention Griddlebone)   40
Are nothing more than agents for the Cat who all the time
Just controls their operations: the Napoleon of Crime!

24 *stifled:* A Pekinese dog is killed.

ALLEN GINSBERG (b. 1926)
America   1956

America I've given you all and now I'm nothing.
America two dollars and twentyseven cents January 17, 1956.
I can't stand my own mind.
America when will we end the human war?
Go fuck yourself with your atom bomb.   5

I don't feel good don't bother me.
I won't write my poem till I'm in my right mind.
America when will you be angelic?
When will you take off your clothes?
When will you look at yourself through the grave?   10
When will you be worthy of your million Trotskyites?°   *American communists*
America why are your libraries full of tears?
America when will you send your eggs to India?
I'm sick of your insane demands.
When can I go into the supermarket and buy what I need with my good
    looks?   15
America after all it is you and I who are perfect not the next world.
Your machinery is too much for me.
You made me want to be a saint.
There must be some other way to settle this argument.
Burroughs° is in Tangiers I don't think he'll come back it's sinister.   20
Are you being sinister or is this some form of practical joke?
I'm trying to come to the point.
I refuse to give up my obsession.
America stop pushing I know what I'm doing.
America the plum blossoms are falling.   25
I haven't read the newspapers for months, everyday somebody goes on trial
    for murder.
America I feel sentimental about the Wobblies.°
America I used to be a communist when I was a kid I'm not sorry.
I smoke marijuana every chance I get.
I sit in my house for days on end and stare at the roses in the closet.   30
When I go to Chinatown I get drunk and never get laid.
My mind is made up there's going to be trouble.
You should have seen me reading Marx.
My psychoanalyst thinks I'm perfectly right.
I won't say the Lord's Prayer.   35
I have mystical visions and cosmic vibrations.
America I still haven't told you what you did to Uncle Max after he came
    over from Russia.

I'm addressing you.
Are you going to let your emotional life be run by Time Magazine?
I'm obsessed by Time Magazine.   40
I read it every week.
Its cover stares at me every time I slink past the corner candystore.
I read it in the basement of the Berkeley Public Library.
It's always telling me about responsibility. Businessmen are serious. Movie
    producers are serious. Everybody's serious but me.
It occurs to me that I am America.   45
I am talking to myself again.

20 *Burroughs:* William Burroughs (b. 1914), author of *Naked Lunch* (1959), who traveled to Tangiers
to avoid prosecution on drug charges.   27 *Wobblies:* Members of the Industrial Workers of the
World (I.W.W.), a militant labor organization.

Asia is rising against me.
I haven't got a chinaman's chance.
I'd better consider my national resources.
My national resources consist of two joints of marijuana millions of genitals
    an unpublishable private literature that goes 1400 miles an hour and
    twentyfive-thousand mental institutions.   50
I say nothing about my prisons nor the millions of underprivileged who
    live in my flowerpots under the light of five hundred suns.
I have abolished the whorehouses of France, Tangiers is the next to go.
My ambition is to be President despite the fact that I'm a Catholic.

America how can I write a holy litany in your silly mood?
I will continue like Henry Ford my strophes are as individual as his auto-
    mobiles more so they're all different sexes.   55
America I will sell you strophes $2500 apiece $500 down on your old strophe
America free Tom Mooney°
America save the Spanish Loyalists°
America Sacco & Vanzetti° must not die
America I am the Scottsboro boys.°   60
America when I was seven momma took me to Communist Cell meet-
    ings they sold us garbanzos a handful per ticket a ticket costs a nickel
    and the speeches were free everybody was angelic and sentimental
    about the workers it was all so sincere you have no idea what a good
    thing the party was in 1835 Scott Nearing was a grand old man a real
    mensch Mother Bloor made me cry I once saw Israel Amter plain.
    Everybody must have been a spy.°
America you don't really want to go to war.
America it's them bad Russians.
Them Russians them Russians and them Chinamen. And them Russians.
The Russia wants to eat us alive. The Russia's power mad. She wants to take
    our cars from out our garages.   65
Her wants to grab Chicago. Her needs a Red Readers' Digest. Her wants
    our auto plants in Siberia. Him big bureaucracy running our filling
    stations.
That no good. Ugh. Him make Indians learn read. Him need big black
    niggers. Hah. Her make us all work sixteen hours a day. Help.
America this is quite serious.
America this is the impression I get from looking in the television set.
America is this correct?   70

---

57 *Tom Mooney:* (1882–1942) A labor organizer convicted of setting off a bomb in a San Francisco crowd; many believed in his innocence. He was released from prison after serving more than twenty years.   58 *Spanish Loyalists:* Resistance fighters who opposed the fascist regime of Francisco Franco.   59 *Sacco & Vanzetti:* Nicola Sacco (1891–1927) and Bartolomeo Vanzetti (1888–1927), anarchists and labor agitators convicted of a payroll robbery and murder for which they were executed. They were widely viewed as victims and political martyrs rather than criminals.   60 *Scottsboro boys:* Another famous court case involving nine blacks falsely accused of raping two white girls in Scottsboro, Alabama.   61 *Everybody . . . spy:* Nearing, Bloor, and Amter were all associated with the Communist party.

I'd better get right down to the job.
It's true I don't want to join the Army or turn lathes in precision parts
    factories, I'm nearsighted and psychopathic anyway.
America I'm putting my queer shoulder to the wheel.

DONALD HALL (b. 1928)
My Son, My Executioner

1955

My son, my executioner,
    I take you in my arms,
Quiet and small and just astir,
    And whom my body warms.

Sweet death, small son, our instrument   5
    Of immortality,
Your cries and hungers document
    Our bodily decay.

We twenty-five and twenty-two,
    Who seemed to live forever,   10
Observe enduring life in you
    And start to die together.

DONALD HALL (b. 1928)
To a Waterfowl

1974

Women with hats like the rear ends of pink ducks
applauded you, my poems.
These are the women whose husbands I meet on airplanes,
who close their briefcases and ask, "What are *you* in?"
I look in their eyes, I tell them I am in poetry,   5

and their eyes fill with anxiety, and with little tears.
"Oh, yeah?" they say, developing an interest in clouds.
"My wife, she likes that sort of thing? Hah-hah?"
I guess maybe I'd better watch my grammar, huh?"
I leave them in airports, watching their grammar,   10

and take a limousine to the Women's Goodness Club
where I drink Harvey's Bristol Cream with their wives,
and eat chicken salad with capers, with little tomato wedges
and I read them "The Erotic Crocodile," and "Eating You."
Ah, when I have concluded the disbursement of sonorities,   15

crooning, "High on thy thigh I cry, Hi!" — and so forth —
they spank their wide hands, they smile like Jell-O,

and they say, "Hah-hah? My goodness, Mr. Hall,
but you certainly do have an imagination, huh?"
"Thank you, indeed," I say; "it brings in the bacon."   20

But now, my poems, now I have returned to the motel,
returned to *l'éternel retour*° of the Holiday Inn,   *endless sameness*
naked, lying on the bed, watching *Godzilla Sucks Mt. Fuji,*
addressing my poems, feeling superior, and drinking bourbon
from a flask disguised to look like a transistor radio.   25

Ah, my poems, it is true,
that with the deepest gratitude and most serene pleasure,
and with hints that I am a sexual Thomas Alva Edison,
and not without collecting an exorbitant fee,
I have accepted the approbation of feathers.   30

And what about you? You, laughing? You, in the bluejeans,
laughing at your mother who wears hats, and at your father
who rides airplanes with a briefcase watching his grammar?
Will you ever be old and dumb, like your creepy parents?
Not you, not you, not you, not you, not you, not you.   35

THOMAS HARDY (1840–1928)
Channel Firing°   April 1914

That night your great guns, unawares,
Shook all our coffins as we lay,
And broke the chancel window squares,°
We thought it was the Judgment-day°

And sat upright. While drearisome   5
Arose the howl of wakened hounds:
The mouse let fall the altar-crumb,°
The worms drew back into the mounds,

The glebe cow° drooled. Till God called, "No;
It's gunnery practice out at sea   10
Just as before you went below;
The world is as it used to be:

"All nations striving strong to make
Red war yet redder. Mad as hatters
They do no more for Christés sake   15
Than you who are helpless in such matters.

Channel Firing: The navy practiced firing guns on the English Channel in the summer of 1914, just
before World War I began.   3 *chancel window squares:* A church's altar window.   4 *Judgment-
day:* In Christian tradition, the day the dead are awakened for judgment.   7 *altar-crumb:* Particle
from the wafer used in the celebration of the Eucharist.   9 *glebe cow:* Parish cow pastured on
church land.

"That this is not the judgment-hour
For some of them's a blessed thing,
For if it were they'd have to scour
Hell's floor for so much threatening . . .   20

"Ha, ha. It will be warmer when
I blow the trumpet (if indeed
I ever do; for you are men,
And rest eternal sorely need)."

So down we lay again. "I wonder,   25
Will the world ever saner be,"
Said one, "than when He sent us under
In our indifferent century!"

And many a skeleton shook his head.
"Instead of preaching forty year,"   30
My neighbor Parson Thirdly said,
"I wish I had stuck to pipes and beer."

Again the guns disturbed the hour,
Roaring their readiness to avenge.
As far inland as Stourton Tower,°   35
And Camelot,° and starlit Stonehenge.°

35 *Stourton Tower:* Eighteenth-century commemoration of King Alfred's ninth-century victory over the Danes in Stourhead Park, Wiltshire.   36 *Camelot:* The legendary castle that housed King Arthur's court, probably located in Cornwall; *Stonehenge:* A circular formation of great stones or monoliths erected about 1800 B.C., associated with religious rituals and perhaps with astronomical calculations, and located on Salisbury Plain, Wiltshire.

THOMAS HARDY (1840–1928)
During Wind and Rain   1917

They sing their dearest songs —
He, she, all of them — yea,
Treble and tenor and bass,
    And one to play;
With the candles mooning each face. . . .   5
    Ah, no; the years O!
How the sick leaves reel down in throngs!

They clear the creeping moss —
Elders and juniors — aye,
Making the pathways neat   10
    And the garden gay;
And they build a shady seat. . . .
    Ah, no; the years, the years;
See, the white storm-birds wing across!

They are blithely breakfasting all —   15
Men and maidens — yea,
Under the summer tree,
    With a glimpse of the bay,
While pet fowl come to the knee. . . .
        Ah, no! the years O!   20
And the rotten rose is ripped from the wall.

They change to a high new house,
He, she, all of them — aye,
Clocks and carpets and chairs
    On the lawn all day,   25
And brightest things that are theirs. . . .
        Ah, no; the years, the years;
Down their carved names the raindrop plows.

THOMAS HARDY (1840–1928)
Hap   1866

If but some vengeful god would call to me
From up the sky, and laugh: "Thou suffering thing,
Know that thy sorrow is my ecstasy,
That thy love's loss is my hate's profiting!"

Then would I bear it, clench myself, and die,   5
Steeled by the sense of ire unmerited;
Half-eased in that a Powerfuller than I
Had willed and meted me the tears I shed.

But not so. How arrives it joy lies slain,
And why unblooms the best hope ever sown?   10
— Crass Casualty obstructs the sun and rain,
And dicing Time for gladness casts a moan. . . .
These purblind Doomsters had as readily strown
Blisses about my pilgrimage as pain.

THOMAS HARDY (1840–1928)
The Man He Killed   1902

Had he and I but met
By some old ancient inn,
We should have sat us down to wet
    Right many a nipperkin!°   *half-pint cup*

But ranged as infantry,   5
And staring face to face,

I shot at him as he at me,
    And killed him in his place.

I shot him dead because —
    Because he was my foe,
Just so: my foe of course he was;
    That's clear enough; although   10

He thought he'd 'list, perhaps,
    Off-hand-like — just as I —
Was out of work — had sold his traps —   15
    No other reason why.

Yes; quaint and curious war is!
    You shoot a fellow down
You'd treat, if met where any bar is,
    Or help to half-a-crown.   20

SEAMUS HEANEY (b. 1939)
Digging   1966

Between my finger and my thumb
The squat pen rests; snug as a gun.

Under my window, a clean rasping sound
When the spade sinks into gravelly ground:
My father, digging. I look down   5

Till his straining rump among the flowerbeds
Bends low, comes up twenty years away
Stooping in rhythm through potato drills
Where he was digging.

The coarse boot nestled on the lug, the shaft   10
Against the inside knee was levered firmly.
He rooted out tall tops, buried the bright edge deep
To scatter new potatoes that we picked
Loving their cool hardness in our hands.

By God, the old man could handle a spade.   15
Just like his old man.

My grandfather cut more turf in a day
Than any other man on Toner's bog.
Once I carried him milk in a bottle
Corked sloppily with paper. He straightened up   20
To drink it, then fell to right away

Nicking and slicing neatly, heaving sods
Over his shoulder, going down and down
For the good turf. Digging.

The cold smell of potato mould, the squelch and slap   25
Of soggy peat, the curt cuts of an edge
Through living roots awaken in my head.
But I've no spade to follow men like them.

Between my finger and my thumb
The squat pen rests.   30
I'll dig with it.

ANTHONY HECHT (b. 1923)
The Dover Bitch°   1968

A Criticism of Life

So there stood Matthew Arnold and this girl
With the cliffs of England crumbling away behind them,
And he said to her, "Try to be true to me,
And I'll do the same for you, for things are bad
All over, etc., etc."   5
Well now, I knew this girl. It's true she had read
Sophocles in a fairly good translation
And caught that bitter allusion to the sea,
But all the time he was talking she had in mind
The notion of what his whiskers would feel like   10
On the back of her neck. She told me later on
That after a while she got to looking out
At the lights across the channel, and really felt sad,
Thinking of all the wine and enormous beds
And blandishments in French and the perfumes.   15
And then she got really angry. To have been brought
All the way down from London, and then be addressed
As a sort of mournful cosmic last resort
Is really tough on a girl, and she was pretty.
Anyway, she watched him pace the room   20
And finger his watch-chain and seem to sweat a bit,
And then she said one or two unprintable things.
But you mustn't judge her by that. What I mean to say is,
She's really all right. I still see her once in a while
And she always treats me right. We have a drink   25
And I give her a good time, and perhaps it's a year
Before I see her again, but there she is,
Running to fat, but dependable as they come.
And sometimes I bring her a bottle of *Nuit d'Amour.*

The Dover Bitch: A parody of Matthew Arnold's poem "Dover Beach" (see p. 72)

GEORGE HERBERT (1593–1633)
The Collar 1633

I struck the board° and cried, "No more;   *table*
    I will abroad!
What? shall I ever sigh and pine?
My lines and life are free, free as the road,
  Loose as the wind, as large as store.°   5
     Shall I be still in suit?°   *serving another*
  Have I no harvest but a thorn
  To let me blood, and not restore
What I have lost with cordial° fruit?   *restorative*
     Sure there was wine   10
Before my sighs did dry it; there was corn
  Before my tears did drown it.
  Is the year only lost to me?
    Have I no bays° to crown it, *triumphal wreaths*
No flowers, no garlands gay? All blasted?   15
    All wasted?
  Not so, my heart; but there is fruit,
    And thou hast hands.
  Recover all thy sigh-blown age
On double pleasures: leave thy cold dispute 20
Of what is fit, and not. Forsake thy cage,
    Thy rope of sands,
Which petty thoughts have made, and made to thee
  Good cable, to enforce and draw,
    And be thy law,   25
While thou didst wink and wouldst not see.
    Away! take heed;
    I will abroad.
Call in thy death's-head° there; tie up thy fears.
    He that forbears   30
    To suit and serve his need,
    Deserves his load."
But as I raved and grew more fierce and wild
    At every word,
Methought I heard one calling, *Child!*   35
    And I replied, *My Lord.*

5 *store:* A storehouse or warehouse. 29 *death's-head:* A skull, reminder of mortality.

M. CARL HOLMAN (1919–1988)
Mr. Z

1967

Taught early that his mother's skin was the sign of error,
He dressed and spoke the perfect part of honor;
Won scholarships, attended the best schools,
Disclaimed kinship with jazz and spirituals;
Chose prudent, raceless views for each situation,   5
Or when he could not cleanly skirt dissension,
Faced up to the dilemma, firmly seized
Whatever ground was Anglo-Saxonized.

In diet, too, his practice was exemplary:
Of pork in its profane forms he was wary;   10
Expert in vintage wines, sauces and salads,
His palate shrank from cornbread, yams and collards.

He was as careful whom he chose to kiss:
His bride had somewhere lost her Jewishness,
But kept her blue eyes; an Episcopalian   15
Prelate proclaimed them matched chameleon.
Choosing the right addresses, here, abroad,
They shunned those places where they might be barred;
Even less anxious to be asked to dine
Where hosts catered to kosher accent or exotic skin.   20

And so he climbed, unclogged by ethnic weights,
An airborne plant, flourishing without roots.
Not one false note was struck — until he died:
His subtly grieving widow could have flayed
The obit writers, ringing crude changes on a clumsy phrase: 25
"One of the most distinguished members of his race."

GERARD MANLEY HOPKINS (1844–1889)
Pied Beauty

1877

Glory be to God for dappled things —
    For skies of couple-color as a brinded cow;
        For rose-moles all in stipple upon trout that swim;
Fresh-firecoal chestnut-falls;° finches' wings;   *fallen chestnut*
    Landscape plotted and pieced — fold, fallow, and plow;   5
        And all trades, their gear and tackle and trim.

All things counter, original, spare, strange;
    Whatever is fickle, freckled (who knows how?)

With swift, slow; sweet, sour; adazzle, dim;
He fathers-forth whose beauty is past change: 10
            Praise him.

GERARD MANLEY HOPKINS (1844–1889)
Spring and Fall   1880

To a Young Child

Márgarét áre you gríeving
Over Goldengrove unleaving?
Leáves, like the things of man, you
With your fresh thoughts care for, can you?
Áh! ás the heart grows older   5
It will come to such sights colder
By and by, nor spare a sigh
Though worlds of wanwood° leafmeal° lie;
And yet you wíll weep and know why.
Now no matter, child, the name: 10
Sórrow's spríngs áre the same.
Nor mouth had, no nor mind, expressed
What heart heard of, ghost° guessed: *soul*
It ís the blight man was born for,
    it is Margaret you mourn for.   15

8 *wanwood:* Gloomy woods; *leafmeal:* Leaves broken up piecemeal.

GERARD MANLEY HOPKINS (1844–1889)
The Windhover°   1877

To Christ Our Lord

I caught this morning morning's minion,° king-   *favorite*
    dom of daylight's dauphin, dapple-dawn-drawn Falcon, in his riding
    Of the rolling level underneath him steady air, and striding
High there, how he rung upon the rein of a wimpling wing
In his ecstasy! then off, off forth on swing,   5
    As a skate's heel sweeps smooth on a bow-bend: the hurl and gliding
    Rebuffed the big wind. My heart in hiding
Stirred for a bird, — the achieve of, the mastery of the thing!

The Windhover: "A name for the kestrel [a kind of small hawk], from its habit of hovering or hanging
with its head to the wind" [OED].

Brute beauty and valour and act, oh, air, pride, plume, here
    Buckle!° AND the fire that breaks from thee then, a billion   10
Times told lovelier, more dangerous, O my chevalier!

    No wonder of it: shéer plód makes plough down sillion°   *furrow*
Shine, and blue-bleak embers, ah my dear,
    Fall, gall themselves, and gash gold-vermilion.

10 *Buckle:* To join, to equip for battle, to crumple.

A. E. HOUSMAN (1859–1936)
Is my team ploughing   1896

"Is my team ploughing,
    That I was used to drive
And hear the harness jingle
    When I was man alive?"

Ay, the horses trample,   5
    The harness jingles now;
No change though you lie under
    The land you used to plough.

"Is football playing
    Along the river shore,
With lads to chase the leather,   10
    Now I stand up no more?"

Ay, the ball is flying,
    The lads play heart and soul;
The goal stands up, the keeper   15
    Stands up to keep the goal.

"Is my girl happy,
    That I thought hard to leave,
And has she tired of weeping
    As she lies down at eve?"   20

Ay, she lies down lightly,
    She lies not down to weep:
Your girl is well contented.
    Be still, my lad, and sleep.

"Is my friend hearty,   25
    Now I am thin and pine,
And has he found to sleep in
    A better bed than mine?"

Yes, lad, I lie easy,
    I lie as lads would choose;   30
I cheer a dead man's sweetheart,
    Never ask me whose.

A. E. HOUSMAN (1859–1936)
Terence,° this is stupid stuff   1896

"Terence, this is stupid stuff:
You eat your victuals fast enough;
There can't be much amiss, 'tis clear,
To see the rate you drink your beer.
But oh, good Lord, the verse you make,   5
It gives a chap the belly-ache.
The cow, the old cow, she is dead;
It sleeps well, the hornèd head:
We poor lads, 'tis our turn now
To hear such tunes as killed the cow.   10
Pretty friendship 'tis to rhyme
Your friends to death before their time
Moping melancholy mad:
Come, pipe a tune to dance to, lad."

Why, if 'tis dancing you would be,   15
There's brisker pipes than poetry.
Say, for what were hop-yards meant,
Or why was Burton built on Trent?°
Oh many a peer of England brews
Livelier liquor than the Muse,   20
And malt does more than Milton can
To justify God's ways to man.°
Ale, man, ale's the stuff to drink
For fellows whom it hurts to think:
Look into the pewter pot   25
To see the world as the world's not.
And faith, 'tis pleasant till 'tis past:
The mischief is that 'twill not last.
Oh I have been to Ludlow fair
And left my necktie God knows where,   30
And carried halfway home, or near,
Pints and quarts of Ludlow beer:
Then the world seemed none so bad,
And I myself a sterling lad;

Terence: Housman's name for himself.   18 *Trent:* Burton-on-Trent, an English city famous for its breweries.   22 *To . . . man:* John Milton's (1608–1674) announced purpose in *Paradise Lost.*

And down in lovely muck I've lain,   35
Happy till I woke again.
Then I saw the morning sky:
Heigho, the tale was all a lie;
The world, it was the old world yet,
I was I, my things were wet,   40
And nothing now remained to do
But begin the game anew.

    Therefore, since the world has still
Much good, but much less good than ill,
And while the sun and moon endure   45
Luck's a chance, but trouble's sure,
I'd face it as a wise man would,
And train for ill and not for good.
'Tis true, the stuff I bring for sale
Is not so brisk a brew as ale: 50
Out of a stem that scored the hand
I wrung it in a weary land.
But take it: if the smack is sour,
The better for the embittered hour;
It should do good to heart and head   55
When your soul is in my soul's stead;
And I will friend you, if I may,
In the dark and cloudy day.

    There was a king reigned in the East:
There, when kings will sit to feast,   60
They get their fill before they think
With poisoned meat and poisoned drink.
He gathered all that springs to birth
From the many-venomed earth;
First a little, thence to more,   65
He sampled all her killing store;
And easy, smiling, seasoned sound,
Sate the king when healths° went round.   *toasts*
They put arsenic in his meat
And stared aghast to watch him eat;   70
They poured strychnine in his cup
And shook to see him drink it up:
They shook, they stared as white's their shirt:
Them it was their poison hurt.
—I tell the tale that I heard told.   75
Mithridates,° he died old.

76 *Mithridates:* King of Pontus in the first century B.C., who took gradually increasing doses of poison
in order to develop a tolerance for them.

A. E. HOUSMAN (1859–1936)
To an Athlete Dying Young

1896

The time you won your town the race
We chaired° you through the marketplace;
Man and boy stood cheering by,
And home we brought you shoulder-high.

Today, the road all runners come,   5
Shoulder-high we bring you home,
And set you at your threshold down,
Townsman of a stiller town.

Smart lad, to slip betimes away
From fields where glory does not stay,   10
And early though the laurel° grows
It withers quicker than the rose.

Eyes the shady night has shut
Cannot see the record cut,
And silence sounds no worse than cheers   15
After earth has stopped the ears:

Now you will not swell the rout
Of lads that wore their honors out,
Runners whom renown outran
And the name died before the man.   20

So set, before its echoes fade,
The fleet foot on the sill of shade,
And hold to the low lintel up
The still-defended challenge-cup.

And round that early-laureled head   25
Will flock to gaze the strengthless dead,
And find unwithered on its curls
The garland briefer than a girl's.

2 *chaired:* Carried on the shoulders in triumphal parade.   11 *laurel:* Flowering shrub traditionally used to fashion wreaths of honor.

LANGSTON HUGHES (1902–1967)

Ballad of the Landlord 1951

Landlord, landlord,
My roof has sprung a leak.
Don't you 'member I told you about it
Way last week?

Landlord, landlord, 5
These steps is broken down.
When you come up yourself
It's a wonder you don't fall down.

Ten Bucks you say I owe you?
Ten Bucks you say is due? 10
Well, that's Ten Bucks more'n I'll pay you
Till you fix this house up new.

What? You gonna get eviction orders?
You gonna cut off my heat?
You gonna take my furniture and 15
Throw it in the street?

Um-huh! You talking high and mighty.
Talk on — till you get through.
You ain't gonna be able to say a word
If I land my fist on you. 20

Police! Police!
Come and get this man!
He's trying to ruin the government
And overturn the land!

Copper's whistle! 25
Patrol bell!
Arrest.

Precinct Station.
Iron cell.
Headlines in press: 30

MAN THREATENS LANDLORD
TENANT HELD NO BAIL
JUDGE GIVES NEGRO 90 DAYS IN COUNTY JAIL

RANDALL JARRELL (1914–1965)
Next Day

Moving from Cheer to Joy, from Joy to All,
I take a box
And add it to my wild rice, my Cornish game hens.
The slacked or shorted, basketed, identical
Food-gathering flocks   5
Are selves I overlook. Wisdom, said William James,°

Is learning what to overlook. And I am wise
If that is wisdom
Yet somehow, as I buy All from these shelves
And the boy takes it to my station wagon,   10
What I've become
Troubles me even if I shut my eyes.

When I was young and miserable and pretty
And poor, I'd wish
What all girls wish: to have a husband,   15
A house and children. Now that I'm old, my wish
Is womanish:
That the boy putting groceries in my car

See me. It bewilders me he doesn't see me.
For so many years   20
I was good enough to eat: the world looked at me
And its mouth watered. How often they have undressed me,
The eyes of strangers!
And, holding their flesh within my flesh, their vile

Imaginings within my imagining,   25
I too have taken
The chance of life. Now the boy pats my dog
And we start home. Now I am good.
The last mistaken,
Ecstatic, accidental bliss, the blind   30

Happiness that, bursting, leaves upon the palm
Some soap and water —
It was so long ago, back in some Gay
Twenties, Nineties, I don't know . . . Today I miss
My lovely daughter   35
Away at school, my sons away at school,

---

6 *William James* (1842–1910): A psychologist and philosopher, author of *Principles of Psychology* (1890).

My husband away at work — I wish for them.
The dog, the maid,
And I go through the sure unvarying days
At home in them. As I look at my life,   40
I am afraid
Only that it will change, as I am changing:

I am afraid, this morning, of my face.
It looks at me
From the rear-view mirror, with the eyes I hate,   45
The smile I hate. Its plain, lined look
Of gray discovery
Repeats to me: "You're old." That's all, I'm old.

And yet I'm afraid, as I was at the funeral
I went to yesterday.   50
My friend's cold made-up face, granite among its flowers,
Her undressed, operated-on, dressed body
Were my face and body.
As I think of her I hear her telling me

How young I seem: I *am* exceptional;   55
I think of all I have.
But really no one is exceptional,
No one has anything, I'm anybody,
I stand beside my grave
Confused with my life, that is commonplace and solitary.   60

BEN JONSON (1573–1637)
On My First Son   1603

Farewell, thou child of my right hand,° and joy.
My sin was too much hope of thee, loved boy;
Seven years thou wert lent to me, and I thee pay,
Exacted by thy fate, on the just day.°   *his birthday*
Oh, could I lose all father° now. For why   *fatherhood*   5
Will man lament the state he should envỳ? —
To have so soon 'scaped world's and flesh's rage,
And, if no other misery, yet age.
Rest in soft peace, and asked, say, "Here doth lie
Ben Jonson his best piece of poetry,"   10
For whose sake henceforth all his vows be such
As what he loves may never like too much.

1 *child of my right hand:* This phrase translates the Hebrew name "Benjamin," Jonson's son.

X. J. KENNEDY (b. 1929)

In a Prominent Bar in Secaucus One Day   1961

To the tune of "The Old Orange Flute" or
the tune of "Sweet Betsy from Pike"

In a prominent bar in Secaucus one day
Rose a lady in skunk with a topheavy sway,
Raised a knobby red finger — all turned from their beer —
While with eyes bright as snowcrust she sang high and clear:

"Now who of you'd think from an eyeload of me   5
That I once was a lady as proud as could be?
Oh I'd never sit down by a tumbledown drunk
If it wasn't, my dears, for the high cost of junk.

"All the gents used to swear that the white of my calf
Beat the down of a swan by a length and a half.   10
In the kerchief of linen I caught to my nose
Ah, there never fell snot, but a little gold rose.

"I had seven gold teeth and a toothpick of gold,
My Virginia cheroot was a leaf of it rolled
And I'd light it each time with a thousand in cash —   15
Why the bums used to fight if I flicked them an ash.

"Once the toast of the Biltmore, the belle of the Taft,
I would drink bottle beer at the Drake, never draft,
And dine at the Astor° on Salisbury steak
With a clean tablecloth for each bite I did take.   20

"In a car like the Roxy° I'd roll to the track,
A steel-guitar trio, a bar in the back,
And the wheels made no noise, they turned over so fast,
Still it took you ten minutes to see me go past.

"When the horses bowed down to me that I might choose,   25
I bet on them all, for I hated to lose.
Now I'm saddled each night for my butter and eggs
And the broken threads race down the backs of my legs.

"Let you hold in mind, girls, that your beauty must pass
Like a lovely white clover that rusts with its grass.   30
Keep your bottoms off barstools and marry you young
Or be left — an old barrel with many a bung.

"For when time takes you out for a spin in his car
You'll be hard-pressed to stop him from going too far
And be left by the roadside, for all your good deeds,   35
Two toadstools for tits and a face full of weeds."

17–19 *Biltmore . . . Astor:* The Biltmore, Taft, Drake, and Astor were elegant hotels in New York
City.   21 *Roxy:* A lush New York theater.

All the house raised a cheer, but the man at the bar
Made a phonecall and up pulled a red patrol car
And she blew us a kiss as they copped her away
From that prominent bar in Secaucus, N.J.   40

ETHERIDGE KNIGHT (b. 1931)
A Watts Mother Mourns While Boiling Beans   1973

The blooming flower of my life is roaming
in the night, and I think surely
that never since he was born
have I been free from fright.
My boy is bold, and his blood   5
grows quickly hot/even now
he could be crawling in the street
bleeding out his life, likely as not.
Come home, my bold and restless son. — Stop
my heart's yearning! But I must quit   10
this thinking — my husband is coming
and the beans are burning.

TED KOOSER (b. 1939)
The Blind Always Come as Such a Surprise   1980

The blind always come as such a surprise,
suddenly filling an elevator
with a great white porcupine of canes,
or coming down upon us in a noisy crowd
like the eye of a hurricane.   5
The dashboards of cars stopped at crosswalks
and the shoes of commuters on trains
are covered with sentences
struck down in mid-flight by the canes of the blind.
Each of them changes our lives,   10
tapping across the bright circles of our ambitions
like cracks traversing the favorite china.

PHILIP LARKIN (1922–1985)
Home Is So Sad

1964

Home is so sad. It stays as it was left,
Shaped to the comfort of the last to go
As if to win them back. Instead, bereft
Of anyone to please, it withers so,
Having no heart to put aside the theft   5

And turn again to what it started as,
A joyous shot at how things ought to be,
Long fallen wide. You can see how it was:
Look at the pictures and the cutlery.
The music in the piano stool. That vase.   10

DENISE LEVERTOV (b. 1923)
News Items

1975

i   America the Bountiful

After the welfare hotel
crumbled suddenly (after repeated warnings)
into the street,

Seventh Day Adventists brought supplies
of clothing to the survivors.   5
" 'Look at this,' exclaimed
Loretta Rollock, 48 years old,
as she held up a green dress
and lingerie. 'I've never worn
such nice clothes. I feel like   10
when I was a kid and my mom
brought me something.' Then
she began to cry."

ii   In the Rubble

For some the hotel's collapse meant
life would have to be started   15
all over again.

Sixty-year-old Charles, on welfare
like so many of the others, who said,
"We are the rootless people," and
"I have no home, no place that I can say I   20
really live in," and,
"I had become used to it here,"
also said:
"I lost

all I ever had,
in the rubble.
I lost my clothes,
I lost the picture of my parents
and I lost my television."

AUDRE LORDE (1934–1992)
Hanging Fire

1978

I am fourteen
and my skin has betrayed me
the boy I cannot live without
still sucks his thumb
in secret   5
how come my knees are
always so ashy
what if I die
before morning
and momma's in the bedroom   10
with the door closed.

I have to learn how to dance
in time for the next party
my room is too small for me
suppose I die before graduation   15
they will sing sad melodies
but finally
tell the truth about me
There is nothing I want to do
and too much   20
that has to be done
and momma's in the bedroom
with the door closed.

Nobody even stops to think
about my side of it   25
I should have been on Math Team
my marks were better than his
why do I have to be
the one
wearing braces   30
I have nothing to wear tomorrow
will I live long enough
to grow up
and momma's in the bedroom
with the door closed.   35

CLAUDE McKAY (1889–1948)
The Harlem Dancer 1917

Applauding youths laughed with young prostitutes
And watched her perfect, half-clothed body sway;
Her voice was like the sound of blended flutes
Blown by black players upon a picnic day.
She sang and danced on gracefully and calm, 5
The light gauze hanging loose about her form;
To me she seemed a proudly-swaying palm
Grown lovelier for passing through a storm.
Upon her swarthy neck black shiny curls
Luxuriant fell; and tossing coins in praise, 10
The wine-flushed, bold-eyed boys, and even the girls,
Devoured her shape with eager, passionate gaze;
But looking at her falsely-smiling face,
I knew her self was not in that strange place.

CHRISTOPHER MARLOWE (1564–1593)
The Passionate Shepherd to His Love c. 1599

Come live with me and be my love,
And we will all the pleasures prove
That valleys, groves, hills, and fields,
Woods, or steepy mountain yields.

And we will sit upon the rocks, 5
Seeing the shepherds feed their flocks,
By shallow rivers to whose falls
Melodious birds sing madrigals.

And I will make thee beds of roses
And a thousand fragrant posies, 10
A cap of flowers, and a kirtle
Embroidered all with leaves of myrtle;

A gown made of the finest wool
Which from our pretty lambs we pull;
Fair lined slippers for the cold, 15
With buckles of the purest gold;

A belt of straw and ivy buds,
With coral clasps and amber studs:
And if these pleasures may thee move,
Come live with me, and be my love. 20

The shepherd swains shall dance and sing
For thy delight each May morning:
If these delights thy mind may move,
Then live with me and be my love.

ANDREW MARVELL (1621–1678)
The Garden

1681

How vainly men themselves amaze°   *become frenzied*
To win the palm, the oak, or bays;°   *awards*
And their incessant labors see
Crowned from some single herb, or tree,
Whose short and narrow-vergèd° shade   *trimmed*   5
Does prudently their toils upbraid;
While all flowers and all trees do close
To weave the garlands of repose!

Fair Quiet, have I found thee here,
And Innocence, thy sister dear!   10
Mistaken long, I sought you then
In busy companies of men.
Your sacred plants, if here below,
Only among the plants will grow;
Society is all but rude   15
To this delicious solitude.

No white nor red was ever seen
So amorous as this lovely green.
Fond lovers, cruel as their flame,
Cut in these trees their mistress' name: 20
Little, alas! they know or heed
How far these beauties hers exceed!
Fair trees! wheres'e'er your barks I wound
No name shall but your own be found.

When we have run our passion's heat,   25
Love hither makes his best retreat.
The gods, that mortal beauty chase,
Still in a tree did end their race;
Apollo hunted Daphne so,
Only that she might laurel grow;   30
And Pan did after Syrinx speed,
Not as a nymph, but for a reed.°

29–32 *Apollo . . . reed:* In Ovid's *Metamorphoses*, Apollo chases Daphne who is turned into a laurel, and Pan chases Syrinx who is turned into a reed.

What wondrous life is this I lead!
Ripe apples drop about my head;
The luscious clusters of the vine   35
Upon my mouth do crush their wine;
The nectarine, and curious° peach,   *exquisite*
Into my hands themselves do reach;
Stumbling on melons, as I pass,
Ensnar'd with flowers, I fall on grass.   40

Meanwhile, the mind, from pleasure less,
Withdraws into its happiness:
The mind, that ocean where each kind
Does straight its own resemblance find;
Yet it creates, transcending these,   45
Far other worlds, and other seas;
Annihilating all that's made
To a green thought in a green shade.

Here at the fountain's sliding foot,
Or at some fruit-tree's mossy root,   50
Casting the body's vest aside,
My soul into the boughs does glide:
There like a bird it sits, and sings,
Then whets° and combs its silver wings;   *grooms*
And, till prepared for longer flight,   55
Waves in its plumes the various light.

Such was that happy garden-state,
While man there walked without a mate:
After a place so pure and sweet,
What other help could yet be meet?°   *appropriate* 60
But 'twas beyond a mortal's share
To wander solitary there:
Two paradises 'twere in one,
To live in paradise alone.

How well the skillful gardener drew   65
Of flowers, and herbs, this dial new;
Where, from above, the milder sun
Does through a fragrant zodiac run;
And, as it works, the industrious bee
Computes its time as well as we.   70
How could such sweet and wholesome hours
Be reckoned but with herbs and flowers!

EDNA ST. VINCENT MILLAY (1892–1950)
I Too beneath Your Moon, Almighty Sex

1939

I too beneath your moon, almighty Sex,
Go forth at nightfall crying like a cat,
Leaving the lofty tower I laboured at
For birds to foul and boys and girls to vex
With tittering chalk; and you, and the long necks   5
Of neighbours sitting where their mothers sat
Are well aware of shadowy this and that
In me, that's neither noble nor complex.
Such as I am, however, I have brought
To what it is, this tower; it is my own;   10
Though it was reared To Beauty, it was wrought
From what I had to build with: honest bone
Is there, and anguish; pride; and burning thought;
And lust is there, and nights not spent alone.

EDNA ST. VINCENT MILLAY (1892–1950)
What Lips My Lips Have Kissed

1923

What lips my lips have kissed, and where, and why,
I have forgotten, and what arms have lain
Under my head till morning; but the rain
Is full of ghosts tonight, that tap and sigh
Upon the glass and listen for reply,   5
And in my heart there stirs a quiet pain
For unremembered lads that not again
Will turn to me at midnight with a cry.
Thus in the winter stands the lonely tree,
Nor knows what birds have vanished one by one,   10
Yet knows its boughs more silent than before:
I cannot say what loves have come and gone,
I only know that summer sang in me
A little while, that in me sings no more.

JOHN MILTON (1608–1674)
On the Late Massacre in Piedmont°

1655

Avenge, O Lord, thy slaughtered saints, whose bones
    Lie scattered on the Alpine mountains cold;

On the Late Massacre . . . . : Milton's protest against the treatment of the Waldenses, members of a Puritan sect living in Piedmont, was not limited to this sonnet. It is thought that he wrote Cromwell's appeals to the duke of Savoy and to others to end the persecution.

Even them who kept thy truth so pure of old,
When all our fathers worshiped stocks and stones,°
Forget not: in thy book record their groans   5
    Who were thy sheep, and in their ancient fold
    Slain by the bloody Piedmontese, that rolled
Mother with infant down the rocks.° Their moans
The vales redoubled to the hills, and they
    To heaven. Their martyred blood and ashes sow   10
O'er all the Italian fields, where still doth sway
    The triple Tyrant;° that from these may grow
    A hundredfold, who, having learnt thy way,
Early may fly the Babylonian woe.°

4 *When . . . stones:* In Milton's Protestant view, English Catholics had worshipped their stone and wooden statues in the twelfth century, when the Waldensian sect was formed.   5–8 *in thy book . . . rocks:* On Easter Day, 1655, 1,700 members of the Waldensian sect were massacred in Piedmont by the duke of Savoy's forces.   12 *triple Tyrant:* The Pope, with his three-crowned tiara, has authority on earth and in Heaven and Hell.   14 *Babylonian woe:* The destruction of Babylon, symbol of vice and corruption, at the end of the world (see Rev. 17–18). Protestants interpreted the "Whore of Babylon" as the Roman Catholic Church.

JOHN MILTON (1608–1674)
When I consider how my light is spent   c. 1655

When I consider how my light is spent,°
    Ere half my days in this dark world and wide,
    And that one talent° which is death to hide
Lodged with me useless, though my soul more bent
To serve therewith my Maker, and present   5
    My true account, lest He returning chide;
    "Doth God exact day-labor, light denied?"
I fondly° ask. But Patience, to prevent   *foolishly*
That murmur, soon replies, "God doth not need
    Either man's work or His own gifts. Who best   10
    Bear His mild yoke, they serve Him best. His state
Is kingly: thousands at His bidding speed,
    And post o'er land and ocean without rest;
    They also serve who only stand and wait."

1 *how my light is spent:* Milton had been totally blind since 1651.   3 *that one talent:* Refers to Jesus's parable of the talents (units of money), in which a servant entrusted with a talent buries it rather than invests it, and is punished upon his master's return (Matt. 25:14–30).

MARIANNE MOORE (1887–1972)
Poetry

1921

I, too, dislike it: there are things that are important beyond all this fiddle.
    Reading it, however, with a perfect contempt for it, one discovers in it
    after all, a place for the genuine.
        Hands that can grasp, eyes
            that can dilate, hair that can rise   5
                if it must, these things are important not because a

high-sounding interpretation can be put upon them but because they are
    useful. When they become so derivative as to become unintelligible,
    the same thing may be said for all of us, that we
        do not admire what
            we cannot understand: the bat   10
                holding on upside down or in quest of something to

eat, elephants pushing, a wild horse taking a roll, a tireless wolf under
    a tree, the immovable critic twitching his skin like a horse that feels a
        flea, the base-
    ball fan, the statistician —   15
        nor is it valid
            to discriminate against "business documents and

school-books"; all these phenomena are important. One must make a
    distinction
    however: when dragged into prominence by half poets, the result is not
        poetry,
    nor till the poets among us can be   20
        "literalists of
            the imagination" — above
                insolence and triviality and can present

for inspection, "imaginary gardens with real toads in them," shall we have
    it. In the meantime, if you demand on the one hand,   25
    the raw material of poetry in
        all its rawness and
        that which is on the other hand
            genuine, you are interested in poetry.

JON MUKAND (b. 1959)
Lullaby

1987

Each morning I finish my coffee,
And climb the stairs to the charts,
Hoping yours will be filed away.
But you can't hear me,
You can't see yourself clamped   5
Between this hard plastic binder:
Lab reports and nurses' notes, a sample
In a test tube. I keep reading
These terse comments: stable as before,
Urine output still poor, respiration normal.   10
And you keep on poisoning
Yourself, your kidneys more useless
Than seawings drenched in an oil spill.
I find my way to your room
And lean over the bedrails   15
As though I can understand
Your wheezed-out fragments.
What can I do but check
Your tubes, feel your pulse, listen
To your heartbeat insistent   20
As a spoiled child who goes on begging?

Old man, listen to me:
Let me take you in a wheelchair
To the back room of the records office,
Let me lift you in my arms   25
And lay you down in the cradle
Of a clean manila folder.

HOWARD NEMEROV (1920–1991)
Life Cycle of Common Man

1960

Roughly figured, this man of moderate habits,
This average consumer of the middle class,
Consumed in the course of his average life span
Just under half a million cigarettes,
Four thousand fifths of gin and about   5
A quarter as much vermouth; he drank
Maybe a hundred thousand cups of coffee,
And counting his parents' share it cost
Something like half a million dollars
To put him through life. How many beasts   10

Died to provide him with meat, belt and shoes
Cannot be certainly said.
                    But anyhow,
It is in this way that a man travels through time,
Leaving behind him a lengthening trail
Of empty bottles and bones, of broken shoes,
Frayed collars and worn out or outgrown
Diapers and dinnerjackets, silk ties and slickers.

Given the energy and security thus achieved,
He did . . . ? What? The usual things, of course,
The eating, dreaming, drinking and begetting,
And he worked for the money which was to pay
For the eating, et cetera, which were necessary
If he were to go on working for the money, et cetera,
But chiefly he talked. As the bottles and bones
Accumulated behind him, the words proceeded
Steadily from the front of his face as he
Advanced into the silence and made it verbal.
Who can tally the tale of his words? A lifetime
Would barely suffice for their repetition;
If you merely printed all his commas the result
Would be a very large volume, and the number of times
He said "thank you" or "very little sugar, please,"
Would stagger the imagination. There were also
Witticisms, platitudes, and statements beginning
"It seems to me" or "As I always say."

Consider the courage in all that, and behold the man
Walking into deep silence, with the ectoplastic
Cartoon's balloon of speech proceeding
Steadily out of the front of his face, the words
Borne along on the breath which is his spirit
Telling the numberless tale of his untold Word°
Which makes the world his apple, and forces him to eat.

42 *Word:* Logos, the controlling principle of the universe.

FRANK O'HARA (1926–1966)
Ave Maria°   1960

Mothers of America
               let your kids go to the movies!
get them out of the house so they won't know what you're up to
it's true that fresh air is good for the body
                           but what about the soul   5
that grows in darkness, embossed by silvery images
and when you grow old as grow old you must
                       they won't hate you
they won't criticize you they won't know
                  they'll be in some glamorous country   10
they first saw on a Saturday afternoon or playing hookey

they may even be grateful to you
                  for their first sexual experience
which only cost you a quarter
                  and didn't upset the peaceful home   15
they will know where candy bars come from
                    and gratuitous bags of popcorn
as gratuitous as leaving the movie before it's over
with a pleasant stranger whose apartment is in the Heaven on Earth Bldg
near the Williamsburg Bridge°   20
              oh mothers you will have made the little tykes
so happy because if nobody does pick them up in the movies
they won't know the difference
                and if somebody does it'll be sheer gravy
and they'll have been truly entertained either way   25
instead of hanging around the yard
              or up in their room
                    hating you
prematurely since you won't have done anything horribly mean yet
except keeping them from the darker joys   30
               it's unforgivable the latter
so don't blame me if you won't take this advice
              and the family breaks up
and your children grow old and blind in front of a TV set
               seeing   35
movies you wouldn't let them see when they were young

Ave Maria: The Catholic prayer Hail Mary, here referred to ironically.   20 *Williamsburg Bridge:*
Links lower Manhattan and Brooklyn, New York.

SIMON J. ORTIZ (b. 1941)

My Father's Song

1976

Wanting to say things,
I miss my father tonight.
His voice, the slight catch,
the depth from his thin chest,
the tremble of emotion   5
in something he has just said
to his son, his song:

    We planted corn one Spring at Acu —
    we planted several times
    but this one particular time   10
    I remember the soft damp sand
    in my hand.

    My father had stopped at one point
    to show me an overturned furrow;
    the plowshare had unearthed   15
    the burrow nest of a mouse
    in the soft moist sand.

    Very gently, he scooped tiny pink animals
    into the palm of his hand
    and told me to touch them.   20
    We took them to the edge
    of the field and put them in the shade
    of a sand moist clod.

    I remember the very softness
    of cool and warm sand and tiny alive mice   25
    and my father saying things.

WILFRED OWEN (1893–1918)

Anthem for Doomed Youth

1917

What passing-bells for these who die as cattle?
Only the monstrous anger of the guns.
Only the stuttering rifles' rapid rattle
Can patter out their hasty orisons.
No mockeries now for them; no prayers nor bells,   5
Nor any voice of mourning save the choirs, —
The shrill, demented choirs of wailing shells;
And bugles calling for them from sad shires.
What candles may be held to speed them all?
Not in the hands of boys, but in their eyes   10
Shall shine the holy glimmers of good-byes.

The pallor of girls' brows shall be their pall;
Their flowers the tenderness of patient minds,
And each slow dusk a drawing-down of blinds.

LINDA PASTAN (b. 1932)
after minor surgery

1982

this is the dress rehearsal
when the body
like a constant lover
flirts for the first time
with faithlessness   5

when the body
like a passenger on a long journey
hears the conductor call out
the name
of the first stop   10

when the body
in all its fear and cunning
makes promises to me
it knows
it cannot keep   15

MARGE PIERCY (b. 1936)
Barbie Doll

1969

This girlchild was born as usual
and presented dolls that did pee-pee
and miniature GE stoves and irons
and wee lipsticks the color of cherry candy.
Then in the magic of puberty, a classmate said: 5
You have a great big nose and fat legs.

She was healthy, tested intelligent,
possessed strong arms and back,
abundant sexual drive and manual dexterity.
She went to and fro apologizing.   10
Everyone saw a fat nose on thick legs.

She was advised to play coy,
exhorted to come on hearty,
exercise, diet, smile and wheedle.
Her good nature wore out   15
like a fan belt.

So she cut off her nose and her legs
and offered them up.
In the casket displayed on satin she lay
with the undertaker's cosmetics painted on,   20
a turned-up putty nose,
dressed in a pink and white nightie.
Doesn't she look pretty? everyone said.
Consummation at last.
To every woman a happy ending.   25

SYLVIA PLATH (1932–1963)
Daddy   1962

You do not do, you do not do
Any more, black shoe
In which I have lived like a foot
For thirty years, poor and white,
Barely daring to breathe or Achoo.   5

Daddy, I have had to kill you.
You died before I had time ——
Marble-heavy, a bag full of God,
Ghastly statue with one gray toe
Big as a Frisco seal   10

And a head in the freakish Atlantic
Where it pours bean green over blue
In the waters off beautiful Nauset.°   *Cape Cod inlet*
I used to pray to recover you.
Ach, du.°   *Oh, you*   15

In the German tongue, in the Polish Town°
Scraped flat by the roller
Of wars, wars, wars.
But the name of the town is common.
My Polack friend   20

Says there are a dozen or two.
So I never could tell where you
Put your foot, your root,
I never could talk to you.
The tongue stuck in my jaw.   25

It stuck in a barb wire snare.
Ich, ich, ich, ich,°   *I, I, I, I*

16 *Polish Town:* Refers to Otto Plath's birthplace, Granbow.

I could hardly speak.
I thought every German was you.
And the language obscene

30

An engine, an engine
Chuffing me off like a Jew.
A Jew to Dachau, Auschwitz, Belsen.°
I began to talk like a Jew.
I think I may well be a Jew.

35

The snows of the Tyrol, the clear beer of Vienna
Are not very pure or true.
With my gypsy-ancestress and my weird luck
And my Taroc° pack and my Taroc pack
I may be a bit of a Jew.

40

I have always been scared of *you,*
With your Luftwaffe,° your gobbledygoo.
And your neat mustache
And your Aryan eye, bright blue.
Panzer-man, panzer-man,° O You —

45

Not God but a swastika
So black no sky could squeak through.
Every woman adores a Fascist,
The boot in the face, the brute
Brute heart of a brute like you.

50

You stand at the blackboard, daddy,
In the picture I have of you,
A cleft in your chin instead of your foot
But no less a devil for that, no not
Any less the black man who

55

Bit my pretty red heart in two.
I was ten when they buried you.
At twenty I tried to die
And get back, back, back to you.
I thought even the bones would do

60

But they pulled me out of the sack,
And they stuck me together with glue.
And then I knew what to do.
I made a model of you,
A man in black with a Meinkampf° look

65

---

33 *Dachau . . . Belsen:* Nazi death camps in World War II.   39 *Taroc:* Or *Tarot,* a pack of cards used to tell fortunes. It is said to have originated among the early Jewish Cabalists, and to have been transmitted to European Gypsies during the Middle Ages.   42 *Luftwaffe:* World War II German air force.   45 *panzer-man:* A member of the panzer division of the German army in World War II, which used armored vehicles and was organized for rapid attack.   65 *Meinkampf:* An allusion to Hitler's autobiography *(My Struggle).*

And a love of the rack and the screw.
And I said I do, I do.
So daddy, I'm finally through.
The black telephone's off at the root,
The voices just can't worm through.   70

If I've killed one man, I've killed two ——
The vampire who said he was you
And drank my blood for a year,
Seven years, if you want to know.
Daddy, you can lie back now.   75

There's a stake in your fat black heart
And the villagers never liked you.
They are dancing and stamping on you.
They always *knew* it was you.
Daddy, daddy, you bastard, I'm through.   80

SYLVIA PLATH (1932–1963)
Metaphors   1960

I'm a riddle in nine syllables,
An elephant, a ponderous house,
A melon strolling on two tendrils.
O red fruit, ivory, fine timbers!
This loaf's big with its yeasty rising.
Money's new-minted in this fat purse.
I'm a means, a stage, a cow in calf.
I've eaten a bag of green apples,
Boarded the train there's no getting off.

EZRA POUND (1885–1972)
The Garden   1913

En robe de parade.
    —Samain°

Like a skein of loose silk blown against a wall
She walks by the railing of a path in Kensington Gardens,
And she is dying piece-meal
    of a sort of emotional anæmia.

En . . . Samain: "Dressed for an outing." From the French *Au Jardin de l'Infante* (1893) by Albert
Samain (1858–1900).

And round about there is a rabble   5
Of the filthy, sturdy, unkillable infants of the very poor.
They shall inherit the earth.

In her is the end of breeding.
Her boredom is exquisite and excessive.
She would like some one to speak to her,   10
And is almost afraid that I
    will commit that indiscretion.

EZRA POUND (1885–1972)
The River-Merchant's Wife: A Letter°   1915

While my hair was still cut straight across my forehead
I played about the front gate, pulling flowers.
You came by on bamboo stilts, playing horse,
You walked about my seat, playing with blue plums.
And we went on living in the village of Chokan: 5
Two small people, without dislike or suspicion.
At fourteen I married My Lord you.
I never laughed, being bashful.
Lowering my head, I looked at the wall.
Called to, a thousand times, I never looked back.   10

At fifteen I stopped scowling,
I desired my dust to be mingled with yours
Forever and forever and forever.
Why should I climb the lookout?

At sixteen you departed,   15
You went into far Ku-to-yen, by the river of swirling eddies,
And you have been gone five months.
The monkeys make sorrowful noise overhead.

You dragged your feet when you went out.
By the gate now, the moss is grown, the different mosses,   20
Too deep to clear them away!
The leaves fall early this autumn, in wind.
The paired butterflies are already yellow with August
Over the grass in the West garden;
They hurt me. I grow older.   25
If you are coming down through the narrows of the river Kiang,
Please let me know before hand,
And I will come out to meet you
    As far as Cho-fu-sa.

The River-Merchant's Wife: A Letter: A free translation of a poem by Li Po (Chinese, 701–762).

SIR WALTER RALEIGH (1554–1618)
The Nymph's Reply to the Shepherd   1600

If all the world and love were young,
And truth in every shepherd's tongue,
These pretty pleasures might me move
To live with thee and be thy love.

Time drives the flocks from field to fold,   5
When rivers rage, and rocks grow cold,
And Philomel° becometh dumb;
The rest complain of cares to come.

The flowers do fade, and wanton fields
To wayward winter reckoning yields: 10
A honey tongue, a heart of gall,
Is fancy's spring, but sorrow's fall.

Thy gowns, thy shoes, thy beds of roses,
Thy cap, thy kirtle, and thy posies
Soon break, soon wither, soon forgotten;   15
In folly ripe, in reason rotten.

Thy belt of straw and ivy buds,
Thy coral clasps and amber studs,
All these in me no means can move
To come to thee and be thy love.   20

But could youth last, and love still breed,
Had joys no date, nor age no need,
Then these delights my mind might move
To live with thee and be thy love.

7 *Philomel:* In Greek mythology, a Greek princess who was changed to a nightingale.

DUDLEY RANDALL (b. 1914)
Ballad of Birmingham   1969

(On the bombing of a church in Birmingham, Alabama, 1963)

"Mother dear, may I go downtown
Instead of out to play,
And march the streets of Birmingham
In a Freedom March today?"

"No, baby, no, you may not go,   5
For the dogs are fierce and wild,
And clubs and hoses, guns and jails
Aren't good for a little child."

"But, mother, I won't be alone.
Other children will go with me,   10
And march the streets of Birmingham
To make our country free."

"No, baby, no, you may not go,
For I fear those guns will fire.
But you may go to church instead   15
And sing in the children's choir."

She has combed and brushed her night-dark hair,
And bathed rose petal sweet.
And drawn white gloves on her small brown hands,
And white shoes on her feet.   20

The mother smiled to know her child
Was in the sacred place,
But that smile was the last smile
To come upon her face.

For when she heard the explosion,   25
Her eyes grew wet and wild.
She raced through the streets of Birmingham
Calling for her child.

She clawed through bits of glass and brick,
Then lifted out a shoe.   30
"Oh, here's the shoe my baby wore,
But, baby, where are you?"

ADRIENNE RICH (b. 1929)
Living in Sin   1955

She had thought the studio would keep itself,
no dust upon the furniture of love.
Half heresy, to wish the taps less vocal,
the panes relieved of grime. A plate of pears,
a piano with a Persian shawl, a cat   5
stalking the picturesque amusing mouse
had risen at his urging.
Not that at five each separate stair would writhe
under the milkman's tramp; that morning light
so coldly would delineate the scraps   10
of last night's cheese and three sepulchral bottles;
that on the kitchen shelf among the saucers
a pair of beetle-eyes would fix her own —
envoy from some black village in the mouldings . . .
Meanwhile, he, with a yawn,   15
sounded a dozen notes upon the keyboard,

declared it out of tune, shrugged at the mirror,
rubbed at his beard, went out for cigarettes;
while she, jeered by the minor demons,
pulled back the sheets and made the bed and found   20
a towel to dust the table-top,
and let the coffee-pot boil over on the stove.
By evening she was back in love again,
though not so wholly but throughout the night
she woke sometimes to feel the daylight coming   25
like a relentless milkman up the stairs.

EDWIN ARLINGTON ROBINSON (1869–1935)
Mr. Flood's Party   1921

Old Eben Flood, climbing alone one night
Over the hill between the town below
And the forsaken upland hermitage
That held as much as he should ever know
On earth again of home, paused warily.   5
The road was his and not a native near;
And Eben, having leisure, said aloud,
For no man else in Tilbury Town to hear:

"Well, Mr. Flood, we have the harvest moon
Again, and we may not have many more;   10
The bird is on the wing, the poet says,°
And you and I have said it here before.
Drink to the bird." He raised up to the light
The jug that he had gone so far to fill,
And answered huskily: "Well, Mr. Flood,   15
Since you propose it, I believe I will."

Alone, as if enduring to the end
A valiant armor of scarred hopes outworn,
He stood there in the middle of the road
Like Roland's ghost winding a silent horn.°   20
Below him, in the town among the trees,
Where friends of other days had honored him,
A phantom salutation of the dead
Rang thinly till old Eben's eyes were dim.

---

11 *The bird . . . says:* Edward Fitzgerald says this of the "Bird of Time" in "The Rubáiyát of Omar Khayyám."   20 *Like Roland's . . . horn:* Roland, hero of French romance, blew his ivory horn to warn his allies of impending attack.

Then, as a mother lays her sleeping child   25
Down tenderly, fearing it may awake,
He set the jug down slowly at his feet
With trembling care, knowing that most things break;
And only when assured that on firm earth
It stood, as the uncertain lives of men   30
Assuredly did not, he paced away,
And with his hand extended paused again:

"Well, Mr. Flood, we have not met like this
In a long time; and many a change has come
To both of us, I fear, since last it was   35
We had a drop together. Welcome home!"
Convivially returning with himself,
Again he raised the jug up to the light;
And with an acquiescent quaver said:
"Well, Mr. Flood, if you insist, I might.   40

"Only a very little, Mr. Flood —
For auld lang syne. No more, sir; that will do."
So, for the time, apparently it did,
And Eben evidently thought so too;
For soon amid the silver loneliness   45
Of night he lifted up his voice and sang,
Secure, with only two moons listening,
Until the whole harmonious landscape rang —

"For auld lang syne." The weary throat gave out,
The last word wavered, and the song being done.   50
He raised again the jug regretfully
And shook his head, and was again alone.
There was not much that was ahead of him,
And there was nothing in the town below —
Where strangers would have shut the many doors   55
That many friends had opened long ago.

THEODORE ROETHKE (1908–1963)
I Knew a Woman   1958

I knew a woman, lovely in her bones,
When small birds sighed, she would sigh back at them;
Ah, when she moved, she moved more ways than one:
The shapes a bright container can contain!
Of her choice virtues only gods should speak,   5
Or English poets who grew up on Greek
(I'd have them sing in chorus, cheek to cheek).

How well her wishes went! She stroked my chin,
She taught me Turn, and Counter-turn, and Stand;°
She taught me Touch, that undulant white skin; 10
I nibbled meekly from her proffered hand;
She was the sickle; I, poor I, the rake,
Coming behind her for her pretty sake
(But what prodigious mowing we did make).

Love likes a gander, and adores a goose: 15
Her full lips pursed, the errant note to seize;
She played it quick, she played it light and loose;
My eyes, they dazzled at her flowing knees;
Her several parts could keep a pure repose,
Or one hip quiver with a mobile nose 20
(She moved in circles, and those circles moved).

Let seed be grass, and grass turn into hay:
I'm martyr to a motion not my own;
What's freedom for? To know eternity.
I swear she cast a shadow white as stone. 25
But who would count eternity in days?
These old bones live to learn her wanton ways:
(I measure time by how a body sways).

9 *Turn* . . . *Stand:* Parts of a Pindaric ode.

CHRISTINA ROSSETTI (1830–1894)
Uphill 1861

Does the road wind uphill all the way?
    Yes, to the very end.
Will the day's journey take the whole long day?
    From morn to night, my friend.

But is there for the night a resting place? 5
    A roof for when the slow dark hours begin.
May not the darkness hide it from my face?
    You cannot miss that inn.

Shall I meet other wayfarers at night?
    Those who have gone before. 10
Then must I knock, or call when just in sight?
    They will not keep you standing at that door.

Shall I find comfort, travel-sore and weak?
    Of labor you shall find the sum.
Will there be beds for me and all who seek? 15
    Yea, beds for all who come.

ANNE SEXTON (1928–1974)
Lobster

1976

A shoe with legs,
a stone dropped from heaven,
he does his mournful work alone,
he is like the old prospector for gold,
with secret dreams of God-heads and fish heads.   5
Until suddenly a cradle fastens round him
and he is trapped as the U.S.A. sleeps.
Somewhere far off a woman lights a cigarette;
somewhere far off a car goes over a bridge;
somewhere far off a bank is held up.   10
This is the world the lobster knows not of.
He is the old hunting dog of the sea
who in the morning will rise from it
and be undrowned
and they will take his perfect green body   15
and paint it red.

WILLIAM SHAKESPEARE (1564–1616)
Not marble, nor the gilded monuments

1609

Not marble, nor the gilded monuments
Of princes, shall outlive this powerful rhyme;
But you shall shine more bright in these conténts
Than unswept stone, besmeared with sluttish time.
When wasteful war shall statues overturn,   5
And broils root out the work of masonry,
Nor Mars his° sword nor war's quick fire shall burn   *possessive of Mars*
The living record of your memory.
'Gainst death and all-oblivious enmity
Shall you pace forth; your praise shall still find room   10
Even in the eyes of all posterity
That wear this world out to the ending doom.
    So, till the judgment that yourself arise,
    You live in this, and dwell in lovers' eyes.

WILLIAM SHAKESPEARE (1564–1616)
Spring°

c. 1595

When daisies pied and violets blue
   And ladysmocks all silver-white
And cuckoobuds of yellow hue
   Do paint the meadows with delight,
The cuckoo then, on every tree,   5
Mocks married men;° for thus sings he,
       Cuckoo;
Cuckoo, cuckoo: Oh word of fear,
Unpleasing to a married ear!

When shepherds pipe on oaten straws,   10
   And merry larks are plowmen's clocks,
When turtles tread,° and rooks, and daws,
   And maidens bleach their summer smocks,
The cuckoo then, on every tree,
Mocks married men; for thus sings he,   15
       Cuckoo;
Cuckoo, cuckoo: Oh word of fear,
Unpleasing to a married ear!

Spring: Song from *Love's Labour's Lost,* V. ii.   6 *Mocks married men:* By singing "cuckoo," which sounds like "cuckold."   12 *turtles tread:* Turtledoves copulate.

WILLIAM SHAKESPEARE (1564–1616)
That time of year thou mayst in me behold

1609

That time of year thou mayst in me behold
When yellow leaves, or none, or few, do hang
Upon those boughs which shake against the cold,
Bare ruined choirs, where late the sweet birds sang.
In me thou see'st the twilight of such day   5
As after sunset fadeth in the west;
Which by and by black night doth take away,
Death's second self,° that seals up all in rest.   *sleep*
In me thou see'st the glowing of such fire,
That on the ashes of his youth doth lie,   10
As the deathbed whereon it must expire,
Consumed with that which it was nourished by.
    This thou perceiv'st, which makes thy love more strong,
    To love that well which thou must leave ere long.

WILLIAM SHAKESPEARE (1564–1616)
When forty winters shall besiege thy brow

1609

When forty winters shall besiege thy brow
And dig deep trenches in thy beauty's field,
Thy youth's proud livery, so gazed on now,
Will be a tattered weed,° of small worth held.   *garment*
Then being asked where all thy beauty lies,   5
Where all the treasure of thy lusty days,
To say within thine own deep-sunken eyes
Were an all-eating shame and thriftless praise.
How much more praise deserved thy beauty's use
If thou couldst answer, "This fair child of mine   10
Shall sum my count and make my old excuse,"
Proving his beauty by succession thine.
    This were to be new made when thou art old,
    And see thy blood warm when thou feel'st it cold.

WILLIAM SHAKESPEARE (1564–1616)
When, in disgrace with Fortune and men's eyes

1609

When, in disgrace with Fortune and men's eyes,
I all alone beweep my outcast state,
And trouble deaf heaven with my bootless cries,
And look upon myself and curse my fate,
Wishing me like to one more rich in hope,   5
Featured like him, like him with friends possessed,
Desiring this man's art, and that man's scope,
With what I most enjoy contented least,
Yet in these thoughts myself almost despising,
Haply I think on thee, and then my state,   10
Like to the lark at break of day arising
From sullen earth, sings hymns at heaven's gate;
    For thy sweet love remembered such wealth brings
    That then I scorn to change my state with kings.

WILLIAM SHAKESPEARE (1564–1616)
Winter°

c. 1595

When icicles hang by the wall
   And Dick the shepherd blows his nail,°
And Tom bears logs into the hall,
   And milk comes frozen home in pail.
When blood is nipped and ways be foul,   5
Then nightly sings the staring owl,
        Tu-who;
Tu-whit, tu-who: a merry note,
While greasy Joan doth keel the pot.°

When all aloud the wind doth blow,   10
   And coughing drowns the parson's saw,°   *maxim*
And birds sit brooding in the snow,
   And Marian's nose looks red and raw,
When roasted crabs° hiss in the bowl,   *crabapples*
Then nightly sings the staring owl,   15
        Tu-who;
Tu-whit, tu-who: a merry note
While greasy Joan doth keel the pot.

Winter: Song from *Love's Labour's Lost,* V. ii.   2 *blows his nail:* Blows on his hands for warmth.
9 *keel the pot:* Cool the contents of the pot by stirring.

PERCY BYSSHE SHELLEY (1792–1822)
Ozymandias°

1818

I met a traveler from an antique land
Who said: Two vast and trunkless legs of stone
Stand in the desert. . . . Near them, on the sand,
Half sunk, a shattered visage lies, whose frown,
And wrinkled lip, and sneer of cold command,   5
Tell that its sculptor well those passions read
Which yet survive, stamped on these lifeless things,
The hand that mocked them, and the heart that fed:
And on the pedestal these words appear:
"My name is Ozymandias, King of Kings: 10

Ozymandias: Greek name for Ramses II, pharaoh of Egypt for sixty-seven years during the 13th century
B.C. His colossal statue lies prostrate in the sands of Luxor. Napoleon's soldiers measured it (56 feet
long, ear 3½ feet long, weight 1,000 tons). Its inscription, according to the Greek historian Diodorus
Siculus, was "I am Ozymandias, King of Kings; if anyone wishes to know what I am and where I lie,
let him surpass me in some of my exploits."

Look on my works, ye Mighty, and despair!"
Nothing beside remains. Round the decay
Of that colossal wreck, boundless and bare
The lone and level sands stretch far away.

SIR PHILIP SIDNEY (1554–1586)
Loving in Truth, and Fain in Verse
My Love to Show   1591

Loving in truth, and fain in verse my love to show,
That she, dear she, might take some pleasure of my pain,
Pleasure might cause her read, reading might make her know,
Knowledge might pity win, and pity grace obtain,
I sought fit words to pain the blackest face of woe,   5
Studying inventions fine, her wits to entertain,
Oft turning others' leaves, to see if thence would flow
Some fresh and fruitful showers upon my sunburnt brain.
But words came halting forth, wanting Invention's stay;
Invention, Nature's child, fled step-dame° Study's blows;   *stepmother* 10
And others' feet still seemed but strangers in my way.
Thus great with child to speak, and helpless in my throes,
Biting my truant pen, beating myself for spite:
"Fool," said my Muse to me, "look in thy heart and write."

LESLIE MARMON SILKO (b. 1948)
Where Mountain Lion Lay Down with Deer   1981

I climb the black rock mountain
  stepping from day to day
                  silently.
I smell the wind for my ancestors
    pale blue leaves   5
    crushed wild mountain smell.
Returning
  up the gray stone cliff
  where I descended
                  a thousand years ago   10
Returning to faded black stone
where mountain lion lay down with deer.
It is better to stay up here
                  watching wind's reflection
                  in tall yellow flowers.   15

The old ones who remember me are gone
              the old songs are all forgotten
and the story of my birth.

How I danced in snow-frost moonlight
              distant stars to the end of the Earth,   20
How I swam away
                    in freezing mountain water
                    narrow mossy canyon tumbling down
                              out of the mountain
                              out of deep canyon stone   25
              down
                    the memory
                              spilling out
                              into the world.

W. D. SNODGRASS (b. 1926)
April Inventory   1959

The green catalpa tree has turned
All white; the cherry blooms once more.
In one whole year I haven't learned
A blessed thing they pay you for.
The blossoms snow down in my hair;   5
The trees and I will soon be bare.

The trees have more than I to spare.
The sleek, expensive girls I teach,
Younger and pinker every year,
Bloom gradually out of reach.   10
The pear tree lets its petals drop
Like dandruff on a tabletop.

The girls have grown so young by now
I have to nudge myself to stare.
This year they smile and mind me how   15
My teeth are falling with my hair.
In thirty years I may not get
Younger, shrewder, or out of debt.

The tenth time, just a year ago,
I made myself a little list   20
Of all the things I'd ought to know,
Then told my parents, analyst,
And everyone who's trusted me
I'd be substantial, presently.

I haven't read one book about   25
A book or memorized one plot.

Or found a mind I did not doubt.
I learned one date. And then forgot.
And one by one the solid scholars
Get the degrees, the jobs, the dollars.

And smile above their starchy collars.
I taught my classes Whitehead's° notions;
One lovely girl, a song of Mahler's.°
Lacking a source-book or promotions,
I showed one child the colors of
A luna moth and how to love.

I taught myself to name my name,
To bark back, loosen love and crying;
To ease my woman so she came,
To ease an old man who was dying.
I have not learned how often I
Can win, can love, but choose to die.

I have not learned there is a lie
Love shall be blonder, slimmer, younger;
That my equivocating eye
Loves only by my body's hunger;
That I have forces, true to feel,
Or that the lovely world is real.

While scholars speak authority
And wear their ulcers on their sleeves,
My eyes in spectacles shall see
These trees procure and spend their leaves.
There is a value underneath
The gold and silver in my teeth.

Though trees turn bare and girls turn wives,
We shall afford our costly seasons;
There is a gentleness survives
That will outspeak and has its reasons.
There is a loveliness exists,
Preserves us, not for specialists.

30

35

40

45

50

55

60

32 *Whitehead:* Alfred North Whitehead (1861–1947), English mathematician and philosopher.
33 *Mahler:* Gustav Mahler (1860–1911), Austrian Post-Romantic composer, known for his songs and symphonies.

GARY SNYDER (b. 1930)
After weeks of watching the roof leak   1967

After weeks of watching the roof leak
      I fixed it tonight
by moving a single board

WALLACE STEVENS (1879–1955)
The Emperor of Ice-Cream   1923

Call the roller of big cigars,
The muscular one, and bid him whip
In kitchen cups concupiscent curds.°
Let the wenches dawdle in such dress
As they are used to wear, and let the boys   5
Bring flowers in last month's newspapers.
Let be be finale of seem.°
The only emperor is the emperor of ice-cream.

Take from the dresser of deal,
Lacking the three glass knobs, that sheet   10
On which she embroidered fantails once
And spread it so as to cover her face.
If her horny feet protrude, they come
To show how cold she is, and dumb.
Let the lamp affix its beam.   15
The only emperor is the emperor of ice-cream.

---

3 *concupiscent curds:* "The words 'concupiscent curds' have no genealogy; they are merely expressive: at least, I hope they are expressive. They express the concupiscence of life, but, by contrast with the things in relation in the poem, they express or accentuate life's destitution, and it is this that gives them something more than a cheap lustre" (Wallace Stevens, *Letters* [New York: Knopf, 1960], p. 500).   7 *Let . . . seem:* "The true sense of 'Let be be the finale of seem' is let being become the conclusion or denouement of appearing to be: in short, ice cream is an absolute good. The poem is obviously not about ice cream, but about being as distinguished from seeming to be" (*Letters,* p. 341).

WALLACE STEVENS (1879–1955)

Sunday Morning

1915

I

Complacencies of the peignoir, and late
Coffee and oranges in a sunny chair,
And the green freedom of a cockatoo
Upon a rug mingle to dissipate
The holy hush of ancient sacrifice.   5
She dreams a little, and she feels the dark
Encroachment of that old catastrophe,°   *the Crucifixion*
As a calm darkens among water-lights.
The pungent oranges and bright, green wings
Seem things in some procession of the dead,   10
Winding across wide water, without sound.
The day is like wide water, without sound,
Stilled for the passing of her dreaming feet
Over the seas, to silent Palestine,
Dominion of the blood and sepulcher.   15

II

Why should she give her bounty to the dead?
What is divinity if it can come
Only in silent shadows and in dreams?
Shall she not find in comforts of the sun,
In pungent fruit and bright, green wings, or else   20
In any balm or beauty of the earth,
Things to be cherished like the thought of heaven?
Divinity must live within herself:
Passions of rain, or moods in falling snow;
Grievings in loneliness, or unsubdued   25
Elations when the forest blooms; gusty
Emotions on wet roads on autumn nights;
All pleasures and all pains, remembering
The bough of summer and the winter branch.
These are the measures destined for her soul.   30

III

Jove° in the clouds had his inhuman birth.
No mother suckled him, no sweet land gave
Large-mannered motions to his mythy mind
He moved among us, as a muttering king,
Magnificent, would move among his hinds,°   *peasant subjects* 35
Until our blood, commingling, virginal,
With heaven, brought such requital to desire
The very hinds discerned it, in a star,°   *of Bethlehem*
Shall our blood fail? Or shall it come to be

31 *Jove:* Jupiter, the supreme Roman god.

The blood of paradise? And shall the earth   40
Seem all of paradise that we shall know?
The sky will be much friendlier then than now,
A part of labor and a part of pain,
And next in glory to enduring love,
Not this dividing and indifferent blue.   45

IV

She says, "I am content when wakened birds,
Before they fly, test the reality
Of misty fields, by their sweet questionings;
But when the birds are gone, and their warm fields
Return no more, where, then, is paradise?"   50
There is not any haunt of prophecy,
Nor any old chimera of the grave,
Neither the golden underground, nor isle
Melodious, where spirits gat° them home,   *got*
Nor visionary south, nor cloudy palm   55
Remote on heaven's hill, that has endured
As April's green endures, or will endure
Like her remembrance of awakened birds,
Or her desire for June and evening, tipped
By the consummation of the swallow's wings.   60

V

She says, "But in contentment I still feel
The need of some imperishable bliss."
Death is the mother of beauty; hence from her,
Alone, shall come fulfillment to our dreams
And our desires. Although she strews the leaves   65
Of sure obliteration on our paths,
The path sick sorrow took, the many paths
Where triumph rang its brassy phrase, or love
Whispered a little out of tenderness,
She makes the willow shiver in the sun   70
For maidens who were wont to sit and gaze
Upon the grass, relinquished to their feet.
She causes boys to pile new plums and pears
On disregarded plate. The maidens taste
And stray impassioned in the littering leaves.   75

VI

Is there no change of death in paradise?
Does ripe fruit never fall? Or do the boughs
Hang always heavy in that perfect sky,
Unchanging, yet so like our perishing earth,
With rivers like our own that seek for seas   80
They never find, the same receding shores
That never touch with inarticulate pang?
Why set the pear upon those river-banks
Or spice the shores with odors of the plum?

Alas, that they should wear our colors there,   85
The silken weavings of our afternoons,
And pick the strings of our insipid lutes!
Death is the mother of beauty, mystical,
Within whose burning bosom we devise
Our earthly mothers waiting, sleeplessly.   90

VII

Supple and turbulent, a ring of men
Shall chant in orgy° on a summer morn   *ritual revelry*
Their boisterous devotion to the sun,
Not as a god, but as a god might be,
Naked among them, like a savage source.   95
Their chant shall be a chant of paradise,
Out of their blood, returning to the sky;
And in their chant shall enter, voice by voice,
The windy lake wherein their lord delights,
The trees, like serafin,° and echoing hills,   100
That choir among themselves long afterward.
They shall know well the heavenly fellowship
Of men that perish and of summer morn.
And whence they came and whither they shall go
The dew upon their feet shall manifest.   105

VIII

She hears, upon that water without sound,
A voice that cries, "The tomb in Palestine
Is not the porch of spirits lingering.
It is the grave of Jesus, where he lay."
We live in an old chaos of the sun,   110
Or old dependency of day and night,
Or island solitude, unsponsored, free,
Of that wide water, inescapable.
Deer walk upon our mountains, and the quail
Whistle about us their spontaneous cries;   115
Sweet berries ripen in the wilderness;
And, in the isolation of the sky,
At evening, casual flocks of pigeons make
Ambiguous undulations as they sink,
Downward to darkness, on extended wings.   120

100 *serafin:* Seraphim, angels having three sets of wings; the highest of the nine orders of angels.

MARK STRAND (b. 1934)
The Continuous Life 1989

What of the neighborhood homes awash
In a silver light, of children hunched in the bushes,
Watching the grownups for signs of surrender,
Signs the irregular pleasures of moving
From day to day, of being adrift on the swell of duty 5
Have run their course? O parents, confess
To your little ones the night is a long way off
And your taste for the mundane grows; tell them
Your worship of household chores has barely begun;
Describe the beauty of shovels and rakes, brooms and mops; 10
Say there will always be cooking and cleaning to do,
That one thing leads to another, which leads to another;
Explain that you live between two great darks, the first
With an ending, the second without one, that the luckiest
Thing is having been born, that you live in a blur 15
Of hours and days, months and years, and believe
It has meaning, despite the occasional fear
You are slipping away with nothing completed, nothing
To prove you existed. Tell the children to come inside,
That your search goes on for something you lost: a name, 20
A book of the family that fell from its own small matter
Into another, a piece of the dark that might have been yours —
You don't really know. Say that each of you tries
To keep busy, learning to lean down close and hear
The careless breathing of earth and feel its available 25
Languor come over you, wave after wave, sending
Small tremors of love through your brief,
Undeniable selves, into your days, and beyond.

ALFRED, LORD TENNYSON (1809–1892)
Crossing the Bar 1889

Sunset and evening star,
    And one clear call for me!
And may there be no moaning of the bar
    When I put out to sea.

But such a tide as moving seems asleep, 5
    Too full for sound and foam,
When that which drew from out the boundless deep
    Turns again home.

Twilight and evening bell,
    And after that the dark!   10
And may there be no sadness of farewell
    When I embark;

For though from out our bourne of Time and Place
    The flood may bear me far,
I hope to see my Pilot face to face   15
    When I have crossed the bar.

ALFRED, LORD TENNYSON (1809–1892)
Ulysses°   1833

    It little profits that an idle king,
By this still hearth, among these barren crags,
Matched with an agèd wife,° I mete and dole   *Penelope*
Unequal laws unto a savage race,
That hoard, and sleep, and feed, and know not me.   5
    I cannot rest from travel; I will drink
Life to the lees. All times I have enjoyed
Greatly, have suffered greatly, both with those
That loved me, and alone; on shore, and when
Through scudding drifts the rainy Hyades°   10
Vexed the dim sea. I am become a name;
For always roaming with a hungry heart
Much have I seen and known — cities of men
And manners, climates, councils, governments,
Myself not least, but honored of them all —   15
And drunk delight of battle with my peers,
Far on the ringing plains of windy Troy.
I am a part of all that I have met;
Yet all experience is an arch wherethrough
Gleams that untraveled world, whose margin fades   20
For ever and for ever when I move.
How dull it is to pause, to make an end,
To rust unburnished, not to shine in use!
As though to breathe were life. Life piled on life
Were all too little, and of one to me   25
Little remains; but every hour is saved
From that eternal silence, something more,
A bringer of new things; and vile it were
For some three suns to store and hoard myself,
And this gray spirit yearning in desire   30

Ulysses: Ulysses, the hero of Homer's epic poem the *Odyssey,* is presented by Dante in *The Inferno,*
XXVI, as restless after his return to Ithaca, and eager for new adventures.   10 *Hyades:* Five stars in
the constellation Taurus, supposed by the ancients to predict rain when they rose with the sun.

To follow knowledge like a sinking star,
Beyond the utmost bound of human thought.

    This is my son, mine own Telemachus,
To whom I leave the scepter and the isle —
Well-loved of me, discerning to fulfill 35
This labor by slow prudence to make mild
A rugged people, and through soft degrees
Subdue them to the useful and the good.
Most blameless is he, centered in the sphere
Of common duties, decent not to fail 40
In offices of tenderness, and pay
Meet adoration to my household gods,
When I am gone. He works his work, I mine.

    There lies the port; the vessel puffs her sail:
There gloom the dark, broad seas. My mariners, 45
Souls that have toiled, and wrought, and thought with me —
That ever with a frolic welcome took
The thunder and the sunshine, and opposed
Free hearts, free foreheads — you and I are old;
Old age hath yet his honor and his toil. 50
Death closes all; but something ere the end,
Some work of noble note, may yet be done,
Not unbecoming men that strove with Gods.
The lights begin to twinkle from the rocks;
The long day wanes; the slow moon climbs; the deep 55
Moans round with many voices. Come, my friends.
'Tis not too late to seek a newer world.
Push off, and sitting well in order smite
The sounding furrows; for my purpose holds
To sail beyond the sunset, and the baths 60
Of all the western stars, until I die.
It may be that the gulfs will wash us down;
It may be we shall touch the Happy Isles,°
And see the great Achilles,° whom we knew.
Though much is taken, much abides; and though 65
We are not now that strength which in old days
Moved earth and heaven, that which we are, we are:
One equal temper of heroic hearts,
Made weak by time and fate, but strong in will
To strive, to seek, to find, and not to yield. 70

63 *Happy Isles:* Elysium, the home after death of heroes and others favored by the gods. It was thought
by the ancients to lie beyond the sunset in the uncharted Atlantic.   64 *Achilles:* The hero of Homer's
Iliad.

DYLAN THOMAS (1914–1953)
Fern Hill

1946

Now as I was young and easy under the apple boughs
About the lilting house and happy as the grass was green,
   The night above the dingle starry,
     Time let me hail and climb
   Golden in the heydays of his eyes,   5
And honored among wagons I was prince of the apple towns
And once below a time I lordly had the trees and leaves
     Trail with daisies and barley
   Down the rivers of the windfall light.

And as I was green and carefree, famous among the barns   10
About the happy yard and singing as the farm was home,
   In the sun that is young once only,
     Time let me play and be
   Golden in the mercy of his means,
And green and golden I was huntsman and herdsman, the calves   15
Sang to my horn, the foxes on the hills barked clear and cold,
     And the sabbath rang slowly
   In the pebbles of the holy streams.

All the sun long it was running, it was lovely, the hay
Fields high as the house, the tunes from the chimneys, it was air   20
   And playing, lovely and watery
     And fire green as grass.
   And nightly under the simple stars
As I rode to sleep the owls were bearing the farm away,
All the moon long I heard, blessed among stables, the nightjars   25
   Flying with the ricks, and the horses
     Flashing into the dark.

And then to awake, and the farm, like a wanderer white
With the dew, come back, the cock on his shoulder; it was all
   Shining, it was Adam and maiden,   30
     The sky gathered again
   And the sun grew round that very day.
So it must have been after the birth of the simple light
In the first, spinning place, the spellbound horses walking warm
   Out of the whinnying green stable   35
     On to the fields of praise.

And honored among foxes and pheasants by the gay house
Under the new made clouds and happy as the heart was long,
   In the sun born over and over,
     I ran my heedless ways,   40
   My wishes raced through the house-high hay
And nothing I cared, at my sky-blue trades, that time allows
In all his tuneful turning so few and such morning songs

Before the children green and golden
    Follow him out of grace, 45

Nothing I cared, in the lamb white days, that time would take me
Up to the swallow-thronged loft by the shadow of my hand,
    In the moon that is always rising,
      Nor that riding to sleep
    I should hear him fly with the high fields 50
And wake to the farm forever fled from the childless land.
Oh as I was young and easy in the mercy of his means,
      Time held me green and dying
    Though I sang in my chains like the sea.

ROBERT WALLACE (b. 1932)
The Double-Play   1961

In his sea lit
distance, the pitcher winding
like a clock about to chime comes down with

the ball, hit
sharply, under the artificial   5
banks of arc-lights, bounds like a vanishing string

over the green
to the shortstop magically
scoops to his right whirling above his invisible

shadows   10
in the dust redirects
its flight to the running poised second baseman

pirouettes
leaping, above the slide, to throw
from mid-air, across the colored tightened interval,   15

to the leaning-
out first baseman ends the dance
drawing it disappearing into his long brown glove

stretches. What
is too swift for deception   20
is final, lost, among the loosened figures

jogging off the field
(the pitcher walks), casual
in the space where the poem has happened.

EDMUND WALLER (1606–1687)
Go, Lovely Rose
1645

  Go, lovely rose,
Tell her that wastes her time and me
  That now she knows,
When I resemble° her to thee,   *compare*
How sweet and fair she seems to be.   5

  Tell her that's young
And shuns to have her graces spied,
  That hadst thou sprung
In deserts where no men abide,
Thou must have uncommended died.   10

  Small is the worth
Of beauty from the light retired:
  Bid her come forth,
Suffer herself to be desired,
And not blush so to be admired.   15

  Then die, that she
The common fate of all things rare
  May read in thee,
How small a part of time they share
That are so wondrous sweet and fair.   20

WALT WHITMAN (1819–1892)
The Dalliance of the Eagles
1880

Skirting the river road, (my forenoon walk, my rest,)
Skyward in air a sudden muffled sound, the dalliance of the eagles,
The rushing amorous contact high in space together,
The clinching interlocking claws, a living, fierce, gyrating wheel,
Four beating wings, two beaks, a swirling mass tight grappling,   5
In tumbling turning clustering loops, straight downward falling,
Till o'er the river poised, the twain yet one, a moment's lull,
A motionless still balance in the air, then parting, talons loosing,
Upward again on slow-firm pinions slanting, their separate diverse flight,
She hers, he his, pursuing.   10

WALT WHITMAN (1819–1892)
One's-Self I Sing

1867

One's-Self I sing, a simple separate person,
Yet utter the word Democratic, the word En-Masse.

Of physiology from top to toe I sing,
Not physiognomy alone nor brain alone is worthy for the Muse, I say the Form
    complete is worthier far,
The Female equally with the Male I sing.

Of Life immense in passion, pulse, and power,
Cheerful, for freest action formed under the laws divine,
The Modern Man I sing.

WALT WHITMAN (1819–1892)
There Was a Child Went Forth

1855

There was a child went forth every day,
And the first object he looked upon, that object he became,
And that object became part of him for the day or a certain part of the day,
Or for many years or stretching cycles of years.

The early lilacs became part of this child,   5
And grass and white and red morning-glories, and white and red clover,
    and the song of the phoebe-bird,
And the Third-month° lambs and the sow's pink-faint litter, and the mare's
    foal and the cow's calf,
And the noisy brood of the barnyard or by the mire of the pond-side,
And the fish suspending themselves so curiously below there, and the
    beautiful curious liquid,
And the water-plants with their graceful flat heads, all became part of him.   10

The field-sprouts of Fourth-month and Fifth-month became part of him,
Winter-grain sprouts and those of the light-yellow corn, and the esculent
    roots of the garden,
And the apple-trees covered with blossoms and the fruit afterward, and
    wood-berries, and the commonest weeds by the road,
And the old drunkard staggering home from the outhouse of the tavern
    whence he had lately risen,
And the schoolmistress that passed on her way to the school,   15
And the friendly boys that passed, and the quarrelsome boys,
And the tidy and fresh-cheeked girls, and the barefoot negro boy and girl,
And all the changes of city and country wherever he went.

7 *Third-month:* March; Whitman is following the Quaker practice of naming the months by their
number in the year's sequence.

436 A Collection of Poems

His own parents, he that had fathered him and she that had conceived him in her womb and birthed him,

They gave this child more of themselves than that,   20

They gave him afterward every day, they became part of him.

The mother at home quietly placing the dishes on the supper-table,

The mother with mild words, clean her cap and gown, a wholesome odor falling off her person and clothes as she walks by,

The father, strong, self-sufficient, manly, mean, angered, unjust,

The blow, the quick loud word, the tight bargain, the crafty lure,   25

The family usages, the language, the company, the furniture, the yearning and swelling heart,

Affection that will not be gainsayed, the sense of what is real, the thought if after all it should prove unreal,

The doubts of day-time and the doubts of night-time, the curious whether and how,

Whether that which appears so is so, or is it all flashes and specks?

Men and women crowding fast in the streets, if they are not flashes and specks what are they?   30

The streets themselves and the facades of houses, and goods in the windows,

Vehicles, teams, the heavy-planked wharves, the huge crossing at the ferries,

The village on the highland seen from afar at sunset, the river between,

Shadows, aureola and mist, the light falling on roofs and gables of white or brown two miles off,

The schooner near by sleepily dropping down the tide, the little boat slack-towed astern,   35

The hurrying tumbling waves, quick-broken crests, slapping,

The strata of colored clouds, the long bar of maroon-tint away solitary by itself, the spread of purity it lies motionless in,

The horizon's edge, the flying sea-crow, the fragrance of salt marsh and shore mud,

These became part of that child who went forth every day, and who now goes, and will always go forth every day.

RICHARD WILBUR (b. 1921)
Love Calls Us to the Things of This World°   1956

The eyes open to a cry of pulleys,°
And spirited from sleep, the astounded soul
Hangs for a moment bodiless and simple
As false dawn.
                Outside the open window   5
The morning air is all awash with angels.

Love Calls Us . . . : From St. Augustine's *Commentary on the Psalms.*   1 *pulleys:* Grooved wheels at each end of a laundry line; clothes are hung on the line and advance as the line is moved.

Some are in bed-sheets, some are in blouses,
Some are in smocks: but truly there they are.
Now they are rising together in calm swells
Of halcyon feeling, filling whatever they wear   10
With the deep joy of their impersonal breathing;
Now they are flying in place, conveying
The terrible speed of their omnipresence, moving
And staying like white water; and now of a sudden
They swoon down into so rapt a quiet   15
That nobody seems to be there.
                              The soul shrinks

                            From all that it is about to remember,
From the punctual rape of every blessèd day,
And cries,   20
        "Oh, let there be nothing on earth but laundry,
Nothing but rosy hands in the rising steam
And clear dances done in the sight of heaven."

Yet, as the sun acknowledges
With a warm look the world's hunks and colors,   25
The soul descends once more in bitter love
To accept the waking body, saying now
In a changed voice as the man yawns and rises,

"Bring them down from their ruddy gallows;
Let there be clean linen for the backs of thieves;   30
Let lovers go fresh and sweet to be undone,
And the heaviest nuns walk in a pure floating
Of dark habits,
           keeping their difficult balance."

RICHARD WILBUR (b. 1921)
The Writer   1976

In her room at the prow of the house
Where light breaks, and the windows are tossed with linden,
My daughter is writing a story.

I pause in the stairwell, hearing
From her shut door a commotion of typewriter-keys   5
Like a chain hauled over a gunwale.

Young as she is, the stuff
Of her life is a great cargo, and some of it heavy:
I wish her a lucky passage.

But now it is she who pauses,   10
As if to reject my thought and its easy figure.
A stillness greatens, in which

The whole house seems to be thinking,
And then she is at it again with a bunched clamor
Of strokes, and again is silent.   15

I remember the dazed starling
Which was trapped in that very room, two years ago;
How we stole in, lifted a sash

And retreated, not to affright it;
And how for a helpless hour, through the crack of the door,   20
We watched the sleek, wild, dark

And iridescent creature
Batter against the brilliance, drop like a glove
To the hard floor, or the desk-top,

And wait then, humped and bloody,   25
For the wits to try it again; and how our spirits
Rose when, suddenly sure,

If lifted off from a chair-back,
Beating a smooth course for the right window
And clearing the sill of the world.   30

It is always a matter, my darling,
Of life or death, as I had forgotten. I wish
What I wished you before, but harder.

MILLER WILLIAMS (b. 1930)

After a Brubeck Concert   1986

Six hundred years ago, more or less,
something more than eight million couples
coupled to have me here at last, at last.
Had not each fondling, fighting, or fumbling pair
conjoined at the exquisitely right time,   5
thirty-four million times, I would be an unborn,
one of the quiet ones who are less than air.
But I will be also, when six hundred years have passed,
one of seventeen million who made love
aiming without aiming to at one   10
barely imaginable, who may then be doing
something no one I know has ever done
or thought of doing, on some distant world
we did not know about when we were here.
Or maybe sitting in a room like this,   15

eating a cheese sandwich and drinking beer,
a small lamp not quite taking the room from the dark,
with someone sitting nearby, humming something
while two dogs, one far away, answer bark for bark.

WILLIAM CARLOS WILLIAMS (1883–1963)
Spring and All   1923

By the road to the contagious hospital
under the surge of the blue
mottled clouds driven from the
northeast — a cold wind. Beyond, the
waste of broad, muddy fields   5
brown with dried weeds, standing and fallen

patches of standing water
and scattering of tall trees

All along the road the reddish
purplish, forked, upstanding, twiggy   10
stuff of bushes and small trees
with dead, brown leaves under them
leafless vines —

Lifeless in appearance, sluggish
dazed spring approaches —   15

They enter the new world naked,
cold, uncertain of all
save that they enter. All about them
the cold, familiar wind —

Now the grass, tomorrow   20
the stiff curl of wildcarrot leaf
One by one objects are defined —
It quickens: clarity, outline of leaf

But now the stark dignity of
entrance — Still, the profound change   25
has come upon them: rooted, they
grip down and begin to awaken

WILLIAM CARLOS WILLIAMS (1883–1963)
This Is Just to Say   1934

I have eaten
the plums
that were in
the icebox

and which   5
you were probably
saving
for breakfast

Forgive me
they were delicious   10
so sweet
and so cold

WILLIAM WORDSWORTH (1770–1850)
I Wandered Lonely as a Cloud   1807

I wandered lonely as a cloud
That floats on high o'er vales and hills,
When all at once I saw a crowd,
A host, of golden daffodils,
Beside the lake, beneath the trees,   5
Fluttering and dancing in the breeze.

Continuous as the stars that shine
And twinkle on the milky way,
They stretched in never-ending line
Along the margin of a bay;   10
Ten thousand saw I at a glance,
Tossing their heads in sprightly dance.

The waves beside them danced, but they
Outdid the sparkling waves in glee;
A poet could not but be gay,   15
In such a jocund company;
I gazed — and gazed — but little thought
What wealth the show to me had brought:

For oft, when on my couch I lie
In vacant or in pensive mood,   20
They flash upon that inward eye
Which is the bliss of solitude;
And then my heart with pleasure fills,
And dances with the daffodils.

WILLIAM WORDSWORTH (1770–1850)
She Dwelt among the Untrodden Ways

1800

She dwelt among the untrodden ways
    Beside the springs of Dove,°
A Maid whom there were none to praise
    And very few to love:

A violet by a mossy stone 5
    Half hidden from the eye!
— Fair as a star, when only one
    Is shining in the sky.

She lived unknown, and few could know
    When Lucy ceased to be; 10
But she is in her grave, and, oh,
    The difference to me!

2 *Dove:* A stream near Wordsworth's home in the Lake District of England.

WILLIAM WORDSWORTH (1770–1850)
A Slumber Did My Spirit Seal

1800

A slumber did my spirit seal;
    I had no human fears —
She seemed a thing that could not feel
    The touch of earthly years.

No motion has she now, no force;
    She neither hears nor sees;
Rolled round in earth's diurnal course.
    With rocks, and stones, and trees.

WILLIAM WORDSWORTH (1770–1850)
The Solitary Reaper°

1807

Behold her, single in the field,
Yon solitary Highland lass!
Reaping and singing by herself;

The Solitary Reaper: Dorothy Wordsworth (William's sister) writes that the poem was suggested by this sentence in Thomas Wilkinson's *Tour of Scotland:* "Passed a female who was reaping alone; she sung in Erse, as she bended over her sickle; the sweetest human voice I ever heard: her strains were tenderly melancholy, and felt delicious, long after they were heard no more."

Stop here, or gently pass!
Alone she cuts and binds the grain,   5
And sings a melancholy strain;
O listen! for the vale profound
Is overflowing with the sound.

No nightingale did ever chaunt
More welcome notes to weary bands   10
Of travelers in some shady haunt
Among Arabian sands.
A voice so thrilling ne'er was heard
In springtime from the cuckoo-bird,
Breaking the silence of the seas   15
Among the farthest Hebrides.

Will no one tell me what she sings? —
Perhaps the plaintive numbers flow
For old, unhappy, far-off things,
And battles long ago.   20
Or is it some more humble lay,
Familiar matter of today?
Some natural sorrow, loss, or pain,
That has been, and may be again?

Whate'er the theme, the maiden sang   25
As if her song could have no ending;
I saw her singing at her work,
And o'er the sickle bending —
I listened, motionless and still;
And, as I mounted up the hill,   30
The music in my heart I bore
Long after it was heard no more.

JAMES WRIGHT (1927–1980)

Lying in a Hammock at William Duffy's Farm in Pine Island, Minnesota   1961

Over my head, I see the bronze butterfly,
Asleep on the black trunk,
Blowing like a leaf in green shadow.
Down the ravine behind the empty house,
The cowbells follow one another   5
Into the distances of the afternoon.
To my right,
In a field of sunlight between two pines,
The droppings of last year's horses
Blaze up into golden stones.   10

I lean back, as the evening darkens and comes on.
A chicken hawk floats over, looking for home.
I have wasted my life.

SIR THOMAS WYATT (1503–1542)
They Flee from Me

1557

They flee from me that sometime did me seek
With naked foot stalking in my chamber.
I have seen them gentle, tame, and meek
That now are wild and do not remember
That sometime they put themselves in danger   5
To take bread at my hand; and now they range
Busily seeking with a continual change.

Thankèd be Fortune, it hath been otherwise
Twenty times better; but once in special,
In thin array after a pleasant guise,   10
When her loose gown from her shoulders did fall,
And she me caught in her arms long and small;°   *narrow*
And therewithall sweetly did me kiss,
And softly said, "Dear heart, how like you this?"

It was no dream; I lay broad waking.   15
But all is turned thorough° my gentleness   *through*
Into a strange fashion of forsaking;
And I have leave to go of her goodness,
And she also to use newfangleness.
But since that I so kindely° am served,   *kindly (ironic)* 20
I fain would know what she hath deserved.

WILLIAM BUTLER YEATS (1865–1939)
Adam's Curse°

1903

We sat together at one summer's end,
That beautiful mild woman, your close friend,
And you and I, and talked of poetry.
I said, "A line will take us hours maybe;
Yet if it does not seem a moment's thought,   5
Our stitching and unstitching has been naught.
Better go down upon your marrow-bones
And scrub a kitchen pavement, or break stones

Adam's Curse: After his fall from grace and eviction from Eden, Adam was cursed with hard work, pain, and death.

Like an old pauper, in all kinds of weather;
For to articulate sweet sounds together
Is to work harder than all these, and yet
Be thought an idler by the noisy set
Of bankers, schoolmasters, and clergymen
The martyrs call the world."
               And thereupon
That beautiful mild woman for whose sake
There's many a one shall find out all heartache
On finding that her voice is sweet and low
Replied, "To be born woman is to know—
Although they do not talk of it at school—
That we must labor to be beautiful."

I said, "It's certain there is no fine thing
Since Adam's fall but needs much laboring.
There have been lovers who thought love should be
So much compounded of high courtesy
That they would sigh and quote with learned looks
Precedents out of beautiful old books;
Yet now it seems an idle trade enough."

We sat grown quiet at the name of love;
We saw the last embers of daylight die,
And in the trembling blue-green of the sky
A moon, worn as if it had been a shell
Washed by time's waters as they rose and fell
About the stars and broke in days and years.

I had a thought for no one's but your ears:
That you were beautiful, and that I strove
To love you in the old high way of love;
That it had all seemed happy, and yet we'd grown
As weary-hearted as that hollow moon.

10

15

20

25

30

35

WILLIAM BUTLER YEATS (1865–1939)
Crazy Jane Talks with the Bishop

1933

I met the Bishop on the road
And much said he and I.
"Those breasts are flat and fallen now,
Those veins must soon be dry;
Live in a heavenly mansion,
Not in some foul sty."

"Fair and foul are near of kin,
And fair needs foul," I cried.
"My friends are gone, but that's a truth

5

Nor grave nor bed denied,   10
Learned in bodily lowliness
And in the heart's pride.

"A woman can be proud and stiff
When on love intent;
But Love has pitched his mansion in   15
The place of excrement;
For nothing can be sole or whole
That has not been rent."

WILLIAM BUTLER YEATS (1865–1939)
The Lake Isle of Innisfree°   1892

I will arise and go now, and go to Innisfree,
And a small cabin build there, of clay and wattles made:
Nine bean-rows will I have there, a hive for the honey-bee,
And live alone in the bee-loud glade.

And I shall have some peace there, for peace comes dropping slow,   5
Dropping from the veils of the morning to where the cricket sings;
There midnight's all a glimmer, and noon a purple glow,
And evening full of the linnet's wings.

I will arise and go now, for always night and day
I hear lake water lapping with low sounds by the shore: 10
While I stand on the roadway, or on the pavements grey,
I hear it in the deep heart's core.

The Lake Isle of Innisfree: An island in Lough (or Lake) Gill, in western Ireland.

WILLIAM BUTLER YEATS (1865–1939)
Leda and the Swan°   1924

A sudden blow: the great wings beating still
Above the staggering girl, her thighs caressed
By the dark webs, her nape caught in his bill,
He holds her helpless breast upon his breast.

How can those terrified vague fingers push   5
The feathered glory from her loosening thighs?
And how can body, laid in that white rush,
But feel the strange heart beating where it lies?

Leda and the Swan: In Greek myth, Zeus in the form of a swan seduced Leda and fathered Helen of
Troy (whose abduction started the Trojan War) and Clytemnestra, Agamemnon's wife and murderer.
Yeats thought of Zeus's appearance to Leda as a type of annunciation, like the angel appearing to
Mary.

A shudder in the loins engenders there
The broken wall, the burning roof and tower   10
And Agamemnon dead.

                    Being so caught up,
So mastered by the brute blood of the air,
Did she put on his knowledge with his power
Before the indifferent beak could let her drop?

WILLIAM BUTLER YEATS (1865–1939)
Sailing to Byzantium°   1927

I
That is no country for old men.° The young
In one another's arms, birds in the trees
— Those dying generations — at their song,
The salmon-falls, the mackerel-crowded seas
Fish, flesh, or fowl, commend all summer long   5
Whatever is begotten, born and dies.
Caught in that sensual music all neglect
Monuments of unaging intellect.

II
An aged man is but a paltry thing,
A tattered coat upon a stick, unless   10
Soul clap its hands and sing, and louder sing
For every tatter in its mortal dress,
Nor is there singing school but studying
Monuments of its own magnificence;
And therefore I have sailed the seas and come   15
To the holy city of Byzantium.

III
O sages standing in God's holy fire
As in the gold mosaic of a wall,
Come from the holy fire, perne in a gyre,°
And be the singing-masters of my soul.   20
Consume my heart away; sick with desire
And fastened to a dying animal
It knows not what it is; and gather me
Into the artifice of eternity.

Byzantium: Old name for the modern city of Istanbul, capital of the Eastern Roman Empire, ancient
artistic and intellectual center. Yeats uses Byzantium as a symbol for "artificial" (and therefore death-
less) art and beauty, as opposed to the beauty of the natural world, which is bound to time and
death.   1 *That . . . men:* Ireland, part of the time-bound world.   19 *perne in a gyre:* Bobbin
making a spiral pattern.

IV

Once out of nature I shall never take   25
My bodily form from any natural thing,
But such a form as Grecian goldsmiths make
Of hammered gold and gold enameling
To keep a drowsy Emperor awake;°
Or set upon a golden bough° to sing   30
To lords and ladies of Byzantium
Of what is past, or passing, or to come.

27–29 *such . . . awake:* "I have read somewhere that in the Emperor's palace at Byzantium was a
tree made of gold and silver, and artificial birds that sang" (Yeats's note).   30 *golden bough:* In
Greek legend, Aeneas had to pluck a golden bough from a tree in order to descend into Hades. As
soon as the bough was plucked, another grew in its place.

WILLIAM BUTLER YEATS (1865–1939)
The Second Coming°   1921

Turning and turning in the widening gyre°
The falcon cannot hear the falconer;
Things fall apart; the center cannot hold;
Mere anarchy is loosed upon the world,
The blood-dimmed tide is loosed, and everywhere   5
The ceremony of innocence is drowned;
The best lack all conviction, while the worst
Are full of passionate intensity.

Surely some revelation is at hand;
Surely the Second Coming is at hand.   10
The Second Coming! Hardly are those words out
When a vast image out of *Spiritus Mundi*°   *Soul of the world*
Troubles my sight: somewhere in sands of the desert
A shape with lion body and the head of a man,
A gaze blank and pitiless as the sun,   15
Is moving its slow thighs, while all about it
Reel shadows of the indignant desert birds.
The darkness drops again; but now I know
That twenty centuries of stony sleep
Were vexed to nightmare by a rocking cradle,   20
And what rough beast, its hour come round at last,
Slouches towards Bethlehem to be born?

The Second Coming: According to Matthew 24:29–44, Christ will return to earth after a time of tribulation to reward the righteous and establish the Millennium of Heaven on earth. Yeats saw his
troubled time as the end of the Christian era, and feared the portents of the new cycle.   1 *gyre:*
Widening spiral of a falcon's flight, used by Yeats to describe the cycling of history.

CLARIBEL ALEGRÍA (Salvadoran/b. 1924)

Born in Estelí, Nicaragua, Claribel Alegría moved with her family to El Salvador within a year of her birth. A 1948 graduate of George Washington University, she considers herself a Salvadoran, and much of her writing reflects the political upheaval of recent Latin American history. In 1978 she was awarded the Casa de las Americas prize for her book *I Survive*. A bilingual edition of her major works, *Flowers from the Volcano,* was published in 1982.

I Am Mirror
TRANSLATED BY ELECTA ARENAL AND MARSHA GABRIELA DREYER

<pre>
Water sparkles
on my skin
and I don't feel it
water streams
down my back   5
I don't feel it
I rub myself with a towel
I pinch myself in the arm
I don't feel
frightened I look at myself in the mirror   10
she also pricks herself
I begin to get dressed
stumbling
from the corners
shouts like lightning bolts   15
tortured eyes
scurrying rats
and teeth shoot forth
although I feel nothing
I wander through the streets: 20
children with dirty faces
ask me for charity
child prostitutes
who are not yet fifteen
the streets are paved with pain   25
tanks that approach
raised bayonets
</pre>

bodies that fall
weeping
finally I feel my arm   30
I am no longer a phantom
I hurt
therefore I exist
I return to watch the scene:
children who run   35
bleeding
women with panic
in their faces
this time it hurts me less
I pinch myself again   40
and already I feel nothing
I simply reflect
what happens at my side
the tanks
are not tanks   45
nor are the shouts
shouts
I am a blank mirror
that nothing penetrates
my surface   50
is hard
is brilliant
is polished
I became a mirror
and I am fleshless   55
scarcely preserving
a vague memory
of pain.

Connections to Other Selections

1. Compare the ways Alegría uses mirror images to reflect life in El Salvador with
   Sylvia Plath's concerns in "Mirror" (p. 98).
2. Write an essay comparing the speaker's voice in this poem and that in William
   Blake's "London" (p. 76). How do the speakers evoke emotional responses to what
   they describe?

KATERINA ANGHELÁKI-ROOKE (Greek/b. 1939)

Athenian Katerina Angheláki-Rooke graduated from the University of
Geneva in 1962. She has been awarded Ford Foundation and Fulbright grants
and has taught at the universities of Iowa and Utah as well as San

Francisco State University and Harvard University. Her works include *Wolves and Clouds* (1963), *Magdalene the Vast Mammal* (1974), and *Counter Love* (1982), which was reprinted as *Being and Things on Their Own*.

Tourism 1975

TRANSLATED BY PHILIP RAMP

My land appeared to me
one morning
like a chunk of bread
tossed in the street
with its doughy crust   5
covered with ants,
countless, black with sunglasses
fidgeting
with their hands and feet.
Loaded with supplies   10
they climb the pine planted hills
the breeze of time blows
withered
while thyme barely breathes
and tightens itself   15
around into empty bottles
and the columns.
Hastily, without passion
they move their hats, antennae
touching whatever fancy   20
they fancy
the post cards, me,
the brown donkey.
Deserted morning
a haze around the keels   25
a mute thoughtful
cleaning fish . . .
Nobody else
empty, me
the ant flocks   30
strolled, shopped . . .
Then empty again.
A far away typewriter
as if from the sea
somebody was dictating   35
the end of the island.
Ant humans
behaving more and more touristically

towards life
they caress without ever
reaching the kernel
insects
they enjoy the luminous intervals
of skin,
but the land is swelling
dropsical
the owl is crippled
while West and East
both blind
poor things
in a ravine
with crows above
excreting on them.
Two old codgers in the countryside
St. Augustine and St. Athanasios°
stammer exorcism, recipes,
their holes draughty with lies
as they tremble from cold.
The consoling lines were broken
the images were transliterated
and were left without glow.

"Strange days down here,"
the foreign girl said,
"no matter how much you suffer
you rejoice with what you see.
The animals emerge from the soil
no hand guides them
they loaf about
they graze colors
and as they stand thoughtful
they are politely swallowed
by night."

40

45

50

55

60

65

70

55 *St. Augustine and St. Athanasios:* The former (354–430) was a Catholic theologian; the latter (293–373) was a Greek patriarch and defender of Catholic teachings.

Connections to Other Selections

1. Discuss the treatment of tourists in this poem and in James Merrill's "Casual Wear" (p. 123).
2. Compare the tone of "Tourism" with that of John Ciardi's "Suburban" (p. 125). How does the speaker of each poem reveal his or her emotions?

ELISABETH EYBERS (South African/b. 1915)

Born in Klerksdorp, South Africa, Elisabeth Eybers grew up speaking Afrikaans but learned English and graduated from the Anglophonic University of the Witwatersrand in 1937. In the early 1960s Eybers left South Africa to live in Holland to protest the political and racial policies of apartheid. She has won several awards, including the Herzog Prize for poetry in 1943 and the Central News Agency Prize for literature in 1973 and 1978. Among her works are *Balance* (1962), *Shelter* (1968), and *Cross of Coin* (1973).

Emily Dickinson   1989

TRANSLATED BY ELISABETH EYBERS

Essential oils are wrung:
The attar from the rose
Is not expressed by suns alone,
It is the gift of screws
                —EMILY DICKINSON

That knowledge which the ruthless screws distil
she could not weigh against the easy truth
that's cheap and readily negotiable:
as time went on, her days grew more aloof.

The years proved meager as they came and went;   5
her narrow, ardent love, commodity
that found no market, still remained unspent:
yearning, forsakenness and ecstasy.

She climbed the scaffolding of loneliness
not to escape from living, but to gain   10
a perilous glimpse into the universe;
and tunneled down into the mind's dark mine,
through tortuous shafts descending to obtain
its flawless fragments, glittering, crystalline.

Connections to Other Selections

1. How is Dickinson's rejection of what Eybers describes as "easy truth" manifested in "I like a look of Agony" (p. 263) and "Tell all the Truth but tell it slant — " (p. 275)?
2. Compare this tribute to Dickinson with Galway Kinnell's tribute to Robert Frost on page 322. Which tribute, in your opinion, is more successful in capturing the essence of its subject? Explain your response in an essay.

FAIZ AHMED FAIZ (Pakistani/1911–1984)

Born in what is now Pakistan, Faiz Ahmed Faiz served in the British Indian Army during World War II. After the war he became a spokesman for Pakistani and Indian rights by editing the *Pakistani Times* and writing poetry in Urdu. Faiz served several jail sentences for his political activism, spending a considerable amount of time in solitary confinement. His poetry is widely known in India and the subcontinent; a translation of some is available as *The True Subject: Selected Poems of Faiz Ahmed Faiz* (1988).

Prison Daybreak   1952
TRANSLATED BY NAOMI LAZARD

Though it was still night
the moon stood beside my pillow and said:
                    "Wake up,
the wine of sleep that was your portion
is finished. The wineglass is empty.   5
Morning is here."
                    I said good-bye to my beloved's image
in the black satin waters of the night
that hung still and stagnant on the world.
                                   Here and there   10
moonlight whirled, the lotus dance commenced;
silver nebulas of stars dropped from the moon's white hand.
They went under, rose again to float, faded and opened.
For a long time night and daybreak swayed,
locked together in each other's arms.   15

              In the prison yard
my comrades' faces, incandescent as candlelight,
flickered through the gloom. Sleep had washed them
with its dew, turned them into gold.
                            For that moment   20
these faces were rinsed clean of grief for our people,
absolved from the pain of separation from their dear ones.
In the distance a gong struck the hour;
wretched footsteps stumbled forward on their rounds,
wasted by near starvation, *maestros* of the morning shuffle,   25
lockstepped, arm in arm with their own terrible laments.
Mutilated voices, broken on the rack, awakened.

              Somewhere a door opened,
another one closed; a chain muttered, grumbled,
shrieked out loud. Somewhere a knife plunged   30

into the gizzard of a lock; a window went mad
and began to beat its own head.

This is the way the enemies of life,
shaken from sleep, showed themselves.
These daemons, hacked from stone and steel,   35
use their great hands to grind down the spirit,
slim as a feather now, of my useless days and nights.
They make it cry out in despair.
                              The prisoners,
all of us, keep watch for our savior   40
who is on his way in the form of a storybook prince,
arrows of hope burning in his quiver,
                ready to let them fly.

Connection to Another Selection

1. Write an essay on the meaning of sleep in Faiz's poem and in Robert Bly's "Waking
   from Sleep" (p. 361). Pay attention to the images that describe sleep in each poem.

VINÍCIUS DE MORAES (Brazilian/1913–1980)

Vinícius de Morales studied law at the University of Brazil and English
Literature at Oxford University in England. In addition to serving as a diplomat in Montevideo, Paris, and New York he was popular as a song lyricist
and wrote the film script for Marcel Camus's *Black Orpheus*. His books
include *My Country* (1949), *Book of Sonnets* (1957), and *Selected Poems*
(1960).

Sonnet of Intimacy   1971

Farm afternoons, there's much too much blue air.
I go out sometimes, follow the pasture track,
Chewing a blade of sticky grass, chest bare,
In threadbare pajamas of three summers back,

To the little rivulets in the riverbed   5
For a drink of water, cold and musical,
And if I spot in the brush a glow of red,
A raspberry, spit its blood at the corral.

The smell of cow manure is delicious.
The cattle look at me unenviously   10
And when there comes a sudden stream and hiss

Accompanied by a look not unmalicious,
All of us, animals, unemotionally
Partake together of a pleasant piss.

Connections to Other Selections

1. Compare the effects of the meter and rhyme scheme in "Sonnet of Intimacy" and Robert Frost's "The Pasture" (p. 297).
2. In an essay discuss the themes of "Sonnet of Intimacy" and William Stafford's "Traveling through the Dark" (p. 118). How is each speaker's relationship to nature established?

PABLO NERUDA (Chilean/1904–1973)

Born in Chile, Pablo Neruda insisted all his life on the connection between poetry and politics. He was an activist and a Chilean diplomat in a number of countries during the 1920s and 1930s and remained politically active until his death. Neruda was regarded as a great and influential poet (he was awarded the Nobel Prize in 1971) whose poetry ranged from specific political issues to the yearnings of romantic love. Among his many works are *Twenty Love Poems and a Song of Despair* (1924), *Residence on Earth* (three series, 1925–45), *Spain in the Heart* (1937), *The Captain's Verses* (1952), and *Memorial of Isla Negra* (1964).

Sweetness, Always ·   1958
TRANSLATED BY ALASTAIR REID

Why such harsh machinery?
Why, to write down the stuff
and people of every day,
must poems be dressed up in gold,
in old and fearful stone?   5

I want verses of felt or feather
which scarcely weigh, mild verses
with the intimacy of beds
where people have loved and dreamed.
I want poems stained   10
by hands and everydayness.

Verses of pastry which melt
into milk and sugar in the mouth,
air and water to drink,
the bites and kisses of love. 15
I long for eatable sonnets,
poems of honey and flour.

Vanity keeps prodding us
to lift ourselves skyward
or to make deep and useless 20
tunnels underground.
So we forget the joyous
love-needs of our bodies.
We forget about pastries.
We are not feeding the world. 25

In Madras a long time since,
I saw a sugary pyramid,
a tower of confectionery —
one level after another,
and in the construction, rubies, 30
and other blushing delights,
medieval and yellow.

Someone dirtied his hands
to cook up so much sweetness.

Brother poets from here 35
and there, from earth and sky,
from Medellín, from Veracruz,
Abyssinia, Antofagasta,
do you know the recipe for honeycombs?

Let's forget all about that stone. 40

Let your poetry fill up
the equinoctial pastry shop
our mouths long to devour —
all the children's mouths
and the poor adults' also. 45
Don't go on without seeing,
relishing, understanding
all these hearts of sugar.

Don't be afraid of sweetness.

With us or without us, 50
sweetness will go on living

and is infinitely alive,
forever being revived,
for it's in a man's mouth,
whether he's eating or singing,   55
that sweetness has its place.

Connections to Other Selections

1. Compare the view of life offered in this poem with that in Robert Frost's "Provide, Provide" (p. 312).
2. Write an essay that discusses Galway Kinnell's "Blackberry Eating" (p. 138) and Helen Chasin's "The Word *Plum*" (p. 155) as the sort of "eatable" poetry the speaker calls for in this poem.

OCTAVIO PAZ (Mexican/b. 1914)

Born in Mexico City, Octavio Paz studied at the National Autonomous University and in 1943 helped found one of Mexico's most important literary reviews, *The Prodigal Son*. He served in the Mexican diplomatic corps in Paris, New Delhi, and New York. Paz's writing reflects the widely traveled poet's Hispanic traditions and European modernism as well as Buddhism. In 1990 he won the Nobel Prize for literature. Paz's major poetic works include *Sun Stone* (1958), *The Violent Season* (1958), *Salamander* (1962), *Blanco* (1966), *Eastern Rampart* (1968), and *Renga* (1971).

The Street

A long silent street.
I walk in blackness and I stumble and fall
and rise, and I walk blind, my feet
stepping on silent stones and dry leaves.
Someone behind me also stepping on stones, leaves: 5
if I slow down, he slows;
if I run, he runs. I turn: nobody.
Everything dark and doorless.
Turning and turning among these corners
which lead forever to the street   10
where nobody waits for, nobody follows me,
where I pursue a man who stumbles
and rises and says when he sees me: nobody.

Connections to Other Selections

1. How does the speaker's anxiety in this poem compare with that in Robert Frost's "Acquainted with the Night" (p. 109)?
2. Write an essay comparing the tone of this poem and that of James Wright's "Lying in a Hammock at William Duffy's Farm in Pine Island, Minnesota" (p. 443). Pay attention to how you read the final lines of each poem.

WOLE SOYINKA (Nigerian/b. 1934)

Born Oluwole Akinwande Soyinka, in the western Nigerian town of Akinwande, Wole Soyinka has embodied in his life and art the contradictions and tensions that can often seem inevitable for the European-educated, English-speaking African writers. Although he has written and published novels and poetry (the following poem is from *A Shuttle in the Crypt* [1972]), Soyinka is most renowned as a playwright whose work embodies his concerns as a political reformer and social critic. His many plays include *The Lion and the Jewel* (1959), *The Strong Bond* (1963), and *Death of the King's Horseman* (1976). His Autobiography *The Man Died* (1973) records his experiences as a political prisoner in Nigeria. In 1986 he was awarded the Nobel Prize for Literature.

Future Plans   1972

The meeting is called
To odium: Forgers, framers
Fabricators Inter-
national. Chairman,
A dark horse, a circus nag turned blinkered sprinter   5

Mach Three°
We rate him — one for the Knife°
Two for 'iavelli,° Three —
Breaking speed
Of the truth barrier by a swooping detention decree   10
Projects in view:
Mao Tse Tung° in league

---

6 *Mach Three:* An air speed of three times the speed of sound.   7 *Knife:* Mack the Knife, an unsavory character from *Threepenny Opera* (1933), by Bertolt Brecht and Kurt Weill.   8 *'iavelli:* Niccolò Machiavelli (1469–1527), an Italian political theorist who described ruthless strategies for gaining power in *The Prince* (1532).   12 *Mao Tse Tung* (1893–1975): Chinese Communist leader.

With Chiang Kai. Nkrumah°
Makes a secret
Pact with Verwood,° sworn by Hastings Banda.°   15
Proven: Arafat°
In flagrante cum
Golda Meir. Castro° drunk
With Richard Nixon°
Contraceptives stacked beneath the papal bunk . . .   20
                        . . . *and more to come*

13 *Chiang Kai. Nkrumah:* Chiang Kai-shek (1887–1975), Nationalist Chinese political leader exiled in Taiwan by Mao Tse Tung; Kwame Nkrumah (1909–1972), first president of Ghana.   15 *Verwood:* Hendrick Verwoerd (1901–1966), former prime minister of South Africa, assassinated in 1966; *Hastings Banda* (b. 1905): African political leader and first president of Malawi.   16 *Arafat:* Yasir Arafat (b. 1929), Palestinian leader.   18 *Golda Meir. Castro:* Golda Meir (1898–1978), former prime minister of Israel; Fidel Castro (b. 1927), Cuban premier since 1959.   19 *Richard Nixon* (1913–1994): Former U.S. president forced to resign in 1974 due to political scandal.

Connections to Other Selections

1. Discuss the political satire in "Future Plans" and in Kenneth Fearing's "AD" (p. 114).
2. Write an essay on whether the leaders alluded to in "Future Plans" are manifestations of the type of leader described in Dylan Thomas's "The Hand That Signed the Paper" (p. 94).

WISLAWA SZYMBORSKA (Polish/b. 1923)

Wislawa Szymborska has lived in Cracow since the age of eight. She steadfastly refuses to reveal biographical details of her life, insisting that her poems should speak for themselves. With the exception of *Sounds, Feelings, Thoughts: Seventy Poems by Wislawa Szymborska* (1981), translated and introduced by Magnus J. Krynski and Robert A. Maguire, only about a score of Szymborska's poems have been translated into English. Two of her later poetry collections — as yet untranslated — are *There But for the Grace* (1972) and *A Great Number* (1976).

The Joy of Writing

TRANSLATED BY MAGNUS J. KRYNSKI AND ROBERT A. MAGUIRE

1981

Where through the written forest runs that written doe?
Is it to drink from the written water,
which will copy her gentle mouth like carbon paper?
Why does she raise her head, is it something she hears?
Poised on four fragile legs borrowed from truth   5
she pricks up her ears under my fingers.
Stillness — this word also rustles across the paper
and parts
the branches brought forth by the word "forest."

Above the blank page lurking, set to spring   10
are letters that may compose themselves all wrong,
besieging sentences
from which there is no rescue.

In a drop of ink there's a goodly reserve
of huntsmen with eyes squinting to take aim,   15
ready to dash down the steep pen,
surround the doe and level their guns.

They forget that this is not real life.
Other laws, black on white, here hold sway.
The twinkling of an eye will last as long as I wish,   20
will consent to be divided into small eternities
full of bullets stopped in flight.
Forever, if I command it, nothing will happen here.
Against my will no leaf will fall
nor blade of grass bend under the full stop of a hoof.   25

Is there then such a world
over which I rule sole and absolute?
A time I bind with chains of signs?
An existence perpetuated at my command?

The joy of writing.   30
The power of preserving.
The revenge of a mortal hand.

Connections to Other Selections

1. Discuss the themes of "The Joy of Writing" and Emily Dickinson's "To make a prairie it takes a clover and one bee" (p. 256). What is the role of the poet's imagination in each poem?
2. Write an essay that considers Szymborska's view of the writer's imagination and John Keats's as expressed in "Keats on the Truth of the Imagination," the Perspective on page 241.

SHINKICHI TAKAHASHI (Japanese/1901–1987)

Born in the fishing village of Shikoku on the smallest of Japan's four main islands, Shinkichi Takahashi dropped out of high school and moved to Tokyo in search of a literary career, educating himself along the way. He became a disciple of a Zen Master and wrote poetry as well as numerous commentaries on Japanese culture. His major collections include *Afterimages* (1970) and *Collected Poems*, which was awarded the Ministry of Education Prize for Art.

Explosion   1973

TRANSLATED BY LUCIEN STRYK AND TAKASHI IKEMOTO

I'm an unthinking dog,
a good-for-nothing cat,
a fog over gutter,
a blossom-swiping rain.

I close my eyes, breathe —   5
radioactive air! A billion years
and I'll be shrunk to half,
pollution strikes my marrow.

So what — I'll whoop at what
remains. Yet scant blood left,   10
reduced to emptiness by nuclear
fission, I'm running very fast.

Connections to Other Selections

1. Discuss the views of nuclear weapons presented in "Explosion" and Denise Levertov's "Gathered at the River" (p. 489).
2. How does the "So what" of line 9 in this poem compare in tone with Pablo Neruda's "Sweetness, Always" (p. 456)?

TOMAS TRANSTROMER (Swedish/b. 1931)

The work of Tomas Transtromer, who was born in Stockholm, is translated more than any other contemporary Scandinavian poet's. He has worked as a psychologist with juvenile offenders and handicapped persons. His collections of poetry include *Night Vision* (1971), *Windows and Stones: Selected Poems* (1972), *Truth Barriers* (1978), and *Selected Poems* (1981). Among his awards are the Petrarch Prize (1981), and a lifetime subsidy from the government of Sweden.

April and Silence 1991
TRANSLATED BY ROBIN FULTON

Spring lies desolate.
The velvet-dark ditch
crawls by my side
without reflections.

The only thing that shines 5
is yellow flowers.

I am carried in my shadow
like a violin
in its black box.

The only thing I want to say 10
glitters out of reach
like the silver
in a pawnbroker's.

Connections to Other Selections

1. Compare the description of spring in this poem with the description in W. D. Snodgrass's "April Inventory" (p. 424).
2. In an essay explain how the dictions used in "April and Silence" and Edna St. Vincent Millay's "Never May the Fruit Be Plucked" (p. 59) contribute to the poems' meanings.

AN ALBUM OF CANADIAN POEMS

MARGARET ATWOOD (b. 1939)

Born in Ottawa, Ontario, Margaret Atwood was educated at the University of Toronto and Harvard University. She has been writing fiction and poetry since she was a child; along the way she has worked odd jobs and been a film writer and a teacher. A prolific novelist, short story writer, and poet (she has published some twelve books of poetry), Atwood has enhanced the appreciation of Canadian literature through her editing of *The New*

Oxford Book of Canadian Verse in English (1982) and The Oxford Book of Canadian Short Stories in English (1986). The following poem is from True Stories (1981).

Spelling

1981

My daughter plays on the floor
with plastic letters,
red, blue & hard yellow,

learning how to spell,
spelling,   5
how to make spells.

     •

I wonder how many women
denied themselves daughters,
closed themselves in rooms,
drew the curtains   10
so they could mainline words.

     •

A child is not a poem,
a poem is not a child.
There is no either / or.
However.   15

     •

I return to the story
of the woman caught in the war
& in labour, her thighs tied
together by the enemy
so she could not give birth.   20

Ancestress: the burning witch,
her mouth covered by leather
to strangle words.

A word after a word
after a word is power.   25

     •

At the point where language falls away
from the hot bones, at the point
where the rock breaks open and darkness
flows out of it like blood, at
the melting point of granite   30
when the bones know
they are hollow & the word

splits & doubles & speaks
the truth & the body
itself becomes a mouth.   35

This is a metaphor.

       •

How do you learn to spell?
Blood, sky & the sun,
your own name first,
your first naming, your first name,   40
your first word.

Connections to Other Selections

1. Compare the use of metaphors in this poem and Marge Piercy's "A Work of Artifice" (p. 63). How do the metaphors serve to develop the themes in each poem?
2. In an essay compare "Spelling" with Audre Lorde's description of poetry in the perspective "Poems Are Not Luxuries" (p. 506). How does each writer make a claim for poetry as a "vital necessity of our existence"?

ROO BORSON (b. 1952)

Originally a Californian, Roo Borson earned an M.F.A. in creative writing at the University of British Columbia and lives in Canada working as a writer in addition to holding a variety of other jobs. Her collections of poems include *Landfall* (1977), *In the Smoky Light of the Fields* (1980), *A Sad Device* (1981), *The Whole Night, Coming Home* (1984), and *The Transparence of November/Snow* (1985).

Talk   1981

The shops, the streets are full of old men
who can't think of a thing to say anymore.
Sometimes, looking at a girl, it
almost occurs to them, but they can't make it out,
they go pawing toward it through the fog.   5

The young men are still jostling shoulders
as they walk along, tussling at one another with words.
They're excited by talk, they can still see the danger.

The old women, thrifty with words,
haggling for oranges, their mouths   10
take bites out of the air. They know the value of oranges.
They had to learn everything
on their own.

The young women are the worst off, no one has bothered
to show them things.   15
You can see their minds on their faces,
they are like little lakes before a storm.
They don't know it's confusion that makes them sad.
It's lucky in a way though, because the young men take
a look of confusion for inscrutability, and this   20
excites them and makes them want to own
this face they don't understand,
something to be tinkered with at their leisure.

Connections to Other Selections

1. Discuss the relationship among the men and women in this poem and Deborah Garrison's "She Was Waiting to Be Told" (p. 483).
2. Write an essay about the problem of people communicating in "Talk" and in Robert Frost's "Home Burial" (p. 300).

GEORGE BOWERING (b. 1935)

Born in Penticon, British Columbia, George Bowering earned degrees at the University of British Columbia and has taught at Simon Fraser University. He is a two-time winner of the Governor General's Award, for poetry (1969) and fiction (1980). Among his collections of poems are *Touch: Selected Poems 1960–1970* (1971), *Particular Accidents: Selected Poems* (1980), and *West Window: The Selected Poetry of George Bowering* (1982).

Grandfather   1962

Grandfather
       Jabez Harry Bowering
strode across the Canadian prairie
hacking down trees

```
                     and building churches                                    5
delivering personal baptist sermons in them
leading Holy holy holy lord god almighty songs in them
red haired man squared off in the pulpit
reading Saul on the road to Damascus at them

Left home                                                                    10
              big walled Bristol town
at age eight
              to make a living
buried his stubby fingers in root snarled earth
for a suit of clothes and seven hundred gruelly meals a year                  15
taking an anabaptist cane across the back every day
for four years till he was whipped out of England

Twelve years old
              and across the ocean alone
to apocalyptic Canada                                                        20
              Ontario of bone bending child labor
six years on the road to Damascus till his eyes were blinded
with the blast of Christ and he wandered west
to Brandon among wheat kings and heathen Saturday nights
young red haired Bristol boy shoveling coal                                   25
in the basement of Brandon college five in the morning

Then built his first wooden church and married
a sick girl who bore two live children and died
leaving several pitiful letters and the Manitoba night

He moved west with another wife and built children and churches             30
Saskatchewan Alberta British Columbia Holy holy holy
lord god almighty
              struck his labored bones with pain
and left him a postmaster prodding grandchildren with crutches
another dead wife and a glass bowl of photographs                            35
and holy books unopened save the bible by the bed

Till he died the day before his eighty fifth birthday
in a Catholic hospital of sheets white as his hair
```

Connections to Other Selections

1. Compare the speaker's attitude toward his grandfather with that of the speaker toward the common man in Howard Nemerov's "Life Cycle of Common Man" (p. 405).
2. In an essay discuss the treatment of religion in this poem and in Emily Dickinson's "Safe in their Alabaster Chambers" (pp. 258–259).

MARILYN BOWERING (b. 1949)

Born in Winnipeg, Marilyn Bowering teaches creative writing at the University of Victoria. Her books include *The Liberation of Newfoundland* (1973), *Many Voices: Contemporary Canadian Indian Poetry* (1977), *The Book of Glass* (1979), *Sleeping with Lambs* (1980), and *The Sunday before Winter: New and Selected Poems* (1984).

Wishing Africa

1980

There's never enough whiskey or rain
when the blood is thin and white,
but oh it was beautiful,
the wind delicate as Queen Anne's lace,
only wild with insects   5
breeding the sponge-green veldt,
and bands of white butterflies
slapping the acacia.
The women's bodies were variable as coral
and men carried snakes on staves.   10

It would do me no good
to go back,
I am threaded
with pale veins,
I am full with dying   15
and ordinary;
but oh if there was a way
of wishing Africa.

When there was planting,
when there was harvesting,   20
I was not far behind
those who first
opened the ground.   .
I stitched in seed,
I grew meat in the earth's blond side.   25
I did it all with little bloody stitches.
What red there was in me
I let out there.
The sun stayed forever
then was gone.   30

I am scented with virus,
I breed flowers for the ochre

my skin was.
There is no sex in it.
I am white as a geisha,   35
my roots indiscriminate
since my bones gave way.
It is a small, personal pruning
that keeps me.
I had a soul,   40
and remember how it hurt
to be greedy and eat.

Connections to Other Selections

1. Discuss the use of sensuality in this poem and Edna St. Vincent Millay's "I Too beneath Your Moon, Almighty Sex" (p. 402). What does it reveal about the speaker in each poem?
2. In an essay compare the themes of "Wishing Africa" and Rainer Maria Rilke's "The Panther" (p. 81).

DAVID DONNELL (b. 1939)

Born in St. Mary's, Ontario, David Donnell writes fiction and poetry. His books include *The Blue Sky* (1977), *Dangerous Crossings* (1980), and *Settlements* (1983), which won the Governor General's Award.

The Canadian Prairies View of Literature   1983

First of all it has to be anecdotal; ideas don't exist;
themes struggle dimly out of accrued material like the shadow
of a slow caterpillar struggling out of a large cocoon;
even this image itself is somewhat urban inasmuch as it suggests
the tree-bordered streets of small southern Ontario towns;   5
towns are alright; Ontario towns are urban; French towns are European;
the action should take place on a farm between April and October;
nature is quiet during winter; when it snows, there's a lot of it;
the poem shimmers in the school-teacher's head like an image
of being somewhere else without a railway ticket to return;   10
the novel shifts its haunches in the hot reporter's head
and surveys the possible relationship between different farms;
sometimes the action happens in the beverage rooms and cheap
hotels area of a small town that has boomed into a new city;
Indians and Metis appear in the novel wearing the marks   15
of their alienation like a sullen confusion of the weather;

the town drunk appears looking haggard and the town mayor
out ward-heeling and smelling women's hands buys him a drink;
a woman gets married and another woman has a child;
the child is not old enough to plow a field and therefore
does not become a focus of interest except as another mouth;   20
they sit around with corn shucks in the head and wonder
who they should vote for, the question puzzles them,
vote for the one with the cracked shoes, he's a good boy,
or the one who jumped over six barrels at a local dance;   25
the fewer buildings they have, the more nationalistic they become
like a man who has stolen all his life accused of cheating;
above all, they dislike the east which at least gives them form
and allows their musings and discontents to flower into rancour;
musing and rancorous, I turn down the small side streets of Galt,   30
Ontario, afternoon light, aged twelve, past South Water Street,
not quite like Rimbaud leaving Charleville,
my hands in my windbreaker pockets like white stones,
and promise myself once again that when I get to the city
everything will happen, I will learn all of its history   35
and become the best writer they have ever dreamed of,
I'll make them laugh and I'll even make them cry,
I'll drink their whiskey and make love to all their wives,
the words tumbling out of my mouth as articulate as the young Hector,
the corn under my shirt awkward a little rough light brown dry   40
and making me itch at times

Connections to Other Selections

1. Compare in an essay Donnell's notions about being a writer with e. e. cummings's
   view in the Perspective "On the Artist's Responsibility" (p. 503).
2. How does this prescription for literature compare with that of Louis Simpson's in
   "American Poetry" (p. 38)?

CAROLYNN HOY (b. 1947)

A native of Kemptville, Ontario, Carolynn Hoy now lives on a farm on
the Bow River in Southern Alberta. She recently studied creative writing at
the University of Calgary. Her poetry has appeared in *Secrets from the Orange
Couch, Ariel,* and *SansCrit.*

In the Summer Kitchen   1993

We speared long wooden spoons
into steaming galvanized tubs

churning and scooping the checked cotton
to feed back and forth
through a wringer   5
from her hand to mine.

And there, on that Monday,
she mentioned Harry, her first born,
my uncle, who died at three months.
That was all,   10
a slip of the tongue
as she hastily turned away.

On the stoop by the clothesline
beyond the screen door,
she snapped our flattened   15
shirts to attention,
shoulders as straight and squared
as her chiselled headstone
I now visit.

That silence.   20

The dignity of it all.

Connections to Other Selections

1. Compare the tone in this poem with Emily Dickinson's "The Bustle in a House"
   (p. 275).
2. Write an essay describing the effects of the images in this poem and in Tess Gallagher's "Black Silk" (p. 128). What emotions does each poem produce for you?

SUSAN MUSGRAVE (b. 1951)

Born in California to Canadian parents, Susan Musgrave was raised on
Vancouver Island. Her poetry volumes include *Selected Strawberries and
Other Poems* (1974), *A Man to Marry, a Man to Bury* (1979), *Tarts and
Muggers: Poems New and Selected* (1982), *Cocktails at the Mausoleum*
(1985), *The Embalmer's Art* (1991), and *Forcing the Narcissus* (1944).

Right through the Heart   1982

and out the other side,
pumping like a bitch in heat,

beast with two backs, the
left and right ventricles.

It has to be love   5
when it goes straight through;
no bone can stop it,
no barb impede its journey.

When it happens you have to bleed,
you want to kiss and hold on   10

despite all the messy blood
you want to embrace it.

You want it to last forever,
you want to own it.
You want to take love's tiny life   15
in your hands

and crush it to death before it dies.

Connections to Other Selections

1. Consider the final lines of this poem and Margaret Atwood's "you fit into me"
   (p. 90). How does the final line of each affect your reading of the poem?
2. In an essay compare the tone of this poem to the tone of Andrew Marvell's "To
   His Coy Mistress" (p. 55), particularly Marvell's lines 33–46.

ALDEN NOWLAN (1933–1983)

Born in Stanley, Nova Scotia, Alden Nowlan served as writer-in-residence
at the University of New Brunswick in Fredericton from 1968 until 1983.
Awarded a Guggenheim fellowship and numerous writing prizes during the
course of his career, Nowlan is the author of *The Early Poems* (1983) and
An Exchange of Gifts: Poems New and Selected (1985).

The Bull Moose   1962

Down from the purple mist of trees on the mountain,
lurching through forests of white spruce and cedar,
stumbling through tamarack swamps,
came the bull moose
to be stopped at last by a pole-fenced pasture.   5

Too tired to turn or, perhaps, aware
there was no place left to go, he stood with the cattle.
They, scenting the musk of death, seeing his great head
like the ritual mask of a blood god, moved to the other end
of the field, and waited.   10

The neighbors heard of it, and by afternoon
cars lined the road. The children teased him
with alder switches and he gazed at them
like an old, tolerant collie. The women asked
if he could have escaped from a Fair.   15

The oldest man in the parish remembered seeing
a gelded moose yoked with an ox for plowing.
The young men snickered and tried to pour beer
down his throat, while their girl friends took their pictures.

And the bull moose let them stroke his tick-ravaged flanks,   20
let them pry open his jaws with bottles, let a giggling girl
plant a little purple cap
of thistles on his head.

When the wardens came, everyone agreed it was a shame
to shoot anything so shaggy and cuddlesome.   25
He looked like the kind of pet
women put to bed with their sons.

So they held their fire. But just as the sun dropped in the river
the bull moose gathered his strength
like a scaffolded king, straightened and lifted his horns   30
so that even the wardens backed away as they raised their rifles.
When he roared, people ran to their cars. All the young men
leaned on their automobile horns as he toppled.

Connections to Other Selections

1. Compare the speaker's attitude and tone in Nowlan's poem with that in Maxine Kumin's "Woodchucks" (p. 52).
2. In an essay discuss the themes in "The Bull Moose" and William Stafford's "Traveling through the Dark" (p. 118).

DAVID SOLWAY (b. 1941)

Montreal-born David Solway has written for the Canadian Broadcasting Corporation and taught at John Abbott College. His books include *Selected Poems* (1982), *The Mulberry Men* (1982), and *Stones and Water* (1983).

Windsurfing

It rides upon the wrinkled hide
of water, like the upturned hull
of a small canoe or kayak
waiting to be righted—yet its law
is opposite to that of boats,   5
it floats upon its breastbone and
brings whatever spine there is to light.
A thin shaft is slotted into place.
Then a puffed right-angle of wind
pushes it forward, out into the bay,   10
where suddenly it glitters into speed,
tilts, knifes up, and for the moment's
nothing but a slim projectile
of cambered fiberglass,
peeling the crests.   15

        The man's
clamped to the mast, taut as a guywire.
Part of the sleek apparatus
he controls, immaculate nerve
of balance, plunge and curvet,   20
he clinches all component movements
into single motion.
It bucks, stalls, shudders, yaws, and dips
its hissing sides beneath the surface
that sustains it, tensing   25
into muscle that nude ellipse
of lunging appetite and power.

And now the mechanism's wholly
dolphin, springing toward its prey
of spume and beaded sunlight,   30
tossing spray, and hits the vertex
of the wide, salt glare of distance,
and reverses.

        Back it comes through
a screen of particles,   35
scalloped out of water, shimmer
and reflection, the wind snapping
and lashing it homeward,
shearing the curve of the wave,
breaking the spell of the caught breath   40
and articulate play of sinew, to enter
the haven of the breakwater
and settle in a rush of silence.

Now the crossing drifts
in the husk of its wake
and nothing's the same again
as, gliding elegantly on a film of water,
the man guides
his brash, obedient legend
into shore.

45

50

Connections to Other Selections

1. Consider the effects of the images in "Windsurfing" and Li Ho's "A Beautiful Girl Combs Her Hair" (p. 39). In an essay explain how these images produce emotional responses in you.
2. Compare the descriptions in "Windsurfing" and Elizabeth Bishop's "The Fish" (p. 19). How does each poet appeal to your senses to describe windsurfing and fishing?

DALE ZIEROTH (b. 1946)

Born in Neepawa, Manitoba, Dale Zieroth has worked as a naturalist, freelance writer, and teacher. His books include *Clearing: Poems from a Journey* (1973) and *Mid-River* (1981).

Time over Earth

1993

Above bank after bank of cloud
and the sudden open hole for rock or snow,
his seat partner
wrestles newspaper into a fold,
and in the cockpit the first officer
fights ennui and gazes into the round faces
of his instruments as they cast upon him
their evening glow, their eagerness
to serve. The steward from first class
offers comments from the passengers
on the delicacy of the flight,
the sureness of the surge, the persuasiveness
of their arc in and out of heaven.

5

10

Meanwhile in seat 16A
the view slips
into darkness once more,
forcing the eyes back from the vista.
His worries resurface

15

in this airy world
of alloy and wine, foam seats and hard-eyed   20
understanding focused in the one-brain
of the crew. A beam, he thinks, will soon
pick them up and lead them down,
and they will stay fastened
to this hope.   25

They rush to smell the new city—or the same one
returned to, which he re-enters
unchanged by time over earth; he knew
the thin light reaching into black
had not touched him   30
when he swept through revolving doors
in no less hurry
than other earthling friends.
Now asleep in his bed
his body still floats   35
across space, trying to arrive
on time, not caught
by the trees reaching up
to tear and throw him open.
Motionless under quilt, on pillow,   40
his eyes repeat all he has seen
and feared to see, each breath
hanging out of his body
in the worst kind of silent air.

Connections to Other Selections

1. Compare the views of the world offered by the speaker in "Time over Earth" and in "Nothing Stays Put" by Amy Clampitt (p. 477).
2. Write an essay comparing the tone in "Time over Earth" and Robert Frost's "Acquainted with the Night" (p. 109).

AN ALBUM OF CONTEMPORARY POEMS

AMY CLAMPITT (b. 1920)

Born in New Providence, Iowa, Amy Clampitt graduated from Grinnell College and now is based primarily in New York City. Her collections of poems include *The Kingfisher* (1983), *What the Light Was Like* (1985), *Archaic Figure* (1987), and *Westward* (1990). She has been writer-in-residence at the College of William and Mary, Amherst College, and Washington University as well as a Phi Beta Kappa Poet at the Harvard Literary Exercises. Among her awards are fellowships from the Guggenheim Foundation and the American Academy of Poets.

Nothing Stays Put   1989

The strange and wonderful are too much with us.
The protea of the antipodes — a great,
globed, blazing honeybee of a bloom —
for sale in the supermarket! We are in
our decadence, we are not entitled.   5
What have we done to deserve
all the produce of the tropics —
this fiery trove, the largesse of it
heaped up like cannonballs, these pineapples, bossed
and crested, standing like troops at attention,   10
these tiers, these balconies of green, festoons
grown sumptuous with stoop labor?

The exotic is everywhere, it comes to us
before there is a yen or a need for it. The green-
grocers, uptown and down, are from South Korea.   15
Orchids, opulence by the pailful, just slightly
fatigued by the plane trip from Hawaii, are
disposed on the sidewalks; alstroemerias, freesias
flattened a bit in translation from overseas; gladioli
likewise estranged from their piercing ancestral crimson;   20
as well as, less altered from the original blue cornflower
of the roadsides and railway embankments of Europe, these
bachelor's buttons. But it isn't the railway embankments
their featherweight wheels of cobalt remind me of — it's
a row of them among prim colonnades of cosmos,   25
snapdragon, nasturtium, bloodsilk red poppies
in my grandmother's garden; a prairie childhood,
the grassland shorn, overlaid with a grid,
unsealed, furrowed, harrowed, and sown with immigrant grasses,
their massive corduroy, their wavering feltings embroidered   30
here and there by the scarlet shoulder patch of cannas
on a courthouse lawn, by a love knot, a cross-stitch
of living matter, sown and tended by women,
nurturers everywhere of the strange and wonderful,
beneath whose hands what had been alien begins,   35
as it alters, to grow as though it were indigenous.

But at this remove what I think of as
strange and wonderful — strolling the side streets of Manhattan
on an April afternoon, seeing hybrid pear trees in blossom,
a tossing, vertiginous colonnade of foam up above —   40

is the white petalfall, the warm snowdrift
of the indigenous wild plum of my childhood.
Nothing stays put. The world is a wheel.
All that we know, that we're
made of, is motion.   45

Connections to Other Selections

1. Clampitt's opening line echoes William Wordsworth's "The World Is Too Much
   with Us" (p. 180) and therefore invites comparison. How does Clampitt's theme
   relate to Wordsworth's? Are their complaints similar or different?
2. Write an essay comparing the speakers' tones in this poem and in Allen Ginsberg's
   "A Supermarket in California" (p. 203). Explain whether Ginsberg's poem might
   also be aptly titled "Nothing Stays Put."

ROBERT CREELEY (b. 1926)

Born in Arlington, Massachusetts, Robert Creely attended Harvard University, which he left in 1944 to serve as an ambulance driver in India and
Burma during World War II. After living in France and Spain in the early
1950s, he returned to the United States and taught at Black Mountain College
in North Carolina (where he founded the *Black Mountain Review*) and at
various colleges and universities throughout the United States and Canada.
His recent publications include *The Collected Poems of Robert Creeley, 1945–
1975* (1983), *Collected Essays* (1989), and his edition of *The Essential Burns*
(1989).

Fathers   1986

Scattered, aslant
faded faces a column
a rise of the packed
peculiar place to a
modest height makes   5
a view of common lots
in winter then, a ground
of battered snow crusted
at the edges under
it all, there under   10
my fathers their
faded women, friends,
the family all echoed,
names trees more tangible

physical place more tangible   15
the air of this place the road
going past to Watertown
or down to my mother's
grave, my father's grave, not
now this resonance of   20
each other one was his, his
survival only, his curious
reticence, his dead state,
his emptiness, his acerbic
edge cuts the hands to   25
hold him, hold on, wants
the ground, *wants* this frozen ground.

Connections to Other Selections

1. Compare the speaker's tone in this poem with that in Donald Hall's "My Son, My Executioner" (p. 379).
2. Write an essay comparing the structures of this poem and Dylan Thomas's "Do not go gentle into that good night" (p. 184). How does the form of each poem contribute to its effects?

LORNA DEE CERVANTES (b. 1954)

Born in San Francisco, California, Lorna Dee Cervantes founded Mango Publications, which publishes mostly Chicano literature and *Mango,* a poetry magazine. In 1978 she received a National Endowment for the Arts fellowship. Her work has appeared in many journals and anthologies and in two volumes of poetry: *Emplumada* (1981) and *From the Cables of Genocide: Poems of Love and Hunger* (1991). She currently teaches creative writing at the University of Colorado, Boulder, where she founded *Red Dirt,* a new poetry magazine.

Poem for the Young White Man Who Asked Me How I, An Intelligent, Well-Read Person Could Believe in the War Between Races   1981

In my land there are no distinctions.
The barbed wire politics of oppression
have been torn down long ago. The only reminder
of past battles, lost or won, is a slight
rutting in the fertile fields.   5

In my land
people write poems about love,
full of nothing but contented childlike syllables.
Everyone reads Russian short stories and weeps.
There are no boundaries.   10
There is no hunger, no
complicated famine or greed.

I am not a revolutionary.
I don't even like political poems.
Do you think I can believe in a war between races?   15

I can deny it. I can forget about it
when I'm safe,
living on my own continent of harmony
and home, but I am not
there.   20

I believe in revolution
because everywhere the crosses are burning,
sharp-shooting goose-steppers round every corner,
there are snipers in the schools . . .
(I know you don't believe this.   25
You think this is nothing
but faddish exaggeration. But they
are not shooting at you.)

I'm marked by the color of my skin.
The bullets are discrete and designed to kill slowly.   30
They are aiming at my children.
These are facts.
Let me show you my wounds: my stumbling mind, my
"excuse me" tongue, and this
nagging preoccupation   35
with the feeling of not being good enough.

These bullets bury deeper than logic.
Racism is not intellectual.
I can not reason these scars away.

Outside my door   40
there is a real enemy
who hates me.

I am a poet
who yearns to dance on rooftops,
to whisper delicate lines about joy   45
and the blessings of human understanding.
I try. I go to my land, my tower of words and
bolt the door, but the typewriter doesn't fade out
the sounds of blasting and muffled outrage.
My own days bring me slaps on the face.   50
Every day I am deluged with reminders

that this is not
my land

and this is my land.

I do not believe in the war between races   55
but in this country
there is war.

Connections to Other Selections

1. Read the Perspective "On 'Hard' Poetry" by Robert Francis (p. 33), and discuss
   whether or not you think Cervantes's poem can be categorized as "hard" or "soft"
   poetry, as defined by Francis.
2. Write an essay on the treatment of life in the United States in Cervantes's poem
   and in Tato Laviera's "AmeRícan" (p. 209). How do you account for the difference
   in tone?

LOUISE ERDRICH (b. 1954)

Born in 1954 in Little Falls, Minnesota, Louise Erdrich grew up as a
member of the Turtle Mountain Band of Chippewa in Wahepton, North
Dakota. After earning degrees at Dartmouth College and Johns Hopkins
University she began her career as a writer. Her first novel *Love Medicine,*
winner of the 1984 National Book Critics Circle Award, is one of an interlocking series concerning Native American life in North Dakota that includes
The Beet Queen (1986), *Tracks* (1988), and *The Bingo Palace* (1994). The
following poem is from her collection of poems, *Jacklight* (1984).

Captivity   1984

*He (my captor) gave me a bisquit, which I put in my pocket, and not daring to eat it,
buried it under a log, fearing he had put something in it to make me love him.*
                     –from the narrative of the captivity of Mrs. Mary Rowlandson,°
                        who was taken prisoner by the Wampanoag when Lancaster,
                                  Massachusetts, was destroyed, in the year 1676.

The stream was swift, and so cold
I thought I would be sliced in two.
But he dragged me from the flood

Mrs. Mary Rowlandson (1637?–1711?): Held captive for three months by a Native-American tribe
during the King Philip's War, Rowlandson recounted her experiences in her *Narrative* (1682).

by the ends of my hair.
I had grown to recognize his face.   5
I could distinguish it from the others.
There were times I feared I understood
his language, which was not human,
and I knelt to pray for strength.

We were pursued! By God's agents   10
or pitch devils I did not know.
Only that we must march.
Their guns were loaded with swan shot.
I could not suckle and my child's wail
put them in danger.   15
He had a woman
with teeth black and glittering.
She fed the child milk of acorns.
The forest closed, the light deepened.

I told myself that I would starve   20
before I took food from his hands
but I did not starve.
One night
he killed a deer with a young one in her
and gave me to eat of the fawn.   25
It was so tender,
the bones like the stems of flowers,
that I followed where he took me.
The night was thick. He cut the cord
that bound me to the tree.   30

After that the birds mocked.
Shadows gaped and roared
and the trees flung down
their sharpened lashes.
He did not notice God's wrath.   35
God blasted fire from half-buried stumps.
I hid my face in my dress, fearing He would burn us all
but this, too, passed.

Rescued, I see no truth in things.
My husband drives a thick wedge   40
through the earth, still it shuts
to him year after year.
My child is fed of the first wheat.
I lay myself to sleep
on a Holland-laced pillowbeer.°   *pillowcase*   45
I lay to sleep.
And in the dark I see myself
as I was outside their circle.

They knelt on deerskins, some with sticks,
and he led his company in the noise   50

until I could no longer bear
the thought of how I was.
I stripped a branch
and struck the earth,
in time, begging it to open   55
to admit me
as he was
and feed me honey from the rock.

Connections to Other Selections

1. Discuss the themes of Erdrich's poem and Paula Gunn Allen's "Pocahontas to Her English Husband, John Rolfe" (p. 344).
2. Write an essay comparing the narrative voice in "Captivity" with that in "Ruby Tells All" (p. 173) by Miller Williams.

DEBORAH GARRISON (b. 1965)

Raised in Ann Arbor, Michigan, Deborah Garrison graduated from Brown University and currently lives in New York City, where she works on the editorial staff of *The New Yorker*. She has not published a collection of poems to date, but her poetry appears regularly in *The New Yorker*.

She Was Waiting to Be Told   1990

For you she learned to wear a short black slip
and red lipstick,
how to order a glass of red wine
and finish it. She learned to reach out
as if to touch your arm and then not   5
touch it, changing the subject.
Didn't you think, she'd begin, or
Weren't you sorry. . . .

To call your best friends
by their schoolboy names   10
and give them kisses good-bye,
to turn her head away when they say
Your wife! So your confidence grows.
She doesn't ask what you want
because she knows.   15

Isn't that what you think?

When actually she was only waiting
to be told *Take off your dress* —
to be stunned, and then do this,
never rehearsed, but perfectly obvious: 20
in one motion up, over, and gone,
the X of her arms crossing and uncrossing,
her face flashing away from you in the fabric
so that you couldn't say if she was
appearing or disappearing.   25

Connections to Other Selections

1. Write an essay comparing the women in "She Was Waiting to Be Told" and John
   Keats's "La Belle Dame sans Merci" (p. 231).
2. Discuss the relationship between the man and woman in Garrison's poem and in
   Richard Wilbur's "A Late Aubade" (p. 58).

MARK HALLIDAY (b. 1949)

Born in Ann Arbor, Michigan, Mark Halliday, who earned a B.A. and an
M.A. from Brown University and a Ph.D. from Brandeis University, is a teacher
at the University of Pennsylvania. His poems have appeared in a variety of
periodicals, including *The Massachusetts Review*, *Michigan Quarterly Review*,
and *The New Republic*. His collection of poems *Little Star* was selected by
The National Poetry Series for publication in 1987. He has also written a
critical study on poet Wallace Stevens titled *Stevens and the Interpersonal*
(1991).

Graded Paper   1991

On the whole this is quite successful work:
your main argument about the poet's ambivalence —
how he loves the very things he attacks —
is mostly persuasive and always engaging.
At the same time,   5

there are spots
where your thinking becomes, for me,
alarmingly opaque, and your syntax seems to jump
backwards through unnecessary hoops,
as on p. 2 where you speak of "precognitive awareness   10
not yet disestablished by the shell that encrusts
each thing that a person actually says"

or at the top of p. 5 where your discussion of
"subverbal undertow miming the subversion of self-belief
woven counter to desire's outreach"   15
leaves me groping for firmer footholds.
(I'd have said it differently,
or rather, said something else.)
And when you say that women "could not fulfill themselves" (p. 6)
"in that era" (only forty years ago, after all!)   20
are you so sure that the situation is so different today?
Also, how does Whitman bluff his way into
your penultimate paragraph? He is the *last* poet
I would have quoted in this context!
What plausible way of behaving   25
does the passage you quote represent? Don't you think
literature should ultimately reveal possibilities for *action*?

Please notice how I've repaired your use of semicolons.

And yet, despite what may seem my cranky response,
I do admire the freshness of
your thinking and your style; there is
a vitality here; your sentences thrust themselves forward
with a confidence as impressive as it is cheeky. . . .
You are not
        me, finally,
and though this is an awkward problem, involving
the inescapable fact that you are so young, so young
it is also a delightful provocation.

Connections to Other Selections

1. Compare the ways in which Halliday reveals the speaker's character in this poem
   with the strategies used by Robert Browning in "My Last Duchess" (p. 126).
2. Write an essay on the professor in this poem and the speaker in Ted Kooser's
   "Selecting a Reader" (p. 35). What are the significant similarities and differences
   between them?

JUDY PAGE HEITZMAN (b. 1952)

    Judy Page Heitzman lives in Marshfield, Massachusetts, and teaches En-
glish at Duxbury High School. She has not published a collection of poems
to date, but her poetry has appeared in *The New Yorker*, *Yankee Magazine*,
Wind, *Yarro*, and *Three Rivers Poetry Journal*.

The Schoolroom on the Second Floor
of the Knitting Mill 1991

While most of us copied letters out of books,
Mrs. Lawrence carved and cleaned her nails.
Now the red and buff cardinals at my back-room window
make me miss her, her room, her hallway,
even the chimney outside   5
that broke up the sky.

In my memory it is afternoon.
Sun streams in through the door
next to the fire escape where we are lined up
getting our coats on to go out to the playground,   10
the tether ball, its towering height, the swings.
She tells me to make sure the line
does not move up over the threshold.
That would be dangerous.
So I stand guard at the door.   15
Somehow it happens
the way things seem to happen when we're not really looking,
or we are looking, just not the right way.
Kids crush up like cattle, pushing me over the line.

Judy is not a good leader is all Mrs. Lawrence says.   20
She says it quietly. Still, everybody hears.
Her arms hang down like sausages.
I hear her every time I fail.

Connections to Other Selections

1. Compare the representations and meanings of being a schoolchild in this poem
   and Emily Dickinson's "From all the Jails the Boys and Girls" (p. 276).
2. Discuss the speaker's tone in Heitzman's poem and in Linda Pastan's "Marks"
   (p. 105).

GALWAY KINNELL (b. 1927)

Born in Providence, Rhode Island, Galway Kinnell earned degrees from
Princeton University and the University of Rochester. He has taught at a
number of universities in the United States and abroad and currently teaches
in the creative writing program at New York University. He has been awarded
fellowships from the Guggenheim, MacArthur, and Rockefeller foundations
as well as a Pulitzer Prize and a National Institute of Arts and Letters award.
His volumes of poetry include *The Avenue Bearing the Initial of Christ into
the New World: Poems 1946–64* (1974); *Mortal Acts, Mortal Words* (1980);

Selected Poems (1982); *The Past* (1985); and *When One Has Lived a Long Time Alone* (1990).

After Making Love We Hear Footsteps 1980

For I can snore like a bullhorn
or play loud music
or sit up talking with any reasonably sober Irishman
and Fergus will only sink deeper
into his dreamless sleep, which goes by all in one flash,   5
but let there be that heavy breathing
or a stifled come-cry anywhere in the house
and he will wrench himself awake
and make for it on the run — as now, we lie together,
after making love, quiet, touching along the length of our bodies,   10
familiar touch of the long-married,
and he appears — in his baseball pajamas, it happens,
the neck opening so small
he has to screw them on, which one day may make him wonder
about the mental capacity of baseball players —   15
and says, "Are you loving and snuggling? May I join?"
He flops down between us and hugs us and snuggles himself to sleep,
his face gleaming with satisfaction at being this very child.

In the half darkness we look at each other
and smile   20
and touch arms across his little, startlingly muscled body —
this one whom habit of memory propels to the ground of his making,
sleeper only the mortal sounds can sing awake,
this blessing love gives again into our arms.

Connections to Other Selections

1. Discuss how this poem helps to bring into focus the sense of loss Robert Frost evokes in "Home Burial" (p. 300).
2. Write an essay comparing the tone and theme of this poem and those of Donald Hall's "My Son, My Executioner" (p. 379), making note of the treatment of the child in each poem.

YUSEF KOMUNYAKAA (b. 1947)

Yusef Komunyakaa, born in Bogalusa, Louisiana, a Vietnam veteran, earned an M.F.A. from the University of California and now teaches creative writing and African-American studies at Indiana University. Among his awards are a National Endowment for the Arts fellowship and a Pulitzer Prize. His volumes of poetry include *Copacetic* (1984), *I Apologize for the Eyes in My Head* (1986), and *Dien Cai Dau* (1989).

Facing It   1988

My black face fades,
hiding inside the black granite.
I said I wouldn't,
dammit: No tears.
I'm stone. I'm flesh.   5
My clouded reflection eyes me
like a bird of prey, the profile of night
slanted against morning. I turn
this way — the stone lets me go.
I turn that way — I'm inside   10
the Vietnam Veterans Memorial
again, depending on the light
to make a difference.
I go down the 58,022 names,
half-expecting to find   15
my own in letters like smoke.
I touch the name Andrew Johnson;
I see the booby trap's white flash.
Names shimmer on a woman's blouse
but when she walks away   20
the names stay on the wall.
Brushstrokes flash, a red bird's
wings cutting across my stare.
The sky. A plane in the sky.
A white vet's image floats   25
closer to me, then his pale eyes
look through mine. I'm a window.
He's lost his right arm
inside the stone. In the black mirror
a woman's trying to erase names: 30
No, she's brushing a boy's hair.

Connections to Other Selections

1. Discuss the speakers' attitudes toward war in "Facing It" and e. e. cummings's "next to of course god america i" (p. 115).
2. In an essay compare the treatment of memory and sorrow in "Facing It" and Wilfred Owen's "Dulce et Decorum Est" (p. 76).

DENISE LEVERTOV (b. 1923)

Born in Essex, England, Denise Levertov was educated at home, served as a nurse during World War II, and in 1948 emigrated to the United States. Levertov has taught at Vassar, Drew, City College of New York, MIT, Tufts, Stanford, and Brandeis and has received awards from the Guggenheim Foundation, the National Institute of Arts and Letters, and the National Endowment for the Arts. Much of her poetry reflects her continuing political activism, which began in the 1960s. Her collections of poems include *Collected Earlier Poems 1940–1960* (1979), *Denise Levertov: Poems 1960–1967* (1983), *Denise Levertov: Poems 1968–1972* (1987), and *A Door in the Hive* (1989).

Gathered at the River   1983

For Beatrice Hawley and John Jagel

As if the trees were not indifferent . . .

A breeze flutters the candles but the trees give off
a sense of listening, of hush.

The dust of August on their leaves.
But it grows dark. Their dark green   5
is something known about, not seen.

But summer twilight takes away
only color, not form. The tree-forms,
massive trunks and the great domed heads,
leaning in towards us, are visible,   10

a half-circle of attention.

They listen because the war
we speak of, the human war with ourselves,

the war against earth,
against nature,   15
is a war against them.

The words are spoken
of those who survived a while,
living shadowgraphs, eyes fixed forever
on witnessed horror,   20
who survived to give
testimony, that no-one
may plead ignorance.
Contra naturam.° The trees,   Against nature (Latin)
the trees are not indifferent.   25

We intone together, *Never again,*

we stand in a circle,
singing, speaking, making vows,

remembering the dead
of Hiroshima,   30
of Nagasaki.

We are holding candles: we kneel to set them
afloat on the dark river
as they do
there in Hiroshima. We are invoking   35

saints and prophets,
heroes and heroines of justice and peace,
to be with us, to help us
stop the torment of our evil dreams . . .

Windthreatened flames bob on the current . . .   40

They don't get far from shore. But none capsizes
even in the swell of a boat's wake.

The waxy paper cups sheltering them
catch fire. But still the candles
sail their gold downstream.   45

And still the trees ponder our strange doings, as if
well aware that if we fail,
we fail for them:
if our resolves and prayers are weak and fail

there will be nothing left of their slow and innocent wisdom,   50

no roots,
no bole nor branch,

no memory
of shade,
of leaf,   55

no pollen.

Connections to Other Selections

1. In her comments on "Gathered at the River" (p. 509), Levertov affirms her "underlying belief in a great design, a potential harmony which can be violated or
   be sustained." How does Robert Frost's "Design" (p. 311) comment on Levertov's
   beliefs? Explain whether you agree with Levertov or not.
2. Levertov also expresses a concern in her essay for the necessity of having "a sense
   of the sacredness of the earthly creation" and mentions that Gerard Manley
   Hopkins has always been one of her favorite poets. Write an essay comparing
   "Gathered at the River" and Hopkins's "God's Grandeur" (p. 144) or "Pied Beauty"
   (p. 386). What significant similarities do you find?

PETER MEINKE (b. 1932)

Peter Meinke, born in Brooklyn, New York, earned a B.A. at Hamilton College, an M.A. at the University of Michigan, and a Ph.D. at the University of Minnesota. In addition to teaching at Eckerd College, he has served as a visiting professor at many colleges and universities and received a number of grants, including National Endowment for the Arts fellowships in 1974 and 1989. Among his poetry collections are *The Rat Poems* (1978), *Trying to Surprise God* (1981), *Night Watch on the Chesapeake* (1986), and *Far from Home* (1988).

The ABC of Aerobics 1983

Air seeps through alleys and our diaphragms
balloon blackly with this mix of
carbon monoxide and the thousand corrosives a city
doles out free to its constituents;
everyone's jogging through Edgemont Park, 5
frightened by death and fatty tissue,
gasping at the maximal heart rate,
hoping to outlive all the others streaming
in the lanes like lemmings lurching toward their last
jump. I join in despair 10
knowing my arteries jammed with
lint and tobacco, lard and bourbon — my
medical history a noxious marsh:
newts and moles slink through the sodden veins,
owls hoot in the lungs' dark branches; 15
probably I shall keel off the john like
queer Uncle George and lie on the bathroom floor
raging about Shirley Clark, my true love in
seventh grade, God bless her wherever she lives
tied to that turkey who hugely 20
undervalues the beauty of her tiny earlobes, one
view of which (either one: they are both perfect)
would add years to my life and I could skip these
x-rays, turn in my insurance card, and trade
yoga and treadmills and jogging and zen and 25
zucchini for drinking and dreaming of her, breathing hard.

Connections to Other Selections

1. Write an essay comparing the way Sharon Olds connects sex and exercise in the next poem, "Sex without Love," with Meinke's treatment here.
2. Compare the voices in this poem and in Galway Kinnell's "After Making Love We Hear Footsteps" (p. 487). Which do you find more appealing? Why?

SHARON OLDS (b. 1942)

Born in San Francisco and educated at Stanford and Columbia, Sharon Olds has received the Lamont award from the Academy of American Poets as well as fellowships from the National Endowment for the Arts and the Guggenheim Foundation. She has taught creative writing at New York University and at Goldwater Hospital for the physically disabled on Roosevelt Island, New York. Her volumes of poems include *Satan Says* (1980), *The Dead and the Living* (1984), and *The Gold Cell* (1987).

Sex without Love   1984

How do they do it, the ones who make love
without love? Beautiful as dancers,
gliding over each other like ice skaters
over the ice, fingers hooked
inside each other's bodies, faces   5
red as steak, wine, wet as the
children at birth whose mothers are going to
give them away. How do they come to the
come to the   come to the   God   come to the
still waters, and not love   10
the one who came there with them, light
rising slowly as steam off their joined
skin? These are the true religious,
the purists, the pros, the ones who will not
accept a false Messiah, love the   15
priest instead of the God. They do not
mistake the lover for their own pleasure,
they are like great runners: they know they are alone
with the road surface, the cold, the wind,
the fit of their shoes, their over-all cardio-   20
vascular health — just factors, like the partner
in the bed, and not the truth, which is the
single body alone in the universe
against its own best time.

Connections to Other Selections

1. How does the treatment of sex and love in Olds's poem compare with that in e. e. cummings's "she being Brand" (p. 47)?
2. Just as Olds describes sex without love, she implies a definition of love in this poem. Consider whether the lovers in Richard Wilbur's "A Late Aubade" (p. 58) fall within Olds's definition.

CATHY SONG (b. 1955)

Born in Hawaii and educated at Wellesley College and Boston University, Cathy Song teaches at the University of Hawaii at Manōa. Her collections of poems include *Picture Bride* (1983), winner of the Yale Series of Younger Poets Award and nominated for a National Book Critics Circle Award, and *Frameless Windows, Squares of Light* (1988).

The White Porch   1983

I wrap the blue towel
after washing,
around the damp
weight of hair, bulky
as a sleeping cat,   5
and sit out on the porch.
Still dripping water,
it'll be dry by supper,
by the time the dust
settles off your shoes,   10
though it's only five
past noon. Think
of the luxury: how to use
the afternoon like the stretch
of lawn spread before me.   15
There's the laundry,
sun-warm clothes at twilight,
and the mountain of beans
in my lap. Each one,
I'll break and snap   20
thoughtfully in half.

But there is this slow arousal.
The small buttons
of my cotton blouse
are pulling away from my body.   25
I feel the strain of threads,
the swollen magnolias
heavy as a flock of birds
in the tree. Already,
the orange sponge cake   30
is rising in the oven.
I know you'll say it makes
your mouth dry
and I'll watch you

drench your slice of it   35
in canned peaches
and lick the plate clean.

So much hair, my mother
used to say, grabbing
the thick braided rope   40
in her hands while we washed
the breakfast dishes, discussing
dresses and pastries.
My mind often elsewhere
as we did the morning chores together.   45
Sometimes, a few strands
would catch in her gold ring.
I worked hard then,
anticipating the hour
when I would let the rope down   50
at night, strips of sheets,
knotted and tied,
while she slept in tight blankets.
My hair, freshly washed
like a measure of wealth,   55
like a bridal veil.
Crouching in the grass,
you would wait for the signal,
for the movement of curtains
before releasing yourself   60
from the shadow of moths.
Cloth, hair and hands,
smuggling you in.

Connections to Other Selections

1. Compare the images used to describe the speaker's "slow arousal" in this poem
   with Sally Croft's images in "Home-Baked Bread" (p. 83). What similarities do you
   see? What makes each description so effective?
2. Write an essay comparing images of sensuality in this poem and Li Ho's "A Beautiful
   Girl Combs Her Hair" (p. 39). Which poem seems more erotic to you? Why?

STEPHEN STEPANCHEV (b. 1915)

Born in New York, Stephen Stepanchev was a professor of English at
Queens College, City University of New York, from 1949 to 1985. His works
include literary criticism and history as well as poetry: *American Poetry Since
1945: A Critical Survey* (1965); *A Man Running in the Rain* (1969); *The Mad
Bomber* (1972); *Mining the Darkness* (1975); *Medusa and Others* (1975); and
Descent (1988).

An oil rose: gold and pink petals flare on the asphalt.
Oil spurts from a sizzling wok. A hot light spits
On the sidewalk. A pigeon struts out of the way
Of a starling. It pecks at a shining black bag.

A blond woman in green jeans, swinging   5
A green purse, cruises past the gang on the corner.
They are watching the girls and the days go by. "Fresh meat,"
Bud says, spitting at the front page of the *News*.

Charley whittles a stick with a machete and grunts,
"Jailbait." Raymond combs his flattop and laughs   10
At his cool image in a plate-glass window.
Sal puts out his hand for an imaginary feel of butt.

A *Watchtower* lady hands out prophetic books.
"The end is near," she says, but the boys can't read.

The sun has dried the oil rose in the street.   15
A Cadillac whistles as its master nears.

Connections to Other Selections

1. Discuss the use of imagery in Stepanchev's poem and Alberto Ríos's "Seniors"
   (p. 34). How do the images contribute to the themes of these poems?
2. Write an essay on the treatment of masculinity in "Cornered on the Corner" and
   Sharon Olds's "Rite of Passage" (p. 207).

C. K. WILLIAMS (b. 1936)

Born in Newark, New Jersey, and educated at Bucknell University and
the University of Pennsylvania, C. K. Williams has worked as a therapist,
editor, and writer and has taught creative writing at a number of schools,
including Boston, Columbia, Drexel, and George Mason universities. He has
received a Guggenheim Fellowship, the National Book Critics Circle Award,
and *The Paris Review*'s Connor Prize. His collections of poetry include *Poems
1963–1988*, and *Flesh and Blood* (1988).

The way these days she dresses with more attention to go out to pass the
    afternoon alone,
shopping or just taking walks, she says, than when they go together to a restau-
    rant or party:
it's such a subtle thing, how even speak of it, how imagine he'd be able to
    explain it to her?
The way she looks for such long moments in the mirror as she gets ready,
    putting on her makeup;
the way she looks so deeply at herself, gazes at her eyes, her mouth, down
    along her breasts: 5
what is he to say, that she's looking at herself in ways he's never seen before,
    more *carnally*?
She would tell him he was mad, or say something else he doesn't want no
    matter what to hear.
The way she puts her jacket on with a flourish, the way she gaily smiles going
    out the door,
the door, the way the door clicks shut, the way its latch clicks shut behind her
    so emphatically.
What is he to think? What is he to say, to whom? The mirror, jacket, latch, the
    awful door?   10
He can't touch the door, he's afraid he'll break the frightening covenant he's
    made with it.
He can't look into the mirror, either, the dark, malicious void: who knows
    what he might see?

Connections to Other Selections

1. Discuss how mirrors reflect more than mere images in this poem and in Sylvia
   Plath's "Mirror" (p. 98).
2. When this poem was originally published in *The New Yorker,* the wider format of
   the magazine page allowed the lines of the poem to be printed without turns
   (that is, the words "afternoon alone" were printed as part of line 1, and so forth).
   This format gave the poem the look of a block of prose. Consider Williams's poem
   as it was originally printed and compare it with George Starbuck's "Japanese Fish"
   (p. 202). What makes these works poetry rather than prose?

13. Perspectives on Poetry

A variety of observations about poetry is presented in this chapter. The pieces offer a wide range of topics related to reading and writing poetry. The perspectives include William Wordsworth on the nature of poetry, Matthew Arnold on classic and popular literature, Ezra Pound on free verse, Dylan Thomas on the words used in poetry, and Denise Levertov on the background and form of one of her poems. In addition, there are poems about poetry by Walt Whitman, Archibald MacLeish, and Robert Francis. These relatively short pieces provide materials to explore some of the topics and issues that readers and writers of poetry have found perennially interesting and challenging.

WILLIAM WORDSWORTH (1770–1850)
On the Nature of Poets and Poetry   1802

Taking up the subject, then, upon general grounds, I ask what is meant by the word "poet"? What is a poet? To whom does he address himself? And what language is to be expected from him? He is a man speaking to men: a man, it is true, endued with more lively sensibility, more enthusiasm and tenderness, who has a greater knowledge of human nature, and a more comprehensive soul, than are supposed to be common among mankind; a man pleased with his own passions and volitions, and who rejoices more than other men in the spirit of life that is in him; delighting to contemplate similar volitions and passions as manifested in the goings-on of the universe, and habitually impelled to create them where he does not find them. To these qualities he has added a disposition to be affected more than other men by absent things as if they were present; an ability of conjuring up in himself passions, which are indeed far from being the same as those produced by real events, yet (especially in those parts of the general sympathy which are pleasing and delightful) do more nearly resemble the passions produced by real events, than anything which, from the motions of their own minds merely, other men are accustomed to feel in themselves; whence, and from practice, he has acquired a greater readiness and power in expressing what he thinks and feels, and especially those thoughts and feelings which, by his own choice, or from the structure of his own mind, arise in him without immediate external excitement. . . .

I have said that poetry is the spontaneous overflow of powerful feelings: it takes its origin from emotion recollected in tranquility: the emotion is contemplated till by a species of reaction the tranquility gradually disappears, and an emotion, kindred to that which was before the subject of contemplation, is gradually produced, and does itself actually exist in the mind. In this mood successful composition generally begins, and in a mood similar to this it is carried on; but the emotion, of whatever kind and in whatever degree, from various causes is qualified by various pleasures, so that in describing any passions whatsoever, which are voluntarily described, the mind will upon the whole be in a state of enjoyment. Now, if nature be thus cautious in preserving in a state of enjoyment a being thus employed, the poet ought to profit by the lesson thus held forth to him, and ought especially to take care, that whatever passions he communicates to his reader, those passions, if his reader's mind be sound and vigorous, should always be accompanied with an overbalance of pleasure. Now the music of harmonious metrical language, the sense of difficulty overcome, and the blind association of pleasure which has been previously received from works of rhyme or meter of the same or similar construction, an indistinct perception perpetually renewed of language closely resembling that of real life, and yet, in the circumstance of meter, differing from it so widely, all these imperceptibly make up a complex feeling of delight, which is of the most important use in tempering the painful feeling which will always be found intermingled with powerful descriptions of the deeper passions. This effect is always produced in pathetic and impassioned poetry; while, in lighter compositions, the ease and gracefulness with which the poet manages his numbers are themselves confessedly a principal source of the gratification of the reader. I might perhaps include all which it is *necessary* to say upon this subject by affirming, what few persons will deny, that, of two descriptions, either of passions, manners, or characters, each of them equally well executed, the one in prose and the other in verse, the verse will be read a hundred times where the prose is read once.

From *Preface to Lyrical Ballads, with Pastoral and Other Poems*

Considerations for Critical Thinking and Writing

1. Discuss Wordsworth's description of a poet's sensibility and "ability of conjuring up in himself passions." What characteristics do you associate with a poetic temperament?

2. Explain why a writer's emotions are (or are not) so much more important in poetry than in prose.

3. Given that Wordsworth describes poetry as "the spontaneous overflow of powerful feelings," why can't his poems be characterized as formless bursts of raw emotion? Consider, for example, "London, 1802" (p. 99), "My Heart Leaps Up" (p. 162), or "The World Is Too Much with Us" (p. 180) to illustrate your response.

PERCY BYSSHE SHELLEY (1792–1822)
On Poets as "Unacknowledged Legislators"

1821

The most unfailing herald, companion, and follower of the awakening of a great people to work a beneficial change in opinion or institution, is poetry. At such periods there is an accumulation of the power of communicating and receiving intense and impassioned conceptions respecting man and nature. The persons in whom this power resides, may often, as far as regards many portions of their nature, have little apparent correspondence with that spirit of good of which they are the ministers. But even whilst they deny and abjure, they are yet compelled to serve, the power which is seated upon the throne of their own soul. It is impossible to read the compositions of the most celebrated writers of the present day without being startled with the electric life which burns within their words. They measure the circumference and sound the depths of human nature with a comprehensive and all-penetrating spirit, and they are themselves perhaps the most sincerely astonished at its manifestations, for it is less their spirit than the spirit of the age. Poets are the hierophants° of an unapprehended inspiration, the mirrors of the gigantic shadows which futurity casts upon the present, the words which express what they understand not; the trumpets which sing to battle, and feel not what they inspire: the influence which is moved not, but moves. Poets are the unacknowledged legislators of the world.

From A Defense of Poetry

hierophants: Interpreters of sacred mysteries.

Considerations for Critical Thinking and Writing

1. What kinds of powers does Shelley attribute to poets?
2. Compare Shelley's view of the poet with Karl Shapiro's (p. 503).

WALT WHITMAN (1819–1892)
When I Heard the Learn'd Astronomer

1865

When I heard the learn'd astronomer,
When the proofs, the figures, were ranged in columns before me,
When I was shown the charts and diagrams, to add, divide, and measure them,
When I sitting heard the astronomer where he lectured with much applause in the lecture-room,
How soon unaccountable I became tired and sick,

Whitman / When I Heard the Learn'd Astronomer **499**

Till rising and gliding out I wander'd off by myself,
In the mystical moist night-air, and from time to time,
Look'd up in perfect silence at the stars.

Considerations for Critical Thinking and Writing

1. How does this poem illustrate the differences between poetry and science?
2. Many people today — rightly or wrongly — continue to regard science and poetry as antithetical. What do you think of their view? Write an essay about the methods and purposes of science and poetry in which you explore the differences and/or similarities between them. Use specific poems as evidence for your argument.

MATTHEW ARNOLD (1822–1888)
On Classic and Popular Literature   1888

The benefit of being able clearly to feel and deeply to enjoy the best, the truly classic, in poetry, — is an end . . . of supreme importance. We are often told that an era is opening in which we are to see multitudes of a common sort of readers, and masses of a common sort of literature; that such readers do not want and could not relish anything better than such literature, and that to provide it is becoming a vast and profitable industry. Even if good literature entirely lost currency with the world, it would still be abundantly worth while to continue to enjoy it by oneself. But it never will lose currency with the world, in spite of momentary appearances; it never will lose supremacy. Currency and supremacy are insured to it, not indeed by the world's deliberate and conscious choice, but by something far deeper, — by the instinct of self-preservation in humanity.

From "The Study of Poetry"

Considerations for Critical Thinking and Writing

1. What, in your opinion, makes a work of literature "truly classic"?
2. What kinds of assumptions does Arnold implicitly make about readers of classics and the "multitudes of a common sort"? Do you agree with his categorizations and assessment of these two kinds of readers? Why or why not?
3. Take a stroll through your local bookstore to get a sense of the amount of space allocated to "classics," science fiction, romances, fantasy, mysteries, cookbooks, health books, and so on. Notice especially the poetry section. Also, check to see what books are on the current best-seller lists (they're usually posted by the cash register). Then write a two-part report: in the first part write up your findings as you think Arnold would describe such a "vast and profitable industry"; in the second explain why you agree or disagree with Arnold's perspective.

EZRA POUND (1885–1972)
On Free Verse
1912

I think one should write vers libre [free verse] when one "must," that is to say, only when the "thing" builds up a rhythm more beautiful than that of set meters, or more real, more a part of the emotion of the "thing," more germane, intimate, interpretative than the measure of regular accentual verse; a rhythm which discontents one with set iambic or set anapestic.

From "Prolegomena," *Poetry Review*

Considerations for Critical Thinking and Writing

1. What implications are there in Pound's statement concerning the relation of a poem's form to its content?
2. Compare this view with Whitman's (p. 499).
3. Select a free verse poem from the text and apply Pound's criteria to it. How are the poem's lines arranged to be "a part of the emotion of the 'thing'"?

ARCHIBALD MacLEISH (1892–1982)
Ars Poetica
1926

A poem should be palpable and mute
As a globed fruit,

Dumb
As old medallions to the thumb,

Silent as the sleeve-worn stone   5
Of casement ledges where the moss has grown —

A poem should be wordless
As the flight of birds.

A poem should be motionless in time
As the moon climbs,   10

Leaving, as the moon releases
Twig by twig the night-entangled trees,

Leaving, as the moon behind the winter leaves,
Memory by memory the mind —

A poem should be motionless in time   15
As the moon climbs.

A poem should be equal to:
Not true.

For all the history of grief
An empty doorway and a maple leaf.   20

For love
The leaning grasses and two lights above the sea —

A poem should not mean
But be.

Considerations for Critical Thinking and Writing

1. The Latin title of this poem is translated as "The Art of Poetry." What is MacLeish's view of good poetry? In what sense can a poem be "wordless"? How do lines 19–20 illustrate that?
2. Explain the final two lines. Does the poem contradict its own announced values?
3. How does MacLeish's attitude toward poetry compare with Robert Francis's view in "Glass" (below)?

ROBERT FRANCIS (1901–1987)
Glass   1949

Words of a poem should be glass
But glass so simple-subtle its shape
Is nothing but the shape of what it holds.

A glass spun for itself is empty,
Brittle, at best Venetian trinket.   5
Embossed glass hides the poem or its absence

Words should be looked through, should be windows.
The best word were invisible.
The poem is the thing the poet thinks.

If the impossible were not   10
And if the glass, only the glass,
Could be removed, the poem would remain.

Considerations for Critical Thinking and Writing

1. How is the form of a poem ideally like glass, according to Francis? Why is that not an achievable ideal?
2. Compare what Francis has to say about the words of a poem with what Dylan Thomas says (p. 504). Although each approaches the topic from a different perspective, do you think they are in basic agreement or disagreement?

e. e. cummings (1894–1962)
On the Artist's Responsibility
1953

So far as I am concerned, poetry and every other art was and is and forever will be strictly and distinctly a question of individuality . . . poetry is being, not doing. If you wish to follow, even at a distance, the poet's calling (and here, as always, I speak from my own totally biased and entirely personal point of view) you've got to come out of the measurable doing universe into the immeasurable house of being. . . . Nobody else can be alive for you; nor can you be alive for anybody else. Toms can be Dicks and Dicks can be Harrys, but none of them can ever be you. There's the artist's responsibility; and the most awful responsibility on earth. If you can take it, take it — and be. If you can't, cheer up and go about other people's business; and do (or undo) till you drop.

From *i: Six Nonlectures*

Considerations for Critical Thinking and Writing

1. What does cummings mean when he says "poetry is being, not doing"? How does this compare with MacLeish's view in "Ars Poetica" (p. 501)?
2. How is cummings's insistence upon individuality reflected in the style of "l(a" (p. 24) and the theme of "next to of course god america i" (p. 115)?

KARL SHAPIRO (b. 1913)
On the Poet's Vision
1960

The poet really does see the world differently, and everything in it. He does not deliberately go into training to sharpen his senses; he is a poet because his senses are naturally open and vitally sensitive. But what the poet sees with his always new vision is not what is "imaginary"; he sees what others have forgotten how to see. The poet is always inadvertently stripping away the veils and showing us his reality. Many poets, as we know, go mad because they cannot bear the worlds of illusion and falsehood in which most human beings spend their lives.

From *In Defense of Ignorance*

Considerations for Critical Thinking and Writing

1. Select a poem from this book that illustrates Shapiro's statement that poets see "what others have forgotten how to see." What "reality" does the poem offer that you had forgotten, overlooked, or hadn't previously apprehended?
2. Do you agree that "most human beings spend their lives" in "worlds of illusion and falsehood"? Why or why not?

DYLAN THOMAS (1914–1953)

On the Words in Poetry

1961

You want to know why and how I just began to write poetry. . . .

To answer . . . this question, I should say I wanted to write poetry in the beginning because I had fallen in love with words. The first poems I knew were nursery rhymes, and before I could read them for myself I had come to love just the words of them, the words alone. What the words stood for, symbolized, or meant, was of very secondary importance. What mattered was the *sound* of them as I heard them for the first time on the lips of the remote and incomprehensible grown-ups who seemed, for some reason, to be living in my world. And these words were, to me, as the notes of bells, the sounds of musical instruments, the noises of wind, sea, and rain, the rattle of milkcarts, the clopping of hooves on cobbles, the fingering of branches on a window pane, might be to someone, deaf from birth, who has miraculously found his hearing. I did not care what the words said, overmuch, not what happened to Jack and Jill and the Mother Goose rest of them; I cared for the shapes of sound that their names, and the words describing their actions, made in my ears; I cared for the colors the words cast on my eyes. I realize that I may be, as I think back all that way, romanticizing my reactions to the simple and beautiful words of those pure poems; but that is all I can honestly remember, however much time might have falsified my memory. I fell in love — that is the only expression I can think of — at once, and am still at the mercy of words, though sometimes now, knowing a little of their behavior very well, I think I can influence them slightly and have even learned to beat them now and then, which they appear to enjoy. I tumbled for words at once. And, when I began to read the nursery rhymes for myself, and, later, to read other verses and ballads, I knew that I had discovered the most important things, to me, that could be ever. There they were, seemingly lifeless, made only of black and white, but out of them, out of their own being, came love and terror and pity and pain and wonder and all the other vague abstractions that make our ephemeral lives dangerous, great, and bearable. Out of them came the gusts and grunts and hiccups and heehaws of the common fun of the earth; and though what the words meant was, in its own way, often deliciously funny enough, so much funnier seemed to me, at that almost forgotten time, the shape and shade and size and noise of the words as they hummed, strummed, jugged, and galloped along. That was the time of innocence; words burst upon me, unencumbered by trivial or portentous association; words were their springlike selves, fresh with Eden's dew, as they flew out of the air. They made their own original associations as they sprang and shone. The words, "Ride a cock-horse to Banbury Cross," were as haunting to me, who did not know then what a cock-horse was nor cared a damn where Banbury Cross might be, as, much later, were such lines as John Donne's, "Go and catch a falling star, Get with child a mandrake root," which also I could not understand when I first read them. And as I read more and more, and it was not all verse, by any means, my love for the real life of words increased until I knew that I must live *with* them and *in* them always. I knew, in fact, that I must be a writer of words, and nothing else. The first thing was to feel and know their sound and substance;

what I was going to do with those words, what use I was going to make of them, what I was going to *say* through them, would come later. I knew I had to know them most intimately in all their forms and moods, their ups and downs, their chops and changes, their needs and demands. (Here, I am afraid, I am beginning to talk too vaguely. I do not like writing *about* words, because then I often use bad and wrong and stale and wooly words. What I like to do is treat words as a craftsman does his wood or stone or what-have-you, to hew, carve, mold, coil, polish, and plane them into patterns, sequences, sculptures, fugues of sound expressing some lyrical impulse, some spiritual doubt or conviction, some dimly-realized truth I must try to reach and realize.)

From Early Prose Writings

Considerations for Critical Thinking and Writing

1. Why does Thomas value nursery rhymes so highly? What nursery rhyme was your favorite as a child? Why were you enchanted by it?
2. Explain what you think Thomas would have to say about Lewis Carroll's "Jabberwocky" (p. 146) or May Swenson's "A Nosty Fright" (p. 135).
3. Consider Thomas's comparison at the end of this passage, in which he likens a poet's work to a craftsman's. In what sense is making poetry similar to sculpting, painting, or composing music? What are some of the significant differences?

SYLVIA PLATH (1932–1963)
On "Headline Poetry"

1962

The issues of our time which preoccupy me at the moment are the incalculable genetic effects of fallout and a documentary article on the terrifying, mad, omnipotent marriage of big business and the military in America. . . . Does this influence the kind of poetry I write? Yes, but in a sidelong fashion. I am not gifted with the tongue of Jeremiah,° though I may be sleepless enough before my vision of the apocalypse. My poems do not turn out to be about Hiroshima, but about a child forming itself finger by finger in the dark. They are not about the terrors of mass extinction, but about the bleakness of the moon over a yew tree in a neighboring graveyard. Not about the testaments of tortured Algerians, but about the night thoughts of a tired surgeon.

In a sense, these poems are deflections. I do not think they are an escape. For me, the real issues of our time are the issues of every time — the hurt and wonder of loving; making in all its forms, children, loaves of bread, paintings, building; and the conservation of life of all people in all places, the jeopardizing of which no abstract doubletalk of "peace" or "implacable foes" can excuse.

I do not think a "headline poetry" would interest more people any more profoundly than the headlines. And unless the up-to-the-minute poem grows out of something closer to the bone than a general, shifting philanthropy and

Jeremiah: (c. 650–585 B.C.) One of the greatest Old Testament prophets.

is, indeed, that unicorn-thing — a real poem — it is in danger of being screwed up as rapidly as the news sheet itself.

From "Context," *London Magazine,* February 1962

Considerations for Critical Thinking and Writing

1. Why does Plath refuse to write "headline poetry"? What kind of poetry does she prefer? Read the Plath poems included in this anthology (see the index) and discuss whether the issues they address "are the issues of every time."
2. Do you agree that the poetry Plath prefers is not "an escape" from contemporary issues? Explain why or why not.
3. Compare Plath's view of poetry with Audre Lorde's perspective (below). Write an essay about the significant similarities and differences you find between the two.

AUDRE LORDE (1934–1992)
Poems Are Not Luxuries   1977

For each of us as women, there is a dark place within where hidden and growing our true spirit rises, "Beautiful and tough as chestnut / Stanchions against our nightmare of weakness" and of impotence. These places of possibility within ourselves are dark because they are ancient and hidden; they have survived and grown strong through darkness. Within these deep places, each one of us holds an incredible reserve of creativity and power, storehouse of unexamined and unrecorded emotion and feeling. The woman's place of power within each of us is neither white nor surface; it is dark, it is ancient, and it is deep.

When we view living, in the european mode, only as a problem to be solved, we rely solely upon our ideas to make us free, for these were what the white fathers told us were precious. But as we become more in touch with our own ancient, black, noneuropean view of living as a situation to be experienced and interacted with, we learn more and more to cherish our feelings, to respect those hidden sources of our power from where true knowledge and therefore lasting action comes. At this point in time, I believe that women carry within ourselves the possibility for fusion of these two approaches as a keystone for survival, and we come closest to this combination in our poetry. I speak here of poetry as the revelation or distillation of experience, not the sterile word play that, too often, the white fathers distorted the word *poetry* to mean — in order to cover their desperate wish for imagination without insight.

For women, then, poetry is not a luxury. It is a vital necessity of our existence. It forms the quality of the light within which we predicate our hopes and dreams toward survival and change, first made into language, then into idea, then into more tangible action. Poetry is the way we help give name to the nameless so it can be thought. The farthest external horizons of our hopes and fears are cobbled by our poems, carved from the rock experiences of our daily lives.

As they become known and accepted to ourselves, our feelings, and the honest exploration of them, become sanctuaries and fortresses and spawning grounds for the most radical and daring of ideas, the house of difference so necessary to change and the conceptualization of any meaningful action. Right now, I could name at least ten ideas I would once have found intolerable or incomprehensible and frightening, except as they came after dreams and poems. This is not idle fantasy, but the true meaning of "It feels right to me." We can train ourselves to respect our feelings and to discipline (transpose) them into a language that catches those feelings so they can be shared. And where that language does not yet exist, it is our poetry which helps to fashion it. Poetry is not only dream or vision, it is the skeleton architecture of our lives.

From "Poems Are Not Luxuries," in *Claims for Poetry,*
edited by Donald Hall

Considerations for Critical Thinking and Writing

1. What distinctions does Lorde make between black culture and "european" culture? How does she describe their different approaches to poetry? Do you agree or disagree with Lorde's assessment?
2. According to Lorde, why can't poetry be regarded as a luxury?
3. Read Lorde's poem "Hanging Fire" (p. 398) and discuss whether you think it fulfills her description of what poetry can do.

MARK STRAND (b. 1934)
On the Audience for Poetry   1977

Interviewer: Are you disturbed by a sense of coterie in recent poetry, by the fact that the audience is so small and ingrown?

Strand: The impression is a little deceptive. The audience for poetry is actually growing bigger, and it constantly changes. A lot of people are interested in poetry for a while, then fall behind and lose interest and get intrigued by other things. But new people are always coming along. The smallness of the audience doesn't bother me. I don't believe poetry is for everyone any more than I believe roast pork is for everyone. Poetry is demanding. It takes a certain amount of getting used to, a period of initiation. Only those people who are willing to spend *time* with it really get anything out of it. No, the lack of audience doesn't bother me. Some poets have 100,000 readers, but I don't believe that many really read poetry. I think if I had that many readers I'd begin to feel that something was *wrong* in my poems.

From an interview by Richard Vine and Robert von Hallberg
in *Chicago Review,* Spring 1977

Considerations for Critical Thinking and Writing

1. What is your impression about the size of audiences for poetry? Are they growing larger or smaller? Explain why.
2. Write an essay in which you agree or disagree with Strand's statement "I don't believe poetry is for everyone any more than I believe roast pork is for everyone."
3. Do you think that if a poet is very popular, there might be something *"wrong"* with his or her poems? Explain why or why not.

GALWAY KINNELL (b. 1927)
The Female and Male Principles of Poetry   1989

If poetry could be divided into two parts, knowing and making, then I would give to knowing the name *the female principle,* and to making I would give the name *the male principle.* Another poet might reverse those names, because these things are myths that just accumulate and we can use them as flexibly as we want. In my own case, you see, I had an Irish mother who brooded and thought and meditated a lot on things and was very articulate. I thought of her as a knower; she really wanted to know. She'd always ask me really hard questions, "Do you really think there's a heaven?" and she would mean it. She wasn't trying to educate me, she wanted to know if there was a heaven. My father, on the other hand, was a maker, he was a carpenter. I spent many hours at his side making things that were solid, had good structure, that wouldn't fall apart, that would last forever.

When I'm writing and I'm doing that beam work and that kind of construction, I always feel that what I'm doing owes a lot to my father, but when I have these moments when I think I know something, which is the most essential thing in poetry, I think that my mother is talking through me. That's why it's worked out that way in my mythology. But I can see how it might be completely different for somebody else.

From "Being with Reality: An Interview with Galway Kinnell,"
Columbia Magazine

Considerations for Critical Thinking and Writing

1. Read Kinnell's "Blackberry Eating" (p. 138) and discuss the poem in terms of Kinnell's ideas about the female principle of knowing and the male principle of making. Can you see evidence of the two principles at work in this poem?
2. One can talk about these principles in relation to reading poetry as well as writing it. Choose three or four poems from Chapter 12 and decide which aspects of the poems you simply know (either by intuition or by a sudden apprehension) and which aspects you must work at to understand. Would you use Kinnell's distinction between female knowing and male making to describe your experience of the poems?

DENISE LEVERTOV (b. 1923)

On "Gathered at the River"

1985

This is the prose of it: Each year on August 6 (and sometimes on August 9 as well) some kind of memorial observance of the bombing of Hiroshima and Nagasaki is held in the Boston/Cambridge area, as in so many other locations. Some years this has consisted of a silent vigil held near Faneuil Hall and other monuments of the American Revolution. Participants stand in a circle facing outward to display signs explaining the theme of the vigil, or pace slowly round, sometimes accompanied by the drums and chanting of attendant Buddhist monks. People stay for varying periods — there may be a constant presence for three days and nights. In 1982 the poet Suzanne Belote (of the Catholic radical peace group Ailanthus) and some others created a variation on this event. Participants (with the usual age range — babes in arms to white-haired old men and women) came to the Cambridge Friends' Meeting House for a brief preparatory assembly, then filed out to receive a candle apiece — thick Jahrzeit candles nailed to pieces of wood and shielded by paper cups — and proceeded to walk in a hushed column along Memorial Drive, beside the Charles River. The sun was low; a long summer day was ending. When we got to the wide grassy area near the Lars Anderson Bridge, where our ceremony was to take place, it was twilight. Shielding flickering flames from the evening breeze, we formed a large circle, into the center of which stepped successive readers of portions from the descriptions recorded (as in the book *Unforgettable Fire*) by survivors of the atomic bombings. A period of silence followed. And then "saints and prophets, heroes and heroines of justice and peace" — including Gandhi, Martin Luther King, A. J. Muste, Emma Goldman, Archbishop Romero, Eugene Debs, Pope John XXIII, Dorothy Day, Saint Francis of Assisi, Saint Thomas More, Prince Kropotkin, Ammon Hennacy, the Prophet Isaiah, and many others I can't remember — were invoked. A form of ritual — an ecumenical liturgy — had been devised for the occasion, and as each such name was uttered by some member of the circle, the rest responded with a phrase that said essentially, "Be with us, great spirits, in this time of great need." The persons conducting the continuum of the liturgy turned slowly as they read the survivors' testimony, or statements of dedication to the cause of peace, so that all could hear at least part of each passage: for we had no microphones, preferring to depend on the unaided human voice for an occasion which had a personal, intimate character for each participant rather than being a PR event. Some music was interspersed among the verbal antiphonies, and the human atmosphere was solemn, harmonious, truly dedicated: from within it I began to feel the strong presence of the trees which half encircled us. Cars passed along Memorial Drive — slowed as drivers craned to see what was happening — passed on. A few blinked their lights in a friendly way, guessing from the date, I suppose, why we were there.

While we earnestly committed — or recommitted — ourselves to do all in our power to prevent nuclear war from ever taking place, it was growing dark. In the soft summer darkness details stood out: hands cupping wicks, small children's gold-illumined faces gazing up in wonder at the crouch and leap of flames, adults' heads bent close to one another as they clustered in twos and threes to relight candles blown out. And now the first part of the ritual was over and it was time to set our candles afloat, as they are set on the river in Hiroshima each year, that river where many drowned in the vain attempt to escape the burning of their own flesh.

People scrambled and helped each other down the short slope of the riverbank to launch the little candle-boats. Oblivious, a motorboat or two sped upriver, and minutes after a big slow wave would reach the shore. The water was black; the candle-boats seemed so fragile, and so tenacious. And all the time the large plane trees (saved from a road-widening project years before, incidentally, by citizens who chained themselves to their trunks in protest), and the other trees and bushes near them, were intensely, watchfully present. I have been asked if I really believe trees can listen. I've always thought our scientific knowledge has made us very arrogant in our assumptions. Wiser and older individuals and cultures have believed other kinds of consciousness and feeling could and did exist alongside of ours; I see no reason to disagree. It is not that I don't know trees have no "gray matter." It is possible that there are other routes to sentience than those with which we consider ourselves familiar.

The form of the poem: The title came from the literal sense of our being gathered there on the shore of the Charles, and also with the cognizance of the Quaker sense of gathering — a *"gathered meeting"* being, to my understanding, one which has not merely acquired the full complement of those who are going to attend it but which has attained a certain level, or quality, of attunement. Then, too, I had a vague memory of the song or hymn from which James Wright took the title of one of his books, and which I presumed must refer to the river of Jordan — "one more river, one more river to cross," as another song says. And though the symbolism there is of heaven lying upon the far shore, yet there is also, in the implication of *lastness,* of a final ordeal, the clear sense of a catastrophic alternative to attaining that shore. (No doubt *Pilgrim's Progress* was in the back of my mind too.) The analogy is obviously not a very close one, since survival of life on earth is a more modest goal than eternal bliss. Yet, relative to the hell proposed by our twentieth-century compound of the ancient vices of greed and love of power with nuclear and other "advanced" technology, mere survival would be a kind of heaven — especially since survival is not a static condition but offers the opportunity, and therefore the hope, of positive change. (For if one hopes for the survival of life on earth, one must logically hope and *intend* also the reshaping of those forces and factors which, unchanged, will only continue to threaten annihilation by one means or another.)

The structure of the poem stems as directly as the title from my experience of the event. The first line stands alone because that perception of the trees as animate and not uninterested presences — witnesses — was the discrete first in a series of heightened perceptions, most of which came in clusters. The following two-line stanza expands the first, more tentative observation, and places the trees' air of attention in the context of a breeze (which does not seem to distract them) and of the fluttering candles, which are thus introduced right at the start. Looking more closely at the trees, I see their late-summer color, but then recognize I am no longer seeing it, for dusk is falling — literally, but also metaphorically. The next stanza notes the largeness (and implied gravity, in both senses) of the trees, which it is not too dark to see, then again in a single line reasserts with more assurance the focus of my own attention: the trees' attentiveness. Following that comes the recognition of why, and for what, they are listening. The Latin words introduced here (echoing Pound's use of them) express the idea that "sin" occurs when humans violate the well-being of their own species and other living things, denying the natural law, the interdependence of all. (That usury belongs in this category, as Pound reemphasized, is not irrelevant to the subject of this poem, recalling the economic underpinning of the arms race and of war itself.)

My underlying belief in a great design, a potential harmony which can be violated or be sustained, probably strikes some people as quaint; but I would be dishonest, as person and artist, if I disowned it. I don't at this stage of my life feel ready for a public discussion of my religious concepts: but I think it must be clear from my writings that I have never been an atheist, and that — given my background and the fact that all my life George Herbert, Henry Vaughan, Thomas Traherne, and Gerard Manley Hopkins have been on my "short list" of favorite poets — whatever degree of belief I might attain would have a Christian context. This in turn implies a concern with the osmosis of "faith and works" and a sense of the sacredness of the earthly creation. That sense, not exclusive to Christianity, and deeply experienced and expressed by, for instance, Native Americans, is linked for Christians to the mystery of the Incarnation. To violate ourselves and our world is to violate the Divine.

The trees' concern, proposed with a tentative "as if" at the beginning, and then as an impression they "give off," is now asserted unequivocally. Once more comes a single line, "We intone together, *Never again*," focused on the purpose of our gathering; and the words "never again" bring together the thought of the Nazi Holocaust with that of the crime committed by the U.S. against Japanese civilians, a crime advocates of the arms race prepare to commit again on a scale vaster than that of any massacre in all of history. This association might carry with it, I would hope, the sense that those who vow to work for prevention of war also are dedicated to political, economic, and racial justice, and understand something of the connections between long-standing oppression, major and "minor" massacres, and the giant shadow of global war and annihilation.

The narration continues, up to the launching of the candle-boats; pauses — a pause indicated by the asterisk — as we hold our breath to watch them go; and continues as they "bob on the current" and, though close to shore, begin to move downstream. Like ourselves, they are few and pitifully small. But at least they don't sink. Like all candles lit for the dead or in prayer, they combine remembrance with aspiration.

Finally the poem returns its regard to the trees, with the feeling that they know what we know — a knowledge those lines state and which it would be silly to paraphrase. The single lines again center on the primary realizations. Indeed, I see that a kind of précis of the entire poem could be extracted by reading the isolated lines alone:

As if the trees were not indifferent   .   .   .
. . . .
a half-circle of attention.
. . . .

We intone together, *Never again.*

. . . .

Windthreatened flames bob on the current . . .

. . . .

there will be nothing left of their slow and innocent wisdom,

. . . .

no pollen,

except that one absolutely essential bone would be missing from that skeleton:
the "if" of "if we fail." The poem, like the ceremony it narrates, and which gives
it its slow, serious *pace* and, I hope, tone, is about interconnection, about dread,
and about hope; that word, *if,* is its core.

> " 'Gathered at the River': Background and Form" in *Singular Voices:*
> *American Poetry Today,* edited by Stephen Berg (Levertov's essay
> was written in response to a request from Berg.)

Considerations for Critical Thinking and Writing

1. In this essay, Levertov describes why and how she wrote "Gathered at the River"
   (p. 489). Does her account of the memorial observance help you to appreciate
   the poem more? Why or why not? Is the background information to the poem
   ("the prose of it") essential for an understanding of it?
2. Why is the word *if* essential to the poem's meaning?
3. Does Levertov exhaust the possibilities for discussing the poem? What can you
   add to her comments?
4. Poets are usually extremely reluctant to comment on their own poetry. Why do
   you think they frequently refuse to talk about the background and form of their
   poems?

ALICE FULTON (b. 1952)
On the Validity of Free Verse   1987

    Until recently, I believed that Pound (along with Blake and Whitman, among
others) had managed to establish beyond all argument the value of *vers libre* as
a poetic medium. I thought that questions concerning the validity of free verse
could be filed along with such antique quarrels as "Is photography Art?" and "Is
abstract art Art?" In the past few years, however, I've heard many people —
professors, poets, readers — speak of free verse as a failed experiment. To these
disgruntled souls, free verse apparently describes an amorphous prosaic spouting, distinguished chiefly by its neglect of meter or rhyme, pattern or plan.
Perhaps the word *free* contributes to the misconception. It's easy to interpret
free as "free from all constraints of form," which lead to "free-for-all." However,
any poet struggling with the obdurate qualities of language can testify that the
above connotations of "free" do not apply to verse.

    Since it's impossible to write unaccented English, free verse has meter. Of
course, rather than striving for regularity, the measure of free verse may change

from line to line, just as the tempo of twentieth-century music may change from bar to bar. As for allegations about formlessness, it seems to me that only an irregular structure with no beginning or end could be described as formless. (If the structure were regular, we could deduce the whole from a part. If irregular and therefore unpredictable, we'd need to see the whole in order to grasp its shape.) By this definition, there are fairly few examples of formless phenomena: certain concepts of God or of the expanding universe come to mind. However, unlike the accidental forms of nature, free verse is characterized by the poet's conscious shaping of content and language: the poet's choices at each step of the creative process give rise to form. Rather than relying on regular meter or rhyme as a means of ordering, the structures of free verse may be based upon registers of diction, irregular meter, sound as analogue for content, syllabics, accentuals, the interplay of chance with chosen elements, theories of lineation, recurring words, or whatever design delights the imagination and intellect. I suspect that the relation between content and form can be important or arbitrary in both metered and free verse. In regard to conventional forms, it's often assumed that decisions concerning content follow decisions concerning form (the add-subject-and-stir approach). However, poets consciously choose different subjects for sonnets than for ballads, thus exemplifying the interdependency of content and form. The reverse assumption is made about free verse: that the subject supersedes or, at best, dictates the form. But this is not necessarily the case. The poet can decide to utilize a structural device, such as the ones suggested previously, and then proceed to devise the content.

When we read a sestina, the form is clearly discernible. This is partly because we've read so many sestinas (familiarity breeds recognition) and partly because it's easy to perceive a highly repetitive pattern. More complex designs, however, often appear to be random until scrutinized closely. Much of what we call free verse tries to create a structure suitable only to itself — a pattern that has never appeared before, perhaps. As in serious modern music or jazz, the repetitions, if they do exist, may be so widely spaced that it takes several readings to discern them. Or the poems' unifying elements may be new to the reader, who must become a creative and active participant in order to appreciate the overall scheme. This is not meant to be a dismissal of the time-honored poetic forms. I admire and enjoy poets who breathe new life into seemingly dead conventions or structures. And I'm intrigued by poetry that borrows its shape from the models around us: poems in the form of TV listings, letters, recipes, and so forth. But I also value the analysis required and the discovery inherent in reading work that invents a form peculiar to itself. I like the idea of varying the meter from line to line so that nuances of tone can find their rhythmic correlative (or antithesis).

From *Ecstatic Occasions, Expedient Forms,* edited by David Lehman

Considerations for Critical Thinking and Writing

1. How does Fulton defend free verse against "allegations about formlessness"?
2. Compare Fulton's comments on the relationship of a poem's form to its content with Walt Whitman's views (p. 499).
3. Browse through Chapter 12 and choose a poem "that invents a form peculiar to itself." Now analyze that poem.

ROBERT J. FOGELIN (b. 1932)

A Case against Metaphors

1988

Recent writers on metaphor often insist, sometimes in extravagant terms, on the power of metaphors. They also complain about the prejudice against metaphor that springs, they suggest, from a narrow, literalist (positivist) conception of language. The fact of the matter is that the vast majority of metaphors are routine and uninteresting. Many metaphors are lame, misleading, overblown, inaccurate, et cetera. Metaphors, in indicating that one thing is like another, so far say very little. Their strength, which they share with comparisons in general, is that their near-emptiness makes them adaptable for use in a wide variety of contexts. On the reverse side, the near-emptiness of metaphors also makes them serviceable for those occasions when we want to avoid saying, and perhaps thinking, what we really mean. Euphemisms are typically couched in metaphors. Metaphors can be evasions — including poetic evasions.

From *Figuratively Speaking*

Considerations for Critical Thinking and Writing

1. Why does Fogelin object to many uses of metaphors? Explain why you agree or disagree with his assessment.
2. Choose a poem from this anthology and write an essay that either supports or refutes Fogelin's assertions.

CRITICAL THINKING AND WRITING

14. Critical Strategies
for Reading

CRITICAL THINKING

Maybe this has happened to you: the assignment is to write an analysis of some aspect of a work, let's say Nathaniel Hawthorne's *The Scarlet Letter,* that interests you and takes into account critical sources that comment on and interpret the work. You cheerfully begin research in the library but quickly find yourself bewildered by several seemingly unrelated articles. The first traces the thematic significance of images of light and darkness in the novel; the second makes a case for Hester Prynne as a liberated woman; the third argues that Arthur Dimmesdale's guilt is a projection of Hawthorne's own emotions; and the fourth analyzes the introduction, "The Custom House," as an attack on bourgeois values. These disparate treatments may seem random and capricious — a confirmation of your worst suspicions that interpretations of literature are hit-or-miss excursions into areas that you know little about or didn't know even existed. But if you understand that the articles are written from different perspectives — formalist, feminist, psychological, and Marxist — and that the purpose of each is to enhance your understanding of the work by discussing a particular element of it, then you can see that their varying strategies represent potentially interesting ways of opening up the text that might otherwise never have occurred to you. There are many ways to approach a text, and a useful first step is to develop a sense of direction, an understanding of how a perspective — your own or a critic's — shapes a discussion of a text.

This chapter offers an introduction to critical approaches to literature by outlining a variety of strategies for reading poetry, fiction, or drama. The emphasis is of course on poetry and to that end the approaches focus on Robert Frost's "Mending Wall" (p. 298); a rereading of that well-known poem will equip you for the discussions that follow. In addition to the emphasis on this poem to illustrate critical approaches, some fiction and drama examples are also included along the way to demonstrate how these critical approaches can be applied to any genre. These strategies include approaches that have long been practiced by readers who have used, for example, the insights gleaned from biography and history to illuminate literary works as well as more recent approaches, such as those used by feminist, reader-response, and deconstructionist critics. Each of these perspectives is sensitive to image, symbol, tone, irony, and other literary elements that you have been studying, but each also casts those elements in a special light. The formalist approach emphasizes how the elements within a work achieve their effects, whereas biographical and psychological approaches lead outward from the work to consider the author's life and other writings. Even broader approaches, such as historical and sociological perspectives, connect the work to historic, social, and economic forces. Mythological readings represent the broadest approach, because they discuss the cultural and universal responses readers have to a work.

Any given strategy raises its own types of questions and issues while seeking particular kinds of evidence to support itself. An awareness of the assumptions and methods that inform an approach can help you to understand better the validity and value of a given critic's strategy for making sense of a work. More important, such an understanding can widen and deepen the responses of your own reading.

The critical thinking that goes into understanding a professional critic's approach to a work is not foreign to you because you have already used essentially the same kind of thinking to understand the work itself. The skills you have developed to produce a literary *analysis* that, for example, describes how a character, symbol, or rhyme scheme supports a theme are also useful for reading literary criticism, because such skills allow you to keep track of how the parts of a critical approach create a particular reading of a literary work. When you analyze a poem, story, or play by closely examining how its various elements relate to the whole, your *interpretation* — your articulation of what the work means to you as supported by an analysis of its elements — necessarily involves choosing what you focus upon in the work. The same is true of professional critics.

Critical readings presuppose choices in the kinds of material that are discussed. An analysis of the setting of Robert Frost's "Home Burial" (p. 300) would probably bring into focus the oppressive environment of the couple's domestic life rather than, say, the economic history of New England farming. The economic history of New England farming might be useful to a Marxist critic concerned with how class is revealed in "Home Burial," but for a formalist critic interested in identifying the unifying structures of the poem such information would be irrelevant.

The Perspectives, Complementary Readings, and Critical Case Study in this anthology offer opportunities to read critics using a wide variety of approaches to analyze and interpret texts. In the Critical Case Study on T. S. Eliot's "The Love Song of J. Alfred Prufrock" (Chapter 11), for instance, Elisabeth Schneider offers a biographical interpretation of Prufrock by suggesting that Eliot shared some of his character's sensibilities. In contrast,

Robert G. Cook argues that Prufrock's character can be explained by the historical influence of Ralph Waldo Emerson's 1841 essay "Self-Reliance." Each of these critics raises different questions, examines different evidence, and employs different assumptions to interpret Prufrock's character. Being aware of those differences — teasing them out so that you can see how they lead to competing conclusions — is a useful way to analyze the analysis itself. What is left out of an interpretation is sometimes as significant as what is included. As you read the critics, it's worth reminding yourself that your own critical thinking skills can help you to determine the usefulness of a particular approach.

The following overview is neither exhaustive in the types of critical approaches covered nor complete in its presentation of the complexities inherent in them, but it should help you to develop an appreciation of the intriguing possibilities that attend literary interpretation. The emphasis in this chapter is on ways of thinking about literature rather than on daunting lists of terms, names, and movements. Although a working knowledge of critical schools may be valuable and necessary for a fully informed use of a given critical approach, the aim here is more modest and practical. This chapter is no substitute for the shelves of literary criticism that can be found in your library, but it does suggest how readers using different perspectives organize their responses to texts.

The summaries of critical approaches that follow are descriptive, not evaluative. Each approach has its advantages and limitations, but those matters are best left to further study. Like literary artists, critics have their personal values, tastes, and styles. The appropriateness of a specific critical approach will depend, at least in part, on the nature of the literary work under discussion as well as on your own sensibilities and experience. However, any approach, if it is to enhance understanding, requires sensitivity, tact, and an awareness of the various literary elements of the text, including, of course, its use of language.

Successful critical approaches avoid eccentric decodings that reveal so-called hidden meanings which are not only hidden but totally absent from the text. For a parody of this sort of critical excess, see "A Reading of 'Stopping by Woods on a Snowy Evening'" (p. 323), in which Herbert R. Coursen, Jr., has some fun with a Robert Frost poem and Santa Claus while making a serious point about the dangers of overly ingenious readings. Literary criticism attempts, like any valid hypothesis, to account for phenomena — the text — without distorting or misrepresenting what it describes.

THE LITERARY CANON:
DIVERSITY AND CONTROVERSY

Before looking at the various critical approaches discussed in this chapter, it makes sense to consider first which literature has been traditionally considered worthy of such analysis. The discussion in the Introduction called The Changing Literary Canon (p. 7) may have already alerted you to the fact that in recent years many more works by women, minorities, and writers from around the world have been considered by scholars, critics, and teachers to merit serious study and inclusion in what is known as the literary canon. This increasing diversity has been celebrated by those who believe that multiculturalism taps new sources for the discovery of great literature while raising significant questions about language, culture, and society. At the same time, others have perceived this diversity as a threat to the established, traditional canon of Western culture.

The debates concerning whose work should be read, taught, and written about have sometimes been acrimonious as well as lively and challenging. Bitter arguments have been waged recently on campuses and in the press over what has come to be called "political correctness." Two camps — roughly — have formed around these debates: liberals and conservatives (the appropriateness of these terms is debatable but the oppositional positioning is unmistakable). The liberals are said to insist upon politically correct views from colleagues and students opening up the curriculum to multicultural texts from Asia, Africa, Latin America, and elsewhere, and to encourage more tolerant attitudes about race, class, gender, and sexual orientation. These revisionists, seeking a change in traditional attitudes, are sometimes accused of intimidating the opposition into silence and substituting ideological dogma for reason and truth. The conservatives are also portrayed as ideologues; in their efforts to preserve what they regard as the best from the past, they refuse to admit that Western classics, mostly written by white male Europeans, represent only a portion of human experience. These traditionalists are seen as advocating values that are neither universal nor eternal but merely privileged and entrenched. Conservatives are charged with refusing to acknowledge that their values also represent a political agenda, which is implicit in their preference for the works of canonical authors such as Homer, Virgil, Shakespeare, Milton, Tolstoy, and Faulkner. The reductive and contradictory nature of this national debate between liberals and conservatives has been neatly summed up by Katha Pollitt: "Read the conservatives' list and produce a nation of sexists and racists — or a nation of philosopher kings. Read the liberals' list and produce a nation of spiritual relativists — or a nation of open-minded world citizens" ("Canon to the Right of Me . . . ," *The Nation,* Sept. 23, 1991, p. 330).

These troubling and extreme alternatives can be avoided, of course, if the issues are not approached from such absolutist positions. Solutions to these issues cannot be suggested in this limited space, and, no doubt, solutions will evolve over time, but we can at least provide a perspective. Books — regardless of what list they are on — are not likely to unite a fragmented nation or to disunite a unified one. It is perhaps more useful and accurate to see issues of canonicity as reflecting political changes rather than being the primary causes of them. This is not to say that books don't have an impact on readers — that *Uncle Tom's Cabin,* for instance, did not galvanize antislavery sentiments in nineteenth-century America — but that book lists do not by themselves preserve or destroy the status quo.

It's worth noting that the curricula of American universities have always undergone significant and, some would say, wrenching changes. Only a little more than one hundred years ago there was strong opposition to teaching English, as well as other modern languages, alongside programs dominated by Greek and Latin. Only since the 1920s has American literature been made a part of the curriculum, and just five decades ago writers such as Emily Dickinson, Robert Frost, W. H. Auden, and Marianne Moore were regarded with the same raised eyebrows that today might be raised about contemporary writers such as Sharon Olds, Galway Kinnell, Rita Dove, or Robert Bly. New voices do not drown out the past; they build on it, and eventually become part of the past as newer writers take their place alongside them. Neither resistance to change nor a denial of the past will have its way with the canon. Though both impulses are widespread, neither is likely to dominate the other, because there are too many reasonable, practical readers and teachers who instead of replacing Shakespeare, Frost, and other canonical writers have supplemented them with neglected writers from Western and other cultures. These readers experience the current debates about the canon not as a binary opposition but as an opportunity to explore important questions about continuity and change in our literature, culture, and society.

FORMALIST STRATEGIES

Formalist critics focus on the formal elements of a work — its language, structure, and tone. A formalist reads literature as an independent work of art rather than as a reflection of the author's state of mind or as a representation of a moment in history. Historic influences on a work, an author's intentions, or anything else outside the work are generally not treated by formalists (this is particularly true of the most famous modern formalists, known as the *New Critics,* who dominated American criticism from the 1940s through the 1960s). Instead, formalists offer intense examinations of the relationship between form and meaning within a work, emphasizing the subtle complexity of how a work is arranged. This kind of close reading pays special attention to what are often described as *intrinsic* matters in a literary work, such as diction, irony, paradox, metaphor, and symbol, as well as larger elements, such as plot, characterization, and narrative technique. Formalists examine how these elements work together to give a coherent shape to a work while contributing to its meaning. The answers to the questions formalists raise about how the shape and effect of a work are related come from the work itself. Other kinds of information that go beyond the text — biography, history, politics, economics, and so on — are typically regarded by formalists as *extrinsic* matters, which are considerably less important than what goes on within the autonomous text.

Poetry especially lends itself to close readings, because a poem's relative brevity allows for detailed analyses of nearly all its words and how they achieve their effects. For a sample formalist reading of how a pervasive sense of death is worked into a poem, see "A Reading of Dickinson's 'There's a certain Slant of light' " (p. 573).

Formalist strategies are also useful for analyzing drama and fiction. In his well-known essay "The World of *Hamlet*," Maynard Mack explores Hamlet's character and predicament by paying close attention to the words and images that Shakespeare uses to build a world in which appearances mask reality and mystery is embedded in scene after scene. Mack points to recurring terms, such as *apparition, seems, assume,* and *put on,* as well as repeated images of acting, clothing, disease, and painting, to indicate the treacherous surface world Hamlet must penetrate to get to the truth. This pattern of deception provides an organizing principle around which Mack offers a reading of the entire play:

> Hamlet's problem, in its crudest form, is simply the problem of the avenger: he must carry out the injunction of the ghost and kill the king. But this problem . . . is presented in terms of a certain kind of world. The ghost's injunction to act becomes so inextricably bound up for Hamlet with the character of the world in which the action must be taken — its mysteriousness, its baffling appearances, its deep consciousness of infection, frailty, and loss — that he cannot come to terms with either without coming to terms with both.

Although Mack places *Hamlet* in the tradition of revenge tragedy, his reading of the play emphasizes Shakespeare's arrangement of language rather than literary history as a means of providing an interpretation that accounts for various elements of the play. Mack's formalist strategy explores how diction reveals meaning and how repeated words and images evoke and reinforce important thematic significances.

A formalist reading of Robert Frost's "Mending Wall" leads to an examination of the tensions produced by the poem's diction, repetitions, and images that take us beyond a merely literal reading. The speaker describes how every spring he and his neighbor walk beside the stone wall bordering their respective farms to replace the stones that have fallen during winter. As they repair the wall, the speaker wonders what purpose the wall serves, given that "My apple trees will never get across / And eat the cones under his pines"; his neighbor, however, "only says, 'Good fences make good neighbors.'" The moment described in the poem is characteristic of the rural

New England life that constitutes so much of Frost's poetry, but it is also typical of how he uses poetry as a means of "saying one thing in terms of another," as he once put it in an essay titled "Education by Poetry."

Just as the speaker teases his neighbor with the idea that the apple trees won't disturb the pines, so too does Frost tease the reader into looking at what it is "that doesn't love a wall." Frost's use of language in the poem does not simply consist of homespun casual phrases enlisted to characterize rural neighbors. From the opening lines, the "Something . . . that doesn't love a wall" and "That sends the frozen-ground swell under it" is, on the literal level, a frost heave that causes the stones to tumble from the wall. But after several close readings of the poem, we can see the implicit pun in these lines which suggest that it is *Frost* who objects to the wall, thus aligning the poet's perspective with the speaker's. A careful examination of some of the other formal elements in the poem supports this reading.

In contrast to the imaginative wit of the speaker who raises fundamental questions about the purpose of any wall, the images associated with his neighbor indicate that he is a traditionalist who "will not go behind his father's saying." Moreover, the neighbor moves "like an old-stone savage" in "darkness" that is attributed to his rigid, tradition-bound, walled-in sensibilities rather than to "the shade of trees." Whereas the speaker's wit and intelligence are manifested by his willingness to question the necessity or desirability of "walling in or walling out" anything, his benighted neighbor can only repeat again that "good fences make good neighbors." The stone-heavy darkness of the neighbor's mind is emphasized by the contrasting light wit and agility of the speaker, who speculates: "Before I built a wall I'd ask to know . . . to whom I was like to give offense." The pun on the final word of this line makes a subtle but important connection between giving "offense" and creating "a fence." Frost's careful use of diction, repetition, and images deftly reveals and reenforces thematic significances suggesting that the stone wall serves as a symbol of isolation, confinement, fear, and even savagery. The neighbor's conservative tradition-bound mindless support of the wall is a foil to the speaker's — read Frost's — poetic, liberal response, which imagines and encourages the possibilites of greater freedom and brotherhood.

Although this brief discussion of some of the formal elements of Frost's poem does not describe all there is to say about how they produce an effect and create meaning, it does suggest the kinds of questions, issues, and evidence that a formalist strategy might raise in providing a close reading of the text itself.

BIOGRAPHICAL STRATEGIES

A knowledge of an author's life can help readers understand his or her work more fully. Events in a work might follow actual events in a writer's life just as characters might be based on people known by the author. Ernest Hemingway's "Soldier's Home" is a story about the difficulties of a World War I veteran named Krebs returning to his small hometown in Oklahoma, where he cannot adjust to the pious assumptions of his family and neighbors. He refuses to accept their innocent blindness to the horrors he has witnessed during the war. They have no sense of the brutality of modern life; instead they insist he resume his life as if nothing has happened. There is plenty of biographical evidence to indicate that Krebs's unwillingness to lie about his war experiences reflects Hemingway's own responses upon his return to Oak Park, Illinois, in 1919. Krebs, like Hemingway, finds he has to leave the sentimentality, repressiveness, and smug complacency that threaten to render his experiences unreal: "the world they were in was not the world he was in."

An awareness of Hemingway's own war experiences and subsequent disillusionment with his hometown can be readily developed through available biographies, letters, and other works he wrote. Consider, for example, this passage from *By Force of Will: The Life and Art of Ernest Hemingway*, in which Scott Donaldson describes Hemingway's response to World War I:

> In poems, as in [*A Farewell to Arms*], Hemingway expressed his distaste for the first war. The men who had to fight the war did not die well:
>
> > Soldiers pitch and cough and twitch —
> > All the world roars red and black;
> > Soldiers smother in a ditch,
> > Choking through the whole attack.
>
> And what did they die for? They were "sucked in" by empty words and phrases —
>
> > King and country,
> > Christ Almighty,
> > And the rest,
> > Patriotism,
> > Democracy,
> > Honor —
>
> which spelled death. The bitterness of these outbursts derived from the distinction Hemingway drew between the men on the line and those who started the wars that others had to fight.

This kind of information can help to deepen our understanding of just how empathetically Krebs is presented in the story. Relevant facts about Hemingway's life will not make "Soldier's Home" a better written story than it is, but such information can make clearer the source of Hemingway's convictions and how his own experiences inform his major concerns as a storyteller.

Some formalist critics — some New Critics, for example — argue that interpretation should be based exclusively on internal evidence rather than on any biographical information outside the work. They argue that it is not possible to determine an author's intention and that the work must stand by itself. Although this is a useful caveat for keeping the work in focus, a reader who finds biography relevant would argue that biography can at the very least serve as a control on interpretation. A reader who, for example, finds Krebs at fault for not subscribing to the values of his hometown would be misreading the story, given both its tone and the biographical information available about the author. Although the narrator never *tells* the reader that Krebs is right or wrong for leaving town, the story's tone sides with his view of things. If, however, someone were to argue otherwise, insisting that the tone is not decisive and that Krebs's position is problematic, a reader familiar with Hemingway's own reactions could refute that argument with a powerful confirmation of Krebs's instincts to withdraw. Hence, many readers find biography useful for interpretation.

However, it is also worth noting that biographical information can complicate a work. For example, readers who interpret "Mending Wall" as a celebration of an iconoclastic sensibility that seeks to break down the psychological barriers and physical walls that separate human beings may be surprised to learn that very few of Frost's other writings support this view. His life was filled with emotional turmoil, a life described by a number of biographers as egocentric and vindictive rather than generous and open to others. He once commented that "I always hold that we get forward as much by hating as by loving." Indeed, many facts about Frost's life — as well as many of the speakers in his poems — are typified by depression, alienation, tension, suspicion, jealous competitiveness, and suicidal tendencies. Instead of challenging wall-builders, Frost more characteristically built walls of distrust around himself among his family, friends, and colleagues. In this biographical context, it is especially worth noting that it is the speaker of "Mending Wall" who alone repairs the damage done to the walls by hunters, and it is he who initiates each spring the rebuilding of the wall. However much he may question its value, the speaker does, after all, rebuild the wall between himself and his neighbor. This biographical approach raises provocative questions about the text. Does the poem suggest that boundaries and walls are, in fact, necessary? Are walls a desirable foundation for relationships between people? Although these and other questions raised by a biographical approach cannot be answered here, this kind of biographical perspective certainly adds to the possibilities of interpretation.

Sometimes biographical information does not change our understanding so much as it enriches our appreciation of a work. It matters, for instance, that much of John Milton's poetry, so rich in visual imagery, was written after he became blind; and it is just as significant — to shift to a musical example — that a number of Ludwig van Beethoven's greatest works, including the Ninth Symphony, were composed after he succumbed to total deafness.

PSYCHOLOGICAL STRATEGIES

Given the enormous influence that Sigmund Freud's psychoanalytic theories have had on twentieth-century interpretations of human behavior, it is nearly inevitable that most people have some familiarity with his ideas concerning dreams, unconscious desires, and sexual repression, as well as his terms for different aspects of the psyche — the id, ego, and superego. Psychological approaches to literature draw upon Freud's theories and other psychoanalytic theories to understand more fully the text, the writer, and the reader. Critics use such approaches to explore the motivations of characters and the symbolic meanings of events, while biographers speculate about a writer's own motivations — conscious or unconscious — in a literary work. Psychological approaches are also used to describe and analyze the reader's personal responses to a text.

Although it is not feasible to explain psychoanalytic terms and concepts in so brief a space as this, it is possible to suggest the nature of a psychological approach. It is a strategy based heavily on the idea of the existence of a human unconscious — those impulses, desires, and feelings about which a person is unaware but which influence emotions and behavior.

Central to a number of psychoanalytic critical readings is Freud's concept of what he called the *Oedipus complex,* a term derived from Sophocles' tragedy *Oedipus the King.* This complex is predicated on a boy's unconscious rivalry with his father for his mother's love and his desire to eliminate his father in order to take his father's place with his mother. The female version of the psychological conflict is known as the *Electra complex,* a term used to describe a daughter's unconscious rivalry for her father. The name comes from a Greek legend about Electra, who avenged the death of her father, Agamemnon, by killing her mother. In *The Interpretation of Dreams,* Freud explains why *Oedipus the King* "moves a modern audience no less than it did the contemporary Greek one." What unites their powerful attraction to the play is an unconscious response:

> There must be something which makes a voice within us ready to recognize the compelling force of destiny in the *Oedipus.* . . . His destiny moves us only because it might have been ours — because the oracle laid the same curse upon us before our birth as upon him. It is the fate of all of us, perhaps, to direct our first sexual impulse towards our mother and our first hatred and our first murderous wish against our father. Our dreams convince us that this is so. King Oedipus, who slew his father Láius and married his mother Jocasta, merely shows us the fulfillment of

our own childhood wishes . . . and we shrink back from him with the whole force of the repression by which those wishes have since that time been held down within us.

In this passage Freud interprets the unconscious motives of Sophocles in writing the play, Oedipus in acting within it, and the audience in responding to it.

A further application of the Oedipus complex can be observed in a classic interpretation of *Hamlet* by Ernest Jones, who used this concept to explain why Hamlet delays in avenging his father's death. This reading has been tightly summarized by Norman Holland, a recent psychoanalytic critic, in *The Shakespearean Imagination*. Holland shapes the issues into four major components:

> One, people over the centuries have been unable to say why Hamlet delays in killing the man who murdered his father and married his mother. Two, psychoanalytic experience shows that every child wants to do just exactly that. Three, Hamlet delays because he cannot punish Claudius for doing what he himself wished to do as a child and, unconsciously, still wishes to do: he would be punishing himself. Four, the fact that this wish is unconscious explains why people could not explain Hamlet's delay.

Although the Oedipus complex is, of course, not relevant to all psychological interpretations of literature, interpretations involving this complex do offer a useful example of how psychoanalytic critics tend to approach a text.

The situation in Frost's "Mending Wall" is not directly related to an Oedipus complex, but the poem has been read as a conflict in which the "father's saying" represents the repressiveness of a patriarchal order that challenges the speaker's individual poetic consciousness. "Mending Wall" has also been read as another kind of struggle with repression. In "Up against the 'Mending Wall': The Psychoanalysis of a Poem by Frost" Edward Jayne offers a detailed reading of the poem as "the overriding struggle to suppress latent homosexual attraction between two men separated by a wall" (*College English* 1973). Jayne reads the poem as the working out of "unconscious homosexual inclinations largely repugnant to Frost and his need to divert and sublimate them." Regardless of whether or not a reader finds these arguments convincing, it is clear that the poem does have something to do with powerful forms of repression. And what about the reader's response? How might a psychological approach account for different responses from readers who argue that the poem calls for either a world that includes walls or one that dismantles them? One needn't be versed in psychoanalytic terms to entertain this question.

HISTORICAL STRATEGIES

Historians sometimes use literature as a window onto the past, because literature frequently provides the nuances of an historic period that cannot be readily perceived through other sources. The characters in Harriet Beecher Stowe's novel *Uncle Tom's Cabin* (1852) display, for example, a complex set of white attitudes toward blacks in mid-nineteenth-century America that is absent from more traditional historic documents such as census statistics or state laws. Another way of approaching the relationship between literature and history, however, is to use history as a means of understanding a literary work more clearly. The plot pattern of pursuit, escape, and capture in nineteenth-century slave narratives had a significant influence on Stowe's plotting of action in *Uncle Tom's Cabin*. This relationship demonstrates that the writing contemporary to an author is an important element of the history that helps to shape a work.

Literary historians shift the emphasis from the period to the work. Hence a literary historian might also examine mid-nineteenth-century abolitionist attitudes toward blacks to determine whether Stowe's novel is representative of those views or significantly to the right or left of them. Such a study might even indicate how closely the book reflects racial attitudes of twentieth-century readers. A work of literature may transcend time to the extent that it addresses the concerns of readers over a span of decades or centuries, but it remains for the literary historian a part of the past in which it was composed, a past that can reveal more fully a work's language, ideas, and purposes.

Literary historians move beyond both the facts of an author's personal life and the text itself to the social and intellectual currents in which the author composed the work. They place the work in the context of its time (as do many critical biographers who write "life and times" studies), and sometimes they make connections with other literary works that may have influenced the author. The basic strategy of literary historians is to illuminate the historic background in order to shed light on some aspect of the work itself.

In Hemingway's "Soldier's Home" we learn that Krebs had been at Belleau Wood, Soissons, the Champagne, St. Mihiel, and the Argonne. Although nothing is said of these battles in the story, they were among the most bloody battles of the war; the wholesale butchery and staggering casualties incurred by both sides make credible the way Krebs's unstated but lingering memories have turned him into a psychological prisoner of war. Knowing something about the ferocity of those battles helps us account for Krebs's response in the story. Moreover, we can more fully appreciate Hemingway's refusal to have Krebs lie about the realities of war for the folks back home if we are aware of the numerous poems, stories, and plays published during World War I that presented war as a glorious, manly, transcendent sacrifice for God and country. Juxtaposing those works with "Soldier's Home" brings the differences into sharp focus.

Similarly, a reading of William Blake's poem "London" (p. 76) is less complete if we do not know of the horrific social conditions — the poverty, disease, exploitation, and hypocrisy — that characterized the city Blake laments in the late eighteenth century.

One last example: The potential historical meaning of the wall that is the subject of Frost's "Mending Wall" might be more distinctly seen if it is placed in the context of its publication date, 1914, when the world was on the verge of collapsing into the violent political landscape of World War I. The insistence that "Good fences make good neighbors" suggests a grim ironic tone in the context of European nationalist hostilities that seemed to be moving inexorably toward war. The larger historical context for the poem would have been more apparent to its readers contemporary with World War I, but a historical reconstruction of the horrific tensions produced by shifting national borders and shattered walls during the war can shed some light on the larger issues that may be at stake in the poem. Moreover, an examination of Frost's attitudes toward the war and America's potential involvement in it could help to produce a reading of the meaning and value of a world with or without walls.

Since the 1960s a development in historical approaches to literature known as *New Historicism* has emphasized the interaction between the historic context of a work and a modern reader's understanding and interpretation of the work. In contrast to many traditional literary historians, however, New Historicists attempt to describe the culture of a period by reading many different kinds of texts that traditional historians might have previously left for sociologists and anthropologists. New Historicists attempt to read a period in all its dimensions, including political, economic, social, and aesthetic concerns. These considerations could be used to explain something about the nature of rural New England life early in the twentieth century. The process of mending the stone wall authentically suggests how this tedious job simultaneously draws the two men together and keeps them apart. Pamphlets and other contemporary writings about farming and maintaining property lines could offer insight into either the necessity or the uselessness of the spring wall-mending rituals. A New Historicist might find useful how advice offered in texts about running a farm reflect or refute the speaker's or neighbor's competing points of view in the poem.

New Historicist criticism acknowledges more fully than traditional historical approaches the competing nature of readings of the past and thereby tends to offer new emphases and perspectives. New Historicism reminds us that there is not only one historic context for "Mending Wall." The year before Frost died, he visited Moscow as a cultural ambassador from the United States. During this 1962 visit — only one year after the Soviet Union's construction of the Berlin Wall — he read "Mending Wall" to his Russian audience. Like the speaker in that poem, Frost clearly enjoyed the "mischief" of that moment, and a New Historicist would clearly find intriguing the way the poem was both intended and received in so volatile a context. By emphasizing that historical perceptions are governed, at least in part, by our own concerns and preoccupations, New Historicists sensitize us to the fact that the history on which we choose to focus is colored by being reconstructed from our own present moment. This reconstructed history affects our reading of texts.

(See "A New Historical Approach to Keats's 'Ode on a Grecian Urn'" by Brook Thomas (p. 549) for an example of this type of criticism.)

SOCIOLOGICAL STRATEGIES, INCLUDING MARXIST AND FEMINIST STRATEGIES

Sociological approaches examine social groups, relationships, and values as they are manifested in literature. These approaches necessarily overlap historical analyses, but sociological approaches to a work emphasize more specifically the nature and effect of the social forces that shape power relationships among groups or classes of people. Such readings treat literature as either a document reflecting social conditions or a product of those conditions. The former view brings into focus the social milieu; the latter emphasizes the work. A sociological reading of Arthur Miller's drama *Death of a Salesman* might, for instance, discuss how the characters' efforts to succeed reflect an increasingly competitive twentieth-century urban sensibility in America. Or it might emphasize how the "American Dream" of success shapes Willy Loman's aspirations and behavior. Clearly, there are numerous ways to talk about the societal aspects of a work. Two sociological strategies that have been especially influential are Marxist and feminist approaches.

Marxist Criticism

Marxist readings developed from the heightened interest in radical reform during the 1930s, when many critics looked to literature as a means of furthering proletarian social and economic goals, based largely on the writings of Karl Marx. *Marxist critics* focus on the ideological content of a work — its explicit and implicit assumptions and values about matters such as culture, race, class, and power. Marxist studies typically aim at not only revealing and clarifying ideological issues but also correcting social injustices. Some Marxist critics have used literature to describe the competing socioeconomic interests that too often advance capitalist money and power rather than socialist morality and justice. They argue that criticism, like literature, is essentially political because it either challenges or supports economic oppression. Even if criticism attempts to ignore class conflicts, it is politicized, according to Marxists, because it supports the status quo.

It is not surprising that Marxist critics pay more attention to the content and themes of literature than to its form. A Marxist critic would more likely be concerned with the exploitive economic forces that cause Willy Loman to feel trapped in Miller's *Death of a Salesman* than with the playwright's use of nonrealistic dramatic techniques to reveal Loman's inner thoughts. Similarly, a Marxist reading of Frost's "Mending Wall" might draw upon the poet's well-known conservative criticisms of President Franklin Delano Roosevelt's New Deal during the 1930s as a means of reading conservative ideology into the poem. Frost's deep suspicions of collective enterprise might suggest to a Marxist that the wall represents the status quo, that is, a capitalist construction that unnaturally divides individuals (in this case, the poem's speaker from his neighbor) and artificially defies nature. Complicit in their own oppression, both farmers, to a lesser and greater degree, accept the idea that "good fences make good neighbors," thereby maintaining and perpetuating an unnatural divisive order that oppresses and is mistakenly perceived as necessary and beneficial. A Marxist reading would see the speaker's and neighbor's conflicts as not only an individual issue but part of a larger class struggle.

Feminist Criticism

Feminist critics would also be interested in examining the status quo in "Mending Wall," because they seek to correct or supplement what they regard as a predominantly male-dominated critical perspective with a feminist consciousness. Like other forms of sociological criticism, feminist criticism places literature in a social context, and, like those of Marxist criticism, its analyses often have sociopolitical purposes, purposes that might explain, for example, how images of women in literature reflect the patriarchal social forces that have impeded women's efforts to achieve full equality with men.

Feminists have analyzed literature by both men and women in an effort to understand literary representations of women as well as the writers and cultures that create them. Related to concerns about how gender affects the way men and women write about each other is an interest in whether women use language differently from the way men do. Consequently, feminist critics' approach to literature is characterized by the use of a broad range of disciplines, including history, sociology, psychology, and linguistics, to provide a perspective sensitive to feminist issues.

A feminist approach to Frost's "Mending Wall" might initially appear to offer few possibilitiess given that no women appear in the poem and that no mention or allusion is made about women. And that is precisely the point: the landscape presented in the poem is devoid of women. Traditional gender roles are evident in the poem because it is men, not women, who work outdoors building walls and who discuss the significance of their work. For a feminist critic, the wall might be read as a symbol of patriarchal boundaries that are defined exclusively by men. If the wall can be seen as a manifestation of the status quo built upon the "father's saying[s]," then mending the wall each year and keeping everything essentially the same — with women securely out of the picture — essentially benefits the established patriarchy. The boundaries are reconstructed and rationalized in the absence of any woman's potential efforts to offer an alternative to the boundaries imposed by the men's rebuilding of the wall. Perhaps one way of considering the value of a feminist perspective on this work can be discerned if a reader imagines the speaker or the neighbor as a woman and how that change might extend the parameters of their conversation about the value of the wall.

MYTHOLOGICAL STRATEGIES

Mythological approaches to literature attempt to identify what in a work creates deep universal responses in readers. Whereas psychological critics interpret the symbolic meanings of characters and actions in order to understand more fully the unconscious dimensions of an author's mind, a character's motivation, or a reader's response, mythological critics (also frequently referred to as archetypal critics) interpret the hopes, fears, and expectations of entire cultures.

In this context myth is not to be understood simply as referring to stories about imaginary gods who perform astonishing feats in the causes of love, jealousy, or hatred. Nor are myths to be judged as merely erroneous, primitive accounts of how nature runs its course and humanity its affairs. Instead, literary critics use myths as a strategy for understanding how human beings try to account for their lives symbolically. Myths can be a window onto a culture's deepest perceptions about itself, because myths attempt to explain what otherwise seems unexplainable: a people's origin, purpose, and destiny.

All human beings have a need to make sense of their lives, whether they are concerned about their natural surroundings, the seasons, sexuality, birth, death, or the very meaning of existence. Myths help people organize their experiences; these systems of belief (less formally held than religious or political tenets but no less important) embody a culture's assumptions and values. What is important to the mythological critic is not the validity or truth of those assumptions and values; what matters is that they reveal common human concerns.

It is not surprising that although the details of mythic stories vary enormously, the essential patterns are often similar, because these myths attempt to explain universal experiences. There are, for example, numerous myths that redeem humanity from permanent death through a hero's resurrection and rebirth. For Christians the resurrection of Jesus symbolizes the ultimate defeat of death and coincides with the rebirth of nature's fertility in spring. Features of this rebirth parallel the Greek myths of Adonis and Hyacinth, who die but are subsequently transformed into living flowers;

there are also similarities that connect these stories to the reincarnation of the Indian Buddha or the rebirth of the Egyptian Osiris. To be sure, important differences exist among these stories, but each reflects a basic human need to limit the power of death and to hope for eternal life.

Mythological critics look for underlying, recurrent patterns in literature that reveal universal meanings and basic human experiences for readers regardless of when or where they live. The characters, images, and themes that symbolically embody these meanings and experiences are called *archetypes.* This term designates universal symbols, which evoke deep and perhaps unconscious responses in a reader because archetypes bring with them the heft of our hopes and fears since the beginning of human time. Surely one of the most powerfully compelling archetypes is the death/rebirth theme that relates the human life cycle to the cycle of the seasons. Many others could be cited and would be exhausted only after all human concerns were catalogued, but a few examples can suggest some of the range of plots, images, and characters addressed.

Among the most common literary archetypes are stories of quests, initiations, scapegoats, meditative withdrawals, descents to the underworld, and heavenly ascents. These stories are often filled with archetypal images: bodies of water that may symbolize the unconscious or eternity or baptismal rebirth; rising suns, suggesting reawakening and enlightenment; setting suns, pointing toward death; colors such as green, evocative of growth and fertility, or black, indicating chaos, evil, and death. Along the way are earth mothers, fatal women, wise old men, desert places, and paradisal gardens. No doubt your own reading has introduced you to any number of archetypal plots, images, and characters.

Mythological critics attempt to explain how archetypes are embodied in literary works. Employing various disciplines, these critics articulate the power a literary work has over us. Some critics are deeply grounded in classical literature, whereas others are more conversant with philology, anthropology, psychology, or cultural history. Whatever their emphases, however, mythological critics examine the elements of a work in order to make larger connections that explain the work's lasting appeal.

A mythological reading of Sophocles' *Oedipus the King,* for example, might focus on the relationship between Oedipus's role as a scapegoat and the plague and drought that threaten to destroy Thebes. The city is saved and the fertility of its fields restored only after the corruption is located in Oedipus. His subsequent atonement symbolically provides a kind of rebirth for the city. Thus, the plot recapitulates ancient rites in which the well-being of a king was directly linked to the welfare of his people. If a leader were sick or corrupt, he had to be replaced in order to guarantee the health of the community.

A similar pattern can be seen in the rottenness that Shakespeare exposes in Hamlet's Denmark. *Hamlet* reveals an archetypal pattern similar to that of *Oedipus the King*: not until the hero sorts out the corruption in his world and in himself can vitality and health be restored in his world. Hamlet avenges his father's death and becomes a scapegoat in the process. When he fully accepts his responsibility to set things right, he is swept away along with the tide of intrigue and corruption that has polluted life in Denmark. The new order — established by Fortinbras at the play's end — is achieved precisely because Hamlet is willing and finally able to sacrifice himself in a necessary purgation of the diseased state.

These kinds of archetypal patterns exist potentially in any literary period. Frost's "Mending Wall," for example, is set in spring, an evocative season that marks the end of winter and earth's renewal. The action in the poem, however, does not lead to a celebration of new life and human community; instead there is for the poem's speaker and his neighbor an annual ritual to "set the wall between us as we go" that separates and divides human experience rather than unifying it. We can see that the rebuilding of the wall runs counter to nature itself because the stones are so round that "We have to use a spell to make them balance." The speaker also resists the wall and sets out to subvert it by toying with the idea of challenging his neighbor's assumption that "good fences make good neighbors," a seemingly ancient belief passed down through one "father's saying" to the next. The speaker, however, does not heroically overcome the neighbor's ritual; he merely points out that the wall is not needed where it is. The speaker's acquiescence results in the continuation of a ritual that confirms the old order rather than overthrowing the "old-stone savage," who demands the dark isolation and separatenesss associated with the "gaps" produced by winter's frost. The neighbor's old order prevails in spite of nature's and the speaker's protestations. From a mythological critic's perspective, the wall might itself be seen as a "gap," an unnatural disruption of nature and the human community.

READER-RESPONSE STRATEGIES

Reader-response criticism, as its name implies, focuses its attention on the reader rather than the work itself. This approach to literature describes what goes on in the reader's mind during the process of reading a text. In a sense, all critical approaches (especially psychological and mythological criticism) concern themselves with a reader's response to literature, but there is a stronger emphasis in reader-response criticism on the reader's active construction of the text. Although many critical theories inform reader-response criticism, all *reader-response critics* aim to describe the reader's experience of a work: in effect we get a reading of the reader, who comes to the work with certain expectations and assumptions, which are either met or not met. Hence the consciousness of the reader — produced by reading the work — is the subject matter of reader-response critics. Just as writing is a creative act, reading is, since it also produces a text.

Reader-response critics do not assume that a literary work is a finished product with fixed formal properties, as, for example, formalist critics do. Instead, the literary work is seen as an evolving creation of the reader's as he or she processes characters, plots, images, and other elements while reading. Some reader-response critics argue that this act of creative reading is, to a degree, controlled by the text, but it can produce many interpretations of the same text by different readers. There is no single definitive reading of a work, because the crucial assumption is that readers create rather than discover meanings in texts. Readers who have gone back to works they had read earlier in their lives often find that a later reading draws very different responses from them. What earlier seemed unimportant is now crucial; what at first seemed central is now barely worth noting. The reason, put simply, is that two different people have read the same text. Reader-response critics are not after the "correct" reading of the text or what the author presumably intended; instead they are interested in the reader's experience with the text.

These experiences change with readers; although the text remains the same, the readers do not. Social and cultural values influence readings, so that, for example, an avowed Marxist would be likely to come away from Miller's *Death of a Salesman* with a very different view of American capitalism than that of, say, a successful sales representative, who might attribute Willy Loman's fall more to his character than to the American economic system. Moreover, readers from different time periods respond differently to texts. An Elizabethan — concerned perhaps with the stability of monarchical rule — might respond differently to Hamlet's problems than would a twentieth-century reader well versed in psychology and concepts of what Freud called the Oedipus complex. This is not to say that anything goes, that Miller's play can be read as an amoral defense of cheating and rapacious business practices or that *Hamlet* is about the dangers of living away from home. The text does, after all, establish some limits that allow us to reject certain readings as erroneous. But reader-response critics do reject formalist approaches that describe a literary work as a self-contained object, the meaning of which can be determined without reference to any extrinsic matters, such as the social and cultural values assumed by either the author or the reader.

Reader-response criticism calls attention to how we read and what influences our readings. It does not attempt to define what a literary work means on the page but rather what it does to an informed reader, a reader who understands the language and conventions used in a given work. Reader-response criticism is not a rationale for mistaken or bizarre readings of works but an exploration of the possibilities for a plurality of readings shaped by the readers' experience with the text. This kind of strategy can help us understand how our responses are shaped by both the text and ourselves.

Frost's "Mending Wall" illustrates how reader-response critical strategies read the reader. Among the first readers of the poem in 1914, those who were eager to see the United States enter World War I might have been inclined to see the speaker as an imaginative thinker standing up for freedom rather than antiquated boundaries and sensibilities that don't know what they are "walling in or walling out." But for someone whose son could be sent to the trenches of France to fight the Germans, the phrase "Good fences make good neighbors" might sound less like an unthinking tradition and more like solid, prudent common sense. In each instance the reader's circumstances could have an effect upon his or her assessment of the value of walls and fences. Certainly the Russians who listened to Frost's reading of "Mending Wall" in 1962, only one year after the construction of the Berlin Wall, had a very different response from the Americans who heard about Frost's reading and who relished the discomfort they thought the reading had caused the Russians.

By imagining different readers we can imagine a variety of responses to the poem that are influenced by the readers' own impressions, memories, or experiences. Such imagining suggests the ways in which reader-response criticism opens up texts to a number of interpretations. As one final example, consider how readers' responses to "Mending Wall" would be affected if it were printed in two different magazines, read in the context of either *Farmer's Almanac* or *The New Yorker*. What assumptions and beliefs would each magazine's readership be likely to bring to the poem? How do you think the respective experiences and values of each magazine's readers would influence their readings?

DECONSTRUCTIONIST STRATEGIES

Deconstructionist critics insist that literary works do not yield fixed, single meanings. They argue that there can be no absolute knowledge about anything because language can never say what we intend it to mean. Anything we write conveys meanings we did not intend, so the deconstructionist argument goes. Language is not a precise instrument but a power whose meanings are caught in an endless web of possibilities that cannot be untangled. Accordingly, any idea or statement that insists on being understood separately can ultimately be "deconstructed" to reveal its relations and connections to contradictory and opposite meanings.

Unlike other forms of criticism, deconstructionism seeks to destabilize meanings instead of establishing them. In contrast to formalists such as the New Critics, who closely examine a work in order to call attention to how its various components interact to establish a unified whole, deconstructionists try to show how a close examination of the language in a text inevitably reveals conflicting, contradictory impulses that "deconstruct" or break down its apparent unity.

Although deconstructionists and New Critics both examine the language of a text closely, deconstructionists focus on the gaps and ambiguities that reveal a text's instability and indeterminacy, whereas New Critics look for patterns that explain how the text's fixed meaning is structured. Deconstructionists painstakingly examine the competing meanings within the text rather than attempting to resolve them into a unified whole.

The questions deconstructionists ask are aimed at discovering and describing how a variety of possible readings are generated by the elements of a text. In contrast to a New Critic's concerns about the ultimate meaning of a work, a deconstructionist's primary interest is in how the use of language — diction, tone, metaphor, symbol, and so on — yields only provisional, not definitive, meanings. Consider, for example, the following excerpt from an American Puritan poet, Anne Bradstreet. The excerpt is from "The Flesh and the Spirit" (1678), which consists of an allegorical debate between two sisters, the body and the soul. During the course of the debate, Flesh, a consummate materialist, insists that Spirit values ideas that do not exist and that her faith in idealism is both unwarranted and insubstantial in the face of the material values that earth has to offer — riches, fame, and physical pleasure. Spirit, however, rejects the materialistic worldly argument that the only ultimate reality is physical reality and pledges her faith in God:

> Mine eye doth pierce the heavens and see
> What is invisible to thee.
> My garments are not silk nor gold,
> Nor such like trash which earth doth hold,
> But royal robes I shall have on,
> More glorious than the glist'ring sun;
> My crown not diamonds, pearls, and gold,
> But such as angels' heads enfold
> The city where I hope to dwell,
> There's none on earth can parallel;
> The stately walls both high and strong,
> Are made of precious jasper stone;
> The gates of pearl, both rich and clear,
> And angels are for porters there;
> The streets thereof transparent gold,
> Such as no eye did e'er behold;
> A crystal river there doth run,
> Which doth proceed from the Lamb's throne.

A deconstructionist would point out that Spirit's language — her use of material images such as jasper stone, pearl, gold, and crystal — cancels the explicit meaning of the passage by offering a supermaterialistic reward to the spiritually faithful. Her language, in short, deconstructs her intended meaning by employing the same images that Flesh would use to describe the rewards of the physical world. A deconstructionist reading, then, reveals the impossibility of talking about the invisible and spiritual worlds without using materialistic (that is, metaphoric) language. Thus Spirit's very language demonstrates a contradiction and conflict in her conviction that the world of here and now must be rejected for the hereafter. Her language deconstructs her meaning.

Deconstructionists look for ways to question and extend the meanings of a text. In Frost's "Mending Wall," for example, the speaker presents himself as being on the side of the imaginative rather than hidebound, rigid responses to life. He seems to value freedom and openness rather than restrictions and narrowly defined limits. Yet his treatment of his Yankee farmer neighbor can be read as condescending and even smug in its superior attitude toward his neighbor's repeating his "father's saying," as if he were "an old-stone savage armed." This condescending attitude hardly suggests a robust sense of community and shared humanity. Moreover, for all the talk about unnecessary conventions and traditions, a deconstructionist would likely be quick to point out that Frost writes the poem in blank verse — unrhymed iambic pentameter — rather than free verse; hence the very regular rhythms of the narrator's speech may be seen to deconstruct its liberationist meaning.

As difficult as it is controversial, deconstructionism is not easily summarized or paraphrased. For an example of deconstructionism in practice and how it differs from New Criticism, see Andrew P. Debicki's "New Criticism and Deconstructionism: Two Attitudes in Teaching Poetry" in Perspectives (p. 546).

SELECTED BIBLIOGRAPHY

Canonical Issues

"The Changing Culture of the University." Special Issue. *Partisan Review* 58 (Spring 1991): 185–410.

Gates, Henry Louis, Jr. *The Signifying Monkey.* New York: Oxford UP, 1988.

Lauter, Paul. *Canons and Contexts.* New York: Oxford UP, 1991.

"The Politics of Liberal Education." Special Issue. *South Atlantic Quarterly* 89 (Winter 1990): 1–234.

Sykes, Charles J. *The Hollow Men: Politics and Corruption in Higher Education.* Washington, D.C.: Regnery Gateway, 1990.

Formalist Strategies

Brooks, Cleanth. *The Well Wrought Urn: Studies in the Structure of Poetry.* New York: Reynal and Hitchcock, 1947.

Crane, Ronald Salmon. *The Languages of Criticism and the Structure of Poetry.* Toronto: U of Toronto P, 1953.

Eliot, Thomas Stearns. *The Sacred Wood: Essays in Poetry and Criticism.* London: Methuen, 1920.

Fekete, John. *The Critical Twilight: Explorations in the Ideology of Anglo-American Literary Theory from Eliot to McLuhan.* London: Routledge, 1977.

Lemon, Lee T., and Marion J. Reis, eds. *Russian Formalist Criticism: Four Essays.* Lincoln: U of Nebraska P, 1965.

Ransom, John Crowe. *The New Criticism.* Norfolk, CT: New Directions, 1941.

Wellek, Rene, and Austin Warren. *Theory of Literature.* New York: Harcourt, Brace and World, 1949.

Biographical and Psychological Strategies

Bleich, David. *Subjective Criticism.* Baltimore: Johns Hopkins UP, 1978.

Bloom, Harold. *The Anxiety of Influence.* New York: Oxford UP, 1975.

Felman, Shoshana. *Writing and Madness (Literature/Philosophy/Psychoanalysis).* Ithaca: Cornell UP, 1985.

Felman, Shoshana, ed. *Literature and Psychoanalysis: The Question of Reading: Otherwise.* Baltimore: Johns Hopkins UP, 1981.

Freud, Sigmund. *The Standard Edition of the Complete Psychological Works.* 24 vols. 1940–1968. London: Hogarth Press and the Institute of Psychoanalysis, 1953.

Holland, Norman. *The Dynamics of Literary Response.* New York: Oxford UP, 1968.

Jones, Ernest. *Hamlet and Oedipus.* New York: Doubleday, 1949.

Lesser, Simon O. *Fiction and the Unconscious.* Chicago: U of Chicago P, 1957.

Skura, Meredith Anne. *The Literary Use of the Psychoanalytic Process.* New Haven: Yale UP, 1981.

Historical and New Historicist Strategies

Dollimore, Jonathan. *Radical Tragedy: Religion, Ideology and Power in the Drama of Shakespeare and His Contemporaries.* Brighton, Eng.: Harvester Press, 1984.

Geertz, Clifford. *The Interpretation of Cultures: Selected Essays.* New York: Basic Books, 1973.

Greenblatt, Stephen. *Renaissance Self-Fashioning: From More to Shakespeare.* Chicago: U of Chicago P, 1980.

Lindenberger, Herbert. *Historical Drama: The Relation of Literature and Reality.* Chicago: U of Chicago P, 1975.

McGann, Jerome. *The Beauty of Inflections: Literary Investigations in Historical Method and Theory.* Oxford: Clarendon P, 1985.

Tennenhouse, Leonard. *Power on Display: The Politics of Shakespeare's Genres.* New York: Methuen, 1986.

White, Hayden. *Tropics of Discourse: Essays in Cultural Criticism.* Baltimore: Johns Hopkins UP, 1978.

Sociological Strategies (Including Marxist and Feminist Strategies)

Adorno, Theodor. *Prisms: Cultural Criticism and Society.* 1955. London: Neville Spearman, 1967.

Beauvoir, Simone de. *The Second Sex.* Trans. H. M. Parshley. New York: Knopf, 1972. Trans. of *Le deuxième sexe.* Paris: Gallimard, 1949.

Benjamin, Walter. *Illuminations.* New York: Harcourt, Brace and World, 1968.

Benstock, Shari, ed. *Feminist Issues and Literary Scholarship.* Bloomington: Indiana UP, 1987.

Cixous, Hélène, and Catherine Clément. *The Newly Born Woman.* Trans. Betsy Wing. Minneapolis: U of Minnesota P, 1986.

Eagleton, Terry. *Criticism and Ideology: A Study in Marxist Literary Theory.* London: New Left Books, 1976.

Fetterley, Judith. *The Resisting Reader: A Feminist Approach to American Fiction.* Bloomington: Indiana UP, 1978.

Frow, John. *Marxist and Literary History.* Cambridge: Harvard UP, 1986.

Gilbert, Sandra M., and Susan Gubar. *The Madwoman in the Attic: The Woman Writer and the Nineteenth-Century Literary Imagination.* New Haven: Yale UP, 1979.

Irigaray, Luce. *This Sex Which Is Not One.* Ithaca: Cornell UP, 1985. Trans. of *Ce sexe qui n'en est pas un.* Paris. Éditions de Minuit, 1977.

Jameson, Fredric. *The Political Unconscious: Studies in the Ideology of Form.* Ithaca: Cornell UP, 1979.

Kolodny, Annette. "Some Notes on Defining a 'Feminist Literary Criticism.'" *Critical Inquiry* 2 (1975): 75–92.

Lukács, Georg. *Realism in Our Time: Literature and the Class Struggle.* 1957. New York: Harper and Row, 1964.

Marx, Karl, and Fredrich Engels. *Marx and Engels on Literature and Art.* St. Louis: Telos Press, 1973.

Millet, Kate. *Sexual Politics.* New York: Avon Books, 1970.

Smith, Barbara. *Toward a Black Feminist Criticism.* New York: Out and Out Books, 1977.

Trotsky, Leon. *Literature and the Revolution.* 1924. Ann Arbor: U of Michigan P, 1960.

Williams, Raymond. *Marxism and Literature.* Oxford: Oxford UP, 1977.

Mythological Strategies

Bodkin, Maud. *Archetypal Patterns in Poetry.* London: Oxford UP, 1934.

Frye, Northrop. *Anatomy of Criticism: Four Essays.* Princeton: Princeton UP, 1957.

Jung, Carl Gustav. *Complete Works.* Eds. Herbert Read, Michael Fordham, and Gerhard Adler. 17 vols. New York: Pantheon, 1953.

Reader-Response Strategies

Booth, Wayne, C. *The Rhetoric of Fiction.* 2nd ed. Chicago: U of Chicago P, 1983.

Eco, Umberto. *The Role of the Reader: Explorations in the Semiotics of Texts.* Bloomington: Indiana UP, 1979.

Escarpit, Robert. *Sociology of Literature.* Painesville, Ohio: Lake Erie College P, 1965.

Fish, Stanley. *Is There a Text in This Class? The Authority of Interpretive Communities.* Cambridge: Harvard UP, 1980.

Freund, Elizabeth. *The Return of the Reader: Reader-Response Criticism.* London: Methuen, 1987.

Holland, Norman N. *5 Readers Reading.* New Haven: Yale UP, 1975.

Iser, Wolfgang. *The Implied Reader: Patterns of Communication in Prose Fiction from Bunyan to Beckett.* Baltimore: Johns Hopkins UP, 1974.

Jauss, Hans Robert. "Literary History as a Challenge to Literary Theory." *Toward an Aesthetics of Reception.* Trans. Timothy Bahti. Minneapolis: U of Minnesota P, 1982. pp. 3–46.

Rosenblatt, Louise. *Literature as Exploration.* 1938. New York: MLA, 1983.

Suleiman, Susan, and Inge Crosman, eds. *The Reader in the Text: Essays on Audience and Interpretation.* Princeton: Princeton UP, 1980.

Tompkins, Jane P., ed. *Reader-Response Criticism: From Formalism to Post-Structuralism.* Baltimore: Johns Hopkins UP, 1980.

Deconstructionist and Other Poststructuralist Strategies

Culler, Jonathan. *On Deconstruction: Theory and Criticism after Structuralism.* Ithaca: Cornell UP, 1982.

de Man, Paul. *Blindness and Insight.* New York: Oxford UP, 1971.

Derrida, Jacques. *Of Grammatology.* 1967. Baltimore: Johns Hopkins UP, 1976.

———. *Writing and Difference.* 1967. Chicago: U of Chicago P, 1978.

Foucault, Michel. *The Order of Things: An Archaeology of the Human Sciences.* 1966. London: Tavistock, 1970.

———. *Language, Counter-Memory, Practice.* Ithaca: Cornell UP, 1977.

Gasche, Rodolphe. "Deconstruction as Criticism." *Glyph* 6 (1979): 177–216.

Hartman, Geoffrey H. *Criticism in the Wilderness.* New Haven: Yale UP, 1980.

Johnson, Barbara. *The Critical Difference: Essays in the Contemporary Rhetoric of Reading.* Baltimore: Johns Hopkins UP, 1980.

Melville, Stephen W. *Philosophy beside Itself: On Deconstruction and Modernism.* Theory and History of Literature 27. Minneapolis: U of Minnesota P, 1986.

Said, Edward W. *The World, the Text, and the Critic.* Cambridge: Harvard UP, 1983.

Smith, Barbara Hernstein. *On the Margins of Discourse: The Relation of Literature to Language.* Chicago: U of Chicago P, 1979.

PERSPECTIVES ON CRITICAL READING

SUSAN SONTAG (b. 1933)
Against Interpretation 1964

Like the fumes of the automobile and of heavy industry which befoul the urban atmosphere, the effusion of interpretations of art today poisons our sensibilities. In a culture whose already classical dilemma is the hypertrophy of the intellect at the expense of energy and sensual capability, interpretation is the revenge of the intellect upon art.

Even more. It is the revenge of the intellect upon the world. To interpret is to impoverish, to deplete the world — in order to set up a shadow world of "meanings." It is to turn *the* world into *this* world. ("This world"! As if there were any other.)

The world, our world, is depleted, impoverished enough. Away with all duplicates of it, until we again experience more immediately what we have. . . .

In most modern instances, interpretation amounts to the philistine refusal to leave the work of art alone. Real art has the capacity to make us nervous. By reducing the work of art to its content and then interpreting *that,* one tames the work of art. Interpretation makes art manageable, conformable.

This philistinism of interpretation is more rife in literature than in any other art. For decades now, literary critics have understood it to be their task to translate the elements of the poem or play or novel or story into something else.

From *Against Interpretation*

Considerations for Critical Thinking and Writing

1. What are Sontag's objections to "interpretation"? Explain whether you agree or disagree with them.
2. In what sense does interpretation make art "manageable" and "conformable"?
3. In an essay explore what you take to be both the dangers of interpretation and its contributions to your understanding of literature.

STANLEY FISH (b. 1938)
On What Makes an Interpretation Acceptable   1980

. . . After all, while "The Tyger" is obviously open to more than one interpretation, it is not open to an infinite number of interpretations. There may be disagreements as to whether the tiger is good or evil, or whether the speaker is Blake or a persona, and so on, but no one is suggesting that the poem is an allegory of the digestive processes or that it predicts the Second World War, and its limited plurality is simply a testimony to the capacity of a great work of art to generate multiple readings. The point is one that Wayne Booth makes when he asks, "Are we *right* to rule out at least some readings?" and then answers his own question with a resounding yes. It would be my answer too; but the real question is what gives us the right so to be right. A pluralist is committed to saying that there is something in the text which rules out some readings and allows others (even though no one reading can ever capture the text's "inexhaustible richness and complexity"). His best evidence is that in practice "we all in fact" do reject unacceptable readings and that more often than not we agree on the readings that are not rejected. . . . Booth concludes that there are justified limits to what we can legitimately do with a text, for "surely we could not go on disputing at all if a core of agreement did not exist." Again, I agree, but if, as I have argued, the text is always a function of interpretation, then the text cannot be the location of the core of agreement by means of which we reject interpretations. We seem to be at an impasse: on the one hand there would seem to be no basis for labeling an interpretation unacceptable, but on the other we do it all the time.

This, however, is an impasse only if one assumes that the activity of interpretation is itself unconstrained; but in fact the shape of that activity is determined by the literary institution which at any one time will authorize only a finite number of interpretative strategies. Thus, while there is no core of agreement *in* the text, there is a core of agreement (although one subject to change) concerning the ways of *producing* the text. Nowhere is this set of acceptable ways written down, but it is a part of everyone's knowledge of what it means to be operating within the literary institution as it is now constituted. A student of mine recently demonstrated this knowledge when, with an air of giving away a trade secret, she confided that she could go into any classroom, no matter what the subject of the course, and win approval for running one of a number of well-defined interpretive routines: she could view the assigned text as an instance of the tension between nature and culture; she could look in the text for evidence of large mythological oppositions; she could argue that the true subject of the text was its own composition, or that in the guise of fashioning a narrative the speaker was fragmenting and displacing his own anxieties and fears. She could not . . . argue that the text was a prophetic message inspired by the ghost of her Aunt Tilly.

My student's understanding of what she could and could not get away with, of the unwritten rules of the literary game, is shared by everyone who plays that game, by those who write and judge articles for publication in learned journals, by those who read and listen to papers at professional meetings, by those who seek and award tenure in innumerable departments of English and comparative literature, by the armies of graduate students for whom knowledge of the rules is the real mark of professional initiation. This does not mean that these rules and the practices they authorize are either monolithic or stable. Within the literary community there are subcommunities. . . . In a classroom whose authority figures include David Bleich and Norman Holland, a student might very well relate a text to her memories of a favorite aunt, while in other classrooms, dominated by the spirit of [Cleanth] Brooks and [Robert Penn] Warren, any such activity would immediately be dismissed as nonliterary, as something that isn't done.

The point is that while there is always a category of things that are not done (it is simply the reverse or flip side of the category of things that *are* done), the membership in that category is continually changing. It changes laterally as one moves from subcommunity to subcommunity, and it changes through time when once interdicted interpretive strategies are admitted into the ranks of the acceptable. Twenty years ago one of the things that literary critics didn't do was talk about the reader, at least in a way that made his experience the focus of the critical act. The prohibition on such talk was largely the result of [W. K.] Wimsatt's and [Monroe] Beardsley's famous essay "The Affective Fallacy," which argued that the variability of readers renders any investigation of their responses ad-hoc and relativistic: "The poem itself," the authors complained, "as an object of specifically critical judgment, tends to disappear." So influential was this essay that it was possible for a reviewer to dismiss a book merely by finding in it evidence that the affective fallacy had been committed. The use of a juridical terminology is not accidental; this was in a very real sense a *legal* finding of activity in violation of understood and institutionalized decorums. Today, however, the affective fallacy, no longer a fallacy but a methodology, is committed all the time, and its practitioners have behind them the full and authorizing weight of a fully articulated institutional apparatus. The "reader in literature" is regularly the subject of forums and workshops at the convention of the Modern Language Association; there is a reader newsletter which reports on the multitudinous labors of a reader industry; any list of currently active schools of literary criticism includes the school of "reader response," and two major university presses have published collections of essays designed both to display the variety of reader-centered criticism (the emergence of factions within a once interdicted activity is a sure sign of its having achieved the status of an orthodoxy) and to detail its history. None of this of course means that a reader-centered criticism is now invulnerable to challenge or attack, merely that it is now recognized as a competing literary strategy that cannot be dismissed simply by being named. It is acceptable not because everyone accepts it but because those who do not are now obliged to argue against it.

From *Is There a Text in This Class?*

Considerations for Critical Thinking and Writing

1. Why *can't* William Blake's "The Tyger" (see p. 170) be read as "an allegory of the digestive processes"? What principle does Fish use to rule out such a reading?
2. What kinds of strategies for reading have you encountered in your classroom experiences? Which have you found to be the most useful? Explain why.
3. Write an essay that describes what you "could and could not get away with" in the literature courses you have taken in high school and college.

ANNETTE KOLODNY (b. 1941)
On the Commitments of Feminist Criticism   1980

If feminist criticism calls anything into question, it must be that dog-eared myth of intellectual neutrality. For what I take to be the underlying spirit or message of any consciously ideologically premised criticism — that is, that ideas are important *because* they determine the ways we live, or want to live, in the world — is vitiated by confining those ideas to the study, the classroom, or the pages of our books. To write chapters decrying the sexual stereotyping of women in our literaure, while closing our eyes to the sexual harassment of our women students and colleagues; to display Katharine Hepburn and Rosalind Russell in our courses on "The Image of the Independent Career Women in Film," while managing not to notice the paucity of female administrators on our own campus; to study the women who helped make universal enfranchisement a political reality, while keeping silent about our activist colleagues who are denied promotion or tenure; to include segments on "Women in the Labor Movement" in our American studies or women's studies courses, while remaining willfully ignorant of the department secretary fired for efforts to organize a clerical workers' union; to glory in the delusions of "merit," "privilege," and "status" which accompany campus life in order to insulate ourselves from the millions of women who labor in poverty — all this is not merely hypocritical; it destroys both the spirit and the meaning of what we are about.

From "Dancing through the Minefield: Some Observations on the Theory, Practice, and Politics of a Feminist Literary Criticism," *Feminist Studies,* 6, 1980

Considerations for Critical Thinking and Writing

1. Why does Kolodny reject "intellectual neutrality" as a "myth"? Explain whether you agree or disagree with her point of view.
2. Kolodny argues that feminist criticism can be used as an instrument for social reform. Discuss the possibility and desirability of her position. Do you think other kinds of criticism can and should be used to create social change?

ANDREW P. DEBICKI (b. 1934)
New Criticism and Deconstructionism: Two Attitudes in Teaching Poetry

1985

[Let's] look at the ways in which a New Critic and a deconstructivist might handle a poem. My first example, untitled, is a work by Pedro Salinas, which I first analyzed many years ago and which I have recently taught to a group of students influenced by deconstruction:

Sand: sleeping on the beach today
and tomorrow caressed
in the bosom of the sea:
the sun's today, water's prize tomorrow.
Softly you yield
to the hand that presses you
and go away with the first
courting wind that appears.
Pure and fickle sand,
changing and clear beloved,
I wanted you for my own,
and held you against my chest and soul.
But you escaped with the waves, the wind, the sun,
and I remained without a beloved,
my face turned to the wind which robbed her,
and my eyes to the far-off sea in which she had
green loves in a green shelter.

My original study of this poem, written very much in the New Critical tradition, focused on the unusual personification of sand as beloved and on the metaphorical pattern that it engendered. In the first part of the work, the physical elusiveness of sand (which slips through one's hand, flies with the wind, moves from shore to sea) evokes a coquettish woman, yielding to her lover and then escaping, running off with a personified wind, moving from one being to another. Watching these images, the reader gradually forgets that the poem is metaphorically describing sand and becomes taken up by the unusual correspondences with the figure of a flirting woman. When in the last part of the poem the speaker laments his loss, the reader is drawn into his lament for a fickle lover who has abandoned him.

Continuing a traditional analysis of this poem, we would conclude that its unusual personification/metaphor takes us beyond a literal level and leads us to a wider vision. The true subject of this poem is not sand, nor is it a flirt who tricks a man. The comparison between sand and woman, however, has made us feel the elusiveness of both, as well as the effect that this elusiveness has had on the speaker, who is left sadly contemplating it at the end of the poem. The poem has used its main image to embody a general vision of fleetingness and its effects.

My analysis, as developed thus far, is representative of a New Critical study. It focuses on the text and its central image, it describes a tension produced within the text, and it suggests a way in which this tension is resolved so as to move the poem beyond its literal level. In keeping with the tenets of traditional

546 Critical Strategies for Reading

analytic criticism, it shows how the poem conveys a meaning that is far richer than its plot or any possible conceptual message. But while it is careful not to reduce the poem to a simple idea or to an equivalent of its prose summary, it does attempt to work all of its elements into a single interpretation which would satisfy every reader . . . : it makes all of the poem's meanings reside in its verbal structures, and it suggests that those meanings can be discovered and combined into a single cohesive vision as we systematically analyze those structures.

By attempting to find a pattern that will incorporate and resolve the poem's tensions, however, this reading leaves some loose ends, which I noticed even in my New Critical perspective — and which I found difficult to explain. To see the poem as the discovery of the theme of fleetingness by an insightful speaker, we have to ignore the fanciful nature of the comparison, the whimsical attitude to reality that it suggests, and the excessively serious lament of the speaker, which is difficult to take at face value — he laments the loss of *sand* with the excessive emotion of a romantic lover! The last lines, with their evocation of the beloved/sand in an archetypal kingdom of the sea, ring a bit hollow. Once we notice all of this, we see the speaker as being somehow unreliable in his strong response to the situation. He tries too hard to equate the loss of sand with the loss of love, he paints himself as too much of a romantic, and he loses our assent when we realize that his rather cliché declarations are not very fitting. Once we become aware of the speaker's limitations, our perspective about the poem changes: we come to see its "meaning" as centered, not on the theme of fleetingness as such, but on a portrayal of the speaker's exaggerated efforts to embody this theme in the image of sand.

For the traditional New Critic, this would pose a dilemma. The reading of the poem as a serious embodiment of the theme of evanescence is undercut by an awareness of the speaker's unreliability. One can account for the conflict between readings, to some extent, by speaking of the poem's use of irony and by seeing a tension between the theme of evanescence and the speaker's excessive concern with an imaginary beloved (which blinds him to the larger issues presented by the poem). That still leaves unresolved, however, the poem's final meaning and effect. In class discussions, in fact, a debate between those students who asserted that the importance of the poem lay in its engendering the theme of fleetingness and those who noted the absurdity of the speaker often ended in an agreement that this was a "problem poem" which never resolved or integrated its "stresses" and its double vision. . . .

The deconstructive critic, however, would not be disturbed by a lack of resolution in the meanings of the poem and would use the conflict between interpretations as the starting point for further study. Noting that the view of evanescence produced by the poem's central metaphor is undercut by the speaker's unreliability, the deconstructive critic would explore the play of signification that the undercutting engenders. Calling into question the attempt to neatly define evanescence, on the one hand, and the speaker's excessive romanticism on the other, the poem would represent, for this critic, a creative confrontation of irresoluble visions. The image of the sand as woman, as well as the portrayal of the speaker, would represent a sort of "seam" in the text, an area of indeterminacy that would open the way to further readings. This image lets us

see the speaker as a sentimental poet, attempting unsuccessfully to define evanescence by means of a novel metaphor but getting trapped in the theme of lost
love, which he himself has engendered; it makes us think of the inadequacy of
language, of the ways in which metaphorical expression and the clichés of a love
lament can undercut each other.

Once we adopt such a deconstructivist perspective, we will find in the text
details that will carry forward our reading. The speaker's statement that he held
"her" against his "chest and his soul" underlines the conflict in his perspective:
it juggles a literal perspective (he rubs sand against himself) and a metaphorical
one (he reaches for his beloved), but it cannot fully combine them — "soul" is
ludicrously inappropriate in reference to the former. The reader, noting the
inappropriateness, has to pay attention to the inadequacy of language as used
here. All in all, by engendering a conflict between various levels and perspectives,
the poem makes us feel the incompleteness of any one reading, the way in
which each one is a "misreading" (not because it is wrong, but because it is
incomplete), and the creative lack of closure in the poem. By not being subject
to closure, in fact, this text becomes all the more exciting: its view of the
possibilities and limitations of metaphor, language, and perspective seems more
valuable than any static portrayal of "evanescence."

The analyses I have offered of this poem exemplify the different classroom
approaches that would be taken by a stereotypical New Critic, on the one hand,
and a deconstructive critic on the other. Imbued with the desire to come to an
overview of the literary work, the former will attempt to resolve its tensions
(and probably remain unsatisfied with the poem). Skeptical of such a possibility
and of the very existence of a definable "work," the latter will focus on the
tensions that can be found in the text as vehicles for multiple readings. Given
his or her attitude to the text, the deconstructive critic will not worry about
going beyond its "limits" (which really do not exist). This will allow, of course,
for more speculative readings; it will also lead to a discussion of ways in which
the text can be extended and "cured" in successive readings, to the fact that it
reflects on the process of its own creation, and to ways in which it will relate to
other texts.

From *Writing and Reading DIFFERENTLY: Deconstruction
and the Teaching of Composition and Literature,*
edited by G. Douglas Atkins and Michael L. Johnson

Considerations for Critical Thinking and Writing

1. Explain how the New Critical and deconstructionist approaches to the Salinas
   poem differ. What kinds of questions are raised by each? What elements of the
   poem are focused on in each approach?
2. Write an essay explaining which reading of the poem you find more interesting.
   In your opening paragraph define what you mean by "interesting."
3. Choose one of the critical strategies for reading discussed in this chapter and
   discuss Salinas's poem from that perspective.

BROOK THOMAS (b. 1947)
A New Historical Approach to Keats's
"Ode on a Grecian Urn"   1987

The traditional reception of the poem invites a discussion of its implied aesthetic. The poem's aesthetic is, however, intricately linked to its attitude to the past. The urn is, after all, Keats's "sylvan historian." To ask what sort of history a piece of art presents to us is, of course, to raise one of the central questions of historical criticism. It also opens up a variety of directions to take in historicizing the teaching of literature. . . .

To ask what history the urn relates to the reader easily leads to a discussion of how much our sense of the past depends upon art and the consequences of that dependency. These are important questions, because even if our students have little knowledge of the past or even interest in it, they do have an attitude toward it. A poem like Keats's "Ode" can help them reflect upon what that attitude is and on how it has been produced.

Such a discussion also offers a way to raise what critics have traditionally seen as the poem's central conflict: that between the temporal world of man and the atemporal world of art. The urn records two different visions of the past, both at odds with what we normally associate with historical accounts. On the one hand, it preserves a beauty that resists the destructive force of time. On the other, it records a quotidian scene populated by nameless people rather than the account of "famous" personages and "important" events our students often associate with traditional histories. Art, Keats seems to suggest, both keeps alive a sense of beauty in a world of change *and* gives us a sense of the felt life of the past. But in its search for a realm in which truth and beauty coexist, art risks freezing the "real" world and becoming a "cold pastoral," cut off from the very felt life it records. In dramatizing this conflict Keats's "Ode" allows students to see both art's power to keep the past alive and its tendency to distort it.

Chances are, however, that not all students share Keats's sense of the relationship between art and history. Rather than demonstrate their lack of "aesthetic appreciation," this difference can open up another direction to pursue in discussing the poem. To acknowledge a difference between our present attitude and the one embodied by Keats's poem is to call into question the conditions that have contributed to the changed attitude. Thus, if the first approach to the poem aims at having students reflect generally upon the influence art has on our attitude toward the past, this approach demands that we look at the specific historical conditions that help shape our general attitude toward both art and the past. In the case of the "Ode," this can lead to a discussion of the economic and political conditions of early nineteenth-century England that helped shape Keats's image of ancient Greece. On the one hand, there was England's self-image as the inheritor of ancient Greece's republican institutions and, on the other, a nostalgia for a harmonious pastoral world in contrast to the present state of industrialized, fragmented British society. Thus, the two versions of the past offered by Keats's sylvan historian — the aesthetic one in which harmony and beauty are preserved and the democratic one in which the life of everyday people is recorded — are related to specific historical conditions at the time Keats wrote. The challenge for our students — and for us — would be to speculate on how our attitudes towards art and history are shaped by our historical moment — how that moment is different from and similar to Keats's.

A third way to teach the poem historically is to concentrate on the urn itself as a historical as well as aesthetic object. "Where," we might ask our students, "would Keats have seen such an urn?" Most likely someone will respond, "A museum." If so, we are ready to discuss the phenomenon of the rise of the art museum in eighteenth- and nineteenth-century Europe, how cultural artifacts from the past were removed from their social setting and placed in museums to be contemplated as art. Seemingly taking us away from Keats's poem, such a discussion might be the best way to help our students understand Keats's aesthetic, for they will clearly see that in Keats's poem an urn that once had a practical social function now sparks aesthetic contemplation about the nature of truth, beauty, and the past. If we ask why the urn takes on this purely aesthetic function in a society that was increasingly practical, our students might start to glimpse how our modern notion of art has been defined in response to the social order.

To consider the urn a historical as well as an aesthetic object is also to raise political questions. For how, we might ask, did a Grecian urn (or the Elgin marbles, if we were to teach another Keats poem) end up in England in the first place? Such a question moves us from Keats's image of ancient Greece to a consideration of Greece in the early nineteenth century, and to how a number of Englishmen who sympathized with its struggle for liberation at the same time pillaged its cultural treasures and set them on display in London to advertise Britain's "advanced" cultural state. Thus, a very simple historical question about Keats's urn can force us to consider the political consequences of our cultural heritage. As Walter Benjamin warned, the cultural treasures that we so love have an origin we should not contemplate without horror: "They owe their existence not only to the efforts of the great minds and talents who have created them, but also to the anonymous toil of their contemporaries. There is no document of civilization which is not at the same time a document of barbarism" ("Theses on the Philosophy of History" in *Illuminations,* 256).

If we consider the task of historical scholarship to re-create the conditions of the past so that we can recover the author's original intention, the questions I have asked about Keats's "Ode" are not valid ones to ask. Clearly my questions are not primarily directed at recovering that intention. Instead, I am treating Keats's poem as social text, one that in telling us about the society that produced it also tells us about the society we inhabit today. This approach is not to say that we should completely abandon the effort to recover Keats's intention, but that, as in the case of formalist criticism, we need to go beyond the traditional historical scholar's efforts. We need to try both to reconstruct the author's intention — for instance, what Keats thought about art and history — and to read against the grain of his intention.

From "The Historical Necessities for — and Difficulties
with — New Historical Analysis in Introductory
Literature Courses," *College English,* September 1987

Considerations for Critical Thinking and Writing

1. Summarize the three historical approaches to "Ode on a Grecian Urn" (p. 237) Thomas describes. Which do you consider the most interesting? Explain why.
2. Write an essay that explores Thomas's claim that "a very simple historical question about the urn can force us to consider the political consequences of our cultural heritage."
3. Choose another poem from this anthology and treat it as a "social text." What kinds of questions can you ask about it that suggest the poem's historical significances?

HARRIET HAWKINS (b. 1939)
Should We Study King Kong *or* King Lear?   1988

> *There is nothing either good or bad, but thinking makes it so.*
> *— Hamlet*

> Troilus: *What's aught but as 'tis valued?*
> Hector: *But value dwells not in particular will:*
>   *It holds its estimate and dignity*
>   *As well wherein 'tis precious of itself*
>   *As in the prizer.*
>   *— Troilus and Cressida*

To what degree is great literature — or bad literature — an artificial category? Are there any good — or bad — reasons why most societies have given high status to certain works of art and not to others? Could Hamlet be right in concluding that there is *nothing* either good or bad but thinking — or criticial or ideological discourse — makes it so? Or are certain works of art so precious, so magnificent — or so trashy — that they obviously ought to be included in the canon or expelled from the classroom? So far as I know, there is not now any sign of a critical consensus on the correct answer to these questions either in England or in the United States.

In England there are, on the one hand, eloquent cases for the defense of the value of traditional literary studies, like Dame Helen Gardner's last book, *In Defence of the Imagination.* On the other hand, there are critical arguments insisting that what really counts is not what you read, but the way that you read it. You might as well study *King Kong* as *King Lear,* because what matters is not the script involved, but the critical or ideological virtues manifested in your own "reading" of whatever it is that you are reading. Reviewing a controversial book entitled *Re-Reading English,* the poet Tom Paulin gives the following account of the issues involved in the debate:

> The contributors are collectively of the opinion that English literature is a dying subject and they argue that it can be revived by adopting a "socialist pedagogy" and introducing into the syllabus "other forms of writing and cultural production than the canon of literature" . . . it is now time to challenge

"hierarchical" and "elitist" conceptions of literature and to demolish the bourgeois ideology which has been "naturalised" as literary value. . . . They wish to develop "a politics of reading" and to redefine the term "text" in order to admit newspaper reports, songs, and even mass demonstrations as subjects for tutorial discussion. Texts no longer have to be books: indeed, "it may be more democratic to study *Coronation Street* [England's most popular soap opera] than *Middlemarch*."

However one looks at these arguments, it seems indisputably true that the issues involved are of paramount critical, pedagogical, and social importance. There are, however, any number of different ways to look at the various arguments. So far as I am, professionally, concerned, they raise the central question, "Why should any of us still study, or teach, Shakespeare's plays (or *Paradise Lost* or *The Canterbury Tales*)?" After all, there are quite enough films, plays, novels, and poems being produced today (to say nothing of all those "other forms of writing," including literary criticism, that are clamoring for our attention) to satisfy anyone interested in high literature, or popular genres, or any form of "cultural production" whatsoever. They also raise the obviously reflexive question: "Assuming that all traditionally 'canonized' works were eliminated, overnight, from the syllabus of every English department in the world, would not comparable problems of priority, value, elitism, ideological pressure, authoritarianism, and arbitrariness almost(?) immediately arise with reference to *whatever* works — of whatsoever kind and nature — were substituted for them?"

If, say, the place on the syllabus currently assigned to *King Lear* were reassigned to *King Kong,* those of us currently debating the relative merits of the Quarto, the Folio, or a conflated version of *King Lear* would, *mutatis mutandis,°* have to decide whether to concentrate classroom attention on the "classic" version of *King Kong,* originally produced in 1933, or to focus on the 1974 remake (which by now has many ardent admirers of its own). Although classroom time might not allow the inclusion of both, a decision to exclude either version might well seem arbitrary or authoritarian and so give rise to grumbles about the "canon." Moreover, comparable questions of "canonization" might well arise with reference to other films excluded from a syllabus that included either version (or both versions) of *King Kong.* For example: why assign class time to *King Kong* and not to (say) *Slave Girls of the White Rhinoceros?* Who, if any, of us has the right to decide whether *King Lear* or *King Kong* or the *Slave Girls* should, or should not, be included on, or excluded from, the syllabus? And can the decision to include, or exclude, any one of them be made, by any one of us, on any grounds whatsoever that do *not* have to do with comparative merit, or comparative value judgments, or with special interests — that is, with the aesthetic or ideological priorities, preferences, and prejudices of the assigners of positions on whatever syllabus there is? And insofar as most, if not all, of our judgments and preferences are comparative, are they not, inevitably, hierarchical?

Is there, in fact, any form of endeavor or accomplishment known to the human race — from sport to ballet to jazz to cooking — wherein comparative standards of excellence comparable to certain "hierarchical" and "elitist" conceptions of literature are nonexistent? Even bad-film buffs find certain bad films more gloriously bad than others. And, perhaps significantly given its compara-

---

mutatis mutandis: Substituting different terms (Latin).

tively short lifetime, the avant-garde cinema has, by now, produced snobs to rival the most elitist literary critic who ever lived, such as the one who thus puts down a friend who likes ordinary Hollywood films:

> Ah that's all right for you, I know the sort you are, but give me a private job that's shot on faded sepia sixteen millimetre stock with non-professional actors . . . no story and dialogue in French *any day of the week.*

What is striking about this snob's assumption is how characteristic it is of a long tradition of critical elitism that has consistently sneered at popular genres (e.g., romance fiction, soap operas, horror films, westerns, etc.) that are tainted by the profit motive and so tend to "give the public what it wants" in the way of sentimentality, sensationalism, sex, violence, romanticism, and the like.

From *"King Lear* to *King Kong* and Back: Shakespeare and Popular Modern Genres" in *"Bad" Shakespeare: Revaluations of the Shakespeare Canon,* edited by Maurice Charney

Considerations for Critical Thinking and Writing

1. Do you agree or disagree that "great literature — or bad literature — [is] an artificial category"? Explain why.
2. Why would problems of "priority, value, elitism, ideological pressure, authoritarianism, and arbitrariness" probably become issues for evaluating any new works that replaced canonized works?
3. Write an essay in which you argue for (or against) studying popular arts (for example popular song lyrics) alongside the works of classic writers such as Shakespeare.

HENRY A. GIROUX (b. 1943)
The Canon and Liberal Arts Education   1990

In the current debate about the importance of constructing a particular canon, the notion of naming and transmitting from one generation to the next what can be defined as "cultural treasure" specifies what has become the central argument for reforming the liberal arts. For that reason, perhaps, it appears as though the debate were reducible to the question of the contents of course syllabi. The notion of critical pedagogy for which I am arguing provides a fundamental challenge to this position: it calls for an argument that transcends the limited focus on the canon, that recognizes the crisis in liberal arts education to be one of historical purpose and meaning, a crisis that challenges us to rethink in a critical fashion the relationship between the role of the university and the imperatives of a democracy in a mass society.

Historically, education in the liberal arts was conceived of as the essential preparation for governing, for ruling — more specifically, the preparation and outfitting of the governing *elite.* The liberal arts curriculum, composed of the "best" that had been said or written, was intended, as Elizabeth Fox-Genovese has observed, "to provide selected individuals with a collective history, culture, and epistemology so that they could run the world effectively."[1] In this context the canon was considered to be a possession of the dominant classes or groups. Indeed, the canon was fashioned as a safeguard to insure that the cultural property of such groups was passed on from generation to generation along with the family estates. Thus, in these terms it seems most appropriate that the literary canon should be subject to revision — as it has been before in the course of the expansion of democracy — such that it might also incorporate and reflect the experience and aspirations of the women, minorities, and children of the working class who have been entering the academy.

Conceived of in this way, a radical vision of liberal arts education is to be found within its elite social origins and purpose. But this does not suggest that the most important questions confronting liberal arts reform lie in merely establishing the content of the liberal arts canon on the model of the elite universities. Instead, the most important questions become [those] of reformulating the meaning and purpose of higher education in ways that contribute to the cultivation and regeneration of an informed citizenry capable of actively participating in the shaping and governing of a democratic society. Within this discourse, the pedagogical becomes political and the notion of a liberal arts canon commands a more historically grounded and critical reading. The pedagogical becomes more political in that it proposes that the way in which students engage and examine knowledge is just as important an issue as the choosing of texts to be used in a class or program. That is, a democratic notion of liberal education rejects those views of the humanities which would treat texts as sacred and instruction as merely transmission. This notion of the canon undermines the possibility for dialogue, argument, and critical thinking; it treats knowledge as a form of cultural inheritance that is beyond considerations regarding how it might be implicated in social practices that exploit, infantilize, and oppress. The canons we have inherited, in their varied forms, cannot be dismissed as simply part of the ideology of privilege and domination. Instead, the privileged texts of the dominant or official canons should be explored with respect to the important role they have played in shaping, for better or worse, the major events of our time. But there are also forms of knowledge that have been marginalized by the official canons. There are noble traditions, histories, and narratives that speak to important struggles by women, blacks, minorities, and other subordinate groups that need to be heard so that such groups can lay claim to their own voices as part of a process of both affirmation and inquiry. At issue here is a notion of pedagogy as a form of cultural politics that rejects a facile restoration of the past, that rejects history as a monologue. A critical pedagogy recognizes that history is constituted in dialogue and that some of the voices that make up that dialogue have been eliminated. Such a pedagogy calls for a public debate regarding the dominant memories and repressed stories that constitute the historical narratives of a social order: in effect, canon formation becomes a matter of both rewriting and reinterpreting the past; canon formation embodies the ongoing "process of reconstructing the 'collective reflexivity' of lived cultural experience . . . which recognizes that the 'notions of the past and future are essentially notions of the

[1]Elizabeth Fox-Genovese, "The Claims of a Common Culture: Gender, Race, Class and the Canon," *Salmagundi* 72 (Fall 1986): 133.

present.'"[2] In this case, such notions are central to the politics of identity and power, and to the memories that structure how experience is individually and collectively authorized and experienced as a form of cultural identity. . . .

A critical pedagogy also rejects a discourse of value neutrality. Without subscribing to a language that polices behavior and desire, it aims at developing pedagogical practices informed by an ethical stance that contests racism, sexism, class exploitation, and other dehumanizing and exploitative social relations as ideologies and social practices that disrupt and devalue public life. This is a pedagogy that rejects detachment, though it does not silence in the name of its own ideological fervor or correctness. It acknowledges social injustices, but examines with care and in dialogue with itself and others how such injustices work through the discourses, experiences, and desires that constitute daily life and the subjectivities of the students who invest in them. It is a pedagogy guided by ethical principles that correspond to a radical practice rooted in historical experience. And it is a pedagogy that comprehends the historical consequences of what it means to take a moral and political position with respect to the horror and suffering of, for example, the Gulag, the Nazi Holocaust, or the Pol Pot regime. Such events not only summon up images of terror, domination, and resistance, but also provide a priori examples of what principles have to be both defended and fought against in the interest of freedom and life. Within this perspective, ethics becomes more than the discourse of moral relativism or a static transmission of reified history. Ethics becomes, instead, a continued engagement in which the social practices of everyday life are interrogated in relation to the principles of individual autonomy and democratic public life — not as a matter of received truth but as a constant engagement. This represents an ethical stance which provides the opportunity for individual capacities to be questioned and examined so that they can serve both to analyze and advance the possibilities inherent in all social forms. At issue is an ethical stance in which community, difference, remembrance, and historical consciousness become central categories as part of the language of public life.

From "Liberal Arts Education and the Struggle for Public Life: Dreaming about Democracy," *South Atlantic Quarterly,* 89, 1990

Considerations for Critical Thinking and Writing

1. Why does Giroux take debates about canonical issues beyond course reading lists? Upon what historical conditions does he base his argument?
2. What kind of teaching — "critical pedagogy" — does Giroux call for? Why?
3. According to Giroux, why should "value neutrality" be rejected by teachers and students?
4. Write an essay in which you agree or disagree that literature should be used to help create an "ethical stance" for its readers.

[2]Gail Guthrie Valaskakis, "The Chippewa and the Other: Living the Heritage of Lac Du Flambeau," *Cultural Studies* 2 (October 1988): 268.

15. Reading and Writing

THE PURPOSE AND VALUE
OF WRITING ABOUT LITERATURE

Introductory literature courses typically include three components: reading, discussion, and writing. Students usually find the readings a pleasure, the class discussions a revelation, and the writing assignments — at least initially — a little intimidating. Writing an analysis of the symbolic use of a wall in Robert Frost's "Mending Wall" (p. 298) or in Herman Melville's "Bartleby, the Scrivener," for example, may seem considerably more daunting than making a case for animal rights or analyzing a campus newspaper editorial that calls for grade reforms. Like Bartleby, you might want to respond with "I would prefer not to." Literary topics are not, however, all that different from the kinds of papers assigned in English composition courses; many of the same skills are required for both. Regardless of the type of paper, you must develop a thesis and support it with evidence in language that is clear and persuasive.

Whether the subject matter is a marketing survey, a political issue, or a literary work, writing is a method of communicating information and perceptions. Writing teaches. But before writing becomes an instrument for informing the reader, it serves as a means of learning for the writer. An essay is a process of discovery as well as a record of what has been discovered. One of the chief benefits of writing is that we frequently realize what we want to say only after trying out ideas on a page and seeing our thoughts take shape in language.

More specifically, writing about a literary work encourages us to be better readers, because it requires a close examination of the elements of a short story, poem, or play. To determine how plot, character, setting, point of view, style, tone, irony, or any number of other literary elements function in a work, we must study them in relation to one another as well as separately. Speed-reading won't do. To read a text accurately and validly — neither ignoring nor distorting significant details — we must return to the work repeatedly to test our responses and interpretations. By paying attention to details and being sensitive to the author's use of language, we develop a clearer understanding of how the work conveys its effects and meanings.

Nevertheless, students sometimes ask why it is necessary or desirable to write about a literary work. Why not allow stories, poems, and plays to speak for themselves? Isn't it presumptuous to interpret Hemingway, Dickinson, or Shakespeare? These writers do, of course, speak for themselves, but they do so indirectly. Literary criticism does not seek to replace the text by explaining it but to enhance our readings of works by calling attention to elements that we might have overlooked or only vaguely sensed.

Another misunderstanding about the purpose of literary criticism is that it crankily restricts itself to finding faults in a work. Critical essays are sometimes mistakenly equated with newspaper and magazine reviews of recently published works. Reviews typically include summaries and evaluations to inform readers about a work's nature and quality, but critical essays assume that readers are already familiar with a work. Although a critical essay may point out limitations and flaws, most criticism — and certainly the kind of essay usually written in an introductory literature course — is designed to explain, analyze, and reveal the complexities of a work. Such sensitive consideration increases our appreciation of the writer's achievement and significantly adds to our enjoyment of a short story, poem, or play. In short, the purpose and value of writing about literature are that doing so leads to greater understanding and pleasure.

READING THE WORK CLOSELY

Know the piece of literature you are writing about before you begin your essay. Think about how the work makes you feel and how it is put together. The more familiar you are with how the various elements of the text convey effects and meanings, the more confident you will be explaining whatever perspective on it you ultimately choose. Do not insist that everything make sense on a first reading. Relax and enjoy yourself; you can be attentive and still allow the author's words to work their magic on you. With subsequent readings, however, go more slowly and analytically as you try to establish relations between characters, actions, images, or whatever else seems important. Ask yourself why you respond as you do. Think as you read, and notice how the parts of a work contribute to its overall nature. Whether the work is a short story, poem, or play, you will read relevant portions of it over and over, and you will very likely find more to discuss in each review if the work is rich.

It's best to avoid reading other critical discussions of a work before you are thoroughly familiar with it. There are several good reasons for following this advice. By reading interpretations before you know a work, you deny yourself the pleasure of discovery. That is a bit like starting with the last chapter in a mystery novel. But perhaps even more important than protecting the surprise and delight that a work might offer is that a premature reading of a critical discussion will probably short-circuit your own responses. You will see the work through the critic's eyes and have to struggle with someone else's perceptions and ideas before you can develop your own.

Reading criticism can be useful, but not until you have thought through your own impressions of the text. A guide should not be permitted to become a tyrant. This does not mean, however, that you should avoid background information about a work, for example, that the title of Diane Ackerman's "A Fine, A Private Place" (p. 65) alludes to Andrew Marvell's earlier *carpe diem* poem, "To His Coy Mistress" (p. 55). Knowing something about the author as well as historic and literary contexts can help to create expectations that enhance your reading.

TAKING NOTES

As you read, get in the habit of making marginal notations in your textbook. If you are working with a library book, use notecards and write down page or line numbers so that you can easily return to annotated passages. Use these cards to record reactions, raise questions, and make comments. They will freshen your memory and allow you to keep track of what goes on in the text.

Taking notes will preserve your initial reactions to the work. Many times first impressions are the best. Your response to a peculiar character, a striking phrase, or a subtle pun might lead to larger perceptions. The student paper on "The Love Song of J. Alfred Prufrock," (p. 330), for example, began with the student making notes in the margins of the text about the disembodied images of eyes and arms that appear in the poem. This, along with the fragmentary thoughts and style of the speaker eventually led her to examine the significance of the images and how they served to characterize Prufrock.

You should take detailed notes only after you've read through the work. If you write too many notes during the first reading, you're likely to disrupt your response. Moreover, until you have a sense of the entire work, it will be difficult to determine how connections can be made among its various elements. In addition to recording your first impressions and noting significant passages, images, diction, and so on, you should consult the Questions for Responsive Reading on page 342. These questions can assist you in getting inside a work as well as organizing your notes.

Inevitably, you will take more notes than you finally use in the paper. Note taking is a form of thinking aloud, but because your ideas are on paper you don't have to worry about forgetting them. As you develop a better sense of a potential topic, your notes will become more focused and detailed.

CHOOSING A TOPIC

If your instructor assigns a topic or offers a choice from among an approved list of topics, some of your work is already completed. Instead of being asked to come up with a topic about Emily Dickinson's poems in this anthology, you may be assigned a three-page essay that specifically discusses "Dickinson's Treatment of Grief in 'The Bustle in a House.'" You also have the assurance that a specified topic will be manageable within the suggested number of pages. Unless you ask your instructor for permission to write on a different or related topic, be certain to address yourself to the assignment. An essay that does not discuss grief but instead describes Dickinson's relationship with her father would be missing the point. Notice too that there is room even in an assigned topic to develop your own approach. One question that immediately comes to mind is whether grief defeats or helps the speaker in the poem. Assigned topics do not relieve you of thinking about an aspect of a work, but they do focus your thinking.

At some point during the course, you may have to begin an essay from scratch. You might, for example, be asked to write about a poem that somehow impressed you or that seemed particularly well written or filled with insights. Before you start considering a topic, you should have a sense of how long the paper will be, because the assigned length can help to determine the extent to which you should develop your topic. Ideally, the paper's length should be based on how much space you deem necessary to present your discussion clearly and convincingly, but if you have any doubts and no specific guidelines have been indicated, ask. The question is important; a topic that might be appropriate for a three-page paper could be too narrow for ten pages. Three pages would probably be adequate for a discussion of the speaker's view of death in John Keats's "To Autumn." Conversely, it would be futile to try to summarize Keats's use of sensuality in his poetry in even ten pages; the topic would have to be narrowed to something like "Images of Sensuality in 'The Eve of St. Agnes.'" Be sure that the topic you choose can be adequately covered in the assigned number of pages.

Once you have a firm sense of how much you are expected to write, you can begin to decide on your topic. If you are to choose what work to write about, select one that genuinely interests you. Too often students pick a poem, because it is mercifully short or seems simple. Such works can certainly be the subjects of fine essays, but simplicity should not be the major reason for selecting them. Choose a work that has moved you so that you have something to say about it. The student who wrote about "The Love Song of J. Alfred Prufrock" was initially attracted to the poem's imagery because she had heard a friend (no doubt an English major) jokingly quote Prufrock's famous lament that "I should have a pair of ragged claws / Scuttling across the floors of silent seas." Her paper then grew out of her curiosity about the meaning of the images. When a writer is engaged in a topic, the paper has a better chance of being interesting to a reader.

After you have settled on a particular work, your notes and annotations of the text should prove useful for generating a topic. The student paper on Prufrock developed naturally from the notes (p. 577) that the student jotted down about the images. If you think with a pen in your hand, you are likely to find when you review your notes that your thoughts have clustered into one or more topics. Perhaps there are patterns of imagery that seem to make a point about life. There may be symbols that are ironically paired or levels of diction that reveal certain qualities about the speaker. Your notes and annotations on such aspects can lead you to a particular effect or impression. Having chuckled your way through Peter Meinke's "The ABC of Aerobics" (p. 491), you may discover that your notations about the poem's humor point to a serious satire of society's values.

DEVELOPING A THESIS

When you are satisfied that you have something interesting to say about a work and that your notes have led you to a focused topic, you can formulate a *thesis,* the central idea of the paper. Whereas the topic indicates what the paper focuses on (the disembodied images in "Prufrock," for example), the thesis explains what you have to say about the topic (the frightening images of eyes, arms, and claws reflect Prufrock's disjointed, fragmentary response to life). The thesis should be a complete sentence (though sometimes it may require more than one sentence) that establishes your topic in clear, un-ambiguous language. The thesis may be revised as you get further into the topic and discover what you want to say about it, but once the thesis is firmly established it will serve as a guide for you and your reader, because all the information and observations in your essay should be related to the thesis.

One student on an initial reading of Andrew Marvell's "To His Coy Mistress" (p. 55) saw that the male speaker of the poem urges a woman to love now before time runs out for them. This reading gave him the impression that the poem is a simple celebration of the pleasures of the flesh, but on subsequent readings he underlined or noted these images: "Time's wingèd chariot hurrying near"; "Deserts of vast eternity"; "marble vault"; "worms"; "dust"; "ashes"; and these two lines: "The grave's a fine and private place, / But none, I think, do there embrace."

By listing these images associated with time and death, he established an inventory that could be separated from the rest of his notes on point of view, character, sounds, and other subjects. Inventorying notes allows patterns to emerge that you might have only vaguely perceived otherwise. Once these images are grouped, they call attention to something darker and more complex in Marvell's poem than a first impression might suggest.

These images may create a different feeling about the poem, but they still don't explain very much. One simple way to generate a thesis about a literary work is to ask the question "why?" Why do these images appear in the poem? Why does the speaker in William Stafford's "Traveling through the Dark" (p. 118) push the dead deer into the river? Why does disorder appeal so much to the speaker in Robert Herrick's "Delight in Disorder" (p. 167)? Your responses to these kinds of questions can lead to a thesis.

Writers sometimes use free writing to help themselves explore possible answers to such questions. It can be an effective way of generating ideas. Free writing is exactly that: the technique calls for nonstop writing without concern for mechanics or editing of any kind. Free writing for ten minutes or so on a question will result in fragments and repetitions, but it can also produce some ideas. Here's an example of a student's response to the question about the images in "To His Coy Mistress":

```
He wants her to make love.  Love poem.  There's little time.
Her crime.  He exaggerates.  Sincere?  Sly?  What's he want?
She says nothing--he says it all.  What about deserts, ashes,
graves, and worms?  Some love poem.  Sounds like an old Vin-
cent Price movie.  Full of sweetness but death creeps in.
Death--hurry hurry!  Tear pleasures.  What passion!  Where's
death in this?  How can a love poem be so ghoulish?  She does
nothing.  Maybe frightened?  Convinced?  Why death?  Love and
death--time--death.
```

This free writing contains several ideas; it begins by alluding to the poem's plot and speaker, but the central idea seems to be death. This emphasis led the student to four potential thesis statements for his essay about the poem:

```
1. "To His Coy Mistress" is a difficult poem.
2. Death in "To His Coy Mistress."
3. There are many images of death in "To His Coy Mistress."
4. On the surface, "To His Coy Mistress" is a celebration of
   the pleasures of the flesh, but this witty seduction is
   tempered by a chilling recognition of the reality of death.
```

The first statement is too vague to be useful. In what sense is the poem difficult? A more precise phrasing, indicating the nature of the difficulty, is needed. The second statement is a topic rather than a thesis. Because it is not a sentence, it does not express a complete idea about how the poem treats death. Although this could be an appropriate title, it is inadequate as a thesis statement. The third statement, like the first one, identifies the topic, but even though it is a sentence, it is not a complete idea that tells us anything significant beyond the fact it states. After these preliminary attempts to develop a thesis, the student remembered his first impression of the poem and incorporated it into his thesis statement. The fourth thesis is a useful approach to the poem because it limits the topic and indicates how it will be treated in the paper: the writer will begin with an initial impression of the poem and then go on to qualify it. An effective thesis, like this one, makes a clear statement about a manageable topic and provides a firm sense of direction for the paper.

Most writing assignments in a literature course require you to persuade readers that your thesis is reasonable and supported with evidence. Papers that report information without comment or evaluation are simply summaries. Similarly, a paper that merely pointed out the death images in "To His Coy Mistress" would not contain a thesis, but a paper that attempted to make a case for the death imagery as a grim reminder of how vulnerable flesh is would involve persuasion. In developing a thesis, remember that you are expected not merely to present information but to argue a point.

ARGUING ABOUT LITERATURE

An argumentative essay is designed to make persuasive your interpretation of a work. Arguing about literature doesn't mean that you're engaged in an angry, antagonistic dispute (though controversial topics do sometimes engender heated debates). Instead, argumentation requires that you present your interpretation of a work (or a portion of it) by supporting your discussion with clearly defined terms, ample evidence, and a detailed analysis of relevant portions of the text.

If you have a choice, it's generally best to write about a topic that you feel strongly about. Even if you don't like cats you might find May Swenson's "The Secret in the Cat" (p. 103) just the sort of dissection that helps explain why you can't warm up to cats. On the other hand, if you're a cat fan, the poem may suggest something essential about cats that you've experienced but have never quite put your finger on. If your essay is to be interesting and convincing, what is important is that it be written from a strong point of view that persuasively argues your evaluation, analysis, and interpretation of a work. It is not enough to say that you like or dislike a work; instead you must give your reader some ideas and evidence that can be accepted or rejected based on the quality of the answers to the questions you raise.

One way to come up with persuasive answers is to generate good questions that will lead you further into the text and to critical issues related to it. Notice how the Perspectives, Complementary Readings, and Critical Case Study in this anthology raise significant questions and issues about texts from a variety of points of view. Moreover, the critical strategies for reading summarized in Chapter 14 can be a resource for raising questions that can be shaped into an argument. The following lists of questions for the critical approaches covered in Chapter 14 should be useful for discovering arguments you might make about a short story, poem, or play. The page number that follows each heading refers to the discussion in the anthology for that particular approach.

Formalist Questions (p. 521)

1. How do various elements of the work — character, point of view, setting, tone, diction, images, symbol, etc. — reinforce its meanings?
2. How are the elements related to the whole?
3. What is the work's major organizing principle? How is its structure unified?
4. What issues does the work raise? How does the work's structure resolve those issues?

Biographical Questions (p. 524)

1. Are there facts about the writer's life relevant to your understanding of the work?
2. Are characters and incidents in the work versions of the writer's own experiences? Are they treated factually or imaginatively?
3. How do you think the writer's values are reflected in the work?

Psychological Questions (p. 526)

1. How does the work reflect the author's personal psychology?
2. What do the speaker's emotions and behavior reveal about his or her psychological state? What type of personality is the speaker?
3. Are psychological matters such as repression, dreams, and desire presented consciously or unconsciously by the author?

Historical Questions (p. 528)

1. How does the work reflect the period in which it is written?
2. How does the work reflect the period it represents?
3. What literary or historical influences helped to shape the form and content of the work?
4. How important is the historical context (both the work's and your own) to interpreting the work?

Marxist Questions (p. 530)

1. How are class differences presented in the work? Are characters aware or unaware of the economic and social forces that affect their lives?
2. How do economic conditions determine the characters' lives?
3. What ideological values are explicit or implicit?

Feminist Questions (p. 531)

1. How are women's lives portrayed in the work? Do the women in the work accept or reject these roles?
2. Is the form and content of the work influenced by the author's gender?

3. What are the relationships between men and women? Are these relationships sources of conflict? Do they provide resolutions to conflicts?

Mythological Questions (p. 532)

1. How does the poem resemble other poems in diction, character, setting, or use of symbols?
2. Are archetypes presented, such as quests, initiations, scapegoats, or withdrawals and returns?
3. Does the protagonist or the speaker undergo any kind of transformation such as a movement from innocence to experience that seems archetypal?

Reader-Response Questions (p. 534)

1. How do you respond to the work?
2. How do your own experiences and expectations affect your reading and interpretation?
3. What is the work's original or intended audience? To what extent are you similar to or different from that audience?

Deconstructionist Questions (p. 536)

1. How are contradictory or opposing meanings expressed in the work?
2. How does meaning break down or deconstruct itself in the language of the text?
3. Would you say that ultimate definitive meanings are impossible to determine and establish in the text? Why? How does that affect your interpretation?

These questions will not apply to all texts; and they are not mutually exclusive. They can be combined to explore a text from several critical perspectives simultaneously. A feminist approach to Paula Gunn Allen's "Pocahontas to Her English Husband, John Rolfe" (p. 344) could also use Marxist concerns about class to make observations about the oppression of women's lives in the historical context of the sixteenth century. Your use of these questions should allow you to discover significant issues from which you can develop an argumentative essay that is organized around clearly defined terms, relevant evidence, and a persuasive analysis.

ORGANIZING A PAPER

After you have chosen a manageable topic and developed a thesis, a central idea about it, you can begin to organize your paper. Your thesis, even if it is still somewhat tentative, should help you decide what information will need to be included and provide you with a sense of direction.

Consider again the sample thesis in the section on developing a thesis:

```
On the surface, "To His Coy Mistress" is a celebration of the
pleasures of the flesh, but this witty seduction is tempered
by a chilling recognition of the reality of death.
```

This thesis indicates that the paper can be divided into two parts: the pleasures of the flesh and the reality of death. It also indicates an order: Because the central point is to show that the poem is more than a simple celebration, the pleasures of the flesh should be discussed first so that another, more complex, reading of the poem can follow. If the paper began with the reality of death, its point would be anticlimactic.

Having established such a broad and informal outline, you can draw upon your underlinings, margin notations, and notecards for the subheadings and evidence required to explain the major sections of your paper. This next level of detail would look like the following:

```
1. Pleasures of the flesh
   Part of the traditional tone of love poetry
2. Recognition of death
   Ironic treatment of love
      Diction
      Images
      Figures of speech
      Symbols
      Tone
```

This list was initially a jumble of terms, but the student arranged the items so that each of the two major sections leads to a discussion of tone. (The student also found it necessary to drop some biographical information from his notes because it was irrelevant to the thesis.) The list indicates that the first part of the paper will establish the traditional tone of love poetry that celebrates the pleasures of the flesh, while the second part will present a more detailed discussion about the ironic recognition of death. The emphasis is on the latter because that is the point to be argued in the paper. Hence, the thesis has helped to organize the parts of the paper, establish an order, and indicate the paper's proper proportions.

The next step is to fill in the subheadings with information from your notes. Many experienced writers find that making lists of information to be included under each subheading is an efficient way to develop paragraphs. For a longer paper (perhaps a research paper), you should be able to develop a paragraph or more on each subheading. On the other hand, a shorter paper may require that you combine several subheadings in a paragraph. You may also discover that while an informal list is adequate for a brief paper, a ten-page assignment could require a more detailed outline. Use the method that is most productive for you. Whatever the length of the essay, your presentation must be in a coherent and logical order that allows your reader to follow the argument and evaluate the evidence. The quality of your reading can be demonstrated only by the quality of your writing.

WRITING A DRAFT

The time for sharpening pencils, arranging your desk, and doing almost anything else instead of writing has ended. The first draft will appear on the page only if you stop avoiding the inevitable and sit, stand up, or lie down to write. It makes no difference how you write, just so you do. Now that you have developed a topic into a tentative thesis, you can assemble your notes and begin to flesh out whatever outline you have made.

Be flexible. Your outline should smoothly conduct you from one point to the next, but do not permit it to railroad you. If a relevant and important idea occurs to you now, work it into the draft. By using the first draft as a means of thinking about what you want to say, you will very likely discover more than your notes originally suggested. Plenty of good writers don't use outlines at all but discover ordering principles as they write. Do not attempt to compose a perfectly correct draft the first time around. Grammar, punctuation, and spelling can wait until you revise. Concentrate on what you are saying. Good writing most often occurs when you are in hot pursuit of an idea rather than in a nervous search for errors.

To make revising easier, leave wide margins and extra space between lines so that you can easily add words, sentences, and corrections. Write on only one side of the paper. Your pages will be easier to keep track of that way, and, if you have to clip a paragraph to place it elsewhere, you will not lose any writing on the other side.

If you are working on a word processor, you can take advantage of its capacity to make additions and deletions as well as move entire paragraphs by making just a few simple keyboard commands. Some software programs can also check spelling and certain grammatical elements in your writing. It's worth remembering, however, that though a clean copy fresh off a printer may look terrific, it will read only as well as the thinking and writing that have gone into it. Many writers prudently store their data on disks and print their pages each time they finish a draft to avoid losing any material because of power failures or other problems. These printouts are also easier to read than the screen when you work on revisions.

Once you have a first draft on paper, you can delete material that is unrelated to your thesis and add material necessary to illustrate your points and make your paper convincing. The student who wrote "Disembodied Images in 'The Love Song of J. Alfred Prufrock'" (p. 578) wisely dropped a paragraph that questioned whether Prufrock displays chauvinistic attitudes toward women. Although this could be an interesting issue, it has nothing to do with the thesis, which explains how the images reflect Prufrock's inability to make a meaningful connection to his world.

Remember that your initial draft is only that. You should go through the paper many times — and then again — working to substantiate and clarify your ideas. You may even end up with several entire versions of the paper. Rewrite. The sentences within each paragraph should be related to a single topic. Transitions should connect one paragraph to the next so that there are no abrupt or confusing shifts. Awkward or wordy phrasing or unclear sentences and paragraphs should be mercilessly poked and prodded into shape.

Writing the Introduction and Conclusion

After you have clearly and adequately developed the body of your paper, pay particular attention to the introductory and concluding paragraphs. It's probably best to write the introduction — at least the final version of it — last, after you know precisely what you are introducing. Because this paragraph is crucial for generating interest in the topic, it should engage the reader and provide a sense of what the paper is about. There is no formula for writing effective introductory paragraphs, because each writing situation is different — depending on the audience, topic, and approach — but if you pay attention to the introductions of the essays you read, you will notice a variety of possibilities. The introductory paragraph to the Prufrock paper, for example, is a straightforward explanation of why the disembodied images are important for understanding Prufrock's character. The rest of the paper then offers evidence to support this point.

Concluding paragraphs demand equal attention because they leave the reader with a final impression. The conclusion should provide a sense of closure instead of starting a new topic or ending abruptly. In the final paragraph about the disembodied images in "Prufrock" the student explains their significance in characterizing Prufrock's inability to think of himself or others as complete and whole human beings. We now see that the images of eyes, arms, and claws are reflections of the fragmentary nature of Prufrock and his world. Of course, the body of your paper is the most important part of your presentation, but do remember that first and last impressions have a powerful impact on readers.

Using Quotations

Quotations can be a valuable means of marshaling evidence to illustrate and support your ideas. A judicious use of quoted material will make your points clearer and more convincing. Here are some guidelines that should help you use quotations effectively.

1. Brief quotations (four lines or fewer of prose or three lines or fewer of poetry) should be carefully introduced and integrated into the text of your paper with quotation marks around them.

According to the narrator, Bertha "had a reputation for strictness." He tells us that she always "wore dark clothes, dressed her hair simply, and expected contrition and obedience from her pupils."

For brief poetry quotations, use a slash to indicate a division between lines.

The concluding lines of Blake's "The Tyger" pose a disturbing question: "What immortal hand or eye / Dare frame thy fearful symmetry?"

Lengthy quotations should be separated from the text of your paper. More than three lines of poetry should be double spaced and centered on the page. More than four lines of prose should be double spaced and indented ten spaces from the left margin, with the right margin the same as for the text. Do *not* use quotation marks for the passage; the indentation indicates that the passage is a quotation. Lengthy quotations should not be used in place of your own writing. Use them only if they are absolutely necessary.

2. If any words are added to a quotation, use brackets to distinguish your addition from the original source.

"He [Young Goodman Brown] is portrayed as self-righteous and disillusioned."

Any words inside quotation marks and not in brackets must be precisely those of the author. Brackets can also be used to change the grammatical structure of a quotation so that it fits into your sentence.

Smith argues that Chekhov "present[s] the narrator in an ambivalent light."

If you drop any words from the source, use an ellipsis (three spaced periods) to indicate the omission.

"Early to bed . . . makes a man healthy, wealthy, and wise."

Use an ellipsis following a period to indicate an omission at the end of a sentence.

"Early to bed and early to rise makes a man healthy. . . ."

Use a single line of spaced periods to indicate the omission of a line or more of poetry or more than one paragraph of prose.

Nothing would sleep in that cellar, dank as a ditch,
Bulbs broke out of boxes hunting for chinks in the dark,
· ·
Nothing would give up life:
Even the dirt kept breathing a small breath.

3. You will be able to punctuate quoted material accurately and confidently if you observe these conventions.

Place commas and periods inside quotation marks.

"Even the dirt," Roethke insists, "kept breathing a small breath."

Even though a comma does not appear after "dirt" in the original quotation, it is placed inside the quotation mark. The exception to this rule occurs when a parenthetical reference to a source follows the quotation.

"Even the dirt," Roethke insists, "kept breathing a small breath" (11).

Punctuation marks other than commas or periods go outside the quotation marks unless they are part of the material quoted.

What does Roethke mean when he writes that "the dirt kept breathing a small breath"?

Yeats asked, "How can we know the dancer from the dance?"

REVISING AND EDITING

Put some distance — a day or so if you can — between yourself and each draft of your paper. The phrase that seemed just right on Wednesday may be revealed as all wrong on Friday. You'll have a better chance of detecting lumbering sentences and thin paragraphs if you plan ahead and give yourself the time to read your paper from a fresh perspective. Through the process of revision, you can transform a competent paper into an excellent one.

Begin by asking yourself if your approach to the topic requires any rethinking. Is the argument carefully thought out and logically presented? Are there any gaps in the presentation? How well is the paper organized? Do the paragraphs lead into one another? Does the body of the paper deliver what the thesis promises? Is the interpretation sound? Are any relevant and important elements of the work ignored or distorted to advance the thesis? Are the points supported with evidence? These large questions should be addressed before you focus on more detailed matters. If you uncover serious problems as a result of considering these questions, you'll probably have quite a lot of rewriting to do, but at least you will have the opportunity to correct the problems — even if doing so takes several drafts.

A useful technique for spotting awkward or unclear moments in the paper is to read it aloud. You might also try having a friend read it aloud to you. If your handwriting is legible, your friend's reading — perhaps accompanied by hesitations and puzzled expressions — could alert you to passages that need reworking. Having identified problems, you can readily correct them on a word processor or on the draft provided you've skipped lines and used wide margins. The final draft you hand in should be neat and carefully proofread for any inadvertent errors.

The following checklist offers questions to ask about your paper as you revise and edit it. Most of these questions will be familiar to you; however, if you need help with any of them, ask your instructor or review the appropriate section in a composition handbook.

Revision Checklist

1. Is the topic manageable? Is it too narrow or too broad?
2. Is the thesis clear? Is it based on a careful reading of the work?
3. Is the paper logically organized? Does it have a firm sense of direction?
4. Is your argument persuasive?
5. Should any material be deleted? Do any important points require further illustration or evidence?
6. Does the opening paragraph introduce the topic in an interesting manner?
7. Are the paragraphs developed, unified, and coherent? Are any too short or long?
8. Are there transitions linking the paragraphs?
9. Does the concluding paragraph provide a sense of closure?
10. Is the tone appropriate? Is it unduly flippant or pretentious?
11. Is the title engaging and suggestive?
12. Are the sentences clear, concise, and complete?
13. Are simple, complex, and compound sentences used for variety?
14. Have technical terms been used correctly? Are you certain of the meanings of all the words in the paper? Are they spelled correctly?
15. Have you documented any information borrowed from books, articles, or other sources? Have you quoted too much instead of summarizing or paraphrasing secondary material?
16. Have you used a standard format for citing sources (see p. 596)?
17. Have you followed your instructor's guidelines for the manuscript format of the final draft?
18. Have you carefully proofread the final draft?

When you proofread your final draft, you may find a few typographical errors that must be corrected but do not warrant retyping an entire page. Provided there are not more than a handful of such errors throughout the page, they can be corrected as shown in the following passage. This example condenses a short paper's worth of errors; no single passage should be this shabby in your essay.

```
To add a letter or word, use a caret on the line where the ad-
                is
dition needed.  To delete a word draw a single line through
        ^
through it.  Run-on words are separated by a vertical line, and
inadvertent spaces are closed like t his.  Transposed letters
are indicated this way.  New paragraphs are noted with the
sign ¶ in front of where the next paragraph is to begin. ¶ Un-
less you . . .
```

These sorts of errors can be minimized by using correction fluid or tape while you type. If you use a word processor, you can eliminate such errors completely by simply entering corrections as you proofread on the screen.

MANUSCRIPT FORM

The novelist and poet Peter De Vries once observed in his characteristically humorous way that he very much enjoyed writing but that he couldn't bear the "paper work." Behind this playful pun is a half-serious impatience with the mechanics of it all. You may feel some of that too, but this is not the time to allow a thoughtful, carefully revised paper to trip over minor details that can be easily accommodated. The final draft you hand in to your instructor should not only read well but look neat. If your instructor does not provide specific instructions concerning the format for the paper, follow these guidelines.

1. Papers (particularly long ones) should be typed on 8½ × 11-inch paper in double space. Avoid transparent paper such as onionskin; it is difficult to read and write comments on. The ribbon should be dark and the letters on the machine clear. If you compose on a word processor with a dot-matrix printer, be certain that the dots are close enough together to be legible. And don't forget to separate your pages and remove the strips of holes on each side of the pages if your printer uses a continuous paper feed. If your instructor accepts handwritten papers, write legibly in ink on only one side of a wide-lined page.

2. Use a one-inch margin at the top, bottom, and sides of each page. Unless you are instructed to include a separate title page, type your name, instructor's name, course number and section, and date on separate lines one inch below the upper-left corner of the first page. Double space between these lines and then center the title below the date. Do not underline or put quotation marks around your paper's title, but do use quotation marks around the titles of poems, short stories, or other brief works, and underline the titles of books and plays (a sample paper title: "Mending Wall" and Other Boundaries in Frost's North of Boston). Begin the text of your paper two spaces below the title. If you have used secondary sources, center the heading "Notes" or "Works Cited" one inch from the top of a separate page and then double space between it and the entries.

3. Number each page consecutively, beginning with page 2, a half inch from the top of the page in the upper-right corner.

4. Gather the pages with a paper clip rather than staples, folders, or some other device. That will make it easier for your instructor to handle the paper.

TYPES OF WRITING ASSIGNMENTS

The types of papers most frequently assigned in literature classes are explication, analysis, and comparison and contrast. Most writing about literature involves some combination of these skills. This section includes a sample explication, an analysis, and a comparison and contrast paper. (For a sample research paper that demonstrates a variety of strategies for documenting outside sources, see p. 603.)

Explication

The purpose of this approach to a literary work is to make the implicit explicit. *Explication* is a detailed explanation of a passage of poetry or prose. Because explication is an intensive examination of a text line by line, it is mostly used to interpret a short poem in its entirety or a brief passage from a long poem, short story, or play. Explication can be used in any kind of paper when you want to be specific about how a writer achieves a certain effect. An explication pays careful attention to language: the connotations of words, allusions, figurative language, irony, symbol, rhythm, sound, and so on. These elements are examined in relation to one another and to the overall effect and meaning of the work.

The simplest way to organize an explication is to move through the passage line by line, explaining whatever seems significant. It is wise to avoid, however, an assembly-line approach that begins each sentence with "In line one. . . ." Instead, organize your paper in whatever way best serves your thesis. You might find that the right place to start is with the final lines, working your way back to the beginning of the poem or passage. The following sample explication on Emily Dickinson's "There's a certain Slant of light" does just that. The student's opening paragraph refers to the final line of the poem in order to present her thesis. She explains that though the poem begins with an image of light, it is not a bright or cheery poem but one concerned with "the look of Death." Since the last line prompted her thesis, that is where she begins the explication.

You might also find it useful to structure a paper by discussing various elements of literature, so that you have a paragraph on connotative words followed by one on figurative language and so on. However your paper is organized, keep in mind that the aim of an explication is not simply to summarize the passage but to comment on the effects and meanings produced by the author's use of language in it. An effective explication (the Latin word *explicare* means "to unfold") displays a text to reveal how it works and what it signifies. Although writing an explication requires some patience and sensitivity, it is an excellent method for coming to understand and appreciate the elements and qualities that constitute literary art.

A STUDENT EXPLICATION

The sample paper by Bonnie Katz is the result of an assignment calling for an explication of about 750 words on any poem by Emily Dickinson. Katz selected "There's a certain Slant of light."

EMILY DICKINSON (1830–1886)
There's a certain Slant of light

c. 1861

There's a certain Slant of light,
Winter Afternoons —
That oppresses, like the Heft
Of Cathedral Tunes —

Heavenly Hurt, it gives us —   5
We can find no scar,
But internal difference,
Where the Meanings, are —

None may teach it — Any —
'Tis the Seal Despair —   10
An imperial affliction
Sent us of the Air —

When it comes, the Landscape listens —
Shadows — hold their breath —
When it goes, 'tis like the Distance   15
On the look of Death —

This essay comments on every line of the poem and provides a coherent reading that relates each line to the speaker's intense awareness of death. Although the essay discusses each stanza in the order that it appears, the introductory paragraph provides a brief overview explaining how the poem's images contribute to its total meaning. In addition, the student does not hesitate to discuss a line out of sequence when it can be usefully connected to another phrase. This is especially apparent in the third paragraph, in her discussion of stanzas 2 and 3. The final paragraph describes some of the formal elements of the poem. It might be argued that this discussion could have been integrated into the previous paragraphs rather than placed at the end, but the student does make a connection in her concluding sentence between the pattern of language and its meaning.

Several other matters are worth noticing. The student works quotations into her own sentences to support her points. She quotes exactly as the words appear in the poem, even Dickinson's irregular use of capital letters.

(Text continues on page 576.)

Bonnie Katz

Professor Quiello

English 109-2

October 26, 19--

A Reading of Dickinson's
"There's a certain Slant of light"

Because Emily Dickinson did not provide titles for her poetry, editors follow the customary practice of using the first line of a poem as its title. However, a more appropriate title for "There's a certain Slant of light," one that suggests what the speaker in the poem is most concerned about, can be drawn from the poem's last line, which ends with "the look of Death." Although the first line begins with an image of light, nothing bright, carefree, or cheerful appears in the poem. Instead, the predominant mood and images are darkened by a sense of despair resulting from the speaker's awareness of death.

In the first stanza, the "certain Slant of light" is associated with "Winter Afternoons," a phrase that connotes the end of a day, a season, and even life itself. Such light is hardly warm or comforting. Not a ray or beam, this slanting light suggests something unusual or distorted and creates in the speaker a certain slant on life that is consistent with the cold, dark mood that winter afternoons can produce. Like the speaker, most of us have seen and felt this sort of light: it "oppresses" and pervades our sense of things when we encounter it. Dickinson uses the senses of hearing and touch as well as sight to describe the overwhelming oppressiveness that the speaker experiences. The light is transformed into sound by a simile that tells us it is "like the Heft / Of Cathedral Tunes." Moreover, the "Heft" of that sound--the slow, solemn measures of tolling church bells and organ music--weighs heavily on our spirits. Through the use of shifting imagery, Dickinson evokes a kind of spiritual numbness that we keenly feel and perceive through our senses.

By associating the winter light with "Cathedral Tunes," Dickinson lets us know that the speaker is concerned about more than the weather. Whatever it is that "oppresses" is related by connotation to faith, mortality, and God. The second and third stanzas offer several suggestions about this connection. The pain caused by the light is a "Heavenly Hurt." This "imperial affliction / Sent us of the Air" apparently comes from God above, and yet it seems to be part of the very nature of life. The oppressiveness we feel is in the air, and it can neither be specifically identified at this point in the poem nor be eliminated, for "None may teach it--Any." All we can know is that existence itself seems depressing under the weight of this "Seal [of] Despair." The impression left by this "Seal" is stamped within the mind or soul rather than externally. "We can find no scar," but once experienced this oppressiveness challenges our faith in life and its "Meanings."

The final stanza does not explain what those "Meanings" are, but it does make clear that the speaker is acutely aware of death. As the winter daylight fades, Dickinson projects the speaker's anxiety onto the surrounding landscape and shadows, which will soon be engulfed by the darkness that follows this light: "The Landscape listens-- / Shadows--hold their breath." This image firmly aligns the winter light in the first stanza with darkness. Paradoxically, the light in this poem illuminates the nature of darkness. Tension is released when the light is completely gone, but what remains is the despair that the "imperial affliction" has imprinted on the speaker's sensibilities, for it is "like the Distance / On the look of Death." There can be no relief from what that "certain Slant of light" has revealed, because what has been experienced is permanent—like the fixed stare in the eyes of someone who is dead.

The speaker's awareness of death is conveyed in a thoughtful, hushed tone. The lines are filled with fluid $\underline{l}$ and smooth $\underline{s}$ sounds that are appropriate for the quiet, meditative voice in the poem. The voice sounds tentative and uncertain—perhaps a little frightened. This seems to be reflected in the slightly irregular meter of the lines. The stanzas are trochaic with the second and fourth lines of each stanza having five syllables, but no stanza is identical because each works a slight variation on the first stanza's seven syllables in the first and third lines. The rhymes also combine exact patterns with variations. The first and third lines of each stanza are not exact rhymes, but the second and fourth lines are exact so that the paired words are more closely related: Afternoons, Tunes; scar, are; Despair, Air; and breath, Death. There is a pattern to the poem, but it is unobtrusively woven into the speaker's voice in much the same way that "the look of Death" is subtly present in the images and language of the poem.

When something is added to a quotation to clarify it, it is enclosed in brackets so that the essayist's words will not be mistaken for the poet's: "Seal [of] Despair." A slash is used to separate line divisions as in "imperial affliction / Sent us of the Air." And, finally, because the essay focuses on a short poem, it is not necessary to include line numbers, though they would be required in a study of a longer work.

Analysis

The preceding sample essay shows how an explication examines in detail the important elements in a work and relates them to the whole. An analysis, however, usually examines only a single element — such as diction, character, point of view, symbol, tone, or irony — and relates it to the entire work. An analytic topic separates the work into parts and focuses on a specific one; you might consider "Point of View in 'The Love Song of J. Alfred Prufrock,'" "Patterns of Rhythm in Robert Browning's 'My Last Duchess,'" or "Irony in 'The Road Not Taken.'" The specific element must be related to the work as a whole or it will appear irrelevant. It is not enough to point out that there are many death images in Andrew Marvell's "To His Coy Mistress"; the images must somehow be connected to the poem's overall effect.

Whether an analytic paper is just a few pages or many, it cannot attempt to discuss everything about the work it is considering. Only those elements that are relevant to the topic can be treated. This kind of focusing makes the topic manageable; this is why most papers that you write will probably be some form of analysis. Explications are useful for a short passage, but a line-by-line commentary on a story, play, or long poem simply isn't practical. Because analysis allows you to consider the central effect or meaning of an entire work by studying a single important element, it is a useful and common approach to longer works.

A STUDENT ANALYSIS

Beth Hart's paper analyzes some of the images in T. S. Eliot's "The Love Song of J. Alfred Prufrock" (the poem appears on p. 330). The assignment simply called for an essay of approximately 750 words on a poem written in the twentieth century. The approach was left to the student.

The idea for this essay began with Hart asking herself why there are so many fragmentary, disjointed images in the poem. The initial answer to this question was that "The disjointed images are important for understanding Prufrock's character." This answer was the rough beginning of a tentative thesis. What still had to be explained, though, was how the images are important. To determine the significance of the disjointed images, Hart jotted down some notes based on her underlinings and marginal notations.

```
Prufrock                      Images
odd name--nervous, timid?     fog
"indecisions," "revisions"    lost, wandering
confessional tone, self       watching eyes
  conscious                   ladies arms
"bald spot"                   polite talk, meaningless talk
"afraid"                      "ragged claws" that scuttle
questioning, tentative        oppressive
"I am not Prince Hamlet"      distorted
"I grow old"                  weary longing
wake--to drown                entrapped--staircase
```

(Text continues on page 581.)

Beth Hart

Professor Lucas

English 110-3

March 30, 19--

Disembodied Images in

"The Love Song of J. Alfred Prufrock"

T. S. Eliot's poem "The Love Song of J. Alfred

Prufrock," addresses the dilemma of a man who finds himself

trapped on the margins of the social world, unable to make

any meaningful interpersonal contact because of his deep-

seated fear of rejection and misunderstanding. Prufrock

feels acutely disconnected from society, which makes him so

self-conscious that he is frightened into a state of social

paralysis. His overwhelming self-consciousness,

disillusionment with social circles, and lack of connection

with those around him are revealed through Eliot's use of

fragmented imagery. Many of the predominant images are

disembodied pieces of a whole, revealing that Prufrock sees

the world not as fully whole or complete, but as disjointed,

fragmented parts of the whole. Eliot's use of frightening

disembodied images such as eyes, arms, and claws reflects

Prufrock's terror at having to face a world to which he feels

no meaningful connection.

Eliot suggests Prufrock's acute self-consciousness

through the fragmentary image of "eyes." Literally, these

eyes merely represent the people who surround Prufrock, but

this disembodied image reveals his obsessive fear of being

watched and judged by others. His confession that "I have

known the eyes already, known them all-- / The eyes that fix

you in a formulated phrase" (lines 55-56) suggests how deeply

he resists being watched, and how uncomfortable he is with

himself, both externally--referring in part to his
sensitivity to the "bald spot in the middle of my hair" (40)
--and internally--his relentless self-questioning "'Do I
dare?' and, 'Do I dare?'" (38). The disembodied eyes force
the reader to recognize the oppression of being closely
watched, and so to share in Prufrock's painful self-
awareness. Prufrock's belief that the eyes have the
terrifying and violent power to trap him like a specimen
insect "pinned and wriggling on the wall" (58), to be
scrutinized in its agony, further reveals the terror of the
floating, accusatory image of the eyes.

The disembodied image of "arms" also reflects Prufrock's
distorted vision of both himself and others around him. His
acknowledgment that he has "known the arms already, known
them all-- / Arms that are braceleted and white and bare"
(62-63) relates to the image of the eyes, yet focuses on a
very different aspect of the people surrounding Prufrock.
Clearly, the braceleted arms belong to women, and that these
arms are attached to a perfumed dress (65) suggests that
these arms belong to upper-class, privileged women. This is
partially what makes the disembodied image of the arms so
frightening for Prufrock: he is incapable of connecting with
a woman the way he, as a man, is expected to. The image of
the arms, close enough to Prufrock reveal their down of
"light brown hair" (64), suggests the potential for reaching
out and possibly touching Prufrock. The terrified self-
consciousness that the image elicits in him leads Prufrock to
wish that he could leave his own body and take on the
characteristics of yet another disembodied image.

Prufrock's despairing declaration, "I should have been a
pair of ragged claws / Scuttling across the floors of silent
seas" (73-74), offers yet another example of his vision of
the world as fragmented and incomplete. The "pair of claws"

that he longs to be not only connotes a complete separation
from the earthly life that he finds so threatening, so
painful, and so meaningless, but also suggests an isolation
from others that would allow Prufrock some freedom and relief
from social pressures. However, this image of the claws as a
form of salvation for Prufrock in fact offers little
suggestion of actual progress from his present circumstances;
crabs can only "scuttle" from side to side and are incapable
of moving directly forward or backward. Similarly, Prufrock
is trapped in a situation in which he feels incapable of
moving either up or down the staircase (39). Thus, this
disembodied image of the claws serves to remind the reader
that Prufrock is genuinely trapped in a life that offers him
virtually no hope of real connection or wholeness.

The fragmented imagery that pervades "The Love Song of
J. Alfred Prufrock" emphasizes and clarifies Prufrock's
vision of the world as disconnected and disjointed. The fact
that Prufrock thinks of people in terms of their individual
component parts (specifically, eyes and arms) suggests his
lack of understanding of people as whole and complete beings.
This reflects his vision of himself as a fragmentary self,
culminating in his wish to be not a whole crab, but merely a
pair of disembodied claws. By use of these troubling images
Eliot infuses the poem with the pain of Prufrock's self-
awareness and his confusion at the lack of wholeness he
feels, in his world.

From these notes Hart saw that the images — mostly fragmented and disjointed — suggested something about Prufrock's way of describing himself and his world. This insight led eventually to the final version of her thesis statement: "Eliot's use of frightening disembodied images such as eyes, arms, and claws reflects Prufrock's terror at having to face a world to which he feels no meaningful connection." Her introductory paragraph concludes with this sentence so that her reader can fully comprehend why she then discusses the images of eyes, arms, and claws that follow.

The remaining paragraphs present details that explain the significance of the images of eyes in the second paragraph, the arms in the third, the claws in the fourth, and in the final paragraph all three images are the basis for concluding that Prufrock's vision of the world is disconnected and disjointed.

Hart's notes certainly do not constitute a formal outline, but they were useful to her in establishing a thesis and recognizing what elements of the poem she needed to cover in her discussion. Her essay is sharply focused, well-organized, and generally well written (though some readers might wish for a more engaging introductory paragraph that captures a glint of Prufrock's "bald spot" or some other small detail in order to generate some immediate interest in his character).

Hart's essay suggests a number of useful guidelines for analytic papers.

1. Only those points related to the thesis are included. In another type of paper the significance of Eliot's epigraph from Dante, for example, might have been more important than the imagery.
2. The analysis keeps the images in focus while at the same time indicating how they are significant in revealing Prufrock's character.
3. The title is a useful lead into the paper; it provides a sense of what the topic is.
4. The introductory paragraph is direct and clearly indicates the paper will argue that the images serve to reveal Prufrock's character.
5. Brief quotations are deftly incorporated into the text of the paper to illustrate points. We are told what we need to know about the poem as evidence is provided to support ideas. There is no unnecessary summary.
6. The paragraphs are well developed, unified, and coherent. They flow naturally from one to another. Notice, for example, the smooth transition worked into the final sentence of the third paragraph and the first sentence of the fourth paragraph.
7. Hart makes excellent use of her careful reading and notes by finding revealing connections among the details she has observed.
8. As events in the poem are described, the present tense is used. This avoids awkward tense shifts and lends an immediacy to the discussion.
9. The concluding paragraph establishes the significance of why the

images should be seen as a reflection of Prufrock's character and provides a sense of closure by relating the images of Prufrock's disjointed world with the images of his fragmentary self.

10. In short, Hart has demonstrated that she has read the work closely, has understood the function of the images in the revelation of Prufrock's sensibilities, and has argued her thesis convincingly by using evidence from the poem.

Comparison and Contrast

Another essay assignment in literature courses often combined with analytic topics is the type that requires you to write about similarities and differences between or within works. You might be asked to discuss "How Sounds Express Meanings in May Swenson's 'A Nosty Fright' and Lewis Carroll's 'Jabberwocky,'" or "Love and Hate in Sylvia Plath's 'Daddy.'" A *comparison* of either topic would emphasize their similarities, while a *contrast* would stress their differences. It is possible, of course, to include both perspectives in a paper if you find significant likenesses and differences. A comparison of Andrew Marvell's "To His Coy Mistress" and Richard Wilbur's "A Late Aubade" would, for example, yield similarities, because each poem describes a man urging his lover to make the most of their precious time together; however, important differences also exist in the tone and theme of each poem that would constitute a contrast. (You should, incidentally, be aware that the term *comparison* is sometimes used inclusively to refer to both similarities and differences. If you are assigned a comparison of two works, be sure that you understand what your instructor's expectations are; you may be required to include both approaches in the essay.)

When you choose your own topic, the paper will be more successful — more manageable — if you write on works that can be meaningfully related to each other. Although Robert Herrick's "To the Virgins, to Make Much of Time" and T. S. Eliot's "The Love Song of J. Alfred Prufrock" both have something to do with hesitation, the likelihood of anyone making a connection between the two that reveals something interesting and important is remote — though perhaps not impossible if the topic were conceived imaginatively and tactfully. Choose a topic that encourages you to ask significant questions about each work; the purpose of a comparison or contrast is to understand the works more clearly for having examined them together.

Choose works to compare or contrast that intersect with each other in some significant way. They may, for example, be written by the same author or about the same subject. Perhaps you can compare their use of some technique, such as irony or point of view. Regardless of the specific topic, be sure to have a thesis that allows you to organize your paper around a central idea that argues a point about the two works. If you merely draw up a list of similarities or differences without a thesis in mind, your paper will be little more than a series of observations with no apparent purpose. Keep in the foreground of your thinking what the comparison or contrast reveals about the works.

There is no single way to organize comparative papers since each topic is likely to have its own particular issues to resolve, but it is useful to be aware of two basic patterns that can be helpful with a comparison, a contrast, or a combination of both. One method that can be effective for relatively short papers consists of dividing the paper in half, first discussing one work and then the other. Here, for example, is a partial informal outline for a discussion of Allen Ginsberg's "America" and Tato Laviera's "AmeRícan"; the topic is a comparison and contrast:

```
"Two Views of America, by Ginsberg and Laviera"
    1. "America"
       a. Diction
       b. Images
       c. Allusions
       d. Themes
    2. "AmeRícan"
       a. Diction
       b. Images
       c. Allusions
       d. Themes
```

This organizational strategy can be effective provided that the second part of the paper combines the discussion of "AmeRícan" with references to "America" so that the thesis is made clear and the paper unified without being repetitive. If the two poems were treated entirely separately, then the discussion would be merely parallel rather than integrated. In a lengthy paper, this organization probably would not work well because a reader would have difficulty remembering the points made in the first half as he or she reads on.

Thus for a longer paper it is usually better to create a more integrated structure that discusses both works as you take up each item in your outline. Here is the second basic pattern using the elements in partial outline just cited.

```
    1. Diction
       a. "America"
       b. "AmeRícan"
    2. Images
       a. "America"
       b. "AmeRícan"
    3. Allusions
       a. "America"
       b. "AmeRícan"
```

4. Themes
    a. "America"
    b. "AmeRícan"

This pattern allows you to discuss any number of topics without requiring that your reader recall what you first said about the diction of "America" before you discuss the diction of "AmeRícan" many pages later. However you structure your comparison or contrast paper, make certain that a reader can follow its elements and keep track of its thesis.

A STUDENT COMPARISON

The following paper is in response to an assignment that required a comparison and contrast — about 1,000 words — of two assigned poems. The student chose to write an analysis of two very different *carpe diem* poems.

Although these two poems are fairly lengthy, Stephanie Smith's brief analysis of them is satisfying because she focuses on the male and female *carpe diem* voices of Andrew Marvell's "To His Coy Mistress" (p. 55) and Diane Ackerman's "A Fine, A Private Place" (p. 65). After introducing the topic in the first paragraph, she takes up the two poems in a pattern similar to the first outline suggested for "Two Views of America, by Ginsberg and Laviera." Notice how Smith works in subsequent references to Marvell's poem as she discusses Ackerman's so that her treatment is integrated and we are reminded why she is comparing and contrasting the two works. Her final paragraph sums up her points without being repetitive and reiterates the thesis with which she began.

Stephanie Smith

English 109-10

Professor Monroe

April 2, 19--

Marvell and Ackerman Seize the Day

In her 1983 poem "A Fine, A Private Place," Diane
Ackerman never mentions Andrew Marvell's 1681 poem "To His
Coy Mistress." However, her one-line allusion to Marvell's
famous argument to his lover is all the reference she needs.
Through a contemporary lens, she firmly qualifies Marvell's
seventeenth-century masculine perspective. Marvell's speaker
attempts to woo a young woman and convince her to have sexual
relations with him. His seize-the-day rhetoric argues that
"his mistress" should let down her conventional purity and
enjoy the moment, his logic being that we are grave-bound
anyway, so why not? Although his poetic pleading is
effective, both stylistically and argumentatively, Marvell's
speaker obviously assumes that the coy mistress will succumb
to his grasps at her sexuality. Further, and most important
for Ackerman, the speaker takes for granted that the female
must be persuaded to love. His smooth talk leaves no room
for a feminine perspective, be it a slap in the face or a
sharing of his carpe diem attitudes. Ackerman accommodates
Marvell's masculine speaker but also deftly takes poetic
license in the cause of female freedom and sensuously lays
out her own fine and private place. Through describing a
personal sexual encounter both sensually and erotically,
Ackerman's female speaker demonstrates that women have just
as many lustful urges as the men who would seduce
them; she presents sex as neither solely a male quest nor a
female sacrifice. "A Fine, A Private Place" takes a female

perspective on sex, and enthusiastically enjoys the pleasure of it.

"To His Coy Mistress" is in a regular rhyme scheme, as each line rhymes with the next—almost like a compilation of couplets. And this, accompanied by traditional iambic tetrameter, lays the foundation for a forcefully flowing speech, a command for the couple to just do it. By the end of the poem the speaker seems to expect his mistress to capitulate. Marvell's speaker declares at the start that if eternity were upon them, he would not mind putting sex aside and paying her unending homage. "Had we but world enough, and time, / This coyness, lady, were no crime. / We would sit down, and think which way / To walk, and pass our long love's day" (lines 1–4). He proclaims he would love her "ten years before the Flood" (8) and concedes that she "should, if you please, refuse / Till the conversion of the Jews" (9–10). This eternal love-land expands as Marvell asserts that his "vegetable love should grow / Vaster than empires, and more slow" (11–12). Every part of her body would be admired for an entire "age" because "lady, you deserve this state, / Nor would I love at lower rate" (19–20). He would willingly wait but, alas, circumstances won't let him. She'll have to settle for the here and now, and he must show her that life is not an eternity but rather an alarm clock.

The speaker laments that "at my back I always hear / Time's wingèd chariot hurrying near" (21–22). He then cleverly draws a picture of what exactly eternity does have in store for them, namely barren "Deserts" where her "beauty shall no more be found" (25) while "worms shall try / That long preserved virginity" (27–28) and her "quaint honor turn to dust" (29). This death imagery is meant to frighten her for not having lived enough. He astutely concedes that "The grave's a fine and private place, / But none, I think, do there embrace" (31-32), thereby making even more vivid the nightmare he has just laid before her. Although he must make his grim argument, he does not want to dampen the mood, so he quickly returns to her fair features.

"Now," the speaker proclaims, "while the youthful hue / Sits on thy skin like morning dew, / And while thy willing soul transpires / At every pore with instant fires, / Now let us sport us while we may" (33-37). The speaker has already made the decision for her. Through sex, their energies will become one—they will "roll" their "strength" and "sweetness up into one ball" (41) as they "tear" their "pleasures with rough strife" (43). If the two of them cannot have eternity and make the "sun / Stand still" (45-46), then they will seize the day, combine and celebrate their humanity, and "make [the sun] run" (46). The speaker makes a vivid case in favor of living for the moment. His elaborate images of the devotion his mistress deserves, the inevitability of death, and the vivaciousness of human life are compelling. Three hundred years later, however, Diane Ackerman demonstrates that women no longer need this lesson, because they share the same desires.

Ackerman's title is taken directly from "To His Coy Mistress." This poet's fine and private place is not the grave, as it was in Marvell's poetic persuasion, but rather her underwater sexual encounter. Ackerman's familiarity with Marvell informs us that she knows about death and its implications. More importantly, her speaker needs no rationale to live fully, she just does. She has sex on her own, willingly, knowingly, and thoroughly.

Unlike "To His Coy Mistress," the poem has no rhyme scheme and has little meter or conventional form. The free verse tells the sexual story in an unconfined, open way. The poem flows together with sensual, sexual images drawn from the mystical, vibrant, undersea world. The speaker and her lover float "under the blue horizon / where long sea fingers / parted like beads / hitched in the doorway / of an opium den" (2–6). Whereas Marvell's lovers race against time, Ackerman's seem to bathe in it. Within this sultry setting the "canyons mazed the deep / reef with hollows, / cul-de-sacs, and narrow boudoirs" (7–10) that evoke erotic images. Her lover's "stroking her arm / with a marine feather / slobbery as aloe pulp" (12–14) constitutes foreplay, and when "the octopus / in his swimsuit / stretch[es] one tentacle / ripple[s] its silky bag" (15–18), she becomes a willing partner. In this "lusty dream" (58), "her hips rolled" (59), "her eyes swam / and chest began to heave" (61–62), and the sea also becomes a willing partner in their love-making as the underwater waves help "drive [his brine] / through petals / delicate as anemone veils / to the dark purpose / of a conch-shaped womb" (68–72).

After "panting ebbed" (75), they return to "shallower realms, / heading back toward/the boat's even keel" (81–83), away from the sensual, wild, sea-world in which they reveled. However, the speaker has not literally or figuratively exhausted the waters yet. The "ocean still petted her / cell by cell, murmuring / along her legs and neck / caressing her / with pale, endless arms" (84–88). Though she emerges from the water and the encounter, the experience stays with her as a satisfying memory.

Her sensual memories of the encounter allow her to savor the moment, in contrast to Marvell's speaker, whose desperate, urgent tone is filled with tension rather than the relief of consummation. In the final section of the poem (106–15), we see that the speaker's sexual encounter is an experience that stays with her "miles / and fathoms away." The erotic language of the sea is in her own voice as she looks out at "minnow snowflakes" while "holding a sponge / idly under [a] tap-gush." As water seems to cascade all around her, the memory of her underwater experience surfaces in the sensuous image of "sinking her teeth / into the cleft / of a voluptuous peach." Ackerman's subject does not have to be persuaded by an excited man to be a sexual being; her sexuality seeps into every day of her life, and we marvel at the depth of her sensuality. Unlike Marvell's speaker, who remains eternally poised to "tear our pleasures," Ackerman's speaker is steeped in those pleasures.

16. The Literary Research Paper

A close reading of a primary source such as a short story, poem, or play can give insights into a work's themes and effects, but sometimes you will want to know more. A published commentary by a critic who knows the work well and is familiar with the author's life and times can provide insights that otherwise may not be available. Such comments and interpretations — known as *secondary sources* — are, of course, not a substitute for the work itself, but they often can take you into a work further than if you made the journey by yourself.

After imagination, good sense, and energy, perhaps the next most important quality for writing a research paper is the ability to organize material. A research paper on a literary topic requires a writer to take account of quite a lot at once: the text, ideas, sources, and documentation techniques all make demands on one's efforts to present a topic clearly and convincingly.

The following list should give you a sense of what goes into creating a research paper. Although some steps on the list can be folded into one another, they offer an overview of the work that will involve you.

1. Choosing a topic
2. Finding sources
3. Evaluating sources
4. Taking notes
5. Developing a thesis
6. Organizing an outline
7. Writing drafts
8. Revising
9. Documenting sources
10. Preparing the final draft and proofreading

Even if you have never written a research paper, you most likely have already had experience choosing a topic, developing a thesis, organizing an outline, and writing a draft that you then revised, proofread, and handed in. Those skills represent six of the ten items on the list. This chapter briefly reviews some of these steps and focuses on the remaining tasks, unique to research paper assignments.

CHOOSING A TOPIC

Chapter 15 discussed the importance of reading a work closely and taking careful notes as a means of generating topics for writing about literature. If you know a work well and record your understanding of it in notes, you'll have impressions and ideas to choose from for potential topics. You may find it useful to review the information on pages 557–558 before reading the advice about putting together a research paper in this chapter.

The student author of the sample research paper "Defining Identity in 'Mending Wall'" (p. 603) was asked to write a five-page paper that demonstrated some familiarity with published critical perspectives on a Robert Frost poem of her choice. Before looking into critical discussions of the poem, she read "Mending Wall" several times, taking notes and making comments in the margin of her textbook on each reading.

What prompted her choice of "Mending Wall" was a class discussion that focused on the poem's speaker's questioning the value and necessity of the wall in contrast to his neighbor's insistence upon it. At one point, however, the boundaries of the discussion opened up to the possibility that the wall is important to both characters in the poem rather than only the neighbor. It is, after all, the speaker, not the neighbor, who repairs the damage to the wall caused by hunters and who initiates the rebuilding of the wall. Why would he do that if he wanted the wall down? Only after having thoroughly examined the poem did the student go to the library to see what professional critics had to say about this question.

FINDING SOURCES

Whether your college library is large or small, its reference librarians can usually help you locate secondary sources about a particular work or author. Unless you choose a very recently published poem about which little or nothing has been written, you should be able to find commentaries about a literary work efficiently and quickly. Here are some useful reference sources that can help you to establish both an overview of a potential topic and a list of relevant books and articles. They are useful for topics on fiction and drama as well as poetry.

Annotated List of References

Baker, Nancy L. *A Research Guide for Undergraduate Students: English and American Literature*. 2nd ed. New York: MLA, 1985. Especially designed for students; a useful guide to reference sources.

Bryer, Jackson, ed. *Sixteen Modern American Authors: A Survey of Research and Criticism*. New York: Norton, 1973. Extensive bibliographic essays on Sherwood Anderson, Willa Cather, Hart Crane, Theodore Dreiser, T. S. Eliot, William Faulkner, F. Scott Fitzgerald, Robert Frost, Ernest Hemingway, Eugene O'Neill, Ezra Pound, Edwin Arlington Robinson, John Steinbeck, Wallace Stevens, William Carlos Williams, and Thomas Wolfe.

Corse, Larry B., and Sandra B. Corse. *Articles on American and British Literature: An Index to Selected Periodicals, 1950–1977*. Athens, OH: Swallow Press, 1981. Specifically designed for students using small college libraries.

Eddleman, Floyd E., ed. *American Drama Criticism: Interpretations, 1890–1977*. 2nd ed. Hamden, CT: Shoe String Press, 1979. Supplement 1984.

Elliot, Emory, et al. *Columbia Literary History of the United States*. New York: Columbia UP, 1988. This updates the discussions in Spiller (below) and reflects recent changes in the canon.

Harner, James L. *Literary Research Guide: A Guide to Reference Sources for the Study of Literature in English and Related Topics*. 2nd ed. New York: MLA, 1993. A selective but extensive annotated guide to important bibliographies, abstracts, data bases, histories, surveys, dictionaries, encyclopedias, and handbooks; an invaluable research tool with extensive, useful indexes.

Holman, C. Hugh, and William Harmon, *A Handbook to Literature*. 6th ed. New York: Macmillan, 1992. A thorough dictionary of literary terms that also provides brief, clear overviews of literary movements such as Romanticism.

Kuntz, Joseph M., and Nancy C. Martinez. *Poetry Explication: A Checklist of Interpretation since 1925 of British and American Poems Past and Present*. Boston: Hall, 1980.

MLA International Bibliography of Books and Articles on Modern Language and Literature. New York: MLA, 1921–. Compiled annually; a major source for articles and books.

The New Cambridge Bibliography of English Literature. 5 vols. Cambridge, Eng.: Cambridge UP, 1967–77. An important source on the literature from A.D. 600 to 1950.

The Oxford History of English Literature. 13 vols. Oxford, Eng.: Oxford UP, 1945–, in progress. The most comprehensive literary history.

The Penguin Companion to World Literature. 4 vols. New York: McGraw-Hill, 1969–71. Covers classical, Oriental, African, European, English, and American literature.

Preminger, Alex, and T. V. F. Brogan, eds. *The New Princeton Encyclopedia of Poetry and Poetics*. Princeton, NJ: Princeton UP, 1993. Includes entries on technical terms and poetic movements.

Rees, Robert, and Earl N. Harbert. *Fifteen American Authors before 1900: Bibliographic Essays on Research and Criticism*. Madison: U of Wisconsin

P, 1971. Among the writers covered are Stephen Crane and Emily
Dickinson.

Spiller, Robert E., et al. *Literary History of the United States.* 4th ed. 2 vols.
New York: Macmillan, 1974. Coverage of literary movements and individual writers from colonial times to the 1960s.

Walker, Warren S. *Twentieth-Century Short Story Explication.* 3rd ed. Hamden, CT: Shoe String Press, 1977. A bibliography of criticism on short
stories written since 1800; supplements appear every few years.

These sources are available in the reference sections of most college libraries; ask a reference librarian to help you locate them.

Computer Searches

Researchers can locate materials in a variety of sources, including card
catalogues, specialized encyclopedias, bibliographies, and indexes to periodicals. Many libraries now also provide computer searches that are linked
to a data base of the libraries' holdings. This can be an efficient way to
establish a bibliography on a specific topic. If your library has such a service,
consult a reference librarian about how to use it and to determine if it is
feasible for your topic. If a computer service is not accessible at your library,
you can still collect the same information from printed sources.

EVALUATING SOURCES AND TAKING NOTES

Evaluate your sources for their reliability and the quality of their evidence. Check to see if an article or book has been superseded by later
studies; try to use up-to-date sources. A popular magazine article will probably not be as authoritative as an article in a scholarly journal. Sources that
are well documented with primary and secondary materials usually indicate
that the author has done his or her homework. Books printed by university
presses and established trade presses are preferable to books privately
printed. But there are always exceptions. If you are uncertain about how to
assess a book, try to find out something about the author. Are there any
other books listed in the catalogue that indicate the author's expertise? What
do book reviews say about the work? Three valuable indexes to book reviews
of literary studies are *Book Review Digest, Book Review Index,* and *Index to
Book Reviews in the Humanities.* Your reference librarian can show you how
to use these important tools for evaluating books. Reviews can be a quick
means to get a broad perspective on writers and their works because re-
viewers often survey previous approaches to the topic under discussion.

As you prepare a list of reliable sources relevant to your topic, record
the necessary bibliographic information so that it will be available when you
make up the list of works cited for your paper. (See the illustration of a
sample bibliography card.) For a book include the author, complete title,
place of publication, publisher, and date. For an article include author,

complete title, name of periodical, volume number, date of issue, and inclusive page numbers.

Once you have assembled a tentative bibliography, you will need to take notes on your readings. If you are not using a word processor, use 3×5, 4×6, or 5×8-inch cards for note taking. They are easy to manipulate and can be readily sorted later on when you establish subheadings for your paper. Be sure to keep track of where the information comes from by writing the author's name and page number on each notecard. If you use more than one work by the same author include a brief title as well as the author's name. (See the illustration of the sample notecard.)

The sample notecard records the source of information (the complete publishing information is on the bibliography card) and provides a heading

> Lynen, John F. The Pastoral
> Art of Robert Frost.
> New Haven: Yale UP,
> 1960.

Sample Bibliography Card for a Book

> Symbolic value of the wall   Lynen 29
>   Lynen describes the wall as
> "the symbol for all kinds of
> man-made barriers."
>
> [Do these barriers have any
> positive value?]

Sample Notecard

594 The Literary Research Paper

that will allow easy sorting later on. Notice that the information is summarized rather than quoted in large chunks. The student also includes a short note asking herself if Lynen's reading could be expanded upon.

Notecards can combine quotations, paraphrases, and summaries; you can also use them to cite your own ideas and give them headings so that you don't lose track of them. As you take notes try to record only points relevant to your topic, though, inevitably, you'll end up not using some of your notes.

DEVELOPING A THESIS AND ORGANIZING THE PAPER

As the notes on "Mending Wall" accumulated, the student sorted them into topics including

```
 1. Publication history of the poem
 2. Frost's experiences as a farmer
 3. Critics' readings of the poem
 4. The speaker's attitude toward the wall
 5. The neighbor's attitude toward the wall
 6. Mythic elements in the poem
 7. Does the wall have any positive value?
 8. How do the speaker and neighbor characterize themselves?
 9. Humor in the poem
10. Frost as a regional poet
```

The student quickly saw that items 1, 2, 6, and 10 were not directly related to her topic concerning why the speaker initiates the rebuilding of the wall. The remaining numbers (3–5, 7–9) are the topics taken up in the paper. The student had begun her reading of secondary sources with a tentative thesis that stemmed from her question about why the poem's speaker helps his neighbor to rebuild the wall. That "why" shaped itself into the expectation that she would have a thesis something like this: "The speaker helps to rebuild the wall because. . . ."

She assumed she would find information that indicated some specific reason. But the more she read the more she discovered that there was no single explanation provided by the poem or by critics' readings of the poem. Instead, through the insights provided by her sources, she began to see that the wall had several important functions in the poem. The perspective she developed into her thesis — that the wall "provided a foundation upon which the men build a personal sense of identity" — allowed her to incorporate a number of the critics' insights into her paper in order to shed light on why the speaker helps to rebuild the wall.

Because the assignment was relatively brief, the student did not write up a formal outline but instead organized her stacks of usable notecards and proceeded to write the first draft from them.

REVISING

After writing your first draft, you should review the advice and revision checklist on pp. 569–570 so that you can read your paper with an objective eye. Two days after writing her next-to-last draft, the writer of "Defining Identity in 'Mending Wall'" realized that she had allotted too much space for critical discussions of the humor in the poem that were not directly related to her approach. She realized that it was not essential to point out and discuss the puns in the poem; hence she corrected this by simply deleting most references to the poem's humor. The point is that she saw this herself after she took some time to approach the paper from a fresh perspective.

DOCUMENTING SOURCES

You must acknowledge the use of a source when you (1) quote someone's exact words, (2) summarize or borrow someone's opinions or ideas, or (3) use information and facts that are not considered to be common knowledge. The purpose of this documentation is to acknowledge your sources, to demonstrate that you are familiar with what others have thought about the topic, and to provide your reader access to the same sources. If your paper is not adequately documented, it will be vulnerable to a charge of *plagiarism* — the presentation of someone else's work as your own. Conscious plagiarism is easy to avoid; honesty takes care of that for most people. However, there is a more problematic form of plagiarism that is often inadvertent. Whether inadequate documentation is conscious or not, plagiarism is a serious matter and must be avoided. Papers can be evaluated only by what is on the page, not by their writers' intentions.

Let's look more closely at what constitutes plagiarism. Consider the following passage quoted from A. R. Coulthard, "Frost's 'Mending Wall,'" *Explicator* 45 (Winter 1987): 40:

> "Mending Wall" has many of the features of an "easy" poem aimed at high-minded readers. Its central symbol is the accessible stone wall to represent separation, and it appears to oppose isolating barriers and favor love and trust, the stuff of Golden Treasury of Inspirational Verse.

Now read this plagiarized version:

> "Mending Wall" is an easy poem that appeals to high-minded readers who take inspiration from its symbolism of the stone wall, which seems to oppose isolating barriers and support trusting love.

Though the writer has shortened the passage and made some changes in the wording, this paragraph is basically the same as Coulthard's. Indeed, several of his phrases are lifted almost intact. (Notice, however, that the plagiarized version seems to have missed Coulthard's irony and, therefore, misinterpreted and misrepresented the passage.) Even if a parenthetical reference had been included at the end of the passage and the source included in "Works Cited," the language of this passage would still be plagiarism because it is presented as the writer's own. Both language and ideas must be acknowledged.

Here is an adequately documented version of the passage:

```
A. R. Coulthard points out that "high-minded readers" mistak-
enly assume that "Mending Wall" is a simple inspirational poem
that uses the symbolic wall to reject isolationism and to sup-
port, instead, a sense of human community (40).
```

This passage makes absolutely clear that the observation is Coulthard's, and it is written in the student's own language with the exception of one quoted phrase. Had Coulthard not been named in the passage, the parenthetical reference would have included his name: (Coulthard 40).

Some mention should be made of the notion of common knowledge before we turn to the standard format for documenting sources. Observations and facts that are widely known and routinely included in many of your sources do not require documentation. It is not necessary to cite a source for the fact that Alfred, Lord Tennyson, was born in 1809 or that Frost writes about New England. Sometimes it will be difficult for you to determine what common knowledge is for a topic that you know little about. If you are in doubt, the best strategy is to supply a reference.

There are two basic ways to document sources. Traditionally, sources have been cited in footnotes at the bottom of each page or in endnotes grouped together at the end of the paper. Here is how a portion of the sample paper on "Mending Wall" would look if footnotes were used instead of parenthetical documentation:

```
It remains one of Frost's more popular poems, and, as Douglas
Wilson notes, "one of the most famous in all of American
poetry."¹
```

```
¹Douglas L. Wilson, "The Other Side of the Wall," Iowa
Review 10 (Winter 1979): 65.
```

Unlike endnotes, which are double spaced throughout under the title of "Notes" on separate pages at the end of the paper, footnotes appear four spaces below the text. They are single spaced with double spaces between notes.

No doubt you will have encountered these documentation methods in your reading. A different style is recommended, however, in the third edition of the Modern Language Association's *MLA Handbook for Writers of Research Papers* (1988). The new style employs parenthetical references within the text of the paper; these are keyed to an alphabetical list of works cited at the end of the paper. This method is designed to be less distracting for the reader. Unless you are instructed to follow the footnote or endnote style for documentation, use the new parenthetical method explained in the next section.

The List of Works Cited

Items in the list of works cited are arranged alphabetically according to the author's last name and indented five spaces after the first line. This allows the reader to locate quickly the complete bibliographic information for the author's name cited within the parenthetical reference in the text. The following are common entries for literature papers and should be used as models. If some of your sources are of a different nature, consult Joseph Gibaldi and Walter S. Achtert, *MLA Handbook for Writers of Research Papers,* 3rd ed. (New York: MLA, 1988); many of the bibliographic possibilities you are likely to need are included in this source.

A Book by One Author

Hendrickson, Robert. <u>The Literary Life and Other Curiosities</u>. New York: Viking, 1981.

Notice that the author's name is in reverse order. This information, along with the full title, place of publication, publisher, and date should be taken from the title and copyright pages of the book. The title is underlined to indicate italics and is also followed by a period. If the city of publication is well known, it is unnecessary to include the state. Use the publication date on the title page; if none appears there use the copyright date (after ©) on the back of the title page.

A Book by Two Authors

Horton, Rod W., and Herbert W. Edwards. <u>Backgrounds of Ameri-</u><u>can Literary Thought</u>. 3rd ed. Englewood Cliffs: Prentice, 1974.

Only the first author's name is given in reverse order. The edition number appears after the title.

A Book with More than Three Authors

Abrams, M. H., et al., eds. <u>The Norton Anthology of English</u>
<u>Literature</u>. 5th ed. 2 vols. New York: Norton, 1986.
Vol. 1.

The abbreviation *et al.* means "and others." It is used to avoid having to list all fourteen editors of this first volume of a two-volume work.

A Work in a Collection by the Same Author

O'Connor, Flannery. "Greenleaf." <u>The Complete Stories</u>. By
O'Connor. New York: Farrar, 1971. 311–34.

Page numbers are given because the reference is to only a single story in the collection.

A Work in a Collection by Different Writers

Frost, Robert. "Design." <u>Poetry: An Introduction</u>.
Ed. Michael Meyer. Boston: Bedford–St. Martin's P, 1995.
311.

The hyphenated publisher's name indicates a publisher's imprint: Bedford Books of St. Martin's Press.

A Translated Book

Grass, Günter. <u>The Tin Drum</u>. Trans. Ralph Manheim. New
York: Vintage–Random, 1962.

An Introduction, Preface, Foreword, or Afterword

Johnson, Thomas H. Introduction. <u>Final Harvest: Emily Dick-</u>
<u>inson's Poems</u>. By Emily Dickinson. Boston: Little,
Brown, 1961. vii–xiv.

This cites the introduction by Johnson. Notice that a colon is used between the book's main title and subtitle. To cite a poem in this book use this method:

Dickinson, Emily. "A Tooth upon Our Peace." <u>Final Harvest:</u>
<u>Emily Dickinson's Poems</u>. Ed. Thomas H. Johnson. Boston:
Little, Brown, 1961. 110.

An Encyclopedia

"Wordsworth, William." The New Encyclopedia Britannica.
        1984 ed.

Because this encyclopedia is organized alphabetically, no page number or other information is given, only the edition number (if available) and date.

An Article in a Magazine

Morrow, Lance.   "Scribble, Scribble, Eh, Mr. Toad." Time 24
        Feb. 1986: 84.

The citation for an unsigned article would begin with the title and be alphabetized by the first word of the title other than "a," "an," or "the."

An Article in a Scholarly Journal with Continuous Pagination beyond a Single Issue

Mahar, William J.   "Black English in Early Blackface Min-
        strelsy: A New Interpretation of the Sources of Minstrel
        Show Dialect." American Quarterly 37 (1985): 260-85.

Because this journal uses continuous pagination instead of separate pagination for each issue, it is not necessary to include the month, season, or number of the issue. Only one of the quarterly issues will have pages numbered 260–85. If you are not certain whether a journal's pages are numbered continuously throughout a volume, supply the month, season, or issue number, as in the next entry.

An Article in a Scholarly Journal with Separate Pagination for Each Issue

Updike, John.   "The Cultural Situation of the American
        Writer." American Studies International 15 (Spring
        1977): 19-28.

By noting the spring issue, the entry saves a reader looking through each issue of the 1977 volume for the correct article on pages 19–28.

An Article in a Newspaper

Ziegler, Philip.   "The Lure of Gossip, the Rules of History."
        New York Times 23 Feb. 1986: sec. 7: 1+.

This citation indicates that the article appears on page 1 of section 7 and continues onto another page.

```
Stern, Milton.  "Melville's View of Law."  English 270 class
     lecture.  University of Connecticut, Storrs, 12 Mar.
     1992.
```

Parenthetical References

A list of works cited is not an adequate indication of how you have used sources in your paper. You must also provide the precise location of quotations and other information by using parenthetical references within the text of the paper. You do this by citing the author's name (or the source's title if the work is anonymous) and the page number.

```
Collins points out that "Nabokov was misunderstood by early
reviewers of his work" (28).
```

or

```
Nabokov's first critics misinterpreted his stories (Collins
28).
```

Either way a reader will find the complete bibliographic entry in the list of works cited under Collins's name and know that the information cited in the paper appears on page 28. Notice that the end punctuation comes after the parentheses.

If you have listed more than one work by the same author, you would add a brief title to the parenthetical reference to distinguish between them. You could also include the full title in your text.

```
Nabokov's first critics misinterpreted his stories (Collins
"Early Reviews" 28).
```

or

```
Collins points out in "Early Reviews of Nabokov's Fiction"
that his early work was misinterpreted by reviewers (28).
```

There can be many variations on what is included in a parenthetical reference, depending on the nature of the entry in the list of works cited. But the general principle is simple enough: provide enough parenthetical information for a reader to find the work in "Works Cited." Examine the sample research paper for more examples of works cited and strategies for including parenthetical references. If you are puzzled by a given situation, ask your reference librarian to show you the *MLA Handbook*.

SAMPLE STUDENT RESEARCH PAPER

The following research paper by Juliana Daniels follows the format described in the *MLA Handbook for Writers of Research Papers* (1988). This format is discussed in the preceding section on Documentation and in Chapter 15, in the section "Manuscript Form" (p. 571). Though the sample paper is short, it illustrates many of the techniques and strategies useful for writing an essay that includes secondary sources. Notice that when you cite poetry lines no abbreviation is used in the parenthetical documentation. Simply use the word *line* or *lines* in that first citation along with the number(s), and then just use the number(s) in subsequent citations after having established that the number(s) refers to lines ("Mending Wall" is reprinted on p. 298.)

Juliana Daniels

Professor Caron

English 109-11

December 6, 19--

Defining Identity in "Mending Wall"

Robert Frost's poem "Mending Wall" has been the object of much critical scrutiny since its publication in 1914. It remains one of Frost's more popular poems, and, as Douglas L. Wilson notes, "one of the most famous in all of American poetry" (65). Perhaps partly as a result of its widespread popularity and frequent inclusion in literature anthologies, critics have tended to treat "Mending Wall" as a fairly straightforward poem that is easily accessible to high school students as well as professional scholars. But over the years there have been decided trends in the critical interpretations of this poem. These trends manifest themselves mostly in debates over which character, the speaker or his neighbor, has a clearer understanding of the real significance of the crumbling stone wall they endeavor to mend. However, scholars have overlooked the important ways that the wall helps each man to define himself in relation to the other. The wall not only offers the men a tangible way to demarcate their property but also affords them a way to clearly define their relationship with each other. Thus the wall does far more than just, as the neighbor asserts, make "good neighbors" (line 27)--it provides a foundation upon which the men may build a personal sense of identity.

This notion of identity as a significant theme in the poem has often been ignored by critics in favor of discussions of the meaning of the wall itself. Many previous interpretations of "Mending Wall" have focused on the speaker's supposed insight, crediting him with the wisdom to recognize the unnaturally limiting and divisive qualities inherent in the wall. After all, it is the speaker who twice mentions that "Something there is that doesn't love a wall" (35), thereby challenging his neighbor's firm defense of the wall as the means of creating "good neighbors" (27). Charles Watson acknowledges the common tendency of readers to interpret the poem as "the meditation of a right-minded man who, even as he participates in the annual wall-mending rite, indulges privately in some gently mocking reflections on his neighbor's mindless adherence to his father's belief in walls" (653). The speaker's apparent "right-mindedness," as well as the appeal of joining him in his supposed aversion to artificial boundaries between people, effectively lulls readers into a mistaken faith in the speaker's negative perception of both the wall and his "recalcitrant and plodding neighbor [who] is a slave to the rituals of the quotidian" (Lentricchia 11).

This original critical trend of favoring the speaker's vision of the wall as meaningless and the neighbor as mindless has been countered by numerous readings of the poem in which the neighbor's point of view is deemed the wiser and more valuable. Fritz Oehlschlaeger, among others, suggests the possibility of interpreting "Mending Wall" in favor of the neighbor's perspective, maintaining that it is the neighbor "who understands both the intransigence of natural fact and the need to limit human ego. This understanding makes the Yankee farmer, not the speaker, the truly neighborly figure in the poem" (244). In this case the neighbor is credited with the understanding that established boundaries provide the necessary foundations for strong and successful relationships between people. His repeated assertion that "Good fences make good neighbors" (27, 45) suggests that walls are "the essential barriers that must exist between man and man if the individual is to preserve his own soul, and mutual understanding is to survive and flourish" (Ward 428).

However, the real wisdom in "Mending Wall" lies not in deciding whose point of view is more admirable but in recognizing that although the wall is perceived differently by the two men, it is essential in defining both of them. That is, the sense of identity that each man has in relation to the other deeply depends upon the existence of the wall that divides them and the way that they conceive of the wall. The neighbor can more readily acknowledge and articulate his desire for the wall to remain in place, but the speaker also does his part to ensure that the wall dividing their property does not crumble. For they each realize, on some level, that if the wall that defines the limits of their land were to disappear, then their sense of the established social order would also disappear, along with their identity as a part of that social order. As James R. Dawes points out, these "men can only interact when reassured by the constructed alienation of the wall" (300). So they work together to keep the wall firmly in place, keeping themselves separated in order to maintain their individual sense of self.

Part of the speaker's sense of identity lies in his role as a questioner, a challenger, a rebel thinker. He twice mentions his recognition that "Something there is that doesn't love a wall" (1, 35), and seems pleased to ally himself with the forces of nature that conspire to destroy that wall which becomes, as John Lynen notes, "the symbol for all kinds of man-made barriers" (29). Yet the speaker's

pleasure at minimizing the importance of the wall results
less from any inherent properties of the actual wall than it
does from the sense of superiority over his neighbor which
this belief affords him. The speaker's created sense of
identity as an insightful, clever "free-thinker" is
corroborated by his belief that "the neighbor's adherence to
his father's saying suggests the narrowness and blind habit
of the primitive" (Lynen 28); it is his opposition to the
neighbor which defines the speaker in the poem. The speaker
declares that he can think of no good reason for maintaining
the wall, as there are no cows to contain and his "apple
trees will never get across / And eat the cones under his
[neighbor's] pines" (25-26). Clearly, his belief in his own
wisdom leads to his sense of superiority over his neighbor,
the "old-stone savage" (40) who "moves in darkness" (41).
Thus, the existence of the wall provides the speaker with the
means to identify himself as superior to his neighbor.

It is revealing to note that in spite of the speaker's
superfluous objections to the rebuilding of the wall, it is
he who initiates its repair each spring. He acknowledges
that "I let my neighbor know beyond the hill; / And on a day
we meet to walk the line / And set the wall between us once
again" (12-14). He also explains how he repeatedly replaces
the stones on the wall after hunters dislodge them: "I have
come after them and made repair / Where they have left not
one stone on a stone / But they would have the rabbit out of
hiding" (6-8). Thus, the speaker's behavior indicates that
he does in fact believe in the importance of the wall,
diligently restoring it whenever the stones are knocked out
of place. This apparent contradiction between the speaker's
actions and his purported beliefs suggests a subtle
recognition of the importance of maintaining the wall. The

speaker fancies himself a genuine liberal, responding to his neighbor's conservative refrain "Good fences make good neighbors" (27) with the question "Why do they make good neighbors?" (30). The answer lies in the reader's understanding that the wall is crucial to maintaining the speaker's own self image. Perhaps the wall is not needed to fence in cows or trees, but it is necessary in order for the speaker to define himself in relation to the way his neighbor conceives of the wall. The speaker's superfluous objections to the wall are nothing more than fancy, for without the wall the speaker would be unable to define himself in opposition to his neighbor.

While the speaker defines his neighbor as a close-minded primitive, thereby validating his notion of himself as much superior to him, the neighbor defines himself as someone who, unlike the speaker, can acknowledge the importance of the wall. He finds it necessary to tell the speaker two separate times that "Good fences make good neighbors" (27, 45), suggesting his recognition that the speaker resists acknowledging the merit of his father's saying. Thus the neighbor is able to define himself in relation to the speaker, believing himself to clearly possess more valuable knowledge about fences and about relationships than his seemingly flighty neighbor does. The humor of this poem lies in the irony that both men consider themselves to have sharper perceptions and broader knowledge than the other, thus contributing to their individual sense of superiority.

Marion Montgomery explains that a "wise person knows that a wall is a point of reference, a touchstone of sanity, and that it must be not only maintained but respected as well" (147). But the wall in "Mending Wall" goes beyond a reference point that protects merely one's privacy and individuality; it actually offers two people the foundation they need in order to be able to relate to each other and to understand themselves. Without the ritual of rebuilding the wall, neither the speaker nor the neighbor would have a way to compare himself to the other and thus reaffirm his own vision of himself. The confrontation between the two men in "Mending Wall" is as much of a ritual as the actual mending of the wall and is maintained as the poem "concludes with the fence having been mended and with the reader expecting the same movement to take place in succeeding years" (Bowen 14). Both the speaker and his neighbor "walk the line" (13) together, each complicit in the rebuilding and re-enforcing of the established barrier that allows them to maintain a sense of personal identity.

Works Cited

Bowen, J. K. "The Persona in Frost's 'Mending Wall': Mended
    or Amended." CEA Critic 31 (November 1968): 14.

Dawes, James R. "Masculinity and Transgression in Robert
    Frost." American Literature 65 (June 1993): 297–312.

Frost, Robert. "Mending Wall." Poetry: An Introduction.
    Ed. Michael Meyer. Boston: Bedford–St. Martin's P,
    1995. 298.

Lentricchia, Frank. "Experience as Meaning: Robert Frost's
    'Mending Wall.'" CEA Critic 34 (May 1972): 8–12.

Lynen, John F. The Pastoral Art of Robert Frost. New Haven:
    Yale UP, 1960. 27–31.

Montgomery, Marion. "Robert Frost and His Use of Barriers:
    Man vs. Nature toward God." Robert Frost: A Collection
    of Critical Essays. Ed. James M. Cox. Englewood
    Cliffs: Prentice, 1962. 138–150.

Oehlschlaeger, Fritz. "Fences Make Neighbors: Process, Iden-
    tity, and Ego in Robert Frost's 'Mending Wall.'" Ari-
    zona Quarterly 40 (Autumn 1984): 242–54.

Ward, William S. "Lifted Pot Lids and Unmended Walls." Col-
    lege English 27 (February 1966): 428–29.

Watson, Charles N. "Frost's Wall: The View from the Other
    Side." New England Quarterly 44 (December 1971): 653–
    56.

Wilson, Douglas L. "The Other Side of the Wall." Iowa Re-
    view 10 (Winter 1979): 65–75.

Acknowledgments *(continued from p. iv)*

Elizabeth Bishop. "Manners," "The Shampoo," "The Fish," "Five Flights Up," and "Sestina" from *The Complete Poems: 1927–1979* by Elizabeth Bishop. Copyright © 1979, 1983 by Alice Helen Methfessel. Reprinted by permission of Farrar, Straus & Giroux, Inc.

Harold Bloom. "On 'Bright Star!'" from *The Visionary Company* by Harold Bloom. Copyright © 1971 by Harold Bloom. Reprinted by permission of the author.

Robert Bly. "Waking from Sleep" from *Silence in the Snowy Fields* by Robert Bly. Copyright © 1962 by Robert Bly. Reprinted by permission of the author.

Louise Bogan. "Single Sonnet" from *The Blue Estuaries* by Louise Bogan. Copyright © 1956 by Charles Scribner's Sons. Renewal Copyright © 1964 by Louise Bogan. Reprinted by permission of Farrar, Straus & Giroux, Inc.

Roo Borson. "Talk" reprinted from *A Sad Device* (Quadrant Editions, 1981).

George Bowering. "Grandfather" from *Touch: Selected Poems 1960–1970* by George Bowering. Used by permission of the Canadian Publishers, McClelland & Stewart, Toronto.

Marilyn Bowering. "Wishing Africa" reprinted by permission of the author.

Anne Bradstreet. "Before the Birth of One of Her Children," "The Author to Her Book," and excerpt from "The Flesh and the Spirit," reprinted by permission of the publishers from *The Works of Anne Bradstreet*, ed. by Jeannine Hensley, Cambridge, Mass.: Harvard University Press, Copyright © 1967 by the President and Fellows of Harvard College.

Cleanth Brooks. "History in 'Ode on a Grecian Urn'" first published in *The Sewanee Review,* vol. 52, no. 1 (Winter 1944). Reprinted with the permission of the editor.

Gwendolyn Brooks. "The Bean Eaters," "We Real Cool," and "The Mother" from *Blacks* by Gwendolyn Brooks. Copyright © 1991 by Gwendolyn Brooks. Reprinted by permission of the author.

Reuben A. Brower. "On the 'Essence of Winter Sleep' in 'After Apple-Picking'" from *The Poetry of Robert Frost: Constellations of Intention* by Reuben A. Brower. Copyright © 1963 by Reuben A. Brower; renewed 1991 by Helen P. Brower. Reprinted by permission of Oxford University Press, Inc.

Michael Cadnum. "Cat Spy," copyright © by Michael Cadnum. First appeared in *Light Year '86*. Reprinted by permission of the author.

Lorna Dee Cervantes. "Poem for the Young White Man Who Asked Me How I, an Intelligent, Well-Read Person Could Believe in the War Between the Races" is reprinted from *Emplumada,* by Lorna Dee Cervantes, by permission of The University of Pittsburgh Press. © 1981 by Lorna Dee Cervantes.

Tracy Chapman. "Fast Car" copyright © 1988 EMI April Music Inc. and Purple Rabbit Music. All rights controlled and administered by EMI April Music Inc. All rights reserved. International copyright secured. Used by permission.

Helen Chasin. "The Word *Plum*" from *Coming Close and Other Poems* by Helen Chasin. Copyright © 1968 by Yale University Press. Reprinted by permission.

John Ciardi. "Suburban." Reprinted from *For Instance* by John Ciardi, with the permission of W. W. Norton & Company, Inc. Copyright © 1979 by John Ciardi.

Amy Clampitt. "Nothing Stays Put" from *Westward* by Amy Clampitt. Copyright © 1990 by Amy Clampitt. Reprinted by permission of Alfred A. Knopf, Inc.

Lucille Clifton. "for deLawd," "come home from the movies," and "the poet," copyright © 1987, by Lucille Clifton. Reprinted from *good woman: poems and a memoir, 1969–1980,* by Lucille Clifton, with the permission of BOA Editions, Ltd., 92 Park Avenue, Brockport, NY 14420.

Leonard Cohen. "Suzanne" copyright 1967 Leonard Cohen Stranger Music, Inc. Used by permission. All rights reserved.

Edmund Conti. "Pragmatist" from *Light Year '86*. Reprinted by permission of the author.

Robert G. Cook. "The Influence of Emerson's 'Self-Reliance' on Prufrock" from "Emerson's 'Self-Reliance,' Sweeney, and Prufrock," *American Literature* 42:2 pp. 221–26. Copyright Duke University Press, 1970. Reprinted with permission.

Herbert R. Coursen, Jr. "A Reading of 'Stopping by Woods on a Snowy Evening,'" excerpt from "The Ghost of Christmas Past: 'Stopping by Woods on a Snowy Evening,'" *College English*, December 1962. Copyright © 1962 by the National Council of Teachers of English. Reprinted with permission.

Robert Creeley. "Fathers" from *Memory Gardens* by Robert Creeley. Copyright © 1986 by Robert Creeley. Reprinted by permission of New Directions Publishing Corporation.

Sally Croft. "Home-Baked Bread" from *Light Year '86*. Reprinted by permission of the author.

Countee Cullen. "For a Lady I Know" and "Saturday's Child" from *Color* by Countee Cullen. Copyright © 1925 by Harper & Brothers; copyright renewed 1953 by Ida M. Cullen. Reprinted by permission of GRM Associates, Inc., Agents for the Estate of Ida M. Cullen.

e. e. cummings. "my sweet old etcetera," "since feeling is first," "she being Brand," "next to of course god america i," "anyone lived in a pretty how town," "l(a," "in Just—," and "Buffalo Bill 's" reprinted from *Complete Poems, 1904–1962,* by e. e. Cummings, Edited by George J. Firmage, by permission of Liveright Publishing Corporation. Copyright © 1923, 1925, 1926, 1931, 1935, 1938, 1939, 1940, 1944, 1945, 1946, 1947, 1948, 1949, 1950, 1951, 1952, 1953, 1954, 1955, 1956, 1957, 1958, 1959, 1960, 1961, 1962 by e. e. Cummings. Copyright © 1961, 1963, 1966, 1967, 1968 by Marion Morehouse Cummings. Copyright © 1972, 1973, 1974, 1975, 1976, 1977, 1978, 1979, 1980, 1981, 1982, 1983, 1984, 1985, 1986, 1987, 1988, 1989, 1990, 1991 by the Trustees for the e. e. Cummings Trust. "On the Artist's Responsibility" reprinted by permission of the publisher from *i: six nonlectures* by e. e. cummings, Cambridge, Mass: Harvard University Press, Copyright © 1953 by e. e. cummings; © 1981 by e. e. Cummings Trust.

H. D. "Garden II" (Heat) from *Collected Poems 1912–1944*. Copyright © 1982 by the Estate of Hilda Doolittle. Reprinted by permission of New Directions Publishing Corporation.

Andrew P. Debicki. "New Criticism and Deconstruction" © 1985 by the University Press of Kansas. Reprinted from *Writing and Reading Differently: Deconstruction and the Teaching of Composition and Literature*, edited by G. Douglas Atkins and Michael L. Johnson.

Peter De Vries. "To His Importunate Mistress," copyright © 1986 by Peter De Vries. This poem first appeared in *The New Yorker*. Reprinted by permission of the author and the Watkins/Loomis Agency.

Emily Dickinson. "After great pain, a formal feeling comes—," "Because I could not stop for Death—," "A Bird came down the Walk," "The Brain—is wider than the Sky," "From all the Jails the Boys and Girls," "'Heaven'—is what I cannot reach!" "I dwell in possibility—," "I heard a Fly buzz—when I died," "A narrow fellow in the Grass," "I never saw a Moor—," "I taste a liquor never brewed—," "If I shouldn't be alive," "I'm Nobody! Who are you?" "Much Madness is divinest Sense," "My Life had stood—a Loaded Gun," "The Robin's my Criterion for Tune," "Shall I take thee, the Poet said," "The Soul Selects her own Society," "Success is counted sweetest," "Tell all the Truth but tell it slant—," "There's a certain Slant of light," reprinted by permission of the publishers and the Trustees of Amherst College from *The Poems of Emily Dickinson,* Thomas H. Johnson, ed., Cambridge, Mass.: The Belknap Press of Harvard University Press, © 1951, 1955, 1983 by the President and Fellows of Harvard College. Also from *The Complete Poems of Emily Dickinson* edited by Thomas H. Johnson. Copyright 1929, 1935 by Martha Dickinson Bianchi; Copyright © renewed 1957, 1963 by Mary L. Hampson. By permission of Little, Brown and Company. "Description of Herself," excerpt from a letter to Thomas Wentworth Higginson, April 25, 1862 reprinted by permission of the publishers from *The Letters of Emily Dickinson* edited by Thomas H. Johnson, Cambridge, Mass.: The Belknap Press of Harvard University Press, Copyright © 1958, 1986 by the President and Fellows of Harvard College.

David Donnell. "The Canadian Prairies View of Literature" from *Settlements* by David Donnell. Used by permission of the Canadian Publishers, McClelland & Stewart, Toronto.

Bernard Duyfhuizen. "'To His Coy Mistress': On How a Female Might Respond," excerpt from "Textual Harassment of Marvell's Coy Mistress: The Institutionalization of Masculine Criticism," *College English*, April 1988. Copyright © 1988 by the National Council of Teachers of English. Reprinted with permission.

Richard Eberhart. "The Groundhog" from *Collected Poems 1930–1986* by Richard Eberhart. Copyright © 1960, 1976, 1988 by Richard Eberhart. Reprinted by permission of Oxford University Press, Inc.

Jane Donahue Eberwein. "On Making Do with Dickinson" from "Doing Without: Dickinson as Yankee Woman Poet" by Jane Donahue Eberwein. Excerpted with permission of G. K. Hall, an imprint of Macmillan Publishing Company, from *Critical Essays on Emily Dickinson*, edited by Paul J. Ferlazzo. Copyright © 1984 by Paul J. Ferlazzo.

T. S. Eliot. "Macavity: The Mystery Cat" from *Old Possum's Book of Practical Cats*, copyright 1939 by T. S. Eliot and renewed 1967 by Esme Valerie Eliot. Reprinted by permission of Harcourt Brace and Company and Faber and Faber Limited.

Louise Erdrich. "Captivity" from *Love Medicine* by Louise Erdrich. Copyright © 1984 by Louise Erdrich. Reprinted by permission of Henry Holt and Company, Inc.

Martín Espada. "Tiburón" from *Trumpets from the Islands of Their Eviction* by Martín Espada. Copyright © 1987 by Bilingual Press/Editorial Bilingüe. Reprinted by permission of Bilingual Press/Editorial Bilingüe, Arizona State University, Tempe, AZ.

Elizabeth Eybers. "Emily Dickinson" from *Longman Anthology of World Literature by Women* edited by Marian Arkin and Barbara Shollar. Copyright © 1989 by Longman Publishing Group.

Ruth Fainlight. "Flower Feet" reprinted by permission; © 1989 Ruth Fainlight. Originally in *The New Yorker*.

Faiz Ahmed Faiz. "Prison Daybreak" from *The True Subject: Selected Poems of Faiz Ahmed Faiz*. Copyright © 1988 by Princeton University Press. Reprinted by permission of Princeton University Press.

Blanche Farley. "The Lover Not Taken" from *Light Year '85*. Reprinted by permission of the author.

Kenneth Fearing. "AD" from *New and Collected Poems* (Indiana University Press, 1956). Reprinted by permission of the Estate of Kenneth Fearing.

Stanley Fish. "On What Makes an Interpretation Acceptable" reprinted by permission of the publishers from *Is There a Text In This Class?* by Stanley Fish, Cambridge, Mass.: Harvard University Press, Copyright © 1980 by the President and Fellows of Harvard College.

F. Scott Fitzgerald. "On the 'Extraordinary Genius' of Keats" from *The Crack-Up*. Copyright 1957 by New Directions Publishing Corp. Reprinted by permission of the New Directions Publishing Corporation.

Robert J. Fogelin. "A Case against Metaphors" from *Figuratively Speaking*, Yale University Press. Copyright © 1988. Reprinted by permission.

Carolyn Forché. "The Colonel" from *The Country Between Us* by Carolyn Forché. Copyright © 1981 by Carolyn Forché. Reprinted by permission of HarperCollins Publishers, Inc.

Robert Francis. "Excellence" and "Glass" reprinted from *Robert Francis: Collected Poems, 1936–1976* (Amherst: University of Massachusetts Press, 1976), copyright © 1976 by Robert Francis. "Hard" from *The Satirical Rogue on Poetry* by Robert Francis. (Amherst: University of Massachusetts Press, 1968). Copyright © 1968 by Robert Francis. Reprinted by permission of University of Massachusetts Press. "Catch" and "The Pitcher," copyright © 1950, 1953 by Robert Francis. Reprinted from *The Orb Weaver*, copyright 1950, 1953 by Robert Francis. Wesleyan University Press by permission of the University Press of New England.

Robert Frost. "Acquainted With The Night," "After Apple-Picking," "Birches," "A Considerable Speck," "Desert Places," "Design," "Fire and Ice," "For Once, Then Something," "The Gift Outright," "Home Burial," "Mending Wall," "Neither Out Far Nor In Deep," "Nothing Gold Can Stay," "Out, Out —," "Oven Bird," "The Pasture," "Provide, Provide," "The Road Not Taken," "The Silken Tent," and "Stopping by Woods on a Snowy Evening" from *The Poetry of Robert Frost* edited by Edward Connery Lathem. Copyright 1936, 1942, 1944, 1951, © 1956, 1958, by Robert Frost. Copyright © 1964, 1967, 1970 by Lesley Frost Ballantine. Copyright 1916, 1923, 1930, 1939, 1967, 1968, 1969 by Henry Holt and Company, Inc. Reprinted by permission of Henry Holt and Company, Inc. "In White" from *The Dimensions of Robert Frost* by Reginald L. Cook. Copyright © 1958 by Reginald Cook. Excerpt from "The Figure a Poem Makes" from *Selected Prose of Robert Frost* edited by Hyde Cox and Edward Connery Lathem. Copyright 1939, © 1967 by Holt, Rinehart, and Winston. All of the above reprinted by permission of Henry Holt and Company, Inc. "On the Living Part of a Poem" reprinted by permission of New York University Press from *A Swinger of Birches: A Portrait of Robert Frost* by Sidney Cox. Copyright © 1957 by New York University Press, Inc. "On the Way to Read a Poem" from "Poetry and School" by Robert Frost in *The Atlantic Monthly*, June, 1951. Reprinted by permission of Peter Gilbert.

Alice Fulton. "On the Validity of Free Verse" from *Ecstatic Occasions, Expedient Forms*, David Lehman, ed. Reprinted by permission of the author.

Tess Gallagher. "Black Silk" copyright © 1987 by Tess Gallagher. Reprinted with the permission of Graywolf Press, Saint Paul, Minnesota.

Deborah Garrison. "She Was Waiting to Be Told" reprinted by permission. © 1990 Deborah Gottlieb Garrison. Originally in *The New Yorker*.

Sandra M. Gilbert and Susan Gubar. "On Dickinson's White Dress" excerpted from *The Madwoman in the Attic* by Gilbert and Gubar. Yale University Press, 1979. Reprinted by permission.

Allen Ginsberg. "America" copyright © 1956, 1959 by Allen Ginsberg. Copyright renewed. "A Supermarket in California" copyright © 1955 by Allen Ginsberg. Both from *Collected Poems 1947–1980* by Allen Ginsberg. Reprinted by permission of HarperCollins Publishers, Inc.

Nikki Giovanni. "Nikki-Rosa" from *Black Feeling, Black Talk, Black Judgment* by Nikki Giovanni. Copyright © 1968, 1970 by Nikki Giovanni. Reprinted by permission of William Morrow & Company, Inc.

Henry A. Giroux. "Liberal Arts Education and the Struggle for Public Life: Dreaming about Democracy" from *South Atlantic Quarterly* 89:1 (1990) and Gless and Hernstein Smith, *The Politics of Liberal Education* (1992), copyright Duke University Press. Reprinted with permission.

Judy Grahn. "She Who Bears It" from *The Work of the Common Woman*, copyright © 1978 by Judy Grahn, published by the Crossing Press, Freedom, CA. Reprinted by permission of the Crossing Press.

Donald J. Greiner. "On What Comes 'After Apple-Picking" from "The Indispensable Robert Frost" by Donald J. Greiner. Excerpted with permission of G. K. Hall & Co., an imprint of Macmillan Publishing Company, from *Critical Essays on Robert Frost* by Philip L. Gerber. Copyright © 1982 by Philip L. Gerber.

Eamon Grennan. "Bat" reprinted by permission; © 1991 Eamon Grennan. Originally in *The New Yorker*.

Donald Hall. "To a Waterfowl" from *The Town of Hill* by Donald Hall. Copyright © 1975 by Donald Hall. Reprinted by permission of David R. Godine, Publisher. "My Son, My Executioner" from *Old and New Poems* by Donald Hall. Copyright © 1990 by Donald Hall. Reprinted by permission of Ticknor & Fields/Houghton Mifflin Co. All rights reserved.

Mark Halliday. "Graded Paper" from *Michigan Quarterly Review*. Reprinted by permission of the author.

William Hathaway. "Oh, Oh" from *Light Year '86*. This poem was originally published in the *Cincinnati Poetry Review*. Reprinted by permission of the author.

Harriet Hawkins. "Should We Study *King Kong* or *King Lear?*" from "*King Lear* to *King Kong* and Back: Shakespeare in Popular Modern Genres" in *"Bad" Shakespeare: Revelations of the Shakespeare Canon*, ed. Maurice Cherney, Fairleigh Dickinson University Press, 1988. Reprinted by permission of Associated University Presses.

Robert Hayden. "Those Winter Sundays." Reprinted from *Those Winter Sundays* by Robert Hayden with the permission of Liveright Publishing Corporation. Copyright © 1966 by Robert Hayden.

Seamus Heaney. "Digging" and "Mid-term Break" from *Poems: 1965–1975* by Seamus Heaney. Copyright © 1966, 1969, 1972, 1975, 1980 by Seamus Heaney. Reprinted by permission of Farrar, Straus & Giroux, Inc. and Faber and Faber Limited.

Anthony Hecht. "The Dover Bitch" from *Collected Earlier Poems* by Anthony Hecht. Copyright © 1990 by Anthony E. Hecht. Reprinted by permission of Alfred E. Knopf, Inc.

Judy Page Heitzman. "The Schoolroom on the Second Floor of the Knitting Mill" reprinted by permission. © 1991 Judy Page Heitzman. Originally in *The New Yorker*.

Thomas Wentworth Higginson. "On Meeting Dickinson for the First Time" reprinted by permission of the publishers from *The Letters of Emily Dickinson*, edited by Thomas H. Johnson, Cambridge, Mass.: The Belknap Press of Harvard University Press, Copyright © 1958, 1986 by the President and Fellows of Harvard College.

Conrad Hilberry. "The Frying Pan" first appeared in *Field* 19 (Fall 1978). Reprinted by permission of Oberlin College.

Edward Hirsch. "Fast Break" from *Wild Gratitude* by Edward Hirsch. Copyright © .1985 by Edward Hirsch. Reprinted by permission of Alfred A. Knopf, Inc.

Margaret Holley. "The Fireflies" copyright © 1991 by Margaret Holley. Reprinted by permission of the author.

M. Carl Holman. "Mr. Z." Reprinted by permission of Mariella A. Holman.

A. E. Housman. "When I was one-and-twenty," "Loveliest of trees, the cherry now," "Is my team ploughing," "Terence, this is stupid stuff," and "To an Athlete Dying Young" from *The Collected Poems of A. E. Housman.* Copyright 1939, 1940, © 1965 by Holt, Rinehart and Winston. Copyright © 1967, 1968 by Robert E. Symons. Reprinted by permission of Henry Holt and Company, Inc.

Carolynn Hoy. "In the Summer Kitchen" from *Ariel,* Vol. 24:2, April 1993. Reprinted by permission of *Ariel* and The University of Calgary, Board of Governors.

Langston Hughes. "Ballad of the Landlord" from *Montage of a Dream Deferred* by Langston Hughes. Copyright 1951 by Langston Hughes. Copyright renewed 1979 by George Houston Bass. Reprinted by permission of Harold Ober Associates Incorporated. "Harlem (A Dream Deferred)" from *The Panther and the Lash* by Langston Hughes. Copyright © 1951 by Langston Hughes. Reprinted by permission of Alfred A. Knopf, Inc.

Paul Humphrey. "Blow" from *Light Year '86.* Reprinted by permission of the author.

Mark Irwin. "Icicles" from *The Halls of Desire* by Mark Irwin. Copyright © 1987. Reprinted by permission of Galileo Press.

Bonnie Jacobson. "On Being Served Apples" from *Stopping for Time* by Bonnie Jacobson. Copyright © 1989. Reprinted by permission of GreenTower Press.

Randall Jarrell. "Next Day" © 1963, 1965 by Randall Jarrell from the book *The Lost World* published in *Randall Jarrell: the Complete Poems,* by Farrar, Straus, & Giroux. Permission by Rhoda Weyr Agency, NY. "The Death of the Ball Turrett Gunner" from *The Complete Poems* by Randall Jarrell. Copyright © 1945, renewal copyright © 1972 by Mrs. Randall Jarrell. Reprinted by permission of Farrar, Straus & Giroux, Inc.

Donald Justice. "Order In the Streets" from *Loser Weepers.* Reprinted by permission of the author. "The Snowfall" from *Summer Anniversaries.* Copyright © 1981 revised edition by Donald Justice. Wesleyan University Press by permission of University Press of New England.

John Keats. "On the Truth of the Imagination," "On Unobtrusive Poetry," "On His Poetic Principles," and "On the Vale of Soul-Making" reprinted by permission of the publishers from *The Letters of John Keats, 1814–1821,* Volumes I & II edited by Hyder Edward Rollins, Cambridge, Mass.: Harvard University Press. Copyright © 1958 by the President and Fellows of Harvard College.

Karl Keller. "Robert Frost on Dickinson" from *The Only Kangaroo Among the Beauty: Emily Dickinson in America.* Copyright © 1979. Reprinted by permission of Johns Hopkins University Press.

X. J. Kennedy. "First Confession" from *Nude Descending a Staircase* by X. J. Kennedy, copyright © 1961 by X. J. Kennedy. "In a Prominent Bar in Secaucus One Day" from *Cross Ties,* © 1985 by X. J. Kennedy. Reprinted by permission of Curtis Brown, Ltd.

Galway Kinnell. "After Making Love, We Hear Footsteps" and "Blackberry Eating" from *Mortal Acts, Mortal Words* by Galway Kinnell. Copyright © 1980 by Galway Kinnell. Excerpt from "For Robert Frost" from *Flower Herding on Mount Monadnock* by Galway Kinnell. Copyright © 1984 by Galway Kinnell. All reprinted by permission of Houghton Mifflin Company. All rights reserved. "The Male and Female Principles of Poetry," from "Being with Reality: an Interview with Galway Kinnell," *Columbia Magazine of Poetry and Prose,* 14 (1989). Reprinted by permission of Galway Kinnell.

Carolyn Kizer. "Food for Love" copyright © 1984, by Carolyn Kizer. Reprinted from *Yin,* by Caroline Kizer, with the permission of BOA Editions, Ltd., 92 Park Ave., Brockport, NY 14420.

Etheridge Knight. "Eastern Guard Tower" from *Poems from Prison* by Etheridge Knight. Copyright © 1968 by Etheridge Knight (Broadside Press). "A Watts Mother Mourns While Boiling Beans" from *Belly Song and Other Poems* by Etheridge Knight. Copyright © 1973 (Broadside Press). Reprinted by permission of the author.

Annette Kolodny. "On the Commitments of Feminist Criticism" excerpted from "Dancing through the Minefield." Copyright © 1979 by Annette Kolodny; all rights reserved. Reprinted with permission of the author.

Yusef Komunyakaa. "Facing It" from *Dien Cai Dau,* copyright © 1988 by Yusef Komunyakaa. Wesleyan University Press by permission of University Press of New England.

Ted Kooser. "The Blind Always Come as Such a Surprise" from *Heartland II: Poets of the Midwest,* edited by Lucien Stryk. Copyright © 1975 by Northern Illinois University Press. Used by permission of the publisher. "Selecting a Reader" from *Sure Signs: New and Selected Poems,* by Ted Kooser, by permission of the University of Pittsburgh Press. Copyright © 1980 by Ted Kooser.

Maxine Kumin. "Woodchucks," copyright © 1971 by Maxine Kumin, "Morning Swim," copyright © 1965 by Maxine Kumin, from *Our Ground Time Here Will Be Brief* by Maxine Kumin. Used by permission of Viking Penguin, a division of Penguin Books USA Inc.

Philip Larkin. "Home Is So Sad" and "A Study of Reading Habits" from *The Whitsun Weddings* by Philip Larkin. Reprinted by permission of Faber and Faber Limited.

Richmond Lattimore. "The Crabs" from *Poems from Three Decades* (Scribner's). Reprinted by permission of Mrs. Richmond Lattimore.

Tato Laviera. "AmeRícan" reprinted from *AmeRícan* (Houston: Arte Publico Press–University of Houston, 1985) with permission of the publisher.

D. H. Lawrence. "Snake" from *The Complete Poems of D. H. Lawrence* by D. H. Lawrence, edited by V. de Sola Pinto & F. W. Roberts. Copyright © 1964, 1971 by Angelo Ravagli and C. M. Weekley, Executors of the Estate of Frieda Lawrence Ravagli. Used by permission of Viking Penguin, a division of Penguin Books USA Inc.

David Lenson. "On the Contemporary Use of Rhyme" from *The Chronicle of Higher Education,* February 24, 1988. Reprinted by permission of the author.

Denise Levertov. "O Taste and See" from *Poems 1960–1967.* Copyright © 1964 by Denise Levertov. "Gathered at the River" from *Oblique Prayers.* Copyright © 1984 by Denise Levertov. "News Items" from *The Freeing of the Dust.* Copyright © 1975 by Denise Levertov. All of these reprinted by permission of New Directions Publishing Corporation. "On 'Gathered at the River'"from "'Gathered at the River': Background and Form" in *Singular Voices: American Poetry Today,* edited by Stephen Berg. Reprinted by permission of Denise Levertov.

Li Ho. "A Beautiful Girl Combs Her Hair," translated by David Young, from *Four T'ang Poets: Field Translation Series #4.* Copyright © Oberlin College Press, 1980. Reprinted by permission.

Audre Lorde. "Hanging Fire." Reprinted from *The Black Unicorn* by Audre Lorde with the permission of W. W. Norton & Company, Inc. Copyright © 1978 by Audre Lorde. Permission to use "Poems Are Not Luxuries" is granted by Audre Lorde.

Robert Lowell. "Skunk Hour" from *Life Studies* by Robert Lowell. Copyright © 1956, 1959 by Robert Lowell. Renewal copyright © 1981, 1986, 1987 by Harriet W. Lowell, Caroline Lowell & Sheridan Lowell. Reprinted by permission of Farrar, Straus & Giroux, Inc.

Katharyn Howd Machan. "Hazel Tells LaVerne" from *Light Year '85.* Reprinted by permission of the author.

Archibald MacLeish. "Ars Poetica" from *Collected Poems 1917–1982* by Archibald MacLeish. Copyright © 1985 by the Estate of Archibald MacLeish. Reprinted by permission of Houghton Mifflin Company. All rights reserved.

Elaine Magarrell. "The Joy of Cooking" from *Sometime the Cow Kick Your Head, Light Year 88/89.* Reprinted by permission of the author.

Nazik al-Mala'ika. "I Am" from *Issues of Contemporary Poetry in Women of the Fertile Crescent: Modern Poetry by Arab Women,* ed. Kamal Boullata. Reprinted by permission of Three Continents Press, Washington, D.C.

David McCord. "Epitaph on a Waiter" from *Odds without Ends.* Reprinted by permission of the author.

Michael McFee. "In Medias Res" from *Light Year '86.* Reprinted by permission of the author.

Claude McKay. "The Harlem Dancer" by permission of the Archives of Claude McKay, Carl Cowl, administrator, from *The Selected Poems of Claude McKay,* Harcourt Brace, 1979.

Peter Meinke. "The ABC of Aerobics" from *Night Watch on the Chesapeake,* by Peter Meinke, by permission of the University of Pittsburgh Press. Copyright © 1987 by Peter Meinke.

James Merrill. "Casual Wear" from *Selected Poems 1946–1985* by James Merrill. Copyright © 1992 by James Merrill. Reprinted by permission of Alfred A. Knopf.

Edna St. Vincent Millay. "Never May the Fruit Be Plucked," "I Too beneath Your Moon, Almighty Sex," and "I Will Put Chaos Into Fourteen Lines" copyright © 1923, 1939, 1951, 1954, 1967, 1982 by Edna St. Vincent Millay and Norma Millay Ellis. From *Collected Poems*, Harper & Row. Reprinted by permission of Elizabeth Barnett, literary executor.

Janice Townley Moore. "To A Wasp" from *Light Year '85*. Reprinted by permission of the author.

Marianne Moore. "The Fish" and "Poetry" reprinted with permission of Macmillan Publishing Company from *Collected Poems of Marianne Moore* by Marianne Moore. Copyright 1935 by Marianne Moore, renewed 1963 by Marianne Moore and T. S. Eliot.

Vinicius de Moraes. "Sonnet of Intimacy" from *The Complete Poems: 1927–1979* by Elizabeth Bishop. Copyright © 1979, 1983 by Alice Helen Methfessel. Reprinted by permission of Farrar, Straus, Giroux, Inc.

Robert Morgan. "On the Shape of a Poem" (*Epoch* Fall/Winter, 1983) reprinted by permission of the author. "Mountain Graveyard" from *Sigodlin*, copyright © 1990 by Robert Morgan. Wesleyan University Press by permission of University Press of New England.

Jon Mukand. "Lullaby" from *Sutured Words: Contemporary Poems About Medicine*, ed. Jon Mukand. Aviva Press, 1987. Copyright © Jon Mukand.

Susan Musgrave. "Right through the Heart" from *Tarts and Muggers: Poems New and Selected* (1982). Reprinted by permission of the author.

Howard Nemerov. "Life Cycle of Common Man" from *The Collected Poems of Howard Nemerov* (University of Chicago Press, 1977) and "The Fourth of July." Both reprinted by permission of Margaret Nemerov, Trustee, the Howard Nemerov Trust.

Pablo Neruda. "Sweetness, Always" from *Extravagaria* by Pablo Neruda. Translation copyright © 1969, 1970, 1972, 1974 by Alastair Reid. Originally published as *Estravagario*, copyright © 1958 by Editorial Losada, S.A., Buenos Aires. Reprinted by permission of Farrar, Straus & Giroux, Inc.

John Frederick Nims. "Love Poem" from *Selected Poems*. Copyright © 1982 by the University of Chicago. All rights reserved.

Alden Nowlan. "The Bull Moose" from *An Exchange of Gifts* by Alden Nowlan. Reprinted with the permission of Staddart Publishing Co., Limited, Don Mills, Ontario.

Frank O'Hara. "Ave Maria" from *The Collected Poems of Frank O'Hara*. Reprinted by permission.

Sharon Olds. "Rite of Passage" and "Sex Without Love" from *The Dead and the Living* by Sharon Olds. Copyright © 1975, 1978, 1979, 1980, 1981, 1982, 1983 by Sharon Olds. Reprinted by permission of Alfred A. Knopf, Inc.

Simon J. Ortiz. "My Father's Song" from *Going for the Rain* by Simon J. Ortiz. Copyright © 1976.

Wilfred Owen. "Dulce et Decorum Est" and "Anthem for Doomed Youth" from *The Collected Poems of Wilfred Owen*, edited by C. Day Lewis. Copyright © 1963 by Chatto & Windus, Ltd. Published by New Directions Publishing Company and The Hogarth Press. Reprinted by permission of New Directions Publishing Corporation, the Estate of Wilfred Owen, and Random Century Limited.

Dorothy Parker. "One Perfect Rose" from *The Portable Dorothy Parker* by Dorothy Parker, Introduction by Brendan Gill. Copyright 1928, renewed © 1956 by Dorothy Parker. Used by permission of Viking Penguin, a division of Penguin Books USA Inc.

Linda Pastan. "after minor surgery." Reprinted from *PM/AM: New and Selected Poems* by Linda Pastan with the permission of W. W. Norton & Company, Inc. Copyright © 1982 by Linda Pastan. "Marks." Reprinted from *The Five Stages of Grief* by Linda Pastan, with the permission of W. W. Norton & Company, Inc. Copyright © 1978 by Linda Pastan.

Octavio Paz. "The street" from *Early Poems 1935–1955*. Reprinted by permission of Indiana University Press.

Laurence Perrine. "The limerick's never averse" from *Light Year '86*. Reprinted by permission of the author.

John B. Pickard. "On 'I heard a Fly buzz — when I died'" from *Emily Dickinson: An Introduction and Interpretation* by John B. Pickard. Copyright © 1967 by Holt, Rinehart and Winston, Inc., reprinted by permission of the publisher.

Marge Piercy. "Barbie Doll," "The Secretary Chant," and "A Work of Artifice" from *Circles on the Water* by Marge Piercy. Copyright © 1969, 1971, 1973 by Marge Piercy. Reprinted by permission of Alfred A. Knopf, Inc.

Sylvia Plath. "Daddy" from *Ariel* by Sylvia Plath. Copyright © 1963 by Ted Hughes. Copyright renewed. "Metaphors" from *Crossing the Water* by Sylvia Plath. Copyright © 1960 by Ted Hughes. Copyright renewed. "Mirror" from *Crossing the Water* by Sylvia Plath. Copyright © 1963 by Ted Hughes. Originally appeared in *The New Yorker*. All reprinted by permission of HarperCollins Publishers, Inc. and Faber and Faber Ltd. "On Headline Poetry" from *Johnny Panic and the Bible of Dreams*. Reprinted by permission of Faber and Faber Ltd.

Ruth Porritt. "Read this Poem from the Bottom Up" originally appeared in *The Laurel Review* and is reprinted by permission of the author.

Ezra Pound. "The Garden," "The River-Merchant's Wife: A Letter," and "In a Station of the Metro" from *Personae*. Copyright 1926 by Ezra Pound. Reprinted by permission of New Directions Publishing Corporation. "On Free Verse" from *The Literary Essays of Ezra Pound*. Copyright 1935 by Ezra Pound. Reprinted by permission of New Directions Publishing Corporation.

Dudley Randall. "Ballad of Birmingham" from *Poem Counter Poem* by Danner and Randall (Broadside Press).

Henry Reed. "Naming of Parts" copyright © The Executor of Henry Reed's Estate 1946, 1947, 1970, and 1991. Reprinted from *Henry Reed: Collected Poems* edited by John Stallworthy (1991) by permission of Oxford University Press.

John Repp. "Cursing the Hole in the Screen, Wondering at the Romance Some Find In Summer." Reprinted by permission of the author.

David S. Reynolds. "Popular Literature and 'Wild Nights — Wild Nights!'" from *Beneath the American Experience* by David S. Reynolds. Copyright © 1988 by David S. Reynolds. Reprinted by permission of Alfred A. Knopf, Inc.

Adrienne Rich. "Living in Sin" is reprinted from *The Fact of a Doorframe: Poems Selected and New, 1950–1984*, by Adrienne Rich, by permission of W. W. Norton & Company, Inc. Copyright © 1984 by Adrienne Rich. Copyright © 1975, 1978 by W. W. Norton & Company, Inc. Copyright © 1981 by Adrienne Rich.

Rainer Maria Rilke. "The Panther" from *The Selected Poetry of Rainer Maria Rilke* by Rainer Maria Rilke, trans. by Stephen Mitchell. Copyright © 1982 by Stephen Mitchell. Reprinted by permission of Random House, Inc.

Alberto Ríos. "Seniors" from *Five Indiscretions*. Copyright © 1985 by Alberto Ríos. Reprinted by permission of the author.

Edwin Arlington Robinson. "Mr Flood's Party" reprinted with permission of Macmillan Publishing Company from *Collected Poems of Edwin Arlington Robinson*. Copyright 1921 by Edwin Arlington Robinson, renewed 1949 by Ruth Nivison.

Theodore Roethke. "I Knew A Woman," copyright 1954 by Theodore Roethke. "Root Cellar," copyright 1943 by Modern Poetry Association, Inc. "My Papa's Waltz," copyright 1942 by Hearst Magazines, Inc. From *The Collected Poems of Theodore Roethke* by Theodore Roethke. Used by permission of Doubleday, a division of Bantam Doubleday Dell Publishing Group, Inc.

Katerina Anghelàki-Rooke. "Tourism" from *Longman Anthology of World Literature by Women* edited by Marian Arkin and Barbara Shollar. Copyright © 1989 by Longman Publishing Group.

Frederick L. Rusch. "Society and Character in 'The Love Song of J. Alfred Prufrock'" from "Approaching Literature Through the Social Psychology of Erich Fromm" in *Psychological Perspectives on Literature: Freudian Dissidents and Non-Freudians*, ed. Joseph Natoli. Copyright © 1984.

Pedro Salinas. "Presagios" from *The Complete Poems of Pedro Salinas*. Reprinted by permission of Mercedes Casanovas, Barcelona.

Sappho. "With his venom" from *Sappho: A New Translation*, trans./ed. Mary Barnard. © 1958, 1984 by Mary Barnard. Reprinted by permission of the University of California Press.

Elisabeth Schneider. "Hints of Eliot in Prufrock." Reprinted by permission of the Modern Language Association of America from "Prufrock and After: The Theme of Change," *PMLA* 87 (1952): 1103–17.

John R. Searle. "Figuring Out Metaphors" from *Expression and Meaning*. Reprinted by permission of Cambridge University Press.

Anne Sexton. "Her Kind" from *To Bedlam and Part Way Back* by Anne Sexton. Copyright © 1960 by Anne Sexton © renewed 1988 by Linda G. Sexton. "Lobster" from *45 Mercy Street* by Anne Sexton. Copyright © 1976 by Linda Gray Sexton and Loring Conant, Jr. Both reprinted by permission of Houghton Mifflin Company. All rights reserved.

Karl Shapiro. "Libraries" from *The Bourgeois Poet* by Karl Shapiro (Random House, 1964). Copyright © 1953, 1985 by Karl Shapiro. Reprinted by arrangement with Wieser & Wieser, Inc. 118 East 25th Street, New York, NY 10010.

Leslie Marmon Silko. "Where Mountain Lion Lay Down with Deer" copyright © 1981 by Leslie Marmon Silko. Reprinted from *Storyteller* by Leslie Marmon Silko, published by Seaver Books, New York, New York. Reprinted by permission of the publisher.

Louis Simpson. "American Poetry" from *At the End of the Open Road* copyright © 1963 by Louis Simpson. Wesleyan University Press by permission of University Press of New England.

David R. Slavitt. "Titanic" from *Big Nose* by David R. Slavitt. Copyright © 1983 by David R. Slavitt. Reprinted by permission of Louisiana State University Press.

Ernest Slyman. "Lightning Bugs" from *Sometime the Cow Kick Your Head, Light Year 88/89*. Reprinted by permission of the author.

Stevie Smith. "Valuable" from *Collected Poems*. Copyright © 1983 by James MacGibbon. Reprinted by permission of New Directions Publishing Corporation.

W. D. Snodgrass. "April Inventory" from *Heart's Needle* by W. D. Snodgrass. Copyright © 1957 by W. D. Snodgrass. Reprinted by permission of Alfred A. Knopf, Inc.

Gary Snyder. "After weeks of watching the roof leak" from "Hitch Haiku" in *The Back Country*. Copyright © 1967 by Gary Snyder. Reprinted by permission of New Directions Publishing Corporation.

David Solway. "Windsurfing" reprinted by permission of the author.

Cathy Song. "The White Porch" from *Picture Bride*. Copyright © 1983 by Cathy Song. Copyright © 1983 by Yale University. Reprinted by permission.

Susan Sontag. "Against Interpretation" from *Against Interpretation* by Susan Sontag. Copyright © 1964 by Susan Sontag. Reprinted by permission of Farrar, Straus, and Giroux, Inc.

Wole Soyinka. "Future Plans" from *A Shuttle in the Crypt* by Wole Soyinka. Copyright © 1972 by Wole Soyinka. Reprinted by permission of Hill & Wang, a division of Farrar, Straus & Giroux, Inc.

William Stafford. "Traveling through the Dark" from *Stories that Could Be True* by William Stafford. Copyright © 1960, 1977 by William Stafford. Reprinted by permission of the author.

George Starbuck. "Japanese Fish" from *Light Year '86*.

Timothy Steele. "Waiting for the Storm" from *Sapphics Against Anger and Other Poems*. Copyright © 1986 by Timothy Steele. Reprinted by permission of the author.

Stephen Stepanchev. "Cornered on the Corner" reprinted by permission; © 1991 Stephen Stepanchev. Originally in *The New Yorker*.

Jim Stevens. "Schizophrenia" first appeared in *Light: The Quarterly of Light Verse* (Spring, 1992). Copyright © 1992 by Jim Stevens. Reprinted by permission.

Wallace Stevens. "The Emperor of Ice-Cream," and "Sunday Morning" from *The Collected Poems of Wallace Stevens* by Wallace Stevens. Copyright 1923 and renewed 1951 by Wallace Stevens. Reprinted by permission of Alfred A. Knopf, Inc.

Jack Stillinger. "On 'The Eve of St. Agnes'" from "The Hoodwinking of Madeline: Skepticism in 'The Eve of St. Agnes',", in *Studies in Philology*, vol. 58, 1961. Copyright © 1961 by the University of North Carolina Press. Used by permission of the publisher.

Mark Strand. "The Continuous Life" from *The Continuous Life* by Mark Strand. Copyright © 1990 by Mark Strand. Reprinted by permission of Alfred A. Knopf, Inc.

Robert H. Swennes. "Fear in 'Home Burial'" from "Man and Wife: the Dialogue of Contraries in Robert Frost's Poetry," *American Literature* 42:3 pp. 363–72. Copyright Duke University Press, 1970. Reprinted with permission.

May Swenson. "A Nosty Fright" copyright © 1984 by May Swenson. Used with permission of the Literary Estate of May Swenson. "The Secret in the Cat" reprinted with permission of Macmillan Publishing Company from *The Complete Poems to Solve* by May Swenson. Copyright © 1993 by The Literary Estate of May Swenson.

Wislawa Szymborska. "The Joy of Writing" from *Sounds, Feelings, Thoughts: Seventy Poems by Wislawa Szymborska*. Copyright © 1981 by Princeton University Press. Reprinted by permission of Princeton University Press.

Shinkichi Takahashi, "Explosion" from *The Penguin Book of Zen Poetry*, ed. and trans. Lucien Stryk and Takashi Ikemoto. Reprinted by permission of Lucien Stryk.

Brook Thomas. Excerpt from "The Historical Necessities for — and Difficulties with — New Historical Analysis in Introductory Literature Courses," *College English*, September 1987. Copyright 1987 by the National Council of Teachers of English. Reprinted with permission.

Dylan Thomas. "Do not go gentle into that good night," "Fern Hill," and "The Hand That Signed the Paper" from *Poems of Dylan Thomas*. Copyright 1939 by New Directions Publishing Corporation, 1945 by the Trustees for the Copyrights of Dylan Thomas, 1952 by Dylan Thomas. Reprinted by permission of New Directions Publishing Corporation and David Higham Associates. "On the Words in Poetry" from *Quite Early One Morning*. Copyright © 1964 by New Directions Publishing Corporation. Reprinted by permission of New Directions Publishing Corporation and David Higham Associates.

Mabel Loomis Todd. "The *Character* of Amherst" from *The Years and Hours of Emily Dickinson*, volume 2, by Jay Leda. Copyright © 1960. Reprinted by permission of Yale University Press.

Jean Toomer. "Reapers." Reprinted from *Cane* by Jean Toomer with the permission of Liveright Publishing Corporation. Copyright 1923 by Boni & Liveright, renewed 1951 by Jean Toomer.

Tomas Transtromer. "April and Silence" translated by Robin Fulton. First published in *The Kenyon Review* New Series, Summer 1991, vol. 13, no. 3. Copyright © 1991 by Kenyon College.

Lionel Trilling. "On Frost As a Terrifying Poet" from *Partisan Review*, Volume 26, Summer 1959. Reprinted by permission of Diana Trilling.

William Trowbridge. "Enter Dark Stranger" from *Enter Dark Stranger* by William Trowbridge. Copyright © 1989. Reprinted by permission of the University of Arkansas Press.

John Updike. "Dog's Death" from *Midpoint and Other Poems* by John Updike. Copyright © 1969 by John Updike. "Player Piano" from *The Carpentered Hen and Other Tame Creatures* by John Updike. Copyright © 1956 by John Updike. Both reprinted by permission of Alfred A. Knopf, Inc.

Alice Walker. "Revolutionary Petunias" from *Revolutionary Petunias and Other Poems*, copyright © 1972 by Alice Walker, reprinted by permission of Harcourt Brace & Company.

Robert Wallace. "The Double-Play" copyright © 1961 by Robert Wallace from *Views of a Ferris Wheel*. Reprinted by permission of the author.

Robert Weisbuch. "On Dickinson's Use of Analogy" from *Emily Dickinson's Poetry* by Robert Weisbuch. Copyright © 1975. Reprinted by permission of The University of Chicago Press.

Richard Wilbur. "Year's End" from *Ceremony and Other Poems*, copyright 1949 and renewed 1977 by Richard Wilbur. "The Writer" from *The Mind Reader*, copyright © 1971 by Richard Wilbur. "Sleepless at Crown Point" from *The Mind Reader*, copyright © 1973 by Richard Wilbur. "Love Calls Us to the Things of This World" from *Things of This World*, copyright © 1956 and renewed 1984 by Richard Wilbur. "A Late Aubade" from *Walking to Sleep: New Poems and Translations*, copyright © 1968 by Richard Wilbur. All reprinted by permission of Harcourt Brace & Company.

C. K. Williams. "The Mirror" from *A Dream of Mind* by C. K. Williams. Copyright © 1992 by C. K. Williams. Reprinted by permission of Farrar, Straus & Giroux, Inc. First published in *The New Yorker*, October 21, 1991.

Miller Williams. "After a Brubeck Concert" and "Ruby Tells All" from *Imperfect Love: Poems by Miller Williams*. Copyright © 1983, 1984, 1985, 1986 by Miller Williams. Reprinted by permission of Louisiana State University Press.

William Carlos Williams. "Poem," "The Red Wheelbarrow," "Spring and All," and "This is Just to Say" from *The Collected Poems of William Carlos Williams, vol. I, 1909–1939*. Copyright 1938 by New Directions Publishing Corp. Reprinted by permission of New Directions Publishing Corporation.

Cynthia Griffin Wolff. "On the Many Voices in Dickinson's Poetry" from *Emily Dickinson* by Cynthia Griffin Wolff. Copyright © 1986 by Cynthia Griffin Wolff. Reprinted by permission of Alfred A. Knopf, Inc.

James Wright. "Lying in a Hammock at William Duffy's Farm in Pine Island, Minnesota" from *The Branch Will Not Break*, copyright 1963 by James Wright. Wesleyan University Press by permission of University Press of New England.

William Butler Yeats. "The Second Coming" reprinted with permission of Macmillan Publishing Company from *The Poems of W. B. Yeats: A New Edition*, edited by Richard J. Finneran. Copyright 1924 by Macmillan Publishing Company, renewed 1952 by Bertha Georgie Yeats. "Leda and the Swan" and "Sailing to Byzantium" reprinted with permission of Macmillan Publishing Company from *The Poems of W. B. Yeats: A New Edition*, edited by Richard J. Finneran. Copyright 1928 by Macmillan Publishing Company, renewed 1956 by Bertha Georgie Yeats. "Crazy Jane Talks with the Bishop" reprinted with permission of Macmillan Publishing Company from *The Poems of W. B. Yeats: A New Edition*, edited by Richard J. Finneran. Copyright 1933 by Macmillan Publishing Company, renewed 1961 by Bertha Georgie Yeats.

Dale Zieroth. "Time over Earth" from *Canadian Literature* 138/139 Fall/Winter, 1993.

Index of First Lines

Index of Authors and Titles

Index of Terms